THE BROADVIEW ANTHOLOGY OF
Victorian Prose
1832–1901

THE BROADVIEW ANTHOLOGY OF
Victorian Prose
1832–1901

edited by
Mary Elizabeth Leighton
and
Lisa Surridge

© 2012 Mary Elizabeth Leighton and Lisa Surridge

All rights reserved. The use of any part of this publication reproduced, transmitted in any form or by any means, electronic, mechanical, photocopying, recording, or otherwise, or stored in a retrieval system, without prior written consent of the publisher—or in the case of photocopying, a licence from Access Copyright (Canadian Copyright Licensing Agency), One Yonge Street, Suite 1900, Toronto, Ontario M5E 1E5—is an infringement of the copyright law.

Library and Archives Canada Cataloguing in Publication

The Broadview anthology of Victorian prose 1832-1901 / edited by Mary Elizabeth Leighton and Lisa Surridge.

Includes bibliographical references.
ISBN 978-1-55111-860-4

1. English literature—19th century. 2. Great Britain—History—Victoria, 1837-1901—Literary collections. I. Leighton, Mary Elizabeth, 1971- II. Surridge, Lisa A. (Lisa Anne), 1963-

PR1145.B76 2012   820.8'008   C2012-902168-7

Broadview Press is an independent, international publishing house, incorporated in 1985.

We welcome comments and suggestions regarding any aspect of our publications—please feel free to contact us at the addresses below or at broadview@broadviewpress.com.

North America   PO Box 1243, Peterborough, Ontario, Canada K9J 7H5
2215 Kenmore Ave., Buffalo, New York, USA 14207
Tel: (705) 743-8990; Fax: (705) 743-8353
email: customerservice@broadviewpress.com

UK, Europe, Central Asia,   Eurospan Group, 3 Henrietta St., London WC2E 8LU, United Kingdom
Middle East, Africa, India,   Tel: 44 (0) 1767 604972; Fax: 44 (0) 1767 601640
and Southeast Asia   email: eurospan@turpin-distribution.com

Australia and New Zealand   NewSouth Books
c/o TL Distribution, 15-23 Helles Ave., Moorebank, NSW, Australia 2170
Tel: (02) 8778 9999; Fax: (02) 8778 9944
email: orders@tldistribution.com.au

www.broadviewpress.com

Broadview Press acknowledges the financial support of the Government of Canada through the Canada Book Fund for our publishing activities.

Copy edited by Michel Pharand

This book is printed on paper containing 50% postconsumer fibre.

PRINTED IN CANADA

CONTENTS

Acknowledgements	9
A Note on the Text	10
Introduction: Victorian Print Media and the Reading Public, *Mary Elizabeth Leighton and Lisa Surridge*	11

LIFE WRITING

Introduction, *David Amigoni*	23
William Dodd, from *A Narrative of the Experience and Sufferings of William Dodd, A Factory Cripple* (1841)	29
Alexander Somerville, from *The Autobiography of a Working Man* (1848)	33
John Stuart Mill, from *Autobiography* (1873)	36
Harriet Martineau, from *Autobiography* (1877)	47
Anthony Trollope, from *An Autobiography* (1883)	51
John Ruskin, from *Praeterita* (1885–89)	55
Annie Besant, from *Annie Besant: An Autobiography* (1893)	63
Oscar Wilde, from *De Profundis* (written 1897; published 1905)	69
Edmund Gosse, from *Father and Son: A Study of Two Temperaments* (1907)	75
Beatrice Webb, from *My Apprenticeship* (1926)	80

THE CONDITION OF ENGLAND: INDUSTRIALIZATION AND SOCIAL REFORM

Introduction, *Dan Bivona*	87
Harriet Martineau, from *Illustrations of Political Economy* (1832–34)	93
Thomas Carlyle, from *Past and Present* (1843)	97
from "Gospel of Mammonism"	98
from "Captains of Industry"	100
Friedrich Engels, from *The Condition of the Working Class in England in 1844* (1845; trans. 1887)	104
Karl Marx and Friedrich Engels, from *Manifesto of the Communist Party* (1848; trans. 1888)	108
Charles Dickens, from "A Walk in a Workhouse" (1850)	115
Henry Mayhew, from *London Labour and the London Poor* (1851)	119
John Stuart Mill, from *On Liberty* (1859)	122
John Ruskin, from *Unto This Last* (1860)	132
Octavia Hill, from "Blank Court; or, Landlords and Tenants" (1871)	141
William Booth, from *In Darkest England and the Way Out* (1890)	144

EDUCATION

Introduction, *Janice Schroeder*	149
Thomas Arnold, from "On the Discipline of Public Schools" (1835)	156
Harriet Martineau, from *Retrospect of Western Travel* (1838)	160
Mary Carpenter, from *Reformatory Schools, for the Children of the Perishing and Dangerous Classes, and for Juvenile Offenders* (1851)	164
John Henry Newman, from *Discourses on the Scope and Nature of University Education Addressed to the Catholics of Dublin* (1852)	169
Henry Morley and Geraldine Jewsbury, from "Instructive Comparisons" (1855)	174
Frederick Denison Maurice, from *Learning and Working: Six Lectures Delivered in Willis's Rooms, London, in June and July, 1854* (1855)	179
Matthew Arnold, from "Art. VIII.—The Functions of Criticism at the Present Time" (1864)	183
Emily Davies, from *The Higher Education of Women* (1866)	192
Henry Maudsley, from "Sex in Mind and in Education" (1874)	197
Elizabeth Garrett Anderson, from "Sex in Mind and Education: A Reply" (1874)	200
John Churton Collins, from "An Educational Crisis, and How to Avert It.—II" (1886)	203
William Morris, from "English at the Universities" (1886)	207
John Addington Symonds, from "English at the Universities.—III." (1886)	208
Walter Pater, from "English at the Universities.—IV." (1886)	209
Matthew Arnold, from "English at the Universities.—IX." (1887)	211
James Anthony Froude, from "English at the Universities.—IX." (1887)	211

AESTHETICS AND CULTURE

Introduction, *Dennis Denisoff*	213
John Ruskin, from *The Stones of Venice* (1851–53)	217
Anna Jameson, from *Legends of the Madonna, as Represented in the Fine Arts* (1852)	226
George Eliot, from *Adam Bede* (1859)	235
Matthew Arnold, from "Culture and Its Enemies" (1867)	238
Walter Pater, from *Studies in the History of the Renaissance* (1873)	249
William Morris, from *Hopes and Fears for Art* (1882)	252
James McNeill Whistler, from *Mr. Whistler's "Ten O'Clock"* (1885)	257
Oscar Wilde, from "The Critic as Artist" (1891)	265
Vernon Lee and Clementina Anstruther-Thomson, from "Beauty and Ugliness" (1897)	277

GENDER AND SEXUALITY

Introduction, *Susan Hamilton*	283
Sarah Stickney Ellis, from *The Women of England: Their Social Duties and Domestic Habits* (1839)	288
Barbara Leigh Smith Bodichon, from *A Brief Summary, in Plain Language, of the Most Important Laws Concerning Women; Together with a Few Observations Thereon* (1854)	292

Florence Nightingale, from *Suggestions for Thought to the Searchers after Truth among the Artizans of England* (1860) — 298
John Ruskin, from *Sesame and Lilies* (1865) — 301
John Stuart Mill, from *The Subjection of Women* (1869) — 309
Thomas Hughes, from *The Manliness of Christ* (1879) — 320
William Thomas Stead, from "The Maiden Tribute of Modern Babylon" (1885) — 324
Mona Caird, from "Marriage" (1888) — 331
John Addington Symonds, from *A Problem in Modern Ethics* (1891) — 340
Havelock Ellis, from *Studies in the Psychology of Sex: Sexual Inversion* (1897) — 343

FAITH AND DOUBT

Introduction, *Catherine Harland* — 349
Thomas Carlyle, from *Sartor Resartus: The Life and Opinions of Herr Teufelsdröckh* (1833–34) — 354
   from "The Everlasting No" — 354
   from "Centre of Indifference" — 358
   from "The Everlasting Yea" — 363
Benjamin Jowett, from "On the Interpretation of Scripture" (1860) — 369
John William Colenso, from *The Pentateuch and Book of Joshua Critically Examined* (1862) — 375
John Henry Newman, from *Apologia pro Vita Sua* (1864) — 381
Leslie Stephen, from "An Agnostic's Apology" (1876) — 391
Vernon Lee, from "The Responsibilities of Unbelief: A Conversation between Three Rationalists" (1883) — 398
Frances Power Cobbe, from "Agnostic Morality" (1883) — 407

SCIENCE

Introduction, *Bernard Lightman* — 413
Charles Lyell, from *Principles of Geology, being an Attempt to Explain the Former Changes of the Earth's Surface, by Reference to Causes Now in Operation* (1830) — 420
Charles Bell, from *The Hand: Its Mechanism and Vital Endowments as Evincing Design* (1833) — 424
Mary Somerville, from *On the Connexion of the Physical Sciences* (1834) — 427
Robert Chambers, from *Vestiges of the Natural History of Creation* (1844) — 432
Herbert Spencer, from *Social Statics: or, The Conditions Essential to Human Happiness Specified, and the First of Them Developed* (1850) — 437
Philip Henry Gosse, from *Evenings at the Microscope* (1859) — 441
Mary Ward, from *Telescope Teachings: A Familiar Sketch of Astronomical Discovery; Combining a Special Notice of Objects Coming within the Range of a Small Telescope, Illustrated by the Author's Original Drawings; with a Detail of the Most Interesting Discoveries Which Have Been Made with the Assistance of Powerful Telescopes, Concerning the Phenomena of the Heavenly Bodies, Including the Recent Comet* (1859) — 445

Charles Darwin, from *On the Origin of Species by Means of Natural Selection, or the Preservation of Favoured Races in the Struggle for Life* (1859)   450
Lydia Becker, from "On the Study of Science by Women" (1869)   459
Francis Galton, from *Hereditary Genius: An Inquiry into Its Laws and Consequences* (1869)   463
Charles Darwin, from *The Descent of Man, and Selection in Relation to Sex* (1871)   468
Richard Proctor, from "A Voyage to the Ringed Planet" (1872)   473
Thomas Henry Huxley, from "The Struggle for Human Existence: A Programme" (1888)   478

TRAVEL AND EXPLORATION

Introduction, *Laura Franey*   483
James Holman, from *A Voyage Round the World Including Travels in Africa, Asia, Australasia, America, etc. etc. from 1827 to 1832* (1834)   488
Charles Darwin, from *Journal of Researches into the Geology and Natural History of the Various Countries Visited by H.M.S. Beagle, under the Command of Captain FitzRoy, R.N. from 1832 to 1836* (1839)   493
Richard F. Burton, from *Personal Narrative of a Pilgrimage to El-Medinah and Meccah* (1855)   498
David Livingstone, from *Missionary Travels and Researches in South Africa* (1857)   504
Henry Walter Bates, from *The Naturalist on the River Amazons, a Record of Adventures, Habits of Animals, Sketches of Brazilian and Indian Life, and Aspects of Nature under the Equator, during Eleven Years of Travel* (1863)   509
Emily Eden, from *"Up the Country": Letters Written to Her Sister from the Upper Provinces of India* (1866)   514
Alfred Russel Wallace, from *The Malay Archipelago: The Land of the Orang-utan, and the Bird of Paradise. A Narrative of Travel, with Studies of Man and Nature* (1869)   518
Henry M. Stanley, from *How I Found Livingstone; Travels, Adventures, and Discoveries in Central Africa; Including Four Months' Residence with Dr. Livingstone* (1872)   522
Anthony Trollope, from *Australia and New Zealand* (1873)   529
Florence Dixie, from *Across Patagonia* (1880)   534
Isabella L. Bird, from *Unbeaten Tracks in Japan: An Account of Travels in the Interior, Including Visits to the Aborigines of Yezo and the Shrines of Nikkô and Isé* (1880)   538
Kate Marsden, from *On Sledge and Horseback to Outcast Siberian Lepers* (1891)   544
Mary H. Kingsley, from *Travels in West Africa Congo Français, Corisco and Cameroon* (1897)   547

Acknowledgements

We are grateful to the many student research assistants who have contributed to our work on this anthology over the years: Brian Beitz, Cameron Butt, Amy Coté, Janis Dawson, Jack Dempster, Jennifer Duggan, Lise Gaston, Dara Greaves, Jane Griffith, Elizabeth Johnston, Treava Kellington, Rachel Krueger, Cara Leitch, Shaun Macpherson, Ryan Munroe, Emily Murphy, Jessica Natale Woollard, Greg Owen, Liam Sarsfield, Danika Sihota, Emily Smith, Evan Stanley, Michael Stevens, and Adam Taylor.

We are also thankful to the many colleagues who kindly responded to our queries: Marina Bettaglio, Laurel Bowman, David Butler, Joe Grossi, Ingrid Holmberg, Lloyd Howard, Janelle Jenstad, Francisco Moises, Harold Munn, Elena Pnevmonidou, Andrew Rippin, Marie Surridge, Helga Thorson, Vanessa Warne, and Adrienne Williams Boyarin.

Katharine Waring in the Department of English General Office at the University of Victoria entered copy at an early stage of the project; we appreciate all her help.

Finally, for their love and support throughout this project (which is older than some of them), we thank our families: John, Michael, and Greg Adams, and Sean, Jacob, and Jessica Hier.

A Note on the Text

Because this anthology emphasizes the confluence of voices in the Victorian press, we have chosen to reproduce texts in their first published form under their original titles. Hence, for example, Matthew Arnold's essay commonly known as "The Function of Criticism at the Present Time" appears in this collection as "The Functions of Criticism at the Present Time," the title under which it first appeared in the *National Review*. Similarly, we reproduce a section of John Henry Newman's *The Idea of a University* under its original title, *Discourses on the Scope of the Nature of University Education Addressed to the Catholics of Dublin*.

We have preserved Victorian authors' original spelling and punctuation except where we found obvious printers' errors; we have silently corrected these. Ellipses indicate places where we have had to cut selections to conserve space.

INTRODUCTION

Victorian Print Media and the Reading Public

Mary Elizabeth Leighton and Lisa Surridge

In an 1840 lecture, Thomas Carlyle hailed the "man of letters" as the "most important modern person" (*Heroes* 155). The "true university," he added, "is a collection of books" (162). In 1852, John Henry Newman similarly upheld periodical reading as a "necessary accomplishment" for the educated man, recommending the "acquaintance with chemistry, and geology, and astronomy, and political economy, and modern history, and biography, and other branches of knowledge, which periodical literature ... diffuse[s] throughout the community" (128). Both Victorian sages recognized that in the nineteenth century, knowledge had become the purview of the press, the book an increasingly accessible source of information, and the periodical a major cultural force. Historians of print media concur, seeing the Victorian period (1837–1901) as heralding the advent of print media, the professional writer, and the mass market.

Carlyle (born in 1795) and Newman (born in 1801) witnessed a revolution in knowledge. At the time of their births, books and newspapers were prohibitively expensive. In 1815, a newspaper cost 7d. and a three-volume novel 31s. 6d., prices beyond the means of middle-class families whose income might average £5 per week (Altick 262, St Clair 194–95).[1] In 1818, a printer told a parliamentary inquiry that "books are a luxury, and the purchase of them has been confined to fewer people" (qtd. in Altick 260). Newspapers, printing paper, and advertisements were all taxed. During the lifetimes of Carlyle and Newman, reading became cheap. Britain witnessed the mechanization of printing; the abolition of newspaper, paper, and advertisement taxes; and widespread distribution of print matter by railroad. In 1854, Victorian publisher Charles Knight celebrated this "great era of cheapness": "It made the essayists. It made the magazines. It made the newspapers" (248).

The Reading Public

Just before this revolution in print production and distribution, a transformation had occurred in reading itself. At the end of the eighteenth century, the number of readers surged: Britain became a "reading nation" (St Clair 13–14). Personal reading habits evolved from the "intensive reading" of a few books for knowledge to "extensive reading" of many books for pleasure (10–13). William St Clair offers a possible explanation for this shift: in 1774, perpetual copyright was eliminated, thereby legalizing cheap reprints of works by established authors. Schools began to use anthologies of English poetry, drama, and prose.

---

1 d stands for pence, s for shilling. Before 1971, there were 12 pence in a shilling, 20 shillings in a pound, and 21 shillings in a guinea. A sovereign is a gold coin worth one pound sterling.

School reading surpassed church reading and, importantly, new readers came to associate books with pleasure. The Romantic period thus saw a "take-off in the nation's reading" (13).

Book historians tend to see this development as positive—"an assertion of freedom against lives that were otherwise all too often miserably constrained" (Bennett 252). However, early nineteenth-century churchmen, politicians, educators, and journalists debated the effects of this new literacy: would it eradicate ignorance? threaten national security? undermine the family? bind the nation? lead to undisciplined imaginations and morality? Farmer Hoskins, a character in Hannah More's *The Sunday School* (1797), voices such fears: "Of all the foolish inventions, and new-fangled devices to ruin the country, that of teaching the poor to read is the very worst" (qtd. in Brantlinger 6).

Such fears buttressed the taxes on newspapers, advertisements, and paper, duties designed to hamper the radical press by pricing reading matter out of the reach of the working class. In 1815, for example, the Stamp Tax added 4d. per copy to all publications; it therefore hit cheap publications the hardest, as a newspaper selling for 1d. was taxed at 400 per cent (St Clair 310). In the same year, the Paper Tax added 3d. to the cost of a pound of paper (Nevett 25). Finally, advertisements—a potential form of revenue for publishers—were taxed at 3s. 6d. each. These taxes drove up the costs of newspapers and books; they also led to small font and cramped formatting because printers crammed as much text as possible onto single sheets of paper. Publishers who refused to pay the Stamp Tax were punished harshly: in the 1820s and 1830s, more than 500 men were jailed for selling unstamped newspapers.

Too expensive for most individuals, newspapers were shared by groups of readers. In 1829, each newspaper was read roughly 30 times (Nevett 51–52). However, towards mid-century, an increasing

"Meeting for the Repeal of the Taxes on Knowledge, at St. Martin's-Hall, Long-Acre."
Illustrated London News (15 March 1851): 220.

number of reformers fought the so-called taxes on knowledge as a bar to working-class education and enlightenment. Under this pressure, the Stamp Tax was dropped to 1d. in 1836 and abolished in 1855. The Paper Tax was dropped to 1½ d. in 1836 (25) and finally abolished in 1861. Its abolition caused such a printing boom that printers ran out of type; they were forced to re-introduce the old-fashioned ſ (long s) that had remained unused for more than fifty years (Altick 357). The abolition of the taxes on knowledge coincided with the first mass readership: in 1864, the popular *London Journal* sold close to 500,000 copies per issue (358).

Important as the taxes on knowledge were, Charles Dickens thought the Window Tax worse. This tax was levied on the number of windows in a building that exceeded six small apertures; it thus effectively taxed daylight and air. Peaking between 1808 and 1823 (Altick 92), it led to bricked-up windows and dark interiors in many working-class homes at a time when newspapers were densely printed and tallow candles provided a weak light source. These conditions resulted in eyestrain and shortened reading hours; as Dickens wrote in 1850 of the poor, "They cannot read without light" (*Letters* 2:205). Alexander Somerville, a self-educated working man, described the Stamp and Window Taxes as "taxes on the light of intelligence and the light of the sun, both the light of heaven" (*Free Trade* 1:146). Somerville's working-class parents carried their own pane of glass from cottage to cottage, shedding light on the family's commitment to reading (Altick 245, Somerville *Autobiography* 2). Many poor readers read by firelight to save candles; the brothers William and Robert Chambers (later well-known publishers) read side by side to save on the cost of borrowing books, one holding the book, the other turning the pages (St Clair 394). Only in 1851 was the Window Tax finally abolished.

Industrialization and Print Production

During the Victorian period, the cost of print materials dropped as machine production, less expensive raw materials, and decreased taxes transformed the industry. At the beginning of the nineteenth century, almost all aspects of printing—papermaking, typesetting, printing, and binding—were done by hand. This changed in 1814 with the *Times*'s first printing by steam press, which more than tripled that newspaper's rate of production from 300 to 1,100 impressions per hour. By the late 1840s, cylinder presses increased the rate again to 12,000 per hour (Raven 326). In book production, the innovation of the durable metal stereotype plate (cast from moveable type) made reprints cheaper. These plates could be stored and reused, ending the era in which type had to be reset for a new print run.[2] Typesetting became mechanized: working by hand, typesetters could set 7,000 letters per day; in the 1850s, composing machines increased this rate to about 7,000 letters per hour (P. Gaskell 274), and from 1886, linotype machines allowed rates of about 10,000 letters per hour (277–78).

Industrialization also modernized and cheapened paper production. When the nineteenth century began, paper was made by hand from rags. Nineteenth-century publisher Knight imagined how the pages of his book might have started life as the "coarse blue shirt of the Italian sailor," the "tattered frock" of a Hungarian shepherd, or the "fustian and buckram, of a London tailor" (256). The cost of hand production plus the Paper Tax meant that paper was extremely valuable during this period. Pages from unsold books

---

[2] Many of the stereotype printing plates that had been stored from the Romantic and Victorian eras were melted down to make munitions for World War I.

"The Illustrated London News Printing Machine at the Inventions Exhibition."
Illustrated London News (8 Aug. 1885): 148.

were not discarded but reused as book bindings, trunk liners, and wrapping for baked goods. George Gordon Byron's letters refer implicitly to this widespread recycling of paper: he claimed to have read James Burgess's poem *Richard the First* on his trunk lining in Malta and mockingly recorded how he read William Wordsworth's remaindered poetry on pastry wrappings:

> Of Turdsworth the great Metaquizzical poet
> A man of great merit amongst those who know it
> Of whose works, as I told Moore last autumn at Mestri
> I owe all I know to my passion for *Pastry*.
> (Marchand 8:66)

Machine production of paper was introduced in France in the late 1790s; by 1900, more than 99 per cent of British paper was machine-made (Altick 262, P. Gaskell 228). Working by hand, one person could produce 60 to 100 pounds of paper per day; mechanization increased this output to 1,000 pounds per day. In the 1850s and 1860s, the raw materials for paper switched from expensive rags to wood pulp and grass. Another factor that lowered paper costs was the reduction of paper taxes, which were halved in 1837 and eliminated in 1861 (Altick 277–78, 306). Between 1846 and 1916, book production rose by 400 per cent while the average book price fell by 50 per cent (Raven 324). These transformations in print production coincided with population growth: Britain's population doubled from 8.9 million in 1801 to 17.9 million at mid-century, nearly doubling again to 32.5 million by 1901 (Altick 81). A mass reading market had been born.

At the same time, the emerging railway network enabled an efficient distribution system for newspapers and periodicals. Before the railway, London newspapers took days or weeks to reach outlying areas of Britain, as Victorian physician and writer Andrew Wynter recollected: "The *Times* in the north was fresh two days after date!" (304). By 1879, fast morning trains from London delivered newly printed papers to every station (Rubery 3). In 1848, bookseller W.H. Smith captured the railway's potential both as distribution network and point of sale (Feather 136). He negotiated the distribution of newspapers by railway as well as securing an exclusive contract for railway bookstalls where he sold cheap editions of popular fiction, which came to be known as "railway novels." Elizabeth Gaskell's *Cranford* (1851–53) neatly captures the link between the Industrial Revolution and the explosion of print media when Captain Brown, an avid reader of Dickens's *Pickwick Papers* (1836–37), dies while saving a child from being hit by a train:

> The Captain was a-reading [*The Pickwick Papers*] ... a-waiting for the down train; and there was a little lass as wanted to come to its mammy, and give its sister the slip, and came toddling across the line. And he looked up sudden at the sound of the train coming, and seed the child, and he darted on the line and cotched it up, and his foot slipped, and the train came over him in no time. (E. Gaskell 23)

This scene captures two inseparable threads of modernity from the 1830s: the railway and affordable print media.

Literacy and Education

The fact that Britain became a reading nation in the early nineteenth century does not mean that all people were literate. Historians have identified three kinds of readers in the era: those who read for pleasure, those who could sign their name or read a document for work, and those who listened to others reading aloud. The latter practice was widespread, revealing how many working-class people were functionally illiterate and—interestingly—how many of these illiterate people avidly consumed print materials, thereby counting as "readers" of a sort (Altick 35, Rubery 6). Early in the century, working-class education was ineffectual and sporadic, including "dame" schools (run in homes by teachers with little formal training), endowed schools (elementary schools funded by charity), Sunday schools (attended by working children), and adult night schools. No public funds were allocated to elementary education until 1833 and money was limited until the 1870s. Only after 1870, when the Forster Act made elementary education mandatory and set up school boards, did literacy rates climb steeply. David Livingstone, who read at his spinning jenny during 12-hour factory workdays, and Henry Stanley, who learned to read in the workhouse, thus beat the considerable odds against working-class literacy.

A major educational innovation were Mechanics' Institutes and Working Men's Colleges, schools for adults inspired by George Birkbeck, who taught science classes for artisans in the first years of the century. Such institutions emphasized lifelong learning for working people, the idea that "[w]orking and learning" could walk "hand in hand" (Maurice 53). Many high-profile authors lectured at these institutions, among them Dickens, Samuel Taylor Coleridge, William Hazlitt, William Morris, D.G. Rossetti, William Gaskell, F.D. Maurice, Ralph Waldo Emerson, Lydia Becker, and John Ruskin. Others learned there, including Walter Henry Bates and Alfred Russel Wallace, the latter later giving lectures at Mechanics' Institutes himself.

After mid-century, especially after the 1870 Education Act, literacy rates in England surged. Estimates of literacy are rough, however, because such information is based on whether people signed their names on the marriage register. Estimates therefore represent only the 90 per cent of the population that got married, and measure those people's ability to write only at the time of marriage—that is, mostly in their twenties, some fifteen years after leaving school (Weedon 50). Further, the signatures tell us how many people could sign their name, not how many could write a letter or read a book. Rough as it is, however, this information indicates that literacy rates shot up after mid-century, from 67 per cent of men and 51 per cent of women in 1841 to 97 per cent of men and 96.8 per cent of women in 1900. The same period also saw multiple printing systems for blind readers, including embossed text and Braille, as well as societies for teaching blind people how to read (Warne). Not only had illiteracy almost vanished, but the literacy gap between men and women had almost closed (Heyck 25; see also Webb, Altick).

The Mass Market

Together with new methods of production and distribution, this new readership created a mass market for print media—one in which large sales of cheap books could turn a profit. In the eighteenth century, publishers produced small print runs for a limited number of wealthy readers. They did not subsequently print cheaper versions of the same book, indicating that they saw no market for such editions. In the Romantic period, too, book prices for new works were extremely high. The long poem, for example, typically sold first in expensive and large quarto format for 25s. or more. After the initial print run, a popular poem would be reissued in the cheaper, smaller octavo format, for 10s. or so. Such prices daunted even the rich: in 1812, for example, Lord Dudley wrote that he would not buy Walter Scott's *The Lord of the Isles* in quarto format for 42s. but would wait for the cheaper octavo edition at 14s. (St Clair 201). In 1825, Scott's publisher, Archibald Constable, recognized that the public would buy books if they were priced affordably: "twelve volumes in the year ... so good that millions must wish to have them, and so cheap that every butcher's callant may have them, if he pleases to let me tax him sixpence a-week!" (qtd. in Lockhart 546). Religious and educational organizations also saw the potential of the new mass market, hoping to reach out to working-class readers with books at unprecedentedly low prices. In 1827, the Society for the Diffusion of Useful Knowledge began publishing its *Library of Useful Knowledge* at 6d. per 32-page part (Altick 269).

However, books remained beyond the means of the working class until well after mid-century. Most working-class homes had a shelf of well-loved books, often limited to the Bible and prayer books, a few chapbooks, and favourites such as Daniel Defoe's *Robinson Crusoe* (1719) and John Bunyan's *Pilgrim's Progress* (1678). In a Kent farming parish in the 1830s, only four out of 51 families owned books besides the Bible, prayer books, and hymnals (Altick 90). Contemporary works were rare in this market because cheap booksellers focused on classics and eighteenth-century materials that were out of copyright and therefore less expensive to reproduce. Wordsworth wrote about leech gatherers and shepherds, but people of such means would not have had access to his poetry. When George Eliot, in *Adam Bede* (1859), put a copy of *Lyrical Ballads* (1798) in the hands of a turn-of-the-century carpenter, she overestimated the penetration of contemporary literature into workers' homes (St Clair 201, 407). As book historian James Raven summarizes, "Many of the writers experienced by working-class readers were dead and unfashionable" (348). Even the middle class found books too expensive to collect in large quantities. Publisher John

Murray noted that in times of financial stress, "the first expense to be curtailed is the purchase of books. That is done (without any outward display of economy) rather than laying down a carriage or dismissing servants" (qtd. in Raven 347).

The high price of books made libraries very important. In 1800, there were 1,000 circulating (subscription) libraries in Great Britain as well as book clubs and reading societies, which shared costs by passing books among members (St Clair 237, 242–47). Starting in 1840, Charles Mudie built an enormous network of circulating libraries, allowing readers to borrow an unlimited number of volumes for an annual fee of one guinea. He bought books in bulk from publishers and stocked new bestsellers as well as classics. He used his business power to control format: he supported the "triple-decker" (three-volume) novel because it allowed him to circulate volumes among more patrons at a time than the single-volume format. As an evangelical, he also sought to control literary content and refused to buy books that violated his sense of middle-class family mores. Because Mudie ordered books in large quantities, sometimes snapping up entire print runs, publishers could not afford to disregard his demands. The growth of free public libraries (established by the 1850 Public Libraries Act) and the fall of the triple-decker led to the fading of Mudie's influence at the century's end, but his force was felt in fiction publishing for much of Victoria's reign.

Newspapers and Periodicals

The nineteenth century inaugurated the reading nation, the book as mass medium, and the age of the newspaper. When the century began, no newspaper commanded a circulation over 5,000: the *Times* printed 2,500 to 3,000 copies, the *Morning Chronicle* 1,500 to 2,000, and the *Morning Post* 1,000 (Nevett 41). Most newspapers published weekly and many were affiliated with specific political parties (Rubery 5). As already mentioned, the taxes on knowledge cramped newspaper layout and put newspaper reading beyond the financial reach of the working and lower middle classes. The elimination of paper, stamp, and advertisement taxes revolutionized the newspaper business and burgeoning revenue from advertisements (after the elimination of the Advertisement Tax in 1853) freed newspapers from partisanship. Between 1856 and 1885, 420 newspaper companies were formed (Lee 80). By 1901, the *Daily Mail* reached almost a million readers (Rubery 6).

Freed from taxes, newspapers became more generous in layout: their readers enjoyed more white space, better fonts, shorter paragraphs, larger headlines, and greater use of illustrations. With its new mass circulation, the newspaper wielded increasing political and cultural clout. As Carlyle remarked in 1842, "the Printing Press is the only, or by far the chief, Pulpit in these days" (*Letters* 259). Frances Power Cobbe, who wrote leaders for the *Echo*, used the newspaper to advocate for feminist causes such as divorce; John Stuart Mill and Harriet Taylor drew attention to spousal abuse by writing letters to the *Morning Chronicle*. The *Times*'s 1854 revelations of hospital conditions in the Crimea, W.T. Stead's 1885 sensational exposé of underage prostitution in London in the *Pall Mall Gazette*, and the marriage debate in the *Daily Telegraph* following Mona Caird's 1888 *Westminster Review* essay on "Marriage" all illustrate the press's power to inspire debate and influence public policy. Newspaper discourse also influenced fiction, as sensation novels borrowed plots from the press, novels imitated documents found in newspaper accounts of trials, and novels featured journalists as protagonists. Not everyone approved of the press's new power, however: as Anthony Trollope complained in 1855, "The newspaper Press is now the rival of the House of Commons" (*New Zealander* 106).

"Newsboys with Latest Accounts of the Prince of Wales." *Illustrated London News* (23 Dec. 1871): 613.

The print explosion also encompassed weekly, monthly, and quarterly periodicals geared for the reading nation's various interests. Between 1824 and 1900, British periodicals proliferated to over 50,000 in number, catering to every taste and budget. They included trade journals such as the *Lancet*, satirical journals such as *Punch*, miscellanies such as the *Penny Magazine* and *Chambers' Edinburgh Journal*, religious journals such as *Good Words*, children's journals such as the *Boy's Own* and *Girl's Own*, women's journals such as *Bow Bells*, literary journals such as the *Cornhill* and *Strand*, and even pornographic journals such as *Peeping Tom* and *Fast Man*. Many Victorian works that are now read and studied in book form originated in periodicals and newspapers: Carlyle's *Sartor Resartus* (1833–34) in *Fraser's*, Henry Mayhew's *London Labour and the London Poor* (1851) in the *Morning Chronicle*, Ruskin's *Unto this Last* (1860) and Matthew Arnold's *Culture and Anarchy* (1869) in the *Cornhill*, Eliot's *Scenes of Clerical Life* (1857) in *Blackwood's Magazine*, and Dickens's *A Tale of Two Cities* (1859) in *All the Year Round*, which he edited. Periodical publication shaped Victorian literature by moulding the novel into serial parts and the essay into compact form, as well as by enabling authors and editors to respond to public opinion of a work as it unfolded.

Not only was nineteenth-century print a mass-market phenomenon, it was also an international one. Because of the very few English-language printers and publishers in the colonies, the British press reached out to Australasia, North America, India, and South Africa (Weedon 38). Between 1828 and 1900, the value of publications exported to British colonies and the United States increased from roughly £35,800 to £1,089,000. Emily Eden's account of reading Dickens's *Pickwick Papers* (1836–37) during her Indian travels in 1837 gives us a glimpse of a reader enjoying British literature in the colonies:

> I wish you would read over again that account of Winkle and the horse which will not go on— "Poor fellow! good old horse!"—and Pickwick saying, "It is like a dream, a horrid dream, to go about all day with a horrid horse that we cannot get rid of." That book makes me laugh till I cry, when I am sitting quite by myself.—There! I thought so. We are aground, and the other steamer is going flourishing by, in grinning delight. (7–8)

For writers included in this anthology, the nineteenth century's print explosion made their careers possible. Authorship was freed from patronage and became a means of earning a respectable living and maintaining a professional identity.[3] Writing in his *Autobiography* (1883), Trollope unabashedly articulated the commercial dimensions of authorship: "In our own century what literary names stand higher than those of Byron, Tennyson, Scott, Dickens, Macaulay, and Carlyle? And I think I may say that none of those great men neglected the pecuniary result of their labours.... Brains that are unbought will never serve the public much" (106–07). Consolidating their professional identity, authors fought for British copyright (under the Copyright Acts of 1814 and 1842) and international copyright (under the Berne Convention of 1886 and the Chace Act of 1891) and formed associations such as the Society of Authors (1884).

Gender

Women participated actively in every aspect of print media, from book binding and typesetting (where they represented 20 per cent of the skilled workforce) to printing. They ran presses (Emily Faithfull), illustrated books (Helen Allingham), served as editors (Eliot, M.E. Braddon, and L.T. Meade), vetted novels (Geraldine Jewsbury), and worked as publishers (Isabella Beeton) and journalists (Cobbe). The bestselling English-language novel of the century, *Uncle Tom's Cabin* (1852), was written by a woman, Harriet Beecher Stowe. While there was a separate feminist press (for example, the Victoria Press, founded by the Langham Place Group), many women published in mainstream media. To study the prose of the Victorian period without including their work is to get merely a partial view of nineteenth-century print culture. This anthology features their voices, including Cobbe's response to Leslie Stephen's agnosticism and Elizabeth Garrett Anderson's riposte to Henry Maudsley's position on the education of women.

Despite women's professional participation in the press, their roles as readers provoked anxiety throughout the Victorian period. Women readers were perceived as impressionable, emotional, and vulnerable to the influence of corrupting books (Flint 4). Byron's poems were deemed too provocative—although women's commonplace books indicate that they read his works anyway (St Clair 227)—and sensation fiction too morally dangerous. Writing in 1859, W.R. Greg expressed his concerns that women readers were more "impressionable" than men, their "feelings are more easily aroused," and their "estimates are more easily influenced" (qtd. in Flint 4). On the other side, authors such as

---

3   For much of the century, however, journals and newspapers published without bylines, meaning that authorship was veiled; literary historians have worked hard to identify authorship for resources such as *The Wellesley Index to Victorian Periodicals* by using authors' and publishers' records.

Matthew Arnold and George Henry Lewes argued that "women's reading practices [constituted] ... a vital indicator of a nation's level of cultural development" (Phegley 109). Journals such as the *Girl's Own Paper* promoted girls' reading by running essay competitions on literary subjects; under Meade's editorship, *Atalanta* (1887–98) ran a Scholarship and Reading Union to promote active literary study by "girl" readers (whose ages ranged into their thirties). Interestingly, an 1881 list of books suitable for a girl's library included many of this anthology's authors: Ruskin, Stephen, Mary Somerville, Herbert Spencer, and Charles Darwin.

Conclusion

From hand-made to machine-produced paper, hand- to steam-driven cylinder presses, from an elite readership to a reading nation, from patronage to the professionalization of authorship, the nineteenth century witnessed a wholesale transformation of print culture. Reading brought to Victorian homes a revolution in knowledge. It introduced visions of unknown peoples, landscapes, and wildlife; it engaged intellectually with contemporary science, religion, and politics; it inspired changes both

"Arrival of the Illustrated Papers" (detail). *Illustrated London News* (30 Jan. 1897): 155.

personal and social. Most importantly, perhaps, reading permitted Victorians to imagine worlds and consciousnesses beyond their own. When, in 1840, Carlyle recognized the man of letters as an emergent hero of culture, he rightly predicted the new power of the author, the newspaper, and the book. Six decades later, Walter Besant, prime mover in the Society of Authors, looked back on this radical change:

> The popular and successful writer of the day may look round him with a telescope and see ... a boundless ocean of faces, eager faces, listening faces, faces played upon by emotions awakened by his own words. That is the main difference between the man of letters of 1750—or him of 1830—and the man of letters of the present day. So great—of such importance—is the enormous revolution that has been brought about during the past fifty years. (31)

Works Cited and Further Reading

Altick, Richard D. *The English Common Reader: A Social History of the Mass Reading Public*. Chicago: U of Chicago P, 1957. Print.

Bennett, Scott. "Revolutions in Thought: Serial Publication and the Mass Market for Reading." *The Victorian Periodical Press: Samplings and Soundings*. Ed. Joanne Shattock and Michael Wolff. Leicester: Leicester UP, 1982. 225–60. Print.

Besant, Walter. *The Pen and the Book*. London: Thomas Burleigh, 1899. Print.

Brantlinger, Patrick. *The Reading Lesson: The Threat of Mass Literacy in Nineteenth-Century British Fiction*. Bloomington: Indiana UP, 1998. Print.

Carlyle, Thomas. *On Heroes, Hero-Worship, and the Heroic in History*. London: Chapman and Hall, 1901. Print.

———. *Letters of Thomas Carlyle to John Stuart Mill, John Sterling and Robert Browning*. Ed. Alexander Carlyle. London: T. Fisher Unwin, 1923. Print.

Dickens, Charles. *The Letters of Charles Dickens*. Ed. Walter Dexter. Vol. 2. Bloomsbury: Nonesuch, 1938. Print.

Eden, Emily. *"Up the Country": Letters Written to Her Sister from the Upper Provinces of India*. Vol. 1. London: Richard Bentley, 1866. Print.

Feather, John. *A History of British Publishing*. London: Routledge, 1988. Print.

Flint, Kate. *The Woman Reader 1837–1914*. Oxford: Clarendon, 1993. Print.

Fredeman, William E. "Emily Faithfull and the Victoria Press: An Experiment in Sociological Biography." *The Library* 5th ser. 19.2 (1974): 139–64. Print.

Gaskell, Elizabeth. *Cranford*. Ed. Patricia Ingham. Harmondsworth: Penguin, 2005. Print.

Gaskell, Philip. *A New Introduction to Bibliography*. New Castle, DE: Oak Knoll, 1995. Print.

Heyck, T.W. *The Transformation of Intellectual Life in Victorian England*. London: Croom Helm, 1982. Print.

Houghton, Walter. "Periodical Literature and the Articulate Classes." *The Victorian Periodical Press: Samplings and Soundings*. Ed. Joanne Shattock and Michael Wolff. Leicester: Leicester UP, 1982. 3–28. Print.

Knight, Charles. *The Old Printer and the Modern Press*. London: John Murray, 1854. Print.

Lee, Alan J. *The Origins of the Popular Press in England, 1885–1914*. London: Croom Helm, 1976. Print.

Lockhart, J.G. *Memoirs of the Life of Sir Walter Scott, Bart*. Edinburgh: Adam and Charles Black, 1852. Print.

Marchand, Leslie A. *Born for Opposition: Byron's Letters and Journals*. Vol. 8. London: John Murray, 1978. Print.

Maurice, Frederick Denison. *Learning and Working: Six Lectures Delivered in Willis's Rooms, London, in June and July, 1854*. Cambridge: MacMillan, 1855. Print.

Nevett, T.R. *Advertising in Britain: A History*. London: Heinemann, 1982. Print.

Newman, John Henry. *The Idea of a University*. Ed. I.T. Ker. London: Oxford UP, 1976. Print.

Phegley, Jennifer. "'I Should No More Think of Dictating What Kinds of Books She Should Read': Images of Woman Readers in Victorian Family Literary Magazines." *Literary Figures and Cultural Icons from the Victorian Age to the Present*. Ed. Janet Badia and Jennifer Phegley. Toronto: U of Toronto P, 2005. 105–28. Print.

Raven, James. *The Business of Books: Booksellers and the English Book Trade 1450–1850*. New Haven: Yale UP, 2007. Print.

Robinson, Solveig. "'Amazed at Our Success': The Langham Place Editors and the Emergence of a Feminist Critical Tradition." *Victorian Periodicals Review* 29.2 (1996): 159–72. Print.

Rose, Jonathan. *The Intellectual Life of the British Working Classes*. New Haven: Yale UP, 2002. Print.

Rubery, Matthew. *The Novelty of Newspapers: Victorian Fiction after the Invention of the News*. Oxford: Oxford UP, 2009. Print.

Somerville, Alexander. *The Autobiography of a Working Man*. Ed. John Carswell. London: Turnstile, 1951. Print.

——. *Free Trade and the League: A Biographic History of the Pioneers of Freedom of Opinion, Commercial Enterprise, and Civilization, in Britain, from the Times of Serfdom to the Age of Free Trade in Manufactures, Food, and Navigation*. Manchester: James Ainsworth, 1853. Print.

St Clair, William. *The Reading Nation in the Romantic Period*. Cambridge: Cambridge UP, 2004. Print.

Trollope, Anthony. *An Autobiography*. London: Oxford UP, 1950. Print.

——. *The New Zealander*. Ed. N. John Hall. Oxford: Clarendon, 1972. Print.

Warne, Vanessa. "'So That the Sense of Touch May Supply the Want of Sight': Blind Reading and Nineteenth-Century British Print Culture." *Image, Sound and Touch in the Nineteenth Century*. Ed. Colette Colligan and Margaret Linley. Surrey: Ashgate, 2011. 43–64. Print.

Webb, R.K. *The British Working Class Reader 1780–1848: Literacy and Social Tension*. New York: Augustus M. Kelly, 1971. Print.

Weedon, Alexis. *Victorian Publishing: The Economics of Book Production for a Mass Market*. Aldershot: Ashgate, 2003. Print.

Wynter, Andrew. *Our Social Bees; or, Pictures of Town and Country Life and Other Papers*. 9th ed. London: Robert Hardwick, 1867. Print.

LIFE WRITING

Introduction
David Amigoni

A considerable expenditure of intellectual and affective energy was devoted to writing and reading about lives throughout the Victorian period and, more broadly, during the nineteenth century. A vibrant self-reflectiveness emerged in early nineteenth-century canonical works, from the poetry of William Wordsworth to the literary criticism of Samuel Taylor Coleridge. Poems such as Wordsworth's "Tintern Abbey" (1798) expressed a complex relationship between the dimensions of present, past, and the inner life of the imagination; Coleridge's *Biographia Literaria* (1817) elaborated acts of criticism that were founded upon such inward acts of self-consciousness. And yet, such reflectiveness had by no means been a dominant feature of the early nineteenth century. In this earlier period, life writing (usually biographies) set about recording the exemplary lives of notables, celebrities, statesmen, and military heroes. One of the great biographical publication successes of this period was Robert Southey's *Life of Nelson* (1813), which commemorated the hero of Trafalgar and was intended as a manual for young readers. Such exemplary life writing formed a central component of an expanding print culture with an educative mission. Steam publication could produce cheap if ephemeral printed material, and middle-class initiatives to organize working-class reading, such as the *Penny Magazine*, made exemplary lives a staple of their output.

As working-class readers became writers, they were able to both adopt the exemplary model and recall literature as the source of new expressions of inwardness. In the working-class Alexander Somerville's account of his early nineteenth-century youth, the pursuit of reading produces a deep, sensuous impression that stimulates his inner life. Somerville recalls a sense of "intellectual ecstacy" derived from hearing stories, as well as "sensations of pleasure" (86, 88) to which encounters with expensive, older, and venerated printed materials gave rise (he compares the tattered leaves of a well-read book to a valuable banknote). By 1848, readers would have recognized that Somerville was writing an autobiography (Southey was important not only for *Life of Nelson* but for making this term current, given that he was the first to use it positively in 1809). Through such writing, Somerville wove important connections between a life lived in a fast-moving, modernizing, and politically turbulent century and the articulation of an inner life. In fact, Somerville's life constitutes an exemplary account of the way in which the resources that nourish inner life can be turned outwards: Somerville made his skill of reading a public one by reading aloud to illiterate co-workers as they ate their meals in the fields.

John Stuart Mill's *Autobiography* has become one of the canonical texts of Victorian autobiography because it narrates the discovery of just such an inner life. Published posthumously in 1873, Mill's narrative describes a powerfully distinctive life formed out of educational experimentation, political and intellectual activism, and a psychological breakdown (of which more in due course). It also records (in the extract reproduced here) the poetical allure of his friend Thomas Carlyle, one of the most important figures in the history of Victorian life writing. Carlyle became an important biographer in his own right, of Oliver Cromwell and Frederick the Great. In 1842, he also delivered a series of lectures *On Heroes, Hero-Worship, and the Heroic in History*. One of those lectures was "The Hero as Man of Letters." While the military hero was an established figure in the national pantheon, Carlyle helped early nineteenth-century culture to enshrine a new hero in the author. One of Carlyle's "heroic exemplars" was the eighteenth-century author and critic Samuel Johnson, whose manner of speaking, acting, and moralizing had been brought vividly to public attention by his biography written by Boswell, published originally in 1791, and by J.W. Croker's new edition of the work, published (and reviewed by Carlyle) in the watershed decade of the 1830s. Despite Carlyle's efforts, however, as authors went on to write autobiographically about their calling, they seldom emerged as heroic in the Carlylean sense. The example of Anthony Trollope, reproduced here, is a good example of dogged professionalism, with writing fitted into the spaces between other professional commitments (in Trollope's case, his work for the Post Office) and undertaken while travelling on the train. Nonetheless, Carlyle fashioned authors and men of letters as modern pilgrims without secure spiritual foundations, as in his biography of John Sterling (1851): in the Victorian period, they and the discourses that they fashioned and had printed for public consumption guided culture as never before.

There is thus a connection between Carlyle's construction of "letters" as a source of heroic questing and the function that poetry performs in John Stuart Mill's autobiography. Mill's autobiography is self-consciously written as a document about changing sensibilities between the eighteenth and the nineteenth centuries. Mill was the leading English philosopher of his day. He had been intensively educated in the early years of the nineteenth century by his father, James Mill, a man shaped by the eighteenth-century rational, secular Enlightenment and the Utilitarian philosophies of Jeremy Bentham. Mill's autobiography can be read as a critique of the doctrine of association, the dominant materialist theory of sensation, mind, and action, which held that the seeking of pleasure and avoidance of pain provided the key to individual motivation, morality, and the organization of a reformed polity. Mill was educated from a very young age to become the public intellectual who would advance the reformist Utilitarian cause. And yet, his account of his breakdown (narrated in detail in the passage extracted here) marks the moment at which inner needs conflicted with this program of action: Mill cannot satisfy himself that if all his father's Benthamite goals of reform were to be achieved, the "dull state of nerves" (133) crippling his emotional state would dissipate. In this crisis, Mill discovers that reading involves him in modes of sympathetic identification and displacement that break his emotional numbness. Indeed, it is his reading of Wordsworth's poetry—Wordsworth was only truly recognized as a canonical author by the early Victorians during the 1830s and 1840s—that leads Mill to value "poetry ... as [an instrument] of human culture" (144) that would shape and develop bodily sensations into complex processes of mental cognition. John Ruskin's *Praeterita* (1885-89), another narrative written in the late nineteenth century about a life formed in its early decades, accords a comparable role to the criticism of the visual arts and architecture as components of an aesthetic education.

It is important to read Victorian texts of self-writing as complex contributions to a nineteenth-century debate about culture that was traversed by discourses of science, religiosity, secularism, and aesthetics; all of these were, in turn, inflected by discourses of gender. Thus, Harriet Martineau was an important woman philosopher, social scientist, and nascent ethnographer. As we see in the extract from her autobiography reproduced here, Martineau wrote her life story in the context of an acute sense of her impending death

Frederick Waddy, "Anthony Trollope." *Cartoon Portraits and Biographical Sketches of Men of the Day* (London: Tinsley, 1873). Facing 68.

Frederick Waddy, "John Ruskin." *Cartoon Portraits and Biographical Sketches of Men of the Day* (London: Tinsley, 1873). Facing 108.

(in reality, Martineau lived another 20 years beyond the writing of her autobiography). Given Martineau's atheism, the work thus becomes a guide to a morally engaged and dignified secular death. The Wordsworths again become exemplary figures here—Martineau was their neighbour in Ambleside—but, in this instance, Martineau identifies not the poetical power of William Wordsworth but instead his wife Mary's domestic skill and the form of moral sociability that follows from it as a source for emulation. Gendered discourses of domesticity could figure ambivalently as impediments to a career in writing in biographies of women writers, as is the case of Elizabeth Gaskell's *Life of Charlotte Brontë* (1857): Gaskell famously reproduces a letter from Robert Southey advising Brontë to abandon her ambition to write and return to domestic tasks. By contrast, in Martineau's autobiography, written self-consciously by a woman of letters, such discourses could figure powerfully and positively for women as sources of social skilfulness and imaginative writing.

Many narratives of self-development, tracing a public career and the acquisition of cultural status, were pre-inscribed by structures of middle-class and aristocratic masculine advantage—namely public schools, universities, and arenas of professional association such as the law, the church, and politics. Thus, even while the Catholic convert John Henry Newman wrote a seemingly defensive "apology" for his religious change of heart of 1845 in his *Apologia pro Vita Sua* (1864) in response to the attack on his intellectual integrity and manliness by Charles Kingsley, Newman could narrate his story of self-development from Anglican religious leader to Catholic convert against the backdrop of universities and the church as arenas of masculine belonging and homosocial disputation. The intense theological and historical education that he had acquired could make the narrative of conversion at once painful and testing, yet also developmentally seamless.

For the younger Beatrice Webb in *My Apprenticeship* (1926), her narrative of self-development was appropriated from the tradition of Victorian intellectual and spiritual autobiography shaped by Newman and others; however, the channels through which this highly intelligent, aspirant middle-class woman worked to become a social investigator were disjointed by the absence, for women, of formal educational opportunities and established patterns of career development. Webb's narrative of self-development is suspended between the tradition of the Victorian man of letters and that of the working-class autodidact. Developed through experiments in observation and writing modelled on Victorian realist fiction, Webb's vocation is given shape by work on Charles Booth's study of poverty, but also by a journey in disguise into the heart of a working-class community in Bacup, Lancashire, a journey narrated as an ethnographic encounter.

In the later part of the nineteenth century, ethnography was one of the discourses of development that filtered into life writing as a way of representing the emergence and growth of the self. Edmund Gosse's *Father and Son* (1907) dramatizes (some would say over-dramatizes) one of the great Victorian intellectual confrontations between evolutionary science and religion. In the extract provided here, Gosse recalls the dramatic effect that the public emergence of Darwin's theory of evolution had on his father, Philip Henry Gosse, a professional naturalist and a devout member of a dissenting Protestant church. Gosse's account of his "'natural magic' practices" as a "savage" child in Devon (114) is also marked by naturalistic ethnographic discourses—shaped by anthropologists such as E.B. Tylor and J.G. Frazer—that constructed a narrative between "savage" stages of the pre-civilized world (conceived as humanity's childhood) and civilization as a mature developmental outcome. Yet Gosse's savage state of childhood is also used to narrate a deeply aesthetic sense of loss: Oddicombe Beach in Devon in the late 1850s is seen by Gosse as very different to the way in which it appears in "these twentieth-century days" when modernizing has rendered "wild beauty ineffectual" (113). Gosse's *Father and Son* took the Victorian life-writing tradition in new directions: it treated relations between parents and children in ways that challenged the reverence that characterized Victorian writing (as practised by Mill, for example) and thus caught the mood of the Edwardian beginning to the new century. Moreover, many readers have been struck positively by the fictive quality of the self, recognizable from traditions of Victorian fiction, which Gosse narrates in the text that he presents as a factual document. Gosse's self is made out of aesthetic impulses, a fiction designed self-consciously to serve an aesthetic drive to self-definition.

To that extent, Gosse's self-writing emerged out of *fin-de-siècle* aestheticism. Oscar Wilde's remarkable autobiographical letter, *De Profundis*, was written in 1897 to his lover Lord Alfred Douglas from Reading Gaol (now H.M. Prison Reading), where Wilde was serving time with hard labour after his conviction for "indecent" (homosexual) acts. This letter is itself a deeply eloquent act of aesthetic self-reckoning as it draws on the languages of development and evolution to produce a self in humility. Wilde's new self evolves out of a previous, flamboyant public self that had been publicly humiliated during his trial for indecency. In his claim that shadow also belongs among the fruits of the world, and allusions to "sack-cloth" and "ashes" (85), Wilde remakes himself from Christian traditions of rhetoric and, indeed, provides the reader with a *tour de force* through many of the languages of self-making that had contributed to Victorian autobiographical traditions. *De Profundis* asserts the power of the inner life to resist the imposition of an identity (in Wilde's case that of the "sodomite") by external authority, legality, and power relations.

At the same time, Wilde's text impels us to recognize pervading contexts of power relations in the framing of all acts of self-writing, from Annie Besant's account of the legal assault on her identity as a mother as she sought to secure a legitimate place for a text about birth control in the public domain to William Dodd's account of himself as a factory child labourer, defined by Victorian labour discipline. Dodd's text does not convey a rich sense of inner life, but the opportunity that Dodd grasped was, nonetheless, literacy's power to create the self that was needed for that occasion through the medium of print.

Works Cited and Further Reading

Amigoni, David, ed. *Life Writing and Victorian Culture*. Aldershot and Vermont: Ashgate, 2006. Print.
"Autobiography." *Oxford English Dictionary*. Oxford UP, 2011. Web.
Boswell, James. *Life of Johnson*. Ed. R.W. Chapman. Oxford: Oxford UP, 1980. Print.
Broughton, Trev Lynn. *Men of Letters, Reading Lives: Masculinity and Literary Auto/Biography in the Late Victorian Period*. London: Routledge, 1999. Print.
Carlyle, Thomas. *Works*. Ed. H.D. Traill. 30 vols. London: Chapman and Hall, 1896–99. Print.
Coleridge, Samuel Taylor. *Biographia Literaria*. London: J.M. Dent, 1906. Print.
Danahay, Martin A. *A Community of One: Masculine Autobiography and Autonomy in Nineteenth-Century Britain*. Albany: SUNY P, 1993. Print.
Gagnier, Regenia. *Subjectivities: A History of Self-Representation in Britain, 1832–1920*. New York: Oxford UP, 1991. Print.
Gaskell, Elizabeth. *Life of Charlotte Brontë*. Ed. Angus Easson. Oxford: Oxford UP, 1996. Print.
Gosse, Edmund. *Father and Son: A Study of Two Temperaments*. London: William Heinemann, 1912. Print.
Mill, John Stuart. *Autobiography*. London: Longmans, Green, Reader, and Dyer, 1873. Print.

Newman, John Henry. *Apologia pro Vita Sua*. London: J.M. Dent, 1912. Print.
Peterson, Linda H. *Traditions of Victorian Women's Autobiography: The Poetics and Politics of Life Writing*. Charlottesville: UP of Virginia, 1999. Print.
Somerville, Alexander. *The Autobiography of a Working Man*. London: Charles Gilpin, 1848. Print.
Southey, Robert. *Life of Horatio, Lord Nelson*. London: J.M. Dent, 1906. Print.
Vincent, David. *Bread, Knowledge and Freedom: A Study of Victorian Working-Class Autobiography*. London: Europa, 1979. Print.
Wilde, Oscar. *De Profundis*. New York and London: G.P. Putnam's Sons, 1905.
Wordsworth, William. *Poetical Works*. Ed. Thomas Hutchinson and Ernest de Selincourt. Rev. ed., 1936. Oxford: Oxford UP, 1981. Print.

William Dodd

from *A Narrative of the Experience and Sufferings of William Dodd, A Factory Cripple* (1841)

Born into a poor family, William Dodd (b. 1804) worked as a card-maker at age five, switching to a textile factory where he worked up to 18 hours daily and became disabled by joint pain. At 16, Dodd became an overseer, verifying the ages of child factory workers; he also undertook clerical work, having learned reading and writing in evening classes. When his joint pain became unbearable, doctors amputated his right arm. Dodd wrote about his experiences as a child worker; Lord Ashley arranged publication in 1841 and employed him to gather information about children's conditions in textile factories, published as *The Factory System: Illustrated* (1842). Both books provoked controversy. When MP John Bright impugned Dodd's character in the House of Commons, Ashley terminated his employment, and Dodd emigrated to the US.

This passage provides a vivid first-hand account of factory labour and its debilitating effects, suggesting the importance of and barriers to working-class literacy.

Dear Reader,—I wish it to be distinctly and clearly understood, that, in laying before you the following sheets, I am not actuated by any motive of ill-feeling to any party with whom I have formerly been connected; on the contrary, I have a personal respect for some of my former masters, and am convinced that, had they been in any other line of life, they would have shone forth as ornaments to the age in which they lived; but having witnessed the efforts of some writers (who can know nothing of the factories by experience) to mislead the minds of the public upon a subject of so much importance, I feel it to be my duty to give to the world a fair and impartial account of the working of the factory system, as I have found it in twenty-five years' experience....

Of four children in our family, I was the only boy; and we were all at different periods, as we could meet with employers, sent to work in the factories. My eldest sister was ten years of age before she went; consequently, she was, in a manner, out of harm's way, her bones having become firmer and stronger than ours, and capable of withstanding the hardships to which she was exposed much better than we could: but her services soon became more valuable in another line of industry. My second sister went at the age of seven years, and, like myself, has been made a cripple for life, and doomed to end her days in the factories or workhouse. My youngest sister also went early, but was obliged to be taken away, like many more, the work being too hard for her! although she afterwards stood a very hard service.

I was born on the 18th of June, 1804; and in the latter part of 1809, being then turned of five years of age, I was put to work at card-making,[1] and about a year after I was sent, with my sisters, to the factories. I was then a fine, strong, healthy, hardy boy, straight in every limb, and remarkably stout and active....

From six to fourteen years of age, I went through a series of uninterrupted, unmitigated suffering, such as very rarely falls to the lot of mortals so early in life, except to those situated as I was, and such as I could not have withstood, had I not been strong, and of a good constitution.

My first place in the factories was that of piecer, or the lowest situation.... It is in this situation of piecer that the greatest number of cripples are made from over-exertion.

The duties of the piecer will not be clearly understood by the reader, unless he is previously made acquainted with the machine for spinning woollen yarn, called a *Billy*.... A billy, then, is a machine somewhat similar in form to the letter H, one side being stationary, and the other moveable, and capable of being pushed close in under the stationary part, almost like the drawer of a side table; the moveable part, or carriage, runs backwards and forwards, by means of six iron wheels, upon three iron rails, as a carriage on a railroad. In this carriage are the spindles, from 70 to 100 in number, all turned by one wheel, which is in the care of the spinner. When the spinner brings the carriage close up under the fixed part of the machine, he is able, by a contrivance for that purpose to obtain a certain length of carding[2] for each spindle, say 10 or 12 inches, which he draws back, and spins into yarn; this done, he winds the yarn round the spindles, brings the carriage close up as before, and again obtains a fresh supply of cardings.... On the top of the cardings, and immediately over the upper roller, runs the billy-roller—the dreaded instrument of punishment for the children. This roller is very easily taken out and put in its place, and is at the full command of the spinner, and, being of great length, it is scarcely possible for the piecer to get out of the way, should the spinner think proper to give him a knock. On these coarse canvas cloths the piecer pieces the ends of the cardings, and prepares them for the spinner.

The cardings are strips of wool 27 inches long, and of equal thickness throughout (generally about as thick as a lady's finger,) except about 2 inches at each end, which are smaller, in order that when two ends are laid one over the other, and rubbed together with the piecer's flat hand, the piecing may not be thicker than any other part of the carding.

These cardings are taken up by the piecer in his left hand, about 20 at a time. He holds them in nearly the same manner as a joiner[3] would hold a bunch of ornamental shavings for a parlour fire-place, about

---

1   Carding involved separating and mixing fibres before spinning; card-making was the process of creating the carding tool (consisting of a leather sheet punched with thousands of holes into which short wire lengths were inserted). The wires and leather were generally prepared by men, while women and children often inserted the wires into the holes.
2   Combed fibres.
3   An artisan who specializes in ornamental woodwork.

4 inches from one end, the other end hanging down; these he takes, with his right hand, one at a time, for the purpose of piecing, and, laying the ends of the cardings about 2 inches over each other, he rubs them together on the canvas cloth with his flat hand. He is obliged to be very expert, in order to keep the spinner well supplied. A good piecer will supply from 30 to 40 spindles with cardings; but this depends, in a great measure, upon the quality of the work to be done, and also whether it is intended for the warp or the weft[4] of the cloth to be made.

The cloths upon which the piecer rubs, or pieces, the ends of the cardings, as above stated, are made of coarse wrappering.[5] The number of cardings a piecer has through his fingers in a day is very great; each piecing requires three or four rubs, over a space of three or four inches; and the continual friction of the hand in rubbing the piecing upon the coarse wrapper wears off the skin, and causes the fingers to bleed. I have had my fingers in this state for weeks together, healing up in the night, and breaking out again in little holes as soon as I commenced work on the following morning.

Another source of pain in the hands of piecers, is their continually swelling from cold in the winter season; and this is an evil which, like the other, cannot altogether be prevented.... [T]he hands get cold, and swell very much; and as there is but little, and in many places no fire allowed, it is next to impossible for them to keep their hands warm; add to this the clothes they have upon their backs, are generally as greasy and comfortless as those upon which they piece, and stick to their arms, legs, and thighs, more like a wet sack than anything intended for warmth and comfort.

The position in which the piecer stands to his work is with his right foot forward, and his right side facing the frame: the motion he makes in going along in front of the frame, for the purpose of piecing, is neither forwards nor backwards, but in a sidling direction, constantly keeping his right side towards the frame. In this position he continues during the day, with his hands, feet, and eyes constantly in motion. It will be easily seen, that the chief weight of his body rests upon his right knee, which is almost always the first joint to give way. The number of cripples with the right knee in, greatly exceed those with the left knee in; a great many have both knees in—such as my own—from this cause.

Another evil resulting from the position in which the piecer stands, is what is termed "splay-foot," which may be explained thus: in a well-formed foot, there is a finely formed arch of bones immediately under the instep and ankle joint. The continual pressure of the body on this arch, before it is sufficiently strong to bear such pressure, (as in the case of boys and girls in the factories,) causes it to give way: the bones fall gradually down, the foot then becomes broad and flat, and the owner drags it after him with the broad side first....

The spinner and the piecer are intimately connected together: the spinner works by the piece, being paid by the stone[6] for the yarn spun; the piecer is hired by the week, and paid according to his abilities. The piecers are the servants of the spinners, and both are under an overlooker, and liable to be dismissed at a week's notice....

In order to induce the piecer to do his work quick and well, the spinner has recourse to many expedients, such as offering rewards of a penny or two-pence for a good week's work—inducing them to sing, which, like the music in the army, has a very powerful effect, and keeps them awake and active

---

4   Lengthwise or crosswise threads of woven cloth.
5   Fabric for wrapping.
6   A unit of weight usually equivalent to 14 pounds but varying by region and commodity.

longer than any other thing; and, as a last resource, when nothing else will do, he takes the strap, or the billy-roller, which are laid on most unmercifully, accompanied by a round volley of oaths; and I pity the poor wretch who has to submit to the inflection of either.

On one occasion, I remember being thrashed with the billy-roller till my back, arms, and legs were covered with ridges as thick as my finger. This was more than I could bear, and, seeing a favourable opportunity, I slipped out, and stole off home, along some by-ways, so as not to be seen. Mother stripped me, and was shocked at my appearance....

A piecer, it will be seen, is an important person in the factories, inasmuch as it is impossible to do without them. Formerly, boys and girls were sent to work in the factories as piecers, at the early age of five or six years—as in my own case—but now, owing to the introduction of some wise laws for the regulation of factories, they cannot employ any as piecers before they have attained the age of 9 years;[7] at which age their bones are comparatively strong, generally speaking, and more able to endure the hardships to which they will be exposed.

They now enjoy many privileges that we had not, such as attending schools, limited hours of labour, &c.; but still it is far from being a desirable place for a child. Formerly, it was nothing but work till we could work no longer. I have frequently worked at the frame till I could scarcely get home, and in this state have been stopped by people in the streets who noticed me shuffling along, and advised me to work no more in the factories: but I was not my own master. Thus year after year passed away, my afflictions and deformities increasing. I could not associate with any body; on the contrary, I sought every opportunity to rest myself, and to shrink into any corner to screen myself from the prying eye of the curious and scornful! During the day, I frequently counted the clock, and calculated how many hours I had still to remain at work; my evenings were spent in preparing for the following day—in rubbing my knees, ankles, elbows, and wrists with oil, &c., and wrapping them in warm flannel! (for everything was tried to benefit me, except the right one—*that of taking me from the work*;) after which, with a *look at*, rather than *eating* my supper, (the bad smells of the factory having generally taken my appetite away,) I went to bed, to cry myself to sleep, and pray that the Lord would take me to himself before morning....

When about 15 years of age, a circumstance occurred to me which does not often fall to the lot of factory children, and which had a great influence on my future life. I happened one day to find an old board laying useless in a corner of the factory. On this board, with a piece of chalk, I was scrawling out, as well as I was able, the initials of my name, instead of attending to my work, as I ought to have been doing. Having formed the letters W.D., I was laying down the board, and turning to my work, when, judge of my surprise, at perceiving one of my masters looking over my shoulder. Of course, I expected a scolding; but the half smile upon his countenance suddenly dispelled my fears. He kindly asked me several questions about my writing and reading, and, after gently chiding me for taking improper opportunities, he gave me two-pence to purchase paper, pens, and ink—which sum he continued weekly for several years, always inspecting my humble endeavours, and suggesting any improvements which he thought necessary. He also (with the approbation of his brother, the other partner in the firm,) allowed me to leave work an hour earlier than the other work-people every evening for a whole winter, in order that I might improve myself; and thus an opportunity was afforded me, which, with a few presents of

---

7   The 1833 Factory Act prohibited child workers under age nine in textile mills and limited the working hours of children under age 12 to 48 per week. The act required that schools be set up in factories and that children attend for two hours per day; such schools were largely ineffective, however.

books, &c. from both masters, were the means, under Providence, of laying the foundation of what I now consider a tolerable education.

This kindness on the part of my masters will never be erased from my memory. It is as fresh to me now as if it had occurred but yesterday.

With this encouragement, and impelled by the activity of my own mind, and an irresistible thirst after knowledge, I set myself earnestly to the acquisition of such branches of education as I thought might better my condition in afterlife; and, although I had still my work to attend, I soon had the happiness to find myself in possession of a tolerable share of mathematics, geography, history, and several branches of natural and experimental philosophy.

So long as I was pursuing these studies, the thoughts of my unhappy condition were in some measure assuaged. But, in proportion as the truths of science were unfolded to my wondering sight, and the mists of ignorance chased from my mind, so the horrors of my situation became daily more and more apparent, and made me, if possible, still more fretful and unhappy! It was evident to me, that I was intended for a nobler purpose than to be a factory slave! and I longed for an opportunity to burst the trammels by which I was kept in bondage!

Alexander Somerville
from *The Autobiography of a Working Man* (1848)

Born into an impoverished Scottish family, Alexander Somerville (1811–85) was home-schooled until age eight. He later attended school and worked as a farmhand and general labourer. As a sawyer in Edinburgh, he attended theatres, listened to preachers and debates, and read widely. In 1832, a year marked by demonstrations in favour of the first Reform Bill, he enlisted with the Scotch Grays; his regiment was sent to Birmingham to support the authorities. In May of that year, Somerville wrote to a newspaper decrying the use of military force at peaceful gatherings; he was court-martialled and received 100 lashes. After his discharge, Somerville promoted reform in London and Glasgow, participated in the Spanish Legion, and began writing for publication in 1847. He emigrated to Canada in 1840, contributing to the transatlantic press until his death.

This excerpt from Somerville's autobiography depicts his fascination with books, which were costly and scarce before mid-century. It also suggests the importance of literacy to Somerville's self-identity and Robert Burns's resonance with working-class readers.

Chapter 7

When I was a boy, the periodicals which are now so common, cheap, and useful in supplying young minds with information, did not exist. Such books of popular instruction as then existed, and might have been useful for me to read, were out of my reach. Not knowing them, I did not seek them, nor feel their absence, and my own loss. My earliest acquaintance with a book subject, one which took a lodgement in me, and remained from its first entrance to this day to receive new comers, and admit them to a place beside it, but never to be dislodged itself, was the story of Joseph and his Brethren. It was told by my mother. My father had been sent to Edinburgh market, a distance of thirty-four miles, with sheep or cattle. On such journeys he was absent a day and night going; a day and night there, and a day to come home. It was one night when he was thus absent that my mother, when we were preparing to go to bed, answered some questions which I put to her, by telling the whole narrative from the selling of Joseph to the Ishmaelites, to the Egyptian bondage of the children of Israel, and their escape to the desert.[8] To this day I remember the very manner of myself and sisters, sitting around her on our cruipy stools[9] on the hearth stone. To this day I can see the fire of logs and coals as it burned behind the bars of the grate; and I see the bars also as they were then, and the fancied figures of Egyptians and Israelites which I then saw in the fire. It was the first time that I felt an intellectual ecstacy....

This occurred in my eighth or ninth year. About three years after, at the end of harvest, on a moonlight evening, when the corn was nearly all in the stackyard, and the carters were still at work in the moonlight, to get the corn carried from the fields while good weather lasted, I was with James Wilson, who was then the stacker, laying the sheaves to his hand as the carter forked them to the stack from his cart. We had some spare time between the departure of the emptied cart, and the arrival of the loaded one; and James Wilson, who was a reader of books, asked me as we sat on the stack together, if I knew Burns's[10] poem of "Halloween." ... I told the stacker that I knew what was meant by Halloween, but not what he meant when he spoke of Burns's poems. What was Burns's poems, was it a book, or a song, or a story?

He said he would tell me; and saying so, he recited all the poem of "Halloween." Seeing that I was delighted with it, he gave me that of "Death and Doctor Hornbook," which pleased me still more. And then he told me some part of Burns's life, which excited an interest in me far stronger than the recital of the two poems had done. He then reminded me that I had heard the songs of "Auld Lang Syne," "Of a' the Airts the Wind can Blaw," "My Nannie O," and some others which he named; and that they were songs made by Burns, and were included in the book called "Burns's Poems," which he would bring with him to-morrow, and lend me to read.

Tired as I was with late work, which had lasted from daylight in the morning until ten at night, I was now so eager to see that famous book, from which he had kindled in me intellectual sensation so new, so delightful, and irrepressibly strong, that I could not go home to supper and to bed, until I had accompanied him to his home, three quarters of a mile distant to get the book; ... It was a volume that had been often read, well read, and well worn. It had been in tatters, and was sewed again together, and I had special charges to take care of it, as it was not every one that it would be lent to. I got it, and if each leaf had been a bank note, I could not have hugged it in my breast pocket more closely and carefully. At first I felt a difficulty with the Scottish dialect of the poems, as I had never seen the dialect in print before; and my education, such as it was, had been exercised only on English reading. Moreover, the dialect of Burns was that of the west of Scotland, while in our every day speech we used that of the Lothians and of Lammermoor in the south-east of Scotland, a dialect differing in many respects from that of the west.

---

8   Genesis 37–50 and Exodus 1–14.
9   Low stools.
10 Robert Burns (1759–96), Scottish vernacular poet.

Yet I was soon able to read the poems with facility; and though I now know that I did not then feel the force of the poetry, I then read them under sensations of pleasure entirely new....

Seeing that I continued to read everything of verse kind which fell in my way, my father resolved to get me a book of poems to read, which he thought would do me good—the *Gospel Sonnets*.[11] It was no small thing for a poor man like him to pay half of a week's wages, and send all the way to Edinburgh for a book of verses for his boy, because he saw that boy eagerly laying hold of every printed poem, song, ballad, or verse, that could be reached, and in the exuberance of his enthusiasm making rhymes for others to listen to. The *Gospel Sonnets* were received and read, but there was something wanting either in me or in them. We stood, the book and I, in positions of respectable friendship, but I rushed not into it to live in it, with it in me, to hold companionship with it in the lonely woods, in the green loaning, or lie with it on the grass and the gowans[12] beside the well, drinking from the well of water when I was thirsty and tired—drinking from the book of poetry always, as in Burns....

The next book which came in my way, and made an impression so strong as to be still unworn and unwearable, was *Anson's Voyage Round the World*.[13] *Gospel Sonnets*, *Burns's Poems*, old ballads, and self-made doggrel, everything gave way to admit the new knowledge of the earth's geography, and the charms of human adventure which I found in those voyages. I had read nothing of the kind before, and knew nothing of foreign countries beyond the glimpses of them opened to me by old James Dawson[14] when he held converse with the personages of history, and the imaginary beings whom he associated with in the solitudes of the Ogle Burn. I got Anson to read in this way:—

James Wilson was at Innerwick smithy one day, getting his horses shod, and his plough irons laid. He saw a thick, aged-looking volume lying on the wall head under the tiles; and taking it down, read parts of it between the heats of the iron, it being his business, as of other men like him at the smithy, to wield the fore-hammer, when the iron was red-hot on the anvil. John Watt, the smith, had borrowed that book, and was reading it at resting hours. In working hours the book lay where James Wilson saw it. The account of it given to me was such as to make me try to get it and surmount all difficulties in the trial. Those difficulties were all the greater that my *blateness* (bashfulness) was at this time oppressive, and almost ridiculous. I was now nearly fourteen years old; but had mingled in no company, and did not know above twenty people, and not even the half of twenty familiarly. If I were going an errand, and saw men at work on the road, laying stones on it, perhaps, I would go half a mile round by some other road, or through fields and over hedges and ditches, rather than pass them. If I had to pass people on the road, I could not look them in the face, nor, if they had asked me a question, could I answer them without my face reddening as if with shame. If my errand was to a private house, I would go past and return again, and pass it once more, and still be unable to muster courage to go in to tell what I wanted. This want of self-confidence, I am sorry to confess, has not been supplanted as it should be unto this day....

Perhaps the writing of this autobiography (and above all its publication, now that I have allowed it to be published) may suggest that if my self-confidence was once weak it abounds in strength now. To this I cannot well reply. I feel that there are other moving causes to this act of publication; but this is not the page on which to write the confession of them.

---

11 Ralph Erskine, *Gospel Canticles, or, Spiritual Songs* (1720).
12 Yellow or white field flowers.
13 This classic of naval literature describes Commodore George Anson's circumnavigation of the globe from 1740 to 1744.
14 An aged blind man in Somerville's neighbourhood.

At all events, whatever I may be now, I was bashful to the extent of being ridiculous when I was younger; and the struggle I had with the desire to go to the owner of Anson's Voyages to borrow the book to read, and the shame of the thought that a boy like I, who only wore corduroy clothes, nailed shoes with thick soles, and a highland bonnet, should presume to go to the house of those who had a back door and a front door,[15] was a war of thoughts that allowed me no peace for several weeks.

But the effort was made. It was successful; and I got the book to read. It was in summer, in the month of July, and I was then one of about ten persons employed in turnip hoeing. The turnips were that year in the large field called the Under Floors. The other workers went home to their dinners,[16] but I carried a bottle of milk with me and a piece of hard bannock of bean and barley meal and would not go home, not though there was the great temptation of new potatoes just come in, or curds and cream, or some of the other summer delicacies which our mother was so pleased to provide for us at that season of the year. I remained in the fields, and lay on the grass under the shadow of the trees and read about the *Centurion*,[17] and all that befel her. When the afternoon work began, I related to the other workers what I had read; and even the grieve[18] began to take an interest in the story. And this interest increased in him and in every one else until they all brought their dinners afield, so that they might remain under the shadow of the trees and hear me read. In the evenings at home I continued the reading, and next day at work put them in possession of the events which I knew in advance of them....

John Stuart Mill
from *Autobiography* (1873)

A progressive philosopher, economist, and women's rights advocate, John Stuart Mill (1806–73) became one of the nineteenth century's most influential public intellectuals. Rigorously educated from age three by his father, the young Mill mixed with his father's radical associates. Reading Jeremy Bentham converted him to utilitarianism, but an 1826–27 mental crisis prompted dissent from Benthamism. Striving for practical reform, Mill spent his professional career at the India Office while editing and writing for periodicals and authoring works on philosophy and on political, economic, and social theory, including *On Liberty* (1859) and *The Subjection of Women* (1869). Mill first encountered the married Harriet Taylor in 1830; they married in 1851 after her first husband died, and Mill credited her collaboration on almost all his mature work.

Composed mainly in the 1850s but published posthumously in 1873, Mill's autobiography traces his intellectual and moral development. In this famous passage, he recounts how he faced a life crisis.

---

15 This detail implies that the occupants have a higher class status than his own: a back door was used for tradespeople and servants, a front door for residents and invited guests.
16 Midday meal.
17 Anson's ship.
18 Farm overseer.

Chapter 5: A Crisis in My Mental History. One Stage Onward

For some years after this time I wrote very little, and nothing regularly, for publication: and great were the advantages which I derived from the intermission. It was of no common importance to me, at this period, to be able to digest and mature my thoughts for my own mind only, without any immediate call for giving them out in print. Had I gone on writing, it would have much disturbed the important transformation in my opinions and character, which took place during those years. The origin of this transformation, or at least the process by which I was prepared for it, can only be explained by turning some distance back.

From the winter of 1821, when I first read Bentham,[19] and especially from the commencement of the Westminster Review,[20] I had what might truly be called an object in life; to be a reformer of the world. My conception of my own happiness was entirely identified with this object. The personal sympathies I wished for were those of fellow labourers in this enterprise. I endeavoured to pick up as many flowers as I could by the way; but as a serious and permanent personal satisfaction to rest upon, my whole reliance was placed on this; and I was accustomed to felicitate myself on the certainty of a happy life which I enjoyed, through placing my happiness in something durable and distant, in which some progress might be always making, while it could never be exhausted by complete attainment. This did very well for several years, during which the general improvement going on in the world and the idea of myself as engaged with others in struggling to promote it, seemed enough to fill up an interesting and animated existence. But the time came when I awakened from this as from a dream. It was in the autumn of 1826. I was in a dull state of nerves, such as everybody is occasionally liable to; unsusceptible to enjoyment or pleasurable excitement; one of those moods when what is pleasure at other times, becomes insipid or indifferent; the state, I should think, in which converts to Methodism[21] usually are, when smitten by their first "conviction of sin." In this frame of mind it occurred to me to put the question directly to myself: "Suppose that all your objects in life were realized; that all the changes in institutions and opinions which you are looking forward to, could be completely effected at this very instant: would this be a great joy and happiness to you?" And an irrepressible self-consciousness distinctly answered, "No!" At this my heart sank within me: the whole foundation on which my life was constructed fell down. All my happiness was to have been found in the continual pursuit of this end. The end had ceased to charm, and how could there ever again be any interest in the means? I seemed to have nothing left to live for.

At first I hoped that the cloud would pass away of itself; but it did not. A night's sleep, the sovereign remedy for the smaller vexations of life, had no effect on it. I awoke to a renewed consciousness of the woful fact. I carried it with me into all companies, into all occupations. Hardly anything had power to cause me even a few minutes' oblivion of it. For some months the cloud seemed to grow thicker and thicker. The lines in Coleridge's "Dejection"[22]—I was not then acquainted with them—exactly describe my case:

---

19 Jeremy Bentham (1748–1832), Utilitarian economist and philosopher.
20 A radical and intellectual journal founded in 1824 by Mill's father, James Mill (1773–1836).
21 A reformist movement within the Church of England founded by John Wesley in the eighteenth century.
22 Samuel Taylor Coleridge, "Dejection: An Ode" (1802).

> A grief without a pang, void, dark and drear,
> A drowsy, stifled, unimpassioned grief,
> Which finds no natural outlet or relief
> In word, or sigh, or tear.

In vain I sought relief from my favourite books; those memorials of past nobleness and greatness from which I had always hitherto drawn strength and animation. I read them now without feeling, or with the accustomed feeling *minus* all its charm; and I became persuaded, that my love of mankind, and of excellence for its own sake, had worn itself out. I sought no comfort by speaking to others of what I felt. If I had loved any one sufficiently to make confiding my griefs a necessity, I should not have been in the condition I was. I felt, too, that mine was not an interesting, or in any way respectable distress. There was nothing in it to attract sympathy. Advice, if I had known where to seek it, would have been most precious. The words of Macbeth to the physician[23] often occurred to my thoughts. But there was no one on whom I could build the faintest hope of such assistance. My father, to whom it would have been natural to me to have recourse in any practical difficulties, was the last person to whom, in such a case as this, I looked for help. Everything convinced me that he had no knowledge of any such mental state as I was suffering from, and that even if he could be made to understand it, he was not the physician who could heal it. My education, which was wholly his work,[24] had been conducted without any regard to the possibility of its ending in this result; and I saw no use in giving him the pain of thinking that his plans had failed, when the failure was probably irremediable, and, at all events, beyond the power of *his* remedies. Of other friends, I had at that time none to whom I had any hope of making my condition intelligible. It was however abundantly intelligible to myself; and the more I dwelt upon it, the more hopeless it appeared.

My course of study had led me to believe, that all mental and moral feelings and qualities, whether of a good or of a bad kind, were the results of association; that we love one thing, and hate another, take pleasure in one sort of action or contemplation, and pain in another sort, through the clinging of pleasurable or painful ideas to those things, from the effect of education or of experience.[25] As a corollary from this, I had always heard it maintained by my father, and was myself convinced, that the object of education should be to form the strongest possible associations of the salutary class; associations of pleasure with all things beneficial to the great whole, and of pain with all things hurtful to it. This doctrine appeared inexpugnable; but it now seemed to me, on retrospect, that my teachers had occupied themselves but superficially with the means of forming and keeping up these salutary associations. They seemed to have trusted altogether to the old familiar instruments, praise and blame, reward and punishment. Now, I did not doubt that by these means, begun early, and applied unremittingly, intense associations of pain and pleasure, especially of pain, might be created, and might produce desires and aversions capable of lasting undiminished to the end of life. But there must always be something artificial and casual in associations thus produced.... All those to whom I looked up, were of opinion that the pleasure of sympathy with human beings, and the feelings which made the good of others, and especially of mankind on a large scale, the object of existence, were the greatest and surest sources of happiness. Of the truth of this I

---

23 "Canst thou not minister to a mind diseased[?]" (*Macbeth* V.iii.40).
24 Believing that the child's mind was a blank slate, James Mill educated his son with great ambition, setting him to learn Greek at the age of three.
25 James Mill trained his son according to associationist ideas, which posited the mind as a blank slate written upon by experience; simple sensations thus formed the building blocks of the self.

was convinced, but to know that a feeling would make me happy if I had it, did not give me the feeling. My education, I thought, had failed to create these feelings in sufficient strength to resist the dissolving influence of analysis, while the whole course of my intellectual cultivation had made precocious and premature analysis the inveterate habit of my mind. I was thus, as I said to myself, left stranded at the commencement of my voyage, with a well-equipped ship and a rudder, but no sail; without any real desire for the ends which I had been so carefully fitted out to work for: no delight in virtue, or the general good, but also just as little in anything else. The fountains of vanity and ambition seemed to have dried up within me, as completely as those of benevolence.... And there seemed no power in nature sufficient to begin the formation of my character anew, and create in a mind now irretrievably analytic, fresh associations of pleasure with any of the objects of human desire.

These were the thoughts which mingled with the dry heavy dejection of the melancholy winter of 1826–7....

In all probability my case was by no means so peculiar as I fancied it, and I doubt not that many others have passed through a similar state; but the idiosyncrasies of my education had given to the general phenomenon a special character, which made it seem the natural effect of causes that it was hardly possible for time to remove. I frequently asked myself, if I could, or if I was bound to go on living, when life must be passed in this manner. I generally answered to myself, that I did not think I could possibly bear it beyond a year. When, however, not more than half that duration of time had elapsed, a small ray of light broke in upon my gloom. I was reading, accidentally, Marmontel's "Memoires,"[26] and came to the passage which relates his father's death, the distressed position of the family, and the sudden inspiration by which he, then a mere boy, felt and made them feel that he would be everything to them—would supply the place of all that they had lost. A vivid conception of the scene and its feelings came over me, and I was moved to tears. From this moment my burden grew lighter. The oppression of the thought that all feeling was dead within me, was gone. I was no longer hopeless: I was not a stock or a stone. I had still, it seemed, some of the material out of which all worth of character, and all capacity for happiness, are made. Relieved from my ever present sense of irremediable wretchedness, I gradually found that the ordinary incidents of life could again give me some pleasure; that I could again find enjoyment, not intense, but sufficient for cheerfulness, in sunshine and sky, in books, in conversation, in public affairs; and that there was, once more, excitement, though of a moderate kind, in exerting myself for my opinions, and for the public good. Thus the cloud gradually drew off, and I again enjoyed life: and though I had several relapses, some of which lasted many months, I never again was as miserable as I had been.

The experiences of this period had two very marked effects on my opinions and character. In the first place, they led me to adopt a theory of life, very unlike that on which I had before acted, and having much in common with what at that time I certainly had never heard of, the anti self-consciousness theory of Carlyle.[27] I never, indeed, wavered in the conviction that happiness is the test of all rules of conduct, and the end of life. But I now thought that this end was only to be attained by not making it the direct end. Those only are happy (I thought) who have their minds fixed on some object other than their own happiness; on the happiness of others, on the improvement of mankind, even on some art or pursuit, followed not as a means, but as itself an ideal end. Aiming thus at something else, they find happiness by

---

26   Jean-François Marmontel, *Mémoires d'un père* (1804).
27   Thomas Carlyle's "Characteristics" (*Edinburgh Review*, December 1831) criticizes his society's intense self-consciousness.

the way. The enjoyments of life (such was now my theory) are sufficient to make it a pleasant thing, when they are taken *en passant*,[28] without being made a principal object. Once make them so, and they are immediately felt to be insufficient. They will not bear a scrutinizing examination. Ask yourself whether you are happy, and you cease to be so. The only chance is to treat, not happiness, but some end external to it, as the purpose of life. Let your self-consciousness, your scrutiny, your self-interrogation, exhaust themselves on that; and if otherwise fortunately circumstanced you will inhale happiness with the air you breathe, without dwelling on it or thinking about it, without either forestalling it in imagination, or putting it to flight by fatal questioning. This theory now became the basis of my philosophy of life. And I still hold to it as the best theory for all those who have but a moderate degree of sensibility and of capacity for enjoyment, that is, for the great majority of mankind.

The other important change which my opinions at this time underwent, was that I, for the first time, gave its proper place, among the prime necessities of human well-being, to the internal culture of the individual. I ceased to attach almost exclusive importance to the ordering of outward circumstances, and the training of the human being for speculation and for action.

I had now learnt by experience that the passive susceptibilities needed to be cultivated as well as the active capacities, and required to be nourished and enriched as well as guided. I did not, for an instant, lose sight of, or undervalue, that part of the truth which I had seen before; I never turned recreant to intellectual culture, or ceased to consider the power and practice of analysis as an essential condition both of individual and of social improvement. But I thought that it had consequences which required to be corrected, by joining other kinds of cultivation with it. The maintenance of a due balance among the faculties, now seemed to me of primary importance. The cultivation of the feelings became one of the cardinal points in my ethical and philosophical creed. And my thoughts and inclinations turned in an increasing degree towards whatever seemed capable of being instrumental to that object.

I now began to find meaning in the things which I had read or heard about the importance of poetry and art as instruments of human culture. But it was some time longer before I began to know this by personal experience. The only one of the imaginative arts in which I had from childhood taken great pleasure, was music.... After the tide had turned, and I was in process of recovery, I had been helped forward by music, but in a much less elevated manner. I at this time first became acquainted with Weber's Oberon,[29] and the extreme pleasure which I drew from its delicious melodies did me good, by showing me a source of pleasure to which I was as susceptible as ever. The good, however, was much impaired by the thought, that the pleasure of music (as is quite true of such pleasure as this was, that of mere tune) fades with familiarity, and requires either to be revived by intermittence, or fed by continual novelty.... And I felt that unless I could see my way to some better hope than this for human happiness in general, my dejection must continue; but that if I could see such an outlet, I should then look on the world with pleasure; content as far as I was myself concerned, with any fair share of the general lot.

This state of my thoughts and feelings made the fact of my reading Wordsworth[30] for the first time (in the autumn of 1828), an important event in my life. I took up the collection of his poems from curiosity, with no expectation of mental relief from it, though I had before resorted to poetry with that hope. In the

---

28 French: in passing.
29 Carl Maria von Weber's opera *Oberon* (1826).
30 William Wordsworth (1770–1850), Romantic poet.

worst period of my depression, I had read through the whole of Byron (then new to me), to try whether a poet, whose peculiar department was supposed to be that of the intenser feelings, could rouse any feeling in me. As might be expected, I got no good from this reading, but the reverse. The poet's state of mind was too like my own....[31] But while Byron was exactly what did not suit my condition, Wordsworth was exactly what did....

In the first place, these poems addressed themselves powerfully to one of the strongest of my pleasurable susceptibilities, the love of rural objects and natural scenery; to which I had been indebted not only for much of the pleasure of my life, but quite recently for relief from one of my longest relapses into depression. In this power of rural beauty over me, there was a foundation laid for taking pleasure in Wordsworth's poetry; the more so, as his scenery lies mostly among mountains, which, owing to my early Pyrenean excursion, were my ideal of natural beauty. But Wordsworth would never have had any great effect on me, if he had merely placed before me beautiful pictures of natural scenery.... What made Wordsworth's poems a medicine for my state of mind, was that they expressed, not mere outward beauty, but states of feeling, and of thought coloured by feeling, under the excitement of beauty. They seemed to be the very culture of the feelings, which I was in quest of. In them I seemed to draw from a source of inward joy, of sympathetic and imaginative pleasure, which could be shared in by all human beings; which had no connexion with struggle or imperfection, but would be made richer by every improvement in the physical or social condition of mankind. From them I seemed to learn what would be the perennial sources of happiness, when all the greater evils of life shall have been removed. And I felt myself at once better and happier as I came under their influence. There have certainly been, even in our own age, greater poets than Wordsworth; but poetry of deeper and loftier feeling could not have done for me at that time what his did. I needed to be made to feel that there was real, permanent happiness in tranquil contemplation. Wordsworth taught me this, not only without turning away from, but with a greatly increased interest in the common feelings and common destiny of human beings. And the delight which these poems gave me, proved that with culture of this sort, there was nothing to dread from the most confirmed habit of analysis. At the conclusion of the Poems came the famous Ode, falsely called Platonic, "Intimations of Immortality:"[32] in which, along with more than his usual sweetness of melody and rhythm, and along with the two passages of grand imagery but bad philosophy so often quoted, I found that he too had had similar experience to mine; that he also had felt that the first freshness of youthful enjoyment of life was not lasting; but that he had sought for compensation, and found it, in the way in which he was now teaching me to find it. The result was that I gradually, but completely, emerged from my habitual depression, and was never again subject to it....

If I am asked, what system of political philosophy I substituted for that which, as a philosophy, I had abandoned, I answer, No system: only a conviction that the true system was something much more complex and many-sided than I had previously had any idea of, and that its office was to supply, not a set of model institutions, but principles from which the institutions suitable to any given circumstances might be deduced. The influences of European, that is to say, Continental, thought, and especially those of the reaction of the nineteenth century against the eighteenth, were now streaming in upon me. They

---

31 George Gordon Byron (1788–1824), Romantic poet; his heroes are typically disaffected.
32 William Wordsworth, "Intimations of Immortality from Recollections of Early Childhood," *Poems by William Wordsworth, Including Lyrical Ballads, and the Miscellaneous Pieces by the Author* (1815).

came from various quarters: from the writings of Coleridge,[33] which I had begun to read with interest even before the change in my opinions; from the Coleridgians with whom I was in personal intercourse; from what I had read of Goethe;[34] from Carlyle's early articles in the Edinburgh and Foreign Reviews,[35] though for a long time I saw nothing in these (as my father saw nothing in them to the last) but insane rhapsody. From these sources, and from the acquaintance I kept up with the French literature of the time, I derived, among other ideas which the general turning upside down of the opinions of European thinkers had brought uppermost, these in particular: That the human mind has a certain order of possible progress, in which some things must precede others, an order which governments and public instructors can modify to some, but not to an unlimited extent: That all questions of political institutions are relative, not absolute, and that different stages of human progress not only *will* have, but *ought* to have, different institutions: that government is always either in the hands, or passing into the hands, of whatever is the strongest power in society, and that what this power is, does not depend on institutions, but institutions on it: that any general theory or philosophy of politics supposes a previous theory of human progress, and that this is the same thing with a philosophy of history. These opinions, true in the main, were held in an exaggerated and violent manner by the thinkers with whom I was now most accustomed to compare notes, and who, as usual with a reaction, ignored that half of the truth which the thinkers of the eighteenth century saw. But though, at one period of my progress, I for some time under-valued that great century, I never joined in the reaction against it, but kept as firm hold of one side of the truth as I took of the other. The fight between the nineteenth century and the eighteenth always reminded me of the battle about the shield, one side of which was white and the other black. I marvelled at the blind rage with which the combatants rushed against one another. I applied to them, and to Coleridge himself, many of Coleridge's sayings about half truths;[36] and Goethe's device, "many-sidedness,"[37] was one which I would most willingly, at this period, have taken for mine.

The writers by whom, more than by any others, a new mode of political thinking was brought home to me, were those of the St. Simonian school[38] in France. In 1829 and 1830 I became acquainted with some of their writings. They were then only in the earlier stages of their speculations. They had not yet dressed out their philosophy as a religion, nor had they organized their scheme of Socialism. They were just beginning to question the principle of hereditary property. I was by no means prepared to go with them even this length; but I was greatly struck with the connected view which they for the first time presented to me, of the natural order of human progress; and especially with their division of all history into organic periods and critical periods. During the organic periods (they said) mankind accept with firm conviction some positive creed, claiming jurisdiction over all their actions, and containing more or less of truth and adaptation to the needs of humanity. Under its influence they make all the progress compatible with the creed, and finally outgrow it; when a period follows of criticism and negation, in which mankind lose their old convictions without acquiring any new ones, of a general or authoritative character, except the

---

33   Samuel Taylor Coleridge (1772–1834), Romantic poet, critic, and philosopher.
34   Johann Wolfgang von Goethe (1749–1832), German writer.
35   These may have included "Signs of the Times" (*Edinburgh Review*, 1829) and *Sartor Resartus* (*Fraser's Magazine*, 1833–34).
36   In his *Biographia Literaria* (1817), Coleridge lamented "a world of power and talent wasted on the support of half truths."
37   The desirable concept of many-sidedness appears in a number of Goethe's works, including Chapter 1 of *Wilhelm Meisters Wanderjahre* (1821; 1829).
38   Followers of French socialist Claude-Henri de Saint-Simon (1760–1825).

conviction that the old are false. The period of Greek and Roman polytheism, so long as really believed in by instructed Greeks and Romans, was an organic period, succeeded by the critical or sceptical period of the Greek philosophers. Another organic period came in with Christianity. The corresponding critical period began with the Reformation, has lasted ever since, still lasts, and cannot altogether cease until a new organic period has been inaugurated by the triumph of a yet more advanced creed. These ideas, I knew, were not peculiar to the St. Simonians; on the contrary, they were the general property of Europe, or at least of Germany and France, but they had never, to my knowledge, been so completely systematized as by these writers, nor the distinguishing characteristics of a critical period so powerfully set forth; for I was not then acquainted with Fichte's Lectures on "The Characteristics of the Present Age."[39] In Carlyle, indeed, I found bitter denunciations of an "age of unbelief,"[40] and of the present age as such, which I, like most people at that time, supposed to be passionate protests in favour of the old modes of belief. But all that was true in these denunciations, I thought that I found more calmly and philosophically stated by the St. Simonians. Among their publications, too, there was one which seemed to me far superior to the rest; in which the general idea was matured into something much more definite and instructive. This was an early work of Auguste Comte,[41] who then called himself, and even announced himself in the title-page as, a pupil of Saint Simon. In this tract M. Comte first put forth the doctrine, which he afterwards so copiously illustrated, of the natural succession of three stages in every department of human knowledge: first, the theological, next the metaphysical, and lastly, the positive stage; and contended, that social science must be subject to the same law; that the feudal and Catholic system was the concluding phasis[42] of the theological state of the social science, Protestantism the commencement, and the doctrines of the French Revolution the consummation of the metaphysical; and that its positive state was yet to come. This doctrine harmonized well with my existing notions, to which it seemed to give a scientific shape. I already regarded the methods of physical science as the proper models for political. But the chief benefit which I derived at this time from the trains of thought suggested by the St. Simonians and by Comte, was, that I obtained a clearer conception than ever before of the peculiarities of an era of transition in opinion, and ceased to mistake the moral and intellectual characteristics of such an era, for the normal attributes of humanity. I looked forward, through the present age of loud disputes but generally weak convictions, to a future which shall unite the best qualities of the critical with the best qualities of the organic periods; unchecked liberty of thought, unbounded freedom of individual action in all modes not hurtful to others; but also, convictions as to what is right and wrong, useful and pernicious, deeply engraven on the feelings by early education and general unanimity of sentiment, and so firmly grounded in reason and in the true exigencies of life, that they shall not, like all former and present creeds, religious, ethical, and political, require to be periodically thrown off and replaced by others.

    M. Comte soon left the St. Simonians, and I lost sight of him and his writings for a number of years. But the St. Simonians I continued to cultivate. I was kept *au courant*[43] of their progress by one of their most enthusiastic disciples, M. Gustave d'Eichthal,[44] who about that time passed a considerable interval

---

39 Johann Gottlieb Fichte, *Der Grundzüge des gegewärtigen Zeitalters* (1806).
40 In "Death of Goethe" (1832), Carlyle wrote, "The whole distracted Existence of man is an age of Unbelief."
41 Auguste Comte, *Système de politique positive* (1824).
42 Phase.
43 French: current.
44 Gustave d'Eichthal (1804–86).

in England. I was introduced to their chiefs, Bazard and Enfantin,[45] in 1830; and as long as their public teachings and proselytism continued, I read nearly everything they wrote. Their criticisms on the common doctrines of Liberalism seemed to me full of important truth; and it was partly by their writings that my eyes were opened to the very limited and temporary value of the old political economy, which assumes private property and inheritance as indefeasible facts, and freedom of production and exchange as the dernier mot[46] of social improvement. The scheme gradually unfolded by the St. Simonians, under which the labour and capital of society would be managed for the general account of the community, every individual being required to take a share of labour either as thinker, teacher, artist, or producer, all being classed according to their capacity, and remunerated according to their works, appeared to me a far superior description of Socialism to Owen's.[47] Their aim seemed to me desirable and rational, however their means might be inefficacious; and though I neither believed in the practicability nor in the beneficial operation of their social machinery, I felt that the proclamation of such an ideal of human society could not but tend to give a beneficial direction to the efforts of others to bring society as at present constituted, nearer to some ideal standard. I honoured them most of all for what they have been most cried down for—the boldness and freedom from prejudice with which they treated the subject of family, the most important of any, and needing more fundamental alterations than remain to be made in any other great social institution, but on which scarcely any reformer has the courage to touch. In proclaiming the perfect equality of men and women, and an entirely new order of things in regard to their relations with one another, the St. Simonians, in common with Owen and Fourier,[48] have entitled themselves to the grateful remembrance of future generations.

In giving an account of this period of my life, I have only specified such of my new impressions as appeared to me, both at the time and since, to be a kind of turning [point], marking a definite progress in my mode of thought. But these few selected points give a very insufficient idea of the quantity of thinking which I carried on respecting a host of subjects during these years of transition. Much of this, it is true, consisted in rediscovering things known to all the world, which I had previously disbelieved, or disregarded. But the rediscovery was to me a discovery, giving me plenary possession of the truths, not as traditional platitudes, but fresh from their source: and it seldom failed to place them in some new light, by which they were reconciled with, and seemed to confirm while they modified, the truths less generally known which lay in my early opinions, and in no essential part of which I at any time wavered. All my new thinking only laid the foundation of these more deeply and strongly, while it often removed misapprehension and confusion of ideas which had perverted their effect. For example, during the later returns of my dejection, the doctrine of what is called Philosophical Necessity[49] weighed on my existence like an incubus.[50] I felt as if I was scientifically proved to be the helpless slave of antecedent circumstances; as if my character and that of all others had been formed for us by agencies beyond our control, and was wholly out of our own power. I often said to myself, what a relief it would be if I could disbelieve the doctrine of the formation of character by circumstances; and remembering the wish of Fox[51] respecting

---

45 Saint-Amand Bazard (1791–1832); Barthélemy-Prosper Enfantin (1796–1864).
46 French: last word.
47 Robert Owen (1771–1858), manufacturer and socialist.
48 (François-Marie-) Charles Fourier (1772–1837), French social theorist.
49 The determination of character by external experience and circumstances.
50 An evil male spirit that descends on women in their sleep, seeking intercourse.
51 Charles James Fox (1749–1806), politician and populist.

the doctrine of resistance to governments, that it might never be forgotten by kings, nor remembered by subjects, I said that it would be a blessing if the doctrine of necessity could be believed by all quoad[52] the characters of others, and disbelieved in regard to their own. I pondered painfully on the subject, till gradually I saw light through it. I perceived, that the word Necessity, as a name for the doctrine of Cause and Effect applied to human action, carried with it a misleading association; and that this association was the operative force in the depressing and paralysing influence which I had experienced: I saw that though our character is formed by circumstances, our own desires can do much to shape those circumstances; and that what is really inspiriting and ennobling in the doctrine of freewill, is the conviction that we have real power over the formation of our own character; that our will, by influencing some of our circumstances, can modify our future habits or capabilities of willing. All this was entirely consistent with the doctrine of circumstances, or rather, was that doctrine itself, properly understood. From that time I drew in my own mind, a clear distinction between the doctrine of circumstances, and Fatalism; discarding altogether the misleading word Necessity. The theory, which I now for the first time rightly apprehended, ceased altogether to be discouraging, and besides the relief to my spirits, I no longer suffered under the burden, so heavy to one who aims at being a reformer in opinions, of thinking one doctrine true, and the contrary doctrine morally beneficial. The train of thought which had extricated me from this dilemma, seemed to me, in after years, fitted to render a similar service to others; and it now forms the chapter on Liberty and Necessity in the concluding Book of my *System of Logic*.[53]

Again, in politics, though I no longer accepted the doctrine of the Essay on Government[54] as a scientific theory; though I ceased to consider representative democracy as an absolute principle, and regarded it as a question of time, place, and circumstance; though I now looked upon the choice of political institutions as a moral and educational question more than one of material interests, thinking that it ought to be decided mainly by the consideration, what great improvement in life and culture stands next in order for the people concerned, as the condition of their further progress, and what institutions are most likely to promote that; nevertheless, this change in the premises of my political philosophy did not alter my practical political creed as to the requirements of my own time and country. I was as much as ever a Radical and Democrat for Europe, and especially for England. I thought the predominance of the aristocratic classes, the noble and the rich, in the English Constitution, an evil worth any struggle to get rid of; not on account of taxes, or any such comparatively small inconvenience, but as the great demoralizing agency in the country. Demoralizing, first, because it made the conduct of the government an example of gross public immorality, through the predominance of private over public interests in the State, and the abuse of the powers of legislation for the advantage of classes. Secondly, and in a still greater degree, because the respect of the multitude always attaching itself principally to that which, in the existing state of society, is the chief passport to power; and under English institutions, riches, hereditary or acquired, being the almost exclusive source of political importance; riches, and the signs of riches, were almost the only things really respected, and the life of the people was mainly devoted to the pursuit of them. I thought, that while the higher and richer classes held the power of government, the instruction and improvement of the mass of the people were contrary to the self-interest of those classes, because tending to render the

---

52 Latin: with respect to.
53 John Stuart Mill, *A System of Logic, Ratiocinative and Inductive* (1843).
54 James Mill, *Essay on Government* (1820).

people more powerful for throwing off the yoke: but if the democracy obtained a large, and perhaps the principal, share in the governing power, it would become the interest of the opulent classes to promote their education, in order to ward off really mischievous errors, and especially those which would lead to unjust violations of property. On these grounds I was not only as ardent as ever for democratic institutions, but earnestly hoped that Owenite, St. Simonian, and all other anti-property doctrines might spread widely among the poorer classes; not that I thought those doctrines true, or desired that they should be acted on, but in order that the higher classes might be made to see that they had more to fear from the poor when uneducated, than when educated.

In this frame of mind the French Revolution of July[55] found me. It roused my utmost enthusiasm, and gave me, as it were, a new existence. I went at once to Paris, was introduced to Lafayette,[56] and laid the groundwork of the intercourse I afterwards kept up with several of the active chiefs of the extreme popular party. After my return I entered warmly, as a writer, into the political discussions of the time; which soon became still more exciting, by the coming in of Lord Grey's Ministry, and the proposing of the Reform Bill.[57] For the next few years I wrote copiously in newspapers. It was about this time that Fonblanque, who had for some time written the political articles in the Examiner, became the proprietor and editor of the paper.[58] It is not forgotten with what verve and talent, as well as fine wit, he carried it on, during the whole period of Lord Grey's Ministry, and what importance it assumed as the principal representative, in the newspaper press, of Radical opinions. The distinguishing character of the paper was given to it entirely by his own articles, which formed at least three-fourths of all the original writing contained in it: but of the remaining fourth I contributed during those years a much larger share than any one else.[59] I wrote nearly all the articles on French subjects, including a weekly summary of French politics, often extending to considerable length; together with many leading articles on general politics, commercial and financial legislation, and any miscellaneous subjects in which I felt interested, and which were suitable to the paper, including occasional reviews of books. Mere newspaper articles on the occurrences or questions of the moment, gave no opportunity for the development of any general mode of thought; but I attempted, in the beginning of 1831, to embody in a series of articles, headed "The Spirit of the Age,"[60] some of my new opinions, and especially to point out in the character of the present age, the anomalies and evils characteristic of the transition from a system of opinions which had worn out, to another only in process of being formed.... Carlyle, then living in a secluded part of Scotland, read them in his solitude, and saying to himself (as he afterwards told me) "here is a new Mystic," inquired on coming to London that autumn respecting their authorship; an inquiry which was the immediate cause of our becoming personally acquainted.

I have already mentioned Carlyle's earlier writings as one of the channels through which I received the influences which enlarged my early narrow creed; but I do not think that those writings, by themselves,

---

55 During the French Revolution of July 1830, King Charles X was overthrown and his cousin Louis-Philippe was crowned king.
56 The Marquis de Lafayette (1757–1834) supported Louis-Philippe in the Revolution of 1830.
57 Lord Grey, a Whig, was elected British prime minister in 1830; the Reform Act of 1832 reformed the electoral system and extended the vote to middle-class males.
58 Albany Fonblanque (1793–1872) controlled the *Examiner* from 1830 to 1847.
59 Mill contributed 210 articles to the *Examiner* between 18 July 1830 and 14 September 1834.
60 Mill's essays on "The Spirit of the Age" were published in the *Examiner* between 6 January and 29 May 1831.

would ever have had any effect on my opinions. What truths they contained, though of the very kind which I was already receiving from other quarters, were presented in a form and vesture less suited than any other to give them access to a mind trained as mine had been. They seemed a haze of poetry and German metaphysics, in which almost the only clear thing was a strong animosity to most of the opinions which were the basis of my mode of thought; religious scepticism, utilitarianism, the doctrine of circumstances, and the attaching any importance to democracy, logic, or political economy. Instead of my having been taught anything, in the first instance, by Carlyle, it was only in proportion as I came to see the same truths through media more suited to my mental constitution, that I recognised them in his writings. Then, indeed, the wonderful power with which he put them forth made a deep impression upon me, and I was during a long period one of his most fervent admirers; but the good his writings did me, was not as philosophy to instruct, but as poetry to animate. Even at the time when our acquaintance commenced, I was not sufficiently advanced in my new modes of thought, to appreciate him fully; a proof of which is, that on his showing me the manuscript of Sartor Resartus, his best and greatest work, which he had just then finished, I made little of it; though when it came out about two years afterwards in Fraser's Magazine[61] I read it with enthusiastic admiration and the keenest delight....

My father's tone of thought and feeling, I now felt myself at a great distance from: greater, indeed, than a full and calm explanation and reconsideration on both sides, might have shown to exist in reality. But my father was not one with whom calm and full explanations on fundamental points of doctrine could be expected, at least with one whom he might consider as, in some sort, a deserter from his standard. Fortunately we were almost always in strong agreement on the political questions of the day which engrossed a large part of his interest and of his conversation. On those matters of opinion on which we differed, we talked little. He knew that the habit of thinking for myself, which his mode of education had fostered, sometimes led me to opinions different from his, and he perceived from time to time that I did not always tell him *how* different. I expected no good, but only pain to both of us, from discussing our differences: and I never expressed them but when he gave utterance to some opinion of feeling repugnant to mine, in a manner which would have made it disingenuousness on my part to remain silent....

Harriet Martineau
from *Autobiography* (1877)

A prolific journalist, historian, and sociologist, Harriet Martineau (1802–76) wrote on such varied subjects as abolition, women's rights, and the Haitian Revolution of the 1790s. Martineau rose to fame and financial success with her *Illustrations of Political Economy* (1832–34), a multivolume series of tales intended to make the principles of political economy understandable to working-class readers. Her virtual deafness by age 20 did not impede her from travelling widely—to America, Egypt, and elsewhere. She wrote travel books, two novels, and an autobiography in addition to publishing widely in the periodical press and regularly for the *Daily News* on social and political issues.

---

61 Thomas Carlyle, *Sartor Resartus* (*Fraser's Magazine*, 1833–34). See Faith and Doubt.

One of the most prominent Victorian women writers, Martineau courted controversy with her atheism and advocacy of mesmerism. The following excerpt from her autobiography—written in 1855, when she believed she was dying of heart failure, but published posthumously in 1877—provides a vivid memoir of an atheist facing death.

∽

Volume 2, Period 6, Section 9: Fatal Illness

... Throughout December and the early part of January, the disturbance on lying down increased, night by night. There was a *creaking* sensation at the heart (the beating of which was no longer to be felt externally;) and, after the creak, there was an intermission, and then a throb. When this had gone on a few minutes, breathing became perturbed and difficult; and I lay till two, three, or four o'clock, struggling for breath. When this process began to spread back into the evening, and then forward into the morning, I was convinced that there was something seriously wrong; and with the approbation of my family, I wrote to consult Dr. Latham; and soon after, went to London to be examined by him.... There Dr. Latham visited and examined me.... It appears that the substance of the heart is deteriorated, so that "it is too feeble for its work;" there is more or less dilatation; and the organ is very much enlarged. Before I left London, the sinking-fits which are characteristic of the disease began to occur; and it has since been perfectly understood by us all that the alternative lies between death at any hour in one of these sinking-fits, or by dropsy,[62] if I live for the disease to run its course.

Though I expected some such account of the case, I was rather surprised that it caused so little emotion in me. I went out, in a friend's carriage, to tell her the result of Dr. Latham's visit; and I also told a cousin who had been my friend since our school-days. When I returned to my lodgings, and was preparing for dinner, a momentary thrill of something like painful emotion passed through me,—not at all because I was going to die, but at the thought that I should never feel health again. It was merely momentary; and I joined the family and Mr. Atkinson, who dined with us, without any indisposition to the merriment which went on during dinner,—no one but my hostess being aware of what had passed since breakfast. In the course of the evening, I told them; and I saw at once what support I might depend on from my friend. I did not sleep at all that night; and many were the things I had to think over; but I never passed a more tranquil and easy night. As soon as my family heard the news, a beloved niece, who had repeatedly requested to be allowed to come to me, joined me in London, and gave me to understand, with her parents' free consent, that she would not leave me again. I sent for my Executor, made a new will, and put him in possession of my affairs, my designs and wishes, as fully as possible, and accepted his escort home to Ambleside. As there was but one possible mode of treatment, and as that could be pursued in one place as well as another, I was eager to get home to the repose and freshness of my own sweet place. It was not only for the pleasure of it; but for the sake of my servants; and because, while prepared, in regard to my affairs, to go at any time, there were things to be done, if I could do them, to which the quiet of home was almost indispensable.... That was three months ago: and during those three months, I have been visited by my family, one by one, and by some dear friends, while my niece has been so constantly with me as to have, in my opinion, prolonged my life by her incomparable nursing. The interval has been employed in writing this Memoir, and in closing

---

62 Now known as edema, a condition caused by fluid buildup under the skin or in body cavities.

all my engagements, so that no interest of any kind may suffer by my departure at any moment. The winter, after long lingering, is gone, and I am still here,—sitting in the sun on my terrace, and at night going out, according to old custom, to look abroad in the moon or star-light.... Never was a dying person more nobly "friended," as the Scotch have it. My days are filled with pleasures, and I have no cares; so that the only thing I have to fear is that, after all the discipline of my life, I should be spoiled at the end of it.

When I learned what my state is, it was my wish ... that my death might take place before long, and by the quicker process: and such is, in an easy sort of way, my wish still. The last is for the sake of my nurse, and of all about me; and the first is mainly because I do not want to deteriorate and get spoiled in the final stage of my life, by ceasing to hear the truth, and the whole truth: and nobody ventures to utter any unpleasant truth to a person with "a heart-complaint." I must take my chance for this; and I have a better chance than most, because my nurse and constant companion knows that I do not desire that any body should "make things pleasant" because I am ill. I should wish, as she knows, to live under complete and healthy moral conditions to the last, if these can be accommodated, by courage and mutual trust, with the physical conditions.—As to the spoiling process,—I have been doubting, for some years past, whether I was not undergoing it. I have lived too long to think of making myself anxious about my state and prospects in any way; but it has occurred to me occasionally, of late years, whether I could endure as I formerly did. I had become so accustomed to ease of body and mind, that it seemed to me doubtful how I might bear pain, or any change;—for it seemed as if any change must be for the worse, as to enjoyment. I remember being struck with a saying of Mrs. Wordsworth's, uttered ten years ago, when she was seventy-six,—that the beauty of our valley made us too fond of life,—too little ready to leave it. Her domestic bereavements since that time have doubtless altered this feeling entirely;[63] but, in many an hour of intense enjoyment on the hills, I have recalled that saying; and, in wonder at my freedom from care, have speculated on whether I should think it an evil to die, then and there. I have now had three months' experience of the fact of constant expectation of death; and the result is, as much regret as a rational person can admit at the absurd waste of time, thought and energy that I have been guilty of in the course of my life in dwelling on the subject of death.... [N]ow that I am awaiting it at any hour, the whole thing seems so easy, simple and natural that I cannot but wonder how I could keep my thoughts fixed upon it when it was far off.... I find death in prospect the simplest thing in the world,—a thing not to be feared or regretted, or to get excited about in any way.—I attribute this very much, however, to the nature of my views of death. The case must be much otherwise with Christians,—even independently of the selfish and perturbing emotions connected with an expectation of rewards and punishments in the next world. They can never be quite secure from the danger that their air-built castle shall dissolve at the last moment, and that they may vividly perceive on what imperfect evidence and delusive grounds their expectation of immortality or resurrection reposes. The mere perception of the incompatibility of immortality and resurrection may be, and often is, deferred till that time; and that is no time for such questions. But, if the intellect be ever so accommodating, there is the heart,—steady to its domestic affections. I, for one, should be heavy-hearted if I were now about to go to the antipodes,[64]—to leave all whom I love, and who are bound up with my daily life,—however cer-

---

63 Mary Wordsworth lived in Ambleside near Martineau; her "domestic bereavements" included the deaths of a grandson (Edward, d. 1845); a nephew of her husband (John, d. 1846); a daughter (Dora, d. 1847); a daughter-in-law (Isabella, d. 1848); her husband (William, d. 1850); and a sister-in-law (Dorothy, d. 1855).
64 The location on the globe directly opposite one's current location.

tain might be the prospect of meeting them again twenty or thirty years hence; and it is no credit to any Christian to be "joyful," "triumphant" and so forth, in going to "glory," while leaving any loved ones behind,—whether or not there may be loved ones "gone before." An unselfish and magnanimous person cannot be solaced, in parting with mortal companions and human sufferers, by personal rewards, glory, bliss, or any thing of the sort. I used to think and feel all this before I became emancipated from the superstition; and I could only submit, and suppose it all right because it was ordained. But now, the release is an inexpressible comfort; and the simplifying of the whole matter has a most tranquillizing effect. I see that the dying (others than the aged) naturally and regularly, unless disturbed, desire and sink into death as into sleep. Where no artificial state is induced, they feel no care about dying, or about living again. The state of their organisation disposes them to rest; and rest is all they think about. We know, by all testimony, that persons who are brought face to face with death by an accident which seems to leave no chance of escape, have no religious ideas or emotions whatever. Where the issue is doubtful, the feeble and helpless cry out to God for mercy, and are in perturbation or calmness according to organisation, training, and other circumstances: but, where escape appears wholly impossible, the most religious men think and feel nothing religious at all,—as those of them who have escaped tell their intimate friends. And again, soldiers rush upon death in battle with utter carelessness,—engrossed in other emotions, in the presence of which death appears as easy and simple a matter as it does to me now.—Conscious as I am of what my anxiety would be if I were exiled to the antipodes,—or to the garden of Eden, if you will,—for twenty or thirty years, I feel no sort of solicitude about a parting which will bring no pain. Sympathy with those who will miss me, I do feel, of course: yet not very painfully, because their sorrow cannot, in the nature of things, long interfere with their daily peace; but to me there is no sacrifice, no sense of loss, nothing to fear, nothing to regret. Under the eternal laws of the universe, I came into being, and, under them, I have lived a life so full that its fullness is equivalent to length. The age in which I have lived is an infant one in the history of our globe and of Man; and the consequence is, a great waste in the years and the powers of the wisest of us; and, in the case of one so limited in powers, and so circumscribed by early unfavourable influences as myself, the waste is something deplorable. But we have only to accept the conditions in which we find ourselves, and to make the best of them; and my last days are cheered by the sense of how much better my later years have been than the earlier; or than, in the earlier, I ever could have anticipated. Some of the terrible faults of my character which religion failed to ameliorate, and others which superstition bred in me, have given way, more or less, since I attained a truer point of view: and the relief from old burdens, the uprising of new satisfactions, and the opening of new clearness,—the fresh air of Nature, in short, after imprisonment in the ghost-peopled cavern of superstition,—has been as favourable to my moral nature as to intellectual progress and general enjoyment. Thus, there has been much in life that I am glad to have enjoyed; and much that generates a mood of contentment at the close. Besides that I never dream of wishing that any thing were otherwise than as it is, I am frankly satisfied to have done with life. I have had a noble share of it, and I desire no more. I neither wish to live longer here, nor to find life again elsewhere. It seems to me simply absurd to expect it.... Nor can I understand why any body should expect me to desire any thing else than this yielding up my place. If we may venture to speak, limited as we are, of any thing whatever being important, we may say that the important thing is that the universe should be full of life, as we suppose it to be, under the eternal laws of the universe: and, if the universe be full of life, I cannot see how it can signify whether the one human faculty of consciousness of identity be preserved and carried forward, when all the rest of the organisation is gone to dust, or so changed as to be in no respect properly the same. In brief, I cannot see how it matters whether my successor be called H.M. or A.B. or Y.Z. I am satisfied that there will always be as much conscious life in the universe as its laws provide for; and that certainty is enough, even for my narrow human conception, which, however, can discern that caring about it at all is a mere human view and emotion. The real and justifiable and honourable subject of interest to human beings, living and dying, is the welfare of their fellows, surrounding them, or surviving them. About this, I do care, and supremely....

Anthony Trollope
from *An Autobiography* (1883)

The prolific Anthony Trollope (1815–82) produced 47 novels as well as short stories, travel books, an autobiography, essays, biographies, histories, and sketches. Preoccupied from childhood with financial insecurity, Trollope gained work as a London postal clerk through the connections of his mother, the writer Frances Trollope. He worked extensively in Ireland before becoming post office surveyor of the eastern district and introduced roadside pillar (mail) boxes in Great Britain before quitting the job in 1867. Trollope started writing novels in his early days at the post office, but his writing career gained traction once he began writing while travelling and maintaining detailed ledgers of how many pages he wrote per day.

In this passage, Trollope describes the composition of his breakthrough novel, *Barchester Towers* (1857). The passage records his careful attention to financial arrangements with publishers and establishes a model of the professional writer.

Chapter 6: "Barchester Towers" and the "Three Clerks." 1855–1858

It was, I think, before I started on my English tours among the rural posts that I made my first attempt at writing for a magazine. I had read, soon after they came out, the two first volumes of Charles Merivale's *History of the Romans under the Empire*,[65] and had got into some correspondence with the author's brother as to the author's views about Cæsar.[66] Hence arose in my mind a tendency to investigate the character of probably the greatest man who ever lived, which tendency in after years produced a little book of which I shall have to speak when its time comes,—and also a taste generally for Latin literature, which has been one of the chief delights of my later life. And I may say that I became at this time as anxious about Cæsar, and as desirous of reaching the truth as to his character, as we have all been in regard to Bismarck[67] in these latter days. I lived in Cæsar, and debated with myself constantly whether he crossed the Rubicon

---

65 Charles Merivale, *History of the Romans under the Empire* (1850–64).
66 Julius Caesar (c. 100–44 BCE), Roman general and politician.
67 Otto von Bismarck (1815–98), Prussian prime minister and first chancellor of the German Empire.

as a tyrant or as a patriot.[68] In order that I might review Mr. Merivale's book without feeling that I was dealing unwarrantably with a subject beyond me, I studied the Commentaries[69] thoroughly, and went through a mass of other reading which the object of a magazine article hardly justified—but which has thoroughly justified itself in the subsequent pursuits of my life. I did write two articles, the first mainly on Julius Cæsar, and the second on Augustus,[70] which appeared in the *Dublin University Magazine*. They were the result of very much labour, but there came from them no pecuniary product. I had been very modest when I sent them to the editor, as I had been when I called on John Forster,[71] not venturing to suggest the subject of money. After a while I did call upon the proprietor of the magazine in Dublin, and was told by him that such articles were generally written to oblige friends, and that articles written to oblige friends were not usually paid for.... Up to the end of 1857 I had received £55 for the hard work of ten years.

It was while I was engaged on *Barchester Towers*[72] that I adopted a system of writing which, for some years afterwards, I found to be very serviceable to me. My time was greatly occupied in travelling, and the nature of my travelling was now changed. I could not any longer do it on horseback. Railroads afforded me my means of conveyance, and I found that I passed in railway-carriages very many hours of my existence. Like others, I used to read,—though Carlyle[73] has since told me that a man when travelling should not read, but "sit still and label his thoughts." But if I intended to make a profitable business out of my writing, and, at the same time, to do my best for the Post Office, I must turn these hours to more account than I could do even by reading. I made for myself therefore a little tablet, and found after a few days' exercise that I could write as quickly in a railway-carriage as I could at my desk. I worked with a pencil, and what I wrote my wife copied afterwards. In this way was composed the greater part of *Barchester Towers* and of the novel which succeeded it,[74] and much also of others subsequent to them....

In the writing of *Barchester Towers* I took great delight. The bishop and Mrs. Proudie were very real to me, as were also the troubles of the archdeacon and the loves of Mr. Slope. When it was done, Mr. W. Longman[75] required that it should be subjected to his reader; and he returned the MS.[76] to me, with a most laborious and voluminous criticism,—coming from whom I never knew. This was accompanied by an offer to print the novel on the half-profit system, with a payment of £100 in advance out of my half-profits,—on condition that I would comply with the suggestions made by his critic.[77] One of these suggestions required that I should cut the novel down to two volumes. In my reply, I went through the criticisms, rejecting one and accepting another, almost alternately, but declaring at last that no consideration should induce me to put out a third of my work.[78] I am at a loss to know how such a task could be performed. I could

---

68 In 49 BCE, Julius Caesar led an army across the Rubicon (a stream separating Gaul and Italy), defying Roman law and prompting civil war.
69 Julius Caesar, *Commentarii de bello Gallico* and *Commentarii de bello civili*.
70 Augustus Caesar (63 BCE–14 CE), first Roman emperor.
71 John Forster (1812–76), writer, editor, and reviewer.
72 Anthony Trollope, *Barchester Towers* (1857).
73 Thomas Carlyle (1795–1881), leading intellectual and social critic. See Condition of England, Faith and Doubt.
74 Anthony Trollope, *Doctor Thorne* (1858).
75 William Longman (1813–77), prominent publisher.
76 Manuscript.
77 In the Victorian half-profit system, publisher and author halved the profits on book sales after the publisher had recouped production and distribution costs.
78 The three-volume (or triple-decker) novel dominated the Victorian book market; its price remained consistent (31 shillings and sixpence) from 1821 to 1894.

burn the MS., no doubt, and write another book on the same story; but how two words out of six are to be withdrawn from a written novel, I cannot conceive. I believe such tasks have been attempted—perhaps performed; but I refused to make even the attempt. Mr. Longman was too gracious to insist on his critic's terms; and the book was published, certainly none the worse, and I do not think much the better, for the care that had been taken with it.

The work succeeded just as *The Warden*[79] had succeeded. It achieved no great reputation, but it was one of the novels which novel readers were called upon to read....

I received my £100, in advance, with profound delight. It was a positive and most welcome increase to my income, and might probably be regarded as a first real step on the road to substantial success. I am well aware that there are many who think that an author in his authorship should not regard money,—nor a painter, or sculptor, or composer in his art. I do not know that this unnatural self-sacrifice is supposed to extend itself further. A barrister, a clergyman, a doctor, an engineer, and even actors and architects, may without disgrace follow the bent of human nature, and endeavour to fill their bellies and clothe their backs, and also those of their wives and children, as comfortably as they can by the exercise of their abilities and their crafts. They may be as rationally realistic, as may the butchers and the bakers; but the artist and the author forget the high glories of their calling if they condescend to make a money return a first object. They who preach this doctrine will be much offended by my theory, and by this book of mine, if my theory and my book come beneath their notice.... All material progress has come from man's desire to do the best he can for himself and those about him, and civilisation and Christianity itself have been made possible by such progress.... Did Titian or Rubens[80] disregard their pecuniary rewards? As far as we know, Shakespeare worked always for money, giving the best of his intellect to support his trade as an actor. In our own century what literary names stand higher than those of Byron, Tennyson, Scott, Dickens, Macaulay,[81] and Carlyle? And I think I may say that none of those great men neglected the pecuniary result of their labours.... Brains that are unbought will never serve the public much. Take away from English authors their copyrights, and you would very soon take away from England her authors.

I say this here, because it is my purpose as I go on to state what to me has been the result of my profession in the ordinary way in which professions are regarded, so that by my example may be seen what prospect there is that a man devoting himself to literature with industry, perseverance, certain necessary aptitudes, and fair average talents, may succeed in gaining a livelihood, as another man does in another profession. The result with me has been comfortable but not splendid, as I think was to have been expected from the combination of such gifts.

I have certainly always had also before my eyes the charms of reputation. Over and above the money view of the question, I wished from the beginning to be something more than a clerk in the Post Office. To be known as somebody,—to be Anthony Trollope if it be no more,—is to me much. The feeling is a very general one, and I think beneficent. It is that which has been called the "last infirmity of noble mind."[82] The infirmity is so human that the man who lacks it is either above or below humanity. I own to the infirmity. But I confess that my first object in taking to literature as a profession was that which is

---

79 Anthony Trollope, *The Warden* (1855).
80 Tiziano "Titian" Vecellio (c. 1488–1576), Italian Renaissance painter; Peter Paul Rubens (1577–1640), Flemish painter.
81 George Gordon Byron (1788–1824), poet; Alfred Tennyson (1809–92), poet; Walter Scott (1771–1832), novelist and poet; Charles Dickens (1812–70), novelist; Thomas Babington Macaulay (1800–59), historian, critic, and poet.
82 John Milton, *Lycidas* (1637).

common to the barrister when he goes to the Bar, and to the baker when he sets up his oven. I wished to make an income on which I and those belonging to me might live in comfort.

If indeed a man writes his books badly, or paints his pictures badly, because he can make his money faster in that fashion than by doing them well, and at the same time proclaims them to be the best he can do,—if in fact he sells shoddy for broadcloth,[83]—he is dishonest, as is any other fraudulent dealer. So may be the barrister who takes money that he does not earn, or the clergyman who is content to live on a sinecure.[84] No doubt the artist or the author may have a difficulty which will not occur to the seller of cloth, in settling within himself what is good work and what is bad,—when labour enough has been given, and when the task has been scamped.[85] It is a danger as to which he is bound to be severe with himself—in which he should feel that his conscience should be set fairly in the balance against the natural bias of his interest. If he do not do so, sooner or later his dishonesty will be discovered, and will be estimated accordingly. But in this he is to be governed only by the plain rules of honesty which should govern us all. Having said so much, I shall not scruple as I go on to attribute to the pecuniary result of my labours all the importance which I felt them to have at the time.

Barchester Towers, for which I had received £100 in advance, sold well enough to bring me further payments—moderate payments—from the publishers. From that day up to this very time in which I am writing, that book and *The Warden* together have given me almost every year some small income. I get the accounts very regularly, and I find that I have received £727, 11s. 3d.[86] for the two. It is more than I got for the three or four works that came afterwards,[87] but the payments have been spread over twenty years.

When I went to Mr. Longman with my next novel, *The Three Clerks*, in my hand, I could not induce him to understand that a lump sum down was more pleasant than a deferred annuity. I wished him to buy it from me at a price which he might think to be a fair value, and I argued with him that as soon as an author has put himself into a position which insures a sufficient sale of his works to give a profit, the publisher is not entitled to expect the half of such proceeds. While there is a pecuniary risk, the whole of which must be borne by the publisher, such division is fair enough; but such a demand on the part of the publisher is monstrous as soon as the article produced is known to be a marketable commodity. I thought that I had now reached that point, but Mr. Longman did not agree with me. And he endeavoured to convince me that I might lose more than I gained, even though I should get more money by going elsewhere. "It is for you," said he, "to think whether our names on your title-page are not worth more to you than the increased payment." This seemed to me to savour of that high-flown doctrine of the contempt of money which I have never admired. I did think much of Messrs. Longman's name, but I liked it best at the bottom of a cheque....

---

83 Fine high-quality cloth used mainly for men's clothing.
84 A paid position with no duties attached.
85 Done in a hurry or without care.
86 727 pounds, 11 shillings, and three pence.
87 Anthony Trollope, *The Three Clerks* (1858), *Doctor Thorne* (1858), *The Bertrams* (1859), *The West Indies and the Spanish Main* (1859).

John Ruskin
from *Praeterita* (1885–89)

Writer and artist John Ruskin (1819–1900) was one of the most influential art and social critics of the Victorian period. Though confirmed as an Anglican while at Oxford, he was not swept up by the Oxford Movement. After Oxford, Ruskin abandoned poetry to write criticism of art and architecture. With his father's financial support, Ruskin launched his writing career by defending artist J.M.W. Turner in *Modern Painters* (1843–60), in which he argued for the apprehension of divinity via contemplation of the beautiful in art. His failed marriage prompted scandal just as he emerged as a public intellectual and proponent of the Pre-Raphaelites. *The Stones of Venice* (1851–53) celebrated Byzantine and Gothic styles and had an impact on Victorian architects. Influenced by Carlyle's *Past and Present* (1843), Ruskin lamented how industrialization reduced craftsmen to machines.

In this selection from *Praeterita* (1885–89), Latin for "past," Ruskin describes travelling to Italy in the mid-1840s to study art and architecture of the Christian tradition.

∽

Chapter 6: The Campo Santo

The summer's work of 1844, so far from advancing the design of "Modern Painters,"[88] had thrown me off it—first into fine botany, then into difficult geology, and lastly, as that entry about the Madonna shows, into a fit of figure study which meant much. It meant, especially, at last some looking into ecclesiastical history,—some notion of the merit of fourteenth century painting, and the total abandonment of Rubens and Rembrandt for the Venetian school.[89] Which, the reader will please observe, signified not merely the advance in sense of colour, but in perception of truth and modesty in light and shade. And on getting home, I felt that in the cyclone of confused new knowledge, this was the thing first to be got firm.

Scarcely any book writing was done that winter,—and there are no diaries; but, for the first time, I took up Turner's "Liber Studiorum"[90] instead of engravings; mastered its principles, practised its method, and by spring-time in 1845 was able to study from nature accurately in full chiaroscuro,[91] with a good frank power over the sepia tinting.

I must have read also, that winter, Rio's "Poésie Chrétienne," and Lord Lindsay's introduction to his "Christian Art."[92] And perceiving thus, in some degree, what a blind bat and puppy I had been, all

---

88 John Ruskin, *Modern Painters* (1843–60).
89 Peter Paul Rubens (1577–1640), Flemish painter; Rembrandt van Rijn (1606–69), Dutch painter; the Venetian school refers to Renaissance art of Venice.
90 J.M.W. Turner, *Liber Studiorum* (1806–19), a series of 70 prints that functioned as a manifesto for his landscape art.
91 In art, contrasts between light and shadow.
92 Alexis-François Rio, *De la Poésie Chrétienne* (1836), a history of Italian art; Alexander William Crawford Lindsay's *Sketches of the History of Christian Art* (1847) surveyed early Italian art history. Ruskin reviewed the work in the *Quarterly Review* in June 1847.

through Italy, determined that at least I must see Pisa and Florence again before writing another word of "Modern Painters."

How papa and mamma took this new vagary, I have no recollection; resignedly, at least: perhaps they also had some notion that I might think differently, and it was to be hoped in a more orthodox and becoming manner, after another sight of the Tribune.[93] At all events, they concluded to give me my own way entirely this time; and what time I chose. My health caused them no farther anxiety;[94] they could trust my word to take care of myself every day, just the same as if I were coming home to tea: my mother was satisfied of Couttet's skill as a physician,[95] and care, if needed, as a nurse;—he was engaged for the summer in those capacities,—and, about the first week in April, I found myself dining on a trout of the Ain, at Champagnole;[96] with Switzerland and Italy at my feet—for to-morrow.

Curiously, the principal opposition to this unprincipled escapade had been made by Turner.[97] He knew that one of my chief objects was to see the motives of his last sketches on the St. Gothard;[98] and he feared my getting into some scrape in the then disturbed state of the cantons.[99] He had probably himself seen some of their doings in 1843, when "la vieille Suisse prit les armes, prévint les Bas Valaisans, qui furent vaincus et massacrés au Pont du Trient, près de Martigny;"[100] and again an expedition of the Corps Francs of the liberal cantons "pour expulser les Jesuits, et renverser le gouvernement,"[101] at Lucerne, had been summarily "renversée"[102] itself by the Lucernois, 8th December, 1844, only three months before my intended start for the Alps. Every time Turner saw me during the winter, he said something to dissuade me from going abroad; when at last I went to say good-bye, he came down with me into the hall in Queen Anne Street, and opening the door just enough for me to pass, laid hold of my arm, gripping it strongly. "Why *will* you go to Switzerland—there'll be such a fidge[103] about you, when you're gone...."

It was no part of my plan, however, as my parents knew, to enter Switzerland in this spring-time: but to do what I could in Italy first. Geneva itself was quiet enough: Couttet met me there, and next day we drove over the ledges of the Salève, all aglow with primrose and soldanelle, down upon Annecy....[104]

At Annecy I made the first careful trial of my new way of work. I herewith reproduce the study; it is very pleasant to me still; and certainly any artist who once accustoms himself to the method cannot afterwards fall into any mean trickery or dull conventionalism. The outline must be made clearly and quietly, conveying as much accurate information as possible respecting the form and structure of the object; then, in washing, the chiaroscuro is lowered from the high lights with extreme care down to the middle tones, and the main masses left in full shade.

---

93 Room 18 of the Uffizi art gallery in Florence, Italy.
94 Ruskin had withdrawn from Oxford in 1840 due to ill health; he was coughing blood.
95 Joseph Couttet served as expedition guide.
96 A town in eastern France on the bank of the River Ain.
97 J.M.W. Turner (1775–1851), landscape painter, whom Ruskin met in 1840 and supported thereafter.
98 Turner painted the Swiss precipices in *The Passage of the St. Gothard* (1804).
99 The 26 cantons of Switzerland comprise the member states of the federation; in the 1830s and 1840s, they were swept by both conservative and radical movements.
100 French: "The Ur-Swiss attacked the inhabitants of Lower Valais, taking them by surprise. The latter were conquered and massacred at the Trient bridge near Martigny": E.H. Gaullieur, *La Suisse Historique* (1855).
101 French: "To expel the Jesuits and overthrow the government."
102 French: overthrown.
103 Fuss.
104 The Salève is a French mountain overlooking Geneva; soldanelle is an alpine plant; Annecy is a town in southeastern France.

A rhyme written to Mont Blanc at Geneva, and another in vituperation of the idle people at Conflans,[105] were, I think, the last serious exertions of my poetical powers. I perceived finally that I could express nothing I had to say, rightly, in that manner; and the "peace of mind" above referred to, which returns to me as the principal character of this opening journey, was perhaps, in part, the result of this extremely wholesome conclusion.

But also, the two full years, since the flash of volcanic lightning at Naples,[106] had brought me into a deeper and more rational state of religious temper. I can scarcely yet call it religious thought; but the steadily read chapters, morning and evening, with the continual comparison between the Protestant and Papal services every Sunday abroad, made me feel that all dogmatic teaching was a matter of chance and habit; and that the life of religion depended on the force of faith, not the terms of it. In the sincerity and brightness of his imagination, I saw that George Herbert represented the theology of the Protestant Church in a perfectly central and deeply spiritual manner: his "Church Porch" I recognised to be blamelessly wise as a lesson to youth; and the exquisitely faithful fancy of the other poems (in the "Temple") drew me into learning most of them by heart,—the "Church Porch," the "Dialogue," "Employment," "Submission," "Gratefulness," and, chief favourite, "The Bag,"—deliberately and carefully.[107] The code of feeling and law written in these verses may be always assigned as a standard of the purest unsectarian Christianity; and whatever has been wisest in thought or happiest in the course of my following life was founded at this time on the teaching of Herbert....

... A little more force was also put on Bible study at this time, because I held myself responsible for George's[108] tenets as well as my own, and wished to set him a discreet example; he being well-disposed, and given to my guidance, with no harm as yet in any of his ways. So I read my chapter with him morning and evening; and if there were no English church on Sundays, the Morning Service, Litany and all, very reverently; after which we enjoyed ourselves, each in our own way, in the afternoons, George being always free, and Couttet, if he chose; but he had little taste for the Sunday promenades in a town, and was glad if I would take him with me to gather flowers, or carry stones. I never, until this time, had thought of travelling, climbing, or sketching on the Sunday:[109] the first infringement of this rule by climbing the isolated peak above Gap,[110] with both Couttet and George, after our morning service, remains a weight on my conscience to this day. But it was thirteen years later before I made a sketch on Sunday.

By Gap and Sisteron to Frejus, along the Riviera to Sestri, where I gave a day to draw the stone-pines now at Oxford; and so straight to my first fixed aim, Lucca,[111] where I settled myself for ten days,—as I supposed. It turned out forty years.

---

105 French for white mountain, Mont Blanc is the Alps' tallest mountain and was a popular destination for nineteenth-century tourists and mountaineers, as well as a popular subject for Romantic writers and artists; Conflans is a medieval town in southeastern France.
106 A southern Italian city.
107 George Herbert, *The Temple* (1633).
108 John Hobbs, a young servant known as "George" to distinguish him from Ruskin and his father, both called John.
109 Ruskin grew up as an evangelical; this refers to his turning away from strict Sabbath observance.
110 A city in southeastern France.
111 Sisteron is an ancient town in southeastern France; settled by Romans, Fréjus is an ancient town in southeastern France; the Riviera is the southeastern French coast that borders the Mediterranean Sea; Sestri is a coastal town in Italy; Lucca is an ancient city in central Italy.

The town is some thousand paces square; the unbroken rampart walk round may be a short three miles. There are upwards of twenty churches in that space, dating between the sixth and twelfth centuries; a ruined feudal palace and tower, unmatched except at Verona: the streets clean—cheerfully inhabited, yet quiet; nor desolate, even now. Two of the churches representing the perfectest phase of round-arched building in Europe, and one of them containing the loveliest Christian tomb in Italy.[112]

The rampart walk, unbroken except by descents and ascents at the gates, commands every way the loveliest ranges of all the Tuscan Apennine:[113] when I was there in 1845, besides the ruined feudal palace, there was a maintained Ducal Palace, with a living Duke in it, whose military band played every evening on the most floral and peaceful space of rampart. After a well-spent day, and a three-course dinner,—military band,—chains, double braided, of amethyst Apennine linked by golden clouds,—then the mountain air of April, still soft as the marble towers grew unsubstantial in the starlight, such the monastic discipline of Lucca to my novitiate mind.

I must stop to think a little how it was that so early as this I could fasten on the tomb of Ilaria di Caretto with certainty of its being a supreme guide to me ever after. If I get tiresome, the reader must skip; I write, for the moment, to amuse myself, and not him. The said reader, duly sagacious, must have felt, long since, that, though very respectable people in our way, we were all of us definitely vulgar people; just as my aunt's dog Towzer was a vulgar dog, though a very good and dear dog. Said reader should have seen also that we had not set ourselves up to have "à tasté" in anything. There was never any question about matching colours in furniture, or having the correct pattern in china. Everything for service in the house was bought plain, and of the best; our toys were what we happened to take a fancy to in pleasant places—a cow in stalactite from Matlock, a fisher-wife doll from Calais, a Swiss farm from Berne, Bacchus and Ariadne from Carrara.[114] But, among these toys, principal on the drawing-room chimney-piece, always put away by my mother at night, and "put out" in the afternoon, were some pieces of Spanish clay, to which, without knowing it, I owed a quantity of strenuous teaching. Native baked clay figures, painted and gilded by untaught persons who had the gift; manufacture mainly practised along the Xeres coast,[115] I believe, and of late much decayed, but then flourishing, and its work as good as the worker could make it. There was a Don Whiskerandos contrabandista,[116] splendidly handsome and good-natured, on a magnificent horse at the trot, brightly caparisoned: everything finely finished, his gun loose in his hand. There was a lemonade seller, a pomegranate seller, a matador with his bull—animate all, and graceful, the colouring chiefly ruddy brown. Things of constant interest to me, and altogether wholesome; vestiges of living sculpture come down into the Herne Hill times, from the days of Tanagra.[117]

---

112 The tomb of Ilaria del Carretto (1379–1405), a marble sarcophagus in the Cathedral of San Martino, Lucca.
113 The central Italian portion of the Apennine mountain range, which runs the length of Italy.
114 Near the English town of Matlock, there are limestone caves where stalactites form as minerals drip from the caves' roofs; Calais is a northern French coastal town that is the main port for English travellers from Dover; Berne is a medieval city in Switzerland; also known as Dionysus, Bacchus was the god of wine and ecstasy; Ariadne was his wife; Carrara is a northern Italian town renowned for its marble quarries.
115 The southwest coast of Spain, where Jerez (the conventional spelling of Xeres) de la Frontera divides the mountains and the sea.
116 Humorous: "Sir Moustachioed Smuggler."
117 Herne Hill is a London neighbourhood; the ancient city of Tanagra in northern Attica was known for its terra cotta sculptures.

For loftier admiration, as before told, Chantrey in Lichfield, Roubilliac in Westminster,[118] were set forth to me, and honestly felt; a scratched white outline or two from Greek vases on the black Derbyshire marble did not interfere with my first general feeling about sculpture, that it should be living, and emotional; that the flesh should be like flesh, and the drapery like clothes; and that, whether trotting contrabandista, dancing girl, or dying gladiator, the subject should have an interest of its own, and not consist merely of figures with torches or garlands standing alternately on their right and left legs. Of "ideal" form and the like, I fortunately heard and thought nothing....

Another influence, no less forcible, and more instantly effective, was brought to bear on me by my first quiet walk through Lucca.

Hitherto, all architecture, except fairy-finished Milan, had depended with me for its delight on being partly in decay. I revered the sentiment of its age, and I was accustomed to look for the signs of age in the mouldering of its traceries, and in the interstices deepening between the stones of its masonry. This looking for cranny and joint was mixed with the love of rough stones themselves, and of country churches built like Westmoreland cottages.

Here in Lucca I found myself suddenly in the presence of twelfth century buildings, originally set in such balance of masonry that they could all stand without mortar; and in material so incorruptible, that after six hundred years of sunshine and rain, a lancet could not now be put between their joints.

Absolutely for the first time I now saw what mediæval builders were, and what they meant. I took the simplest of all façades for analysis, that of Santa Maria Foris-Portam,[119] and thereon literally *began* the study of architecture.

In the third—and, for the reader's relief, last—place in these technical records, Fra Bartolomeo's picture of the Magdalene, with St. Catherine of Siena,[120] gave me a faultless example of the treatment of pure Catholic tradition by the perfect schools of painting.

And I never needed lessoning more in the principles of the three great arts. After those summer days of 1845, I advanced only in knowledge of individual character, provincial feeling, and details of construction or execution. Of what was primarily right and ultimately best, there was never more doubt to me, and my art-teaching, necessarily, in its many local or personal interests partial, has been from that time throughout consistent, and progressing every year to more evident completion.

The full happiness of that time to me cannot be explained except to consistently hard workers; and of those, to the few who can keep their peace and health. For the world appeared to me now exactly right. Hills as high as they should be, rivers as wide, pictures as pretty, and masters and men as wise—as pretty and wise could be. And I expected to bring everybody to be of my opinion, as soon as I could get out my second volume; and drove down to Pisa in much hope and pride, though grave in both.

For now I had read enough of Cary's Dante, and Sismondi's "Italian Republics," and Lord Lindsay, to feel what I had to look for in the Campo Santo.[121] Yet at this moment I pause to think what it was that I found.

---

118 The sculptures by Sir Francis Legatt Chantrey (1781–1841) in Lichfield Cathedral and by Louis-François Roubiliac (1702–62) in Westminster Abbey.
119 The church of Santa Maria Forisportam in Lucca, begun in the thirteenth century.
120 Fra Bartolomeo, *God the Father with SS. Catherine of Siena and Mary Magdalen* (1509).
121 Henry Francis Cary's complete translation of Dante's *Divina Commedia* was first published in 1814; Léonard Simond de Sismondi, *L'Histoire des républiques italiennes du Moyen-Âge* (1809–18); Latin for the Holy Field, the Campo Santo is an enclosed burial ground in Pisa.

Briefly, the entire doctrine of Christianity, painted so that a child could understand it. And what a child cannot understand of Christianity, no one need try to.

In these days of the religion of this and that,—briefly let us say, the religion of Stocks and Posts[122] in order to say a clear word of the Campo Santo, one must first say a firm word concerning Christianity itself. I find numbers, even of the most intelligent and amiable people, not knowing what the word means; because they are always asking how much is true, and how much they like, and never ask, first, what *was* the total meaning of it, whether they like it or not.

The total meaning was, and is, that the God who made earth and its creatures, took at a certain time upon the earth, the flesh and form of man; in that flesh sustained the pain and died the death of the creature He had made; rose again after death into glorious human life, and when the date of the human race is ended, will return in visible human form, and render to every man according to his work. Christianity is the belief in, and love of, God thus manifested. Anything less than this, the mere acceptance of the sayings of Christ, or assertion of any less than divine power in His Being, may be, for aught I know, enough for virtue, peace, and safety; but they do not make people Christians, or enable them to understand the heart of the simplest believer in the old doctrine. One verse more of George Herbert will put the height of that doctrine into less debateable, though figurative, picture than any longer talk of mine:—

Hast thou not heard that my Lord Jesus died?
Then let me tell thee a strange story.
The God of Power, as he did ride
In his majestic robes of glory,
    Resolved[123] to light; and so, one day
    He did descend, undressing all the way.

The stars his tire of light, and rings, obtained,
The cloud his bow, the fire his spear,
The heavens[124] his azure mantle gained,
And when they asked what he would wear,
    He smiled, and said as he did go,
    "He had new clothes a-making, here, below."[125]

I write from memory; the lines have been my lesson, ever since 1845, of the noblesse of thought which makes the simplest word best.

And the Campo Santo of Pisa is absolutely the same in painting as these lines in word. Straight to its purpose, in the clearest and most eager way; the purpose, highest that can be; the expression, the best possible to the workman according to his knowledge. The several parts of the gospel of the Campo Santo are written by different persons; but all the original frescoes are by men of honest genius. No matter for their names;[126] the contents of this wall-scripture are these....

---

122 Of money and book-keeping (posts are ledger entries).
123 "Reserv'd" in the original.
124 "Sky" in the original.
125 George Herbert, "The Bag," *The Temple* (1633).
126 The frescoes of the Campo Santo were begun c. 1330; many are by unknown artists.

Meantime, my own first business was evidently to read what these Pisans had said of it, and take some record of the sayings; for at that time the old-fashioned ravages were going on, honestly and innocently. Nobody cared for the old plaster, and nobody pretended to. When any dignitary of Pisa was to be buried, they peeled off some Benozzo Gozzoli,[127] or whatever else was in the way, and put up a nice new tablet to the new defunct; but what was left was still all Benozzo, (or repainting of old time, not last year's restoration). I cajoled the Abbé Rosini into letting me put up a scaffold level with the frescoes; set steadily to work with what faculty in outline I had; and being by this time practised in delicate curves, by having drawn trees and grass rightly, got far better results than I had hoped, and had an extremely happy fortnight of it! For as the triumph of Death was no new thought to me, the life of hermits was no temptation; but the stories of Abraham, Job, and St. Ranier, well told, were like three new—Scott's novels,[128] I was going to say, and will say, for I don't see my way to anything nearer the fact, and the work on them was pure delight. I got an outline of Abraham's parting with the last of the three angels;[129] of the sacrifice of Job;[130] of the three beggars, and a fiend or two, out of the Triumph of Death;[131] and of the conversion of St. Ranier,[132] for which I greatly pitied him.

For he is playing, evidently with happiest skill, on a kind of zithern-harp,[133] held upright as he stands, to the dance of four sweet Pisan maids, in a round, holding each other only by the bent little fingers of each hand. And one with graver face, and wearing a purple robe, approaches him, saying—I knew once what she said, but forget now; only it meant that his joyful life in that kind was to be ended. And he obeys her, and follows, into a nobler life.

I do not know if ever there was a real St. Ranier; but the story of him remained for truth in the heart of Pisa as long as Pisa herself lived.

I got more than outline of this scene: a coloured sketch of the whole group, which I destroyed afterwards, in shame of its faults, all but the purple-robed warning figure; and that is lost, and the fresco itself now lost also, all mouldering and ruined by what must indeed be a cyclical change in the Italian climate: the frescoes exposed to it of which I made note before 1850, seem to me to have suffered more in the twenty years since, than they had since they were painted: those at Verona alone excepted, where the art of fresco seems to have been practised in the fifteenth century in absolute perfection, and the colour to have been injured only by violence, not by time.

There was another lovely cloister in Pisa, without fresco, but exquisite in its arched perspective and central garden, and noble in its unbuttressed height of belfry tower;—the cloister of San Francesco:[134] in these, and in the meadow round the baptistery, the routine of my Italian university life was now fixed for a good many years in main material points.

---

127 Benozzo Gozzoli (c. 1421–97) painted frescoes in the Campo Santo, focusing on stories from the Old Testament.
128 The Campo Santo frescoes include a depiction of the *Triumph of Death* by an unknown fourteenth-century artist; the frescoes also include a life cycle of Saint Rainerius, patron saint of Pisa; the novels of Walter Scott (1771–1832) entranced early nineteenth-century readers with their vivid depictions of historical events.
129 In Genesis 18:1–8, three angels visit Abraham; they tell him that his wife, Sarah, will give birth to a child and that God will destroy Sodom and Gomorrah, where Abraham's nephew lives.
130 In the Bible, Job regularly offers God burnt offerings in order to atone for his sons' sins; he also refuses to curse God's name even when his children and belongings are destroyed.
131 See 1 Corinthians 15:26.
132 Son of a wealthy Pisan merchant, Saint Rainerius converted to Christianity after conversing with a holy man.
133 A musical instrument with 30 to 40 strings, played by hand.
134 The San Francesco de' Ferri is a church in Pisa dating from the thirteenth century.

In summer I have been always at work, or out walking, by six o'clock, usually awake by half-past four; but I keep to Pisa for the present, where my monkish discipline arranged itself thus. Out, any how, by six, quick walk to the field, and as much done as I could, and back to breakfast at half-past eight. Steady bit of Sismondi over bread and butter, then back to Campo Santo, draw till twelve; quick walk to look about me and stretch my legs, in shade if it might be, before lunch, on anything I chanced to see nice in a fruit shop, and a bit of bread. Back to lighter work, or merely looking and thinking, for another hour and a half, and to hotel for dinner at four. Three courses and a flask of Aleatico, (a sweet, yet rather astringent, red, rich for Italian, wine—provincial, and with lovely basket-work round the bottle). Then out for saunter with Couttet; he having leave to say anything he had a mind to, but not generally communicative of his feelings; he carried my sketch-book, but in the evening there was too much always to be hunted out, of city; or watched, of hills, or sunset; and I rarely drew,—to my sorrow, now. I wish I knew less, and had drawn more.

Homewards, from wherever we had got to, the moment the sun was down, and the last clouds had lost their colour. I avoided marshy places, if I could, at all times of the day, because I didn't like them; but I feared neither sun nor moon, dawn nor twilight, malaria nor anything else malefic, in the course of work, except only draughts and ugly people. I never would sit in a draught for half a minute, and fled from some sorts of beggars; but a crowd of the common people round me only made me proud, and try to draw as well as I could; mere rags or dirt I did not care an atom for.

As early as 1835, and as late as 1841, I had been accustomed, both in France and Italy, to feel that the crowd behind me was interested in my choice of subjects, and pleasantly applausive of the swift progress under my hand of street perspectives, and richness of surface decoration, such as might be symbolized by dextrous zigzags, emphatic dots, or graceful flourishes. I had the better pleasure, now, of feeling that my really watchful delineation, while still rapid enough to interest any stray student of drawing who might stop by me on his way to the Academy, had a quite unusual power of directing the attention of the general crowd to points of beauty, or subjects of sculpture, in the buildings I was at work on, to which they had never before lifted eyes, and which I had the double pride of first discovering for them, and then imitating—not to their dissatisfaction.

And well might I be proud; but how much more ought I to have been pitiful, in feeling the swift and perfect sympathy which the "common people"—companion-people I should have said, for in Italy there is no commonness—gave me, in Lucca, or Florence, or Venice, for every touch of true work that I laid in their sight.... How much more, I say, should it have been pitiful to me, to recognize their eager intellect, and delicate senses, open to every lesson and every joy of their ancestral art, far more deeply and vividly than in the days when every spring kindled them into battle, and every autumn was red with their blood: yet left now, alike by the laws and lords set over them, less happy in aimless life than of old in sudden death; never one effort made to teach them, to comfort them, to economize their industries, animate their pleasures, or guard their simplest rights from the continually more fatal oppression of unprincipled avarice, and unmerciful wealth.

But all this I have felt and learned, like so much else, too late. The extreme seclusion of my early training[135] left me long careless of sympathy for myself; and that which I gave to others never led me into any hope of being useful to them, till my strength of active life was past. Also, my mind was not yet

---

135 Ruskin was educated at home by his parents and private tutors.

catholic[136] enough to feel that the Campo Santo belonged to its own people more than to me; and indeed, I had to read its lessons before I could interpret them. The world has for the most part been of opinion that I entered on the task of philanthropy too soon rather than too late: at all events, my conscience remained at rest during all those first times at Pisa, in mere delight in the glory of the past, and in hope for the future of Italy, without need of my becoming one of her demagogues. And the days that began in the cloister of the Campo Santo usually ended by my getting upon the roof of Santa Maria della Spina,[137] and sitting in the sunlight that transfused the warm marble of its pinnacles, till the unabated brightness went down beyond the arches of the Ponte-a-Mare,[138]—the few footsteps and voices of the twilight fell silent in the streets, and the city and her mountains stood mute as a dream, beyond the soft eddying of Arno.

Annie Besant
from *Annie Besant: An Autobiography* (1893)

Social reformer Annie Besant (1847–1933) advocated for the distribution of birth control information, unionization of unskilled workers, free speech, people's right to public demonstration, and Indian independence. Having lost her faith, Besant chose "expulsion" over "hypocrisy" when her clergyman husband demanded church attendance. In the 1880s, she helped factory match-girls organize for better pay and working conditions; got elected to the London School Board; and joined the Fabian Society. She spoke publicly on theosophy, an unorthodox belief system, and became Theosophical Society president in 1907. In India (her eventual home), Besant founded schools and newspapers and formed the Home Rule for India League in 1916.

In the following selections from her autobiography, Besant describes the publication of "The Knowlton Pamphlet" and her resulting trial on obscenity charges. The memoir records Besant as an activist and mother and identifies the high cost of political activism: custody of her daughter.

Chapter 9: The Knowlton Pamphlet

The year 1877 dawned, and in its early days began a struggle which, ending in victory all along the line, brought with it pain and anguish that I scarcely care to recall. An American physician, Dr. Charles Knowlton, convinced of the truth of the teaching of the Rev. Mr. Malthus,[139] and seeing that that teach-

---

136 All-embracing.
137 A small thirteenth-century church in Pisa, a renowned example of Gothic architecture.
138 A bridge over the Arno River.
139 Thomas Robert Malthus (1766–1834) theorized that human populations would outstrip food supply and advocated birth control as a way to limit population growth.

ing had either no practical value or tended to the great increase of prostitution, unless married people were taught to limit their families within their means of livelihood—wrote a pamphlet on the voluntary limitation of the family.[140] It was published somewhere in the Thirties—about 1835, I think—and was sold unchallenged in England as well as in America for some forty years. Philosophers of the Bentham[141] school, like John Stuart Mill,[142] endorsed its teachings, and the bearing of population on poverty was an axiom in economic literature. Dr. Knowlton's work was a physiological treatise, advocating conjugal prudence and parental responsibility; it argued in favour of early marriage, with a view to the purity of social life; but as early marriage between persons of small means generally implies a large family, leading either to pauperism or to lack of necessary food, clothing, education, and fair start in life for the children, Dr. Knowlton advocated the restriction of the number of the family within the means of subsistence, and stated the methods by which this restriction could be carried out. The book was never challenged till a disreputable Bristol bookseller put some copies on sale to which he added some improper pictures, and he was prosecuted and convicted.[143] The publisher of the *National Reformer*[144] and of Mr. Bradlaugh's[145] and my books and pamphlets had taken over a stock of Knowlton's pamphlets among other literature he bought, and he was prosecuted and, to our great dismay, pleaded guilty. We at once removed our publishing from his hands, and after careful deliberation we decided to publish the incriminated pamphlet in order to test the right of discussion on the population question, when, with the advice to limit the family, information was given as to how that advice could be followed. We took a little shop,[146] printed the pamphlet, and sent notice to the police that we would commence the sale at a certain day and hour, and ourselves sell the pamphlet, so that no one else might be endangered by our action.... Our position as regarded the pamphlet was simple and definite; had it been brought to us for publication, we stated, we should not have published it, for it was not a treatise of high merit; but, prosecuted as immoral because it advised the limitation of the family, it at once embodied the right of publication....

We were not blind to the danger to which this defiance of the authorities exposed us, but it was not the danger of failure, with the prison as penalty, that gave us pause. It was the horrible misconceptions that we saw might arise; the odious imputations on honour and purity that would follow.... To Mr. Bradlaugh it meant, as he felt, the almost certain destruction of his Parliamentary position, the forging by his own hands of a weapon that in the hands of his foes would be well-nigh fatal. To me it meant the loss of the pure reputation I prized, the good name I had guarded—scandal the most terrible a woman could face. But I had seen the misery of the poor, of my sister-women with children crying for bread; the wages of the workmen were often sufficient for four, but eight or ten they could not maintain. Should I set my own safety, my own good name, against the helping of these? ...

---

140 Charles Knowlton's *The Fruits of Philosophy: or the Private Companion of Young Married People* (1832) provided information about birth control methods.
141 Jeremy Bentham (1748–1832), Utilitarian economist and philosopher, advocated social policies that promoted the greatest good for the greatest number.
142 John Stuart Mill (1806–73), influential intellectual. See Life Writing, Condition of England, Gender and Sexuality.
143 Under the Obscene Publications Act (1857).
144 Charles Watts (1836–1906), journalist, publisher, and bookseller.
145 Charles Bradlaugh (1833–91), atheist and radical MP.
146 Rented a shop.

The day before the pamphlet was put on sale we ourselves delivered copies to the Chief Clerk of the Magistrates at Guildhall, to the officer in charge at the City Police Office in Old Jewry, and to the Solicitor for the City of London. With each pamphlet was a notice that we would attend and sell the book from 4 to 5 p.m. on the following day, Saturday, March 24th.... [W]arrants were issued against us and we were arrested on April 6th. Letters of approval and encouragement came from the most diverse quarters, including among their writers General Garibaldi, the well-known economist, Yves Guyot, the great French constitutional lawyer, Emile Acollas,[147] together with letters literally by the hundred from poor men and women thanking and blessing us for the stand taken. Noticeable were the numbers of letters from clergymen's wives, and wives of ministers of all denominations....

The trial commenced on June 18th before the Lord Chief Justice of England and a special jury, Sir Hardinge Giffard, the Solicitor-General of the Tory Government, leading against us, and we defending ourselves. The Lord Chief Justice "summed up strongly for an acquittal," as a morning paper said; he declared that "a more ill-advised and more injudicious proceeding in the way of a prosecution was probably never brought into a court of justice," and described us as "two enthusiasts who have been actuated by a desire to do good in a particular department of society." ... Every one in court thought that we had won our case, but they had not taken into account the religious and political hatred against us and the presence on the jury of such men as Mr. Walter, of the *Times*.[148] After an hour and thirty-five minutes of delay the verdict was a compromise: "We are unanimously of opinion that the book in question is calculated to deprave public morals, but at the same time we entirely exonerate the defendants from any corrupt motive in publishing it." The Lord Chief Justice looked troubled, and said that he should have to translate the verdict into one of guilty ... so the foreman's "Guilty" passed, and the judge set us free, on Mr. Bradlaugh's recognisances to come up for judgment that day week.

On that day we moved to quash the indictment and for a new trial, partly on a technical ground and partly on the ground that the verdict, having acquitted us of wrong motive, was in our favour, not against us. On this the Court did not agree with us, holding that the part of the indictment alleging corrupt motive was superfluous. Then came the question of sentence, and on this the Lord Chief Justice did his best to save us; we were acquitted of any intent to violate the law; would we submit to the verdict of the jury and promise not to sell the book? No, we would not; we claimed the right to sell, and meant to vindicate it. The judge pleaded, argued, finally got angry with us, and, at last, compelled to pass sentence, he stated that if we would have yielded he would have let us go free without penalty, but that as we would set ourselves against the law, break it and defy it ... he could only pass a heavy sentence on each of six months' imprisonment, a fine of £200, and recognisances of £500 for two years, and this, as he again repeated, upon the assumption "that they do intend to set the law at defiance." ... Then, as Mr. Bradlaugh stated that we should move for a writ of error, he liberated us on Mr. Bradlaugh's recognisance for £100, the queerest comment on his view of the case and of our characters, since we were liable jointly to £1,400 under the sentence, to say nothing of the imprisonment. But prison and money penalties vanished into thin air, for the writ of error was granted, proved successful, and the verdict was quashed.[149]

---

147 Giuseppe Garibaldi (1807–82), Italian patriot, soldier, and advocate for the unification of Italy; Yves Guyot (1843–1928), French lawyer, economist and politician; Emile Acollas (1826–91), French socialist and jurist.
148 John Walter III (1818–94), proprietor of the *Times*.
149 Besant's and Bradlaugh's appeals were granted in February 1878.

Then ensued a somewhat anxious time. We were resolute to continue selling; were our opponents equally resolved to prosecute us? We could not tell. I wrote a pamphlet entitled "The Law of Population,"[150] giving the arguments which had convinced me of its truth, the terrible distress and degradation entailed on families by overcrowding and the lack of the necessaries of life, pleading for early marriages that prostitution might be destroyed, and limitation of the family that pauperism might be avoided; finally, giving the information which rendered early marriage without these evils possible. This pamphlet was put in circulation as representing our view of the subject, and we again took up the sale of Knowlton's....

But the worst part of the fight, for me, was to come. Prosecution of the "Law of Population" was threatened, but never commenced; a worse weapon against me was in store. An attempt had been made in August, 1875, to deprive me of the custody of my little girl by hiding her away when she went on her annual visit of one month to her father, but I had promptly recovered her by threatening to issue a writ of *habeas corpus*.[151] Now it was felt that the Knowlton trial might be added to the charges of blasphemy that could be urged against me, and that this double-barrelled gun might be discharged with effect. I received notice in January, 1878, that an application was to be made to the High Court of Chancery to deprive me of the child, but the petition was not filed till the following April. Mabel was dangerously ill with scarlet fever at the time, and though this fact was communicated to her father I received a copy of the petition while sitting at her bedside. The petition alleged that, "The said Annie Besant is, by addresses, lectures, and writings, endeavouring to propagate the principles of Atheism, and has published a book entitled 'The Gospel of Atheism.'[152] She has also associated herself with an infidel lecturer and author named Charles Bradlaugh in giving lectures and in publishing books and pamphlets, whereby the truth of the Christian religion is impeached, and disbelief in all religion inculcated."

It further alleged against me the publication of the Knowlton pamphlet, and the writing of the "Law of Population." Unhappily, the petition came for hearing before the then Master of the Rolls, Sir George Jessel, a man animated by the old spirit of Hebrew bigotry, to which he had added the time-serving morality of a "man of the world," sceptical as to all sincerity, and contemptuous of all devotion to an unpopular cause. The treatment I received at his hands on my first appearance in court told me what I had to expect. I had already had some experience of English judges, the stately kindness and gentleness of the Lord Chief Justice, the perfect impartiality and dignified courtesy of the Lords Justices of Appeal. My astonishment, then, can be imagined when, in answer to a statement by Mr. Ince, Q.C., that I appeared in person, I heard a harsh, loud voice exclaim:

"Appear in person? A lady appear in person? Never heard of such a thing! Does the lady really appear in person?"...

This encouraging beginning may be taken as a sample of the case.... Mr. Ince declared that Mabel, educated by me, would "be helpless for good in this world," and "hopeless for good hereafter, outcast in this life and damned in the next." Mr. Bardswell implored the judge to consider that my custody of her "would be detrimental to the future prospects of the child in society, to say nothing of her eternal prospects." Had not the matter been to me of such heart-breaking importance, I could have laughed at

---

150 The first instalment of Besant's popular text was published in the *National Reformer* in October 1877; the 48-page pamphlet cost sixpence and had sold about 40,000 copies by 1880.
151 The legal demand to "produce the body" of the person in court, usually in cases of public or private detention.
152 Besant published her pamphlet *The Gospel of Atheism: A Lecture* in 1877.

the mixture of Mrs. Grundy,[153] marriage establishment, and hell, presented as an argument for robbing a mother of her child....

... I distinctly said I was an Atheist, that I had withdrawn the child from religious instruction at the day-school she attended, that I had written various anti-Christian books, and so on; but I claimed the child's custody on the ground that the deed of separation distinctly gave it to me, and had been executed by her father after I had left the Christian Church, and that my opinions were not sufficient to invalidate it. It was admitted on the other side that the child was admirably cared for, and there was no attempt at attacking my personal character. The judge stated that I had taken the greatest possible care of the child, but decided that the mere fact of my refusing to give the child religious instruction was sufficient ground for depriving me of her custody....

... Sir George Jessel was all-powerful in his own court, and he deprived me of my child, refusing to stay the order even until the hearing of my appeal against his decision. A messenger from the father came to my house, and the little child was carried away by main force, shrieking and struggling, still weak from the fever, and nearly frantic with fear and passionate resistance. No access to her was given me, and I gave notice that if access were denied me, I would sue for a restitution of conjugal rights,[154] merely that I might see my children. But the strain had been too great, and I nearly went mad, spending hours pacing up and down the empty rooms, striving to weary myself to exhaustion that I might forget.

The loneliness and silence of the house, of which my darling had always been the sunshine and the music, weighed on me like an evil dream; I listened for the patter of the dancing feet, and merry, thrilling laughter that rang through the garden, the sweet music of the childish voice; during my sleepless nights I missed in the darkness the soft breathing of the little child.... At last health broke down, and fever struck me, and mercifully gave me the rest of pain and delirium instead of the agony of conscious loss.... When recovered, I took steps to set aside an order obtained by Mr. Besant during my illness, forbidding me to bring any suit against him, and even the Master of the Rolls, on hearing that all access had been denied to me, and the money due to me stopped, uttered words of strong condemnation of the way in which I had been treated. Finally the deed of separation executed in 1873 was held to be good as protecting Mr. Besant from any suit brought by me, whether for divorce or for restitution of conjugal rights, while the clauses giving me the custody of the child were set aside. The Court of Appeal in April, 1879, upheld the decision, the absolute right of the father as against a married mother being upheld. This ignoring of all right to her children on the part of the married mother is a scandal and a wrong that has since been redressed by Parliament,[155] and the husband has no longer in his grasp this instrument of torture, whose power to agonise depends on the tenderness and strength of the motherliness of the wife....

One thing I gained in the Court of Appeal. The Court expressed a strong view as to my right of access, and directed me to apply to Sir George Jessel for it, adding that it could not doubt he would grant it. Under cover of this I applied to the Master of the Rolls, and obtained liberal access to the children; but I found that my visits kept Mabel in a continual state of longing and fretting for me, while the ingenious forms of petty insult that were devised against me and used in the children's presence would soon become palpable to them and cause continual pain. So, after a painful struggle with myself, I resolved to give up the right

---

153 A character in Thomas Morton's *Speed the Plough* (1789) whose name became synonymous with social propriety.
154 The spouse's legal right to have sexual intercourse with the other spouse.
155 The Infant Custody Act (1886) made the wife guardian of her children if she survived her husband. Previously, the law had presumed the father's right to the custody of his children, including the right to decide guardianship after his death.

of seeing them.... Resolutely I turned my back on them that I might spare them trouble, and determined that, robbed of my own, I would be a mother to all helpless children I could aid, and cure the pain at my own heart by soothing the pain of others.

As far as regards this whole struggle over the Knowlton pamphlet, victory was finally won all along the line. Not only did we, as related, recover all our seized pamphlets, and continue the sale till all prosecution and threat of prosecution were definitely surrendered; but my own tract had an enormous sale, so that when I withdrew it from sale in June, 1891, I was offered a large sum for the copyright, an offer which I, of course, refused. Since that time not a copy has been sold with my knowledge or permission, but long ere that the pamphlet had received a very complete legal vindication. For while it circulated untouched in England, a prosecution was attempted against it in New South Wales, but was put an end to by an eloquent and luminous judgment by the senior puisne judge of the Supreme Court,[156] Mr. Justice Windmyer, in December, 1888. This judge, the most respected in the great Australian colony, spoke out plainly and strongly on the morality of such teaching.

"Take the case," he said, "of a woman married to a drunken husband.... Where is the immorality, if, already broken in health from unresting maternity, having already a larger family than she can support when the miserable breadwinner has drunk himself to death, the woman avails herself of the information given in this book, and so averts the consequences of yielding to her husband's brutal insistence on his marital rights?["][157] ...

... ["]I do not believe that it was ever meant that the Obscene Publication[s] Act[158] should apply to cases of this kind, but only to the publication of such matter as all good men would regard as lewd and filthy, to lewd and bawdy novels, pictures and exhibitions, evidently published and given for lucre's sake. It could never have been intended to stifle the expression of thought by the earnest-minded on a subject of transcendent national importance like the present, and I will not strain it for that purpose. As pointed out by Lord Cockburn in the case of the Queen v. Bradlaugh and Besant, all prosecutions of this kind should be regarded as mischievous, even by those who disapprove the opinions sought to be stifled, inasmuch as they only tend more widely to diffuse the teaching objected to. To those, on the other hand, who desire its promulgation, it must be a matter of congratulation that this, like all attempted persecutions of thinkers, will defeat its own object, and that truth, like a torch, 'the more it's shook it shines.'"[159] ...

... The judgment was spoken of at the time in the English press as a "brilliant triumph for Mrs. Besant," and so I suppose it was; but no legal judgment could undo the harm wrought on the public mind in England by malignant and persistent misrepresentation. What that trial and its results cost me in pain no one but myself will ever know; on the other hand, there was the passionate gratitude evidenced by letters from thousands of poor married women—many from the wives of country clergymen and curates—thanking and blessing me for showing them how to escape from the veritable hell in which they lived.... To me, indeed, it meant the losing of all that made life dear, but for them it seemed to be the gaining of all that gave hope of a better future. So how could I hesitate—I whose heart had been fired by devotion to an ideal Humanity, inspired by that Materialism that is of love and not of hate? ...

---

156 The most senior judge other than the head of the court.
157 The same as conjugal rights.
158 The Obscene Publications Act (1857) authorized the search and seizure and destruction by police of publications deemed by a magistrate to be obscene.
159 Sir William Hamilton, *Discussion on Philosophy and Literature, Education and University Reform* (1852).

Oscar Wilde
from *De Profundis*[160] (written 1897; published 1905)

Prolific essayist, novelist, playwright, poet, editor, and lecturer Oscar Wilde (1854–1900) advocated art's importance for the sake of beauty rather than social or moral engagement. His views were influenced by John Ruskin (see Life Writing, Condition of England, Aesthetics and Culture, Gender and Sexuality) and Walter Pater (see Education, Aesthetics and Culture). Prominent in the Aesthetic movement, Wilde was satirized for his flamboyant dress and mannerisms—a criticism he embraced. His works include poetry, a novel, stories, plays, prose treaties and dialogues on aesthetic and political theory, and a term as editor of *Woman's World*. In a series of highly publicized 1895 trials, Wilde was convicted of gross indecency and sentenced to two years in prison with hard labour for homosexual acts.

While serving his sentence, Wilde composed a letter to his former lover Lord Alfred Douglas, affectionately referred to as "Bosie." Posthumously named *De Profundis*, the letter records Wilde's fall from literary fame to public humiliation and his efforts to combat despair in prison. In 1905, Wilde's executor, Robert Ross, published the expurgated version reproduced here, in which he removed all references to Douglas.

... I have lain in prison for nearly two years. Out of my nature has come wild despair; an abandonment to grief that was piteous even to look at; terrible and impotent rage; bitterness and scorn; anguish that wept aloud; misery that could find no voice; sorrow that was dumb. I have passed through every possible mood of suffering. Better than Wordsworth himself I know what Wordsworth meant when he said:

"Suffering is permanent, obscure, and dark,
And has the nature of infinity."[161]

But while there were times when I rejoiced in the idea that my sufferings were to be endless, I could not bear them to be without meaning. Now I find hidden somewhere away in my nature something that tells me that nothing in the whole world is meaningless, and suffering least of all. That something hidden away in my nature, like a treasure in a field,[162] is Humility.

It is the last thing left in me, and the best: the ultimate discovery at which I have arrived, the starting-point for a fresh development. It has come to me right out of myself, so I know that it has come at the proper time. It could not have come before, nor later. Had any one told me of it, I would have rejected it. Had it been brought to me, I would have refused it. As I found it, I want to keep it. I must do so. It is

---

160 Latin: "Out of the depths." Psalm 130.
161 William Wordsworth, *The Borderers* (1842).
162 Matthew 13:44.

the one thing that has in it the elements of life, of a new life, a *Vita Nuova*[163] for me. Of all things it is the strangest. One cannot acquire it, except by surrendering everything that one has. It is only when one has lost all things, that one knows that one possesses it.

Now I have realised that it is in me, I see quite clearly what I ought to do; in fact, must do. And when I use such a phrase as that, I need not say that I am not alluding to any external sanction or command. I admit none. I am far more of an individualist than I ever was. Nothing seems to me of the smallest value except what one gets out of oneself. My nature is seeking a fresh mode of self-realisation. That is all I am concerned with. And the first thing that I have got to do is to free myself from any possible bitterness of feeling against the world.

I am completely penniless, and absolutely homeless. Yet there are worse things in the world than that. I am quite candid when I tell you that rather than go out from this prison with bitterness in my heart against the world, I would gladly and readily beg my bread from door to door. If I got nothing from the house of the rich I would get something at the house of the poor. Those who have much are often greedy; those who have little always share. I would not a bit mind sleeping in the cool grass in summer, and when winter came on sheltering myself by the warm close-thatched rick, or under the pent-house of a great barn, provided I had love in my heart. The external things of life seem to me now of no importance at all. You can see to what intensity of individualism I have arrived—or am arriving rather, for the journey is long, and "where I walk there are thorns."[164]

Of course I know that to ask alms on the highway is not to be my lot, and that if ever I lie in the cool grass at night-time it will be to write sonnets to the moon. When I go out of prison, R——[165] will be waiting for me on the other side of the big iron-studded gate, and he is the symbol, not merely of his own affection, but of the affection of many others besides. I believe I am to have enough to live on for about eighteen months at any rate,[166] so that if I may not write beautiful books, I may at least read beautiful books; and what joy can be greater? After that, I hope to be able to recreate my creative faculty....

I need not say that my task does not end there. It would be comparatively easy if it did. There is much more before me. I have hills far steeper to climb, valleys much darker to pass through. And I have to get it all out of myself. Neither religion, morality, nor reason can help me at all.

Morality does not help me. I am a born antinomian.[167] I am one of those who are made for exceptions not for laws. But while I see that there is nothing wrong in what one does, I see that there is something wrong in what one becomes. It is well to have learned that.

Religion does not help me. The faith that others give to what is unseen, I give to what one can touch, and look at. My gods dwell in temples made with hands; and within the circle of actual experience is my creed made perfect and complete....

Reason does not help me. It tells me that the laws under which I am convicted are wrong and unjust laws, and the system under which I have suffered a wrong and unjust system. But, somehow, I have got to make both of these things just and right to me. And exactly as in Art one is only concerned with what a

---

163 Dante Alighieri, *La Vita Nuova* (c. 1293), which describes Dante's love for Beatrice and signifies a new start after emotional difficulty.
164 Oscar Wilde, *A Woman of No Importance* (1893).
165 Robert Ross (1869–1918), Wilde's first male lover, most loyal supporter after his trials, and literary executor.
166 The trials bankrupted Wilde, whose home was seized and possessions auctioned to pay debts.
167 Someone who contests the supremacy of moral law.

particular thing is at a particular moment to oneself, so it is also in the ethical evolution of one's character. I have got to make everything that has happened to me good for me. The plank bed, the loathsome food, the hard ropes shredded into oakum till one's finger tips grow dull with pain,[168] the menial offices with which each day begins and finishes, the harsh orders that routine seems to necessitate, the dreadful dress that makes sorrow grotesque to look at, the silence, the solitude, the shame—each and all of these things I have to transform into a spiritual experience. There is not a single degradation of the body which I must not try and make into a spiritualising of the soul.

I want to get to the point when I shall be able to say quite simply, and without affectation, that the two great turning points in my life were when my father sent me to Oxford, and when society sent me to prison. I will not say that prison is the best thing that could have happened to me; for that phrase would savour of too great bitterness towards myself. I would sooner say, or hear it said of me, that I was so typical a child of my age, that in my perversity, and for that perversity's sake, I turned the good things of my life to evil, and the evil things of my life to good....

The fact of my having been the common prisoner of a common gaol I must frankly accept, and, curious as it may seem, one of the things I shall have to teach myself is not to be ashamed of it. I must accept it as a punishment, and if one is ashamed of having been punished, one might just as well never have been punished at all. Of course there are many things of which I was convicted that I had not done, but then there are many things of which I was convicted that I had done, and a still greater number of things in my life for which I was never indicted at all. And as the gods are strange, and punish us for what is good and humane in us as much as for what is evil and perverse, I must accept the fact that one is punished for the good as well as for the evil that one does. I have no doubt that it is quite right one should be. It helps one, or should help one, to realise both, and not to be too conceited about either. And if I then am not ashamed of my punishment, as I hope not to be, I shall be able to think, and walk, and live with freedom.

Many men on their release carry their prison about with them into the air, and hide it as a secret disgrace in their hearts, and at length, like poor poisoned things, creep into some hole and die. It is wretched that they should have to do so, and it is wrong, terribly wrong of society that it should force them to do so. Society takes upon itself the right to inflict appalling punishment on the individual, but it also has the supreme vice of shallowness, and fails to realise what it has done. When the man's punishment is over, it leaves him to himself; that is to say, it abandons him at the very moment when its highest duty towards him begins. It is really ashamed of its own actions, and shuns those whom it has punished, as people shun a creditor whose debt they cannot pay, or one on whom they have inflicted an irreparable, an irredeemable wrong. I can claim on my side that if I realise what I have suffered, society should realise what it has inflicted on me; and that there should be no bitterness or hate on either side.

Of course I know that from one point of view things will be made different for me than for others; must indeed, by the very nature of the case be made so. The poor thieves and outcasts who are imprisoned here with me are in many respects more fortunate than I am. The little way in grey city or green field that saw their sin is small; to find those who know nothing of what they have done they need go no farther than a bird might fly between the twilight and the dawn; but for me the world is shrivelled to a hand's-

---

168 Oakum picking (picking apart old hemp rope to make caulking for wooden ships) was common in Victorian prisons and workhouses.

breadth,[169] and everywhere I turn my name is written on the rocks in lead. For I have come, not from obscurity to the momentary notoriety of crime, but from a sort of eternity of fame to a sort of eternity of infamy, and sometimes seem to myself to have shown, if indeed it required showing, that between the famous and the infamous there is but one step, if as much as one.

Still, in the very fact that people will recognise me wherever I go, and know all about my life, as far as its follies go, I can discern something good for me. It will force on me the necessity of again asserting myself as an artist, and as soon as I possibly can. If I can produce only one beautiful work of art I shall be able to rob malice of its venom, and cowardice of its sneer, and to pluck out the tongue of scorn[170] by the roots. And if life be, as it surely is, a problem to me, I am no less a problem to life. People must adopt some attitude towards me, and so pass judgment both on themselves and me. I need not say I am not talking of particular individuals. The only people I would care to be with now are artists and people who have suffered: those who know what beauty is, and those who know what sorrow is: nobody else interests me. Nor am I making any demands on life. In all that I have said I am simply concerned with my own mental attitude towards life as a whole; and I feel that not to be ashamed of having been punished is one of the first points I must attain to, for the sake of my own perfection, and because I am so imperfect.

Then I must learn how to be happy. Once I knew it, or thought I knew it, by instinct. It was always springtime once in my heart. My temperament was akin to joy. I filled my life to the very brim with pleasure, as one might fill a cup to the very brim with wine. Now I am approaching life from a completely new standpoint, and even to conceive happiness is often extremely difficult for me. I remember during my first term at Oxford reading in Pater's *Renaissance*[171]—that book which has had such a strange influence over my life—how Dante places low in the Inferno those who wilfully live in sadness; and going to the college library and turning to the passage in the *Divine Comedy* where beneath the dreary marsh lie those who were "sullen in the sweet air," saying for ever and ever through their sighs,—

"Tristi fummo
Nell aer dolce che dal sol s'allegra."[172]

I knew the Church condemned *accidia*,[173] but the whole idea seemed to me quite fantastic, just the sort of sin, I fancied, a priest who knew nothing about real life would invent. Nor could I understand how Dante, who says that "sorrow remarries us to God,"[174] could have been so harsh to those who were enamoured of melancholy, if any such there really were. I had no idea that some day this would become to me one of the greatest temptations of my life.

While I was in Wandsworth prison I longed to die. It was my one desire. When after two months in the infirmary I was transferred here, and found myself growing gradually better in physical health, I was filled with rage.[175] I determined to commit suicide on the very day on which I left prison. After a time

---

169 Oscar Wilde, *A Woman of No Importance* (1893).
170 William Julius Mickle, "The Neglect of Poetry" (1776).
171 Walter Pater, *Studies in the History of the Renaissance* (1873). See Aesthetics and Culture.
172 Italian: "Sullen were we / in the air made sweet by the Sun": Dante Alighieri, *Inferno*, *La Divina Commedia* (c. 1308–21).
173 Latin: sloth or listlessness.
174 Dante Alighieri, *Purgatorio*, *La Divina Commedia* (c. 1308–21).
175 Wilde spent a month in Pentonville Prison, nearly five months in Wandsworth Prison, and the rest of his sentence in the smaller Reading Gaol.

that evil mood passed away, and I made up my mind to live, but to wear gloom as a King wears purple: never to smile again: to turn whatever house I entered into a house of mourning: to make my friends walk slowly in sadness with me: to teach them that melancholy is the true secret of life: to maim them with an alien sorrow: to mar them with my own pain. Now I feel quite differently. I see it would be both ungrateful and unkind of me to pull so long a face that when my friends came to see me they would have to make their faces still longer in order to show their sympathy; or, if I desired to entertain them, to invite them to sit down silently to bitter herbs[176] and funeral baked meats. I must learn how to be cheerful and happy.

The last two occasions on which I was allowed to see my friends here, I tried to be as cheerful as possible, and to show my cheerfulness, in order to make them some slight return for their trouble in coming all the way from town to see me. It is only a slight return, I know, but it is the one, I feel certain, that pleases them most. I saw R—— for an hour on Saturday week, and I tried to give the fullest possible expression of the delight I really felt at our meeting. And that, in the views and ideas I am here shaping for myself, I am quite right is shown to me by the fact that now for the first time since my imprisonment I have a real desire for life.

There is before me so much to do that I would regard it as a terrible tragedy if I died before I was allowed to complete at any rate a little of it. I see new developments in art and life, each one of which is a fresh mode of perfection. I long to live so that I can explore what is no less than a new world to me. Do you want to know what this new world is? I think you can guess what it is. It is the world in which I have been living.

Sorrow, then, and all that it teaches one, is my new world....

This New Life, as through my love of Dante I like sometimes to call it, is of course no new life at all, but simply the continuance, by means of development, and evolution, of my former life. I remember when I was at Oxford saying to one of my friends as we were strolling round Magdalen's narrow bird-haunted walks one morning in the year before I took my degree,[177] that I wanted to eat of the fruit of all the trees in the garden of the world,[178] and that I was going out into the world with that passion in my soul. And so, indeed, I went out, and so I lived. My only mistake was that I confined myself so exclusively to the trees of what seemed to me the sun-lit side of the garden, and shunned the other side for its shadow and its gloom. Failure, disgrace, poverty, sorrow, despair, suffering, tears even, the broken words that come from lips in pain, remorse that makes one walk on thorns, conscience that condemns, self-abasement that punishes, the misery that puts ashes on its head,[179] the anguish that chooses sack-cloth for its raiment[180] and into its own drink puts gall:[181]—all these were things of which I was afraid. And as I had determined to know nothing of them, I was forced to taste each of them in turn, to feed on them, to have for a season, indeed, no other food at all.

I don't regret for a single moment having lived for pleasure. I did it to the full, as one should do everything that one does. There was no pleasure I did not experience. I threw the pearl of my soul into

---

176 Exodus 12:8.
177 Wilde studied classics at Magdalen College, Oxford from 1874 to 1878.
178 Genesis 3.
179 2 Samuel 13:19.
180 A symbol of mourning and penance; see Genesis 37:34 and 2 Samuel 3:31.
181 Gall is an ancient term for venom or poison, which was offered to Jesus on the cross by soldiers but he refused it; see Matthew 27:34.

a cup of wine.[182] I went down the primrose path[183] to the sound of flutes.[184] I lived on honeycomb.[185] But to have continued the same life would have been wrong because it would have been limiting. I had to pass on. The other half of the garden had its secrets for me also....

I am to be released, if all goes well with me, towards the end of May, and hope to go at once to some little seaside village abroad with R—— and M——....[186]

I hope to be at least a month with my friends, and to gain peace and balance, and a less troubled heart, and a sweeter mood. I have a strange longing for the great simple primeval things, such as the sea, to me no less of a mother than the Earth....

... I tremble with pleasure when I think that on the very day of my leaving prison both the laburnum and the lilac will be blooming in the gardens, and that I shall see the wind stir into restless beauty the swaying gold of the one, and make the other toss the pale purple of its plumes so that all the air shall be Arabia for me. Linnaeus[187] fell on his knees and wept for joy when he saw for the first time the long heath of some English upland made yellow with the tawny aromatic blossoms of the common furze, and I know that for me, to whom flowers are part of desire, there are tears waiting in the petals of some rose. It has always been so with me from my boyhood. There is not a single colour hidden away in the chalice of a flower, or the curve of a shell, to which, by some subtle sympathy with the very soul of things, my nature does not answer. Like Gautier, I have always been one of those *pour qui le monde visible existe*.[188]

Still, I am conscious now that behind all this beauty, satisfying though it may be, there is some spirit hidden of which the painted forms and shapes are but modes of manifestation, and it is with this spirit that I desire to become in harmony. I have grown tired of the articulate utterances of men and things. The Mystical in Art, the Mystical in Life, the Mystical in Nature—this is what I am looking for. It is absolutely necessary for me to find it somewhere.

All trials are trials for one's life, just as all sentences are sentences of death; and three times have I been tried. The first time I left the box to be arrested, the second time to be led back to the house of detention, the third time to pass into a prison for two years.[189] Society, as we have constituted it, will have no place for me, has none to offer; but Nature, whose sweet rains fall on unjust and just alike,[190] will have clefts in the rocks[191] where I may hide, and secret valleys in whose silence I may weep undisturbed. She will hang the night with stars so that I may walk abroad in the darkness without stumbling, and send the

---

182 According to Pliny the Elder, Cleopatra melted a pearl in a glass of wine and drank it.
183 Shakespeare, *Hamlet* (I.iii.46–51).
184 In *Studies in the History of the Renaissance* (1873), Pater describes the Mona Lisa's worldly experiences: "all this has been to her but as the sound of lyres and flutes."
185 Matthew 3:4.
186 Robert Ross and William More Adey (1858–1942), Robert Ross's friend and Wilde's legal consultant.
187 Swedish botanist Carolus Linnaeus (1707–78) visited England in 1736.
188 French: "for whom the visible world exists." In their 1857 journal, French authors the Goncourt brothers recorded the use of this term by French poet, novelist, and critic Théophile Gautier (1811–72); Gautier insisted on the consolation of beauty in a transient world and articulated his "art for art's sake doctrine" in his 1830s works. Wilde also used Gautier's phrase to describe Dorian in *The Picture of Dorian Gray* (1890, 1891).
189 Wilde was involved in three legal trials in 1895. First, he charged the Marquess of Queensberry, father of Lord Alfred Douglas, with libel in a trial that began on 3 April; he dropped the charges but was himself arrested on 5 April. He was subsequently charged with gross indecency in a trial that opened on 26 April and resulted in a mistrial on 1 May. He was convicted of gross indecency in a final trial that took place between 20 and 25 May.
190 Matthew 5:45.
191 Isaiah 2:21.

wind over my footprints so that none may track me to my hurt: she will cleanse me in great waters, and with bitter herbs make me whole.[192]

Edmund Gosse
from *Father and Son: A Study of Two Temperaments* (1907)

Edmund Gosse (1849–1928) hoped to be a poet but distinguished himself instead as an essayist and biographer. Gosse left home at 17 to clerk in the British Museum library. His little-circulated first poetry book brought recognition from Dante Gabriel Rossetti and Algernon Charles Swinburne, though success came from his biographies of John Donne, Henrik Ibsen, Swinburne, and others. Delivering the Cambridge Clark lectures, Gosse was pilloried by John Churton Collins (see Education) for factual errors but escaped London's opprobrium due to his friendships with literary figures, many of whom were depicted in his transatlantic magazine essays. Appointed House of Lords librarian in 1904, Gosse influenced such literary matters as Cambridge's new English chair and the choice of Poet Laureate.

Father and Son (1907), his most enduring work, recounts Gosse's efforts to break free from his zoologist father, Philip Henry Gosse, a fundamentalist Christian (see Science). The memoir captures an Edwardian generation striving to transcend its forebears' Victorianism, thus embodying the movement into Modernism.

Chapter 5

... The village, on the outskirts of which we had taken up our abode, was built parallel to the cliff-line above the shore, but half a mile inland. For a long time after the date I have now reached, no other form of natural scenery than the sea had any effect upon me at all. The tors[193] of the distant moor might be drawn in deep blue against the pallor of our morning or our evening sky, but I never looked at them. It was the Sea, always the sea, nothing but the sea. From our house, or from the field at the back of our house, or from any part of the village itself, there was no appearance to suggest that there could lie anything in an easterly direction to break the infinitude of red ploughed fields. But on that earliest morning, how my heart remembers! we hastened,—Miss Marks, the maid, and I between them,—along a couple of high-walled lanes, when suddenly, far below us, in an immense arc of light, there stretched the enormous plain of waters. We had but to cross a step or two of downs, when the hollow sides of the great limestone cove yawned at our feet, descending, like a broken cup, down, down to the moon of snow-white shingle and the expanse of blue-green sea.

---

192 Psalms 32:6 and 93:4; Ezekiel 27:26; Exodus 12:3.
193 High rocky peaks or hills.

In these twentieth-century days, a careful municipality has studded the down with rustic seats and has shut its dangers out with railings, has cut a winding carriage-drive round the curves of the cove down to the shore, and has planted sausage-laurels at intervals in clearings made for that aesthetic purpose. When last I saw the place, thus smartened and secured, with its hair in curl-papers and its feet in patent-leathers, I turned from it in anger and disgust, and could almost have wept. I suppose that to those who knew it in no other guise, it may still have beauty. No parish councils, beneficent and shrewd, can obscure the lustre of the waters or compress the vastness of the sky. But what man could do to make wild beauty ineffectual, tame and empty, has amply been performed at Oddicombe.

Very different was it fifty years ago, in its uncouth majesty. No road, save the merest goat-path, led down its concave wilderness, in which loose furze-bushes and untrimmed brambles wantoned into the likeness of trees, each draped in audacious tissue of wild clematis. Through this fantastic maze the traveller wound his way, led by little other clue than by the instinct of descent. For me, as a child, it meant the labour of a long, an endless morning, to descend to the snow-white pebbles, to sport at the edge of the cold, sharp sea, and then to climb up home again, slipping in the sticky red mud, clutching at the smooth boughs of the wild ash, toiling, toiling upwards into flat land out of that hollow world of rocks.

On the first occasion, I recollect, our Cockney housemaid, enthusiastic young creature that she was, flung herself down upon her knees, and drank of the salt waters. Miss Marks, more instructed in phenomena, refrained, but I, although I was perfectly aware what the taste would be, insisted on sipping a few drops from the palm of my hand. This was a slight recurrence of what I have called my "natural magic" practices, which had passed into the background of my mind, but had not quite disappeared. I recollect that I thought I might secure some power of walking on the sea, if I drank of it—a perfectly irrational movement of mind, like those of savages.

My great desire was to walk out over the sea as far as I could, and then lie flat on it, face downwards, and peer into the depths....

It was not with Miss Marks, however, but with my Father, that I became accustomed to make the laborious and exquisite journeys down to the sea and back again. His work as a naturalist eventually took him, laden with implements, to the rock-pools on the shore, and I was in attendance as an acolyte. But our earliest winter in South Devon was darkened for us both by disappointments, the cause of which lay, at the time, far out of my reach. In the spirit of my Father were then running, with furious velocity, two hostile streams of influence. I was standing, just now, thinking of these things, where the Cascine[194] ends in the wooded point which is carved out sharply by the lion-coloured swirl of the Arno on the one side and by the pure flow of the Mugnone on the other. The rivers meet, and run parallel, but there comes a moment when the one or the other must conquer, and it is the yellow vehemence that drowns the purer tide.

So, through my Father's brain, in that year of scientific crisis, 1857, there rushed two kinds of thought, each absorbing, each convincing, yet totally irreconcilable. There is a peculiar agony in the paradox that truth has two forms, each of them indisputable, yet each antagonistic to the other. It was this discovery, that there were two theories of physical life, each of which was true, but the truth of each incompatible with the truth of the other, which shook the spirit of my Father with perturbation. It was not, really, a paradox, it was a fallacy, if he could only have known it, but he allowed the turbid volume of superstition to drown the delicate stream of reason. He took one step in the service of truth, and then he drew back in an agony, and accepted the servitude of error.

---

194 A large public park in Florence, Italy, situated between the Arno and the Mugnone Rivers.

This was the great moment in the history of thought when the theory of the mutability of species was preparing to throw a flood of light upon all departments of human speculation and action. It was becoming necessary to stand emphatically in one army or the other. Lyell[195] was surrounding himself with disciples, who were making strides in the direction of discovery. Darwin had long been collecting facts with regard to the variation of animals and plants. Hooker and Wallace, Asa Gray and even Agassiz,[196] each in his own sphere, were coming closer and closer to a perception of that secret which was first to reveal itself clearly to the patient and humble genius of Darwin. In the year before, in 1856, Darwin, under pressure from Lyell, had begun that modest statement of the new revelation, that "abstract of an essay," which developed so mightily into "The Origin of Species." Wollaston's "Variation of Species"[197] had just appeared, and had been a nine days' wonder in the wilderness.

On the other side, the reactionaries, although never dreaming of the fate which hung over them, had not been idle. In 1857 the astounding question had for the first time been propounded with contumely, "What, then, did we come from an orang-outang?" The famous "Vestiges of Creation"[198] had been supplying a sugar-and-water panacea for those who could not escape from the trend of evidence, and who yet clung to revelation. Owen[199] was encouraging reaction by resisting, with all the strength of his prestige, the theory of the mutability of species.

In this period of intellectual ferment, as when a great political revolution is being planned, many possible adherents were confidentially tested with hints and encouraged to reveal their bias in a whisper. It was the notion of Lyell, himself a great mover of men, that before the doctrine of natural selection was given to a world which would be sure to lift up at it a howl of execration, a certain body-guard of sound and experienced naturalists, expert in the description of species, should be privately made aware of its tenour. Among those who were thus initiated, or approached with a view towards possible illumination, was my Father. He was spoken to by Hooker, and later on by Darwin, after meetings of the Royal Society in the summer of 1857.

My Father's attitude towards the theory of natural selection was critical in his career, and, oddly enough, it exercised an immense influence on my own experience as a child. Let it be admitted at once, mournful as the admission is, that every instinct in his intelligence went out at first to greet the new light. It had hardly done so, when a recollection of the opening chapter of Genesis checked it at the outset. He consulted with Carpenter,[200] a great investigator, but one who was fully as incapable as himself of remodelling his ideas with regard to the old, accepted hypotheses. They both determined, on various grounds, to have nothing to do with the terrible theory, but to hold steadily to the law of the fixity of species. It was exactly at this juncture that we left London, and the slight and occasional, but always extremely salutary personal intercourse with men of scientific leading which my Father had enjoyed at

---

195 Charles Lyell (1797–1875), geologist and author of *Principles of Geology* (1830). See Science.
196 Charles Darwin (1809–82), naturalist and geologist, author of *On the Origin of Species* (1859); see Science. Joseph Dalton Hooker (1817–1911), a botanist, encouraged Darwin's work on natural selection; in 1858, naturalist Alfred Russel Wallace (1823–1913) (see Travel and Exploration) sent Darwin an essay that set out the basic theory of evolution; Asa Gray (1810–88), American botanist and correspondent of Darwin, accepted the theory of natural selection; Louis Agassiz (1807–73), naturalist and geologist, studied fish fossils and glacier activity.
197 Thomas Vernon Wollaston, *On the Variation of Species, with Especial Reference to the Insecta Followed by an Inquiry into the Nature of Genera* (1856).
198 Robert Chambers, *Vestiges of the Natural History of Creation* (1844). See Science.
199 Richard Owen (1804–92), distinguished palaeontologist and vehement opponent of Darwin's theories.
200 Philip Carpenter (1819–77), naturalist, conchologist, and minister.

the British Museum and at the Royal Society came to an end. His next act was to burn his ships, down to the last beam and log out of which a raft could have been made. By a strange act of wilfulness, he closed the doors upon himself for ever.

My Father had never admired Sir Charles Lyell. I think that the famous "Lord Chancellor manner" of the geologist intimidated him, and we undervalue the intelligence of those whose conversation puts us at a disadvantage. For Darwin and Hooker, on the other hand, he had a profound esteem, and I know not whether this had anything to do with the fact that he chose, for his impetuous experiment in reaction, the field of geology, rather than that of zoology or botany. Lyell had been threatening to publish a book on the geological history of Man, which was to be a bomb-shell flung into the camp of the catastrophists. My Father, after long reflection, prepared a theory of his own,[201] which, as he fondly hoped, would take the wind out of Lyell's sails, and justify geology to godly readers of "Genesis." It was, very briefly, that there had been no gradual modification of the surface of the earth, or slow development of organic forms, but that when the catastrophic act of creation took place, the world presented, instantly, the structural appearance of a planet on which life had long existed.

The theory, coarsely enough, and to my Father'[s] great indignation, was defined by a hasty press as being this—that God hid the fossils in the rocks in order to tempt geologists into infidelity. In truth, it was the logical and inevitable conclusion of accepting, literally, the doctrine of a sudden act of creation; it emphasised the fact that any breach in the circular course of nature could be conceived only on the supposition that the object created bore false witness to past processes, which had never taken place. For instance, Adam would certainly possess hair and teeth and bones in a condition which it must have taken many years to accomplish, yet he was created full-grown yesterday. He would certainly—though Sir Thomas Browne denied it—display an *omphalos*,[202] yet no umbilical cord had ever attached him to a mother.

Never was a book cast upon the waters with greater anticipations of success than was this curious, this obstinate, this fanatical volume. My Father lived in a fever of suspense, waiting for the tremendous issue. This "Omphalos" of his, he thought, was to bring all the turmoil of scientific speculation to a close, fling geology into the arms of Scripture, and make the lion eat grass with the lamb. It was not surprising, he admitted, that there had been experienced an ever-increasing discord between the facts which geology brings to light and the direct statements of the early chapters of "Genesis." Nobody was to blame for that. My Father, and my Father alone, possessed the secret of the enigma; he alone held the key which could smoothly open the lock of geological mystery. He offered it, with a glowing gesture, to atheists and Christians alike. This was to be the universal panacea; this the system of intellectual therapeutics which could not but heal all the maladies of the age. But, alas! atheists and Christians alike looked at it, and laughed, and threw it away.

In the course of that dismal winter, as the post began to bring in private letters, few and chilly, and public reviews, many and scornful, my Father looked in vain for the approval of the churches, and in vain for the acquiescence of the scientific societies, and in vain for the gratitude of those "thousands of thinking persons," which he had rashly assured himself of receiving. As his reconciliation of Scripture statements and geological deductions was welcomed nowhere; as Darwin continued silent, and the youthful Hux-

---

201 Philip Henry Gosse, *Omphalos; An Attempt to Untie the Geological Knot* (1857).
202 Greek: navel. Sir Thomas Browne (1605-82) argued in *Pseudodoxia epidemica* (1646) that Adam and Eve (having been created, not born) could not have possessed navels.

ley[203] was scornful, and even Charles Kingsley,[204] from whom my Father had expected the most instant appreciation, wrote that he could not "give up the painful and slow conclusion of five and twenty years' study of geology, and believe that God has written on the rocks one enormous and superfluous lie,"—as all this happened or failed to happen, a gloom, cold and dismal, descended upon our morning teacups....

During that grim season, my Father was no lively companion, and circumstance after circumstance combined to drive him further from humanity. He missed more than ever the sympathetic ear of my Mother; there was present to support him nothing of that artful, female casuistry which insinuates into the wounded consciousness of a man the conviction that, after all, he is right and all the rest of the world is wrong. My Father used to tramp in solitude round and round the red ploughed field which was going to be his lawn, or sheltering himself from the thin Devonian rain, pace up and down the still-naked verandah where blossoming creepers were to be. And I think that there was added to his chagrin with all his fellow mortals a first tincture of that heresy which was to attack him later on. It was now that, I fancy, he began, in his depression, to be angry with God. How much devotion had he given, how many sacrifices had he made, only to be left storming round this red morass with no one in all the world to care for him except one pale-faced child with its cheek pressed to the window!...

The key is lost by which I might unlock the perverse malady from which my Father's conscience seemed to suffer during the whole of this melancholy winter. But I think that a dislocation of his intellectual system had a great deal to do with it. Up to this point in his career, he had, as we have seen, nourished the delusion that science and revelation could be mutually justified, that some sort of compromise was possible. With great and ever greater distinctness, his investigations had shown him that in all departments of organic nature there are visible the evidences of slow modification of forms, of the type developed by the pressure and practice of æons. This conviction had been borne in upon him until it was positively irresistible. Where was his place, then, as a sincere and accurate observer? Manifestly, it was with the pioneers of the new truth, it was with Darwin, Wallace and Hooker. But did not the second chapter of "Genesis" say that in six days the heavens and earth were finished, and the host of them, and that on the seventh day God ended his work which he had made?[205]

Here was a dilemma! Geology certainly *seemed* to be true, but the Bible, which was God's word, *was* true. If the Bible said that all things in Heaven and Earth were created in six days, created in six days they were,—in six literal days of twenty-four hours each. The evidences of spontaneous variation of form, acting, over an immense space of time, upon ever-modifying organic structures, *seemed* overwhelming, but they must either be brought into line with the six-day labour of creation, or they must be rejected. I have already shown how my Father worked out the ingenious "Omphalos" theory in order to justify himself as a strictly scientific observer who was also a humble slave of revelation. But the old convention and the new rebellion would alike have none of his compromise.

To a mind so acute and at the same time so narrow as that of my Father—a mind which is all logical and positive without breadth, without suppleness and without imagination—to be subjected to a check of this kind is agony. It has not the relief of a smaller nature, which escapes from the dilemma by some foggy formula; nor the resolution of a larger nature to take to its wings and surmount the obstacle. My

---

203 T.H. Huxley (1825–95), known as "Darwin's Bulldog," was an important defender of evolutionary theory. See Science.
204 Charles Kingsley (1819–75), Church of England clergyman and novelist.
205 See Genesis 2:1–2.

Father, although half-suffocated by the emotion of being lifted, as it were, on the great biological wave, never dreamed of letting go his clutch of the ancient tradition, but hung there, strained and buffeted. It is extraordinary that he—an "honest hodman[206] of science," as Huxley once called him—should not have been content to allow others, whose horizons were wider than his could be, to pursue those purely intellectual surveys for which he had no species of aptitude. As a collector of facts and marshaller of observations, he had not a rival in that age; his very absence of imagination aided him in this work. But he was more an attorney than a philosopher, and he lacked that sublime humility which is the crown of genius. For, this obstinate persuasion that he alone knew the mind of God, that he alone could interpret the designs of the Creator, what did it result from if not from a congenital lack of that highest modesty which replies "I do not know" even to the questions which Faith, with menacing finger, insists on having most positively answered?

Beatrice Webb
from *My Apprenticeship* (1926)

Leftist intellectual Beatrice Webb (1858–1943) participated in the Fabian Society and Labour Party and helped found the London School of Economics. In almost 40 publications (including 18 books), nearly all co-authored with her husband, Sidney Webb, she focused on social issues, including the cooperative movement, trade unionism, industrial legislation, and local government. Initially opposed to women's suffrage, she adopted feminism as the suffrage movement expanded to comprise a wider range of women's concerns.

Webb was also an exceptional diarist and autobiographer: *My Appenticeship* (1926) recounts early efforts to find meaningful work, and *Our Partnership* (1948) describes her political work with her husband after their 1892 marriage. The following selection records Webb's conflicting allegiances to her ailing father and her progressive principles. The passage also narrates the author's nascent romance and intellectual partnership with Sidney Webb based on their shared political views.

Chapter 7: Why I Became a Socialist

The Passage from Life

The enquiry into the Co-operative Movement[207] was carried out under the deepening gloom of my father's last illness;[208] and at times I despaired of completing my task. In the pages of my diary, during the autumn

---

206 A worker who brings supplies to those actually doing construction; a literary hack.
207 Webb's independent study of the Cooperative Movement began in 1883, when she went to Bacup, East Lancashire, disguised as a Welsh farmer's daughter in order to observe working-class life.
208 Webb's father had a stroke in 1885; she cared for him until his death in 1892.

of 1889, I watch myself falling back for encouragement on a growing faith in the possibility of reorganising society by the application of the scientific method directed by the religious spirit.

Unfit for work: alone with poor dear father and his shadowlike mind and irresponsible character. Depressed, I take up a volume of Matthew Arnold's[209] poems and read these words as the expression of the ideal life towards which I constantly strive:

> Of toil unsevered from tranquility!
> Of labour, that in lasting fruit outgrows
> Far noisier schemes, accomplished in repose
> Too great for haste, too high for rivalry![210]

This state of toil unsevered from tranquility I sometimes feel I have attained. Still, one is troubled (alas, too often troubled) with the foolish dreams of personal success and with a deep depression of personal failure. I love my work; that is my salvation; I delight in this slow stepping towards truth. Search after truth by the careful measurement of facts is the enthusiasm of my life. And of late this has been combined with a realisation of the common aim of the great army of truth-seekers: the ennobling of human life. It has been enriched by the consciousness of the supreme unity of science, art, morality; the eternal trinity of the good, the beautiful and the true; knit together in the ideal towards which humanity is constantly striving, knowingly or unknowingly, with failure or success according to the ebb and flow of pure motive and honest purpose [MS.[211] diary, August 17, 1889].

Constantly during the last week, as I have eagerly read every detail of the Strike, (the famous Dock Strike of August 1889)[212] I have been depressed by my own powerlessness to suggest any way out of the difficulty; I have been disheartened by a consciousness that my little mite of knowledge is not of much avail—that the great instinctive movements of the mass are perhaps, after all, more likely to effect than the carefully reasoned judgements of the scientific (or pseudo-scientific?) observer.... Then I have realised that if we are to get a basis for action through knowledge of facts, that knowledge must be far more complete and exhaustive than it is ever likely to be in my time; certainly than it is likely to be in my case. For instance, the little knowledge I gained of the London Docks is practically useless. In order to offer an opinion of any value, one would need to thoroughly master the facts about trade at the docks; to realise exactly the methods of management; to compare these with other methods of management so as to discover deficiencies and possibilities. Is that kind of exhaustive knowledge, even granting the opportunity and the ability and the strength to acquire it, open to a mere observer? Is it not the exclusive opportunity of the great organiser? On the other hand, this realisation of the extent of the knowledge required shows me that in my desire to master commercial and financial facts as a key to the labour problem

---

209 Matthew Arnold (1822–88), poet and social critic. See Education, Aesthetics and Culture.
210 Matthew Arnold, "Quiet Work" (1849).
211 Manuscript.
212 In the 1889 London Dock Strike, workers won a pay increase to sixpence an hour and inspired other unskilled workers to unionize.

I was guided by a true instinct; that on my capacity to master these facts will rest my power to influence for good the condition of my people [MS. diary, August 31, 1889]....

The final entry in the diary for the year 1889 was written during a crisis in my father's illness which we all thought would be the last ...[:]

And now that he lies helpless, the vitality flickering to extinction: his limbs motionless, his breathing laboured, the last pleasure in his sleep, food and cigarette gone, he still brightens up to welcome his "bright-eyed daughter"; to compliment a middle-aged married woman on her good looks: to enquire how each husband is doing; to ask how much he will leave to his children. In the long hours of restlessness he broods over the success of his children, and finds reason for peace and satisfaction. "I want one more son-in-law" (a proof that he feels near his end, as he has discouraged the idea of matrimony for me, put it off as something I could easily attain), "a woman is happier married: I should like to see my little Bee married to a good strong fellow", and the darling old father dreams of the "little Bee" of long ago; he does not realise that she has passed away, leaving the strong form and determined features of the "glorified spinster"[213] bending over him as a mother bends over her sick child [MS. diary, November 26, 1889].

"The Other One"

My father lingered on for another two years, barely conscious of his surroundings. But within a few weeks of his call for "one more son-in-law" there came "The Other One"!

This culminating event of my life—for did it not lead to the rapid transformation of "My Apprenticeship" into "Our Partnership",[214] and therefore to the ending of this book?—clearly deserves a preface. And this preface shall consist in a recollection of a mysterious penumbra,[215] making me aware of a new and significant Presence in my environment at least a year before I was introduced to the little figure with a big head who was to become the man of my destiny, the source of unhoped-for happiness; and, be it added, the predominant partner of the firm of Webb!

It was, I think, in the spring of 1888 that my friend J.J. Dent, at that time General Secretary of the (working men's) Club and Institute Union, talked to me, in tones of mingled admiration and suspicion, about a group of clever young men who, with astonishing energy and audacity, were haranguing the London Radical clubs; contributing innumerable articles and paragraphs, signed or unsigned, to the *Star* and the *Daily Chronicle*, and distributing, far and wide, "Facts for Socialists", and other subversively plausible pamphlets.... "There are among them", said he, "some very clever speakers, but the man who organises the whole business, drafts the resolutions and writes the tracts, is Sidney Webb."[216] ...

It was certainly surprising that, given all these activities of the Fabian Society[217] during 1888–89, and absorbed as I was in political and economic problems, I failed to become known to any of the fu-

---

213 An unsigned article by Frances Martin in *Macmillan's Magazine* (May 1888) described a "new species", "The Glorified Spinster," who embraces political activism and a single life. The *Saturday Review* and *Woman* carried identically titled articles at around the same time.
214 Webb followed *My Apprenticeship* (1926) with *Our Partnership* (1948).
215 The partly shaded area around the shadow of an opaque body; the extended influence of a person or thing beyond itself.
216 Socialist Sidney Webb (1859–1947), Beatrice's future husband and partner in political activism.
217 A socialist society founded around 1883.

ture Fabian essayists (apart from a slight acquaintance with Mrs. Annie Besant,[218] then at the zenith of her power as a great popular orator) until January 1890. The explanation is, that I had entered the field of controversy from the stand point of big enterprise, party politics and metropolitan philanthropy, and was biased against socialist solutions of political and economic problems; whilst the Fabians entered this same field as Radicals and rebels, drawn, by a vision of a new social order, from every vocation and many parts of the country. Further, my craft being that of an investigator, I was seeking enlightenment, not from socialist lecturers and theoretical pamphlets, but from an objective study of the Co-operative Movement and of Trade Unionism, the leaders of which were at that time contemptuous of the socialism that they knew. The great Dock Strike of August 1889, led, as it was, by three socialist workmen—John Burns, Tom Mann and Ben Tillett—together with the emergence of the "New Unionism,"[219] with its reliance on political changes, altered the orientation of the Labour Movement itself. Meanwhile, I had realised, as already described, that the working-class Co-operative Movement, as distinguished from the middle-class projects of self-governing workshops, industrial partnerships and schemes of profit-sharing, was essentially "collectivist" in character and aims, having for its object the elimination from industry of profit and the profit-maker, by the substitution of an open democracy, managing by the instrumentality of salaried officials the services that it desired. Hence when, in October 1889, a friend forwarded to me the recently published *Fabian Essays*[220] as the true gospel of distinctively British socialism, I read this daintily-turned-out volume from cover to cover. In passing it on to J.C. Gray of the Co-operative Union, I find that I incidentally remarked (in a letter which he afterwards returned to me) that "by far the most significant and interesting essay is the one by Sidney Webb; *he has the historic sense*"....

The reason for our meeting in the first days of January 1890 was in itself a presage of our future comradeship in work. The critical phase of my father's illness having once again passed away, my sister Kate begged me to return with her husband to London for a week's rest and recreation, a welcome opportunity to get material I urgently needed for the first chapter of my forthcoming book. For whilst planning out my analysis of the Co-operative Movement of that day, I became aware that I lacked historical background. As was my wont, I applied for help to the best available authority: in this case to a London acquaintance, the distinguished historian of the eighteenth century, W.E.H. Lecky.[221] "Why was there no working-class association in these years of turmoil and change?" I innocently and ignorantly asked. The answer to this incorrect assertion, disguised as a question, was a courteous, kindly and lengthy explanation of the "reason why", meant to be helpful. But seeing that my mistaken assumption was apparently accepted as the starting-point of the answer, the professional historian led me nowhere. Not satisfied, I was on the look-out for another guide. "Sidney Webb, one of the Fabian Essayists, is your man," casually remarked a friendly woman journalist. "He knows everything: when you go out for a walk with him he literally pours out information." An interview was arranged during my short stay in London. A list of sources,

---

218 Annie Besant (1847–1933), social reformer and birth control advocate. See Life Writing.
219 John Burns (1858–1943), labour leader and politician; Thomas Mann (1856–1941), trade unionist and communist; Benjamin Tillett (1860–1943), dock worker and trade unionist who rose to fame during the London Dock Strike of 1889. The Dock Strike spurred unionization, including the formation of the Transport and General Workers' Union, which became the largest British labour union.
220 George Bernard Shaw, ed., *Fabian Essays in Socialism* (1889).
221 W.E.H. Lecky (1838–1903), author of *History of England in the Eighteenth Century* (1878–90).

accessible at the British Museum, including the then little known Place manuscripts,[222] various State trials, old Chartist[223] periodicals, and autobiographies of working-class agitators, was swiftly drafted, then and there, in a faultless handwriting, and handed to me. A few days later brought the first token of personal regard in the shape of a newly published pamphlet by the Fabian on the Rate of Interest, thus opening up a regular correspondence.

I give a few from many entries from the MS. diary revealing the new ferment at work.

Already one month of the New Year past. Father lying in a half-conscious, motionless state, recognising his children but not realising ideas or feelings; his life a flickering shadow which at times seems to disappear, then to gather substance, and for a while you imagine that it is the dear familiar spirit lighting up the worn-out frame.

I am, in the meantime, so long as life lasts, chained to his side; all my plans for this six months of the year indefinitely postponed.... Sometimes I feel discouraged. Not only am I baulked in carrying out my work, but with the lack of all accomplishment I begin to doubt my ability to do it. Continuous reading makes me feel a mere learner, entangled in my own growth, helpless before this ever-accumulating mass of facts, which must be carved into some intelligible shape indicative of its main characteristics. At present, the facts are heaped up around me, oppressing me with their weight.

I feel, too, exiled from the world of thought and action of other men and women. London is in a ferment: strikes are the order of the day; the new Trade Unionism, with its magnificent conquest of the docks, is striding along with an arrogance rousing employers to a keen sense of danger, and to a determination to strike against strikes. The socialists, led by a small set of able young men (Fabian Society) are manipulating London radicals, ready, at the first checkmate of Trade Unionism, to voice a growing desire for state action; and I, from the peculiarity of my social position, should be in the midst of all parties, sympathetic with all, allied with none, in a true vantage ground for impartial observation of the forces at work. Burnett[224] and the older Trade Unionists on the one side; Tom Mann, Tillett and Burns on the other; round about me co-operators of all schools, together with new acquaintances among the leading socialists. And as a background, all those respectable and highly successful men, my brothers-in-law, typical of the old reign of private property and self-interested action.... And the whole seems a whirl of contending actions, aspirations and aims, out of which I dimly see the tendency towards a socialist community, in which there will be individual freedom and public property, instead of class slavery and private possession of the means of subsistence of the whole people. At last I am a socialist! [MS. diary, February 1, 1890].

Sidney Webb, the socialist, dined here [Devonshire House Hotel] to meet the Booths.[225] A remarkable little man with a huge head and a tiny body, a breadth of forehead quite sufficient to

---

222 The manuscripts of Francis Place (1771–1854), radical and freethinker.
223 Supporters of the *People's Charter* (1838), a demand for six points of electoral reform.
224 John Burnett (1842–1914), trade unionist and civil servant.
225 Social investigator Charles Booth (1840–1916), Beatrice's cousin by marriage, and his wife, Mary (1847–1939).

account for the encyclopædic character of his knowledge. A Jewish nose, prominent eyes and mouth[,] black hair, somewhat unkempt, spectacles and a most bourgeois black coat shiny with wear. But I like the man. There is a directness of speech, an open-mindedness, an imaginative warm-heartedness which will carry him far. He has the self-assurance of one who is always thinking faster than his neighbours; who is untroubled by doubts, and to whom the acquisition of facts is as easy as the grasping of things; but he has no vanity and is totally unself-conscious. Hence his absence of consciousness as to treading on his neighbours' corns. Above all, he is utterly disinterested, and is, I believe, genuine in his Faith that collective control and collective administration will diminish, if not abolish, poverty [MS. diary, February 14, 1890].

Every day my social views take a more decidedly socialist turn, every hour reveals fresh instances of the curse of gain without labour; the endless perplexities of the rich, the never-failing miseries of the poor. In this household [there are] ten persons living on the fat of the land in order to minister to the supposed comfort of one poor old man.... We feed our servants well, keep them in luxurious slavery, because we hate to see discomfort around us. But they and we are consuming the labour of others and giving nothing in return, except useless service to a dying life past serving ... [MS. diary, April 22, 1890].

Glasgow Co-operative Congress. Exquisite Whitsun[226] weather....
   In the evening S.W. and I wandered through the Glasgow streets. A critical twenty-four hours, followed by another long walk by glorious sunset through the crowded streets, knocking up against drunken Scots. With glory in the sky and hideous bestiality on the earth, two socialists came to a working compact. "You understand you promise me to realise that the chances are a hundred to one that nothing follows but friendship ..." [Glasgow, MS. diary, Whitsun 1890].

A day out in Epping Forest: "When I left you yesterday [said he] (we had travelled up from Haslemere, where I had stayed at the Frederic Harrisons,[227] and he with the Pearsall Smiths[228]) I went straight home; found two urgent letters, one from O'Brien begging me to write the London articles for the *Speaker*;[229] the other from Massingham[230] telling me I must review Marshall's new book[231] for the *Star*.... [I]t is a great book, it will supersede Mill.[232] But it will not make an epoch in Economics. Economics has still to be re-made. Who is to do it? Either you must help me to do it; or I must help you ..." [MS. diary, July 27, 1890].

Throughout the remaining months of 1890 we saw little of each other. When not in attendance on my father, I was staying in Glasgow, Manchester, Leeds, Leicester and other big industrial centres,

---

226 The seventh Sunday after Easter.
227 Frederic Harrison (1831–1923), writer and positivist.
228 (Lloyd) Logan Pearsall Smith (1865–1946), writer and literary critic.
229 Richard Barry O'Brien (1847–1918) served on the editorial staff of the *Speaker*, the weekly rival to the *Spectator*.
230 Henry William Massingham (1860–1924), editor of the *Star*.
231 Alfred Marshall, *The Principles of Economics* (1890).
232 John Stuart Mill, *Principles of Political Economy* (1848).

completing the co-operative enquiry and starting the investigation into Trade Unionism. But letters in the faultless handwriting followed me wherever I went, suggesting new sources of information, or telling me of the doings of the Fabians.... In the spring of 1891 I sent my newly-found counsellor proofs of my forthcoming book on the Co-operative Movement. "I am disappointed", he wrote with commendable sincerity; "this book ought to have taken six weeks to write, not seven months. Why not let me help you in the investigation into Trade Unionism? Whilst you interview officials and attend Trade Union meetings, I can rush through reports and MS. minutes at the Trade Union offices."

"I am a piece of steel", I warn my friend. "One and one placed close together, in a sufficiently integrated relationship, make not two but eleven", he answered unconcernedly....

The Lincoln Co-operative Congress of 1891 found us journeying down together. "I cannot tell how things will settle themselves", I write in my diary; "I think probably in his way. His resolute, patient affection, his constant care for my welfare—helping and correcting me—a growing distrust of a self-absorbed life and the egotism of successful work, done on easy terms and reaping more admiration than it deserves—all these feelings are making for our eventual union. Meanwhile father lingers on, and while he lives, nothing can be decided" [MS. diary, May 1891]. In the course of the summer The Other One and I became definitely but secretly betrothed, my father's state making disclosure, even to my own family, undesirable....

> We are both of us [I write in my diary, July 7] second-rate minds; but we are curiously combined. I am the investigator and he the executant; between us we have a wide and varied experience of men and affairs. We have also an unearned salary. These are unique circumstances. A considerable work should be the result if we use our combined talents with a deliberate and persistent purpose....

On the first of January 1892 my father died; and six months later we were married.

Here ends "My Apprenticeship" and opens "Our Partnership": a working comradeship founded in a common faith and made perfect by marriage; perhaps the most exquisite, certainly the most enduring, of all the varieties of happiness.

THE CONDITION OF ENGLAND: INDUSTRIALIZATION AND SOCIAL REFORM

Introduction

Dan Bivona

No event had a more disruptive impact on nineteenth-century British society than the Industrial Revolution. In the middle of the eighteenth century, the British began the unprecedented experiment of applying new machinery and production techniques to manufactured goods—mainly cotton textiles at first—on a vast scale. Beginning in northern England, around the growing city of Manchester, the Industrial Revolution spread throughout Britain, ultimately reshaping the politics and the landscape, inducing millions to move from the country to take up factory work in industrial cities, blackening the skies with coal soot, challenging the authority of the landed aristocracy, and accelerating the growth and influence of the middle class and, eventually, the industrial working class. By the 1830s, many had recognized individual efforts to apply steam power to production processes as part of a large historical movement—the Industrial Revolution—profoundly transforming work and social relationships across the country.

Delighted by new economic opportunities, many celebrated this transformation and embraced a characteristic Victorian faith in the inevitability of material and social progress. Others, however, doubted that progress was inevitable, for along with the successes came disturbing events that shook such faith: disrupted families; periodic starvation; men, women, and children as young as six forced to work long hours in the mines and factories; the twin plagues of soot-filled air in the cities and cotton dust in the factories; and periodic strikes, layoffs, and reduced pay for the working class. By the beginning of the 1840s, many feared that industrial Britain would always be plagued by periods of high unemployment and social unrest and, worse, that prosperity might never be shared throughout society. The working-class movement known as Chartism arose from dissatisfaction at workers' lack of social and political power: more than a million people signed an 1839 petition to parliament demanding universal manhood suffrage and salaries for MPs, among other reforms designed to distribute power more equally in society. When the House of Commons rejected the Chartists' demands in 1839 (and again in 1842 and 1848), there were strikes and leaders of the movement were jailed. Writing in the early 1840s, in the midst of one of the earliest modern economic recessions, the Victorian "sage" Thomas Carlyle captured the mood when he said, "The condition of England ... is justly regarded as one of the most ominous, and one of the

"The Brummagem Frankenstein." Punch (8 Sept. 1866): 103.

strangest ever seen in this world. England is full of wealth, of multifarious produce, supply for human want in every kind; yet England is dying of inanition" (1: 1). This dawning awareness of the fundamental contradiction of industrialism—that the best system ever designed for producing wealth seemed also to generate unprecedented poverty and misery—would henceforth make many British people ambivalent about their own economic success.

The writers represented in this section range from influential socialist critics of industrialization (Marx and Engels) to dedicated defenders of capitalism (Martineau) and individual energy and enterprise (Mill) to Victorian sages preoccupied with the moral, physical, and psychological ravages of the new social order (Carlyle and Ruskin) to journalists (Mayhew), novelists (Dickens), and crusading social reformers (Booth), all of whom sounded alarms about the plight of those suffering under the new industrial order. We should note that many of these writers personally benefited from this new order, as an increasingly large, prosperous, and literate middle class guaranteed a growing audience for their published work; however, the awareness that they were living in a time of unprecedented rapid and psychologically destabilizing social change accounts for the note of apocalyptic alarm often found in the most influential writings about the "condition of England."

Shortly after Harriet Martineau began a series of narrative "illustrations" of the principles of political economy in the early 1830s, the first major parliamentary reform act passed in 1832, granting the vote to a significant portion of the male middle class for the first time and beginning the shift of political power to the rapidly growing industrial cities. Many in Britain swelled with pride because they had just weathered a dangerous political crisis through means of electoral reform rather than violent revolution. Sensing that this was the moment to interest readers in narrative "illustrations" of abstract economic laws, Martineau set to work on her popular didactic stories. As the chapter "Night and Morning" suggests, Martineau's main intentions were threefold: (1) to assuage fears of rapid economic change, (2) to teach that capitalism can benefit all social classes because of its unequalled ability to generate new wealth, and (3) to suggest that the suffering accompanying rapid social change is mandated by economic necessity to which individuals must submit.

Of the critics of the new industrial order, the Victorian "sages" Carlyle and John Ruskin are among the harshest. In *Past and Present* (1843), Carlyle idealistically anchors his criticism of what he calls the "Gospel of Mammonism" (the greed motivating industrial Britain's wealthy classes) in the vision of a neo-medieval social order governed by concern for the poor. Like many nineteenth-century critics of industrialism from the political right (Benjamin Disraeli, for example), Carlyle yearns for the values of an imagined feudal era in which the harshness of class difference was supposedly tempered by an ethical demand that the wealthy care for the needy.

The major art critic of the Victorian period, Ruskin was strongly influenced by the social mission outlined in *Past and Present*. When he began writing essays on "the condition of England" in the *Cornhill Magazine* in 1860, his ideas were guided by both outrage at what he considered the impoverished view of human life trumpeted by political economists and a determination to broaden the discussion of social duty to embrace the need to nurture "the soul." By the 1880s, Ruskin's influence as a social critic at least equalled his influence as a pioneering art historian. The first holder of the Slade Professorship in Art at Oxford University, where his lectures were heard by many of the upper-class elite, he inspired a diverse group of thinkers about the social question in the late nineteenth century. He supported the work of Octavia Hill's Charity Organisation Society, the first modern social work institution in Britain, and Hill's attempts to broaden opportunities for the poor to live in decent housing and to access public open space. In 1874, Ruskin enlisted a group of Oxford undergraduates—including Oscar Wilde, Alfred Milner, and Arnold Toynbee—in helping to reconstruct the road from Oxford to Hinksey. In the case of Toynbee, this event inspired a determination to create institutional opportunities for idealistic Oxford and Cambridge students to live among and serve the poor. Toynbee Hall in the East End of London, named in his honour, was the most admired and emulated of nineteenth-century "settlement" houses in Britain. Ruskin's ideas placed him politically in both right and left camps. Both his extreme Toryism and his passionate belief in the value of service to the less well off are on display in the excerpt included here. His words would have a major impact in the twentieth century as other admirers, particularly the founders of the Labour Party, Beatrice and Sidney Webb, sought to embody at least some of his ideas in political institutions dedicated to addressing the problem of poverty.

On the political left, stand Karl Marx and Friedrich Engels, whose lifelong intellectual and financial collaboration began in 1844. While Engels's *The Condition of the Working Class in England in 1844* (1845) critically examines the impact of rapid economic change on the British working class, both men welcome what twentieth-century economist Joseph Schumpeter would call the "creative destruction" (81) of capitalism in action. Insisting as much as Martineau on the extreme importance of economic laws, both thinkers looked forward to a utopian communistic future in which a militant working class would have overthrown a bourgeois capitalistic order. Neither had any faith that returning to an idealized feudal order would solve nineteenth-century social problems. Marx and Engels rested their analysis of capitalism on an

"Interior of a Dorsetshire Labourer's Cottage." *Illustrated London News* (5 Sept. 1846): 156.

awareness that it is finally a progressive force, remaking social relationships and thus ultimately creating the preconditions for the triumph of the working class. Eric Hobsbawm has described *The Communist Manifesto* as an "irresistible combination of utopian confidence, moral passion, hard-edged analysis, and—not least—a dark literary eloquence [that] was eventually to become perhaps the best-known and certainly the most widely translated pamphlet of the nineteenth century" ("Marx" n.pag.). Published just before much of continental Europe erupted in revolution in 1848, it stirringly merges the promise of political freedom with that of economic justice for the masses, predicting a widespread social revolution that failed to materialize in the nineteenth century.

One of the premier legislative accomplishments of the first "reformed" parliament elected in 1832 was the New Poor Law of 1834, which replaced the old system of parish relief for the poor with a new system: workhouse relief. Designed according to principles of political economy, the workhouses contained a built-in incentive for inhabitants to find employment outside the workhouse: they paid very low wages and offered meagre accommodations for what was often brutal work. Unlike the older parish relief system, which had allowed families to stay in their own homes, the workhouse system separated the sexes, sending women to lodge in separate workhouses from men in accordance with the Malthusian principle—that the only way to slow poverty is to prevent the breeding of more poor people. The workhouse system attracted heated criticism for its inhumanity, none more acerbic than that of Charles Dickens, the most beloved novelist of his era. While many of his novels decry the pathologies of poverty, his early novel *Oliver Twist* (1837–39) offers a grim depiction of organized criminality in the city of London and a darkly satirical, if somewhat inaccurate, treatment of the system of workhouse relief. His account of a visit in 1850 to a London workhouse is included here.

The city of London, the political and financial capital of Great Britain, was not an "industrial" city in the same sense that Manchester or Leeds were in the nineteenth century. While London's growing class of bankers, merchants, and traders played a crucial role in Britain's industrialization, London lacked steam-powered mills and heavy industry, as well as the large industrial working class, that were such prominent features of Britain's industrial landscape elsewhere. Instead, the London economy was dominated by a great number of small employers and retailers, who often hired "casual" labourers. The 1840s marked the historical moment when a number of London journalists presented to a growing middle-class readership, in vividly compelling narratives, the daily lives of casual labourers along with sometimes sensationalized accounts of the poor who led a brutal existence in the city warrens. Henry Mayhew's account of the watercress girl in *London Labour and the London Poor* (1851) offers a largely sympathetic portrayal of a London practitioner of small-bore capitalism. William Booth, the founder of the Salvation Army, was committed to ameliorating the harsh lives of the London poor and wrote sensationalized accounts of the lives of poor Londoners in order to generate support among middle-class readers for the Army's work. These writers shared a keen awareness that they were opening the eyes of middle-class readers to the daily lives of the poor and working classes and, in many cases, a sense that these lives had been misshapen by nineteenth-century social and economic changes. A keen awareness of the paradox of poverty in the midst of growing plenty, cast in the form of increasingly sensationalized narratives, marks the literature of social investigation of nineteenth-century London.

Crucial to the growth of nineteenth-century capitalism was the philosophy of individual rights. In the hands of political economists, this often came down to the so-called doctrine of laissez-faire capitalism—a political argument for freeing entrepreneurs from government interference so that they could make money. In the case of popular writers such as Samuel Smiles, the author of the well-known *Self-Help* (1859), this ideology expressed itself in triumphant narratives of business successes that bless those who exercise their individual powers to imagine and invent. Although anything but a simple spokesman for unfettered individualism, John Stuart Mill nonetheless offered a powerfully compelling philosophical justification of individual rights—in particular, the right to speak freely—in his *Essay on Liberty* (1859). Interestingly, much of his argument discusses the limits on individual freedom that must be observed in order to protect the rights of others.

Ranging in tone from optimistically celebratory to bitter and satirical, the sample of writings on the "condition of England" included here reflects the wide span of reactions by the members of the Victorian intellectual class to the rapid social changes precipitated by the Industrial Revolution.

Works Cited and Further Reading

Bivona, Daniel, and Roger B. Henkle. *The Imagination of Class: Masculinity and the Victorian Urban Poor*. Columbus: Ohio State UP, 2006. Print.

Carlyle, Thomas. *Past and Present*. New York: Wiley and Putnam, 1847. Print.

Dickens, Charles. *Oliver Twist. The Works of Dickens*. Riverside ed. New York: Hurd and Houghton, 1867. Print.

Engels, Frederick. *The Condition of the Working Class in England in 1844*. Trans. Florence Kelly Wischnewetzky. London: Swan, Sonnenschein and Co., 1892. Print.

Freedgood, Elaine, ed. *Factory Production in Nineteenth-Century Britain*. New York: Oxford UP, 2003. Print.

Hewison, Robert. "Ruskin, John (1819–1900)." *Oxford Dictionary of National Biography*. Oxford UP, Jan. 2010. Web.

Hobsbawm, E.J. *The Age of Capital, 1848–1875*. New York: Scribner, 1975. Print.

——. *The Age of Empire, 1875–1914*. London: Weidenfeld and Nicholson, 1987. Print.

——. *The Age of Revolution, Europe 1789–1848*. New York: Praeger, 1969. Print.

——. "Marx, Karl Heinrich (1818–1883)." *Oxford Dictionary of National Biography*. Oxford UP, 2004. Web.

Jones, Gareth Stedman. *Languages of Class: Studies in English Working Class History, 1832–1982*. Cambridge: Cambridge UP, 1983. Print.

Koven, Seth. *Slumming: Sexual and Social Politics in Victorian London*. Princeton: Princeton UP, 2004. Print.

Schumpeter, Joseph. *Capitalism, Socialism, and Democracy*. New York: Taylor and Francis, 2003. Print.

Smiles, Samuel. *Self-Help; with Illustrations of Character and Conduct*. New York: Harper and Bros., 1860. Print.

Thompson, E.P. *The Making of the English Working Class*. New York: Pantheon, 1963. Print.

Williams, Raymond. *The Country and the City*. New York: Oxford UP, 1973. Print.

——. *Culture and Society, 1780–1950*. New York: Columbia UP, 1958. Print.

Harriet Martineau
from *Illustrations of Political Economy* (1832–34)

A prolific journalist, historian, and sociologist, Harriet Martineau (1802–76) wrote on such varied subjects as abolition, women's rights, and the Haitian revolution of the 1790s. Martineau rose to fame and financial success with her *Illustrations of Political Economy* (1832–34), a multivolume series of tales intended to make the principles of political economy understandable to working-class readers. Her virtual deafness by age 20 did not impede her from travelling widely—to America, Egypt, and elsewhere. In addition to publishing widely in the periodical press and regularly for the *Daily News* on social and political issues, she wrote books based on her foreign travels, two novels, and an autobiography.

Martineau's work *Illustrations of Political Economy* displays her commitment to social reform and indebtedness to Thomas Malthus and James Mill. In this excerpt, she depicts a child's factory labour and the father's involvement in a strike to illustrate theories of wage labour.

∽

A Manchester Strike. A Tale.

Chapter 6: Night and Morning

"How is Martha?" was Allen's first inquiry on meeting his wife at the head of the stairs. Martha had been asleep when he had returned in the middle of the day; for it was now her turn for night-work at the factory, and what rest she had, must be taken in the day. Her mother said that her lameness was much the same; that she had seen Mr. Dawson, the apothecary, who pronounced that rest was what her weak limbs most required; and that as perfect rest was out of the question, her mother must bandage the joints while the child was at her work, and keep her laid on her bed at home. Here was the difficulty, her mother said, especially while Hannah was with her, for they were both fond of play when poor Martha was not too tired to stir. She was now gone to her work for the night.

The little girl repaired to the factory, sighing at the thought of the long hours that must pass before she could sit down or breathe the fresh air again. She had been as willing a child at her work as could be, till lately; but since she had grown sickly, a sense of hardship had come over her, and she was seldom happy. She was very industrious, and disposed to be silent at her occupation; so that she was liked by her employers, and had nothing more to complain of than the necessary fatigue and disagreeableness of the work. She would not have minded it for a few hours of the day; but to be shut up all day, or else all night, without any time to nurse the baby or play with her companions, was too much for a little girl of eight years old. She had never been so sensible of this as since her renewed acquaintance with Hannah. This night, when the dust from the cotton made her cough, when the smell and the heat brought on sickness and faintness, and the incessant whizzing and whirling of the wheels gave her the feeling of being in a dream, she remembered that a part of Hannah's business was to walk on broad roads or through green fields by her father's side, listening to the stories he amused her with, and to sit on a stile or under a tree to practice a new tune, or get a better dinner than poor Martha often saw. She forgot that Hannah was sometimes wet through, or scorched by the sun, as her complexion, brown as a gipsy's, showed; and that Hannah had no home and no mother, and very hard and unpleasant work to do at fairs, and on particular occasions. About midnight, when Martha remembered that all at home were probably sound asleep, she could not resist the temptation of resting her aching limbs, and sat down, trusting to make up afterwards for lost time, and taking care to be on her feet when the overlooker passed, or when any one else was likely to watch her.... She fairly fell asleep after a time, and dreamed that she was attending very diligently to her work; and so many things besides passed through her mind during the two minutes that she slept, that when the overlooker laid his hand upon her shoulder, she started and was afraid she was going to be scolded for a long fit of idleness. But she was not harshly spoken to.

"Come, come, child; how long have you been asleep?"

"I don't know. I thought I was awake all the time." And Martha began to cry.

"Well, don't cry. I was past just now, and you were busy enough; but don't sit down; better not, for fear you should drop asleep again."

Martha thought she had escaped very well; and winking and rubbing her eyes, she began to limp forwards and use her trembling hands. The overlooker watched her for a few moments, and told her she was so industrious in general that he should be sorry to be hard upon her; but she knew that if she was seen flagging over her work, the idle ones would make it an excuse to do so too. Martha curtsied, and put new vigour into her work at this praise. Before he went on in his rounds, the overlooker pointed to the window and told her morning was come.

It was a strange scene that the dawn shone upon. As the grey light from the east mingled with the flickering, yellow glare of the lamps, it gave a mottled, dirty appearance to every thing; to the pale-faced children, to the unshaved overlooker, to the loaded atmosphere, and even to the produce of the wheels.

When a bright sunbeam shone in through the window, thickened with the condensed breath of the work-people, and showed the oily steam rising through the heated room, the lamps were extinguished, to the great relief of those who found the place growing too like an oven to be much longer tolerable. The sunbeams rested now on the ceiling, and Martha knew that they must travel down to the floor and be turned full on her frame and some way past it, before she could be released; but still it was a comfort that morning was come.

She observed that the overlooker frequently went out and came back again, and that there was a great deal of consultation among her betters as the hours drew on. A breath of fresh air came in now and then from below, and news went round that the gates were already open, two hours earlier than usual. Presently the tramp of heavy feet was heard, like that of the weavers and spinners coming to their daily work. Martha looked up eagerly to the clock, supposing that the time had passed quicker than she had been aware of; but it was only four o'clock. What could bring the people to their work so early? ... More news went round. Those who had arrived had barely escaped being waylaid and punished for coming to work after a strike had been proclaimed. They had been pursued to the gates and very nearly caught, and must now stay where they were till nightfall, as they could not safely appear in broad daylight, going to and returning from their dinners. Many wondered that they had ventured at all, and all prophecied that they must give up to the will of the Union if they wished to be safe. The overlooker, finding much excitement prevailing on the circulation of the news, commanded silence, observing that it was no concern of any of the children present. There was no strike of the children, and they would be permitted to go and come without hinderance. Martha determined to get away the first moment she could, and to meet her father, if possible, that he might not encounter any troublesome people for her sake.

Allen was watching the moment of release as anxiously for his little daughter as she could have done for herself, and he was to the full as weary as she. On the previous evening he had carried home paper and pens, preferring to write the necessary letters at his own dwelling to spending the night at the Spread Eagle. He got his wife to clear and wipe down the deal table,[1] when she had put all the children to bed; and then he sat down to compose a pattern letter,[2] stating the circumstances which had led to a strike, and urging an appeal to their fellow-workmen in distant places for aid in the struggle which might be deemed a peculiarly important one. Having tolerably well satisfied himself that the letter was the proper thing, he read it to his admiring wife, who by turns smiled because she was proud of her husband.... She then went to bed and was soothed to sleep by the scratching of his nicely-mended pen....

When nearly twenty copies of his letter had been written, each varying a little from the original, according to the differing circumstances of those to whom it was addressed, Allen was so weary that he could write no longer without some refreshment. He put out his light, and opened the window for a minute to breathe the fresh air. The pattering of the rain wakened his wife, who roused herself to fret over the weather and wonder how Martha was to get home. Her husband told her he meant to go for the child, and would carry a shawl to wrap her up in. If Mary had known what lions were in her husband's path, she would not have let him go.

There was but one man visible when Allen went forth, and he was walking rapidly at some distance. It was Hare,—who, having never been well disposed towards a turn-out, and being supported in his dislike of it by his wife, hoped to avoid mischief and continue his earnings by going to the factory before people should be looking for him, and doing his work as usual, without talking about wages to anybody. Such devices did not suit the purposes of the Union, and were guarded against, as in all similar cases. Hare thought it just possible that he might meet with opposition, and looked as far before him as his eyes could reach; but he did not suspect an ambush on either hand. When he continued in the same direction, however, so as to render it certain that he was making for the factory, six men issued, one by one, from opposite alleys, and formed a line across the street....

... [T]hey coolly told their trembling fellow-workman that as he had not the pretence of any contract, and was nevertheless going to work at an unfair price, he must be ducked.[3] They had a rope ready, and would deliver him up to be dragged through the river.

Hare turned from one to another with as large a variety of excuses as he could invent at the moment. Among the rest, he vowed that he came to watch who would be wicked enough to go to work at this same factory after having sworn to strike. He was laughed at, let off with a roll in the kennel[4] and with being hunted part of the way home, whither he ran to seek refuge with his wife in panting terror, and presenting a woeful spectacle of disgrace....

Allen proceeded at his best pace while this judgment was being inflicted on Hare, never supposing that he could be suspected of taking work unfairly; but, like all eminent men, he had his enemies, and these chose to take for granted that he could not be going to the factory with any honest design. He was seized, girded with the dreadful rope, and hauled towards the river, though he produced the shawl, demanded

---

1 Fir or pine table.
2 An example or model.
3 Submerged briefly in water.
4 Gutter.

time to call witnesses, and used all the eloquence he could command. His last resource was to explain that the supplies from a distance must be delayed if any harm happened to him. This occasioned a short pause, during which the night-children came forth from the factory. One of the ambush, who had some sense of justice, and wished to find out the truth about Allen, ran up to Martha, as soon as she appeared, and before she could know what had happened, and asked her whether her father was not late in coming to work this morning?

"He is not coming to work at all," said the child; "but he said he would come for me. Perhaps the rain made him stay at home."

This testimony released Allen, and disappointed some of the lads who stood round of a frolic, which they had desired to fill up the time till they could proceed to a frolic of a different kind. They looked up at the clouds, and hoped the rain would not make the parson cheat them. They were going to be married. Several had begun to think of this some time before (as lads and lasses that work together in factories are wont to do); and this seemed the very time, when they had a holiday they did not know what to do with, and were sure, they believed, of ten shillings a week as long as the turn-out should last. So, amid the warning looks of elderly friends, and the remonstrances of parents who justly thought this the worst possible time to take new burdens upon them, several thoughtless young couples went laughing through the rain to the altar, and snapped their fingers at the clergyman behind his back[5] because his careful enquiries brought to light no cause why the solemnization of matrimony[6] should not proceed....

Summary of Principles illustrated in this volume.

COMMODITIES, being produced by capital and labour, are the joint property of the capitalist and labourer.

The capitalist pays in advance to the labourers their share of the commodity, and thus becomes its sole owner.

The portion thus paid is WAGES.

REAL WAGES are the articles of use and consumption that the labourer receives in return for his labour.

NOMINAL WAGES are the portion he receives of these things reckoned in money.

The fund from which wages are paid in any country consists of the articles required for the use and consumption of labourers which that country contains.

THE PROPORTION OF THIS FUND RECEIVED BY INDIVIDUALS MUST MAINLY DEPEND ON THE NUMBER AMONG WHOM THE FUND IS DIVIDED.

The rate of wages in any country depends, therefore, not on the wealth which that country contains, but on the proportion between its capital and its population.

As population has a tendency to increase faster than capital, wages can be prevented from falling to the lowest point only by adjusting the proportion of population to capital.

The lowest point to which wages can be permanently reduced is that which affords a bare subsistence to the labourer.

---

5   A sign of contempt.
6   Marriage service, *Book of Common Prayer*.

The highest point to which wages can be permanently raised is that which leaves to the capitalist just profit enough to make it worth his while to invest his capital.

The variations of the rate of wages between these extreme points depending mainly on the supply of labour offered to the capitalist, the rate of wages is mainly determined by the sellers, not the buyers of labour.

Combinations of labourers[7] against capitalists (whatever other effects they may have) cannot secure a permanent rise of wages unless the supply of labour falls short of the demand;—in which case, strikes are usually unnecessary.

Nothing can permanently affect the rate of wages which does not affect the proportion of population to capital.

Legislative interference does not affect this proportion, and is therefore useless.

Strikes affect it only by wasting capital, and are therefore worse than useless.

Combinations may avail or not, according to the reasonableness of their objects.

Whether reasonable or not, combinations are not subjects for legislative interference; the law having no cognizance of their causes.

Disturbance of the peace being otherwise provided against, combinations are wisely therefore now left unregarded by the law.[8]

The condition of labourers may be best improved,—

1st. By inventions and discoveries which create capital.

2d. By husbanding instead of wasting capital:—for instance, by making savings instead of supporting strikes.

3d. BY ADJUSTING THE PROPORTION OF POPULATION TO CAPITAL.

Thomas Carlyle
from *Past and Present* (1843)

Thomas Carlyle (1795–1881), an influential social critic, helped to introduce German literature and philosophy to England in the early to mid-nineteenth century. His debt to Germanic thought found expression in translations of Goethe and Teutonic phrasings known as "Carlylese." *Sartor Resartus* (1833–34, 1838) and *History of the French Revolution* (1837) established him as the "Sage of Chelsea," though he depended financially on lectures, including *On Heroes, Hero-Worship, and the Heroic in History* (1841). In *Chartism* (1841) and *Past and Present* (1843), Carlyle attacked laissez-faire policies and sympathized with the working poor. He rejected democracy for leadership by elites in *Latter-Day Pamphlets* (1850) and other works. His almost 40-year marriage to Jane Welsh Carlyle gained notoriety after his death, when J.A. Froude (see Education) published material suggesting their marital unhappiness.

---

7   Unions of workers.
8   The Combination Acts (1799 and 1800) that made trade unionism illegal were repealed in 1824.

In these selections from *Past and Present*, Carlyle decries the cash nexus as a basis for social relations and calls upon industrial leaders to become "captains" in rebuilding society on more compassionate grounds.

Book 3, Chapter 2: Gospel of Mammonism[9]

Reader, even Christian Reader as thy title goes, hast thou any notion of Heaven and Hell? I rather apprehend, not. Often as the words are on our tongue, they have got a fabulous or semi-fabulous character for most of us, and pass on like a kind of transient similitude, like a sound signifying little.

Yet it is well worth while for us to know, once and always, that they are not a similitude, nor a fable nor semi-fable; that they are an everlasting highest fact! "No Lake of Sicilian[10] or other sulphur burns now anywhere in these ages," sayest thou? Well, and if there did not! Believe that there does not; believe it if thou wilt, nay hold by it as a real increase, a rise to higher stages, to wider horizons and empires. All this has vanished, or has not vanished; believe as thou wilt as to all this. But that an Infinite of Practical Importance, speaking with strict arithmetical exactness, an *Infinite*, has vanished or can vanish from the Life of any Man: this thou shalt not believe! O brother, the Infinite of Terror, of Hope, of Pity, did it not at any moment disclose itself to thee, indubitable, unnameable? ... The Infinite is more sure than any other fact. But only men can discern it; mere building beavers, spinning arachnes much more the predatory vulturous and vulpine species,[11] do not discern it well!—

"The word Hell," says Sauerteig,[12] "is still frequently in use among the English people: but I could not without difficulty ascertain what they meant by it. Hell generally signifies the Infinite Terror, the thing a man *is* infinitely afraid of, and shudders and shrinks from, struggling with his whole soul to escape from it. There is a Hell therefore, if you will consider, which accompanies man, in all stages of his history, and religious or other development: but the Hells of men and Peoples differ notably. With Christians it is the infinite terror of being found guilty before the Just Judge. With old Romans, I conjecture, it was the terror not of Pluto,[13] for whom probably they cared little, but of doing unworthily, doing unvirtuously, which was their word for un*man*fully.[14] And now what is it, if you pierce through his Cants, his oft-repeated Hearsays, what he calls his Worships and so forth,—what is it that the modern English soul does, in very truth, dread infinitely, and contemplate with entire despair? What *is* his Hell; after all these reputable, oft-repeated Hearsays, what is it? With hesitation, with astonishment, I pronounce it to be: The terror of 'Not succeeding;' of not making money, fame, or some other figure in the world,—chiefly of not making money! Is not that a somewhat singular Hell?"

Yes, O Sauerteig, it is very singular.... But indeed this Hell belongs naturally to the Gospel of Mammonism, which also has its corresponding Heaven. For there *is* one Reality among so many Phantasms;

---

9 Love of wealth.
10 Brimstone (enflamed sulphur); see Revelations 19:20. Most European sulphur was imported from Sicily.
11 Carlyle distinguishes "men" from those who focus solely on industry.
12 Carlyle invents the voice of Gottfried Sauerteig, a fictional tourist.
13 Roman god of the underworld.
14 The Latin *virtus* (manliness or worth) derives from *vir* (man).

about one thing we are entirely in earnest: The making of money. Working Mammonism does divide the world with idle game-preserving Dilettantism:—thank Heaven that there is even a Mammonism, *any*thing we are in earnest about! Idleness is worst, Idleness alone is without hope: work earnestly at anything, you will by degrees learn to work at almost all things. There is endless hope in work, were it even work at making money.

True, it must be owned, we for the present, with our Mammon-Gospel, have come to strange conclusions. We call it a Society; and go about professing openly the totalest separation, isolation. Our life is not a mutual helpfulness; but rather, cloaked under due laws-of-war, named "fair competition" and so forth, it is a mutual hostility. We have profoundly forgotten everywhere that *Cash-payment* is not the sole relation of human beings; we think, nothing doubting, that *it* absolves and liquidates all engagements of man. "My starving workers?" answers the rich mill-owner: "Did not I hire them fairly in the market? Did I not pay them, to the last sixpence, the sum covenanted for? What have I to do with them more?"—Verily Mammon-worship is a melancholy creed. When Cain, for his own behoof, had killed Abel, and was questioned, "Where is thy brother?" he too made answer, "Am I my brother's keeper?"[15] Did I not pay my brother *his* wages, the thing he had merited from me?

O sumptuous Merchant-Prince, illustrious game-preserving Duke,[16] is there no way of "killing" thy brother but Cain's rude way!... To a deadened soul, seared with the brute Idolatry of Sense, to whom going to Hell is equivalent to not making money, all "promises," and moral duties, that cannot be pleaded for in Courts of Requests,[17] address themselves in vain. Money he can be ordered to pay, but nothing more. I have not heard in all Past History, and expect not to hear in all Future History, of any Society anywhere under God's Heaven supporting itself on such Philosophy. The Universe is not made so; it is made otherwise than so. The man or nation of men that thinks it is made so, marches forward nothing doubting, step after step; but marches—whither we know! In these last two centuries of Atheistic Government (near two centuries now, since the blessed restoration of his Sacred Majesty, and Defender of the Faith, Charles Second),[18] I reckon that we have pretty well exhausted what of "firm earth" there was for us to march on;—and are now, very ominously, shuddering, reeling, and let us hope trying to recoil, on the cliff's edge!—

For out of this that we call Atheism come so many other *isms* and falsities, each falsity with its misery at its heels!—A SOUL is not like wind (*spiritus*, or breath) contained within a capsule; the ALMIGHTY MAKER is not like a Clockmaker that once, in old immemorial ages, having *made* his Horologe[19] of a Universe, sits ever since and sees it go! Not at all. Hence comes Atheism; come, as we say, many other *isms*; and as the sum of all, comes Valetism, the *reverse* of Heroism; sad root of all woes whatsoever.... For the faith in an Invisible, Unnameable, Godlike, present everywhere in all that we see and work and suffer, is the essence of all faith whatsoever; and that once denied, or still worse, asserted with lips only, and out of bound prayerbooks only, what other thing remains believable? That Cant well-ordered is marketable Cant; that Heroism means gas-lighted Histrionism; that seen with "clear eyes" (as they call Valet-eyes), no man

---

15   Genesis 4:9.
16   Carlyle implies here that the aristocracy is more interested in preserving game animals for sport than in caring for the nation's poor.
17   Local courts dealing with small debts.
18   Carlyle implies here that the last Christian ruler of Britain was Oliver Cromwell (1599–1658).
19   Clock.

is a Hero, or ever was a Hero, but all men are Valets and Varlets.[20] The accursed practical quintessence of all sorts of Unbelief! For if there be now no Hero, and the Histrio[21] himself begin to be seen into, what hope is there for the seed of Adam here below? ... Alas, the Atheist world, from its utmost summits of Heaven and Westminster-Hall,[22] downwards through poor seven-feet Hats[23] and "Unveracities fallen hungry,"[24] down to the lowest cellars and neglected hunger-dens of it, is very wretched.

One of Dr. Alison's[25] Scotch facts struck us much. A poor Irish Widow, her husband having died in one of the Lanes of Edinburgh, went forth with her three children, bare of all resource, to solicit help from the Charitable Establishments of that City. At this Charitable Establishment and then at that she was refused; referred from one to the other, helped by none;—till she had exhausted them all; till her strength and heart failed her: she sank down in typhus-fever; died, and infected her Lane with fever, so that "seventeen other persons" died of fever there in consequence. The humane Physician asks thereupon, as with a heart too full for speaking, Would it not have been *economy* to help this poor Widow? She took typhus-fever, and killed seventeen of you!—Very curious. The forlorn Irish Widow applies to her fellow-creatures, as if saying, "Behold I am sinking, bare of help: ye must help me! I am your sister, bone of your bone;[26] one God made us: ye must help me!" They answer, "No; impossible: thou art no sister of ours." But she proves her sisterhood; her typhus-fever kills *them*: they actually were her brothers, though denying it! Had man ever to go lower for a proof?

For, as indeed was very natural in such case, all government of the Poor by the Rich has long ago been given over to Supply-and-demand, Laissez-faire and suchlike, and universally declared to be "impossible." "You are no sister of ours; what shadow of proof is there? Here are our parchments, our padlocks, proving indisputably our money-safes to be *ours*, and you to have no business with them. Depart! It is impossible!"—Nay, what wouldst thou thyself have us do? cry indignant readers. Nothing, my friends,—till you have got a soul for yourselves again. Till then all things are "impossible." Till then I cannot even bid you buy, as the old Spartans[27] would have done, two-pence worth of powder and lead, and compendiously shoot to death this poor Irish Widow: even that is "impossible" for you. Nothing is left but that she prove her sisterhood by dying, and infecting you with typhus. Seventeen of you lying dead will not deny such proof that she *was* flesh of your flesh; and perhaps some of the living may lay it to heart....

Book 4, Chapter 4: Captains of Industry

If I believed that Mammonism with its adjuncts was to continue henceforth the one serious principle of our existence, I should reckon it idle to solicit remedial measures from any Government, the disease being insusceptible of remedy. Government can do much, but it can in no wise do all. Government, as the most

---

20 Pun: a valet is a servant; a varlet, a rogue.
21 A player of farces.
22 Westminster Hall is the oldest English parliamentary building.
23 Carlyle mocks a contemporary hatter's advertisement: a huge wheeled lath-and-plaster hat, seven feet high; see "Captains of Industry."
24 Earlier in *Past and Present*, Carlyle contrasts "God-Veracities" and "Devil-Falsities."
25 William Pulteney Alison, *Observations on the Management of the Poor in Scotland and its Effect on the Health of the Great Towns* (1840).
26 Genesis 2:23.
27 Spartans practised euthanasia, believing that anyone in ill health or not of service to the state was better off dead.

conspicuous object in Society, is called upon to give signal of what shall be done; and, in many ways, to preside over, further, and command the doing of it. But the Government cannot do, by all its signaling and commanding, what the Society is radically indisposed to do. In the long-run every Government is the exact symbol of its People, with their wisdom and unwisdom; we have to say, Like People like Government.—The main substance of this immense Problem of Organising Labour, and first of all of Managing the Working Classes, will, it is very clear, have to be solved by those who stand practically in the middle of it; by those who themselves work and preside over work. Of all that can be enacted by any Parliament in regard to it, the germs[28] must already lie potentially extant in those two Classes, who are to obey such enactment. A Human Chaos *in* which there is no light, you vainly attempt to irradiate by light shed *on* it: order never can arise there.

But it is my firm conviction that the "Hell of England" will *cease* to be that of "not making money;" that we shall get a nobler Hell and a nobler Heaven! I anticipate light *in* the Human Chaos, glimmering, shining more and more; under manifold true signals from without That light shall shine. Our deity no longer being Mammon,—O Heavens, each man will then say to himself: "Why such deadly haste to make money? I shall not go to Hell, even if I do not make money! There is another Hell, I am told!" Competition, at railway-speed, in all branches of commerce and work will then abate:—good felt-hats for the head, in every sense, instead of seven-feet lath-and-plaster hats on wheels,[29] will then be discoverable! Bubble-periods,[30] with their panics and commercial crises, will again become infrequent; steady modest industry will take the place of gambling speculation. To be a noble Master, among noble Workers, will again be the first ambition with some few; to be a rich Master only the second. How the Inventive Genius of England, with the whirr of its bobbins and billy-rollers[31] shoved somewhat into the backgrounds of the brain, will contrive and devise, not cheaper produce exclusively, but fairer distribution of the produce at its present cheapness! By degrees, we shall again have a Society with something of Heroism in it, something of Heaven's Blessing on it; we shall again have, as my German friend asserts,[32] "instead of Mammon-Feudalism with unsold cotton-shirts[33] and Preservation of the Game,[34] noble just Industrialism and Government by the Wisest!"

It is with the hope of awakening here and there a British man to know himself for a man and divine soul, that a few words of parting admonition, to all persons to whom the Heavenly Powers have lent power of any kind in this land, may now be addressed. And first to those same Master-Workers, Leaders of Industry; who stand nearest, and in fact powerfulest, though not most prominent, being as yet in too many senses a Virtuality rather than an Actuality.

The Leaders of Industry, if Industry is ever to be led, are virtually the Captains of the World; if there be no nobleness in them, there will never be an Aristocracy more.... Captains of Industry are the true Fighters, henceforth recognisable as the only true ones: Fighters against Chaos, Necessity and the

---

28 Rudiments of a new organism.
29 Carlyle mocks a contemporary hatter's advertisement: a huge wheeled lath-and-plaster hat, seven feet high; see "Gospel of Mammonism."
30 Periods of financial speculation.
31 Heavy rods, part of industrial machines.
32 Carlyle invents the voice of Gottfried Sauerteig, a fictional tourist.
33 The main product of industrial Manchester was cotton.
34 Game animals.

Devils and Jötuns;[35] and lead on Mankind in that great, and alone true, and universal warfare; the stars in their courses fighting for them, and all Heaven and all Earth saying audibly, Well-done![36] Let the Captains of Industry retire into their own hearts, and ask solemnly, If there is nothing but vulturous hunger, for fine wines, valet reputation and gilt carriages, discoverable there? Of hearts made by the Almighty God I will not believe such a thing. Deep-hidden under wretchedest god-forgetting Cants, Epicurisms,[37] Dead-Sea Apisms;[38] forgotten as under foulest fat Lethe[39] mud and weeds, there is yet, in all hearts born into this God's-World, a spark of the Godlike slumbering. Awake, O nightmare sleepers; awake, arise, or be forever fallen![40] This is not playhouse poetry; it is sober fact. Our England, our world cannot live as it is. It will connect itself with a God again, or go down with nameless throes and fire-consummation to the Devils. Thou who feelest aught of such a Godlike stirring in thee, any faintest intimation of it as through heavy-laden dreams, follow *it*, I conjure thee. Arise, save thyself, be one of those that save thy country.

Bucaniers, Chactaw Indians,[41] whose supreme aim in fighting is that they may get the scalps, the money, that they may amass scalps and money: out of such came no Chivalry, and never will! Out of such came only gore and wreck, infernal rage and misery; desperation quenched in annihilation. Behold it, I bid thee, behold there, and consider! What is it that thou have a hundred thousand-pound bills laid-up in thy strong-room, a hundred scalps hung up in thy wigwam? I value not them or thee. Thy scalps and thy thousand-pound bills are as yet nothing, if no nobleness from within irradiate them; if no Chivalry, in action, or in embryo ever struggling towards birth and action, be there.

Love of men cannot be bought by cash-payment; and without love, men cannot endure to be together. You cannot lead a Fighting World without having it regimented, chivalried: the thing, in a day, becomes impossible; all men in it, the highest at first, the very lowest at last, discern consciously, or by a noble instinct, this necessity. And can you any more continue to lead a Working World unregimented, anarchic? I answer, and the Heavens and Earth are now answering, No!... Yes, when fathers and mothers, in Stockport hunger-cellars,[42] begin to eat their children, and Irish widows have to prove their relationship by dying of typhus-fever;[43] and amid Governing "Corporations of the Best and Bravest," busy to preserve their game by "bushing,"[44] dark millions of God's human creatures start up in mad Chartisms,[45] impracticable Sacred-Months,[46] and Manchester Insurrections;[47]—and there is a virtual Industrial Aristocracy as yet only half-alive, spell-bound amid money-bags and ledgers; and an actual Idle Aristocracy seemingly near

---

35   Giants in Scandinavian mythology.
36   Matthew 25:23.
37   Epicurianism is the pursuit of pleasure.
38   Elsewhere in the text, Carlyle refers to a story from the Koran in which a tribe near the Dead Sea ignores Moses' advice and is transformed into apes.
39   A river in Hades causing forgetfulness.
40   John Milton, *Paradise Lost* (1667).
41   A buccaneer is a pirate or sea robber; the Choctaws are a tribe of North American Indians originally from the southeastern United States.
42   Earlier in *Past and Present*, Carlyle tells the story of a Stockport couple who poisoned their children to defraud a burial insurance society.
43   See "Gospel of Mammonism."
44   Protecting game by placing bushes at intervals to prevent the sweep of poachers' nets.
45   Movement supporting the *People's Charter* (1838), a demand for six points of electoral reform.
46   A general strike proposed by the Chartists.
47   On 24 September 1838, a mass Chartist demonstration took place on Kersal Moor near Manchester.

dead in somnolent delusions, in trespasses and double-barrels; "sliding," as on inclined-planes, which every new year they *soap* with new Hansard's-jargon[48] under God's sky, and so are "sliding" ever faster, towards a "scale" and balance-scale whereon is written *Thou art found Wanting*:[49]—in such days, after a generation or two, I say, it does become, even to the low and simple, very palpably impossible! No Working World, any more than a Fighting World, can be led on without a noble Chivalry of Work, and laws and fixed rules which follow out of that,—far nobler than any Chivalry of Fighting was. As an anarchic multitude on mere Supply-and-demand, it is becoming inevitable that we dwindle in horrid suicidal convulsion, and self-abrasion, frightful to the imagination, into *Chactaw* Workers. With wigwam and scalps,—with palaces and thousand-pound bills; with savagery, depopulation, chaotic desolation! Good Heavens, will not one French Revolution and Reign of Terror[50] suffice us, but must there be two? There will be two if needed; there will be twenty if needed; there will be precisely as many as are needed. The Laws of Nature will have themselves fulfilled. That is a thing certain to me.

Your gallant battle-hosts and work-hosts, as the others did, will need to be made loyally yours; they must and will be regulated, methodically secured in their just share of conquest under you;—joined with you in veritable brotherhood, sonhood, by quite other and deeper ties than those of temporary day's wages! How would mere red-coated regiments, to say nothing of chivalries, fight for you, if you could discharge them on the evening of the battle, on payment of the stipulated shillings,—and they discharge you on the morning of it! Chelsea Hospitals,[51] pensions, promotions, rigorous lasting covenant on the one side and on the other, are indispensable even for a hired fighter. The Feudal Baron, much more,—how could he subsist with mere temporary mercenaries round him, at sixpence a day; ready to go over to the other side, if sevenpence were offered? He could not have subsisted;—and his noble instinct saved him from the necessity of even trying! The Feudal Baron had a Man's Soul in him; to which anarchy, mutiny, and the other fruits of temporary mercenaries, were intolerable: he had never been a Baron otherwise, but had continued a Chactaw and Bucanier. He felt it precious, and at last it became habitual, and his fruitful enlarged existence included it as a necessity, to have men round him who in heart loved him; whose life he watched over with rigour yet with love; who were prepared to give their life for him, if need came. It was beautiful; it was human! Man lives not otherwise, nor can live contented, anywhere or anywhen. Isolation is the sum-total of wretchedness to man.... To have neither superior, nor inferior, nor equal, united manlike to you. Without father, without child, without brother. Man knows no sadder destiny.... It was not a God that did this; no!

Awake, ye noble Workers, warriors in the one true war: all this must be remedied. It is you who are already half-alive, whom I will welcome into life; whom I will conjure in God's name to shake off your enchanted sleep, and live wholly! Cease to count scalps, gold-purses; not in these lies your or our salvation. Even these, if you count only these, will not long be left. Let bucaniering be put far from you; alter, speedily abrogate all laws of the bucaniers, if you would gain any victory that shall endure. Let God's justice, let pity, nobleness and manly valour, with more gold-purses or with fewer, testify themselves in this your brief Life-transit to all the Eternities, the Gods and Silences. It is to you I call; for ye are not dead, ye are already half-alive: there is in you a sleepless dauntless energy, the prime-matter of all nobleness

---

48   Records of British parliamentary debates are published in *Hansard*.
49   Daniel 5:27.
50   During the French Revolution (1789–99), the Reign of Terror (1793–94) saw the arrest of approximately 300,000 prisoners and 17,000 executions.
51   Chelsea Hospital is a retirement home for British soldiers.

in man. Honour to you in your kind. It is to you I call: ye know at least this, That the mandate of God to His creature man is: Work! The future Epic of the World rests not with those that are near dead, but with those that are alive, and those that are coming into life.

Look around you. Your world-hosts are all in mutiny, in confusion, destitution; on the eve of fiery wreck and madness! They will not march farther for you, on the sixpence a day and supply-and-demand principle: they will not; nor ought they, nor can they. Ye shall reduce them to order, begin reducing them. To order, to just subordination; noble loyalty in return for noble guidance. Their souls are driven nigh mad; let yours be sane and ever saner. Not as a bewildered bewildering mob; but as a firm regimented mass, with real captains over them, will these men march any more. All human interests, combined human endeavours, and social growths in this world, have, at a certain stage of their development, required organising: and Work, the grandest of human interests, does now require it.

God knows, the task will be hard: but no noble task was ever easy. This task will wear away your lives, and the lives of your sons and grandsons: but for what purpose, if not for tasks like this, were lives given to men? ...

Friedrich Engels
from *The Condition of the Working Class in England in 1844* (1845, trans. 1887)

Born in Germany, Friedrich Engels (1820–95) became famous for his collaboration with fellow communist theorist Karl Marx; however, Engels's early involvement with radical political movements and his writing on working-class England established him as a social theorist well before this collaboration. Engels's double life—as a bourgeois business man and as a revolutionary—led him to one of the most important analyses of English industrial society. After a stint at his father's Manchester textile mills (1842–44), Engels published *The Condition of the Working Class in England in 1844* (1845) (see Condition of England). The book made him famous in Germany and was translated into English in 1887.

In this selection from "The Great Towns," Engels vividly depicts the slums of London, decrying the degradation and squalor wrought by industrialization. For Engels, the "Great Towns" represent the typical sites of capitalism, which has created "social war" in which the "stronger treads the weaker under foot."

∼

The Great Towns

A town, such as London, where a man may wander for hours together without reaching the beginning of the end, without meeting the slightest hint which could lead to the inference that there is open country within reach, is a strange thing. This colossal centralization, this heaping together of two and a half millions of human beings at one point, has multiplied the power of this two and a half millions a hundred fold; has raised London to the commercial capital of the world, created the giant docks and assembled the thousand vessels that continually cover the Thames. I know nothing more imposing than the view which the Thames offers during the ascent from the sea to London Bridge. The masses of buildings, the wharves on both sides, especially from Woolwich upwards, the countless ships along both shores, crowding ever closer and closer together until, at last, only a narrow passage remains in the middle of the river, a passage through which hundreds of steamers shoot by one another; all this is so vast, so impressive, that a man cannot collect himself, but is lost in the marvel of England's greatness before he sets foot upon English soil.

But the sacrifices which all this has cost become apparent later. After roaming the streets of the capital a day or two, making headway with difficulty through the human turmoil and the endless lines of vehicles, after visiting the slums of the metropolis, one realises for the first time that these Londoners have been forced to sacrifice the best qualities of their human nature, to bring to pass all the marvels of civilization which crowd their city; that a hundred powers which slumbered within them have remained inactive, have been suppressed in order that a few might be developed more fully and multiply through union with those of others. The very turmoil of the streets has something repulsive, something against which human nature rebels. The hundreds of thousands of all classes and ranks crowding past each other, are they not all human beings with the same qualities and powers, and with the same interest in being happy? ... The brutal indifference, the unfeeling isolation of each in his private interest becomes the more repellant and offensive, the more these individuals are crowded together within a limited space. And however much one may be aware that this isolation of the individual, this narrow self-seeking is the fundamental principle of our society everywhere, it is nowhere so shamelessly barefaced, so selfconscious as just here in the crowding of the great city....

Hence it comes, too, that the social war, the war of each against all, is here openly declared. Just as in Stirner's recent book,[52] people regard each other only as useful objects; each exploits the other, and the end of it all is, that the stronger treads the weaker under foot, and that the powerful few, the capitalists, seize everything for themselves, while to the weak many, the poor, scarcely a bare existence remains.

What is true of London, is true of Manchester, Birmingham, Leeds, is true of all great towns. Everywhere barbarous indifference, hard egotism on one hand and nameless misery on the other, everywhere social warfare, every man's house in a state of siege, everywhere reciprocal plundering under the protection of the Law, and all so shameless, so openly avowed that one shrinks before the consequences of our social state as they manifest themselves here undisguised, and can only wonder that the whole crazy fabric still hangs together.

Since capital, the direct or indirect control of the means of subsistence and production, is the weapon with which this social warfare is carried on, it is clear that all the disadvantages of such a state must fall upon the poor.... Cast into the whirlpool, [the poor man] must struggle through as well as he can. If he is so happy as to find work, *i.e.*, if the bourgeoisie does him the favor to enrich itself by means of him, wages await him which scarcely suffice to keep body and soul together; if he can get no work he may steal, if he is not afraid of the police, or starve, in which case the police will take care that he does so in a quiet and inoffensive manner. During my residence in England, at least twenty to thirty persons have died of simple starvation under the most revolting circumstances, and a jury has rarely been found possessed

---

52   Max Stirner, *Der Einzige und sein Eigentum* (1845).

of the courage to speak the plain truth in the matter.... The bourgeoisie dare not speak the truth in these cases, for it would speak its own condemnation. But indirectly, far more than directly, many have died of starvation, where long continued want of proper nourishment has called forth fatal illness, when it has produced such debility that causes which might otherwise have remained inoperative, brought on severe illness and death. The English workingmen call this "social murder," and accuse our whole society of perpetrating this crime perpetually. Are they wrong?

True, it is only individuals who starve, but what security has the working man that it may not be his turn to-morrow? Who assures him employment, who vouches for it, that, if for any reason or no reason his lord and master discharges him to-morrow, he can struggle along with those dependent upon him until he may find some one else "to give him bread?"[53] Who guarantees that willingness to work shall suffice to obtain work, that uprightness, industry, thrift, and the rest of the virtues recommended by the bourgeoisie, are really his road to happiness? No one.... He knows that every breeze that blows, every whim of his employer, every bad turn of trade may hurl him back into the fierce whirlpool from which he has temporarily saved himself, and in which it is hard and often impossible to keep his head above water. He knows that, though he may have the means of living to-day, it is very uncertain whether he shall to-morrow.

Meanwhile, let us proceed to a more detailed investigation of the position in which the social war has placed the non-possessing class. Let us see what pay for his work society does give the workingman in the form of dwelling, clothing, food, what sort of subsistence it grants those who contribute most to the maintenance of society; and, first, let us consider the dwellings.

Every great city has one or more slums where the working class is crowded together. True, poverty often dwells in hidden alleys close to the palaces of the rich; but, in general, a separate territory has been assigned to it, where, removed from the sight of the happier classes, it may struggle along as it can. These slums are pretty equally arranged in all the great towns of England, the worst houses in the worst quarters of the towns; usually one or two-storied cottages in long rows, perhaps with cellars used as dwellings, almost always irregularly built. These houses of three or four rooms and a kitchen form, throughout England, some parts of London excepted, the general dwellings of the working class. The streets are generally unpaved, rough, dirty, filled with vegetable and animal refuse, without sewers or gutters, but supplied with foul stagnant pools instead. Moreover, ventilation is impeded by the bad, confused method of building of the whole quarter, and since many human beings here live crowded into a small space, the atmosphere that prevails in these working-mens' quarters may readily be imagined....

Let us investigate some of the slums in their order. London comes first, and in London the famous rookery[54] of St. Giles which is now, at last, about to be penetrated by a couple of broad streets. St. Giles is in the midst of the most populous part of the town, surrounded by broad, splendid avenues in which the gay world of London idles about, in the immediate neighborhood of Oxford Street, Regent Street, of Trafalgar Square and the Strand. It is a disorderly collection of tall, three or four-storied houses, with narrow, crooked, filthy streets in which there is quite as much life as in the great thoroughfares of the town except that, here, people of the working class only are to be seen. A vegetable market is held in the street, baskets with vegetables and fruits, naturally all bad and hardly fit to use, obstruct the sidewalk still further, and from these, as well as from the fish dealers' stalls, arises a horrible smell. The houses are

---

53   Proverbs 25:21.
54   A crowded lower-class tenement.

occupied from cellar to garret, filthy within and without, and their appearance is such that no human being could possibly wish to live in them. But all this is nothing in comparison with the dwellings in the narrow courts and alleys between the streets, entered by covered passages between the houses, in which the filth and tottering ruin surpass all description. Scarcely a whole window pane can be found, the walls are crumbling, doorposts and window frames loose and broken, doors of old boards nailed together or altogether wanting in this thieves' quarter where no doors are needed, there being nothing to steal. Heaps of garbage and ashes lie in all directions, and the foul liquids emptied before the doors gather in stinking pools. Here live the poorest of the poor, the worst paid workers with thieves, and the victims of prostitution indiscriminately huddled together, the majority Irish or of Irish extraction, and those who have not yet sunk in the whirlpool of moral ruin which surrounds them, sinking daily deeper, losing daily more and more of their power to resist the demoralizing influence of want, filth and evil surroundings....

The most extensive working people's district lies east of the Tower in White Chapel and Bethnal Green, where the greatest masses of London working people live. Let us hear Mr. G. Alston, preacher of St. Philip's, Bethnal Green, on the condition of his parish. He says:

> ... I believe that before the Bishop of London called attention to this most poverty-stricken parish, people at the West End knew as little of it as of the savages of Australia or the South Sea Isles. And if we make ourselves acquainted with these unfortunates, through personal observation, if we watch them at their scanty meal and see them bowed by illness and want of work, we shall find such a mass of helplessness and misery, that a nation like ours must blush, that these things can be possible. I was rector near Huddersfield during the three years in which the mills were at their worst, but I have never seen such complete helplessness of the poor as since then in Bethnal Green. Not one father of a family in ten in the whole neighborhood has other clothing than his working suit, and that is as bad and tattered as possible; many indeed, have no other covering for the night than these rags, and no bed, save a sack of straw and shavings.

The foregoing description furnishes an idea of the aspect of the interiors of the dwellings. But let us follow the English officials who occasionally stray thither, into one or two of these workingmen's homes.

On the occasion of an inquest held Nov. 14th, 1843, by Mr. Carter, coroner for Surrey, upon the body of Ann Galway, aged 45 years, the newspapers[55] related the following particulars concerning the deceased: She had lived at No. 3 White Lion Court, Bermondsey Street, London, with her husband and a nineteen year-old son in a little room, in which neither a bedstead nor any other furniture was to be seen. She lay dead beside her son upon a heap of feathers which were scattered over her almost naked body, there being neither sheet nor coverlet. The feathers stuck so fast over the whole body that the physician could not examine the corpse until it was cleansed, and then found it starved and scarred from the bites of vermin. Part of the floor of the room was torn up, and the hole used by the family as a privy....

I am far from asserting that *all* London working people live in such want.... I know very well that ten are somewhat better off, where one is so totally trodden under foot by society; but I assert that thousands of industrious and worthy people—far worthier and more to be respected than all the rich of London—do find themselves in a condition unworthy of human beings; and that every proletarian, everyone without exception, is exposed to a similar fate without any fault of his own and in spite of every possible effort.

---

55 See, for example, "Appalling Destitution," *Lloyd's Weekly London Newspaper* (19 Nov. 1843).

But in spite of all this, they who have some kind of a shelter are fortunate, fortunate in comparison with the utterly homeless. In London fifty thousand human beings get up every morning, not knowing where they are to lay their heads at night. The luckiest of this multitude, those who succeed in keeping a penny or two until evening, enter a lodging-house, such as abound in every great city, where they find a bed. But, what a bed! These houses are filled with beds from cellar to garret, four, five, six beds in a room; as many as can be crowded in. Into every bed four, five or six human beings are piled, as many as can be packed in, sick and well, young and old, drunk and sober, men and women, just as they come, indiscriminately.... And those who cannot pay for such a refuge? They sleep where they find a place, in passages, arcades,[56] in corners where the police and the owners leave them undisturbed. A few individuals find their way to the refuges which are managed, here and there, by private charity, others sleep on the benches in the parks close under the windows of Queen Victoria....

Karl Marx and Friedrich Engels
from *Manifesto of the Communist Party* (1848; trans. 1888)

Born in Germany, socialist theorist Friedrich Engels (1820–95) became famous for his career-long collaboration with fellow theorist Karl Marx (1818–83), a Prussian of Jewish descent; however, Engels's early involvement with radical political societies and his writing on working-class England had established him as a social theorist well before this collaboration. Indeed, Engels's double life—as a bourgeois business man and revolutionary advocate for the proletariat—led him to publish *The Condition of the Working Class in England in 1844* (1845; translated into English 1887). In Paris, in 1844, Engels met revolutionary intellectual Karl Marx; their productive collaboration resulted in *The Communist Manifesto* (1848) and Engels's completion of Marx's *Capital* (3 vols., 1867–94). As a wealthy factory owner's son, Engels supported Marx financially and provided important contacts with labour activists.

Commissioned at the Communist Workers' Educational Club to draft a manifesto, Marx and Engels completed *The Communist Manifesto* just ahead of the continental revolutions of 1848. The most widely translated nineteenth-century pamphlet, the *Manifesto* presents communism as the inevitable culmination of capitalism.

A spectre is haunting Europe—the spectre of Communism. All the Powers of old Europe have entered into a holy alliance to exorcise this spectre; Pope and Czar, Metternich[57] and Guizot,[58] French Radicals and German police-spies.

---

56 Covered passageways.
57 Klemens Fürst von Metternich (1773–1859), conservative Austrian statesman.
58 François Guizot (1787–1874), French politician and leader of the constitutional monarchists during the July Monarchy (1830–48).

Where is the party in opposition that has not been decried as communistic by its opponents in power? Where the Opposition that has not hurled back the branding reproach of Communism, against the more advanced opposition parties, as well as against its re-actionary adversaries?

Two things result from this fact.

I. Communism is already acknowledged by all European Powers to be itself a Power.

II. It is high time that Communists should openly, in the face of the whole world, publish their views, their aims, their tendencies, and meet this nursery tale of the Spectre of Communism with a Manifesto of the party itself.

To this end, Communists of various nationalities have assembled in London, and sketched the following manifesto, to be published in the English, French, German, Italian, Flemish and Danish languages.

Chapter 1: Bourgeois and Proletarians. (a)[59]

The history of all hitherto existing society (b)[60] is the history of class struggles.

Freeman and slave, patrician and plebeian, lord and serf, guild-master (c)[61] and journeyman, in a word, oppressor and oppressed, stood in constant opposition to one another, carried on an uninterrupted, now hidden, now open fight, a fight that each time ended, either in a revolutionary re-constitution of society at large, or in the common ruin of the contending classes.

In the earlier epochs of history, we find almost everywhere a complicated arrangement of society into various orders, a manifold gradation of social rank. In ancient Rome we have patricians, knights, plebeians, slaves; in the middle ages, feudal lords, vassals, guild-masters, journeymen, apprentices, serfs; in almost all of these classes, again, subordinate gradations.

The modern bourgeois society that has sprouted from the ruins of feudal society has not done away with class antagonisms. It has but established new classes, new conditions of oppression, new forms of struggle in place of the old ones.

Our epoch, the epoch of the bourgeoisie, possesses, however, this distinctive feature; it has simplified the class antagonisms. Society as a whole is more and more splitting up into two great hostile camps, into two great classes, directly facing each other: Bourgeoisie and Proletariat.

From the serfs of the Middle Ages sprang the chartered burghers of the earliest towns. From these burgesses the first elements of the bourgeoisie were developed.

---

59   Authors' note: (a) By bourgeoisie is meant the class of modern Capitalists, owners of the means of social production and employers of wage-labour. By proletariat, the class of modern wage-labourers who, having no means of production of their own, are reduced to selling their labour-power in order to live.

60   Authors' note: (b) That is, all written history. In 1847, the pre-history of society, the social organization existing previous to recorded history, was all but unknown. Since then, Haxthausen discovered common ownership of land in Russia, Maurer proved it to be the social foundation from which all Teutonic races started in history, and by and bye village communities were found to be, or to have been the primitive form of society everywhere from India to Ireland. The inner organization of this primitive Communistic society was laid bare, in its typical form, by Morgan's crowning discovery of the true nature of the gens and its relation to the tribe. With the dissolution of these primæval communities society begins to be differentiated into separate and finally antagonistic classes. I have attempted to retrace this process of dissolution in: "Die Ursprung der Familie, des Privateigenthums und des Staats," 2nd edit., Stuttgart 1886.

61   Authors' note: (c) Guild-master, that is a full member of a guild, a master within, not a head of, a guild.

The discovery of America, the rounding of the Cape,[62] opened up fresh ground for the rising bourgeoisie. The East-Indian and Chinese markets, the colonisation of America, trade with the colonies, the increase in the means of exchange and in commodities generally, gave to commerce, to navigation, to industry, an impulse never before known, and thereby, to the revolutionary element in the tottering feudal society, a rapid development.

The feudal system of industry, under which industrial production was monopolised by close guilds,[63] now no longer sufficed for the growing wants of the new markets. The manufacturing system took its place. The guild-masters were pushed on one side by the manufacturing middle-class; division of labour between the different corporate guilds vanished in the face of division of labour in each single workshop.

Meantime the markets kept ever growing, the demand ever rising. Even manufacture no longer sufficed. Thereupon, steam and machinery revolutionised industrial production. The place of manufacture was taken by the giant, Modern Industry, the place of the industrial middle-class, by industrial millionaires, the leaders of whole industrial armies, the modern bourgeois.

Modern Industry has established the world-market, for which the discovery of America paved the way. This market has given an immense development to commerce, to navigation, to communication by land....

We see, therefore, how the modern bourgeoisie is itself the product of a long course of development, of a series of revolutions in the modes of production and of exchange.

Each step in the development of the bourgeoisie was accompanied by a corresponding political advance of that class. An oppressed class under the sway of the feudal nobility, an armed and self-governing association in the mediæval commune (d),[64] here independent urban republic (as in Italy and Germany), there taxable "third estate" of the monarchy (as in France), afterwards, in the period of manufacture proper, serving either the semi-feudal or the absolute monarchy as a counterpoise against the nobility, and, in fact, corner stone of the great monarchies in general, the bourgeoisie has at last, since the establishment of Modern Industry and of the world-market, conquered for itself, in the modern representative State, exclusive political sway. The executive of the modern State is but a committee for managing the common affairs of the whole bourgeoisie.

The bourgeoisie, historically, has played a most revolutionary part.

The bourgeoisie, wherever it has got the upper hand, has put an end to all feudal, patriarchal, idyllic relations. It has pitilessly torn asunder the motley feudal ties that bound man to his "natural superiors," and has left remaining no other nexus between man and man than naked self-interest, than callous "cash payment." It has drowned the most heavenly ecstasies of religious fervour, of chivalrous enthusiasm, of philistine sentimentalism, in the icy water of egotistical calculation. It has resolved personal worth into exchange value, and in place of the numberless indefeasible chartered freedoms, has set up that single, unconscionable freedom—Free Trade. In one word, for exploitation, veiled by religious and political illusions, it has substituted naked, shameless, direct, brutal exploitation.

---

62 Rounding the Cape of Good Hope (South Africa) led trading ships to the rich markets of India and Asia.
63 Medieval trade guilds brought together people practising the same craft to protect their common interests.
64 Authors' note: (d) "Commune" was the name taken, in France, by the nascent towns even before they had conquered from their feudal lords and masters, local self-government and political rights as "the Third Estate." Generally speaking, for the economical development of the bourgeoisie, England is here taken as the typical country; for its political development, France.

The bourgeoisie has stripped of its halo every occupation hitherto honoured and looked up to with reverent awe. It has converted the physician, the lawyer, the priest, the poet, the man of science, into its paid wage-labourers.

The bourgeoisie has torn away from the family its sentimental veil, and has reduced the family relation to a mere money relation.

The bourgeoisie has.... been the first to shew what man's activity can bring about. It has accomplished wonders far surpassing Egyptian pyramids, Roman aqueducts, and Gothic cathedrals; it has conducted expeditions that put in the shade all former Exoduses of nations and crusades.

The bourgeoisie cannot exist without constantly revolutionising the instruments of production, and thereby the relations of production, and with them the whole relations of society. Conservation of the old modes of production in unaltered form, was, on the contrary, the first condition of existence for all earlier industrial classes. Constant revolutionising of production, uninterrupted disturbance of all social conditions, everlasting uncertainty and agitation distinguish the bourgeois epoch from all earlier ones....

The need of a constantly expanding market for its products chases the bourgeoisie over the whole surface of the globe. It must nestle everywhere, settle everywhere, establish connexions everywhere.

The bourgeoisie has through its exploitation of the world-market given a cosmopolitan character to production and consumption in every country. To the great chagrin of Re-actionists, it has drawn from under the feet of industry the national ground on which it stood. All old-established national industries have been destroyed or are daily being destroyed.... In place of the old wants, satisfied by the productions of the country, we find new wants, requiring for their satisfaction the products of distant lands and climes. In place of the old local and national seclusion and self-sufficiency, we have intercourse in every direction, universal inter-dependence of nations. And as in material, so also in intellectual production. The intellectual creations of individual nations become common property. National one-sidedness and narrow-mindedness become more and more impossible, and from the numerous national and local literatures, there arises a world-literature.

The bourgeoisie, by the rapid improvement of all instruments of production, by the immensely facilitated means of communication, draws all, even the most barbarian, nations into civilisation. The cheap prices of its commodities are the heavy artillery with which it batters down all Chinese walls, with which it forces the barbarians' intensely obstinate hatred of foreigners to capitulate. It compels all nations, on pain of extinction, to adopt the bourgeois mode of production; it compels them to introduce what it calls civilisation into their midst, *i.e.*, to become bourgeois themselves. In one word, it creates a world after its own image.[65]

The bourgeoisie has subjected the country to the rule of the towns. It has created enormous cities, has greatly increased the urban population as compared with the rural, and has thus rescued a considerable part of the population from the idiocy of rural life. Just as it has made the country dependent on the towns, so it has made barbarian and semi-barbarian countries dependent on the civilised ones, nations of peasants on nations of bourgeois, the East on the West.

The bourgeoisie keeps more and more doing away with the scattered state of the population, of the means of production, and of property. It has agglomerated population, centralised means of production,

---

65 Genesis 1:27.

and has concentrated property in a few hands. The necessary consequence of this was political centralisation....

The bourgeoisie, during its rule of scarce one hundred years, has created more massive and more colossal productive forces than have all preceding generations together....

We see then: the means of production and of exchange, on whose foundation the bourgeoisie built itself up, were generated in feudal society. At a certain stage in the development of these means of production and of exchange, the conditions under which feudal society produced and exchanged, the feudal organisation of agriculture and manufacturing industry, in one word, the feudal relations of property became no longer compatible with the already developed productive forces; they became so many fetters. They had to be burst asunder; they were burst asunder.

Into their place stepped free competition, accompanied by a social and political constitution adapted to it, and by the economical and political sway of the bourgeois class.

A similar movement is going on before our own eyes. Modern bourgeois society with its relations of production, of exchange and of property, a society that has conjured up such gigantic means of production and of exchange, is like the sorcerer, who is no longer able to control the powers of the nether world whom he has called up by his spells. For many a decade past the history of industry and commerce is but the history of the revolt of modern productive forces against modern conditions of production, against the property relations that are the conditions for the existence of the bourgeoisie and of its rule. It is enough to mention the commercial crises that by their periodical return put on its trial, each time more threateningly, the existence of the entire bourgeois society. In these crises a great part not only of the existing products, but also of the previously created productive forces, are periodically destroyed. In these crises there breaks out an epidemic that, in all earlier epochs, would have seemed an absurdity—the epidemic of over-production.... The productive forces at the disposal of society no longer tend to further the development of the conditions of bourgeois property; on the contrary, they have become too powerful for these conditions, by which they are fettered, and so soon as they overcome these fetters, they bring disorder into the whole of bourgeois society, endanger the existence of bourgeois property. The conditions of bourgeois society are too narrow to comprise the wealth created by them. And how does the bourgeoisie get over these crises? On the one hand by enforced destruction of a mass of productive forces; on the other, by the conquest of new markets, and by the more thorough exploitation of the old ones. That is to say, by paving the way for more extensive and more destructive crises, and by diminishing the means whereby crises are prevented.

The weapons with which the bourgeoisie felled feudalism to the ground are now turned against the bourgeoisie itself.

But not only has the bourgeoisie forged the weapons that bring death to itself; it has also called into existence the men who are to wield those weapons—the modern-working class—the proletarians.

In proportion as the bourgeoisie, *i.e.*, capital, is developed, in the same proportion is the proletariat, the modern-working class, developed, a class of labourers, who live only so long as they find work, and who find work only so long as their labour increases capital. These labourers, who must sell themselves piecemeal, are a commodity, like every other article of commerce, and are consequently exposed to all the vicissitudes of competition, to all the fluctuations of the market.

Owing to the extensive use of machinery and to division of labour, the work of the proletarians has lost all individual character, and, consequently, all charm for the workman. He becomes an appendage of the machine, and it is only the most simple, most monotonous, and most easily acquired knack, that is required of him....

Modern industry has converted the little workshop of the patriarchal master, into the great factory of the industrial capitalist. Masses of labourers, crowded into the factory, are organised like soldiers. As privates of the industrial army they are placed under the command of a perfect hierarchy of officers and sergeants. Not only are they slaves of the bourgeois class, and of the bourgeois State, they are daily and hourly enslaved by the machine, by the over-looker, and, above all, by the individual bourgeois manufacturer himself. The more openly this despotism proclaims gain to be its end and aim, the more petty, the more hateful and the more embittering it is.

The less the skill and exertion of strength implied in manual labour, in other words, the more modern industry becomes developed, the more is the labour of men superseded by that of women. Differences of age and sex have no longer any distinctive social validity for the working class. All are instruments of labour, more or less expensive to use, according to their age and sex.

No sooner is the exploitation of the labourer by the manufacturer, so far, at an end, that he receives his wages in cash, than he is set upon by the other portions of the bourgeoisie, the landlord, the shopkeeper, the pawnbroker, etc....

The proletariat goes through various stages of development. With its birth begins its struggle with the bourgeoisie. At first the contest is carried on by individual labourers, then by the workpeople of a factory, then by the operatives of one trade, in one locality, against the individual bourgeois who directly exploits them. They direct their attacks not against the bourgeois conditions of production, but against the instruments of production themselves; they destroy imported wares that compete with their labour, they smash to pieces machinery, they set factories ablaze, they seek to restore by force the vanished status of the workman of the Middle Ages.

At this stage the labourers still form an incoherent mass scattered over the whole country, and broken up by their mutual competition. If anywhere they unite to form more compact bodies, this is not yet the consequence of their own active union, but of the union of the bourgeoisie, which class, in order to attain its own political ends, is compelled to set the whole proletariat in motion, and is moreover yet, for a time able to do so. At this stage, therefore, the proletarians do not fight their enemies, but the enemies of their enemies, the remnants of absolute monarchy, the landowners, the non-industrial bourgeois, the petty bourgeoisie. Thus the whole historical movement is concentrated in the hands of the bourgeoisie; every victory so obtained is a victory for the bourgeoisie.

But with the development of industry the proletariat not only increases in number; it becomes concentrated in greater masses, its strength grows, and it feels that strength more. The various interests and conditions of life within the ranks of the proletariat are more and more equalised, in proportion as machinery obliterates all distinctions of labour, and nearly everywhere reduces wages to the same low level. The growing competition among the bourgeois, and the resulting commercial crises, make the wages of the workers ever more fluctuating. The unceasing improvement of machinery, ever more rapidly developing, makes their livelihood more and more precarious; the collisions between individual workmen and individual bourgeois take more and more the character of collisions between two classes. Thereupon the workers begin to form combinations (Trades' Unions) against the bourgeois; they club together in order to keep up the rate of wages; they found permanent associations in order to make provision beforehand for these occasional revolts. Here and there the contest breaks out into riots.

Now and then the workers are victorious, but only for a time. The real fruit of their battles lies, not in the immediate result, but in the ever expanding union of the workers. This union is helped on by the improved means of communication that are created by modern industry, and that place the workers of different localities in contact with one another. It was just this contact that was needed to centralise the numerous local struggles, all of the same character, into one national struggle between classes. But every class struggle is a political struggle. And that union, to attain which the burghers of the Middle Ages, with their miserable highways, required centuries, the modern proletarians, thanks to railways, achieve in a few years....

Of all the classes that stand face to face with the bourgeoisie to-day, the proletariat alone is a really revolutionary class. The other classes decay and finally disappear in the face of modern industry; the proletariat is its special and essential product.

The lower middle-class, the small manufacturer, the shopkeeper, the artisan, the peasant, all these fight against the bourgeoisie, to save from extinction their existence as fractions of the middle class. They are therefore not revolutionary, but conservative. Nay more, they are reactionary, for they try to roll back the wheel of history. If by chance they are revolutionary, they are so, only in view of their impending transfer into the proletariat, they thus defend not their present, but their future interests, they desert their own standpoint to place themselves at that of the proletariat.

The "dangerous class," the social scum, that passively rotting mass thrown off by the lowest layers of old society, may, here and there, be swept into the movement by a proletarian revolution; its conditions of life, however, prepare it far more for the part of a bribed tool of reactionary intrigue.

In the conditions of the proletariat, those of old society at large are already virtually swamped. The proletarian is without property; his relation to his wife and children has no longer anything in common with the bourgeois family-relations; modern industrial labour, modern subjection to capital, the same in England as in France, in America as in Germany, has stripped him of every trace of national character. Law, morality, religion, are to him so many bourgeois prejudices, behind which lurk in ambush just as many bourgeois interests.

All the preceding classes that got the upper hand, sought to fortify their already acquired status by subjecting society at large to their conditions of appropriation. The proletarians cannot become masters of the productive forces of society, except by abolishing their own previous mode of appropriation, and thereby also every other previous mode of appropriation. They have nothing of their own to secure and to fortify; their mission is to destroy all previous securities for, and insurances of, individual property.

All previous historical movements were movements of minorities, or in the interest of minorities. The proletarian movement is the self-conscious, independent movement of the immense majority, in the interest of the immense majority. The proletariat, the lowest stratum of our present society, cannot stir, cannot raise itself up, without the whole superincumbent strata of official society being sprung into the air....

In depicting the most general phases of the development of the proletariat, we traced the more or less veiled civil war, raging within existing society, up to the point where that war breaks out into open revolution, and where the violent overthrow of the bourgeoisie, lays the foundation for the sway of the proletariat.

Hitherto, every form of society has been based, as we have already seen, on the antagonism of oppressing and oppressed classes. But in order to oppress a class, certain conditions must be assured to it under which it can, at least, continue its slavish existence. The serf, in the period of serfdom, raised himself to membership in the commune, just as the petty bourgeois, under the yoke of feudal absolutism, managed to develop into a bourgeois. The modern labourer, on the contrary, instead of rising with the progress of industry, sinks deeper and deeper below the conditions of existence of his own class. He becomes a pauper, and pauperism develops more rapidly than population and wealth. And here it becomes evident, that the bourgeoisie is unfit any longer to be the ruling class in society, and to impose its conditions of existence upon society as an over-riding law. It is unfit to rule because it is incompetent to assure an existence to its slave within his slavery, because it cannot help letting him sink into such a state, that it has to feed him, instead of being fed by him. Society can no longer live under this bourgeoisie, in other words, its existence is no longer compatible with society.

The essential condition for the existence, and for the sway of the bourgeois class, is the formation and augmentation of capital[;] the condition for capital is wage-labour. Wage-labour rests exclusively on competition between the labourers. The advance of industry, whose involuntary promoter is the bourgeoisie, replaces the isolation of the labourers, due to competition, by their revolutionary combination, due to association. The development of Modern Industry, therefore, cuts from under its feet the very foundation on which the bourgeoisie produces and appropriates products. What the bourgeoisie therefore produces, above all, is its own grave-diggers. Its fall and the victory of the proletariat are equally inevitable.

Charles Dickens
from "A Walk in a Workhouse"[66] (1850)

Novelist Charles Dickens (1812–70) captured the public imagination with his fiction and journalism, much of which drew attention to social issues such as child labour and neglect, poverty, and prostitution. He began his writing career as a parliamentary reporter for the *Morning Chronicle*, soon distinguishing himself with articles on London street scenes. The creation of Mr. Pickwick, whose adventures Dickens recounted in 20 parts (1836–37), achieved great popularity and consolidated the serial format for Victorian fiction. Dickens edited three weekly magazines, published many Christmas books and periodical essays, and wrote over 13 novels, including *Oliver Twist* (1837–39), *David Copperfield* (1849–50), *Bleak House* (1852–53), and *Great Expectations* (1860–61).

Published in *Household Words*, the weekly magazine Dickens edited from 1850 to 1859, "A Walk in a Workhouse" (1850) illustrates some characteristic strategies of his journalism and fiction: scenes of pathos, keen character description, and indignation at inhumane government institutions.

---

66 Under the 1834 Poor Law, workhouses were established to provide minimal food and accommodation for the poor; those able to work were required to do so.

A few Sundays ago, I formed one of the congregation assembled in the chapel of a large metropolitan Workhouse. With the exception of the clergyman and clerk, and a very few officials, there were none but paupers present. The children sat in the galleries; the women in the body of the chapel, and in one of the side aisles; the men in the remaining aisle.... The usual supplications were offered, with more than the usual significancy in such a place, for the fatherless children and widows, for all sick persons and young children, for all that were desolate and oppressed, for the comforting and helping of the weak-hearted, for the raising-up of them that had fallen; for all that were in danger, necessity, and tribulation.[67] The prayers of the congregation were desired "for several persons in the various wards, dangerously ill;" and others who were recovering returned their thanks to Heaven.

Among this congregation, were some evil-looking young women, and beetle-browed[68] young men; but not many—perhaps that kind of characters kept away. Generally, the faces (those of the children excepted) were depressed and subdued, and wanted colour. Aged people were there, in every variety. Mumbling, blear-eyed, spectacled, stupid, deaf, lame; vacantly winking in the gleams of sun that now and then crept in through the open doors, from the paved yard; shading their listening ears, or blinking eyes, with their withered hands; poring over their books, leering at nothing, going to sleep, crouching and drooping in corners.... Upon the whole, it was the dragon, Pauperism, in a very weak and impotent condition; toothless, fangless, drawing his breath heavily enough, and hardly worth chaining up.

When the service was over, I walked with the humane and conscientious gentleman whose duty it was to take that walk, that Sunday morning, through the little world of poverty enclosed within the workhouse walls. It was inhabited by a population of some fifteen hundred or two thousand paupers, ranging from the infant newly born or not yet come into the pauper world, to the old man dying on his bed.

In a room opening from a squalid yard, where a number of listless women were lounging to and fro, trying to get warm in the ineffectual sunshine of the tardy May morning—in the "Itch Ward,"[69] not to compromise the truth—a woman such as Hogarth[70] has often drawn, was hurriedly getting on her gown, before a dusty fire. She was the nurse, or wardswoman, of that insalubrious department—herself a pauper—flabby, raw-boned, untidy—unpromising and coarse of aspect as need be. But, on being spoken to about the patients whom she had in charge, she turned round, with her shabby gown half on, half off, and fell a crying with all her might.... [She was] sobbing most bitterly, wringing her hands, and letting fall abundance of great tears, that choked her utterance. What was the matter with the nurse of the itch-ward? Oh, "the dropped child" was dead! Oh, the child that was found in the street, and she had brought up ever since, had died an hour ago, and see where the little creature lay, beneath this cloth! The dear, the pretty dear!

The dropped child seemed too small and poor a thing for Death to be in earnest with, but Death had taken it; and already its diminutive form was neatly washed, composed, and stretched as if in sleep upon a box. I thought I heard a voice from Heaven saying, It shall be well for thee,[71] O nurse of the itch-ward, when some less gentle pauper does those offices to thy cold form, that such as the dropped child are the angels who behold my Father's face!

---

67 See the Litany, *Book of Common Prayer*.
68 With prominent eyebrows; associated with surliness.
69 Skin disease ward.
70 William Hogarth (1697–1764), artist known for his (mostly satirical) engravings of everyday life.
71 See Isaiah 3:10.

In another room, were several ugly old women crouching, witch-like, round a hearth, and chattering and nodding, after the manner of the monkies. "All well here? And enough to eat?" A general chattering and chuckling; at last an answer from a volunteer. "Oh yes gentleman! Bless you gentleman! Lord bless the parish of St. So-and-So! It feed the hungry, Sir, and give drink to the thusty,[72] and it warm them which is cold, so it do, and good luck to the parish of St. So-and-So, and thankee gentleman!" Elsewhere, a party of pauper nurses were at dinner. "How do *you* get on?" "Oh pretty well Sir! We works hard, and we lives hard—like the sodgers!"[73]

In another room, a kind of purgatory or place of transition, six or eight noisy madwomen were gathered together, under the superintendence of one sane attendant. Among them was a girl of two or three and twenty, very prettily dressed, of most respectable appearance and good manners, who had been brought in from the house where she had lived as domestic servant (having, I suppose, no friends), on account of being subject to epileptic fits....

If this girl had stolen her mistress's watch, I do not hesitate to say she would, in all probability, have been infinitely better off. Bearing in mind, in the present brief description of this walk, not only the facts already stated in this Journal, in reference to the Model Prison at Pentonville,[74] but the general treatment of convicted prisoners under the associated silent system[75] too, it must be once more distinctly set before the reader, that we have come to this absurd, this dangerous, this monstrous pass, that the dishonest felon is, in respect of cleanliness, order, diet, and accommodation, better provided for, and taken care of, than the honest pauper.

And this conveys no special imputation on the workhouse of the parish of St. So-and-So, where, on the contrary, I saw many things to commend. It was very agreeable ... to find the pauper children in this workhouse looking robust and well, and apparently the objects of very great care. In the Infant School—a large, light, airy room at the top of the building—the little creatures, being at dinner, and eating their potatoes heartily, were not cowed by the presence of strange visitors, but stretched out their small hands to be shaken, with a very pleasant confidence. And it was comfortable to see two mangey pauper rocking-horses rampant in a corner. In the girls' school, where the dinner was also in progress, everything bore a cheerful and healthy aspect. The meal was over, in the boys' school, by the time of our arrival there and the room was not yet quite re-arranged; but the boys were roaming unrestrained about a large and airy yard, as any other schoolboys might have done. Some of them had been drawing large ships upon the schoolroom wall; and if they had a mast with shrouds and stays[76] set up for practice (as they have in the Middlesex House of Correction), it would be so much the better. At present, if a boy should feel a strong impulse upon him to learn the art of going aloft, he could only gratify it, I presume, as the men and women paupers gratify their aspirations after better board and lodging, by smashing as many workhouse windows as possible, and being promoted to prison.

In one place, the Newgate[77] of the Workhouse, a company of boys and youths were locked up in a yard alone; their day-room being a kind of kennel where the casual poor used formerly to be littered

---

72 Matthew 25:35.
73 Soldiers.
74 See "Pet Prisoners [Pentonville Prison]," *Household Words* (27 Apr. 1850).
75 Under the silent system, prisoners were permitted to work together but not to communicate.
76 A ship's rigging.
77 Newgate Prison, London.

down at night. Divers of them had been there some long time. "Are they never going away?" was the natural enquiry. "Most of them are crippled, in some form or other," said the Wardsman, "and not fit for anything." They slunk about, like dispirited wolves or hyænas; and made a pounce at their food when it was served out, much as those animals do. The big-headed idiot shuffling his feet along the pavement, in the sunlight outside, was a more agreeable object everyway.

Groves of babies in arms; groves of mothers and other sick women in bed; groves of lunatics; jungles of men in stone-paved down-stairs day-rooms, waiting for their dinners; longer and longer groves of old people, in upstairs Infirmary wards, wearing out life, God knows how—this was the scenery through which the walk lay, for two hours. In some of these latter chambers, there were pictures stuck against the wall, and a neat display of crockery and pewter on a kind of sideboard; now and then it was a treat to see a plant or two; in almost every ward, there was a cat.

In all of these Long Walks of aged and infirm, some old people were bed-ridden, and had been for a long time; some were sitting on their beds half-naked; some dying in their beds; some out of bed, and sitting at a table near the fire. A sullen or lethargic indifference to what was asked, a blunted sensibility to everything but warmth and food, a moody absence of complaint as being of no use, a dogged silence and resentful desire to be left alone again, I thought were generally apparent....

As we turn to go out at the door, another previously invisible old man, a hoarse old man in a flannel gown, is standing there, as if he had just come up through the floor.

"I beg your pardon, Sir, could I take the liberty of saying a word?"

"Yes; what is it?"

"I am greatly better in my health, Sir; but what I want, to get me quite round," with his hand on his throat, "is a little fresh air, Sir. It has always done my complaint so much good, Sir. The regular leave for going out, comes round so seldom, that if the gentlemen, next Friday, would give me leave to go out walking, now and then—for only an hour or so, Sir!—"

Who could wonder, looking through those weary vistas of bed and infirmity, that it should do him good to meet with some other scenes, and assure himself that there was something else on earth? Who could help wondering why the old men lived on as they did; what grasp they had on life; what crumbs of interest or occupation they could pick up from its bare board....

The morsel of burnt child, lying in another room, so patiently, in bed, wrapped in lint and looking steadfastly at us with his bright quiet eyes when we spoke to him kindly, looked as if the knowledge of these things, and of all the tender things there are to think about, might have been in his mind—as if he thought, with us, that there was a fellow-feeling in the pauper nurses which appeared to make them more kind to their charges than the race of common nurses in the hospitals—as if he mused upon the Future of some older children lying around him in the same place, and thought it best, perhaps, all things considered, that he should die—as if he knew, without fear, of those many coffins, made and unmade, piled up in the store below—and of his unknown friend, "the dropped child," calm upon the box-lid covered with a cloth. But there was something wistful and appealing, too, in his tiny face, as if, in the midst of all the hard necessities and incongruities he pondered on, he pleaded, in behalf of the helpless and the aged poor, for a little more liberty—and a little more bread.

Henry Mayhew
from *London Labour and the London Poor* (1851)

Editor and journalist Henry Mayhew (1812–87) also wrote plays, collaborated on several novels, and produced travel literature and children's books. He co-founded and co-edited the popular weekly *Figaro in London* and, in 1841, co-founded *Punch*, the successful satirical weekly. Mayhew's most enduring contribution to Victorian journalism was *London Labour and the London Poor*. Published in the *Morning Chronicle* as 82 articles (1849–50), it proved enormously popular, prompting correspondence from interested readers and the creation of a Labour and the Poor fund. Mayhew retooled the articles, publishing *London Labour and the London Poor* first in serial form (1850–52), then in two illustrated volumes (1851), and again with additions in the early 1860s. Mayhew's sketches influenced Victorian representations of working-class people, from characters in Dickens's novels to music-hall songs.

In this famous interview with a young street vendor, Mayhew exposes the lives of labouring children.

Watercress[78] Girl

The little watercress girl who gave me the following statement, although only eight years of age, had entirely lost all childish ways, and was, indeed, in thoughts and manner, a woman. There was something cruelly pathetic in hearing this infant, so young that her features had scarcely formed themselves, talking of the bitterest struggles of life, with the calm earnestness of one who had endured them all. I did not know how to talk with her. At first I treated her as a child, speaking on childish subjects; so that I might, by being familiar with her, remove all shyness, and get her to narrate her life freely. I asked her about her toys and her games with her companions; but the look of amazement that answered me soon put an end to any attempt at fun on my part. I then talked to her about the parks, and whether she ever went to them. "The parks!" she replied in wonder, "where are they?" I explained to her, telling her that they were large open places with green grass and tall trees, where beautiful carriages drove about, and people walked for pleasure, and children played. Her eyes brightened up a little as I spoke; and she asked, half doubtingly, "Would they let such as me go there—just to look?" All her knowledge seemed to begin and end with watercresses, and what they fetched. She knew no more of London than that part she had seen on her rounds, and believed that no quarter of the town was handsomer or pleasanter than it was at Farringdon-market or at Clerkenwell, where she lived. Her little face, pale and thin with privation, was wrinkled where the dimples ought to have been, and she would sigh frequently. When some hot dinner was offered to her, she would not touch it, because, if she eat too much, "it made her sick," she said; "and she wasn't used to meat, only on a Sunday."

---

78 A small green plant used in salads.

The poor child, although the weather was severe, was dressed in a thin cotton gown, with a threadbare shawl wrapped round her shoulders. She wore no covering to her head, and the long rusty hair stood out in all directions. When she walked she shuffled along, for fear that the large carpet slippers that served her for shoes should slip off her feet.

"I go about the streets with water-creases, crying, 'Four bunches a penny, water-creases.' I am just eight years old—that's all, and I've a big sister, and a brother and a sister younger than I am. On and off, I've been very near a twelvemonth in the streets. Before that, I had to take care of a baby for my aunt. No, it wasn't heavy—it was only two months old; but I minded it for ever such a time—till it could walk. It was a very nice little baby, not a very pretty one; but, if I touched it under the chin, it would laugh. Before I had the baby, I used to help mother, who was in the fur trade; and, if there was any slits in the fur, I'd sew them up. My mother learned me to needle-work and to knit when I was about five. I used to go to school, too; but I wasn't there long. I've forgot all about it now, it's such a time ago; and mother took me away because the master whacked me, though the missus use'n't to never touch me. I didn't like him at all. What do you think? he hit me three times, ever so hard, across the face with his cane, and made me go dancing down stairs; and when mother saw the marks on my cheek, she went to blow him up, but she couldn't see him—he was afraid. That's why I left school.

"The creases is so bad now, that I haven't been out with 'em for three days. They're so cold, people won't buy 'em; for when I goes up to them, they say, 'They'll freeze our bellies.' Besides, in the market, they won't sell a ha'penny handful now—they're ris to a penny and tuppence. In summer there's lots, and 'most as cheap as dirt; but I have to be down at Farringdon-market between four and five, or else I can't get any creases, because everyone almost—especially the Irish—is selling them, and they're picked up so quick. Some of the saleswomen—we never calls 'em ladies—is very kind to us children, and some of them altogether spiteful. The good one will give you a bunch for nothing, when they're cheap; but the others, cruel ones, if you try to bate them a farden[79] less than they ask you, will say, 'Go along with you, you're no good.' ... When we've bought a lot, we sits down on a door-step, and ties up the bunches. We never goes home to breakfast till we've sold out; but, if it's very late, then I buys a penn'orth of pudden,[80] which is very nice with gravy.... We children never play down there, 'cos we're thinking of our living. No; people never pities me in the street—excepting one gentleman, and he says, says he, 'What do you do out so soon in the morning?' but he gave me nothink—he only walked away.

"It's very cold before winter comes on reg'lar—specially getting up of a morning. I gets up in the dark by the light of the lamp in the court. When the snow is on the ground, there's no creases. I bears the cold—you must; so I puts my hands under my shawl, though it hurts 'em to take hold of the creases, especially when we takes 'em to the pump to wash 'em. No; I never see any children crying—it's no use.

"Sometimes I make a great deal of money. One day I took 1s. 6d.,[81] and the creases cost 6d.; but it isn't often I get such luck as that. I oftener makes 3d. or 4d. than 1s.; and then I'm at work, crying, 'Creases, four bunches a penny, creases!' from six in the morning to about ten....

"I always give mother my money, she's so very good to me. She don't often beat me; but, when she do, she don't play with me. She's very poor, and goes out cleaning rooms sometimes, now she don't work

---

79 Farthing (a quarter-penny).
80 Not dessert, but either a savoury boiled pudding or a stuffed sausage.
81 One shilling (s), sixpence (d).

at the fur. I ain't got no father, he's a father-in-law.[82] No; mother ain't married again—he's a father-in-law. He grinds scissors, and he's very good to me. No; I dont mean by that that he says kind things to me, for he never hardly speaks. When I gets home, after selling creases, I stops at home. I puts the room to rights: mother don't make me do it, I does it myself. I cleans the chairs, though there's only two to clean. I takes a tub and scrubbing-brush and flannel, and scrubs the floor—that's what I do three or four times a week.

"I don't have no dinner.[83] Mother gives me two slices of bread-and-butter and a cup of tea for breakfast, and then I go till tea,[84] and has the same. We has meat of a Sunday, and, of course, I should like to have it every day. Mother has just the same to eat as we has, but she takes more tea—three cups, sometimes. No; I never has no sweet-stuff; I never buy none—I don't like it. Sometimes we has a game of 'honey-pots'[85] with the girls in the court, but not often. Me and Carry H—— carries the little 'uns. We plays, too, at 'kiss-in-the-ring.'[86] I knows a good many games, but I don't play at 'em, 'cos going out with creases tires me. On a Friday night, too, I goes to a Jew's house till eleven o'clock on Saturday night. All I has to do is to snuff the candles and poke the fire. You see they keep their Sabbath then, and they won't touch anything; so they gives me my wittals[87] ... and 1½d., and I does it for 'em. I have a reg'lar good lot to eat. Supper of Friday night, and tea after that, and fried fish of a Saturday morning, and meat for dinner, and tea, and supper, and I like it very well.

"Oh, yes; I've got some toys at home. I've a fire-place, and a box of toys, and a knife and fork, and two little chairs. The Jews gave 'em to me where I go to on a Friday, and that's why I said they was very kind to me. I never had no doll; but I misses little sister—she's only two years old. We don't sleep in the same room; for father and mother sleeps with little sister in the one pair,[88] and me and brother and other sister sleeps in the top room. I always goes to bed at seven, 'cos I has to be up so early.

"I am a capital hand at bargaining—but only at buying watercreases. They can't take me in. If the woman tries to give me a small handful of creases, I says, 'I ain't a goin' to have that for a ha'porth,'[89] and I go to the next basket, and so on, all round. I know the quantities very well. For a penny I ought to have a full market hand, or as much as I could carry in my arms at one time, without spilling. For 3d. I has a lap full, enough to earn about a shilling; and for 6d. I gets as many as crams my basket. I can't read or write, but I knows how many pennies goes to a shilling, why, twelve, of course, but I don't know how many ha'pence there is, though there's two to a penny. When I've bought 3d. of creases, I ties 'em up into as many little bundles as I can. They must look biggish, or the people won't buy them, some puffs them out as much as they'll go. All my money I earns I puts in a club[90] and draws it out to buy clothes with. It's better than spending it in sweet-stuff, for them as has a living to earn. Besides it's like a child to care for sugar-sticks, and not like one who's got a living and vittals to earn. I aint a child, and I shan't be a woman

---

82   Stepfather.
83   Midday meal.
84   Late-afternoon meal.
85   A game in which a player called a "honey pot" sits with hands clasped under the legs; the player is lifted under the arms by the "honey sellers," carried to "market," and shaken in an attempt to dislodge his or her legs.
86   A game in which boys and girls stand in a ring with hands joined; one runs around outside the ring and tags someone of the opposite sex. This person then breaks out of the ring and they chase each other, kissing whomever is caught.
87   Food.
88   A room located one pair of stairs above the ground floor.
89   Halfpenny-worth.
90   Savings club.

till I'm twenty, but I'm past eight, I am. I don't know nothing about what I earns during the year, I only know how many pennies goes to a shilling, and two ha'pence goes to a penny, and four fardens goes to a penny. I knows, too, how many fardens goes to tuppence—eight. That's as much as I wants to know for the markets." ...

John Stuart Mill
from *On Liberty* (1859)

A progressive philosopher, economist, and women's rights advocate, John Stuart Mill (1806–73) became one of the nineteenth century's most influential public intellectuals. Rigorously educated from age three by his father, the young Mill mixed with his father's radical associates. Reading Jeremy Bentham converted him to utilitarianism, but a mental crisis in 1826–27 prompted dissent from Benthamism. Striving for practical reform, Mill spent his professional career at the India Office while editing and writing for periodicals and authoring works on philosophy and on political, economic, and social theory, including *On Liberty* (1859) and *The Subjection of Women* (1869). Mill first encountered the married Harriet Taylor in 1830; they married in 1851 after her first husband died, and Mill credited her collaboration on almost all his mature work.

In this passage from *On Liberty*, Mill argues vehemently for freedom of speech, insisting that ideas must be tested by questions and opposition to ensure their truth.

Chapter 2: Of the Liberty of Thought and Discussion

The time, it is to be hoped, is gone by, when any defence would be necessary of the "liberty of the press" as one of the securities against corrupt or tyrannical government. No argument, we may suppose, can now be needed, against permitting a legislature or an executive, not identified in interest with the people, to prescribe opinions to them, and determine what doctrines or what arguments they shall be allowed to hear. This aspect of the question, besides, has been so often and so triumphantly enforced by preceding writers, that it needs not be specially insisted on in this place.... Let us suppose, therefore, that the government is entirely at one with the people, and never thinks of exerting any power of coercion unless in agreement with what it conceives to be their voice. But I deny the right of the people to exercise such coercion, either by themselves or by their government. The power itself is illegitimate. The best government has no more title to it than the worst. It is as noxious, or more noxious, when exerted in accordance with public opinion, than when in opposition to it. If all mankind minus one, were of one opinion, and only one person were of the contrary opinion, mankind would be no more justified in silencing that one person, than he, if he had the power, would be justified in silencing mankind. Were an opinion a personal possession of no value except to the owner; if to be obstructed in the enjoyment of it were simply a private injury, it would make some difference whether the injury was inflicted only on a few persons or on many. But the peculiar evil of silencing the expression of an opinion is, that it is robbing the human race; posterity as well as the existing generation; those who dissent from the opinion, still more than those who hold it. If the opinion is right, they are deprived of the opportunity of exchanging error for truth: if wrong, they lose, what is almost as great a benefit, the clearer perception and livelier impression of truth, produced by its collision with error.

It is necessary to consider separately these two hypotheses, each of which has a distinct branch of the argument corresponding to it. We can never be sure that the opinion we are endeavouring to stifle is a false opinion; and if we were sure, stifling it would be an evil still.

First: the opinion which it is attempted to suppress by authority may possibly be true. Those who desire to suppress it, of course deny its truth; but they are not infallible. They have no authority to decide the question for all mankind, and exclude every other person from the means of judging. To refuse a hearing to an opinion, because they are sure that it is false, is to assume that *their* certainty is the same thing as *absolute* certainty. All silencing of discussion is an assumption of infallibility. Its condemnation may be allowed to rest on this common argument, not the worse for being common.

Unfortunately for the good sense of mankind, the fact of their fallibility is far from carrying the weight in their practical judgment, which is always allowed to it in theory; for while every one well knows himself to be fallible, few think it necessary to take any precautions against their own fallibility, or admit the supposition that any opinion of which they feel very certain, may be one of the examples of the error to which they acknowledge themselves to be liable. Absolute princes, or others who are accustomed to unlimited deference, usually feel this complete confidence in their own opinions on nearly all subjects. People more happily situated, who sometimes hear their opinions disputed, and are not wholly unused to be set right when they are wrong, place the same unbounded reliance only on such of their opinions as are shared by all who surround them, or to whom they habitually defer: for in proportion to a man's want of confidence in his own solitary judgment, does he usually repose, with implicit trust, on the infallibility of "the world" in general. And the world, to each individual, means the part of it with which he comes in contact; his party, his sect, his church, his class of society: the man may be called, by comparison, almost liberal and large-minded to whom it means anything so comprehensive as his own country or his own age. Nor is his faith in this collective authority at all shaken by his being aware that other ages, countries, sects, churches, classes, and parties have thought, and even now think, the exact reverse. He devolves upon his own world the responsibility of being in the right against the dissentient worlds of other people; and it never troubles him that mere accident has decided which of these numerous worlds is the object of his reliance, and that the same causes which make him a Churchman in London, would have made him a Buddhist or a Confucian in Pekin. Yet it is as evident in itself as any amount of argument can make it, that ages are no more infallible than individuals; every age having held many opinions which subsequent ages have deemed not only false but absurd; and it is as certain that many opinions, now general, will be rejected by future ages, as it is that many, once general, are rejected by the present....

... It is the duty of governments, and of individuals, to form the truest opinions they can; to form them carefully, and never impose them upon others unless they are quite sure of being right. But when they are sure (such reasoners may say), it is not conscientiousness but cowardice to shrink from acting on their opinions, and allow doctrines which they honestly think dangerous to the welfare of mankind, either in this life or in another, to be scattered abroad without restraint, because other people, in less enlightened times, have persecuted opinions now believed to be true. Let us take care, it may be said, not to make the same mistake: but governments and nations have made mistakes in other things, which are not denied to be fit subjects for the exercise of authority: they have laid on bad taxes, made unjust wars. Ought we therefore to lay on no taxes, and, under whatever provocation, make no wars? Men, and governments, must act to the best of their ability. There is no such thing as absolute certainty, but there is assurance sufficient for the purposes of human life. We may, and must, assume our opinion to be true for the guidance of our own conduct: and it is assuming no more when we forbid bad men to pervert society by the propagation of opinions which we regard as false and pernicious.

I answer, that it is assuming very much more. There is the greatest difference between presuming an opinion to be true, because, with every opportunity for contesting it, it has not been refuted, and assuming its truth for the purpose of not permitting its refutation. Complete liberty of contradicting and disproving our opinion, is the very condition which justifies us in assuming its truth for purposes of action; and on no other terms can a being with human faculties have any rational assurance of being right.

When we consider either the history of opinion, or the ordinary conduct of human life, to what is it to be ascribed that the one and the other are no worse than they are? Not certainly to the inherent force of the human understanding; for, on any matter not self-evident, there are ninety-nine persons totally incapable of judging of it, for one who is capable; and the capacity of the hundredth person is only comparative; for the majority of the eminent men of every past generation held many opinions now known to be erroneous, and did or approved numerous things which no one will now justify. Why is it, then, that there is on the whole a preponderance among mankind of rational opinions and rational conduct? If there really is this preponderance—which there must be, unless human affairs are, and have always been, in an almost desperate state—it is owing to a quality of the human mind, the source of everything respectable in man, either as an intellectual or as a moral being, namely, that his errors are corrigible. He is capable of rectifying his mistakes by discussion and experience. Not by experience alone. There must be discussion, to show how experience is to be interpreted. Wrong opinions and practices gradually yield to fact and argument: but facts and arguments, to produce any effect on the mind, must be brought before it. Very few facts are able to tell their own story, without comments to bring out their meaning. The whole strength and value, then, of human judgment, depending on the one property, that it can be set right when it is wrong, reliance can be placed on it only when the means of setting it right are kept constantly at hand. In the case of any person whose judgment is really deserving of confidence, how has it become so? Because he has kept his mind open to criticism of his opinions and conduct. Because it has been his practice to listen to all that could be said against him; to profit by as much of it as was just, and expound to himself, and upon occasion to others, the fallacy of what was fallacious. Because he has felt, that the only way in which a human being can make some approach to knowing the whole of a subject, is by hearing what can be said about it by persons of every variety of opinion, and studying all modes in which it can be looked at by every character of mind. No wise man ever acquired his wisdom in any mode but this; nor is it in the nature of human intellect to become wise in any other manner....

It is not too much to require that what the wisest of mankind, those who are best entitled to trust their own judgment, find necessary to warrant their relying on it, should be submitted to by that miscellaneous collection of a few wise and many foolish individuals, called the public.... The beliefs which we have most warrant for, have no safeguard to rest on, but a standing invitation to the whole world to prove them unfounded. If the challenge is not accepted, or is accepted and the attempt fails, we are far enough from certainty still; but we have done the best that the existing state of human reason admits of; we have neglected nothing that could give the truth a chance of reaching us: if the lists[91] are kept open, we may hope that if there be a better truth, it will be found when the human mind is capable of receiving it; and in the meantime we may rely on having attained such approach to truth, as is possible in our own day. This is the amount of certainty attainable by a fallible being, and this the sole way of attaining it....

In the present age—which has been described as "destitute of faith, but terrified at scepticism,"[92]—in which people feel sure, not so much that their opinions are true, as that they should not know what to do without them—the claims of an opinion to be protected from public attack are rested not so much on its truth, as on its importance to society. There are, it is alleged, certain beliefs, so useful, not to say indispensable to well-being, that it is as much the duty of governments to uphold those beliefs, as to protect any other of the interests of society. In a case of such necessity, and so directly in the line of their duty, something less than infallibility may, it is maintained, warrant, and even bind, governments, to act on their own opinion, confirmed by the general opinion of mankind. It is also often argued, and still oftener thought, that none but bad men would desire to weaken these salutary beliefs; and there can be nothing wrong, it is thought, in restraining bad men, and prohibiting what only such men would wish to practise. This mode of thinking makes the justification of restraints on discussion not a question of the truth of doctrines, but of their usefulness; and flatters itself by that means to escape the responsibility of claiming to be an infallible judge of opinions. But those who thus satisfy themselves, do not perceive that the assumption of infallibility is merely shifted from one point to another. The usefulness of an opinion is itself matter of opinion: as disputable, as open to discussion and requiring discussion as much, as the opinion itself. There is the same need of an infallible judge of opinions to decide an opinion to be noxious, as to decide it to be false, unless the opinion condemned has full opportunity of defending itself. And it will not do to say that the heretic may be allowed to maintain the utility or harmlessness of his opinion, though forbidden to maintain its truth. The truth of an opinion is part of its utility. If we would know whether or not it is desirable that a proposition should be believed, is it possible to exclude the consideration of whether or not it is true? In the opinion, not of bad men, but of the best men, no belief which is contrary to truth can be really useful: and can you prevent such men from urging that plea, when they are charged with culpability for denying some doctrine which they are told is useful, but which they believe to be false? Those who are on the side of received opinions, never fail to take all possible advantage of this plea; you do not find *them* handling the question of utility as if it could be completely abstracted from that of truth: on the contrary, it is, above all, because their doctrine is "the truth," that the knowledge or the belief of it is held to be so indispensable. There can be no fair discussion of the question of usefulness, when an argument so vital may be employed on one side, but not on the other. And in point of fact, when law or public feeling do not permit the truth of an opinion to be disputed, they are just as little tolerant of a denial of its usefulness. The utmost they allow is an extenuation of its absolute necessity or of the positive guilt of rejecting it....

---

91 Spaces for combat.
92 Thomas Carlyle, "Sir Walter Scott" (1838).

To pass from this to the only other instance of judicial iniquity, the mention of which, after the condemnation of Socrates,[93] would not be an anti-climax: the event which took place on Calvary[94] rather more than eighteen hundred years ago. The man who left on the memory of those who witnessed his life and conversation, such an impression of his moral grandeur, that eighteen subsequent centuries have done homage to him as the Almighty in person, was ignominiously put to death, as what? As a blasphemer. Men did not merely mistake their benefactor; they mistook him for the exact contrary of what he was, and treated him as that prodigy of impiety, which they themselves are now held to be, for their treatment of him. The feelings with which mankind now regard these lamentable transactions, especially the later of the two, render them extremely unjust in their judgment of the unhappy actors. These were, to all appearance, not bad men—not worse than men most commonly are, but rather the contrary; men who possessed in a full, or somewhat more than a full measure, the religious, moral, and patriotic feelings of their time and people: the very kind of men who, in all times, our own included, have every chance of passing through life blameless and respected. The high-priest who rent his garments when the words were pronounced, which, according to all the ideas of his country, constituted the blackest guilt,[95] was in all probability quite as sincere in his horror and indignation, as the generality of respectable and pious men now are in the religious and moral sentiments they profess; and most of those who now shudder at his conduct, if they had lived in his time and been born Jews, would have acted precisely as he did. Orthodox Christians who are tempted to think that those who stoned to death the first martyrs must have been worse men than they themselves are, ought to remember that one of those persecutors was Saint Paul....[96]

Let us now pass to the second division of the argument, and dismissing the supposition that any of the received opinions may be false, let us assume them to be true, and examine into the worth of the manner in which they are likely to be held, when their truth is not freely and openly canvassed. However unwillingly a person who has a strong opinion may admit the possibility that his opinion may be false, he ought to be moved by the consideration that however true it may be, if it is not fully, frequently, and fearlessly discussed, it will be held as a dead dogma, not a living truth.

There is a class of persons (happily not quite so numerous as formerly) who think it enough if a person assents undoubtingly to what they think true, though he has no knowledge whatever of the grounds of the opinion, and could not make a tenable defence of it against the most superficial objections. Such persons, if they can once get their creed taught from authority, naturally think that no good, and some harm, comes of its being allowed to be questioned.... This is not knowing the truth. Truth, thus held, is but one superstition the more, accidentally clinging to the words which enunciate a truth.

If the intellect and judgment of mankind ought to be cultivated, a thing which Protestants at least do not deny, on what can these faculties be more appropriately exercised by any one, than on the things which concern him so much that it is considered necessary for him to hold opinions on them? If the cultivation of the understanding consists in one thing more than in another, it is surely in learning the grounds of one's own opinions. Whatever people believe, on subjects on which it is of the first importance

---

93 Socrates was condemned to death in 399 BCE by a jury of his fellow citizens on charges of impiety and corrupting the youth of Athens.
94 The site of Jesus' crucifixion.
95 The high priest tears his clothes when he asks Jesus if he is the son of God and Jesus replies, "I am" (Mark 14:61–63).
96 See Acts 9:1–4, which describes Saul's (Paul's) persecution of Christians before his conversion.

to believe rightly, they ought to be able to defend against at least the common objections.... He who knows only his own side of the case, knows little of that.... Nor is it enough that he should hear the arguments of adversaries from his own teachers, presented as they state them, and accompanied by what they offer as refutations. That is not the way to do justice to the arguments, or bring them into real contact with his own mind. He must be able to hear them from persons who actually believe them; who defend them in earnest, and do their very utmost for them. He must know them in their most plausible and persuasive form; he must feel the whole force of the difficulty which the true view of the subject has to encounter and dispose of, else he will never really possess himself of the portion of truth which meets and removes that difficulty.... So essential is this discipline to a real understanding of moral and human subjects, that if opponents of all important truths do not exist, it is indispensable to imagine them and supply them with the strongest arguments which the most skilful devil's advocate can conjure up.

To abate the force of these considerations, an enemy of free discussion may be supposed to say, that there is no necessity for mankind in general to know and understand all that can be said against or for their opinions by philosophers and theologians. That it is not needful for common men to be able to expose all the misstatements or fallacies of an ingenious opponent. That it is enough if there is always somebody capable of answering them, so that nothing likely to mislead uninstructed persons remains unrefuted. That simple minds, having been taught the obvious grounds of the truths inculcated on them, may trust to authority for the rest, and being aware that they have neither knowledge nor talent to resolve every difficulty which can be raised, may repose in the assurance that all those which have been raised have been or can be answered, by those who are specially trained to the task.

Conceding to this view of the subject the utmost that can be claimed for it by those most easily satisfied with the amount of understanding of truth which ought to accompany the belief of it; even so, the argument for free discussion is no way weakened. For even this doctrine acknowledges that mankind ought to have a rational assurance that all objections have been satisfactorily answered; and how are they to be answered if that which requires to be answered is not spoken? or how can the answer be known to be satisfactory, if the objectors have no opportunity of showing that it is unsatisfactory? ... If the teachers of mankind are to be cognisant of all that they ought to know, everything must be free to be written and published without restraint....

... We have hitherto considered only two possibilities: that the received opinion may be false, and some other opinion, consequently, true; or that, the received opinion being true, a conflict with the opposite error is essential to a clear apprehension and deep feeling of its truth. But there is a commoner case than either of these; when the conflicting doctrines, instead of being one true and the other false, share the truth between them; and the nonconforming opinion is needed to supply the remainder of the truth, of which the received doctrine embodies only a part. Popular opinions, on subjects not palpable to sense, are often true, but seldom or never the whole truth. They are a part of the truth; sometimes a greater, sometimes a smaller part, but exaggerated, distorted, and disjoined from the truths by which they ought to be accompanied and limited. Heretical opinions, on the other hand, are generally some of these suppressed and neglected truths, bursting the bonds which kept them down, and either seeking reconciliation with the truth contained in the common opinion, or fronting it as enemies, and setting themselves up, with similar exclusiveness, as the whole truth. The latter case is hitherto the most frequent, as, in the human mind, one-sidedness has always been the rule, and many-sidedness the exception. Hence, even in revolutions of opinion, one part of the truth usually sets while another rises. Even progress, which ought to superadd, for the most part only substitutes one partial and incomplete truth for another; improvement consisting chiefly in this, that the new fragment of truth is more wanted, more adapted to the needs of the time, than that which it displaces. Such being the partial character of prevailing opinions, even when resting on a true foundation; every opinion which embodies somewhat of the portion of truth which the common opinion omits, ought to be considered precious, with whatever amount of error and confusion that truth may be blended. No sober judge of human affairs will feel bound to be indignant because those who force on our notice truths which we should otherwise have overlooked, overlook some of those which we see. Rather, he will think that so long as popular truth is one-sided, it is more desirable than otherwise that unpopular truth should have onesided asserters too; such being usually the most energetic, and the most likely to compel reluctant attention to the fragment of wisdom which they proclaim as if it were the whole.

Thus, in the eighteenth century, when nearly all the instructed, and all those of the uninstructed who were led by them, were lost in admiration of what is called civilization, and of the marvels of modern science, literature, and philosophy, and while greatly overrating the amount of unlikeness between the men of modern and those of ancient times, indulged the belief that the whole of the difference was in their own favour; with what a salutary shock did the paradoxes of Rousseau[97] explode like bombshells in the midst, dislocating the compact mass of onesided opinion, and forcing its elements to recombine in a better form and with additional ingredients. Not that the current opinions were on the whole farther from the truth than Rousseau's were; on the contrary, they were nearer to it; they contained more of positive truth, and very much less of error. Nevertheless there lay in Rousseau's doctrine, and has floated down the stream of opinion along with it, a considerable amount of exactly those truths which the popular opinion wanted; and these are the deposit which was left behind when the flood subsided. The superior worth of simplicity of life, the enervating and demoralizing effect of the trammels and hypocrisies of artificial society, are ideas which have never been entirely absent from cultivated minds since Rousseau wrote; and they will in time produce their due effect, though at present needing to be asserted as much as ever, and to be asserted by deeds, for words, on this subject, have nearly exhausted their power.

In politics, again, it is almost a commonplace, that a party of order or stability, and a party of progress or reform, are both necessary elements of a healthy state of political life; until the one or the other shall have so enlarged its mental grasp as to be a party equally of order and of progress, knowing and distinguishing what is fit to be preserved from what ought to be swept away. Each of these modes of thinking derives its utility from the deficiencies of the other; but it is in a great measure the opposition of the other that keeps each within the limits of reason and sanity. Unless opinions favorable to democracy and to aristocracy, to property and to equality, to co-operation and to competition, to luxury and to abstinence, to sociality and individuality, to liberty and discipline, and all the other standing antagonisms of practical life, are expressed with equal freedom, and enforced and defended with equal talent and energy, there is no chance of both elements obtaining their due; one scale is sure to go up, and the other down. Truth, in the great practical concerns of life, is so much a question of the reconciling and combining of opposites, that very few have minds sufficiently capacious and impartial to make the adjustment with an approach to correctness, and it has to be made by the rough process of a struggle between combatants fighting under hostile banners. On

---

[97] Swiss-born French philosopher Jean-Jacques Rousseau (1712–78) argued that civilization had not improved humanity; humans were, he contended, most pure in the state of noble savagery.

any of the great open questions just enumerated, if either of the two opinions has a better claim than the other, not merely to be tolerated, but to be encouraged and countenanced, it is the one which happens at the particular time and place to be in a minority. That is the opinion which, for the time being, represents the neglected interests, the side of human well-being which is in danger of obtaining less than its share. I am aware that there is not, in this country, any intolerance of differences of opinion on most of these topics. They are adduced to show, by admitted and multiplied examples, the universality of the fact, that only through diversity of opinion is there, in the existing state of human intellect, a chance of fair play to all sides of the truth. When there are persons to be found, who form an exception to the apparent unanimity of the world on any subject, even if the world is in the right, it is always probable that dissentients have something worth hearing to say for themselves, and that truth would lose something by their silence.

It may be objected, "But *some* received principles, especially on the highest and most vital subjects, are more than half-truths. The Christian morality, for instance, is the whole truth on that subject and if any one teaches a morality which varies from it, he is wholly in error." As this is of all cases the most important in practice, none can be fitter to test the general maxim. But before pronouncing what Christian morality is or is not, it would be desirable to decide what is meant by Christian morality. If it means the morality of the New Testament, I wonder that any one who derives his knowledge of this from the book itself, can suppose that it was announced, or intended, as a complete doctrine of morals. The Gospel always refers to a pre-existing morality, and confines its precepts to the particulars in which that morality was to be corrected, or superseded by a wider and higher; expressing itself, moreover, in terms most general, often impossible to be interpreted literally, and possessing rather the impressiveness of poetry or eloquence than the precision of legislation. To extract from it a body of ethical doctrine, has never been possible without eking it out from the Old Testament, that is, from a system elaborate indeed, but in many respects barbarous, and intended only for a barbarous people. St. Paul, a declared enemy to this Judaical mode of interpreting the doctrine and filling up the scheme of his Master, equally assumes a pre-existing morality, namely, that of the Greeks and Romans....[98] What is called Christian, but should rather be termed theological, morality, was not the work of Christ or the Apostles, but is of much later origin, having been gradually built up by the Catholic church of the first five centuries, and though not implicitly adopted by moderns and Protestants, has been much less modified by them than might have been expected. For the most part, indeed, they have contented themselves with cutting off the additions which had been made to it in the middle ages, each sect supplying the place by fresh additions, adapted to its own character and tendencies. That mankind owe[s] a great debt to this morality, and to its early teachers, I should be the last person to deny; but I do not scruple to say of it, that it is, in many important points, incomplete and onesided, and that unless ideas and feelings, not sanctioned by it, had contributed to the formation of European life and character, human affairs would have been in a worse condition than they now are. Christian morality (so called) has all the characters of a reaction; it is, in great part, a protest against Paganism. Its ideal is negative rather than positive; passive rather than active; Innocence rather than Nobleness; Abstinence from Evil, rather than energetic Pursuit of Good: in its precepts (as has

---

98 St. Paul, a Jew and a Roman citizen, preached mainly in Greek centres; he was well-educated (probably in Damascus) and would have been aware of Greek and Roman intellectual issues, although modern scholars consider these influences less central to his thought than Mill suggests. Modern scholars have also overturned Mill's view that Paul's thought is a renunciation of Judaism.

been well said) "thou shalt not" predominates unduly over "thou shalt."[99] ... It is essentially a doctrine of passive obedience; it inculcates submission to all authorities found established; who indeed are not to be actively obeyed when they command what religion forbids, but who are not to be resisted, far less rebelled against, for any amount of wrong to ourselves. And while, in the morality of the best Pagan nations, duty to the State holds even a disproportionate place, infringing on the just liberty of the individual; in purely Christian ethics that grand department of duty is scarcely noticed or acknowledged. It is in the Koran, not the New Testament, that we read the maxim—"A ruler who appoints any man to an office, when there is in his dominions another man better qualified for it, sins against God and against the State."[100] What little recognition the idea of obligation to the public obtains in modern morality, is derived from Greek and Roman sources, not from Christian; as, even in the morality of private life, whatever exists of magnanimity, high-mindedness, personal dignity, even the sense of honor, is derived from the purely human, not the religious part of our education, and never could have grown out of a standard of ethics in which the only worth, professedly recognised, is that of obedience.

I am as far as any one from pretending that these defects are necessarily inherent in the Christian ethics, in every manner in which it can be conceived, or that the many requisites of a complete moral doctrine which it does not contain, do not admit of being reconciled with it. Far less would I insinuate this of the doctrines and precepts of Christ himself. I believe that the sayings of Christ are all, that I can see any evidence of their having been intended to be; that they are irreconcilable with nothing which a comprehensive morality requires; that everything which is excellent in ethics may be brought within them, with no greater violence to their language than has been done to it by all who have attempted to deduce from them any practical system of conduct whatever. But it is quite consistent with this, to believe that they contain and were meant to contain, only a part of the truth; that many essential elements of the highest morality are among the things which are not provided for, nor intended to be provided for, in the recorded deliverances of the Founder of Christianity, and which have been entirely thrown aside in the system of ethics erected on the basis of those deliverances by the Christian Church. And this being so, I think it a great error to persist in attempting to find in the Christian doctrine that complete rule for our guidance, which its author intended it to sanction and enforce, but only partially to provide. I believe, too, that this narrow theory is becoming a grave practical evil, detracting greatly from the value of the moral training and instruction, which so many well-meaning persons are now at length exerting themselves to promote. I much fear that by attempting to form the mind and feelings on an exclusively religious type, and discarding those secular standards (as for want of a better name they may be called) which heretofore co-existed with and supplemented the Christian ethics, receiving some of its spirit, and infusing into it some of theirs, there will result, and is even now resulting, a low, abject, servile type of character, which, submit itself as it may to what it deems the Supreme Will, is incapable of rising to or sympathizing in the conception of Supreme Goodness. I believe that other ethics than any which can be evolved from exclusively Christian sources, must exist side by side with Christian ethics to produce the moral regeneration of mankind; and that the Christian system is no exception to the rule that in an imperfect state of the human mind, the interests of truth require a diversity of opinions. It is not necessary that in ceasing to ignore the moral truths not contained in Christianity, men should ignore

---

99 See the Ten Commandments: Exodus 20:2–17.
100 George Sale's 1734 translation of the Koran, the sole translation available at the time, does not include this maxim.

any of those which it does contain. Such prejudice, or oversight, when it occurs, is altogether an evil; but it is one from which we cannot hope to be always exempt, and must be regarded as the price paid for an inestimable good. The exclusive pretension made by a part of the truth to be the whole, must and ought to be protested against, and if a reactionary impulse should make the protestors unjust in their turn, this onesidedness, like the other, may be lamented, but must be tolerated. If Christians would teach infidels to be just to Christianity, they should themselves be just to infidelity. It can do truth no service to blink the fact, known to all who have the most ordinary acquaintance with literary history, that a large portion of the noblest and most valuable moral teaching has been the work, not only of men who did not know, but of men who knew and rejected, the Christian faith.

I do not pretend that the most unlimited use of the freedom of enunciating all possible opinions would put an end to the evils of religious or philosophical sectarianism. Every truth which men of narrow capacity are in earnest about, is sure to be asserted, inculcated, and in many ways even acted on, as if no other truth existed in the world, or at all events none that could limit or qualify the first. I acknowledge that the tendency of all opinions to become sectarian is not cured by the freest discussion, but is often heightened and exacerbated thereby; the truth which ought to have been, but was not, seen, being rejected all the more violently because proclaimed by persons regarded as opponents. But it is not on the impassioned partisan, it is on the calmer and more disinterested bystander, that this collision of opinions works its salutary effect. Not the violent conflict between parts of the truth, but the quiet suppression of half of it, is the formidable evil: there is always hope when people are forced to listen to both sides; it is when they attend only to one that errors harden into prejudices, and truth itself ceases to have the effect of truth, by being exaggerated into falsehood. And since there are few mental attributes more rare than that judicial faculty which can sit in intelligent judgment between two sides of a question, of which only one is represented by an advocate before it, truth has no chance but in proportion as every side of it, every opinion which embodies any fraction of the truth, not only finds advocates, but is so advocated as to be listened to.

We have now recognised the necessity to the mental well-being of mankind (on which all their other well-being depends) of freedom of opinion, and freedom of the expression of opinion, on four distinct grounds; which we will now briefly recapitulate.

First, if any opinion is compelled to silence, that opinion may, for aught we can certainly know, be true. To deny this is to assume our own infallibility.

Secondly, though the silenced opinion be an error, it may, and very commonly does, contain a portion of truth; and since the general or prevailing opinion on any subject is rarely or never the whole truth, it is only by the collision of adverse opinions that the remainder of the truth has any chance of being supplied.

Thirdly, even if the received opinion be not only true, but the whole truth; unless it is suffered to be, and actually is, vigorously and earnestly contested, it will, by most of those who receive it, be held in the manner of a prejudice, with little comprehension or feeling of its rational grounds. And not only this, but, fourthly, the meaning of the doctrine itself will be in danger of being lost, or enfeebled, and deprived of its vital effect on the character and conduct: the dogma becoming a mere formal profession, inefficacious for good, but cumbering the ground, and preventing the growth of any real and heartfelt conviction, from reason or personal experience....

John Ruskin
from *Unto This Last*[101] (1860)

Writer and artist John Ruskin (1819–1900) was one of the most influential art and social critics of the Victorian period. Though confirmed as an Anglican while at Oxford, he was not swept up by the Oxford Movement. After Oxford, Ruskin abandoned poetry to write criticism of art and architecture. With his father's financial support, Ruskin launched his writing career by defending artist J.M.W. Turner in *Modern Painters* (1843–60), in which he argued for the apprehension of divinity via contemplation of the beautiful in art. His failed marriage prompted scandal just as he emerged as a public intellectual and proponent of the Pre-Raphaelites. *The Stones of Venice* (1851–53) celebrated Byzantine and Gothic styles and had an impact on Victorian architects. Influenced by Carlyle's *Past and Present* (1843), Ruskin lamented how industrialization reduced craftsmen to machines.

In "The Roots of Honour" (*Cornhill Magazine*, 1860), a chapter of *Unto This Last* (1860), Ruskin argues against "political economy" and in favour of a commerce not based purely on self-interest.

1: The Roots of Honour

Among the delusions which at different periods have possessed themselves of the minds of large masses of the human race, perhaps the most curious—certainly the least creditable—is the modern *soi-disant*[102] science of political economy, based on the idea that an advantageous code of social action may be determined irrespectively of the influence of social affection.

Of course, as in the instances of alchemy, astrology, witchcraft, and other such popular creeds, political economy has a plausible idea at the root of it. "The social affections," says the economist, "are accidental and disturbing elements in human nature; but avarice and the desire of progress are constant elements. Let us eliminate the inconstants, and, considering the human being merely as a covetous machine, examine by what laws of labour, purchase, and sale, the greatest accumulative result in wealth is obtainable. Those laws once determined, it will be for each individual afterwards to introduce as much of the disturbing affectionate element as he chooses, and to determine for himself the result on the new conditions supposed."

This would be a perfectly logical and successful method of analysis, if the accidentals afterwards to be introduced were of the same nature as the powers first examined. Supposing a body in motion to be influenced by constant and inconstant forces, it is usually the simplest way of examining its course to trace it first under the persistent conditions, and afterwards introduce the causes of variation. But the disturbing elements in the social problem are not of the same nature as the constant ones; they alter the essence of the creature under examination the moment they are added; they operate, not mathematically,

---

101 Author's note: "I will give unto this last, even as unto thee."—Matt. xx. 14.
102 French: so-called.

but chemically, introducing conditions which render all our previous knowledge unavailable. We made learned experiments upon pure nitrogen, and have convinced ourselves that it is a very manageable gas; but, behold! the thing which we have practically to deal with is its chloride, and this, the moment we touch it on our established principles, sends us and our apparatus through the ceiling.[103]

Observe, I neither impugn nor doubt the conclusions of the science if its terms are accepted. I am simply uninterested in them, as I should be in those of a science of gymnastics which assumed that men had no skeletons. It might be shown, on that supposition, that it would be advantageous to roll the students up into pellets, flatten them into cakes, or stretch them into cables; and that when these results were effected, the re-insertion of the skeleton would be attended with various inconveniences to their constitution. The reasoning might be admirable, the conclusions true, and the science deficient only in applicability. Modern political economy stands on a precisely similar basis. Assuming, not that the human being has no skeleton, but that it is all skeleton, it founds an ossifiant[104] theory of progress on this negation of a soul; and having shown the utmost that may be made of bones, and constructed a number of interesting geometrical figures with death's-heads and humeri,[105] successfully proves the inconvenience of the reappearance of a soul among these corpuscular[106] structures. I do not deny the truth of this theory: I simply deny its applicability to the present phase of the world.

This inapplicability has been curiously manifested during the embarrassment caused by the late strikes of our workmen.[107] Here occurs one of the simplest cases, in a pertinent and positive form, of the first vital problem which political economy has to deal with (the relation between employer and employed); and, at a severe crisis, when lives in multitudes and wealth in masses are at stake, the political economists are helpless—practically mute; no demonstrable solution of the difficulty can be given by them, such as may convince or calm the opposing parties. Obstinately the masters take one view of the matter. Obstinately the operatives[108] another; and no political science can set them at one.

It would be strange if it could, it being not by "science" of any kind that men were ever intended to be set at one. Disputant after disputant vainly strives to show that the interests of the masters are, or are not, antagonistic to those of the men: none of the pleaders ever seeming to remember that it does not absolutely or always follow that the persons must be antagonistic because their interests are. If there is only a crust of bread in the house, and mother and children are starving, their interests are not the same. If the mother eats it, the children want it; if the children eat it, the mother must go hungry to her work. Yet it does not necessarily follow that there will be "antagonism" between them, that they will fight for the crust, and that the mother, being strongest, will get it, and eat it. Neither, in any other case, whatever the relations of the persons may be, can it be assumed for certain that, because their interests are diverse, they must necessarily regard each other with hostility, and use violence or cunning to obtain the advantage.

---

103 French chemist Pierre-Louis Dulong discovered nitrogen trichloride in 1813; subsequent experiments on the explosive compound injured his hand and destroyed his vision in one eye.
104 Becoming bone-like.
105 Plural of humerus, a bone in the upper arm that runs from shoulder to elbow.
106 Composed of corpuscles or atoms.
107 Probably a reference to the 1859–60 struggle of London building workers, recognized by historians as one of the major labour struggles of the century.
108 Workers.

Even if this were so, and it were as just as it is convenient to consider men as actuated by no other moral influences than those which affect rats or swine, the logical conditions of the question are still indeterminable. It can never be shown generally either that the interests of master and labourer are alike, or that they are opposed; for, according to circumstances, they may be either. It is, indeed, always the interest of both that the work should be rightly done, and a just price obtained for it; but, in the division of profits, the gain of the one may or may not be the loss of the other. It is not the master's interest to pay wages so low as to leave the men sickly and depressed, nor the workman's interest to be paid high wages if the smallness of the master's profit hinders him from enlarging his business, or conducting it in a safe and liberal way....

And the varieties of circumstances which influence these reciprocal interests are so endless, that all endeavour to deduce rules of action from balance of expediency is in vain. And it is meant to be in vain. For no human actions ever were intended by the Maker of men to be guided by balances of expediency, but by balances of justice. He has therefore rendered all endeavours to determine expediency futile for evermore. No man ever knew, or can know, what will be the ultimate result to himself, or to others, of any given line of conduct. But every man may know, and most of us do know, what is a just and unjust act. And all of us may know also, that the consequences of justice will be ultimately the best possible, both to others and ourselves, though we can neither say what *is* the best, or how it is likely to come to pass.

I have said balances of justice, meaning, in the term justice, to include affection,—such affection as one man *owes* to another. All right relations between master and operative, and all their best interests, ultimately depend on these.

We shall find the best and simplest illustration of the relations of master and operative in the position of domestic servants.

We will suppose that the master of a household desires only to get as much work out of his servants as he can, at the rate of wages he gives. He never allows them to be idle; feeds them as poorly and lodges them as ill as they will endure, and in all things pushes his requirements to the exact point beyond which he cannot go without forcing the servant to leave him. In doing this, there is no violation on his part of what is commonly called "justice." He agrees with the domestic for his whole time and service, and takes them;—the limits of hardship in treatment being fixed by the practice of other masters in his neighbourhood; that is to say, by the current rate of wages for domestic labour. If the servant can get a better place, he is free to take one, and the master can only tell what is the real market value of his labour, by requiring as much as he will give.

This is the politico-economical view of the case, according to the doctors of that science; who assert that by this procedure the greatest average of work will be obtained from the servant, and therefore the greatest benefit to the community, and through the community, by reversion, to the servant himself.

That, however, is not so. It would be so if the servant were an engine of which the motive power was steam, magnetism, gravitation, or any other agent of calculable force. But he being, on the contrary, an engine whose motive power is a Soul, the force of this very peculiar agent, as an unknown quantity, enters into all the political economist's equations, without his knowledge, and falsifies every one of their results. The largest quantity of work will not be done by this curious engine for pay, or under pressure, or by help of any kind of fuel which may be supplied by the chaldron.[109] It will be done only when the

---

109 A measure used for coal.

motive force, that is to say, the will or spirit of the creature, is brought to its greatest strength by its own proper fuel; namely, by the affections.

It may indeed happen, and does happen often, that if the master is a man of sense and energy, a large quantity of material work may be done under mechanical pressure, enforced by strong will and guided by wise method; also it may happen, and does happen often, that if the master is indolent and weak (however good-natured), a very small quantity of work, and that bad, may be produced by the servant's undirected strength, and contemptuous gratitude. But the universal law of the matter is that, assuming any given quantity of energy and sense in master and servant, the greatest material result obtainable by them will be, not through antagonism to each other, but through affection for each other; and that if the master, instead of endeavouring to get as much work as possible from the servant, seeks rather to render his appointed and necessary work beneficial to him, and to forward his interests in all just and wholesome ways, the real amount of work ultimately done, or of good rendered, by the person so cared for, will indeed be the greatest possible.

Observe, I say, "of good rendered," for a servant's work is not necessarily or always the best thing he can give his master. But good of all kinds, whether in material service, in protective watchfulness of his master's interest and credit, or in joyful readiness to seize unexpected and irregular occasions of help.

Nor is this one whit less generally true because indulgence will be frequently abused, and kindness met with ingratitude. For the servant who, gently treated, is ungrateful, treated ungently, will be revengeful; and the man who is dishonest to a liberal master will be injurious to an unjust one.

In any case, and with any person, this unselfish treatment will produce the most effective return. Observe, I am here considering the affections wholly as a motive power; not at all as things in themselves desirable or noble, or in any other way abstractedly good. I look at them simply as an anomalous force, rendering every one of the ordinary political economist's calculations nugatory; while, even if he desired to introduce this new element into his estimates, he has no power of dealing with it; for the affections only become a true motive power when they ignore every other motive and condition of political economy. Treat the servant kindly, with the idea of turning his gratitude to account, and you will get, as you deserve, no gratitude, nor any value for your kindness; but treat him kindly without any economical purpose, and all economical purposes will be answered; in this, as in all other matters, whosoever will save his life shall lose it, whoso loses it shall find it....[110]

The next clearest and simplest example of relation between master and operative is that which exists between the commander of a regiment and his men.

Supposing the officer only desires to apply the rules of discipline so as, with least trouble to himself, to make the regiment most effective, he will not be able, by any rules or administration of rules, on this selfish principle, to develop the full strength of his subordinates. If a man of sense and firmness, he may, as in the former instance, produce a better result than would be obtained by the irregular kindness of a weak officer; but let the sense and firmness be the same in both cases, and assuredly the officer who has the most direct personal relations with his men, the most care for their interests, and the most value for their lives, will develop their effective strength, through their affection for his own person, and trust in his character, to a degree wholly unattainable by other means. The law applies still more stringently as the

---

110 See Luke 9:24; Luke 17:33; Matthew 16:25.

numbers concerned are larger; a charge may often be successful, though the men dislike their officers; a battle has rarely been won, unless they loved their general.

Passing from these simple examples to the more complicated relations existing between a manufacturer and his workmen, we are met first by certain curious difficulties, resulting, apparently, from a harder and colder state of moral elements. It is easy to imagine an enthusiastic affection existing among soldiers for the colonel. Not so easy to imagine an enthusiastic affection among cotton-spinners for the proprietor of the mill. A body of men associated for purposes of robbery (as a Highland clan in ancient times) shall be animated by perfect affection, and every member of it be ready to lay down his life for the life of his chief. But a band of men associated for purposes of legal production and accumulation is usually animated, it appears, by no such emotions, and none of them are in any-wise willing to give his life for the life of his chief. Not only are we met by this apparent anomaly, in moral matters, but by others connected with it, in administration of system. For a servant or a soldier is engaged at a definite rate of wages, for a definite period; but a workman at a rate of wages variable according to the demand for labour, and with the risk of being at any time thrown out of his situation by chances of trade. Now, as, under these contingencies, no action of the affections can take place, but only an explosive action of disaffections, two points offer themselves for consideration in the matter.

The first.—How far the rate of wages may be so regulated as not to vary with the demand for labour.

The second.—How far it is possible that bodies of workmen may be engaged and maintained at such fixed rate of wages (whatever the state of trade may be), without enlarging or diminishing their number, so as to give them permanent interest in the establishment with which they are connected, like that of the domestic servants in an old family, or an *esprit de corps*,[111] like that of the soldiers in a crack regiment.

The first question is, I say, how far it may be possible to fix the rate of wages, irrespectively of the demand for labour.

Perhaps one of the most curious facts in the history of human error is the denial by the common political economist of the possibility of thus regulating wages; while, for all the important, and much of the unimportant labour on the earth, wages are already so regulated.

We do not sell our prime-ministership by Dutch auction;[112] nor, on the decease of a bishop, whatever may be the general advantages of simony,[113] do we (yet) offer his diocese to the clergyman who will take the episcopacy at the lowest contract. We (with exquisite sagacity of political economy!) do indeed sell commissions,[114] but not openly, generalships: sick, we do not inquire for a physician who takes less than a guinea;[115] litigious, we never think of reducing six-and-eight-pence to four-and-sixpence; caught in a shower, we do not canvass the cabmen, to find one who values his driving at less than sixpence a mile.

It is true that in all these cases there is, and in every conceivable case there must be, ultimate reference to the presumed difficulty of the work, or number of candidates for the office. If it were thought that the labour necessary to make a good physician would be gone through by a sufficient number of students with the prospect of only half-guinea fees, public consent would soon withdraw the unnecessary half-guinea.

---

111 French: the feeling of individual group members for the honour of the whole group.
112 An auction at which items are offered for sale at prices higher than their actual value; prices are gradually lowered until someone agrees to pay the amount.
113 Buying or selling of church appointments.
114 Warrants appointing army and navy officers.
115 Twenty-one shillings.

In this ultimate sense, the price of labour is indeed always regulated by the demand for it; but, so far as the practical and immediate administration of the matter is regarded, the best labour always has been, and is, as *all* labour ought to be, paid by an invariable standard.

"What!" the reader perhaps answers amazedly: "pay good and bad workmen alike?"

Certainly. The difference between one prelate's[116] sermons and his successor's—or between one physician's opinion and another's,—is far greater, as respects the qualities of mind involved, and far more important in result to you personally, than the difference between good and bad laying of bricks (though that is greater than most people suppose). Yet you pay with equal fee, contentedly, the good and bad workmen upon your soul, and the good and bad workmen upon your body; much more may you pay, contentedly, with equal fees, the good and bad workmen upon your house.... The natural and right system respecting all labour is, that it should be paid at a fixed rate, but the good workman employed, and the bad workman unemployed. The false, unnatural, and destructive system is when the bad workman is allowed to offer his work at half-price, and either take the place of the good, or force him by his competition to work for an inadequate sum.

This equality of wages, then, being the first object toward which we have to discover the directest available road—the second is, as above stated, that of maintaining constant numbers of workmen in employment, whatever may be the accidental demand for the article they produce.

I believe the sudden and extensive inequalities of demand, which necessarily arise in the mercantile operations of an active nation, constitute the only essential difficulty which has to be overcome in a just organization of labour. The subject opens into too many branches to admit of being investigated in a paper of this kind; but the following general facts bearing on it may be noted.

The wages which enable any workman to live are necessarily higher if his work is liable to intermission than if it is assured and continuous; and however severe the struggle for work may become, the general law will always hold, that men must get more daily pay if, on the average, they can only calculate on work three days a week than they would require if they were sure of work six days a week. Supposing that a man cannot live on less than a shilling a day, his seven shillings he must get, either for three days' violent work, or six days' deliberate work. The tendency of all modern mercantile operations is to throw both wages and trade into the form of a lottery, and to make the workman's pay depend on intermittent exertion, and the principal's profit on dexterously used chance.

In what partial degree, I repeat, this may be necessary in consequence of the activities of modern trade, I do not here investigate; contenting myself with the fact, that in its fatalest aspects it is assuredly unnecessary, and results merely from love of gambling on the part of the masters, and from ignorance and sensuality in the men. The masters cannot bear to let any opportunity of gain escape them, and frantically rush at every gap and breach in the walls of Fortune, raging to be rich, and affronting, with impatient covetousness, every risk of ruin, while the men prefer three days of violent labour, and three days of drunkenness, to six days of moderate work and wise rest. There is no way in which a principal, who really desires to help his workmen, may do it more effectually than by checking these disorderly habits both in himself and them; keeping his own business operations on a scale which will enable him to pursue them securely, not yielding to temptations of precarious gain; and, at the same time, leading his workmen into regular habits of labour and life, either by inducing them rather to take low wages in

---

116 High-ranking clergyman.

the form of a fixed salary, than high wages, subject to the chance of their being thrown out of work; or, if this be impossible, by discouraging the system of violent exertion for nominally high day wages, and leading the men to take lower pay for more regular labour.

In effecting any radical changes of this kind, doubtless there would be great inconvenience and loss incurred by all the originators of movement. That which can be done with perfect convenience and without loss, is not always the thing that most needs to be done, or which we are most imperatively required to do.

I have already alluded to the difference hitherto existing between regiments of men associated for purposes of violence, and for purposes of manufacture; in that the former appear capable of self-sacrifice—the latter, not; which singular fact is the real reason of the general lowness of estimate in which the profession of commerce is held, as compared with that of arms. Philosophically, it does not, at first sight, appear reasonable (many writers have endeavoured to prove it unreasonable) that a peaceable and rational person, whose trade is buying and selling, should be held in less honour than an unpeaceable and often irrational person, whose trade is slaying. Nevertheless, the consent of mankind has always, in spite of the philosophers, given precedence to the soldier.

And this is right.

For the soldier's trade, verily and essentially, is not slaying, but being slain. This, without well knowing its own meaning, the world honours it for. A bravo's[117] trade is slaying; but the world has never respected bravos more than merchants: the reason it honours the soldier is, because he holds his life at the service of the State.... [P]ut him in a fortress breach, with all the pleasures of the world behind him, and only death and his duty in front of him, he will keep his face to the front; and he knows that his choice may be put to him at any moment, and has beforehand taken his part,—virtually takes such part continually—does, in reality, die daily.

Not less is the respect we pay to the lawyer and physician, founded ultimately on their self-sacrifice. Whatever the learning or acuteness of a great lawyer, our chief respect for him depends on our belief that, set in a judge's seat, he will strive to judge justly, come of it what may. Could we suppose that he would take bribes, and use his acuteness and legal knowledge to give plausibility to iniquitous decisions, no degree of intellect would win for him our respect. Nothing will win it, short of our tacit conviction, that in all important acts of his life justice is first with him; his own interest, second.

In the case of a physician, the ground of the honour we render him is clearer still. Whatever his science, we should shrink from him in horror if we found him regard his patients merely as subjects to experiment upon; much more, if we found that, receiving bribes from persons interested in their deaths, he was using his best skill to give poison in the mask of medicine.

Finally, the principle holds with utmost clearness as it respects clergymen. No goodness of disposition will excuse want of science in a physician, or of shrewdness in an advocate;[118] but a clergyman, even though his power of intellect be small, is respected on the presumed ground of his unselfishness and serviceableness.

Now, there can be no question but that the tact, foresight, decision, and other mental powers, required for the successful management of a large mercantile concern, if not such as could be compared with those of a great lawyer, general, or divine, would at least match the general conditions of mind required in the

---

117 Paid killer or mercenary.
118 Lawyer.

subordinate officers of a ship, or of a regiment, or in the curate of a country parish. If, therefore, all the efficient members of the so-called liberal professions are still, somehow, in public estimate of honour, preferred before the head of a commercial firm, the reason must lie deeper than in the measurement of their several powers of mind.

And the essential reason for such preference will be found to lie in the fact that the merchant is presumed to act always selfishly. His work may be very necessary to the community; but the motive of it is understood to be wholly personal. The merchant's first object in all his dealings must be (the public believe) to get as much for himself, and leave as little to his neighbour (or customer) as possible. Enforcing this upon him, by political statute, as the necessary principle of his action; recommending it to him on all occasions, and themselves reciprocally adopting it; proclaiming vociferously, for law of the universe, that a buyer's function is to cheapen, and a seller's to cheat,—the public, nevertheless, involuntarily condemn the man of commerce for his compliance with their own statement, and stamp him for ever as belonging to an inferior grade of human personality.

This they will find, eventually, they must give up doing. They must not cease to condemn selfishness; but they will have to discover a kind of commerce which is not exclusively selfish.... They will find that commerce is an occupation which gentlemen will every day see more need to engage in, rather than in the businesses of talking to men, or slaying them; that, in true commerce, as in true preaching, or true fighting, it is necessary to admit the idea of occasional voluntary loss;—that sixpences have to be lost, as well as lives, under a sense of duty; that the market may have its martyrdoms as well as the pulpit; and trade its heroisms as well as war....

The fact is, that people never have had clearly explained to them the true functions of a merchant with respect to other people. I should like the reader to be very clear about this.

Five great intellectual professions, relating to daily necessities of life, have hitherto existed—three exist necessarily, in every civilized nation:

The Soldier's profession is to *defend* it.

The Pastor's to *teach* it.

The Physician's to *keep it in health*.

The Lawyer's to *enforce justice* in it.

The Merchant's to *provide* for it.

And the duty of all these men is, on due occasion, to *die* for it.

"On due occasion," namely:—

The Soldier, rather than leave his post in battle.

The Physician, rather than leave his post in plague.

The Pastor, rather than teach Falsehood.

The Lawyer, rather than countenance Injustice.

The Merchant—what is *his* "due occasion" of death?

It is the main question for the merchant, as for all of us. For, truly, the man who does not know when to die, does not know how to live.

Observe, the merchant's function (or manufacturer's, for in the broad sense in which it is here used the word must be understood to include both) is to provide for the nation. It is no more his function to get profit for himself out of that provision than it is a clergyman's function to get his stipend. This stipend is a due and necessary adjunct, but not the object of his life, if he be a true clergyman, any more than his fee (or *honorarium*) is the object of life to a true physician. Neither is his fee the object of life to a true merchant. All three, if true men, have a work to be done irrespective of fee—to be done even at any cost, or for quite the contrary of fee; the pastor's function being to teach, the physician's to heal, and the merchant's, as I have said, to provide. That is to say, he has to understand to their very root the qualities of the thing he deals in, and the means of obtaining or producing it; and he has to apply all his sagacity and energy to the producing or obtaining it in perfect state, and distributing it at the cheapest possible price where it is most needed.

And because the production or obtaining of any commodity involves necessarily the agency of many lives and hands, the merchant becomes in the course of his business the master and governor of large masses of men in a more direct, though less confessed way, than a military officer or pastor; so that on him falls, in great part, the responsibility for the kind of life they lead: and it becomes his duty, not only to be always considering how to produce what he sells in the purest and cheapest forms, but how to make the various employments involved in the production, or transference of it, most beneficial to the men employed.

And as into these two functions, requiring for their right exercise the highest intelligence, as well as patience, kindness, and tact, the merchant is bound to put all his energy, so for their just discharge he is bound, as soldier or physician is bound, to give up, if need be, his life, in such way as it may be demanded of him. Two main points he has in his Providing function to maintain: first, his engagements (faithfulness to engagements being the real root of all possibilities in commerce); and secondly, the perfectness and purity of the thing provided; so that, rather than fail in any engagement, or consent to any deterioration, adulteration, or unjust and exorbitant price of that which he provides, he is bound to meet fearlessly any form of distress, poverty, or labour, which may, through maintenance of these points, come upon him.

Again: in his office as governor of the men employed by him, the merchant or manufacturer is invested with a distinctly paternal authority and responsibility. In most cases, a youth entering a commercial establishment is withdrawn altogether from home influence; his master must become his father, else he has, for practical and constant help, no father at hand: in all cases the master's authority, together with the general tone and atmosphere of his business, and the character of the men with whom the youth is compelled in the course of it to associate, have more immediate and pressing weight than the home influence, and will usually neutralize it either for good or evil; so that the only means which the master has of doing justice to the men employed by him is to ask himself sternly whether he is dealing with such subordinate as he would with his own son, if compelled by circumstances to take such a position. Supposing the captain of a frigate saw it right, or were by any chance obliged, to place his own son in the position of a common sailor: as he would then treat his son, he is bound always to treat every one of the men under him. So, also, supposing the master of a manufactory saw it right, or were by any chance obliged, to place his own son in the position of an ordinary workman; as he would then treat his son, he is bound always to treat every one of his men. This is the only effective, true, or practicable RULE which can be given on this point of political economy.

And as the captain of a ship is bound to be the last man to leave his ship in case of wreck, and to share his last crust with the sailors in case of famine, so the manufacturer, in any commercial crisis or distress, is bound to take the suffering of it with his men, and even to take more of it for himself than he allows his men to feel; as a father would in a famine, shipwreck, or battle, sacrifice himself for his son.

All which sounds very strange: the only real strangeness in the matter being, nevertheless, that it should so sound. For all this is true, and that not partially nor theoretically, but everlastingly and practically: all other doctrine than this respecting matters political being false in premises, absurd in deduction, and impossible in practice, consistently with any progressive state of national life; all the life which we now possess as a nation showing itself in the resolute denial and scorn, by a few strong minds and faithful hearts, of the economic principles taught to our multitudes, which principles, so far as accepted, lead straight to national destruction....

Octavia Hill

from "Blank Court;[119] or, Landlords and Tenants" (1871)

Reformer Octavia Hill (1838–1912) became important in Victorian housing debates by modelling successful housing reform. Her mother's work with a co-operative crafts guild exposed Hill to the London poor; she also thereby met Christian socialist F.D. Maurice (see Education) and John Ruskin (see Life Writing, Condition of England, Aesthetics and Culture, Gender and Sexuality). She taught women's classes at the Working Men's College and helped Barbara Leigh Smith Bodichon (see Gender and Sexuality) collect signatures on a petition supporting married women's control over property. (Hill opposed women's suffrage but supported women's local political involvement.) Shocked by London slums, Hill undertook a housing reform scheme with Ruskin's financial backing: she renovated dwellings, employed tenants, and built playgrounds. With Beatrice Webb (see Life Writing), she joined the Royal Commission for the Poor Law in 1905. She also campaigned for public spaces; many of her principles are now embodied in the National Trust.

Hill described her successful housing reforms in articles such as this one on "Blank Court" (*Macmillan's Magazine*, 1871).

... How this relation of landlord and tenant might be established in some of the lowest districts of London, and with what results, I am about to describe by relating what has been done in the last two years in Blank Court.

... In many of the houses the dustbins[120] were utterly unapproachable, and cabbage leaves, stale fish and every sort of dirt were lying in the passages and on the stairs; in some the back kitchen had been used as a dustbin, but had not been emptied for years, and the dust filtered through into the front kitchens, which were the sole living and sleeping rooms of some families; in some, the kitchen stairs were many inches thick with dirt, which was so hardened that a shovel had to be used to get it off; in some there was hardly any water to be had; the wood was eaten away, and broken away; windows were smashed, and the

---

119 Hill gave the pseudonym "Blank Court" to Barrett's Court; it was later renamed St. Christopher's Place.
120 Garbage cans.

rain was coming through the roofs. At night it was still worse; and during the first winter I had to collect the rents chiefly then, as the inhabitants, being principally costermongers,[121] were out nearly all day, and they were afraid to entrust their rent to their neighbours. It was then that I saw the houses in their most dreadful aspect. I well remember wet, foggy Monday nights, when I turned down the dingy court, past the brilliantly lighted public-house at the corner, past the old furniture outside the shops, and dived into the dark, yawning passage ways. The front doors stood open day and night, and as I felt my way down the kitchen stairs, broken, and rounded by the hardened mud upon them, the foul smells which the heavy, foggy air would not allow to rise, met me as I descended, and the plaster rattled down with a hollow sound as I groped along. It was truly appalling to think that there were human beings who lived habitually in such an atmosphere, with such surroundings. Sometimes I had to open the kitchen door myself, after knocking several times in vain, when a woman, quite drunk, would be lying on the floor on some black mass which served as a bed; sometimes, in answer to my knocks, a half-drunken man would swear, and thrust the rent-money out to me through a chink of the door, placing his foot against it, so as to prevent it from opening wide enough to admit me. Always it would be shut again without a light being offered to guide me up the pitch-dark stairs. Such was Blank Court in the winter of 1869. Truly, a wild, lawless, desolate little kingdom to come to rule over.

On what principles was I to rule these people? On the same that I had already tried, and tried with success, in other places, and which I may sum up as the two following: firstly, to demand a strict fulfilment of their duties to me,—one of the chief of which would be the punctual payment of rent; and secondly, to endeavour to be so unfailingly just and patient that they should learn to trust the rule that was over them.

With regard to details, I would make a few improvements at once—such, for example, as the laying on of water and repairing of dustbins, but, for the most part, improvements should be made only by degrees, as the people became more capable of valuing them and not abusing them. I would have the rooms distempered, and thoroughly cleansed, as they became vacant, and then they should be offered to the more cleanly of the tenants. I would have such repairs as were not immediately needed, used as a means of giving work to the men in times of distress. I would draught the occupants of the underground kitchens into the upstair rooms, and would ultimately convert the kitchens into bath-rooms and wash-houses. I would have the landlady's portion of the house—*i.e.* the stairs and passages—at once repaired and distempered,[122] and they should be regularly scrubbed, and, as far as possible, made models of cleanliness, for I knew, from former experience, that the example of this would, in time, silently spread itself to the rooms themselves, and that payment for this work would give me some hold over the elder girls. I would collect savings personally, not trust to their being taken to distant banks or saving clubs. And finally, I knew that I should learn to feel these people as my friends, and so should instinctively feel the same respect for their privacy and their independence, and should treat them with the same courtesy that I should show towards any other personal friends. There would be no interference, no entering their rooms uninvited, no offer of money or the necessaries of life. But when occasion presented itself, I should give them any help I could, such as I might offer without insult to other friends—sympathy in their distresses; advice, help and counsel in their difficulties; introductions that might be of use to them; means of education; visits to the country; a lent book when not able to work; a bunch of flowers brought on purpose; an invitation

---

121 Street vendors who sold fruit.
122 Painted with an early type of primer.

to any entertainment, in a room built at the back of my own house, which would be likely to give them pleasure. I am convinced that one of the evils of much that is done for the poor, springs from the want of delicacy felt, and courtesy shown, towards them, and that we cannot beneficially help them in any spirit different to that in which we help those who are better off. The help may differ in amount, because their needs are greater. It should not differ in kind.

... I have learnt to know that people are ashamed to abuse a place they find cared for. They will add dirt to dirt till a place is pestilential, but the more they find done for it, the more they will respect it, till at last order and cleanliness prevail. It is this feeling of theirs, coupled with the fact that they do not like those whom they have learned to love and whose standard is higher than their own, to see things which would grieve them, which has enabled us to accomplish nearly every reform of outward things that we have achieved; so that the surest way to have any place kept clean is to go through it often yourself.

... Amongst the many benefits which the possession of the houses enables us to confer on the people, perhaps one of the most important is our power of saving them from neighbours who would render their lives miserable. It is a most merciful thing to protect the poor from the pain of living in the next room to drunken, disorderly people. "I am dying," said an old woman to me the other day: "I wish you would put me where I can't hear S—— beating his wife. Her screams are awful. And B——, too, he do come in so drunk. Let me go over the way to No. 30." Our success depends on duly arranging the inmates: not too many children in any one house, so as to overcrowd it; not too few, so as to overcrowd another; not two bad people side by side, or they drink together; not a terribly bad person beside a very respectable one....

It appears to me then to be proved by practical experience, that when we can induce the rich to undertake the duties of landlords in poor neighbourhoods, and ensure a sufficient amount of the wise, personal supervision of educated and sympathetic people acting as their representatives, we achieve results which are not attainable in any other way....

... I would call upon those who may possess cottage property in large towns, to consider the immense power they thus hold in their hands and the large influence for good they may exercise by the wise use of that power. When they have to delegate it to others, let them take care to whom they commit it; and let them beware lest, through the widely prevailing system of subletting, this power ultimately abide with those who have neither the will nor the knowledge which would enable them to use it beneficially....

... It is on these things and their faithful execution that the life of the whole matter depends, and by which steady progress is ensured. It is the small things of the world that colour the lives of those around us, and it is on persistent efforts to reform these that progress depends; and we may rest assured that they who see with greater eyes than ours have a due estimate of the service, and that if we did but perceive the mighty principles underlying these tiny things we should rather feel awed that we are entrusted with them at all, than scornful and impatient that they are no larger. What are we that we should ask for more than that God should let us work for Him among the tangible things which He created to be fair, and the human which He redeemed to be pure? From time to time He lifts a veil[123] and shows us, even while we struggle with imperfections here below, that towards which we are working,—shows us how, by governing and ordering the tangible things one by one we may make of this earth a fair dwelling-place. And far better still, how by cherishing human beings He will let us help Him in His work of building up temples

---

123 Exodus 34:33–35.

meet for Him to dwell in—faint images of that best temple of all, which He promised that He would raise up on the third day, though men might destroy it.[124]

William Booth
from *In Darkest England and the Way Out* (1890)

Salvation Army founder William Booth (1829–1912) converted to Methodism after his impoverished family terminated his education, apprenticing him to a pawnbroker. He established a reputation as a travelling preacher but was attacked for his vehement rhetoric. Supported by his wife, Catherine, he rejected Methodism for religious independence, founding the Christian Mission (which later became the Salvation Army) in London's slums. Militaristic titles and uniforms distinguished the Army, which boasted 100,000 "soldiers" by 1900 and encouraged equality for female workers. Rejecting religious doctrine, science, and philosophy in favour of non-sacramental worship and hands-on work, Booth pitied the poor and believed that non-Christians faced eternal punishment.

Written largely by W.T. Stead (see Gender and Sexuality) but incorporating Booth's ideas, *In Darkest England and the Way Out* (1890) included advice for helping the homeless and the unemployed. Referring to the African exploration narrative of Henry Morton Stanley (see Travel and Exploration), Booth compares "Darkest" Africa and England, arguing for Christian philanthropy at home in "Darkest London."

Chapter 1: Why "Darkest England"?

This summer the attention of the civilised world has been arrested by the story which Mr. Stanley has told of "Darkest Africa" and his journeyings across the heart of the Lost Continent.[125] In all that spirited narrative of heroic endeavour, nothing has so much impressed the imagination, as his description of the immense forest, which offered an almost impenetrable barrier to his advance. The intrepid explorer, in his own phrase, "marched, tore, ploughed, and cut his way for one hundred and sixty days through this inner womb of the true tropical forest." The mind of man with difficulty endeavours to realise this immensity of wooded wilderness, covering a territory half as large again as the whole of France, where the rays of the sun never penetrate, where in the dark, dank air, filled with the steam of the heated morass, human beings dwarfed into pygmies and brutalised into cannibals lurk and live and die....

"We entered the forest," says Mr. Stanley, "with confidence; forty pioneers in front with axes and bill hooks to clear a path through the obstructions, praying that God and good fortune would lead us." But before the conviction of the forest dwellers that the forest was without end, hope faded out of the hearts

---

124 John 2:19.
125 Henry Morton Stanley (see Travel and Exploration), *In Darkest Africa* (1890).

of the natives of Stanley's company. The men became sodden with despair, preaching was useless to move their brooding sullenness, their morbid gloom.

The little religion they knew was nothing more than legendary lore, and in their memories there dimly floated a story of a land which grew darker and darker as one travelled towards the end of the earth and drew nearer to the place where a great serpent lay supine and coiled round the whole world. Ah! then the ancients must have referred to this, where the light is so ghastly, and the woods are endless, and are so still and solemn and grey; to this oppressive loneliness, amid so much life, which is so chilling to the poor distressed heart; and the horror grew darker with their fancies; the cold of early morning, the comfortless grey of dawn, the dead white mist, the ever-dripping tears of the dew, the deluging rains, the appalling thunder bursts and the echoes, and the wonderful play of the dazzling lightning. And when the night comes with its thick palpable darkness, and they lie huddled in their damp little huts, and they hear the tempest overhead, and the howling of the wild winds, the grinding and groaning of the storm-tost trees, and the dread sounds of the falling giants, and the shock of the trembling earth which sends their hearts with fitful leaps to their throats, and the roaring and a rushing as of a mad overwhelming sea—oh, then the horror is intensified! ...

That is the forest. But what of its denizens? They are comparatively few; only some hundreds of thousands living in small tribes from ten to thirty miles apart, scattered over an area on which ten thousand million trees put out the sun from a region four times as wide as Great Britain. Of these pygmies there are two kinds; one a very degraded specimen with ferretlike eyes, close-set nose, more nearly approaching the baboon than was supposed to be possible, but very human; the other very handsome, with frank open innocent features, very prepossessing. They are quick and intelligent, capable of deep affection and gratitude, showing remarkable industry and patience. A pygmy boy of eighteen worked with consuming zeal; time with him was too precious to waste in talk. His mind seemed ever concentrated on work. Mr. Stanley said:

"When I once stopped him to ask him his name, his face seemed to say, 'Please don't stop me. I must finish my task.'

"All alike, the baboon variety and the handsome innocents, are cannibals. They are possessed with a perfect mania for meat. We were obliged to bury our dead in the river, lest the bodies should be exhumed and eaten, even when they had died from smallpox."

Upon the pygmies and all the dwellers of the forest has descended a devastating visitation in the shape of the ivory raiders of civilisation. The race that wrote the Arabian Nights, built Bagdad and Granada, and invented Algebra, sends forth men[126] with the hunger for gold in their hearts, and Enfield muskets in their hands, to plunder and to slay. They exploit the domestic affections of the forest dwellers in order to strip them of all they possess in the world. That has been going on for years. It is going on to-day. It has come to be regarded as the natural and normal law of existence....

It is a terrible picture, and one that has engraved itself deep on the heart of civilisation. But while brooding over the awful presentation of life as it exists in the vast African forest, it seemed to me only too vivid a picture of many parts of our own land. As there is a darkest Africa is there not also a darkest England? Civilisation, which can breed its own barbarians, does it not also breed its own pygmies? May we not find a parallel at our own doors, and discover within a stone's throw of our cathedrals and palaces similar horrors to those which Stanley has found existing in the great Equatorial forest?

---

126 Arab traders.

The more the mind dwells upon the subject, the closer the analogy appears. The ivory raiders who brutally traffic in the unfortunate denizens of the forest glades, what are they but the publicans who flourish on the weakness of our poor? The two tribes of savages, the human baboon and the handsome dwarf, who will not speak lest it impede him in his task, may be accepted as the two varieties who are continually present with us—the vicious, lazy lout, and the toiling slave. They, too, have lost all faith of life being other than it is and has been. As in Africa, it is all trees, trees, trees with no other world conceivable; so is it here—it is all vice and poverty and crime. To many the world is all slum, with the Workhouse[127] as an intermediate purgatory before the grave. And just as Mr. Stanley's Zanzibaris lost faith, and could only be induced to plod on in brooding sullenness of dull despair, so the most of our social reformers, no matter how cheerily they may have started off, with forty pioneers swinging blithely their axes as they force their way in to the wood, soon become depressed and despairing. Who can battle against the ten thousand million trees? Who can hope to make headway against the innumerable adverse conditions which doom the dweller in Darkest England to eternal and immutable misery? What wonder is it that many of the warmest hearts and enthusiastic workers feel disposed to repeat the lament of the old English chronicler, who, speaking of the evil days which fell upon our forefathers in the reign of Stephen, said "It seemed to them as if God and his Saints were dead."[128]

An analogy is as good as a suggestion; it becomes wearisome when it is pressed too far. But before leaving it, think for a moment how close the parallel is, and how strange it is that so much interest should be excited by a narrative of human squalor and human heroism in a distant continent, while greater squalor and heroism not less magnificent may be observed at our very doors.

The Equatorial Forest traversed by Stanley resembles that Darkest England of which I have to speak, alike in its vast extent—both stretch, in Stanley's phrase, "as far as from Plymouth to Peterhead;" its monotonous darkness, its malaria and its gloom, its dwarfish de-humanized inhabitants, the slavery to which they are subjected, their privations and their misery. That which sickens the stoutest heart, and causes many of our bravest and best to fold their hands in despair, is the apparent impossibility of doing more than merely to peck at the outside of the endless tangle of monotonous undergrowth; to let light into it, to make a road clear through it, that shall not be immediately choked up by the ooze of the morass and the luxuriant parasitical growth of the forest—who dare hope for that? At present, alas, it would seem as though no one dares even to hope! It is the great Slough of Despond[129] of our time.

And what a slough it is no man can gauge who has not waded therein, as some of us have done, up to the very neck for long years. Talk about Dante's Hell,[130] and all the horrors and cruelties of the torture-chamber of the lost! The man who walks with open eyes and with bleeding heart through the shambles of our civilisation needs no such fantastic images of the poet to teach him horror. Often and often, when I have seen the young and the poor and the helpless go down before my eyes into the morass, trampled underfoot by beasts of prey in human shape that haunt these regions, it seemed as if God were no longer in His world, but that in His stead reigned a fiend, merciless as Hell, ruthless as the grave. Hard it is, no

---

127 An institution where a parish's paupers were lodged; those able to work were required to do so.
128 The Peterborough Manuscript of the Anglo-Saxon Chronicle for the year 1137 so describes the period of anarchy under King Stephen.
129 In John Bunyan's *Pilgrim's Progress* (1678), the Slough of Despond engulfs the protagonist, Christian, in fears, doubts, and discouragement.
130 Dante Alighieri, *Inferno, La Divina Commedia* (c. 1308–21).

doubt, to read in Stanley's pages of the slave-traders coldly arranging for the surprise of a village, the capture of the inhabitants, the massacre of those who resist, and the violation of all the women; but the stony streets of London, if they could but speak, would tell of tragedies as awful, of ruin as complete, of ravishments as horrible, as if we were in Central Africa; only the ghastly devastation is covered, corpselike, with the artificialities and hypocrisies of modern civilisation.

The lot of a negress in the Equatorial Forest is not, perhaps, a very happy one, but is it so very much worse than that of many a pretty orphan girl in our Christian capital? We talk about the brutalities of the dark ages, and we profess to shudder as we read in books of the shameful exaction of the rights of feudal superior. And yet here, beneath our very eyes, in our theatres, in our restaurants, and in many other places, unspeakable though it be but to name it, the same hideous abuse flourishes unchecked. A young penniless girl, if she be pretty, is often hunted from pillar to post by her employers, confronted always by the alternative—Starve or Sin.[131] And when once the poor girl has consented to buy the right to earn her living by the sacrifice of her virtue, then she is treated as a slave and an outcast by the very men who have ruined her. Her word becomes unbelievable, her life an ignominy, and she is swept downward ever downward, into the bottomless perdition of prostitution. But there, even in the lowest depths, excommunicated by Humanity and outcast from God, she is far nearer the pitying heart of the One true Saviour than all the men who forced her down, aye, and than all the Pharisees and Scribes[132] who stand silently by while these fiendish wrongs are perpetrated before their very eyes.

The blood boils with impotent rage at the sight of these enormities, callously inflicted, and silently borne by these miserable victims. Nor is it only women who are the victims, although their fate is the most tragic. Those firms which reduce sweating[133] to a fine art, who systematically and deliberately defraud the workman of his pay, who grind the faces of the poor, and who rob the widow and the orphan, and who for a pretence make great professions of public spirit and philanthropy, these men nowadays are sent to Parliament to make laws for the people. The old prophets sent them to Hell—but we have changed all that. They send their victims to Hell, and are rewarded by all that wealth can do to make their lives comfortable. Read the House of Lords' Report on the Sweating System,[134] and ask if any African slave system, making due allowance for the superior civilisation, and therefore sensitiveness, of the victims, reveals more misery.

Darkest England, like Darkest Africa, reeks with malaria. The foul and fetid breath of our slums is almost as poisonous as that of the African swamp. Fever is almost as chronic there as on the Equator. Every year thousands of children are killed off by what [are] called defects of our sanitary system. They are in reality starved and poisoned, and all that can be said is that, in many cases, it is better for them that they were taken away from the trouble to come.

Just as in Darkest Africa it is only a part of the evil and misery that comes from the superior race who invade the forest to enslave and massacre its miserable inhabitants, so with us, much of the misery of those whose lot we are considering arises from their own habits. Drunkenness and all manner of uncleanness, moral and physical, abound. Have you ever watched by the bedside of a man in delirium tremens?[135]

---

131 Starve or engage in prostitution.
132 Matthew 23:13.
133 Sweatshop labour.
134 Reports from the Select Committee of the House of Lords on the Sweating System (1888–90); sweatshop practices were widespread in the sewing and tailoring industries.
135 Delirium brought on by withdrawal from alcohol.

Multiply the sufferings of that one drunkard by the hundred thousand, and you have some idea of what scenes are being witnessed in all our great cities at this moment. As in Africa streams intersect the forest in every direction, so the gin-shop stands at every corner with its River of the Water of Death flowing seventeen hours out of the twenty-four for the destruction of the people. A population sodden with drink, steeped in vice, eaten up by every social and physical malady, these are the denizens of Darkest England amidst whom my life has been spent, and to whose rescue I would now summon all that is best in the manhood and womanhood of our land.

But this book is no mere lamentation of despair. For Darkest England, as for Darkest Africa, there is a light beyond. I think I see my way out, a way by which these wretched ones may escape from the gloom of their miserable existence into a higher and happier life. Long wandering in the Forest of the Shadow of Death[136] at our doors, has familiarised me with its horrors; but while the realisation is a vigorous spur to action it has never been so oppressive as to extinguish hope. Mr. Stanley never succumbed to the terrors which oppressed his followers. He had lived in a larger life, and knew that the forest, though long, was not interminable. Every step forward brought him nearer his destined goal, nearer to the light of the sun, the clear sky, and the rolling uplands of the grazing land[.] Therefore he did not despair. The Equatorial Forest was, after all, a mere corner of one quarter of the world. In the knowledge of the light outside, in the confidence begotten by past experience of successful endeavour, he pressed forward; and when the 160 days' struggle was over, he and his men came out into a pleasant place where the land smiled with peace and plenty, and their hardships and hunger were forgotten in the joy of a great deliverance.

So I venture to believe it will be with us. But the end is not yet. We are still in the depths of the depressing gloom. It is in no spirit of light-heartedness that this book is sent forth into the world as if it was written some ten years ago.

If this were the first time that this wail of hopeless misery had sounded on our ears the matter would have been less serious. It is because we have heard it so often that the case is so desperate. The exceeding bitter cry of the disinherited has become to be as familiar in the ears of men as the dull roar of the streets or as the moaning of the wind through the trees. And so it rises unceasing, year in and year out, and we are too busy or too idle, too indifferent or too selfish, to spare it a thought. Only now and then, on rare occasions, when some clear voice is heard giving more articulate utterance to the miseries of the miserable men, do we pause in the regular routine of our daily duties, and shudder as we realise for one brief moment what life means to the inmates of the Slums. But one of the grimmest social problems of our time should be sternly faced, not with a view to the generation of profitless emotion, but with a view to its solution.

Is it not time? There is, it is true, an audacity in the mere suggestion that the problem is not insoluble that is enough to take away the breath. But can nothing be done? If, after full and exhaustive consideration, we come to the deliberate conclusion that nothing can be done, and that it is the inevitable and inexorable destiny of thousands of Englishmen to be brutalised into worse than beasts by the condition of their environment, so be it. But if, on the contrary, we are unable to believe that this "awful slough," which engulfs the manhood and womanhood of generation after generation, is incapable of removal; and if the heart and intellect of mankind alike revolt against the fatalism of despair, then, indeed, it is time, and high time, that the question were faced in no mere dilettante spirit, but with a resolute determination to make an end of the crying scandal of our age....

---

136 Psalm 23:4.

EDUCATION

Introduction
Janice Schroeder

Of the many massive reform projects the Victorians tackled, education was perhaps the most broadly encompassing. The "ragged schools" of the urban slums, the governess-ruled middle-class nursery, and the cloistered colleges of Oxford and Cambridge—all were subject to the quest to improve and expand educational opportunities for the nation. Questions about how to educate women, the poor, and the sons of the elite were debated in nearly every print format. As educational institutions were founded and existing ones transformed, Victorians revised pedagogical techniques and classroom management, revisions that demanded the re-imagination of many social categories, including childhood, poverty, gender, disability, and culture.

At the century's beginning, there was no consensus either that education was a social right or that the state should assume a leading role in ensuring that all children receive basic literacy and numeracy training. Many perceived the education of women and the poor as not only unnecessary but dangerous to the nation's stability. For much of the century, education for those without means consisted of a patchwork of voluntary and charity schools run by Christian organizations or private individuals. The industrial school that Henry Morley and Geraldine Jewsbury describe in "Instructive Comparisons" (1855) was one of many hundreds of ad hoc training schools administered by well-meaning (often ill-qualified) individuals. Funded by charitable donations, the schools' mandate was to transmit moral lessons, religious instruction, and vocational training. In descriptions of these schools by sympathetic middle-class observers, the "inmates" (213) are often hybrid figures—part prisoner, part trainee, part moral patient—reflecting a general belief that poverty both caused and resulted from crime and disease. In *Reformatory Schools* (1851) and elsewhere, Mary Carpenter, one of the most influential educational reformers of the century, exhorts readers to see pauper children as "future actors in the world's theatre" (58) and "coheirs with ourselves of an eternal existence" (73). For Carpenter, "love" should replace fear as the "ruling sentiment" (74) of the reform school—a controversial approach. Similarly, in her assessment of American schools for deaf and blind children, Harriet Martineau urges English readers to resist stereotypes of children with disabilities as either "brutish" (3:93) or a "sacred, favoured class" (3:95). All three writers regarded the poor and disadvantaged not as moral criminals or lost souls but as products of unhealthy environments and social ignorance. It fell to middle-class teachers to help shape such children into individuals responsible for their own governance.

The question of how to mould Britain's future leaders preoccupied Thomas Arnold, headmaster of Rugby, one of the country's elite public schools. So-called because they had been founded centuries

"Work-School for the Blind, Euston-Road." *Illustrated London News* (24 April 1858): 428.

earlier to train young men for posts in the church and public service, by the nineteenth century, "public" schools such as Eton, Winchester, and Rugby had become private boarding schools for sons of the rising middle class. Their curriculum consisted mainly of classics, preparing students for entry into Oxford or Cambridge, but more crucial training in the habits of authority and gentlemanly conduct took place in dormitories and on sports fields. In "The Discipline of Public Schools" (1835), Arnold defended corporal punishment and physical pain as promoting manly courage while preventing bad behaviour. The fagging system—in which junior boys performed chores for senior ones—had come under criticism for seeming to sanction the physical, mental, and sexual abuse of young boys at the hands of their adolescent "superiors" (1835). Yet Arnold endorsed fagging at Rugby because it inculcated a sense of orderly advancement through the ranks (or forms) as well as a sense of duty to others, qualities that would prepare boys to become leaders of the nation and empire.

"It has been said that the end of education is 'to form a nation of living, orderly men,'" noted Emily Davies ruefully in *The Higher Education of Women* (1866), her treatise on education and the Victorian feminine ideal (71). Indeed, until the second half of the century, formal education for girls and women was neglected and unsystematized. Middle-class girls were typically educated at home by governesses and at private boarding schools run by gentlewomen, both in which "feminine accomplishments" such as music, French, drawing, and decorative needlework were emphasized above academic subjects. These skills would effectively prepare a girl for marriage and her supposedly natural role as wife and mother. After the 1850s, feminist reformers, including Davies, began to denounce the weakness of female education, women's "idleness" within the home, and women's lack of access to male-only educational institutions. By 1870, Davies had founded Girton College, the first women's college at Cambridge—a significant achievement in a culture still hostile or indifferent to women's higher education. Indeed, even as educational and professional opportunities for women increased from 1850 onward, feminists contended with the "sex in mind" debates, in which medical experts warned that intellectual study would harm women's reproductive health and the future of "the race." As Henry Maudsley argued in 1874, "whatever aspirations of an intellectual kind [women] may have, they cannot be relieved from the performance of those offices [reproductive functions] so long as it is thought necessary that mankind should continue on earth" (471). Maudsley's argument equated menstruation with illness, an assumption that feminist physician Elizabeth Garrett Anderson corrected in her 1874 response by identifying its class bias.

If middle-class women's "delicate" bodily constitution was thought incompatible with serious intellectual work, so too was the manual labour of working-class men. In his definition of a liberal scholar, John Henry Newman classified "servile work," "bodily labour," and "mechanical employment" as ungentlemanly and therefore inimical to a liberal education (175). Yet even a working-class man could achieve a gentlemanly character—if not a gentleman's formal education—through self-directed study and by attending lectures at the Working Men's Colleges founded by Frederick Maurice and others in the Christian Socialist movement. Propelled by a strong Victorian belief in adult education and self-instruction, the Working Men's Colleges (and later women's colleges) promoted a broad liberal education for working-class adults. Anticipating the approaches of twentieth-century pedagogy, Maurice called for a "fellowship" between teachers and learners—a classroom in which teachers would also learn from students—which would, he hoped, lead to greater understanding between social classes: "If we can by any means assist in forming men, for which end we must teach them, and learn from them, not patronize them, that surely will be a better and more healthful work for our age and for the ages to come" (69).

Maurice criticized the education men received in universities, not only because universities excluded most of the population, but also because he felt that their education did not apply to the real world. At the beginning of the nineteenth century, English universities emphasized mental and moral discipline through the study of classics and mathematics in preparation for careers in law or the clergy. Secularization, the growing status of natural science, and the need to make higher education more responsive to business and industry all prompted widespread reform at the ancient universities and the founding of many new provincial universities. Yet John Henry Newman cautioned in 1852 against the notion that education should serve a practical goal, a debate that continues to inform universities today. Newman envisaged the university as a "moral atmosphere" (236) in which men pursued knowledge for its own sake, independently of material and political constraints. A liberal education, Newman argued, cultivated the taste and refined conduct through its emphasis on critical distance and abstract contemplation; knowledge was "valuable" as a "presence" (172) and a "habit" (187) rather than as a conduit to something else.

A decade after Newman's lectures on the university, Matthew Arnold, eldest son of Thomas Arnold, made similar claims about knowledge in "The Functions of Criticism at the Present Time" (1864). Writing before English literature became a university discipline, Arnold called for the professionalization of literary criticism and the establishment of a literary canon, or what he called "the best that is known and thought in the world" (239). Arguing that criticism could prompt new ideas in a literary culture that, in his view, had become stagnant and vulgar, Arnold insisted that criticism refrain from politics and practicalities, claiming instead "a disinterested love of a free play of the mind on all subjects, for its own sake" (238). The literary critic—"one of a very small circle" (244)—would "see things as they are" (244) and help to elevate English culture from what Arnold called its "Philistin[ism]" (249).

Decades later, Arnold contributed to a debate in the *Pall Mall Gazette* about the teaching of English as a university discipline at Oxford. While welcoming the idea, he remained pessimistic about English literature's institutionalization in the university. As the debate demonstrates, those such as John Churton Collins felt that English literature should be taught alongside Greek and Latin texts for its aesthetic properties—"its structure ... characters ... its ethical, its metaphysical, its poetic, its dramatic interest" (11). Arnold, Walter Pater, and John Addington Symonds all agreed that English literature warranted a space in Oxford's curriculum, but worried about how to balance it with a traditional classical education and how to ensure its rigour as a subject, with William Morris offering the cynical prediction that "the result would be merely vague talk about literature, which would teach nothing" (2). Like "The Functions of Criticism," the debate about English at Oxford in the 1880s constitutes a foundational text in the history of English literary study, demonstrating the power struggles waged in the disciplinary emergence and professionalization of what we now call literary criticism.

By the end of the century, the principles of a universal education system were enshrined in the Education Act of 1870, literacy rates had increased, teacher training colleges were established across the country, specialized education for deaf and blind people became compulsory, and women could obtain

"Free Education—A Difficult Problem." *Illustrated London News* (3 Oct. 1891): 385.

INTRODUCTION 153

"A London School Board Capture" (detail). *Illustrated London News* (9 Sept. 1871): 221.

a university education at both Oxford and Cambridge (although they could not graduate with degrees). Much had changed, not least of which was the improved status of the teaching profession itself. In the process, the Victorian liberal state was transformed as the public acknowledged the centrality of education to the nation's political and economic stability.

"Annual Inspection of the Middlesex Industrial School at Feltham."
Illustrated London News (20 July 1865): 97.

Works Cited and Further Reading

Altick, Richard. *The English Common Reader: A Social History of the Mass Reading Public, 1800–1900.* 2nd ed. Columbus: U of Ohio P, 1988. Print.

Arnold, Matthew. "Art. VIII.—The Functions of Criticism at the Present Time." *National Review* (Nov. 1864): 230–51. Print.

Borsay, Anne. *Disability and Social Policy in Britain since 1750: A History of Exclusion.* Houndmills: Palgrave Macmillan, 2005. Print.

Brantlinger, Patrick. *The Reading Lesson: The Threat of Mass Literacy in Nineteenth-Century British Fiction.* Bloomington: Indiana UP, 1998. Print.

Burstyn, Joan. *Victorian Education and the Ideal of Womanhood.* London: Croom Helm, 1980. Print.

Carpenter, Mary. *Reformatory Schools, for the Children of the Perishing and Dangerous Classes, and for Juvenile Offenders.* London: C. Gilpin, 1851. Print.

Collins, John Churton. "An Educational Crisis, and How to Avert It.—II." *Pall Mall Gazette* (31 May 1886): 11–12. Print.

Davies, Emily. *The Higher Education of Women.* London: Alexander Strahan, 1866. Print.

Digby, Anne, and Peter Searby. *Children, School and Society in Nineteenth-Century England.* London: Macmillan, 1981. Print.

Dyhouse, Carol. *No Distinction of Sex? Women in British Universities, 1870–1939.* London: UCL, 1995. Print.

Garland, Martha. *Cambridge before Darwin: The Ideal of a Liberal Education, 1800–1860.* Cambridge: Cambridge UP, 1980. Print.

Holmes, Martha Stoddard. *Fictions of Affliction: Physical Disability in Victorian Culture.* Ann Arbor: U of Michigan P, 2004. Print.

Honey, John Raymond De Symons. *Tom Brown's Universe: The Development of the English Public School in the Nineteenth Century.* New York: Quadrangle, 1977. Print.

Hunter, Ian. *Culture and Government: The Emergence of Literary Education.* Hampshire: Macmillan, 1988. Print.

Martineau, Harriet. *Retrospect of Western Travel.* 3 vols. London: Saunders and Otley, 1838. Print.

Maudsley, Henry. "Sex in Mind and in Education." *Fortnightly Review* (April 1874): 466–83. Print.

Maurice, Frederick Denison. *Learning and Working: Six Lectures Delivered in Willis's Rooms, London, in June and July, 1854.* Cambridge: Macmillan, 1855. Print.

Morley, Henry, and Geraldine Jewsbury. "Instructive Comparisons." *Household Words* (29 Sept. 1855): 211–14. Print.

Morris, William. "English Literature at the Universities. VI.—By Mr. William Morris." *Pall Mall Gazette* (1 Nov. 1886): 1–2. Print.

Newman, John Henry. *Discourses on the Scope and Nature of University Education Addressed to the Catholics of Dublin.* Dublin: James Duffy, 1852. Print.

Pedersen, Joyce Senders. *The Reform of Girls' Secondary and Higher Education in Victorian England.* New York: Garland, 1987. Print.

Purvis, June. *Hard Lessons: The Lives and Education of Working-Class Women in Nineteenth-Century England.* Cambridge: Polity, 1989. Print.

Russett, Cynthia Eagle. *Sexual Science: The Victorian Construction of Womanhood.* Cambridge, MA: Harvard UP, 1989. Print.

Smelser, Neil J. *Social Paralysis and Social Change: British Working-Class Education in the Nineteenth Century.* Berkeley: U of California P, 1991. Print.

Tullberg, Rita McWilliams. *Women at Cambridge.* Rev. ed. Cambridge: Cambridge UP, 1998. Print.

Thomas Arnold
from "On the Discipline of Public Schools" (1835)

As headmaster of Rugby School, Thomas Arnold (1795–1842) influenced English public school education, reforming Rugby from a state of decline to a model public school. He accomplished this through governance—he improved the school's moral character by expelling students for misbehaviour, winning staff members' loyalty by improving their status, implementing term exams and report cards, and starting a prefect system in which sixth-form boys monitored younger students. Arnold's pedagogical vision was grounded in his Christian faith. The father of Matthew Arnold (see Education, Aesthetics and Culture), Arnold published five volumes of sermons and various historical studies, among other writings.

In this 1835 response to an article in the *Quarterly Review of Education* that attacked flogging and fagging in Winchester School, Arnold defends corporal punishment on the principle that it be used only where inculcation of moral values has failed. He also advocates the system of fagging, whereby younger boys serve and emulate boys in the sixth form, as a form of school governance.

... "Corporal punishment," it is said, "is degrading." I well know of what feeling this is the expression; it originates in that proud notion of personal independence which is neither reasonable nor Christian, but essentially barbarian. It visited Europe in former times with all the curses of the age of chivalry,[1] and is threatening us now with those of Jacobinism.[2] For so it is, that the evils of ultra-aristocracy[3] and ultra-popular principles spring precisely from the same source—namely, from selfish pride—from an idolatry of personal honour and dignity in the aristocratical form of the disease—of personal independence in its modern and popular form. It is simply impatience of inferiority and submission—a feeling which must be more frequently wrong or right, in proportion to the relative situation and worthiness of him who entertains it, but which cannot be always or generally right except in beings infinitely more perfect than man. Impatience of inferiority felt by a child towards his parents, or by a pupil towards his instructors, is merely wrong, because it is at variance with the truth: there exists a real inferiority in the relation, and it is an error, a fault, a corruption of nature, not to acknowledge it.

Punishment, then, inflicted by a parent or a master for the purposes of correction, is in no true sense of the word degrading; nor is it the more degrading for being corporal. To say that corporal punishment is an appeal to personal fear is a mere abuse of terms. In this sense all bodily pain or inconvenience is an appeal to personal fear; and a man should be ashamed to take any pains to avoid the tooth-ache or the

---

1 The idea of chivalry as the honourable behaviour expected of knights peaked in the twelfth and thirteenth centuries.
2 Extreme political radicalism; during the French Revolution, Jacobins advocated democracy and equality to the point of imprisoning and executing aristocrats and their sympathizers.
3 French ultra-royalists (1815–30) opposed the French Revolution's democratic principles, instead supporting landowners, aristocrats, and clergy.

gout. Pain is an evil; and the fear of pain, like all other natural feelings, is of a mixed character, sometimes useful and becoming, sometimes wrong and mischievous. I believe that we should not do well to extirpate any of these feelings, but to regulate and check them by cherishing and strengthening such as are purely good. To destroy the fear of pain altogether, even if practicable, would be but a doubtful good, until the better elements of our nature were so perfected as wholly to supersede its use. Perfect love of good is the only thing which can profitably cast out all fear. In the meanwhile, what is the course of true wisdom? Not to make a boy insensible to bodily pain, but to make him dread moral evil more; so that fear will do its proper and appointed work, without so going beyond it as to become cowardice. It is cowardice to fear pain or danger more than neglect of duty, or than the commission of evil; but it is useful to fear them, when they are but the accompaniments or the consequences of folly and of faults....

With regard to the highest forms,[4] indeed, it is well known that corporal punishment is as totally out of the question in the practice of our schools as it is at the universities; and I believe that there could nowhere be found a set of young men amongst whom punishment of any kind was less frequent, or by whom it was less required. The real point to be considered is merely, whether corporal punishment is in all cases unfit to be inflicted on boys under fifteen, or on those who, being older in years, are not proportionably advanced in understanding or in character, who must be ranked in the lower part of the school, and who are little alive to the feeling of self-respect, and little capable of being influenced by moral motives. Now, with regard to young boys, it appears to me positively mischievous to accustom them to consider themselves insulted or degraded by personal correction. The fruits of such a system were well shown in an incident which occurred in Paris during the three days of the revolution of 1830.[5] A boy of twelve years old, who had been forward in insulting the soldiers, was noticed by one of the officers; and though the action was then raging, the officer, considering the age of the boy, merely struck him with the flat part of his sword, as the fit chastisement for boyish impertinence. But the boy had been taught to consider his person sacred, and that a blow was a deadly insult; he therefore followed the officer, and having watched his opportunity, took deliberate aim at him with a pistol, and murdered him.... At an age when it is almost impossible to find a true, manly sense of the degradation of guilt or faults, where is the wisdom of encouraging a fantastic sense of the degradation of personal correction? What can be more false, or more adverse to the simplicity, sobriety, and humbleness of mind which are the best ornament of youth, and offer the best promise of a noble manhood? There is an essential inferiority in a boy as compared with a man, which makes an assumption of equality on his part at once ridiculous and wrong; and where there is no equality, the exercise of superiority implied in personal chastisement cannot in itself be an insult or a degradation....

The beau-ideal[6] of school discipline with regard to young boys would appear to be this—that whilst corporal punishment was retained on principle as fitly answering to, and marking the naturally inferior state of, boyhood, morally and intellectually, and therefore as conveying no peculiar degradation to persons in such a state, we should cherish and encourage to the utmost all attempts made by the several boys as individuals to escape from the natural punishment of their age by rising above its naturally low tone of principle. While we told them that, as being boys, they were not degraded by being punished as

---

4   School levels or grades.
5   The French Revolution of July 1830. After three days of fighting, Charles X abdicated the throne and Louis-Philippe was crowned king.
6   French: the perfect model of beauty or excellence.

boys, we should tell them also, that in proportion as we saw them trying to anticipate their age morally, so we should delight to anticipate it also in our treatment of them personally—that every approach to the steadiness of principle shown in manhood should be considered as giving a claim to the respectability of manhood—that we should be delighted to forget the inferiority of their age, as they laboured to lessen their moral and intellectual inferiority. This would be a discipline truly generous and wise, in one word, truly Christian—making an increase of dignity the certain consequence of increased virtuous effort, but giving no countenance to that barbarian pride which claims the treatment of a freeman and an equal, while it cherishes all the carelessness, the folly, and the low and selfish principle of a slave.

With regard to older boys, indeed, who yet have not attained that rank in the school which exempts them from corporal punishment, the question is one of greater difficulty. In this case the obvious objections to such a punishment are serious; and the truth is, that if a boy above fifteen is of such a character as to require flogging, the essentially trifling nature of school correction is inadequate to the offence. But in fact boys, after a certain age, who cannot keep their proper rank in a school, ought not to be retained at it; and if they do stay, the question becomes only a choice of evils. For the standard of attainment at a large school being necessarily adapted for no more than the average rate of capacity, a boy who, after fifteen, continues to fall below it, is either intellectually incapable of deriving benefit from the system of the place, or morally indisposed to do so, and in either case he ought to be removed from it.... Now it is superfluous to say, that in these cases corporal punishment should be avoided wherever it is possible; and perhaps it would be best, if for such grave offences as would fitly call for it in younger boys, older boys whose rank in the school renders them equally subject to it, were at once to be punished by expulsion. As it is, the long-continued use of personal correction as a proper school punishment renders it possible to offer the alternative of flogging to an older boy, without subjecting him to any excessive degradation, and his submission to it marks appropriately the greatness and disgraceful character of his offence, while it establishes, at the same time, the important principle, that as long as a boy remains at school, the respectability and immunities of manhood must be earned by manly conduct and a manly sense of duty.

It seems to me, then, that the complaints commonly brought against our system of school discipline are wrong either in their principle or as to the truth of the fact. The complaint against *all* corporal punishment, as degrading and improper, goes, I think, upon a false and mischievous principle: the complaint against governing boys by fear, and mere authority, without any appeal to their moral feelings, is perfectly just in the abstract, but perfectly inapplicable to the actual state of schools in England. I now proceed to make a few remarks upon another part of the system of public schools, which is even less understood than the subject already considered,—I mean the power of fagging.[7]

Now by "the power of fagging," I understand a power given by the supreme authorities of a school to the boys of the highest class or classes in it, to be exercised by them over the lower boys for the sake of securing the advantages of regular government amongst the boys themselves, and avoiding the evils of anarchy,—in other words, of the lawless tyranny of physical strength. This is the simple statement of the nature and ends of public school fagging—an institution which, like all other government, has been often

---

7   A system of service whereby a young schoolboy performs tasks for a particular senior; Arnold believed that such pairings would result in a sense of emulation in the younger and mentorship in the older boy.

abused, and requires to be carefully watched, but which is as indispensable to a multitude of boys living together, as government, in like circumstances, is indispensable to a multitude of men.

I have said that fagging is necessary for a multitude of boys when *living together*; for this will show how the system may be required in the public schools of England, and yet be wholly needless in those of Scotland.... In the Scotch schools the boys *live* at their own homes, and are under the government of their own relations; they only meet at school for a certain definite object during a certain portion of the day. But in England the boys, for nearly nine months of the year, live with one another in a distinct society; their school life occupies the whole of their existence; at their studies and at their amusements, by day and by night, they are members of one and the same society, and in closer local neighbourhood with one another than is the case with the ordinary society of grown men. At all those times, then, when Scotch boys are living at home with their respective families, English boys are living together amongst themselves alone; and for this their habitual living they require a government. It is idle to say that the masters form, or can form, this government; it is impossible to have a sufficient number of masters for the purpose; for, in order to obtain the advantages of home government, the boys should be as much divided as they are at their respective homes.... And hence, if you have a large *boarding*-school, you cannot have it adequately governed without a system of fagging.

Now, a government among the boys themselves being necessary, the actual constitution of public schools places it in the best possible hands. Those to whom the power is committed, are not simply the strongest boys, nor the oldest, nor yet the cleverest; they are those who have risen to the highest form in the school—that is to say, they will be probably at once the oldest, and the strongest, and the cleverest; and further, if the school be well ordered, they will be the most respectable in application and general character—those who have made the best use of the opportunities which the school affords, and are most capable of entering into its objects. In short, they constitute a real aristocracy, a government of the most worthy, their rank itself being an argument of their deserving. And their business is to keep order amongst the boys; to put a stop to improprieties of conduct, especially to prevent that oppression and ill-usage of the weaker boys by the stronger which is so often ignorantly confounded with a system of fagging. For all these purposes a general authority over the rest of the school is given them; and in some schools they have the power, like the masters, of enforcing this authority by impositions, that is, by setting tasks to be written out or learnt by heart for any misbehaviour. And this authority is exercised over all those boys who are legally subject to it, that is, over all below a certain place in the school, whatever be their age or physical strength; so that many boys who, if there were no regular fagging, would by mere physical force be exercising power over their schoolfellows, although from their idleness, ignorance, and low principle they might be most unfit to do so, are now not only hindered from tyrannizing over others, but are themselves subject to authority—a most wholesome example, and one particularly needed at school, that mere physical strength, even amongst boys, is not to enjoy an ascendancy. Meanwhile this governing part of the school, thus invested with great responsibility, treated by the masters with great confidence and consideration, and being constantly in direct communication with the head-master, and receiving their instruction almost exclusively from him, learn to feel a corresponding self-respect in the best sense of the term; they look upon themselves as answerable for the character of the school, and by the natural effect of their position acquire a manliness of mind and habits of conduct infinitely superior, generally speaking, to those of young men of the same age who have not enjoyed the same advantages....

Harriet Martineau
from *Retrospect of Western Travel* (1838)

A prolific journalist, historian, and sociologist, Harriet Martineau (1802–76) wrote on such varied subjects as abolition, women's rights, and the Haitian Revolution of the 1790s. Martineau rose to fame and financial success with her *Illustrations of Political Economy* (1832–34), a multivolume series of tales intended to make the principles of political economy understandable to working-class readers. Her virtual deafness by age 20 did not impede her from travelling widely—to America, Egypt, and elsewhere. She wrote books based on her foreign travels, two novels, and an autobiography, in addition to publishing widely in the periodical press and regularly for the *Daily News* on social and political issues.

While correcting the notion that deaf people have extraordinary perception, Martineau advocates for dedicated schools to educate them; she also enters the Victorian controversy surrounding print for blind readers, here promoting a system of raised print rather than Braille.

∼

Volume 2: Mutes and Blind

... Some weeping philosophers of the present day are fond of complaining of the mercenary spirit of the age, and insist that men are valued (and treated accordingly), not as men, but as producers of wealth; that the age is so mechanical, that individuals who cannot act as parts of a machine for creating material comforts and luxuries are cast aside to be out of the way of the rest. What do such complainers make of the lot of the helpless in these days? How do they contrive to overlook or evade the fact that misery is recognised as a claim to protection and solace, not only in individual cases, which strike upon the sympathies of a single mind, but by wholesale; unfortunates, as a class, being cared for on the ground of their misfortunes? Are deformed and deficient children now cast out into the wastes to perish? Is any one found in this age who is of Aristotle's[8] opinion, that the deaf and dumb must remain wholly brutish? Does any one approve the clause of the code of Justinian[9] by which deaf-mutes are deprived of their civil rights?... If every one living is wiser than to believe these things, he owes his wisdom to the benevolent investigation which has been made into the condition of these isolated and helpless beings; an investigation purely benevolent, as it proceeded on the supposition that they were irremediably deficient. The testimony of their best benefactors goes to prove this....

The benevolence which undertook the care of this class of unfortunates, when their condition was esteemed hopeless, has, in many cases, through a very natural delight at its own success, passed over into a new and opposite error, particularly in America, where the popular philosophy of mind comes in aid

---

8   Aristotle (384–22 BCE), Greek philosopher.
9   Laws developed under Byzantine emperor Justinian I (483–565).

of the delusion. From fearing that the deaf and dumb had hardly any capacities, too many of their friends have come to believe them a sort of sacred, favoured class, gifted with a keener apprehension, a more subtle reason, and a purer spirituality than others, and shut out from little but what would defile and harden their minds. Such a belief may not be expressed in propositions or allowed on a full statement; but much of the conversation on the condition of the class proceeds on such an idea; and, in my own opinion, the education of deaf-mutes is and will be materially impaired by it. Not only does it give rise to mistakes in their treatment, but there is reason to fear bad effects from the disappointment which must sooner or later be occasioned....

... A very superficial view of the case of the class shows something of what the privation really is, and, consequently, furnishes hints as to the treatment by which it may be in part supplied. Many kindhearted people in America, and not a few in Europe, cry out, "They are only deprived of one sense and one means of expression. They have the infinite human spirit within them, active and irrepressible, with infinite objects in its view. They lose the pleasures of the ear; they lose one great opportunity of spiritual action, both on the world of matter and on human minds; but this is compensated for by the activity of the soul in other regions of thought and emotion; and their contemplation of their own objects is undisturbed, in comparison with what it would be if they were subject to the vulgar associations with which we have to contend."

It is true that the deaf from birth are deficient in one sense only, while they are possessed of four; but the one in which they are deficient is, beyond all estimate, the most valuable in the formation of mind. The eye conveys, perhaps, more immediate and vivid pleasures of sense, and is more requisite to external and independent activity; so that, in the case of the loss of a sense after the period of education, the privation of sight is a severer misfortune, generally speaking, than the loss of hearing. But, in the case of deficiency from birth, the deaf are far more unfortunate than the blind, from the important power of abstraction being in them very feeble in its exercise, and sadly restricted in the material on which it has to work....

The case of the deaf from birth is as precisely opposite as can be imagined, and much less favourable. They labour under an equal privation of elementary experience; and, in addition, under an almost total absence of the means of forming correct abstractions of the most important kinds. Children in general learn far less of the most essential things by express teaching than by what comes to them in the course of daily life. Their wrong ideas are corrected, their partial abstractions are rectified and enriched by the incessant unconscious action of other minds upon theirs. Of this kind of discipline the deaf-mute is deprived, and the privation seems to be fatal to a healthy intellectual and moral growth. He is taught expressly what he knows of intellectual and moral growth. He is taught expressly what he knows of intellectual and moral affairs; of memory, imagination, science, and sagacity; of justice, fortitude, emotion, and conscience. And this through imperfect means of expression. Children, in general, learn these things unconsciously better than they learn anything by the most complete express teaching. So that we find that the deaf-mute is ready at defining what he little understands, while the ordinary child feelingly understands what he cannot define.... The most watchful person may live in the same house with a deaf-mute for weeks and months, conversing on a plain subject from time to time, with every conviction of understanding and being understood, and find at length a blank ignorance, or an astounding amount of mistake existing in the mind of his dumb companion, while the language had been fluent and correct, and every appearance of doubt and hesitation excluded.... A pupil at Paris, who was considered to have been effectually instructed in the first principles of religion, was discovered, after a lapse of years, to have understood that God was a venerable old man living in the clouds; that the Holy Spirit was a dove surrounded with light; and that the devil was a monster dwelling in a deep place....

It is often said that, if the blind have the advantage of communication with other minds by conversation, the deaf have it by books. This is true; but, alas! to books must be brought the power of understanding them. The grand disadvantage of the deaf is sustained antecedently to the use of books; and, though they gain much knowledge of facts and other advantages by reading, books have no power to remedy the original faulty generalization by which the minds of deaf-mutes are kept narrow and superficial. If a remedy be ever found, it seems as if it must be by rendering their intercourse by the finger-alphabet and writing much more early than it is, and as nearly as possible general.... But the finger-alphabet is not yet practised, or likely to be practised beyond the sufferers themselves and their teachers and families; and before a deaf and dumb child can be taught reading and writing, the mischief to his mind is done.

As for the general intellectual and moral characteristics of deaf-mutes, they are precisely what good reasoners would anticipate. The wisest of the class have some originality of thought, and most have much originality of combination[.] They are active, ingenious, ardent, impressible, and strongly affectionate towards individuals; but they are superficial, capricious, passionate, selfish, and vain. They are like a coterie of children, somewhat spoiled by self-importance, and prejudiced and jealous with regard to the world in whose intercourses they do not share....

The first efforts towards erecting an institution for the education of the deaf and dumb in America were made in 1815, at Hartford, Connecticut. This institution, called the American Asylum, from its having been aided by the general government, has always enjoyed a high reputation.... The Pennsylvania Institution followed in 1821; and the New-York Asylum, opened in 1818, began to answer the hopes of its founders only in 1830. These two I visited....

The number of deaf-mutes in Pennsylvania was, at the period of the last census, seven hundred and thirty; six hundred and ninety-four being whites, and thirty-six persons of colour. As usual, it is discovered on inquiry that, in a large majority of cases, the hearing was lost in childhood, and not deficient from birth; so that it is to the medical profession that we must look for a diminution of this class of unfortunates. The number of pupils in the Institution in 1833 was seventy-four, thirty-seven of each sex; and of deaf-mute assistants six. The buildings, gardens, and arrangements are admirable, and the pupils look lively and healthy.

They went through some of their school exercises in the ordinary manner for our benefit. Many of them were unintelligible to us, of course; but when they turned to their large slates, we could understand what they were about. A teacher told a class of them, by signs, a story of a Chinese who had fish in his pond, and who summoned the fish by ringing a bell, and then fed them by scattering rice. All told it differently as regarded the minor particulars, and it was evident that they did not understand the connexion of the bell with the story. One wrote that the fishes came at the *trembling* of the bell; but the main circumstances were otherwise correct. They all understood that the fishes got the rice. When they were called upon to write what *smooth* meant, and to describe what things were smooth, they instanced marble, the sky, the ocean, and *eloquence*. This was not satisfactory; the generalization was imperfect, and the word eloquence meaningless to them. Nor did they succeed much better in introducing certain phrases, such as "on account of," "at the head of," into sentences; but one showed that he knew that the president was at the head of the United States. Then the word "glorious" was given, and their bits of chalk began to work with great rapidity. One youth thought that a woman governing the United States would be glorious; and others declared Lord Brougham to be glorious. The word "cow" was given; and out of a great number of exercises, there was not one which mentioned milk. Milk seemed almost the only idea which a cow did not call up. The ideas appeared so arbitrarily connected as to put all our associations at fault....

In the girls' workroom there were rows of knitters, straw-platters, and needle-women. The ingenuity they put into their work is great. The nicety of the platting of dolls' straw-bonnets cannot be surpassed; and I am in possession of a pair of worsted gloves, double knitted, of the size of my thumb-nail, of which every finger is perfect in its proportions. Perhaps this may be the class of American society destined to carry on the ingenuity of handiworks to perfection, as the Shakers seem to be appointed to show how far neatness can go. One little girl who was knitting in the workroom is distinguished from the rest by being able to speak. So the poor little thing understands the case. She can speak two words, "George" and "brother," having become deaf when she had learned this much of language. She likes being asked to speak, and gives the two words in a plaintive tone, much like the inarticulate cry of a young animal....

The education of the blind is a far more cheering subject than that of the deaf and dumb. The experiments which have been made in regard to it are so splendid, and their success so complete, that it almost seems as if little improvement remained to be achieved. It appears doubtful whether the education of the blind has ever been carried on so far as at present in the United States; and there is one set of particulars, at least, in which we should do well to learn from the new country.

I am grieved to find in England, among some who ought to inform themselves fully on the subject, a strong prejudice against the discovery by which the blind are enabled to read, for their own instruction and amusement. The method of printing for the blind, with raised and sharp types, on paper thicker and more wetted than in the ordinary process of printing, is put to full and successful use at the fine institution at Boston. Having seen the printing and the books, heard the public readings, and watched the private studies of the blind, all the objections brought to the plan by those who have not seen its operation appear to me more trifling than I can express....

The common letters are used, and not any abbreviated language. I think this is wise; for thus the large class of persons who become blind after having been able to read are suited at once; and it seems desirable to make as little difference as possible in the instrument of communication used by the blind and the seeing. It appears probable that, before any very long time, all valuable literature may be put into the hands of the blind; and the preparation will take place with much more ease if the common alphabet be used, than if works have to be translated into a set of arbitrary signs....

The best friends and most experienced teachers of the blind lay down, as their first principle in the education of their charge, that the blind are to be treated in all possible respects like other people; and these respects are far more numerous than the inexperienced would suppose. One of the hardest circumstances in the lot of a blind child is that his spirits are needlessly depressed, and his habits made needlessly dependant. From his birth, or from the period of his loss of sight, he never finds himself addressed in the every-day human voice. He hears words of pity from strangers, uttered in tones of hesitating compassion; and there is a something in the voices of his parents when they speak to him which is different from their tone towards their other children. Everything is done for him. He is dressed, he is fed, he is guided. If he attempts to walk alone, some one removes every impediment which lies in his way. A worse evil than even helplessness arises out of this method of treatment. The spirits and temper are injured.... The experienced students of the case of the blind hint at worse consequences still arising from this pernicious indulgence of the blind at home. Unless the mind be fully and independently exercised, and unless the blind be drawn off from the contemplation of himself as an isolated and unfortunate, if not injured being, the animal nature becomes too strong for control, and some species of sensual vice finishes the destruction which ill-judged indulgence began....

The generosity of American society, already so active and extensive, will continue to be exerted in behalf of sufferers from the privation of the senses, till all who need it will be comprehended in its care. No one doubts that the charity will be done. The fear is lest the philosophy which should enlighten and guide the charity should be wanting. Such sufferers are apt to allure the observer, by means of his tenderest sympathies, into the imaginative regions of philosophy. Science and generosity equally demand that the allurement should be resisted. If observers will put away all mere imaginations respecting their charge; if they will cease to approach them as superior beings in disguise, and look upon them as a peculiar class of children more than ordinarily ignorant, and ignorant in a remarkable direction, facts may be learned relative to the formation of mind and the exercise of intellect which may give cause to the race of ordinary men to look upon their infirm brethren with gratitude and love, as the medium through which new and great blessings have been conferred. By a union of inquirers and experimenters, by the speculative and practical cordially joining to work out the cases of human beings with four senses, the number might perhaps be speedily lessened of those who, seeing, see not, and who, hearing, hear not nor understand.[10]

Mary Carpenter
from *Reformatory Schools, for the Children of the Perishing and Dangerous Classes, and for Juvenile Offenders* (1851)

Educator, penal reformer, and Unitarian Mary Carpenter (1807–77) was among the most important Victorian advocates for poor and delinquent children. Her work in the Bristol slums led her to protest the courts' harsh punishment of child criminals. Her influential books on juvenile offenders—*Reformatory Schools, for the Children of the Perishing and Dangerous Classes, and for Juvenile Offenders* (1851) and *Juvenile Delinquents, their Condition and Treatment* (1853)—contributed to the creation of the Youthful Offenders Act of 1854, which established and partly funded reformatory schools run by volunteers. She travelled widely—to Canada, the US, and India—writing *Six Months in India* in 1868. She also promoted female education, fought for the repeal of the Contagious Diseases Acts, and met with Queen Victoria to discuss Indian education.

---

10 Matthew 13:13.

> In this selection from *Reformatory Schools* (1851), Carpenter proposes that reform schools rehabilitate juvenile offenders and, inspired by Christian values, manifests her belief in love as a reforming force.

Chapter 1: Condition of the Children of the "Perishing and Dangerous" Classes—Fundamental Principles to be Adopted in Schools for Them

Having now, it is hoped, shown the necessity of applying a system of sound moral and religious training to the children of the dangerous classes, we proceed to consider the principles on which [Reformatory] Schools adapted to such a purpose should be established.

Let us, however, first endeavour to gain some insight into the real position and character of the children whom we desire to rescue from their moral degradation.

The external aspect of these poor children is calculated to excite compassion in any heart not rendered callous by absorption in the world's selfish interests;—their tattered garments, their bare feet, their starved look, their mean and degraded aspect, on which the parent's vice has imprinted legible characters even in infancy,[11]—must touch even those who regard them only as young beings, susceptible as our own children of privation and suffering. But let us look at them as the future actors in the world's theatre, destined to increase the vast amount of evil now existing if their course is not arrested,—and still more as the heirs of an immortality the condition of which is dependent on their life on earth,—and the painful external aspect loses its horrors in comparison with the infinitely greater dangers which attack the immortal spirits of these young creatures....

Let us select a few out of the many pictures drawn by eye-witnesses, of the scenes that present themselves to those who attempt the work of juvenile reformation.

The following is from the diary of the master of a London Ragged School,[12] and is extracted from the *Sunday School Teacher's Magazine*, April 1850.

> *October 29*,—On the way to the school this morning in company with——, who has been appointed to act as my assistant, we were saluted by women and boys as we went along, in a most singular manner.... It was a dismal scene—no appearance of thrift or industry, nothing but squalid wretchedness and dirt and idleness;—the lanes leading to the school were full of men, women, and children, shouting, gossiping, swearing and laughing in a most discordant and unnatural manner. The whole population seemed to be on the eve of a great outbreak of one kind or another; ready for anything but work. These lanes are a moral hell.... No school can possibly be worse than this....

The following is a specimen of the ordinary Police Reports of a weekly paper in a large town.—[*Bristol Mercury*, Feb. 15, 1851.]

---

11 Many Victorians took literally the idea that the sins of the parents would be inherited by their children.
12 Starting in the 1840s, free or "ragged" schools were established for the education of the poor; the number of such schools diminished after the Education Act (1870).

J.S., a boy about thirteen years of age, was committed for a month, for stealing a piece of bacon from a shop. The prisoner said that his father had been killed by a railway accident, and his mother had deserted him. It being his first offence, the Magistrates remitted the whipping, which generally forms a portion of the punishment of juvenile offenders....

The preceding sketches will fail to give any adequate idea of the reality to those who have not witnessed similar cases; but they contain important elements on which to base the principles which should guide Reformatory Schools, and they are types of various subdivisions of the classes for whom we destine them. These we shall briefly describe, as on the peculiar characteristics of each must depend the nature of the Schools appropriated to them.

In this review of the "perishing and dangerous classes" of children, we shall not here include those who have already subjected themselves to the grasp of the law, and who are inmates of our prisons ... but we shall comprehend in it all those children who are *absolutely unable*, whether from poverty or vice, to receive instruction in the existing Schools, and who, without instruction gratuitously given, must grow up utterly destitute of it, and will most probably become a burden to the State, either as paupers or criminals.

First, then, are the children of those parents whom extreme poverty prevents from sending their children to School, but who yet desire education for them. This poverty may be the result, to them unavoidable, of external circumstances; it may be directly caused by their own vicious habits; in either case it is soul-crushing and degrading, and unless a hand is stretched out to save the children, they will sink into still lower depths of society.... [T]hese very children are raised and stimulated by the education given in a good free School, so far superior to what they were imbibing in the streets. The influence of such an education has been often seen to be most valuable, not only preparing the child to gain an honest livelihood, but indirectly stimulating the parents to exertions for their children which they before felt useless, and inducing a self-respect which is the first step to improvement....

Next, are the offspring of parents low and ignorant, who are perfectly careless about the spiritual welfare of their children, and heed their physical condition no more than absolute necessity compels them to do. They have themselves felt no need of education; they are too debased even to understand what it means; they have, like the lower animals, been satisfied with obtaining, as honestly as they have been compelled to do by the laws of society, that food only which perisheth,[13] and they leave their children to do the same. Were there not an indestructible germ of a divine nature in these unhappy little beings, their case would be indeed hopeless; *they* must be first lured to School, and patiently borne with for many a toilsome hour and long day, before the seed of life perceptibly springs up; but the happy influences of a School conducted in the spirit of "love, and of power, and of a sound mind,"[14] will be at length perceptible in them also....

Another and entirely separate class is formed by the Irish population, with whom our sea-port towns abound. They possess very distinctive peculiarities, both in habit and character; the worst parts of the national features are, of course, developed in them; indolent contentment with their condition, however low, excitability, unstableness of purpose, and a jealous yet blind attachment to the Catholic religion,— render it very difficult permanently to act on them; while their warmth of affection, grateful feeling, and quickness of apprehension, make them most interesting scholars when their faults are conquered. When

---

13   John 6:27.
14   2 Timothy 1:7.

Irish families become permanently settled in our cities, and can be induced to send their children to a School where no interference with their religion is attempted ... the surest step is taken for correcting the national faults, and for softening the strong prejudice which now places a barrier between those inhabiting the same street, or even the same house.

For these three classes, good Free Day Schools will generally prove most valuable; and here, as elsewhere, the language of theory is not used, but of actual experience and observation. But it is utterly unavailable to those children of whom examples have been given, who are homeless, and friendless, who are barely maintaining themselves from day to day by hawking[15] and jobbing.[16] There are many among these of fine and noble spirits, early trained to independence and acuteness of intellect, whom the instruction given in the Evening Ragged School has led to a right direction of their energies ... ; but for the greater part of them, nothing can be anticipated but that they must fall into the two last classes, the thieves and the beggars, and for these nothing can prove an effective preservation from vice but Feeding Industrial Schools,[17] to which all shall be *compelled* to go, who from inability or from vicious inclination do not attend the Free Day School, and are addicted to vagrant habits.

We usually regard the juvenile thieves as a distinct class ... ; but there are a large number of boys in our large cities who merely fall into the practice from sheer idleness, or from that love of enterprize so natural to boys, and often lauded in the children of gentlemen;—a few, but comparatively few, are driven to the practice by sheer destitution. The thieves, as a class, would then be speedily diminished, and so marked as to impair their strength, if such a system were pursued as we are advocating;—and the determined culprits could then be submitted more readily to stringent reformatory discipline.

But the last class is even more difficult to deal with, because there is one stamp of degradation on them all, which must make them an hereditary burden to the country, if the young children are not early trained to a different course of life. This they will never adopt *voluntarily*; their present mode of life is so lucrative and so pleasant, that they will not exchange it for another apparently presenting far greater advantages. Their filth and rags are no annoyances to them, for they are the implements of their trade; the cold and hunger which they continually endure are most amply compensated by an occasional luxurious meal. The close and noisome dens in which they are stowed at night presents nothing revolting to their feelings, and they prefer them to a clean abode where they must resign their occupation and some portion of their liberty. The elasticity of spirit, the activity of youth, is changed for a degrading and dependent servility, which destroys all wish to rise. We have not known even a solitary instance in which a child who has been accustomed to beg has been induced to attend a Day School regularly, even though allured by promises of an improved condition;—and if the children of beggars are induced to come they are soon withdrawn by the parents, except in very few cases.

This sketch is imperfect and faint. All who would more truly know these children must visit them in their homes, watch them unobserved in their daily goings, see them in groups planning evil, enter the "gaffs,"[18] the sweetmeat shops, where they are early initiated into the mysteries of gambling,—the penny theatres, where, with all the accompaniments that excite the imagination and feelings, many have learnt

---

15　Selling goods in the street.
16　Performing odd jobs.
17　Schools where impoverished children learned trades.
18　Cheap theatres or music halls.

their first lesson in crime,—the singing rooms,[19] the nature of which, as given by Mr. Clay in his last Report,[20] is too revolting to describe here,—and even the public-houses[21] for children, for such there are, where the young rival the old in vice. Or they may read details of these things in the Reports of the Ragged School Union,[22] and in the valuable Essays that have appeared on Juvenile Depravity.[23] Enough has been said of their condition to prepare for a statement of general principles which must guide us in all Schools for their reformation, and which are essential to the success of our efforts.

First, and above all, there must be in the minds of those who plan, and of those who carry out the work, a strong faith in the immortality of the human soul, the universal and parental government of God, and the equal value in His sight of each one of these poor perishing young creatures with the most exalted of our race. We must feel even a reverence, blended with that intense pity which can never be separated from love, for these children, coheirs with ourselves of an eternal existence, and be able to discern under the most degraded exterior the impress of God's creative Spirit, one of those for whom Christ died....[24] [T]his must be the direct and avowed object of Reformatory Schools, or they will fail in their design, and will have but a short-lived existence. It is the Spirit only that quickeneth.[25]

Secondly. Love must be the ruling sentiment of all who attempt to influence and guide these children.... Love draws with human cords far stronger than chains of iron. While in the education of the young generally this element is a most essential ingredient, yet if wanting in the School, it may be supplied in the home;—but here?—if these poor children have a home, it is but too often one to crush rather than cherish any feeling of affection; and towards society in general, at any rate the more favoured portion of it, we have already seen that "their hand is against every man, and every man's hand against them."[26] ... Would we teach them to respect the law of man, and reverence the law of God, it will not be by imposing on them a severe pressure, from which their elastic spirits will rise up more vigorous for evil whenever it is shaken off,—but by making them *feel* the brotherhood of man, and after teaching them to love man whom they have seen, they will learn easily to love God whom they have not seen, and to desire to obey His laws. It is love only which is the "fulfilling of the law."[27] Love to the teacher will make what belongs to *him* sacred to the child who has hitherto thought all lawful booty; the same feeling is soon extended to the whole School property, which has been found secure when surrounded by young thieves: a desire to please the teacher will inspire a higher moral tone in his presence, and this, enlarged and strengthened by wise instruction, becomes a principle of action. Love to the teacher may be made the means also of awakening the spiritual affections towards the Heavenly Father....

These are the two fundamental principles which must pervade all our Schools of Reformation.

---

19 Singing saloons provided food, alcohol, and popular entertainment, including singers, dancers, and chorus singing by the audience.
20 John Clay (1796–1858), prison chaplain and reformer. Clay's annual reports were reproduced in the parliamentary papers from 1824 onwards.
21 Pubs.
22 The Ragged School Union was established in 1844 to promote ragged schools.
23 Possibly Rev. H. Worsley, *The Prize Essay on Juvenile Depravity* (1849); Thomas Beggs, *An Inquiry into the Extent and Causes of Juvenile Depravity* (1849).
24 1 Corinthians 15:3.
25 John 6:63.
26 Genesis 16:12.
27 Romans 13:10.

John Henry Newman
from *Discourses on the Scope and Nature of University Education Addressed to the Catholics of Dublin* (1852)

Catholic intellectual John Henry Newman (1801–90) began his career as an important Anglican theologian. Educated at Trinity College, Oxford, he became a fellow of Oriel College and vicar of the Anglican church of St. Mary's, Oxford, where his sermons enraptured audiences. In 1833, Newman (with clergymen John Keble, Edward Bouverie Pusey, Richard Hurrell Froude, and others) founded the Oxford Movement, which promoted seventeenth-century High Church tradition in opposition to Broad-Church liberalism and state involvement in the church. *Tracts for the Times* (1833–41), the movement's pamphlet series, aroused particular controversy with Newman's *Tract 90* (1841), which proposed that the Church of England's 39 Articles were compatible with Catholicism. Oxford authorities banned the tracts; Newman resigned from St. Mary's in 1843. In 1845, he became Catholic, eventually becoming a priest (1847) and a cardinal (1879).

In 1851, Newman became the first president of the new Catholic University of Ireland (now University College, Dublin), delivering five lectures in 1852 that advocated liberal education, later published as *The Idea of a University* (1873).

Discourse 6: Philosophical Knowledge its Own End

… When then I am asked what is the end of a Liberal or a University Education, and of the Liberal or Philosophical Knowledge which I conceive it to impart, I answer, that it has a very tangible, real, and sufficient end, but that the end cannot be divided from that knowledge itself. Knowledge is capable of being its own end. Such is the constitution of the human mind, that any kind of knowledge, if it be really such, is its own reward. And if this is true of all knowledge, it is true of that special Philosophy, which I have made to consist in a comprehensive view of truth in all its branches, of the relations of science to science, of their mutual bearings, and their respective values. What the worth of such an acquirement is, compared with other objects which we seek,—wealth or power or honour or the conveniences and comforts of life, I do not profess here to discuss; but I would maintain, and mean to show, that it is an object, in its own nature so really and undeniably good, as to be the compensation of a great deal of thought in compassing, and a great deal of trouble in attaining.

Now, when I say that Knowledge is, not merely a means to something beyond it, or the preliminary of certain arts into which it naturally resolves, but an end sufficient to rest in and to pursue for its own sake, surely I am uttering no paradox, for I am stating what is both intelligible in itself, and has ever been the common judgment of philosophers and the ordinary feeling of mankind.… I am but saying what whole volumes have been written to illustrate, by a "selection from the records of Philosophy, Literature, and Art, in all ages and countries, of a body of examples, to show how the most unpropitious circumstances have been unable to conquer an ardent desire for the acquisition of knowledge."[28] That further advantages accrue to us and redound to others, by its possession, over and above what it is in itself, I am very far indeed from denying; but, independent of these, we are satisfying a direct need of our nature in its very acquisition; and, whereas our nature, unlike that of the inferior creation, does not at once reach its perfection, but depends in order to it on a number of external aids and appliances, Knowledge, as one of those principal gifts or accessories, by which it is completed, is valuable for what its very presence in us does for us by a sort of *opus operatum*,[29] even though it be turned to no further account, nor subserve any direct end.

Hence it is that Cicero, in enumerating the various heads of mental excellence, lays down the pursuit of knowledge for its own sake, as the first of them.... [H]e considers Knowledge the very first object to which we are attracted, after the supply of our physical wants. After the calls and duties of our animal existence, as they may be termed, as regards ourselves, our family, and our neighbours, follows, he tells us, "the search after truth. Accordingly, as soon as we escape from the pressure of necessary cares, forthwith we desire to see, to hear, to learn; and consider the knowledge of what is hidden or is wonderful a condition of our happiness."[30]

This passage, though it is but one of many similar passages in a multitude of authors, I take for the very reason that it is so familiarly known to us; and I wish you to observe, Gentlemen, how distinctly it separates the pursuit of Knowledge from those ulterior objects to which certainly it can be made to conduce, and which are, I suppose, solely contemplated by the persons who would ask of me the use of a University or Liberal Education....

This was the ground of the opposition, which the elder Cato made to the introduction of Greek Philosophy among his countrymen, when Carneades and his companions, on occasion of their embassy, were charming the Roman youth with their eloquent expositions of it.[31] A fit representative of a practical people, he estimated every thing by what it produced; whereas the Pursuit of Knowledge promised nothing beyond Knowledge itself. It was as fatal, he considered, to attempt to measure the advantages of Philosophy by a Utilitarian[32] standard, as to estimate a point of taste by a barometer, or to trace out an emotion by an equation. Cato knew at the time as little of what is meant by refinement or enlargement of mind, as the busy every-day world now knows of the operations of grace. He despised what he had never felt.

Things, which can bear to be cut off from everything else and yet persist in living, must have life in themselves; pursuits, which issue in nothing, and still maintain their ground for ages, which are regarded as admirable, though they have not as yet proved themselves to be useful, must have their sufficient end in themselves, whatever it turn out to be. And we are brought to the same conclusion by considering the force of the epithet, by which the knowledge under consideration is popularly designated. It is common to speak of "*liberal* knowledge", of the "*liberal* arts and studies", and of a "*liberal* education", as the especial characteristic or property of a University and of a gentleman; what is meant by the word? Now, first, in its grammatical sense it is opposed to *servile*; and by "servile work" is understood, as our catechisms inform us, bodily labour, mechanical employment, and the like, in which the mind has little or no part.... As far as this contrast may be considered as a guide into the meaning of the word, liberal knowledge and liberal pursuits are such as belong to the mind, not to the body.

---

28 George Craik and Francis Wayland, *The Pursuit of Knowledge under Difficulties, Illustrated by Anecdotes* (1831).
29 Latin: spiritual effect.
30 Cicero, *De Officiis* (44 BCE).
31 See Plutarch, *Life of Cato the Elder* (late first to early second century).
32 Based on the principle of the greatest good for the greatest number of people.

But we want something more for its explanation, for there are bodily exercises which are liberal, and mental exercises which are not so. For instance, in ancient times the practitioners in medicine were commonly slaves; yet it was an art as intellectual in its nature, in spite of the low magic or empiricism with which it might then, as now, be debased, as it was heavenly in its aim. And so in like manner, we contrast a liberal education with a commercial education or a professional; yet no one can deny that commerce and the professions afford scope for the highest and most diversified powers of mind. There is then a great variety of intellectual exercises, which are not technically called "liberal"; on the other hand, I say, there are exercises of the body which do receive that appellation. Such, for instance, was the palæstra,[33] in ancient times; such the Olympic games, in which strength and dexterity of body as well as of mind gained the prize.... War, too, however rough a profession, has ever been accounted liberal, unless in cases when it becomes heroic, which would introduce us to another subject.

Now comparing these instances together, we shall have no difficulty in determining the principle of this apparent variation in the application of the term which I am examining. Manly games, or games of skill, or military prowess, though bodily, are, it seems, accounted liberal; on the other hand, what is merely professional, though highly intellectual, nay, though liberal in comparison of trade and manual labour, is not simply called liberal, and mercantile occupations are not liberal at all. Why this distinction? because that alone is liberal knowledge, which stands on its own pretensions, which is independent of sequel, expects no complement, refuses to be *informed* (as it is called) by any end, or absorbed into any art, in order duly to present itself to our contemplation. The most ordinary pursuits have this specific character, if they are self-sufficient and complete; the highest lose it, when they minister to something beyond them. It is absurd to balance a treatise on reducing[34] fractures with a game of cricket or a fox-chase; yet of the two the bodily exercise has that quality which we call "liberal," and the intellectual has it not. And so of the learned professions altogether, considered merely as professions; though the one of them be the most popularly beneficial, and another the most politically important, and the third the most intimately divine of all human pursuits, yet the very greatness of their end, the health of the body, or of the commonwealth, or of the soul, diminishes, not increases, their claim to the appellation in question, and that still more, if they are cut down to the strict exigencies of that end....

All that I have been now saying is summed up in a few characteristic words of the great Philosopher. "Of possessions," he says, "those rather are useful which bear fruit; those *liberal, which tend to enjoyment*. By fruitful, I mean, which yield revenue; by enjoyable, where *nothing accrues of consequence beyond the use*."[35] ...

I consider then, that I am chargeable with no paradox, when I speak of a Knowledge which is its own end, when I call it liberal knowledge, or a gentleman's knowledge, when I educate for it, and make it the scope of a University. And still less am I incurring such a charge, when I make this acquisition consist, not in Knowledge in a vague and ordinary sense, but in that knowledge which I have especially called Philosophy or, in an extended sense of the word, Science; for whatever claims Knowledge has to be considered as a good, these it has in a higher degree when it is viewed not vaguely, not popularly, but precisely and transcendently as Philosophy. Knowledge, I say, is especially liberal, or needs no end beside itself, when and so far as it is philosophical; and this I proceed to show.

---

33   In ancient Greece and Rome, the palaestra was a forum for both public teaching and athletic exercises.
34   Setting.
35   Aristotle, *Rhetoric* (c. 350 BCE).

You may recollect, Gentlemen, that, in my forgoing Discourse, I said that systematising, or taking general views of all departments of thought, or what I called Philosophy, was but a modification of the mental condition which we designate by the name of science, or was a Science of sciences; now bear with me, if what I am about to say, has at first sight a fanciful appearance. Philosophy then or Science is related to Knowledge in this way:—Knowledge is called by the name of Science or Philosophy, when it is acted upon, informed, or, if I may use a strong figure, impregnated by Reason. Reason is the principle of that intrinsic fecundity of Knowledge, which, to those who possess it, is its especial value, and which dispenses with the necessity of their looking abroad for any end to rest upon external to itself. Knowledge indeed, when thus exalted into a scientific form, is also power; not only is it excellent in itself, but whatever such excellence may be, it is something more, it has a result beyond itself. Doubtless; but that is a further consideration, with which I am not concerned. I only say that, prior to its being a power, it is a good; that it is, not only an instrument, but an end. I know well it may resolve itself into an art, and terminate in a mechanical process, and in tangible fruit; but it also may fall back upon reason, and resolve itself into philosophy. In the one case it is called Useful Knowledge, in the other Liberal.... You see then, Gentlemen, here are two methods of Education; the one aspires to be philosophical, the other to be mechanical; the one rises towards ideas, the other is exhausted upon what is particular and external. Let me not be thought to deny the necessity, or to decry the benefit, of such attention to what is particular and practical, of the useful or mechanical arts; life could not go on without them; we owe our daily welfare to them; their exercise is the duty of the many, and we owe to the many a debt of gratitude for fulfilling it. I only say that Knowledge, in proportion as it tends more and more to be particular, ceases to be Knowledge.... When I speak of Knowledge, I mean something intellectual, something which grasps what it perceives through the senses; something which takes a view of things; which sees more than the senses convey; which reasons upon what it sees, and while it sees; which invests it with an idea. It expresses itself, not in a mere enunciation, but by an enthymeme:[36] it is of the nature of science from the first, and in this consists its dignity. The principle of real dignity in Knowledge, its worth, its desirableness, considered irrespectively of its results, is this germ within it of a scientific or a philosophical process. This is how it comes to be an end in itself; this is why it is called Liberal. Not to know the relative disposition of things is the state of slaves or children; to have mapped out the Universe is the boast of Philosophy....

... Such knowledge is not a mere extrinsic or accidental advantage, which is ours to-day and another's to-morrow, which may be got up from a book, and easily forgotten again, which we can command or communicate at our pleasure, which we can borrow for the occasion, carry about in our hand, and take into the market; it is an acquired illumination, it is a habit, a personal possession, and an inward endowment. And this is the reason, why it is more correct, as well as more usual, to speak of a University as a place of education, than of instruction, though, when knowledge is concerned, instruction would at first sight have seemed the more appropriate word. We are instructed, for instance, in manual exercises, in the fine and useful arts, in trades, and in ways of business; for these are methods, which have little or no effect upon the mind itself, are contained in rules committed to memory, tradition, or use, and bear upon an end external to themselves. But education is a higher word; it implies an action upon our mental nature, and the formation of a character; it is something individual and permanent, and is commonly spoken of in connexion with religion and virtue. When then we speak of the communication of Knowledge as being Education,

---

36 An argument based on probability; a syllogism that omits one premise.

we thereby really imply that that Knowledge is a state or condition of mind; and since cultivation of mind is surely worth seeking for its own sake, we are thus brought once more to the conclusion, which the word "Liberal" and the word "Philosophy" have already suggested, that there is a Knowledge, which is desirable, though nothing come of it, as being of itself a treasure, and a sufficient remuneration of years of labour....

Useful Knowledge then certainly has done its work; and Liberal Knowledge as certainly has not done its work: supposing, as the objectors assume, its direct end, like Religious Knowledge, is to make men better; but this I will not for an instant allow. For all its friends, or its enemies, may say, I insist upon it, that it is as real a mistake to implicate it with virtue or religion, as with the arts. Its direct business is not to steel the soul against temptation or to console it in affliction, any more than to set the loom in motion, or to direct the steam carriage; be it ever so much, the means or the condition of both material and moral advancement, still, taken by and in itself, it as little mends our hearts, as it improves our temporal circumstances. And if its eulogists claim for it such a power, they commit the very same kind of encroachment on a province not their own, as the political economist who should maintain that his science educated him for casuistry or diplomacy. Knowledge is one thing, virtue is another; good sense is not conscience, refinement is not humility, nor is largeness and justness of view faith. Philosophy, however enlightened, however profound, gives no command over the passions, no influential motives, no vivifying principles. Liberal Education makes not the Christian, not the Catholic, but the gentleman. It is well to be a gentleman, it is well to have a cultivated intellect, a delicate taste, a candid, equitable, dispassionate mind, a noble and courteous bearing in the conduct of life;—these are the connatural qualities of a large knowledge; they are the objects of a University; I am advocating, I shall illustrate and insist upon them; but still, I repeat, they are no guarantee for sanctity or even for conscientiousness, they may attach to the man of the world, to the profligate, to the heartless,—pleasant, alas, and attractive as he seems when decked out in them. Taken by themselves, they do but seem to be what they are not; they look like virtue at a distance, but they are detected by close observers, and on the long run; and hence it is that they are popularly accused of pretence and hypocrisy, not, I repeat, from their own fault, but because their professors and their admirers persist in taking them for what they are not, and are officious in arrogating for them a praise to which they have no claim. Quarry the granite rock with razors, or moor the vessel with a thread of silk; then may you hope with such keen and delicate instruments as human knowledge and human reason to contend against those giants, the passion and the pride of man.

Surely we are not driven to theories of this kind, in order to vindicate the value and dignity of Liberal Knowledge. Surely the real grounds on which its pretensions rest, are not so very subtle or abstruse, so very strange or improbable. Surely it is very intelligible to say, and that is what I say here, that Liberal Education, viewed in itself, is simply the cultivation of the intellect, as such, and its object is nothing more or less than intellectual excellence. Every thing has its own perfection, be it higher or lower in the scale of things; and the perfection of one is not the perfection of another. Things animate, inanimate, visible, invisible, all are good in their kind, and have a *best* of themselves, which is an object of pursuit. Why do you take such pains with your garden or your park? You see to your walks and turf and shrubberies; to your trees and drives; not as if you meant to make an orchard of the one, or corn or pasture land of the other, but because there is a special beauty in all that is goodly in wood, water, plain, and slope, brought all together by art into one shape, and grouped into one whole. Your cities are beautiful, your palaces, your public buildings, your territorial mansions, your churches; and their beauty leads to nothing beyond itself. There is a physical beauty and a moral: there is a beauty of person, there is a beauty of our moral being, which is natural virtue; and in like manner there is a beauty, there is a perfection, of the intellect. There is an ideal perfection in these various subject matters, towards which individual instances are seen to rise, and which are the standards for all instances whatever. The Greek divinities and demigods, as the statuary has moulded them, with their symmetry of figure, and their high forehead and their regular features, are the perfection of physical beauty. The heroes, of whom history tells, Alexander, or Cæsar, or Scipio, or Saladin,[37] are the representatives of that magnanimity or self mastery which is the greatness of human nature. Christianity too has its heroes, and in the supernatural order, and we call them Saints. The artist puts before him beauty of feature and form; the poet, beauty of mind; the preacher, the beauty of grace: then intellect too, I repeat, has its beauty, and it has those who aim at it. To open the mind, to correct it, to refine it, to enable it to know, and to digest, master, rule, and use its knowledge, to give it power over its own faculties, application, flexibility, method, critical exactness, sagacity, resource, address, eloquent expression, is an object as intelligible (for here we are inquiring, not what the object of a Liberal Education is worth, nor what use the Church makes of it, but what it is in itself,) I say, an object as intelligible as the cultivation of virtue, while, at the same time it is absolutely distinct from it.

This indeed is but a temporal object, and a transitory possession; but so are other things in themselves which we make much of and pursue. The moralist will tell us, that man, in all his functions, is but a flower which blossoms and fades, except so far as a higher principle breathes upon him, and makes him and what he is, immortal. Body and mind are carried on into an eternal state of being by the gifts of Divine Munificence; but at first they do but fail in a failing world; and, if the powers of intellect decay, the powers of the body have decayed before them, and, if an Hospital or an Almshouse, though its end be secular, may be sanctified to the service of Religion, so surely may an University, were it nothing more than I have as yet described it. We attain to heaven by using this world well, though it is to pass away; we perfect our nature, not by undoing it, but by adding to it what is more than nature, and directing it towards aims higher than its own.

Henry Morley and Geraldine Jewsbury
from "Instructive Comparisons" (1855)

Journalist Henry Morley (1822–94) trained in medicine before working as a private tutor and establishing a school, where (contrary to Victorian conventions) he refused to use corporal punishment. His medical knowledge provided the basis for several articles on public health and the cholera epidemic of 1848. These publications led Charles Dickens (see Condition of England) to invite him to contribute articles on sanitation to *Household Words*, whose staff Morley joined in 1851 as the sole member with a university degree. Morley wrote widely for the periodical press (including "Ground in the Mill" [1854],

---

37 Alexander the Great (356–23 BCE), king of Macedonia; Julius Caesar (c. 100–44 BCE), Roman general and dictator; Scipio Africanus the Elder (236–183 BCE), Roman general; Salah al-Din Yusuf ibn Ayyub (c. 1137/38–93), Muslim hero and conqueror of Jerusalem in 1187.

an exposé of insufficient safety regulations in factories) and served as editor of the daily *Examiner* (1861–67). He also wrote several biographies, taught evening extension courses, and supported women students' admission at University College London once appointed professor of English language and literature.

Journalist and novelist Geraldine Jewsbury (1812–80) exerted much influence on Victorian literature as a publisher's reader of novels (recommending and discouraging publication of submitted manuscripts) and a book reviewer for the weekly *Athenaeum* (reviewing over 2,000 books from 1849 to 1880). She also wrote fiction—including novels, children's books, and short stories—as well as translations and an article on spiritual struggles. Noted for her animated personality and for her smoking habit (unconventional for women), Jewsbury enjoyed a wide circle of friends including the Huxleys (see Science), the Brownings, the Rossettis, Frances Power Cobbe (see Faith and Doubt), and John Ruskin (see Life Writing, Condition of England, Aesthetics and Culture, Gender and Sexuality). A lifelong associate of the Carlyles (see Condition of England, Faith and Doubt), Jewsbury was Jane Welsh Carlyle's closest friend.

In "Instructive Comparisons," published in *Household Words*, Morley and Jewsbury note the advantages of a school without religious affiliation. They also suggest the potential of teaching trades to former child criminals and assisting them with emigration.

There are in Edinburgh two industrial schools, both very well conducted, though founded upon opposite theories of education for the poor. A local pamphlet that has found its way into our hands, analyses the results that have in each case been obtained by matter-of-fact comparison between the last annual reports of the two institutions. The evidence obtained in this way is, we think, so far as it goes, of a kind likely to be useful to the public.

Of the two institutions thus compared, one, known as the Original Ragged School,[38] is by some years the elder.... The management of this school, resting mainly in the hands of free churchmen,[39] and entirely in the hands of pious Protestants, it follows that Protestant teachers, the Protestant version of the Bible, Protestant commentaries, have been made essential parts of the school system. Now, it is known very generally, that the wynds[40] and closes of such places as the Cowgate and the Grass Market at Edinburgh, contain throngs of miserable Irish families; and that of all the ragged children whom these schools are meant to bless, no inconsiderable portion is supplied by Roman Catholics. Many persons of influence in the town considered it, in the case of the Original Ragged School, a serious objection that it was not practically open to all classes of the poor; and ... they set on foot another ragged school in consonance with their own sense of what is liberal and just: which other school exists under the name of the United Industrial. In the United Industrial School, it is made necessary that religious teaching should be given, in hours set apart for that purpose; but it is not furnished by the school itself, which is content to open

---

38   Starting in the 1840s, free or "ragged" schools were established for the education of the poor; the number of such schools diminished after the Education Act (1870).
39   Members of a church free from state control; that is, of a non-conformist church.
40   Narrow lanes or alleys.

its doors to the various religious instructors chosen for the pupils by their friends. For the last eight years the respective merits of these systems have been eagerly discussed in Edinburgh ... ; and so, taking the report of each school for the present year, and comparing the results proclaimed by each, we adopt the question, What have they to show? ...

The managers of the United Industrial School, keeping in view the children whom they have taken from the streets and put into decent ways of life, can account for about one hundred and forty out of one hundred and sixty boys who have gone to situations.[41] Ninety of these are still in their first places.[42] It can account, also, for ninety-two girls, who, out of a hundred and six finding employment, still keep up a friendship with their teachers. Thirty-four of these are still in their first places. The parents who send children to this school, having their religious feelings openly respected, are content; and from this school, accordingly, all straying away of pupils is extremely rare. On the other hand, the report of the school hampered by a too zealous orthodoxy, giving an account of its year's work, has to record that, while out of two hundred and seventy-five pupils, not more than forty-nine (or eighteen and a-half per cent) went to employments, nearly an equal number (forty-nine) deserted, or would not return, or could not be found; that of the remaining number, twenty-two seceded to Roman Catholic exclusive schools, twenty-two went to parishes on which they had a claim, twenty-nine left Edinburgh without employment, and ten were taken away by their parents. Thus, about half the number entering the more sectarian school was lost by desertions and removals; and the other school, with not more than half the resources, sent out into the world, last year, an absolutely larger number—a number larger by one-fourth—of ragged boys and girls converted into useful and industrious young men and women. It has also sent them out, not merely instructed in the religion of their fathers, but taught by daily habit the important lesson, that no difference of creed should part young playfellows, or divide the interests of men and women in the common work of life.

As for the filth and crime among our wretched classes, who does not know that it is too often at bottom a question of position? The other day a young thief, apparently in full sincerity, when sentenced to four years' imprisonment, begged for fifteen of transportation.[43] If he were locked up for four years, and let loose again among his own companions, he could only thieve, as of old. Punish crime by all means—punish it severely while you pity the condition that produced it—but do not forget that there are thousands of poor devils plundering and begging, who cry, "Gentlemen, what else are we to do?" Such schools as those we have described just now, are good precisely in proportion to the means they offer for the manufacture of the raw material of thieves into honest artisans. And it is not only by ragged schools that this is done. Even while we write, our mind contains the fresh impressions of a visit to an unobtrusive London institution, at which a great deal of the same kind of good is done in another way. The pupils in this school are not simply the children of the wretched poor, many of whom have only a life of crime before them, but already convicted thieves. The place itself is a den of thieves—happily penitent.

We have walked up and down the New Road many hundreds of times; but it was only the other day—because we made a special search for it—that we noticed the name of the Preventive and Reformatory Institution, painted in white, at the corner of Gower Street North. At the locality that had been indicated to us we saw nothing but a rather handsome cabinetmaker's shop, with customers in it. A beadle,[44] in

---

41 A job for wages.
42 Places of employment.
43 Penal transportation was a legal sentence; convicts were sent to a penal colony, such as Australia.
44 Parish constable.

awful array of cocked hat, staff, and gold-laced coat, was standing over the way. We crossed, and diffidently requested him, as an official person, to direct us to Mr. Bowyer's Preventive and Reformatory Institution. He knew nothing about it. We described it as a place where ill-conducted boys and young thieves were taken in to be mended. No; he had never heard of it. And the stupid creature, with the uniform on his asinine person blazing in the sunshine, looked at us as though we had insulted the majesty of the law by mentioning a thief to him. A respectable tradesman, to whom we next applied, seemed to have a better opinion of the place, and pointed it out with alacrity. The cabinetmaker's shop itself was the establishment we sought.

Passing through the shop, we were conducted into a workroom behind, where several young men were at work upon different articles of cabinet ware, similar to those exposed for sale, which were also of their workmanship. They all touched their caps as we entered, and looked like respectable artisans. "But where are the thieves?"—"They are here," replied our conductor; "all whom you see have been in prison; and that boy," pointing to a bright-looking, intelligent lad, "was a regularly trained thief, and one of the best hands at that trade in London." A friend with us remarked upon the intelligence of their faces. "Why, yes," he replied, slightly laughing, "they have all lived by their wits till they are somewhat sharper than is needful." We were then conducted to a carpenters' shed, where heavier work was going on. One little fellow, who was sitting outside upon a bench, with a log before him, into which he was driving a chisel with great zeal, looked up at us with a comical twinkle in his eyes, as much as to say, "Arn't it a fine lark to think of me coming here!" He too was an old acquaintance with the police. From the carpenters' we went to the smiths' place, where everything bespoke great activity; and the sweat was pouring down the men's faces in a way that answered for the vigour of their labour. There are tailors and shoemakers also in the establishment, but we did not visit them.

We went into the kitchen, and there we learnt that everything, from the kettles to the kitchen range, had been made on the premises. We then mounted up to one of the sleeping-rooms. It contained more beds than was absolutely desirable, but that could not in the present state of things have been avoided. Each inmate has a separate iron bed; everything is clean; and the room is airy and well-ventilated. We visited, last, the refectory and school-room: a long, whitewashed apartment. Wooden benches and tables, and bookshelves containing some well-chosen books, completed the furniture. Here we sat down and began to ask questions. What are the rules? and how is the time spent?

The inmates rise at half-past five, and are allowed to go out of doors where they please until seven. Then they meet in the school-room, and have instruction in reading and writing, &c., until a quarter to eight o'clock, which is the time for prayers and breakfast. From half-past eight until one, they are kept hard at work. They have an hour for dinner and amusement; then follows hard work again until six o'clock, when there is an hour allowed for tea and recreation. After seven, there is secular instruction until it is time for prayers and bed. The day ends at a quarter to ten. A very good mixture, on the whole, of

> Books and work and healthful play,

as good Doctor Watts sings.[45] Admission into the society is not difficult to any who apply for it. The only limitations are the funds of the establishment. The inmates are of all ages above sixteen. They come entirely with their own consent, and there is nothing to prevent their leaving at any moment if they please. They consist of convicted criminals—thieves, who, from attendance at the ragged schools, or any other cause, acquire a wish to leave their ugly mode of life, and try a handsomer. Some are youths struggling

---

45   Isaac Watts, "How doth the Little Bee," *Divine Songs for the Use of Children* (1715).

on the brink of vice and wishing to keep honest. Of late years, notices of this institution have been put up in different prisons, in order that prisoners desiring to lead an honest life may know where to apply. Sometimes the candidates are chosen by the chaplains, and with these pupils of industry the government pays five shillings a-week. As soon as a boy enters, he is put to a given trade; if he shows no aptness for that, he is put to another.

As for the discipline, the boys themselves are appealed to, and depended upon, to observe the rules of the establishment; and their self-respect is re-instated in every possible way. During the periods of recreation no surveillance is exercised; indeed, from the nature of the premises, which consist of several houses in a densely crowded neighbourhood, it would be impossible to set up anything like bounds. Nevertheless they are not found to consort with their old companions—they are placed above them, and consider they have made a step upward in life. Mr. Bowyer tells us, that the appeal to their self-respect is his strong-hold over them all, and that he frequently entrusts boys who have been in the Institution for some time, with rather large sums of money to pay bills, &c.; that by so doing he had never once been made to suffer, never met with a breach of trust. To our anxious inquiry, How do you dispose of your inmates, when you have reformed them? he replied, "Most of them emigrate. Connected with the Institution there is a fund to enable us to send them out. All we have sent out have done well. Others again are draughted into the army and navy, and we have received excellent characters of them from their officers. Some, who are good workmen, have obtained situations in this immediate neighbourhood. There is a disposition to employ them, and a character from us is a sufficient recommendation. Each inmate remains two years, by which time his good habits have taken root. Every boy who enters, has to undergo a fortnight's separation from his companions, and a bread and water diet. This is a test of his sincerity; and is not introduced until some weeks after he has joined; because, it is thought, when he has once enjoyed for a time the benefits of the Institution, his solitude is more likely to be profitable. If he wishes to work in his solitude, he is allowed to have his tools."

The expression of the boys' faces we found to be, with few exceptions, good. Mr. Bowyer tells us, that the improvement which becomes visible in that respect is so great, that after the lapse of a few weeks he can sometimes scarcely recognise a new-comer for the same lad who entered. The exceptions remarked by us proved to be all of them new-comers, and we were assured that they would alter their expression in the course of a short time. Much of the success that has attended the working of this institution is undoubtedly owing to the present influence of the manager over the inmates. He has evidently a liking for his work. Another advantage is, the simplicity and directness of the effect; there is no waste of power; no cumbrous machinery stands between the programme and the performance; there is no philanthropic routine to be set in motion; what has to be done, can always be done at once. The expenses of the Institution are incurred only for things of the strictest necessity. Nothing is wasted upon appearances: consequently great good has been effected with comparatively little money. Mr. Bowyer, who is founder of the Institution, was not a rich man when he undertook the work. His income was decidedly limited, and his time much occupied by his employment; but he was interested in the ragged schools; many boys came to him, and said, if they had a refuge and the chance of doing better, they would thankfully leave their evil courses. Then, at his own expense, he engaged rooms and began with eight boys, giving them at all events a home. Friends have since gathered round the good Samaritan;[46] a list of noble patrons gives to his enterprise

---

46 Luke 10:30–35.

the prestige of their names; the value of his work is recognised by a free-hearted and free-handed public; and there is now every reason to believe that it will go on, increase, and prosper.

Frederick Denison Maurice
from *Learning and Working: Six Lectures Delivered in Willis's Rooms, London, in June and July, 1854* (1855)

Anglican clergyman and theologian [John] Frederick Denison Maurice (1805–72) led the mid-century Christian Socialist movement, which provided education and fostered cooperative associations for working men. Educated at Cambridge and Oxford, Maurice became professor of English literature, history, and theology at King's College London, where he co-founded Queen's College for women. His most enduring work, *The Kingdom of Christ* (1838), departed from his Tractarian contemporaries (see Newman, Education, Faith and Doubt) by emphasizing Christian unity. *Theological Essays* (1853) aroused controversy for its repudiation of eternal damnation, prompting Maurice's dismissal from King's College. Maurice founded the London Working Men's College in 1854; other teachers included Dante Gabriel Rossetti and John Ruskin (see Life Writing, Condition of England, Aesthetics and Culture, Gender and Sexuality). Maurice became a professor of philosophy at Cambridge in 1866.

In "Learning and Leisure," the second lecture published in *Learning and Working: Six Lectures Delivered in Willis's Rooms, London, in June and July, 1854* (1855), Maurice advocates the value of life experience as a preparation for learning, as well as the value of combining education with life experience.

Lecture 2: Learning and Leisure

The maxim, that all hope for the improvement of our country lies in the education of her youth, was examined in my last Lecture. I pointed out some of the difficulties which those experience who try to carry it into practice. The children of the poor, and of some who are not absolutely poor, are taken away for the business of the world, before they have acquired more than a smattering of knowledge from the school. That smattering of knowledge is not found to be of any great avail afterwards: the complaint has gone forth, that they have not cultivated the faculty or obtained the information which fit them to be serviceable citizens. Either they are awkward in the business to which they devote themselves, or in the pursuit of it they forget most of the little lore which they have brought with them. These statements may be much exaggerated; if they are true, there must be innumerable exceptions. But the evidence for them is too strong not to shake terribly the expectations which we had most of us built on our schools for boys and girls.

Is it possible, then, to found schools for men? If we cannot keep the young from business, may we teach the full-grown who are already busy? May we endeavour to give parents an interest in the education of their children by educating *them*? At first sight the difficulties in the way of such a project seem far greater than those which we are encountering now—the materials which we have to mould are so much harder and less pliable. But it is not always safe to act upon first impressions. What is the testimony of history on the subject? I endeavoured to trace the intellectual growth of Europe, but especially of England, through a series of ages, dwelling not upon events that happened in a corner, or that looked important to an individual or a party, but on those which were admitted by all to be of deep and wide significance. The inference appeared irresistible. Schools, according to the original force of the word, had not a direct application to children. They were places for preserving and expanding the studies which belong especially to men. They were intended to make men conscious that they had other organs besides the organs of sense, and that these had their proper objects and exercises.... Adult education was always taking precedence of juvenile education, determining its objects and for the most part its form, exercising an influence over the whole of society which that could never have exercised. In due time we saw the Grammar-school[47] arising; but it arose in connexion with the College, the College itself being under the shadow of the University. Gradually these schools for boys obtained an independent importance; their connexion with the adult teaching was not as obvious as it had been....

A conclusion honestly deduced from facts so various and so inconsistent as these, has some right to be considered of weight. Yet I can conceive that it may still appear to many quite incredible. It would appear so to me—scarcely any amount of historical evidence would induce me to accept it—if I felt that it really contradicted the principle which the champions of early education are asserting. They are certain that a full-grown man who has been without education all his life, must be in a more hopeless condition for receiving it than a child or a boy. There can, I conceive, be no doubt of that proposition. The question is, whether this is the condition in which our forefathers found those to whom they imparted their lessons; whether this is the condition in which we shall find the working-men of our day. The people of Kent and Northumbria might perhaps have seen no Christian Missionaries till Augustine[48] or Paulinus[49] came among them. But surely it would be a prodigious mistake to say that they had had no teaching which prepared them for that of the Missionaries, none but what interfered with it. They had the sun and moon and stars over their heads; they had the earth which they were trying to cultivate; they had the ocean on which they were sailing. They had children, brothers, wives, husbands. They had affections and sorrows; they had life and death. These were school-masters that had been at work upon them, and without whose aid Augustine and Paulinus, I apprehend, would not have done much....

The simple teaching of Alfred[50] in geography and history was addressed to people living in an island, and often seeing ships which came to them from other countries with strange things and stranger men; to people who had come to know that they were members of a nation, and therefore cared to know what the nation had been doing before they were born. If you wonder that in the centuries which followed, this kind of teaching seemed to be less prized than that which had no native associations, that which, as we

---

47 A type of school founded in or before the sixteenth century for teaching Latin; these later became known as secondary schools.
48 Augustine, first archbishop of Canterbury (d. c. 604), founder of the Christian church in the south of England.
49 Saint Paulinus, (c. 584–644), missionary who converted Northumbria to Christianity.
50 Alfred the Great (849–99), king of Wessex, promoted learning and literacy among his subjects.

are wont to say consisted only in verbal subtleties, I must ask you again to remember that words have as much to do with human beings as swords and ingots[51] have; that words were the special weapons of the scholar as distinguished from the warrior and the merchant, though all three were obliged to use them; that to enter into the force and conditions of these words and the relations in which they stood to things, did not look like trifling, but like a very solemn and serious occupation indeed....

There was, then, a previous education and discipline which led men in these ages to seek for certain kinds of intellectual food. They received the food if it met the particular hunger which had been awakened in them; if any other had been provided, it would have been rejected. Are we to suppose that it is altogether otherwise in our day? Have our working people received no education for which they are not indebted to us? They have, at all events, some of those books out of which their forefathers read. They see the sun and stars occasionally, even in London and Manchester; often enough to remove any scepticism as to their continued existence. They have brothers, wives, sons; they have to fight with sorrows, inward and outward—with life and death. They converse with each other in words, as men did in other days, as men do still in other classes. Their words follow certain laws, understood or misunderstood. They belong to a nation richer by a thousand years in history than it was when Alfred reigned. The government under which they live affects them for good or evil as his did the inhabitants of Wessex and the more distant provinces out of which our England was only beginning to form itself. I speak of that which they have in common with those who discovered that the lore of the schools concerned them. We are wont to boast that our century has immeasurable advantages which theirs could not dream of. We talk of our cheap books, magazines, newspapers. We delight to remember that our people throw shuttles, work engines, transmit lightning messages.[52] Can it be that they crave less for intellectual nourishment than those did upon whom we look almost with contempt, or that they have not the same organs for masticating and digesting it? ...

No one has ever doubted that the monastic life and discipline are closely connected with European civilization. If any Protestant is afraid to confess this fact, he must be an exceedingly bad Protestant; one who acts upon the maxim which in words he repudiates, that truth may be concealed, and that we may lie for God; one who is ignorant to what men we owe the first impulses towards reformation. It is, in fact, the denial of the worth of the monastic life which has led to a monstrous exaggeration of its worth, to the fancy which many in our day are cherishing, that it has a merit in itself, that it is less liable to abuse than other kinds of life, that it is desirable for all countries and all times; notions which the testimonies of monks and the histories of orders would much more completely refute than any criticisms or commentaries of ours upon them. The history of this life in the west,—for the monastic life of the east has quite a different meaning and character,—begins with the foundation of the monastery near Monte Casino in the middle of the sixth century. Thither came young Benedict in the year 528. There he established his order,[53] there he proclaimed the rule which became the model for all subsequent rules,[54] the standard which the restorers of discipline, after it had decayed, were always seeking to brin[g] back. The Benedictines of the congregation of St. Maur,[55] who in the seventeenth century were the most learned men in Europe, always maintained, that in devoting themselves to study they were following out the intentions of their

---

51 Metal (often gold or silver) bars.
52 Telegraph messages.
53 Around 529, St. Benedict of Nursia established the Abbey of Monte Cassino, source of the Benedictine Order.
54 *The Rule of Saint Benedict* (c. 530-47) laid out directions for monastic living, covering both spiritual and material aspects.
55 Order of French Benedictine monks founded in 1618.

founder.... What [Benedict] did was to lead men away from their farms and their merchandise, that they might become the teachers of nations, the asserters of a spiritual and divine foundation for the culture of western Europe. Now the following passage is taken from the Benedictine rule; it embodies a maxim, which you will perceive could not be merely a maxim, but was worked into the system.

> Idleness is the enemy of the soul. Therefore, at certain times the brethren must be occupied in the labour of the hands, and again at certain hours in divine study. We think that both ends may be accomplished by this arrangement. From Easter till the Calends[56] of October, let them go out in the morning, and from the first hour till nearly the fourth let them labour for the procuring of that which is necessary. Again, from the fourth hour to about the sixth let them be at leisure for reading. Rising from the table after the sixth hour, let them have an interval of rest upon their beds, or if any one should wish to read, let him so read that he may not disturb his neighbour. At the ninth hour let them again work till the evening if the necessity of the place or their poverty require it, and let them gather the fruits of the earth, seeing that those are true monks who live by the labour of their hands, as our fathers and the Apostles did. But let all things be done moderately and in measure on account of those that are feeble. From the Calends of October till the beginning of Lent, let them be at leisure for reading till the second hour, then from the third to the ninth hour let all labour at the work which is enjoined them. In the days of Lent, let them be at leisure for their readings from the early morning to the third hour, from thence to the eleventh let them do the work which is enjoined them.[57]

I quote this passage that you may see what principles were recognised as fundamental in this discipline. Working and learning so far, not learning and leisure, went hand in hand. Or rather, for this is the phrase which the Benedictine rule adopts, the reading was the leisure. The work of the hands demanded this to quicken and sustain it. The reading demanded equally the work of the hands as the condition of its being healthy and nutritive to the mind.... [L]et learning try to exist by itself and it dies; let common industry try to exist by itself and it dies. The ease to which each gives birth murders its parent....

All I have endeavoured to do in this Lecture is, to show you that the hindrances to this result do not arise from the fact that Work and Learning have a natural antipathy to each other. The practical difficulties in the present condition of society which hinder their union, which threaten to make the separation wider and more hopeless, I propose to consider hereafter. I shall conclude what I have been saying to-day, by alluding to the subject of which I was speaking at the end of the last Lecture. You may think that my remarks have had an almost exclusive reference to *men*,—that there was something ominous in my beginning from the monastery. On the contrary, I believe that the persons who have reconciled the schools with the world, the life of thought with the life of action, have been women, and most of all, the women of England. An attempt was made to unite them in the monastery, but it failed, as every attempt must fail ultimately, to do that by our methods which God has done by his methods. Looking at the best female literature of our own and of former days, this, as it seems to me, has been its great function, to claim that all thought shall bear upon action and express itself in action, that it shall not dwell apart in a region of its own. I believe there is another task equally necessary, which it falls, perhaps, more within

---

56 The first day of the month.
57 *The Rule of Saint Benedict* (c. 530–47).

our province to perform, to show that there cannot be action without thought, that the power to rule the world without must come from the world within. If each sex fulfils its own calling, there will be a blessing of which others besides those whom we call the working-people will be the inheritors. If either fails, both will suffer, and suffer in a worse way than by the loss of any material advantages. The question has been greatly discussed in our day, what is the force of the apostolical injunction, "If a man will not work, neither let him eat,"[58] and under what limitations it is applicable to us. There is a more terrible sentence still, of which we should seek diligently to avert the execution upon ourselves and upon those who have all they need of outward consolations—"If a man will not work, neither let him think."

Matthew Arnold
from "Art. VIII.—The Functions of Criticism at the Present Time" (1864)

Initially known for his poetry, in the 1860s and 1870s Matthew Arnold (1822–88) became England's leading critic with essays on literary, religious, social, and educational issues. The son of Thomas Arnold (see Education), he was educated at Winchester, Rugby, and Oxford. Beginning in 1851, Arnold worked as a school inspector for 35 years, observing the social conditions of education. In his criticism, Arnold denounced "Philistinism," his term for middle-class people's lack of liberal culture (see Arnold in Aesthetics and Culture); he argued for intellectual curiosity and openness, qualities he lauded in European educational models.

Arnold wrote "The Functions of Criticism at the Present Time" (1864) during his tenure as Professor of Poetry at Oxford University. First published in the *National Review* (the version excerpted here), the essay also appeared in Arnold's *Essays in Criticism* (1865) under the title "The Function of Criticism at the Present Time." In this passage, Arnold asserts the value of "disinterested" criticism in encouraging a vibrant moral culture.

Many objections have been made to a proposition which, in some remarks of mine on translating Homer,[59] I ventured to put forth; a proposition about criticism, and its importance at the present day. I said "of the literature of France and Germany, as of the intellect of Europe in general, the main effort, for now many years, has been a critical effort; the endeavor, in all branches of knowledge, theology, philosophy, history, art, science, to see the object as in itself it really is." I added, that owing to the operation in English literature of certain causes, "almost the last thing for which one would come to English literature was just that very thing which now Europe most desires—criticism;" and that the power and value of English

---

58 2 Thessalonians 3:10.
59 Homer (c. eighth century BCE), Greek poet thought to be the author of the *Iliad* and the *Odyssey*; Arnold published *On Translating Homer* in 1861.

literature was thereby impaired. More than one rejoinder declared that the importance I here assigned to criticism was excessive, and asserted the inherent superiority of the creative effort of the human spirit over its critical effort. And the other day, having been led by an excellent notice of Wordsworth[60] ... to turn again to his biography,[61] I found, in the words of this great man, whom I, for one, must always listen to with the profoundest respect, a sentence passed on the critic's business, which seems to justify every possible disparagement of it. Wordsworth says in one of his letters:

"The writers in these publications" (the Reviews),[62] "while they prosecute their inglorious employment, cannot be supposed to be in a state of mind very favourable for being affected by the finer influences of a thing so pure as genuine poetry."

... [E]verybody would admit that a false or malicious criticism had better never have been written. Everybody, too, would be willing to admit, as a general proposition, that the critical faculty is lower than the inventive. But is it true that criticism is really, in itself, a baneful and injurious employment; is it true that all time given to writing critiques on the works of others would be much better employed if it were given to original composition, of whatever kind this may be? ...

The critical power is of lower rank than the creative. True; but in assenting to this proposition, one or two things are to be kept in mind. It is undeniable that the exercise of a creative power, that a free creative activity, is the true function of man; it is proved to be so by his finding in it his true happiness. But it is undeniable, also, that men may have the sense of exercising this free creative activity in other ways than in producing great works of literature or art; ... they may have it in well-doing, they may have it in learning, they may have it even in criticising. This is one thing to be kept in mind. Another is, that the exercise of the creative power in the production of great works of literature or art, however high this exercise of it may rank, is not at all epochs and under all conditions possible; and that therefore labour may be vainly spent in attempting it, and may with more fruit be used in preparing for it, in rendering it possible. This creative power works with elements, with materials; what if it has not those materials, those elements, ready for its use? In that case it must surely wait till they are ready. Now in literature ... the elements with which the creative power works are ideas; the best ideas, on every matter which literature touches, current at the time; at any rate we may lay it down as certain that in modern literature no manifestation of the creative power not working with these can be very important or fruitful. And I say current at the time, not merely accessible at the time; for creative literary genius does not principally show itself in discovering new ideas; that is rather the business of the philosopher; the grand work of literary genius is a work of synthesis and exposition, not of analysis and discovery; its gift lies in the faculty of being happily inspired by a certain intellectual and spiritual atmosphere, by a certain order of ideas, when it finds itself in them; of dealing divinely with these ideas, presenting them in the most effective and attractive combinations, making beautiful works with them, in short. But it must have the atmosphere, it must find itself amidst the order of ideas, in order to work freely; and these it is not so easy to command. This is why great creative epochs in literature are so rare; this is why there is so much that is unsatisfactory in the productions of many men of real genius; because for the creation of a master-work of literature two powers must concur, the power of the man and the power of the moment, and the man

---

60 William Wordsworth (1770–1850), poet.
61 Christopher Wordsworth, *Memoirs of William Wordsworth* (1851).
62 Periodical magazines.

is not enough without the moment; the creative power has, for its happy exercise, appointed elements, and those elements are not in its own control.

Nay, they are more within the control of the critical power. It is the business of the critical power, as I said in the words already quoted, "in all branches of knowledge, theology, philosophy, history, art, science, to see the object as in itself it really is." Thus it tends, at last, to make an intellectual situation of which the creative power can profitably avail itself. It tends to establish an order of ideas, if not absolutely true, yet true by comparison with that which it displaces; to make the best ideas prevail. Presently these new ideas reach society, the touch of truth is the touch of life, and there is a stir and growth everywhere; out of this stir and growth come the creative epochs of literature....

It has long seemed to me that the burst of creative activity in our literature, through the first quarter of this century, had about it, in fact, something premature; and that from this cause its productions are doomed, most of them, in spite of the sanguine hopes which accompanied and do still accompany them, to prove hardly more lasting than the productions of far less splendid epochs. And this prematureness comes from its having proceeded without having its proper data, without sufficient materials to work with. In other words, the English poetry of the first quarter of this century, with plenty of energy, plenty of creative force, did not know enough. This makes Byron so one-toned, Shelley so incoherent,[63] Wordsworth even, profound as he is, yet so wanting in completeness and variety. Wordsworth cared little for books, and disparaged Goethe.[64] I admire Wordsworth, as he is, so much that I cannot wish him different; and it is vain, no doubt, to imagine such a man different from what he is, to suppose that he could have been different; but surely the one thing wanting to make Wordsworth an even greater poet than he is,—his thought richer, and his influence of wider application,—was that he should have read more books, among them, no doubt, those of that Goethe whom he disparaged without reading him. But to speak of books and reading may easily lead to a misunderstanding here. It was not really books and reading that lacked to our poetry, at this epoch; Shelley had plenty of reading, Coleridge had immense reading. Pindar and Sophocles[65]—as we all say so glibly, and often with so little discernment of the real import of what we are saying—had not many books; Shakespeare was no deep reader. True; but in the Greece of Pindar and Sophocles, in the England of Shakespeare, the poet lived in a current of ideas in the highest degree animating and nourishing to the creative power; society was, in the fullest measure, permeated by fresh thought, intelligent and alive; and this state of things is the true basis for the creative power's exercise, in this it finds its data, its materials, truly ready for its hand; all the books and reading in the world are only valuable as they are helps to this.... In the England of the first quarter of this century there was neither a national glow of life and thought, such as we had in the age of Elizabeth,[66] nor yet a culture and a force of learning and criticism such as were to be found in Germany. Therefore the creative power of poetry wanted for success in the highest sense, materials and a basis; a thorough interpretation of the world was necessarily denied to it.

... Ideas cannot be too much prized in and for themselves, cannot be too much lived with; but to transport them abruptly into the world of politics and practice, violently to revolutionise this world to

---

63 George Gordon Byron (1788–1824), poet; Percy Bysshe Shelley (1792–1822), poet.
64 Johann Wolfgang von Goethe (1749–1832), German poet and intellectual.
65 Samuel Taylor Coleridge (1772–1834), poet and critic; Pindar (c. 518–438 BCE), Greek poet; Sophocles (c. 496–06 BCE), Greek playwright.
66 Elizabeth I (1533–1603) ruled England from 1558 to 1603.

their bidding, that is quite another thing. There is the world of ideas and there is the world of practice; the French are often for suppressing one and the English the other; but neither is to be suppressed.... Joubert has said beautifully: "C'est la force et le droit qui règlent toutes choses dans le monde; la force en attendant le droit."[67] Force and right are the governors of this world; force till right is ready. *Force till right is ready*; and till right is ready, force, the existing order of things, is justified, is the legitimate ruler. But right is something moral, and implies inward recognition, free assent of the will; we are not ready for right—right, so far as we are concerned, is not ready—until we have attained this sense of seeing it and willing it. The way in which for us it may change and transform force, the existing order of things, and become, in its turn, the legitimate ruler of the world, will depend on the way in which, when our time comes, we see it and will it. Therefore for other people enamoured of their own newly discerned right, to attempt to impose it upon us as ours, and violently to substitute their right for our force, is an act of tyranny, and to be resisted. It sets at nought the second great half of our maxim, *force till right is ready*. This was the grand error of the French Revolution,[68] and its movement of ideas, by quitting the intellectual sphere and rushing furiously into the political sphere, ran, indeed, a prodigious and memorable course, but produced no such intellectual fruit as the movement of ideas of the Renaissance,[69] and created, in opposition to itself, what I may call an *epoch of concentration*....

... The Englishman has been called a political animal, and he values what is political and practical so much that ideas easily become objects of dislike in his eyes, and thinkers "miscreants," because ideas and thinkers have rashly meddled with politics and practice. This would be all very well if the dislike and neglect confined themselves to ideas transported out of their own sphere, and meddling rashly with practice; but they are inevitably extended to ideas as such, and to the whole life of intelligence; practice is everything, a free play of the mind is nothing. The notion of the free play of the mind upon all subjects being a pleasure in itself, being an object of desire, being an essential provider of elements without which a nation's spirit, whatever compensations it may have for them, must, in the long run, die of inanition, hardly enters into an Englishman's thoughts. It is noticeable that the word *curiosity*, which in other languages is used in a good sense, to mean, as a high and fine quality of man's nature, just this disinterested love of a free play of the mind on all subjects, for its own sake—it is noticeable, I say, that this word has in our language no sense of the kind, no sense but a rather bad and disparaging one. But criticism, real criticism, is essentially the exercise of this very quality; it obeys an instinct prompting it to try to know the best that is known and thought in the world, irrespectively of practice, politics, and everything of the kind; and to value knowledge and thought as they approach this best, without the intrusion of any other considerations whatever. This is an instinct for which there is, I think, little original sympathy in the practical English nature, and what there was of it has undergone a long benumbing period of check and suppression in the epoch of concentration which followed the French Revolution.

But epochs of concentration cannot well endure forever; epochs of expansion, in the due course of things, follow them. Such an epoch of expansion seems to be opening in this country. In the first place all danger of a hostile forcible pressure of foreign ideas upon our practice has long disappeared; like

---

67 French: Arnold's translation follows in the next sentence. Joseph Joubert, *Pensées* (1838).
68 During the French Revolution (1789-99), the French monarchy was deposed in favour of short-lived and bloody republics.
69 During the European Renaissance of the fifteenth and sixteenth centuries, interest in Greek and Roman traditions prompted the flourishing of art, literature, architecture, and politics.

the traveller in the fable, therefore, we begin to wear our cloak a little more loosely.[70] Then, with a long peace, the ideas of Europe steal gradually and amicably in, and mingle, though in infinitesimally small quantities at a time, with our own notions. Then, too, in spite of all that is said about the absorbing and brutalizing influence of our passionate material progress, it seems to me indisputable that this progress is likely, though not certain, to lead in the end to an apparition of intellectual life, and that man, after he has made himself perfectly comfortable and has now to determine what to do with himself next, may begin to remember that he has a mind, and that the mind may be made the source of great pleasure. I grant it is mainly the privilege of faith, at present, to discern this end to our railways, our business, and our fortune-making; but we shall see if, here as elsewhere, faith is not in the end the true prophet.... Flutterings of curiosity, in the foreign sense of the word, appear amongst us; and it is in these that criticism must look to find its account. Criticism first; a time of true creative activity, perhaps—which, as I have said, must inevitably be preceded amongst us by a time of criticism—hereafter, when criticism has done its work.

It is of the last importance that English criticism should clearly discern what rule for its course, in order to avail itself of the field now opening to it, and to produce fruit for the future, it ought to take. The rules may be given in one word; by being *disinterested*. And how is it to be disinterested? By keeping aloof from practice; by resolutely following the law of its own nature, which is to be a free play of the mind on all subjects which it touches; by steadily refusing to lend itself to any of those ulterior, political, practical considerations about ideas which plenty of people will be sure to attach to them, which perhaps ought often to be attached to them, which in this country at any rate are certain to be attached to them quite sufficiently, but which criticism has really nothing to do with. Its business is, as I have said, simply to know the best that is known and thought in the world, and, by in its turn making this known, to create a current of true and fresh ideas. Its business is to do this with inflexible honesty, with due ability; but its business is to do no more, and to leave alone all questions of practical consequences and applications, questions which will never fail to have due prominence given to them.... No other criticism will ever attain any real authority or make any real way towards its end—the creating a current of true and fresh ideas.

It is because criticism has so little kept in the pure intellectual sphere, has so little detached itself from practice, has been so directly polemical and controversial, that it has so ill accomplished, in this country, its true spiritual work; which is to keep man from a self-satisfaction which is retarding and vulgarizing, to lead him towards perfection, by making his mind dwell upon what is excellent in itself, and the absolute beauty and fitness of things. A polemical practical criticism makes men blind even to the ideal imperfection of their practice, makes them willingly assert its ideal perfection, in order the better to secure it against attack; and clearly this is narrowing and baneful for them. If they were reassured on the practical side, speculative considerations of ideal perfection they might be brought to entertain, and their spiritual horizon would thus gradually widen. Mr. Adderley[71] says to the Warwickshire farmers:

"Talk of the improvement of breed! Why, the race we ourselves represent, the men and women, the old Anglo-Saxon race, are the best breed in the whole world ...[72] The absence of a too enervating[73]

---

70 Aesop, "The North Wind and the Sun" (c. sixth century BCE).
71 Charles Bowyer Adderley (1814–1905), politician and social reformer.
72 Ellipsis in original.
73 Weakening.

climate, too unclouded skies, and a too luxurious nature, has produced so vigorous a race of people, and has rendered us so superior to all the world."

... They have in view opponents whose aim is not ideal, but practical, and in their zeal to uphold their own practice against these innovators, they go so far as even to attribute to this practice an ideal perfection. Somebody has been wanting to introduce a six-pound franchise,[74] or to abolish church-rates,[75] or to collect agricultural statistics by force, or to diminish local self-government. How natural, in reply to such proposals, very likely improper or ill-timed, to go a little beyond the mark, and to say stoutly: "Such a race of people as we stand, so superior to all the world! The old Anglo-Saxon race, the best breed in the whole world! I pray that our unrivalled happiness may last! I ask you whether, the world over or in past history, there is anything like it." And so long as criticism answers this dithyramb[76] by insisting that the old Anglo-Saxon race would be still more superior to all others if it had no church-rates, or that our unrivalled happiness would last yet longer with a six-pound franchise, so long will the strain, "The best breed in the whole world!" swell louder and louder, everything ideal and refining will be lost out of sight, and both the assailed and their critics will remain in a sphere, to say the truth, perfectly unintelligent, a sphere in which spiritual progression is impossible. But let criticism leave church-rates and the franchise alone, and in the most candid spirit, without a single lurking thought of practical innovation, confront with our dithyramb this paragraph on which I stumbled in a newspaper ... —

"A shocking child murder has just been committed at Nottingham. A girl named Wragg left the Workhouse[77] there on Saturday morning with her young illegitimate child. The child was soon afterwards found dead on Mapperly Hills,[78] having been strangled. Wragg is in custody."

Nothing but that; but ... how eloquent, how suggestive are those few lines! "Our old Anglo-Saxon breed, the best in the whole world!"—how much that is harsh and ill-favoured there is in this best. Wragg! ... In Ionia and Attica[79] they were luckier in this respect than "the best race in the world;" by the Ilissus[80] there was no Wragg, poor thing! And "our unrivalled happiness"—what an element of grimness, bareness, and hideousness mixes with it and blurs it; the workhouse, the dismal Mapperly Hills,—how dismal those who have seen them will remember;—the gloom, the smoke, the cold, the strangled illegitimate child! ... And the final touch—short, bleak, and inhuman: *Wragg is in custody*. The sex lost in the confusion of our unrivalled happiness; or, shall I say, the superfluous Christian name[81] lopped off by the straightforward vigour of our old Anglo-Saxon breed? There is profit for the spirit in such contrasts as these; criticism serves the cause of perfection by establishing them. By eluding sterile conflict, by refusing to remain in the sphere where alone narrow and relative conceptions have any worth and validity, criticism may diminish

---

74 The 1832 Reform Act extended the franchise to propertied adult males holding a lease of more than ten pounds per year; the six-pound franchise would lower this requirement, thus enabling more men to vote.
75 A tax imposed on churchgoers to maintain the church and its functions.
76 An emphatic speech.
77 Under the 1834 Poor Law, workhouses were established to provide minimal food and accommodation for the poor; those able to work were required to do so.
78 Mapperley forms part of Nottingham in the East Midlands.
79 Ionia was a region, including the west coast of present-day Turkey and the Aegean islands, colonized by Greece, Persia, and Rome; Attica was the region in Greece that included Athens.
80 A stream just outside Athens.
81 First name.

its momentary importance, but only in this way has it a chance of gaining admittance for those wider and more perfect conceptions to which all its duty is really owed....

It will be said that it is a very subtle and indirect action which I am thus prescribing for criticism, and that by embracing in this manner the Indian virtue of detachment[82] and abandoning the sphere of practical life, it condemns itself to a slow and obscure work. Slow and obscure it may be, but it is the only proper work of criticism. The mass of mankind will never have any ardent zeal for seeing things as they are; very inadequate ideas will always satisfy them.... The rush and roar of practical life will always have a dizzying and attracting effect upon the most collected spectator, and tend to draw him into its vortex; most of all will this be the case where that life is so powerful as it is in England. But it is only by remaining collected, and refusing to lend himself to the point of view of the practical man, that the critic can do the practical man any service; and it is only by the greatest sincerity in pursuing his own course, and by at last convincing even the practical man of his sincerity, that he can escape misunderstandings which perpetually threaten him.

For the practical man is not apt for fine distinctions, and yet in these distinctions truth and the highest culture greatly find their account. But it is not easy to lead a practical man,—unless you reassure him as to your practical intentions you have no chance of leading him—to see that a thing which he has always been used to look at from one side only, which he greatly values, and which, looked at from that side more than deserves, perhaps, all the prizing and admiring which he bestows upon it—that this thing looked at from another side may appear much less beneficent and beautiful, and yet retain all its claims to our practical allegiance. Where shall we find language innocent enough, how shall we make the spotless purity of our intentions evident enough, to enable us to say to the political Englishman that the British constitution itself, which seen from the practical side, looks such a magnificent organ of progress and virtue, seen from the speculative side,—with its compromises, its love of facts, its horror of theory, its studied avoidance of clear thoughts,—that seen from this side, our august constitution sometimes looks—forgive me, shade of Lord Somers![83]—a colossal machine for the manufacture of Philistines.[84] How is Cobbett[85] to say this and not be misunderstood, blackened as he is with the smoke of a lifelong conflict in the field of political practice? how is Mr. Carlyle to say it and not be misunderstood, after his furious raid into this field with his *Latter-Day Pamphlets*?[86] how is Mr. Ruskin, after his pugnacious political economy?[87] I say the critic must keep out of the region of immediate practice in the political, social, humanitarian sphere, if he wants to make a beginning for that more free speculative treatment of things, which may perhaps one day make its benefits felt even in this sphere, but in a natural and thence irresistible manner....

How serious a matter it is to try and resist, I had ample opportunity of experiencing when I ventured some time ago to criticise the celebrated first volume of Bishop Colenso.[88] The echoes of the storm which

---

82 In both Hinduism and Buddhism, detachment from the world and from the material self is perceived as virtuous.
83 John Somers (1651–1716), politician, helped to draft the Bill of Rights.
84 Enemies of the Israelites in the Old Testament; a term used in the nineteenth century to refer to someone ignorant or uncultured.
85 William Cobbett (1763–1835), political advocate and writer.
86 Thomas Carlyle (1795–1881), writer. See Condition of England, Faith and Doubt; *Latter-Day Pamphlets* (1850).
87 John Ruskin (1819–1900), critic. See Life Writing, Condition of England, Aesthetics and Culture, Gender and Sexuality.
88 John William Colenso (1814–83), South African bishop and scholar; the first volume of *The Pentateuch and Book of Joshua Critically Examined* (1862) was heavily criticized for stating that the Bible "is not historically true," for example in Matthew Arnold, "The Bishop and the Philosopher" (1863). See Faith and Doubt.

was then raised I still, from time to time, hear grumbling round me. That storm arose out of a misunderstanding almost inevitable. It is a result of no little culture to attain to a clear perception that science and religion are two wholly different things; the multitude will for ever confound them, but happily that is of no great real importance, for while it imagines itself to live by its false science it does really live by its true religion. Dr. Colenso, however, in his first volume did all he could to strengthen the confusion, and to make it dangerous.... I criticised Bishop Colenso's speculative confusion. Immediately there was a cry raised: "What is this? here is a liberal attacking a liberal. Do not you belong to the movement? are not you a friend of truth. Is not Bishop Colenso in pursuit of truth? then speak with proper respect of his book ..."

But criticism cannot follow this coarse and indiscriminate method. It is unfortunately possible for a man in pursuit of truth to write a book which reposes upon a false conception. Even the practical consequences of a book are to genuine criticism no recommendation of it, if the book is, in the highest sense, blundering....

In criticism these are elementary laws; but they never can be popular, and in this country they have been very little followed, and one meets immense obstacles in following them. That is a reason for asserting them again and again. Criticism must maintain its independence of the practical spirit and its aims. Even with well-meant efforts of the practical spirit it must express dissatisfaction if in the sphere of the ideal they seem impoverishing and limiting. It must not hurry on to the goal because of its practical importance. It must be patient, and know how to wait; and flexible, and know how to attach itself to things and how to withdraw from them. It must be apt to study and praise elements that for the fulness of spiritual perfection are wanted, even though they belong to a power which in the practical sphere may be maleficent. It must be apt to discern the spiritual shortcomings or illusions of powers that in the practical sphere may be beneficent. And this without any notion of favoring or injuring, in the practical sphere, one power or the other; without any notion of playing off, in this sphere, one power against the other. When one looks, for instance, at the English Divorce Court—an institution which no doubt has its practical conveniences, but which in the ideal sphere is so hideous; an institution which neither makes separation impossible nor makes it decent, which allows a man to get rid of his wife, or a wife of her husband, but makes them drag one another first, for the public edification, through a mire of unutterable infamy[89]—when one looks at this charming institution, I say, with its crowded benches, its newspaper reports, and its money-compensations, this institution in which the gross unregenerate British Philistine has indeed stamped an image of himself—one may be permitted to find the marriage-theory of Catholicism refreshing and elevating.

... Let us think of quietly enlarging our stock of true and fresh ideas, and not, as soon as we get an idea or half an idea, be running out with it into the street and trying to make it rule there. Our ideas will, in the end, shape the world all the better for maturing a little....

If I have insisted so much on the course which criticism must take where politics and religion are concerned, it is because, where these burning matters are in question, it is most likely to go astray. In general its course is determined for it by the idea which is the law of its being; the idea of a disinterested endeavor to learn and propagate the best that is known and thought in the world, and thus to establish a

---

89   Opened in 1858 after the 1857 Matrimonial Causes Act, the Divorce Court could grant divorces to husbands on the basis of adultery and to wives on the basis of adultery plus another matrimonial offence, such as cruelty, bestiality, sodomy, bigamy, or incest. Newspapers publicized court proceedings, which provided salacious details of people's private lives.

current of fresh and true ideas. By the very nature of things, as England is not all the world, much of the best that is known and thought in the world cannot be of English growth, must be foreign ... ; the English critic, therefore, must dwell much on foreign thought, and with particular heed on any part of it, which, while significant and fruitful in itself, is for any reason likely to escape him. Judging is often spoken of as the critic's one business; and so in some sense it is; but the judgment which almost insensibly forms itself in a fair and clear mind, along with fresh knowledge, is the valuable one; and thus knowledge, and ever fresh knowledge, must be his great concern for himself, and it is by communicating fresh knowledge, and letting his own judgment pass along with it,—but insensibly, and in the second place not the first, as a sort of companion and clue, not as an abstract law-giver,—that he will generally do most good to his readers. Sometimes, no doubt, for the sake of establishing an author's place in literature, and his relation to a central standard, (and if this is not done how are we to get at our *best in the world*) criticism may have to deal with a subject-matter so familiar that fresh knowledge is out of the question, and then it must be all judgment; an enunciation and detailed application of principles. Here the great safeguard is never to let oneself become abstract, always to retain an intimate and lively consciousness of what one is saying, and, the moment this fails us, to be sure that something is wrong. But under all circumstances this mere judgment and application of principles is, in itself, not the most satisfactory work to the critic; like Mathematics it is tautological,[90] and cannot well give us, like fresh learning, the sense of creative activity. To have this sense, is as I said at the beginning, the great happiness and the great proof of being alive, and it is not denied to criticism to have it; but then criticism must be sincere, simple, flexible, ardent, ever widening its knowledge. Then it may have in no contemptible measure, a joyful sense of creative activity: a sense which a man of insight and conscience will prefer to what he might derive from a poor, starved, fragmentary, inadequate creation. And at some epochs no other creation is possible.

Still, in full measure, the sense of creative activity belongs only to genuine creation; in literature we must never forget that. But what true man of letters ever can forget it? It is no such common matter for a gifted nature to come into possession of a current of true and living ideas, and to produce amidst the inspiration of them, that we are likely to underrate it. The epochs of Æschylus[91] and Shakespeare make us feel their pre-eminence. In an epoch like those, is, no doubt, the true life of a literature; there is the promised land[92] towards which criticism can only beckon. That promised land it will not be ours to enter, and we shall die in the wilderness: but to have desired to enter it, to have saluted it from afar, is already, perhaps, the best distinction among contemporaries; it will certainly be the best title to esteem with posterity.

---

90 That is, it repeats a statement in order to prove it.
91 Aeschylus (c. 525–456 BCE), Greek playwright.
92 See Exodus 12:25.

Emily Davies
from *The Higher Education of Women* (1866)

Emily Davies (1830–1921) campaigned for women's suffrage and admission to universities and professions. She also edited the *English Woman's Journal* and the *Victoria Magazine* with members of the Langham Place Group and co-founded Girton, the first women's college at Cambridge University. Davies lobbied for the inclusion of girls' education in the Schools Inquiry Commission of 1864, giving evidence (the first time a woman had served as an expert before a Royal Commission). With Barbara Leigh Smith Bodichon (see Gender and Sexuality), Helen Taylor, Frances Power Cobbe (see Faith and Doubt), and others, she helped obtain almost 1,500 signatures on a petition for women's suffrage, which John Stuart Mill (see Life Writing, Condition of England, Gender and Sexuality) presented to parliament in 1866.

In the following passage from *The Higher Education of Women* (1866), her earliest and most renowned book, Davies criticizes inadequate educational opportunities for women and articulates women's desire for wider "scope for action."

~

Chapter 3: Things as They Are

Whether it is owing to the prevailing confusion of ideas as to the objects of female education, or to whatever cause it may be attributed, there can be little doubt that the thing itself is held in slight esteem. No one indeed would go so far as to say that it is not worth while to educate girls at all. *Some* education is held to be indispensable, but how much is an open question; and the general indifference operates in the way of continually postponing it to other claims, and, above all, in shortening the time allotted to systematic instruction and discipline. Parents are ready to make sacrifices to secure a tolerably good and complete education for their sons; they do not consider it necessary to do the same for their daughters. Or perhaps it would be putting it more fairly to say, that a very brief and attenuated course of instruction, beginning late and ending early, is believed to constitute a good and complete education for a woman.

It is usually assumed that when a boy's school education has once begun, which it does at a very early age, it is to go on steadily till he is a man. A boy who leaves school at sixteen or eighteen, either enters upon some technical course of training for a business or profession, or he passes on to the University, and from thence to active work of some sort or other. In other words, he is *in statu pupillari*[93] until general education and professional instruction are superseded by the larger education supplied by the business of life. In the education of girls no such regular order appears. A very usual course seems to be for girls to spend their early years in a haphazard kind of way, either at home, or in not very regular attendance at an inferior school; after which they are sent for a year or two to a school or

---

93 Latin: in a state of pupilage.

college to finish.[94] The heads of schools complain with one voice that they are called upon to "finish" what has never been begun, and that to attempt to give anything like a sound education, in the short time at their disposal, is perfectly hopeless. But, to take the most favourable case,—that of a girl so well prepared that she is able to make good use of the teaching provided in a first-rate school,—just at the moment when she is making real, substantial progress, she is taken away. At sixteen, seventeen, or eighteen, as the case may be, her education comes to an abrupt pause. When she marries, it may be said to begin again; but between leaving school and marriage there is usually an interval of at least three or four years, if not a much longer period. These years a youth spends, as has been before said, in preparation for his future career. In the case of girls, no such preparation seems to be considered necessary.

Is this reasonable? Apart from immediate pecuniary necessity, is it desirable that the regular education of women should be considered as finished at the age of eighteen? ...

So fixed and wide-spread a custom must have had, at some time or other, even if it has not now, a meaning and a justification. And this may perhaps be found in the fact that our mothers and our grandmothers were accustomed to undergo at home, after leaving school, what was in fact an apprenticeship to household management. It seems indeed at one time to have been customary to apprentice girls of what we now call the middle class, to trades,—as we find George Herbert urging his Country Parson not to put his children "into vain trades and unbefitting the reverence of their father's calling, such as are taverns for men and lacemaking for women,"[95]—but even where there was no apprenticeship to a specific business, the round of household labours would supply a very considerable variety of useful occupation. An active part in these labours would naturally devolve upon the daughters of the house, who would thus be forming habits of industry and order invaluable in after life.

Probably a great many fathers, profoundly ignorant as they are of the lives of women, cherish a vague imagination that the same kind of thing is going on still. If Providence should at any time lead them to spend a week in the society of their daughters, under ordinary circumstances—not when illness has altered the usual current of affairs—they would find that this is very far from being the case. That great male public, which spends its days in chambers and offices and shops, knows little of what is going on at home. Writers in newspapers and magazines are fond of talking about the nursery, as if every household contained a never-ending supply of young children, on whom the grown-up daughters might be practising the art of bringing up. Others have a great deal to say about the kitchen, assuming it to be desirable that the ladies of the house should supersede, or at least assist, the cook. In that case, where there is a mother with two or three daughters, we should have four or five cooks. The undesirableness of such a multiplication of artists need scarcely be pointed out.... Needlework, again, occupies a much larger space in the imagination of writers than it does in practical life. Except in families where there are children, there is very little plain needlework to be done, and what there is, many people make a point of giving out, on the ground that it is better to pay a half-starved needlewoman for work done, than to give her the money in the form of alms.

---

94 Finishing schools for girls provided a year or two of education in late adolescence; most focused on cultural subjects and social skills such as painting, drawing, modern languages, and music.
95 George Herbert, *A Priest to the Temple* (1652).

Having mentioned needlework, cookery, and the care of children, we seem to have come to an end of the household work in which ladies are supposed to take part. If young women of eighteen and upwards are learning anything in their daily life at home, it must be something beside and beyond the acquirement of dexterity in ordinary domestic arts.

Many fathers, however, are no doubt aware that their daughters have very little to do. But that seems to them anything but a hardship. They wish they had a little less to do themselves, and can imagine all sorts of interesting pursuits to which they would betake themselves if only they had a little more leisure. Ladies, it may be said, have their choice, and they must evidently prefer idleness, or they would find something to do. If this means that half-educated young women do not choose steady work when they have no inducement whatever to overcome natural indolence, it is no doubt true. Women are not stronger-minded than men, and a commonplace young woman can no more work steadily without motive or discipline than a commonplace young man....

How true this is, the friends and counsellors of girls could abundantly testify. There is no point on which schoolmistresses are more unanimous and more emphatic than on the difficulty of knowing what to do with girls after leaving school. People who have not been brought into intimate converse with young women have little idea of the extent to which they suffer from perplexities of conscience. "The discontent of the modern girl" is not mere idle self-torture. Busy men and women—and people with disciplined minds—can only, by a certain strain of the imagination, conceive the situation. If they at all entered into it, they could not have the heart to talk as they do. For the case of the modern girl is peculiarly hard in this, that she has fallen upon an age in which idleness is accounted disgraceful. The social atmosphere rings with exhortations to act, act in the living present. Everywhere we hear that true happiness is to be found in work—that there can be no leisure without toil—that people who do nothing are unfruitful fig-trees which cumber the ground. And in this atmosphere the modern girl lives and breathes. She is not a stone, and she does not live underground. She hears people talk—she listens to sermons—she reads books....

... She is bidden to "look around her"—to do the duty that lies nearest[96]—to teach in the schools, or visit the poor—to take up a pursuit—to lay down a course of study and stick to it. She looks around her, and sees no particular call to active exertion. The duties that lie in the way are swallowed up by an energetic mother or elder sister; very possibly she has no vocation for philanthropy—and the most devoted philanthropists are the most urgent in warning off people who lack the vocation—or she lives in a village where the children are better taught than she could teach them, and the poor are already too much visited by the clergy-man's family; she feels no sort of impulse to take up any particular pursuit, or to follow out a course of study; and so long as she is quiet and amiable, and does not get out of health, nobody wants her to do anything.... Ought we to wonder if, in the great majority of cases, girls let themselves go drifting down the stream, despising themselves, but listlessly yielding to what seems to be their fate?

An appeal to natural guides is most often either summarily dismissed, or received with reproachful astonishment. It is considered a just cause for surprise and disappointment, that well brought up girls, surrounded with all the comforts of home, should have a wish or a thought extending beyond its precincts. And, perhaps, it is only natural that parents should be slow to encourage their daughters in aspirations after any duties and interests besides those of ministering to their comfort and pleasure. In taking for

---

96 Thomas Carlyle, *Sartor Resartus* (1833–34). See Faith and Doubt.

granted that this is the only object, other than that of marriage, for which women were created, they are but adopting the received sentiment of society. No doubt, too, they honestly believe that, in keeping their daughters to themselves till they marry, they are doing the best thing for them, as well as pleasing themselves. If the daughters take a different view, parents think it is because they are young and inexperienced, and incompetent to judge.... No doubt young people are ignorant, and want guidance. But they should be helped and advised, not silenced. Parents take upon themselves a heavy responsibility when they hastily crush the longing after a larger and more purposeful life.

That such an impulse is worthy of respect can scarcely be denied. The existence of capacities is in itself an indication that they are intended for some good purpose.... To have a soul which can be satisfied with vanities is not eminently virtuous and Christian, but the reverse. To be awake to responsibilities, sensitive in conscience, quickly responsive to all kindling influences, is a sign that education has, so far, done a good work. A flowing river is no doubt more troublesome to manage than a tranquil pool; but pools, if let alone too long, are apt to become noxious, as well as useless. The current may require to be wisely directed; but that there should be a current of being, wanting to set itself somewhere, is surely a cause for thankful rejoicing....

The representation here given is, of course, not universally applicable. It is quite possible that in some senses, and to some persons, an apparently empty life may be easier, and even richer, than one of toil. There are people to whom the Happy Valley[97] kind of life is by no means intolerable; and even earnest-minded and conscientious girls, urged by a strong sense of the heinousness of discontent, often manage to crush troublesome aspirations, and make themselves happy. There is something undignified in being miserable, without a just and intelligible cause to show for it; and many young women, capable of higher things, accommodate themselves with a considerable degree of cheerfulness to a narrow and unsatisfying round of existence. Nor is it intended to represent ladies as habitually doing nothing. On the contrary, they have many resources. Among them are various arts and handicrafts, gardening, letter-writing, and much reading. Of these, the last is perhaps the most popular and the most delusive. A girl who is "very fond of reading" is considered to be happily suited with never-failing occupation, and no thought is taken as to what is to come of her reading. On this subject, the observations of Miss Aikin, herself an experienced reader, are worth considering. "Continual reading," she says, "if desultory, and without a definite object, favours indolence, unsettles opinions, and of course enfeebles the mental and moral energies."[98] ...

The same might be said of all merely *dilettante* occupation. Its fault is simply that it *is dilettante*—literally a pastime. It may as well be done, if nothing else turns up, and that is all. And this drawback, belonging to nearly all the ordinary work of young women, they are by themselves unable to overcome. Of course, the case is partly in their own hands, and those who are by nature abnormally energetic, will make a career for themselves in spite of difficulties. Where the inward impulse is irrepressible, it becomes a lantern to the feet, and a lamp unto the path,[99] making the way of duty plain and unmistakable. But for the few whose course is thus illumined, there will be the many hovering in uneasy doubt, their consciences and intellects just lively enough to make them restless and unhappy, not sufficiently clear in their minds as to right and wrong, either to be nerved for vigorous action, or to accept contentedly the conventional duty of

---

97 In Samuel Johnson's *Rasselas* (1759), the protagonist grows weary of the Happy Valley, where the inhabitants know only "the soft vicissitudes of pleasure and repose."
98 Lucy Aikin, *Memoirs, Miscellanies and Letters: Of the Late Lucy Aikin* (1864).
99 Psalm 119:105.

quiescence. There must be something wrong in social regulations which make a demand for exceptional wisdom and strength on the part of any particular class; and that such a demand is made upon average young women is sufficiently clear. What society says to them seems to be something to this effect. Either you have force enough to win a place in the world, in the face of heavy discouragement, or you have not. If you have, the discipline of the struggle is good for you; if you have not, you are not worth troubling about. Is not this a hard thing to say to commonplace girls, not professing to be better or stronger than their neighbours? ... More than any other class, at the same age, they are exempted from direction and control—liberally gifted with the kind of freedom enjoyed by the denizens of a village pound. Within their prescribed sphere, they may wander at will, and if they "there small scope for action see," it is explained to them that they must not "for this give room to discontent;" nor let their time "be spent in idly dreaming" how they might be

> More free
> From outward hindrance or impediment.
> For presently this hindrance thou shalt find
> That without which all goodness were a task
> So slight, that virtue never could grow strong.[100]

In reply to such admonitions they are tempted to inquire what task, other than that of dreaming, is set before them—what virtue, always excepting that one virtue of passive submission, has any chance of growing strong under such conditions. The "slow," who sink into dull inertia, and the "fast,"[101] who get rid of their superfluous energy in silly extravagances, have alike the excuse, that at the moment when they need the support of a routine explained and justified by a reasonable purpose, discipline and stimulus are at once withdrawn, leaving in their place no external support beyond the trivial demands and restraints of conventional society.

It may seem that an exaggerated importance is here attached to the interval between school and marriage; and if the considerations brought forward had reference to this period only, the charge would be just. But rightly to estimate the value of these years, we must bear in mind that they are the spring-time of life.... It is then that an impress is given to character which lasts through life. Opportunities then thrown away or misused can scarcely be recovered in later years. And it has seemed necessary to dwell upon the existing tenour of young women's lives, because, in dealing with the question of extending the duration of female education, we must be largely influenced by our conception of the alternative involved in leaving things as they are. It has been said that the end of education is "to form a nation of living, orderly men."[102] If it has been shown that the course now pursued tends to make a large part of the nation inanimate and disorderly, a case would seem to be established for urging efforts at improvement.

---

100 Richard Chenevix Trench, "Thou cam'st not to thy place by accident" (1835).
101 Without regard for decorum.
102 F.D. Maurice, *Has the Church, or the State, the Power to Educate the Nation? A Course of Lectures* (1839).

Henry Maudsley
from "Sex in Mind and in Education" (1874)

Henry Maudsley (1835–1918) achieved fame as a prominent "alienist," or doctor who treats mental illnesses. After studying medicine, he pursued a career in psychiatry, superintending the Manchester Royal Lunatic Asylum (1859–62) and eventually donating £30,000 to establish London's Maudsley Hospital in 1914 for treating, researching, and teaching about mental illness. Maudsley co-edited the *Journal of Mental Science* (1863–78), lectured on insanity at St. Mary's Hospital (1868–81), taught medical jurisprudence at University College London (1869–79), and wrote 11 books and almost 80 articles and pamphlets. In works such as the well-regarded *Physiology and Pathology of Mind* (1867), he stressed the physical underpinnings of mental illness and emphasized ideas of inheritance and degeneration.

In the following selection from "Sex in Mind and in Education," published in the *Fortnightly Review*, Maudsley argues that essential physiological differences (especially the menstrual cycle) mean that women are physically and psychologically unfit for the kind of education given to men.

Those who view without prejudice, or with some sympathy, the movements for improving the higher education of women, and for throwing open to them fields of activity from which they are now excluded, have a hard matter of it sometimes to prevent a feeling of reaction being aroused in their minds by the arguments of the most eager of those who advocate the reform. Carried away by their zeal into an enthusiasm which borders on or reaches fanaticism, they seem positively to ignore the fact that there are significant differences between the sexes, arguing in effect as if it were nothing more than an affair of clothes, and to be resolved, in their indignation at woman's wrongs, to refuse her the simple rights of her sex. They would do better in the end if they would begin by realising the fact that the male organization is one, and the female organization another, and that, let come what come may in the way of assimilation of female and male education and labour, it will not be possible to transform a woman into a man....

It is quite evident that many of those who are foremost in their zeal for raising the education and social status of woman, have not given proper consideration to the nature of her organization, and to the demands which its special functions make upon its strength. These are matters which it is not easy to discuss out of a medical journal; but, in view of the importance of the subject at the present stage of the question of female education, it becomes a duty to use plainer language than would otherwise be fitting in a literary journal. The gravity of the subject can hardly be exaggerated. Before sanctioning the proposal to subject woman to a system of mental training which has been framed and adapted for men, and under which they have become what they are, it is needful to consider whether this can be done without serious injury to her health and strength. It is not enough to point to exceptional instances of women who have undergone such a training, and have proved their capacities when tried by the same standard as men; without doubt there are women who can, and will, so distinguish themselves, if stimulus be applied and opportunity given; the question is, whether they may not do it at a cost which is too large a demand upon the resources of their nature. Is it well for them to contend on equal terms with men for the goal of man's ambition?

Let it be considered that the period of the real educational strain will commence about the time when, by the development of the sexual system, a great revolution takes place in the body and mind, and an extraordinary expenditure of vital energy is made, and will continue through those years after puberty when, by the establishment of periodical functions,[103] a regularly recurring demand is made upon the resources of a constitution that is going through the final stages of its growth and development. The energy of a human body being a definite and not inexhaustible quantity, can it bear, without injury, an excessive mental drain as well as the natural physical drain which is so great at that time? Or, will the profit of the one be to the detriment of the other? It is a familiar experience that a day of hard physical work renders a man incapable of hard mental work, his available energy having been exhausted. Nor does it matter greatly by what channel the energy be expended; if it be used in one way it is not available for use in another. When Nature spends in one direction, she must economise in another direction.... The time of puberty and the years following it are therefore justly acknowledged to be a critical time for the female organization. The real meaning of the physiological changes which constitute puberty is, that the woman is thereby fitted to conceive and bear children, and undergoes the bodily and mental changes that are connected with the development of the reproductive system. At each recurring period there are all the preparations for conception, and nothing is more necessary to the preservation of female health than that these changes should take place regularly and completely. It is true that many of them are destined to be fruitless so far as their essential purpose is concerned, but it would be a great mistake to suppose that on that account they might be omitted or accomplished incompletely, without harm to the general health. They are the expressions of the full physiological activity of the organism. Hence it is that the outbreak of disease is so often heralded, or accompanied, or followed by suppression or irregularity of these functions. In all cases they make a great demand upon the physiological energy of the body; they are sensitive to its sufferings, however these be caused; and, when disordered, they aggravate the mischief that is going on.

When we thus look the matter honestly in the face, it would seem plain that women are marked out by nature for very different offices in life from those of men, and that the healthy performance of her special functions renders it improbable she will succeed, and unwise for her to persevere, in running over the same course at the same pace with him.... Nor is it a sufficient reply to this argument to allege, as is sometimes done, that there are many women who have not the opportunity of getting married, or who do not aspire to bear children; for whether they care to be mothers or not, they cannot dispense with those physiological functions of their nature that have reference to that aim, however much they might wish it, and they cannot disregard them in the labor of life without injury to their health. They cannot choose but to be women; cannot rebel successfully against the tyranny of their organization, the complete development and function whereof must take place after its kind. This is not the expression of prejudice nor of false sentiment; it is the plain statement of a physiological fact. Surely, then, it is unwise to pass it by; first or last it must have its due weight in the determination of the problem of woman's education and mission; it is best to recognize it plainly, however we may conclude finally to deal with it....

---

103 Menstruation.

If the foregoing reflections be well grounded, it is plain we ought to recognise sex in education, and to provide that the method and aim of mental culture should have regard to the specialties of woman's physical and mental nature. Each sex must develope after its kind; and if education in its fundamental meaning be the external cause to which evolution is the internal answer, if it be the drawing out of the internal qualities of the individual into their highest perfection by the influence of the most fitting external conditions, there must be a difference in the method of education of the two sexes answering to differences in their physical and mental natures. Whether it be only the statement of a partial truth, that "for valour he" is formed, and "for beauty she and sweet attractive grace,"[104] or not, it cannot be denied that they are formed for different functions, and that the influence of those functions pervades and affects essentially their entire beings. There is sex in mind and there should be sex in education.

Let us consider, then, what an adapted education must have regard to. In the first place, a proper regard to the physical nature of women means attention given, in their training, to their peculiar functions and to their foreordained work as mothers and nurses of children. Whatever aspirations of an intellectual kind they may have, they cannot be relieved from the performance of those offices so long as it is thought necessary that mankind should continue on earth.... Moreover, [those offices] are work which, like all work, may be well or ill done, and which, in order to be done well, cannot be done in a perfunctory manner, as a thing by the way. It will have to be considered whether women can scorn delights, and live laborious days of intellectual exercise and production, without injury to their functions as the conceivers, mothers, and nurses of children. For it would be an ill thing, if it should so happen, that we got the advantages of a quantity of female intellectual work at the price of a puny, enfeebled, and sickly race. In this relation, it must be allowed that women do not and cannot stand on the same level as men.

In the second place, a proper regard to the mental nature of women means attention given to those qualities of mind which correlate the physical differences of her sex.... [W]omen are manifestly endowed with qualities of mind which specially fit them to stimulate and foster the first growths of intelligence in children, while the intimate and special sympathies which a mother has with her child as a being which, though individually separate, is still almost a part of her nature, give her an influence and responsibilities which are specially her own. The earliest dawn of an infant's intelligence is its recognition of its mother as the supplier of its wants, as the person whose near presence is associated with the relief of sensations of discomfort, and with the production of feelings of comfort; while the relief and pleasure which she herself feels in yielding it warmth and nourishment strengthens, if it was not originally the foundation of, that strong love of offspring which, with unwearied patience, surrounds its wayward youth with a thousand ministering attentions. It can hardly be doubted that if the nursing of babies were given over to men for a generation or two, they would abandon the task in despair or in disgust, and conclude it to be not worth while that mankind should continue on earth. But "can a woman forget her sucking child, that she should not have compassion on the son of her womb?"[105] Those can hardly be in earnest who question that woman's sex is represented in mind, and that the mental qualities which spring from it qualify her specially to be the successful nurse and educator of infants and young children....

---

104 "For contemplation he and valor formed / For softness she and sweet attractive grace; / He for God only, she for God in him": John Milton, *Paradise Lost* (1667).
105 Isaiah 49:15.

Elizabeth Garrett Anderson
from "Sex in Mind and Education: A Reply" (1874)

Physician Elizabeth Garrett Anderson (1836–1917) was the first woman to be licensed by the Society of the Apothecaries (1865), awarded an MD from the University of Paris (1870), granted membership of the British Medical Association (1873), or elected mayor in England (1908). Having struggled for medical education and professional status, Garrett Anderson fought for women's access to education, especially in medicine. She founded the New Hospital for Women (1871), the first British hospital with only women as medical staff, and taught at the London School of Medicine for Women (established in 1874), where she became dean in 1883. In 1870, she was elected to the London School Board (1870). Her writings include a medical textbook and newspaper articles on medical and women's issues.

In this excerpt, published in the *Fortnightly Review*, Garrett Anderson refutes Henry Maudsley's argument that people should be educated according to gender. She contends that a woman's physical and mental health is not disabled by her physiological make-up.

... Dr. Maudsley's paper consists mainly of a protest against the assimilation of the higher education of men and women, and against the admission of women to new careers; and this protest is founded upon a consideration of the physiological peculiarities of women. It derives much of its importance from the assumption that what is now being tried in England has already been tried in America, and that it has there produced the results which Dr. Maudsley thinks are inevitable. When, however, we turn to Dr. Clarke's book[106] (from which the American evidence quoted by Dr. Maudsley is taken) we find that the American system is, in many important features, and especially in those most strongly condemned by Dr. Clarke and the other witnesses, widely different from that now being advocated in England.... We shall show later on in what the difference between the American and English systems consists, but it is necessary, first of all, to warn readers of Dr. Maudsley's article that his use of American evidence is misleading and is not confirmed by reference to Dr. Clarke's book.

One other preliminary statement needs to be made before entering upon the consideration of Dr. Maudsley's argument.... He says, and in one form or another he repeats the charge again and again, that their aim is to change women into men, or, as he puts it, "to assimilate the female to the male mind." ... To meet such charges is difficult on account of their vagueness. We can but ask with unfeigned surprise what ground Dr. Maudsley can conceive that he has for them? We ask, what body of persons associated together in England for the purpose of promoting the education of women has made any statement, in any form or degree implying such aims? ... The single aim of those anxious to promote a higher and more serious education for women is to make the best they can of the materials at their disposal, and if they fail, it assuredly will not be from thinking that the masculine type of excellence includes all that can be desired in humanity.

---

106 Edward H. Clarke, *Sex in Education; or, A Fair Chance for the Girls* (1873).

The position Dr. Maudsley has undertaken to defend is this, that the attempt now being made in various directions to assimilate the mental training of men and women is opposed to the teachings of physiology, and more especially, that women's health is likely to be seriously injured if they are allowed or encouraged to pursue a system of education laid down on the same lines, following the same method, and having the same ends in view, as a system of education for men.

He bases his opinion on the fact that just at the age when the real educational strain begins, girls are going through an important phase of physiological development,[107] and that much of the health of their after-life depends upon the changes proper to this age being effected without check and in a normal and healthy manner. Moreover, the periodical recurrence of the function thus started, is attended, Dr. Maudsley thinks, with so great a withdrawal of nervous and physical force, that all through life it is useless for women to attempt, with these physiological drawbacks, to pursue careers side by side with men.

We have here two distinct assertions to weigh and verify: 1st, that the physiological functions started in girls between the ages of fourteen and sixteen are likely to be interfered with or interrupted by pursuing the same course of study as boys, and by being subjected to the same examinations; and, 2nd, that even when these functions are in good working order and the woman has arrived at maturity, the facts of her organization interfere periodically to such an extent with steady and serious labour of mind or body that she can never hope to compete successfully with men in any career requiring sustained energy. Both with girls and women, however, it is the assimilation of their education and the equality of their aim with those of boys and men which, in Dr. Maudsley's eyes, call for special condemnation. And in each case he grounds his objection on the fact that physiologically important differences are found in the two sexes. He says, "It would seem plain that as women are marked out by nature for very different offices from those of men, the healthy performance of her special functions renders it improbable she will succeed, and unwise for her to persevere in running over the same course at the same pace with him." But surely this argument contains a *non sequitur*.[108] The question depends upon the nature of the course and the quickness of the pace, and upon the fitness of both for women; not at all on the amount of likeness or unlikeness between men and women. So far as education is concerned it is conceivable, and indeed probable that, were they ten times as unlike as they are, many things would be equally good for both. If girls were less like boys than the anthropomorphic apes, nothing but experience would prove that they would not benefit by having the best methods and the best tests applied to their mental training....

The educational methods followed by boys being admitted to be better than those hitherto applied to girls, it is necessary to show that these better methods would in some way interfere with the special functions of girls. This Dr. Maudsley has not done. He has not attempted to show how the adoption of a common standard of examination for boys and girls, allowing to each a considerable range in the choice of subjects, is likely to interfere more with a girl's health than passing an inferior examination for girls only. Either would hurt her if unwisely pressed, if the stimulus of competition were unduly keen, or if in the desire for mental development the requirements of her physical nature were overlooked.

What we want to know is what exactly these requirements are, and especially how much consideration girls and women ought to show to the fact of the periodic and varying functions of their organization. In considering this point, we ought not to overlook the antecedent improbability of any organ or set of organs

---

107 The onset of menstruation.
108 A statement that does not follow logically from what has preceded it.

requiring exceptional attention; the rule certainly being that, when people are well, their physiological processes go on more smoothly without attention than with it. Are women an exception to this rule? When this is settled we shall be in a position to speculate upon how far in education or in after-life they will be able to work side by side with men without overtaxing their powers.

And first, with regard to adults. Is it true, or is it a great exaggeration, to say that the physiological difference between men and women seriously interferes with the chances of success a woman would otherwise possess? We believe it to be very far indeed from the truth. When we are told that in the labour of life women cannot disregard their special physiological functions without danger to health, it is difficult to understand what is meant, considering that in adult life healthy women do as a rule disregard them almost completely.... Among poor women, where all the available strength is spent upon manual labour, the daily work goes on without intermission, and, as a rule, without ill effects. For example, do domestic servants, either as young girls or in mature life, show by experience that a marked change in the amount of work expected from them must be made at these times unless their health is to be injured? It is well known that they do not.

With regard to mental work it is within the experience of many women that that which Dr. Maudsley speaks of as an occasion of weakness, if not of temporary prostration, is either not felt to be such or is even recognised as an aid, the nervous and mental power being in many cases greater at those times than at any other. This is confirmed by what is observed when this function is prematurely checked, or comes naturally to an end.[109] In either case its absence usually gives rise to a condition of nervous weakness unknown while the regularity of the function was maintained. It is surely unreasonable to assume that the same function in persons of good health can be a cause of weakness when present, and also when absent. If its performance made women weak and ill, its absence would be a gain, which it is not. Probably the true view of the matter is this. From various causes the demand made upon the nutritive processes is less in women than in men, while these processes are not proportionally less active; nutrition is thus continually a little in excess of what is wanted by the individual, and there is a margin ready for the demand made in childbearing. Till this demand arises it is no loss, but quite the reverse, to get rid of the surplus nutritive material, and getting rid of it involves, when the process is normal, no loss of vigour to the woman....

The case is, we admit, very different during early womanhood, when rapid growth and the development of new functions have taxed the nutritive powers more than they are destined to be taxed in mature life. At this age a temporary sense of weakness is doubtless much more common than it is later in life, and where it exists wise guardians and teachers are in the habit of making allowance for it, and of encouraging a certain amount of idleness. This is, we believe, as much the rule in the best English schools as it is in private schoolrooms and homes. No one wishes to dispute the necessity for care of this kind; but in our experience teachers, as a rule, need a warning on the point even less than parents....

It must not be overlooked, that the difficulties which attend the period of rapid functional development are not confined to women, though they are expressed differently in the two sexes. Analogous changes take place in the constitution and organization of young men, and the period of immature manhood is frequently one of weakness, and one during which any severe strain upon the mental and nervous powers is productive of more mischief than it is in later life. It is possible that the physiological demand thus made is lighter than that made upon young women at the corresponding age, but on the

---

109 That is, by surgery or menopause.

other hand it is certain that, in many other ways unknown to women, young men still further tax their strength, *e.g.* by drinking, smoking, unduly severe physical exercise, and frequently by late hours and dissipation generally. Whether, regard being had to all these varying influences, young men are much less hindered than young women in intellectual work by the demands made upon their physical and nervous strength during the period of development, it is probably impossible to determine. All that we wish to show is that the difficulties which attend development are not entirely confined to women, and that in point of fact great allowance ought to be made, and has already been made, for them in deciding what may reasonably be expected in the way of intellectual attainment from young men. It is not much to the point to prove that men could work harder than women, if the work demanded from either is very far from overtaxing the powers of even the weaker of the two. If we had no opportunity of measuring the attainments of ordinary young men, or if they really were the intellectual athletes Dr. Maudsley's warnings would lead us to suppose them to be, the question, "Is it well for women to contend on equal terms with men for the goal of man's ambition?" might be as full of solemnity to us as it is to Dr. Maudsley. As it is, it sounds almost ironical. Hitherto most of the women who have "contended with men for the goal of man's ambition" have had no chance of being any the worse for being allowed to do so on equal terms. They have had all the benefit of being heavily handicapped. Over and above their assumed physical and mental inferiority, they have had to start in the race without a great part of the training men have enjoyed, or they have gained what training they have been able to obtain in an atmosphere of hostility, to remain in which has taxed their strength and endurance far more than any amount of mental work could tax it....

John Churton Collins
from "An Educational Crisis, and How to Avert It.—II" (1886)

Educated at Oxford, John Churton Collins (1848–1908) championed the academic study of English literature. Fourteen years of tutoring candidates for the Indian civil service examinations developed his teaching method and consolidated his passionate commitment to English literature. Collins wrote for newspapers and such prestigious periodicals as the *Cornhill Magazine* and *Quarterly Review*, and lectured (more than 10,000 times between 1880 and 1907) for university extension programs. His popularizing zeal arguably kept him out of coveted endowed positions in universities' newly formed English departments until his appointment at Birmingham in 1904.

After applying unsuccessfully for the Merton Professorship of English Language and Literature at Oxford in 1885, Collins launched a public discussion in the *Pall Mall Gazette* on the place of English literature at Oxford, recruiting such luminaries as Matthew Arnold (see Education, Aesthetics and Culture), Walter Pater (see Education, Aesthetics and Culture), and J.A. Froude (see Education) to comment on the role of university English. The following selections are excerpted from this series.

The pedantry which has degraded the Greek and Roman classics into mere material for verbal criticism has degraded the English classics in the same way. I would exhort any one who is interested in education to turn to the Clarendon Press[110] editions of Milton and Shakspeare. I will take their "Hamlet," as it happens to be at hand. We there find 117 pages of text printed in large type and 159 pages of introduction and notes printed in very small type. In this stupendous mass of commentary, satisfactory, no doubt, from a philological point of view, there is, if we except a short paragraph quoted from "Wilhelm Meister,"[111] a single line dealing with the play as a work of art, not a word about its structure, about the characters, about its ethical, its metaphysical, its poetic, its dramatic interest. Anything more sickening and depressing, anything more calculated to make the name of Shakspeare stink in the nostrils of the youth of the English-speaking world, it would be impossible for man to devise. And this work, or some work precisely similar to it, is inflicted on every student who presents himself for examination in what university and Government boards are pleased to denominate English literature. At the beginning of last year there was some hope that our own literature at least would be rescued from this degradation, and that Oxford would confer on this country the great boon of placing that study on a proper footing. A chair of English Literature was founded, and liberally endowed. A board of electors was appointed. As there was already a chair of Celtic, a chair of Anglo-Saxon, a chair of Comparative Philology, and as therefore the philological study of English was amply provided for, no one entertained the smallest doubt that the choice of the electors would fall on the sort of person contemplated by the university when the professorship was founded. What was the result? Availing themselves of a wretched quibble on the word language—for the statute authorizing the foundation of the chair chanced to couple the word "language" with "literature"—the board of electors, ignoring the purpose for which the chair was founded, succeeded in inflicting, at a permanent salary of about £900 a year, a fourth professor of philology on the university. And so, in the ensuing term, Oxford presented the edifying spectacle of two professors, the new Professor of "English Literature"[112] and the old Professor of Anglo-Saxon, lecturing simultaneously to empty benches on Beowulf.[113] It is, however, some consolation to think that pedantry has now done its worst, that the *reductio ad absurdum*[114] of the present system is at last complete. That there should be no less than four chairs for the philological study of literature, that ample provision should be made for the interpretation of Cædmon[115] and Beowulf, for the interpretation of the Gododin and the Taîn Bo,[116] for the interpretation of Robert of Gloucester and William of Shoreham,[117] but that the study of English literature, as represented by the English classics, should be absolutely unprovided for, is an anomaly so extraordinary, or, to speak plainly, so scandalous, that it can scarcely fail to strike even university legislators. What is to be devoutly hoped is that the Board of Studies will see that the true solution of the problem before them is the obvious one. A little reflection will show them that the insufficiency of the present system lies in its not recognizing the distinction between

---

110 The imprint of learned books published by Oxford University Press.
111 Johann Wolfgang von Goethe, *Wilhelm Meisters Lehrjahre* (1795–96).
112 Arthur Sampson Napier (1853–1916), philologist and first Merton Professor of English Language and Literature at Oxford University.
113 *Beowulf*, an Old English epic poem dating from between the eighth and tenth centuries.
114 Latin: reducing to the absurd.
115 Caedmon (fl. 658–80), poet and monk.
116 "Y Gododdin," a medieval Welsh poem; "Táin Bó Cuailnge" (Cattle Raid of Cooley), an early Irish prose epic.
117 Robert of Gloucester (fl. 1260–1300), chronicler, known for his contribution to the metrical history of England, "The Chronicle of Robert of Gloucester" (c. 1300); William of Shoreham (fl. fourteenth century), poet.

the study of literature regarded merely as a monument of language and the study of literature regarded as the expression of genius and art.... What is needed is provision for an enlarged and enlightened study of the classics of Greece and Rome side by side with a similar study of our own classics. It is as critics of life and as consummate artists that the Athenian dramatists are of interest and value. Let them be so studied; let their theology, let their ethics, be interpreted; let their characters, their plots, their structure, be analysed and discussed, as modern philosophical criticism analyses and discusses those of Shakspeare. It is not by worrying youths about the doctrine of the digamma,[118] and about the authorship of the "Iliad,"[119] but by teaching them to understand what constitutes its pre-eminence among epic poems that the study of "Iliad" will be of benefit.... To be able to construe Pindar and Horace[120] accurately is all perhaps that need to be required of a youth so long as he remains a schoolboy, but if he quits the university without understanding why the one towers over all the lyric poets in the world, and why it is that the other has won his way to the heart of the world, it is certain that he has not made much progress in a liberal education, and it is almost equally certain that in a year or two, unless he happens to be a schoolmaster, he will cease to be able to construe them.... [I]f the Poetics, the Rhetoric, the Treatise on the Sublime,[121] a work which, incredible to relate, is not even recognized at either of the universities, and the Institutes of Quintilian,[122] were applied to the purpose for which they were intended—were so treated, that is to say, as to form a running commentary on the poets and prose-writers of antiquity—the secret of literary immortality would be understood, and criticism would be taught not only where to find its touchstones and its standards but how to apply them.

It may, perhaps, be objected that such a study of the classics would involve the sacrifice of that accurate scholarship on which our universities justly pride themselves, and without which the study of languages which are no longer spoken would be worse than useless. It may be urged that to talk of studying the poetry, the oratory, the criticism, of the ancients without the nicest appreciation of the weight and force of every word, and of every collocation of words in the original would be ridiculous. The reply to this is that there is not the smallest necessity for lowering the standard of scholarship. All that is required is to confine it to its proper sphere, to apply it to its proper use. If the time which is now given to composition, to unnecessarily minute grammatical analysis, to the platitudes and paradoxes of rival commentators, to the controversies of textual critics, were devoted to translation at sight, to the principles of syntax, to the careful study of each leading classic in an edition where the text is settled, where the notes, brief and pertinent, confine themselves to the elucidation of the text, and lectures conducted on the same principle supplemented such a course of reading, any youth of average intelligence who had been well grounded at school would, in three years, not only be able to read Greek and Latin with ease and comfort, but with scholarly accuracy.

And this brings me to the last point. I have submitted that in such a School of Literature as would be worthy of our universities, in such a school as is imperatively needed, our own classics should be studied side by side with those of Greece and Rome, and should be studied on the same principle and with the same object. And the reason for this is obvious. The three literatures are radically and essentially connected. What the literature of Greece is to that of Rome, the literatures of Greece and Rome are to that

---

118 The sixth letter of the Greek alphabet; it fell into disuse as its sound disappeared from the language.
119 Ancient Greek poem usually attributed to Homer, a figure about whom little is known except that his name was associated with the poem by the Greeks themselves.
120 Pindar (c. 518–438 BCE), Greek lyric poet; Horace (65–8 BCE), Latin poet and satirist.
121 Aristotle, *Poetics* and *Rhetoric*; *On the Sublime* (probably from the first century), usually attributed to Longinus.
122 Quintilian, *Institutio oratoria* (c. 95).

of England. A scholar would at once see the absurdity of separating the study of Roman literature from that of Greece, for the simple reason that without a knowledge of the latter the former is unintelligible. Imagine a lecturer professing to interpret the Ænied[123] without an adequate acquaintance with the Homeric poems, with the Attic drama, with the poetry of Alexandria, or a man setting up to expound the odes of Horace, or to comment on the style of Sallust and Tacitus, who was ignorant of Greek lyric poetry and of Thucydides.[124] Now the absurdity of separating the study of our own classics from the study of the Greek and Roman classics is equally great. Not only have most of our poets and all our best prose writers, as well in the present age as in former ages, been nourished on the literature of Greece and Rome, not only has the form of at least two-thirds of our best poetry and our best prose derived its distinctive features from those literatures, not only has the influence of those literatures alternately modifying and moulding our own determined its course and its characteristics, but a large portion what is most valuable in our poetry is as historically unintelligible apart from the Greek and Roman classics as the epic poetry of Rome is apart from the epic poetry of Greece. Take, for example, the poetry of Milton. Could anything be more preposterous than for a man to undertake to comment on "Paradise Lost," on "Paradise Regained," on "Comus," on "Samson Agonistes,"[125] who was unacquainted with the literatures which were to Milton's genius what the soil is to a plant, and which determined not merely his character as an artist, but exercised an influence on his intellect and temper scarcely less powerful than hereditary instincts and contemporary history? And what applies to Milton applies equally to Gray,[126] and to innumerable others. The key to the peculiarities of Dryden and Pope[127] is to be found, and to be found only, in the Roman satirists. The best commentary on Shakspeare is Sophocles, as the best commentary on Burke is Cicero.[128] And yet so entirely is this truth, this self-evident truth, ignored that the teaching of English is in all our schools and institutes separated on principle from the classical curriculum, and it is almost entirely in the hands of men who make no pretension to classical learning, or, if they possess it, never dream of applying it to the interpretation of English.... Nothing, for example, is more common than for a youth to be "instructed" in such works as Johnson's London, Milton's Samson, Gray's Bard, Wordsworth's great Ode, without a single allusion being made to Juvenal, to the Greek plays, to Pindar, to Plato.[129] For this wretched standard of teaching, which would not be tolerated in any other subject, the universities, and the universities only, are to blame.

If the Board of Studies would only provide for such a School of Literature as I have suggested there would be little danger of the supremacy of the classics being shaken; for their historical importance

---

123 Virgil, *Aeneid* (c. 30–19 BCE).
124 Sallust (86–35/4 BCE), Roman historian; Tacitus (56–120), Roman historian; Thucydides (c. 460–404 BCE), Greek historian.
125 John Milton, *Paradise Lost* (1667), *Paradise Regained* (1671), *A Maske Presented at Ludlow Castle, 1634: On Michaelmasse Night, before the Right Honorable John Earl of Bridgewater, Lord President of Wales* [*Comus*] (1637), and *Samson Agonistes* (1671).
126 Thomas Gray (1716–71), poet.
127 John Dryden (1631–1700), playwright, essayist, and poet; Alexander Pope (1688–1744), poet, satirist, and translator of Homer.
128 Sophocles (496–06 BCE), Greek playwright; Edmund Burke (1729–97), essayist, statesman, and political theorist; Cicero (106–43 BCE), Roman statesman, orator, and expert on rhetoric.
129 Samuel Johnson, *London* (1738); Thomas Gray, *The Bard* (1757); William Wordsworth, "Intimations of Immortality from Recollections of Early Childhood" (1807); Juvenal (c. 55–127), Roman satirical poet; Plato (428/27–348/47 BCE), Greek philosopher.

whenever literature shall be adequately taught is as great as their intrinsic value. The study of the poetry, the oratory, the criticism, of Greece and Rome pursued side by side with that of our own would at once place the study of the classics on the only footing on which in modern times it is possible to justify it, and at the same time raise the study of English literature to its proper level in education. As it is, at the "Centres of Culture"—as they are absurdly termed—the only subjects which are neglected are what chiefly contribute to culture; the only class of students unprovided for—the class which is most entitled to consideration—the poets, the critics, the men of letters of the future. To this obstinate and stupid indifference of the universities to the interests of literary culture is to be attributed in a large measure the present degraded condition of our national literature. No feature of our time is so striking as the contrast between the thoroughness and conscientiousness with which scientific men do their work, and the flimsiness and unsubstantiality of the work done in literature—between the "rang'd Empire" over which Professor Huxley presides and the wretched anarchy over which Mr. Matthew Arnold mourns.[130]

William Morris
from "English at the Universities" (1886)

William Morris (1834–96) rose to prominence as a poet, artist, and designer of home furnishings. Having encountered reformist politics—especially the writings of Ruskin (see Life Writing, Condition of England, Aesthetics and Culture, Gender and Sexuality) and Carlyle (see Condition of England, Faith and Doubt)—at Oxford, Morris affirmed the joy of labour in artistic production. In 1861, he founded the influential design company, later Morris and Co., and in 1891, the Kelmscott Press, which produced high-quality illustrated books. Morris's philosophy ("Have nothing in your houses that you do not know to be useful or believe to be beautiful") inspired the Arts and Crafts movement. Despite the critical failure of *The Defence of Guinevere, and Other Poems* (1858), in the mid-1860s, Morris was as popular as Browning, Tennyson, and Swinburne. A socialist, Morris wrote the utopian *News from Nowhere* (1890) and edited the Socialist League's *The Commonweal*.

In this letter to the *Pall Mall Gazette* (part of the series prompted by John Churton Collins), Morris derides teaching literary criticism as opposed to literary history.

I expect I shall be in a minority among those who answer your letter as to the proposed Professorship of English Literature, for I think the Universities had better let it alone. Those disasters the Slade Professorships of Art,[131] ought to warn them off establishing chairs whose occupiers would have necessarily to

---

130 Shakespeare, *Antony and Cleopatra* (I.i.34); Thomas Henry Huxley (1825–95) (see Science), biologist and scientist, president of the Royal Society (1883–85), and a senator at London University (1883–95); Matthew Arnold, *Culture and Anarchy* (1869) (see Aesthetics and Culture).
131 In 1871, the Slade Professorships of Fine Art were founded at Oxford, Cambridge, and London (University College).

deal vaguely with great subjects; and this all the more as the Slade Professors chosen have been the best that offered, one a man of genius,[132] and the rest men of talent. Need I mention that queer absurdity the Oxford Chair of Poetry[133] as a further warning? As to the Merton Professorship, which you mention in your note, I think the University did all it could in the matter, because philology can be taught, but "English literature" cannot.[134] Neither can I admit that there is any analogy between the proposed study of English literature and the way that the Universities have dealt with the classics: their study implies that of the language and history of civilized antiquity; they are not taught as literature, not criticized as literature, at any rate. If the function of the proposed chair were to be, or could be, the historical evolution of English literature, including, of course, the English language, it might be well enough; but I do not think that this is intended, judging by the outcry raised about the filling of the Merton Professorship. I fear that most professors would begin English literature with Shakspeare, not with Beowulf. What *is* intended seems to me a Chair of *Criticism*; and against the establishment of such a Chair I protest emphatically. For the result would be merely vague talk about literature, which would teach nothing. Each succeeding professor would strive to outdo his predecessor in "originality" on subjects whereon nothing original remains to be said. Hyper-refinement and paradox would be the order of the day, and the younger students would be confused by the literary polemics which would be sure to flourish round such a Chair; and all this would have the seal of authority set upon it, and probably would not seldom be illustrated by some personal squabble like the one which your note mentions. Pray, Sir, change your mind, and do your best to deliver us from two (or more) Professors of Criticism....

John Addington Symonds
from "English at the Universities.—III." (1886)

Trained in classics at Oxford, John Addington Symonds (1840–93) became an author and an early proponent of sexual reform. He wrote almost 40 books, including the *Renaissance in Italy* (seven volumes, 1875–86), which consisted of his own poetry as well as translations from Greek and Italian, and collections of travel essays. Married in 1864, he nevertheless acknowledged his homosexuality, advocating legal reform and recognition of homosexuality as innate. His death in 1893 ended his early collaboration with Havelock Ellis (see Gender and Sexuality) on *Sexual Inversion* (1897), which includes a case study of Symonds, and two pamphlets on homosexuality that Ellis partly reproduced. Symonds's fragile health, including his tuberculosis, prompted long stays in alpine climates.

---

132 John Ruskin (1819–1900) (see Life Writing, Condition of England, Aesthetics and Culture, Gender and Sexuality) held the Slade Professorship at Oxford several times between 1869 and 1885.
133 The Oxford Chair of Poetry was founded in 1708; in the mid-nineteenth century, it became a platform for theological disputes.
134 The first Merton Professor of English Language and Literature at Oxford University was Arthur Sampson Napier (1853–1916), a philologist.

In this letter to the *Pall Mall Gazette* (part of a series prompted by John Churton Collins), Symonds depicts English literature as a necessary component of undergraduate university education and recommends that it be studied alongside classics.

∼

I should heartily welcome any sound scheme for introducing the study of English literature into our Universities. Nothing is more striking than the comparative ignorance and indifference which even accomplished Greek and Latin scholars from Oxford and Cambridge often display with regard to our own authors. But I do not believe that the object is to be attained merely by the foundation of new professorships or by the establishment of a new "school" or "tripos"[135] for English. Were this subject left to the option of individuals, the best teaching both at public schools and at colleges in the Universities would follow the old routine, and the best talents of the students would still be attracted almost exclusively to Literæ Humaniores[136] and mathematics. What is wanted is some plan whereby the study of English should be combined with the study of classical literature, and become a necessary element in the education of every undergraduate who aspires to honours or reads for a degree. English, in my opinion, ought to enter as a subject into the examinations of each student on whom the mark of the University is stamped, if it is to be made a serious branch of our higher intellectual training. Short of this, it might just as well be left to take its chance, according to the present system.

Walter Pater
from "English at the Universities.—IV." (1886)

Walter Pater (1839–94) was a leader in the fin-de-siècle Aesthetic movement. Educated at Oxford, Pater became a fellow of Brasenose College (in classics), where he tutored Gerard Manley Hopkins. Influenced by the Pre-Raphaelites, he later advocated "aesthetic poetry." Pater's earliest periodical publications focused on Samuel Taylor Coleridge (1866), Johann Winckelmann (1867), and William Morris (see Education, Aesthetics and Culture) (1868); he drew upon these in *Studies in the History of the Renaissance* (1873) (see Aesthetics and Culture). This controversial volume redirected attention away from the object per se (see Arnold, Aesthetics and Culture) and toward personal impressions of art, cultivated in a seemingly hedonistic spirit. This approach inspired Oxford undergraduates and aesthetes, including Oscar Wilde (see Life Writing, Aesthetics and Culture), who adopted Pater's injunction to "burn always with this hard gem-like flame."

In this letter to the *Pall Mall Gazette* (part of a series prompted by John Churton Collins), Pater advocates studying English literature in conjunction with the classics and opposes any system that might turn the "fine flower" of English poetry into a "cram."

---

135 Final honours examination.
136 Known at Oxford as "Greats"; the study of Greek and Roman literature, philosophy, and history.

∼

You have asked me to express an opinion on a proposal to establish here a School of English Literature. I have long had an interest in the teaching of young men at Oxford, and in the study of English literature; and proposals similar to this have from time to time occurred to me. The university has done little for English literature by way of direct teaching. Its indirect encouragement of what is best in English literature has, I think, been immense, as regards both the appreciation of what is old and the initiation of what is new. The university has been enabled to exercise this influence mainly as a consequence of its abundant and disinterested devotion, in the face of much opposition, to Greek and Latin literature—to the study of those literary productions wherein lie the sources of all our most salutary literary traditions, and which must always remain typical standards in literature, of a stirring interest in the matter together with absolute correctness in the form. I should, therefore, be no advocate for any plan of introducing English literature into the course of university studies which seemed likely to throw into the background that study of classical literature which has proved so effective for the maintenance of what is excellent in our own. On the other hand, much probably might be done for the expansion and enlivening of classical study itself by a larger infusion into it of those literary interests which modern literature, in particular, has developed; and a closer connection of it, if this be practicable, with the study of great modern works (classical literature and the literature of modern Europe having, in truth, an organic unity); above all, by the maintenance, at its highest possible level, of the purely literary character of those literary exercises in which the classical examination mainly consists.

An examination seems to run the risk of two opposite defects. Many of those who most truly enjoy this or that special study are jealous of examinations in it. The "fine flower"[137] of English poetry, or Latin oratory, or Greek art, might fade for them, in the long, pedantic, mechanical discipline (perhaps the "cram"[138]) which is the necessary accompaniment of a system of examination; indispensable as that may nevertheless be for certain purposes. Intelligent Englishmen resort naturally for a liberal pleasure to their own literature. Why transform into a difficult exercise what is natural virtue in them? On the other hand, there are those who might give the preference to these studies for their fancied easiness, and welcome such a change in the interest of that desire to facilitate things, at any cost, the tendency of which is to suppress every kind of excellence born of strenuous labor, and, in literature especially, to promote what is lax and slipshod, alike in thought and expression....

---

137 See Pindar, *Isthmian Odes* and "Hymn 2."
138 Information memorized hastily for an examination.

Matthew Arnold
from "English at the Universities.—IX." (1887)

Initially known for his poetry, in the 1860s and 1870s Matthew Arnold (1822–88) became England's leading literary critic with essays on literary, religious, social, and educational issues. The son of Thomas Arnold (see Education), he was educated at Winchester, Rugby, and Oxford. Beginning in 1851, Arnold worked as a school inspector for 35 years, observing the social conditions of education. In his criticism, Arnold denounced "Philistinism," his term for middle-class people's lack of liberal culture (see Arnold in Education, Aesthetics and Culture); he argued for intellectual curiosity and openness, qualities he lauded in European educational models.

In this letter to the *Pall Mall Gazette*, Arnold identifies England as unique in not teaching its national literature and advocates teaching English alongside Greek and Latin literary classics.

I have no difficulty in saying that I should like to see standard English authors joined to the standard authors of Greek and Latin literature who have to be taken up for a pass, or for honours, at the universities. I should be sorry to see a separate school, with degrees and honours, for the modern languages as such, although it is desirable that the professors and teachers of those languages should give certificates of fitness to teach them. I would add no literature except that of our own country to the classical literature taken up for the degree, whether with or without honours in Arts. These seem to me to be elementary propositions, when one is laying down what is desirable in respect to the university degree in Arts. The omission of the mother tongue and its literature in school and university instruction is peculiar, so far as I know, to England. You do a good work in urging us to repair that omission....

James Anthony Froude
from "English at the Universities.—IX." (1887)

Writer and historian James Anthony Froude (1818–94) achieved fame with his popular histories of England. At Oxford, during the controversies excited by John Henry Newman (see Education, Faith and Doubt), Froude was ordained as a minister but came to question his faith. His skeptical novel, *The Nemesis of Faith* (1849), scandalized Oxford, prompting Froude to resign his fellowship. Froude thenceforth wrote to support his family, publishing a review, in 1854, of the poetry of Matthew Arnold (see Education, Aesthetics and Culture), the *History of England* (1856–70), and works on the politics of Ireland, South Africa, and the West Indies, as well as editing *Fraser's Magazine* (1860–74). As the friend and literary executor of Thomas Carlyle (see Condition of England, Faith and Doubt),

Froude published controversial biographical material that revealed the Carlyles' unhappy marriage. Froude became Regius Professor of Modern History at Oxford in 1892.

In this letter to the *Pall Mall Gazette*, Froude argues that while writers may succeed without a thorough knowledge of Greek or Latin, critics and scholars cannot.

~

I will answer your questions as briefly as I can.

1. Should English literature be included in the University curriculum? This depends on what Universities undertake to do. In my time there was one special curriculum (or two, including mathematics) which was insisted on for all. It did not include English literature, nor could it have done so in my opinion without impairing the excellence of the teaching which it actually gave. If, on the other hand, the English Universities are to revert to their original character as places where all learning is taught, and the students are to select their special branches, then I think that English literature certainly ought to form one of those branches.

2. I hesitate to say that an understanding of English literature is impossible without a knowledge of Greek and Latin literature. Many of our very best writers knew little or no Greek and Latin. Shakspeare had "small Latin and less Greek."[139] Pope translated Homer,[140] but was a poor scholar. De Foe, Bunyan, Burns, Byron, Carlyle, Cobbett, Charles Lamb[141]—these and many other names occur to me which disprove the position, as it concerns writers; and I think you might find very good students of English literature also equally ignorant. The Scandinavian literature, not the classical, was the cradle of our own. At the same time I regard the Greek and Latin literature as the best in the world, as superior to the modern as Greek sculpture is superior to the schools of England and France; and that no one can be a finished scholar and critic (I do not say writer) who is ignorant of it. Our national taste and the tone of the national intellect will suffer a serious decline if it ceases to be studied among us.

---

139 Ben Jonson, "To the Memory of My Beloved, The Author Mr. William Shakespeare, and What He Hath Left Us" (1623).
140 Alexander Pope (1688–1744) translated Homer's *Iliad* (1715–20) and *Odyssey* (1725–26).
141 Daniel Defoe (1660–1731), novelist and essayist; John Bunyan (1628–88), author of *The Pilgrim's Progress* (1678); Robert Burns (1759–96), poet; George Gordon Byron (1788–1824), poet; Thomas Carlyle (1795–1881) (see Condition of England, Faith and Doubt), essayist, historian, biographer, and social critic; William Cobbett (1763–1835), political writer, newspaper editor, and defender of rural England; Charles Lamb (1775–1834), essayist.

AESTHETICS AND CULTURE

Introduction
Dennis Denisoff

During the Victorian era, the British grew increasingly unsure of many of their most prominent cultural institutions, including their dominant religious traditions, their imperialist exploits, and the colonialist mindset that buttressed their government's industrialist ethos. The realm of aesthetics, conversely, gained broader recognition and influence, making it, by the end of the century, a formidable cultural force. As Max Nordau declared in *Degeneration* (1892; trans. 1895), one might dare attack "the Church" or "rulers and governments," but "grievous is the fate of him who has the audacity to characterize æsthetic fashions as forms of mental decay" (vi). Nordau was being only slightly ironic in implying that aesthetics had, by the end of the century, become the era's significant authority. Artists and art theorists were indeed now readily recognized as cultural leaders. More subtly, people's personal choices in fashion and home design functioned as signs of their aesthetic taste, class status, wealth, and intellectual competence—in short, of their very identities.

By the end of the century, Victorians viewed aesthetics not only as a philosophy of beauty and taste but as a source of cultural identity. The artist became a social icon, as "high" art became commercialized and affordable periodicals offered a popular education in art and literature. Some artists took advantage of these new opportunities for self-promotion and notoriety. In her essay "Silly Novels by Lady Novelists" (1856), George Eliot speculated that three-quarters of female novelists become prose writers out of sheer vanity. The same motivation was partly responsible for the newfound popularity of the bohemian artist. This is not to say that artists and art scholars were insincere in the philosophies they espoused on aesthetics (the study of the pleasure one derives from the sensory experience of nature and cultural objects). But Victorian commentaries on the subject often as earnestly addressed writers' interests either in their own special qualities and rights as artists or in seemingly non-aesthetic issues. The period's prose reveals that Victorians recognized aesthetics as not just a philosophy but also a reflection of the concerns of the dominant cultural spokespeople of the era.

One can see the political potency of aesthetics in the works of influential poet and theorist Matthew Arnold. His discussions of beauty—that which gives pleasure to one's senses or mind—are situated within the context of culture, which he saw as the most important pursuit of any society. In *Culture and Anarchy* (1869), Arnold argues that, although the full benefits of culture are not available to everybody, if people are driven by "the moral and social passion for doing good" (8), the general collective will enjoy the highest quality of life. In his view, the best culture and people are formed through the pursuit of beauty and intelligence, which he refers to respectively as "sweetness and light" (47). First published in the *Cornhill Magazine*, Arnold's arguments encouraged a sense of aesthetics as a social duty; in his formulation, aesthetics sustained a strong moral purpose but also made people responsible for enhancing their personal experiences of beauty. The moral implications in Arnold's writings are coupled with sensitivity to the situation of the poor and working classes. Culture could only fulfill its mandate if the poorest of Victorians were lifted into a better quality of life along with the more privileged. These interests are equally strong in the works of other scholars of the period. Anna Jameson, for example, argues that images of the Madonna, as "consoler of the afflicted" (37), have proven "extremely effective as an appeal to the popular feelings" (39), and in *Adam Bede* (1859), George Eliot advocates the use of fictional realism to inspire readers' "pity" and "love" for fellow mortals (178). Meanwhile, John Ruskin, perhaps the most influential Victorian commentator on aesthetics, similarly roots his aesthetic position in beauty as a sign of the divine. Thus, when modern industrial development curtails the experience of beauty, it demoralizes workers and results in uninspiring products and unjust social structures: "Unless you provide some elements of beauty for your workmen to be surrounded by, you will find that no elements of beauty can be invented by them" (61). Ruskin's essay "The Nature of Gothic" captures in poetic language the sense of the divine in all living things and a respect for the artistic sensitivity of the craftsperson.

For Nordau, Ruskin was misled in thinking that beauty is innately divine; he blamed Ruskin's influence for what he perceived as the flawed artistic development known as the Pre-Raphaelite movement. Founded in 1848, the Pre-Raphaelite Brotherhood (PRB) included James Collinson, William Holman Hunt, John Everett Millais, Dante Gabriel Rossetti, William Michael Rossetti, Frederic George Stephens, and Thomas Woolner. Although the members of the brotherhood were not especially cohesive in their aesthetics or politics, they ranked among the nineteenth century's most influential artists. Of them, Dante Gabriel Rossetti had the greatest impact. He emphasized that art should capture imaginative thought; the artist must therefore create from within the thought itself: "The motive powers of art reverse the requirement of science, and demand first of all an *inner* standing-point. The heart of such a mystery as this must be plucked from the very world in which it beats or bleeds" (217). The sway of Rossetti and the PRB extended beyond philosophic views, concerns over modern production methods, and the erasure of the craftsperson to include changes in hairstyles, clothing, popular colours, and interior design.

A close colleague of the Pre-Raphaelites, writer, socialist, and designer William Morris was particularly forceful in his critique of mass production—his efforts becoming a key impetus of the Arts and Crafts movement. By creating such things as furniture, wallpaper, and carpets aimed at celebrating the same craft-based values articulated by Ruskin, Morris extended Ruskin's philosophy of beauty into middle-class households. Although women equalled, if not surpassed, men in the output of these "lesser arts" (as Morris called them), he and the Pre-Raphaelites strongly emphasized male production. The term "Pre-Raphaelite women" is still used as often to refer to the females in the PRB's works as to the actual women in the community. With some exceptions (such as the poet Christina Rossetti), most of these women served primarily as models for or lovers of the Pre-Raphaelite men, rather than as artists in their own right. Although many authors stressed the importance of craftsmanship as a source of beauty, craftswomen without high-art affiliations or aspirations remained virtually unacknowledged in nineteenth-century essays on aesthetics.

The idea that such everyday objects as wallpaper and milk jugs should embody aesthetic principles was also voiced by contributors to the Aesthetic movement, which began around the same time as the Pre-Raphaelite and Arts and Crafts movements. While the three developments overlapped considerably, aesthetes centred their ideas less on crafts and working-class issues and more on the importance of taste in all aspects of life. Aestheticism's most influential early spokesperson, Walter Pater, summarized his philosophy in the conclusion to his *Studies in the History of the Renaissance* (1873). Pater proposed that the main purpose in life is to maximize one's immediate pleasure. The best source of such pleasure is "the poetic passion, the desire of beauty, the love of art for its own sake," because "art comes to you proposing frankly to give nothing but the highest quality to your moments as they pass, and simply for those moments' sake" (224). Pater's language harkens back to that of the Romantic sublime and, on first glance, appears not to address any political concerns, yet his works were attacked and satirized more forcefully than those of almost any other Victorian writing on the topic of aesthetics. Many interpreted his conclusion—his students at Oxford delightedly and more responsible individuals anxiously—as glorifying irresponsibility and perhaps even immorality. The celebration of "art for art's sake" had been initiated decades earlier by the French novelist Théophile Gautier in the preface to *Mademoiselle de Maupin* (1835), his novel recounting the life of a cross-dressing, bisexual opera singer. Gautier rails against reviewers who find pleasure in searching through art for hints of sexual immorality. Pater thus chose to paraphrase language already carrying connotations of impropriety. By coupling this insinuation with words such as "passion" and "desire," Pater ensured that his ideas and the Aesthetic movement would be associated with immorality and unconventional sexualities and

"Nincompoopiana." *Punch* (4 June 1879): 266.

sexes such as homosexuality and hermaphroditism; however, both Gautier and Pater insisted that the morality of aesthetics was not absent but essential, existing beyond the ethical claims of a society at a particular historical moment.

During this time, the growing commodification of lifestyles and identities resulted in the rise of a fashion for self-display. Aestheticism—which built on Pater's *Renaissance* and tapped into France's more salacious Decadent movement—offered the most vibrant opportunities for such gestures. Oscar Wilde, who performed the image of the dandy aesthete both in London and in North America (during his lecture tour in the early 1880s), quickly became a lightning rod for those wishing to criticize and mock the Aesthetic movement. As one among a growing number of writers and artists aiming for fame or notoriety, Wilde took advantage of the publicity to advance his career. As the aesthete character Gilbert declares, in Wilde's essay-in-dialogue "The Critic as Artist" (1890, revised 1891), the two "supreme and highest arts" are "Life and Literature, life and the perfect expression of life" (1016). Repeated three times, "life" gets top billing here—but only life that is self-conscious and individualist. For Wilde, the ideal artwork is the artist who uses imagination to create a reality that had not previously existed. In this aesthetic model, ideal citizens do not merely dress and act eccentrically, but consciously turn themselves fully into art for the consumption of others.

Because it is spoken by a character rather than in the author's voice, Wilde's flippant declaration encourages us to question his sincerity. Indeed, this uncertainty around issues of beauty, identity, and morality is part of his point. Other contributors to the Aesthetic movement, such as Vernon Lee and Clementina Anstruther-Thomson, however, describe a more scientific and rationalist investigation of beauty. In contrast to the aesthetes' penchant for artifice and performance, these women searched for physical signs of an innate pleasure-response to art and nature. They did so by conducting experiments—standing in front of art objects and recording any physiological effects that the encounter with beauty had on their bodies, such as changes in temperature or breathing. In their essay "Beauty and Ugliness" (1897), they conclude that aesthetic experience depends on how the object's form affects a person's respiration and equilibrium. Here we find an early articulation of the formalist aesthetic theory central to the high Modernism of the early twentieth century.

Although the aesthetics of Wilde, Lee, and Anstruther-Thomson might appear unconventional and removed from the everyday concerns of most late Victorians, their writings reflected the rise of the middle class's cultural and economic authority. The spiritual and moral values that were championed at the start of the period by the likes of Arnold and Ruskin continued to resonate strongly among the middle class, but notions of the individual as art or as a receptacle and embodiment of beauty effectively complemented the commodity culture through which this segment of society had begun defining itself and others.

Works Cited and Further Reading

Arnold, Matthew. *Culture and Anarchy*. London: Smith, Elder and Co., 1869. Print.
Corbett, David Peters, and Lara Perry, eds. *English Art, 1860–1914: Modern Artists and Identity*. Manchester: Manchester UP, 2000. Print.
Dowling, Linda. *The Vulgarity of Art: Victorians and Aesthetic Democracy*. Charlottesville: U of Virginia P, 1996. Print.
Eliot, George. *Adam Bede*. 1859. Harmondsworth: Penguin, 1985. Print.

———. "Silly Novels by Lady Novelists." *Westminster Review* 66 (1856): 442–61. Print.
Gautier, Théophile. *Mademoiselle de Maupin*. 1835. Paris: Bibliothèque-Charpentier, 1924. Print.
Jameson, Anna. *Legends of the Madonna, as Represented in the Fine Arts*. London: Longman, Brown, Green, and Longmans, 1852. Print.
Lee, Vernon, and Clementina Anstruther-Thomson. *Beauty and Ugliness and Other Studies in Psychological Aesthetics*. London: John Lane, 1912. Print.
Macleod, Dianne Sachko. *Art and the Victorian Middle Class: Money and the Making of Cultural Identity*. Cambridge: Cambridge UP, 1996. Print.
Nordau, Max. *Degeneration*. 1892. Lincoln: U of Nebraska P, 1993. Print.
Pater, Walter. *Studies in the History of the Renaissance*. 1873. New York: Meridian, 1967. Print.
Prettejohn, Elizabeth. *Art for Art's Sake: Aestheticism in Victorian Painting*. New Haven: Yale UP, 2007. Print.
Rossetti, Dante Gabriel. "The *Contemporary Review* and the Stealthy School of Criticism: A Letter to Robert Buchanan, Esq. (Alias Thomas Maitland, Esq.)." London, 1871. Rpt. in *Victorian Poetry* 41.2 (2003): 207–27. Print.
Ruskin, John. *The Two Paths: Being Lectures on Art and Its Application to Decoration and Manufacture*. 1859. West Lafayette, IN: Parlor, 2004. Print.
Teukolsky, Rachel. *The Literate Eye: Victorian Art Writing and Modernist Aesthetics*. Oxford: Oxford UP, 2009. Print.
Wilde, Oscar. *The Complete Works of Oscar Wilde*. New York: Harper and Row, 1989. Print.

John Ruskin
from *The Stones of Venice* (1851–53)

Writer and artist John Ruskin (1819–1900) was one of the most influential art and social critics of the Victorian period. Though confirmed as an Anglican while at Oxford, he was not swept up by the Oxford Movement. After Oxford, Ruskin abandoned poetry to write criticism of art and architecture. With his father's financial support, Ruskin launched his writing career by defending artist J.M.W. Turner in *Modern Painters* (1843–60), in which he argued for the apprehension of divinity via contemplation of the beautiful in art. His failed marriage prompted scandal just as he emerged as a public intellectual and proponent of the Pre-Raphaelites.

The Stones of Venice (1851–53) celebrated Byzantine and Gothic styles and had an impact on Victorian architects. Influenced by Carlyle's *Past and Present* (1843), Ruskin lamented how industrialization reduced craftsmen to machines. In this selection, Ruskin suggests that the liberated artist's creative and imaginative capacity is revealed through the variations in Gothic architecture.

Volume 2, Chapter 6: The Nature of Gothic

... [W]e are now about to enter upon the examination of that school of Venetian architecture which forms an intermediate step between the Byzantine and Gothic forms; but which I find may be conveniently considered in its connexion with the latter style. In order that we may discern the tendency of each step of this change, it will be wise in the outset to endeavour to form some general idea of its final result. We know already what the Byzantine architecture is from which the transition was made, but we ought to know something of the Gothic architecture into which it led. I shall endeavour therefore to give the reader in this chapter an idea, at once broad and definite, of the true nature of *Gothic* architecture, properly so called; not of that of Venice only, but of universal Gothic....

The principal difficulty in doing this arises from the fact that every building of the Gothic period differs in some important respect from every other; and many include features which, if they occurred in other buildings, would not be considered Gothic at all; so that all we have to reason upon is merely, if I may be allowed so to express it, a greater or less degree of *Gothicness* in each building we examine. And it is this Gothicness,—the character which, according as it is found more or less in a building, makes it more or less Gothic,—of which I want to define the nature; and I feel the same kind of difficulty in doing so which would be encountered by any one who undertook to explain, for instance, the nature of Redness, without any actually red thing to point to, but only orange and purple things. Suppose he had only a piece of heather and a dead oak-leaf to do it with. He might say, the colour which is mixed with the yellow in this oak-leaf, and with the blue in this heather, would be red, if you had it separate; but it would be difficult, nevertheless, to make the abstraction perfectly intelligible: and it is so in a far greater degree to make the abstraction of the Gothic character intelligible, because that character itself is made up of many mingled ideas, and can consist only in their union. That is to say, pointed arches do not constitute Gothic, nor vaulted roofs, nor flying buttresses,[1] nor grotesque sculptures; but all or some of these things, and many other things with them, when they come together so as to have life.

Observe also, that, in the definition proposed, I shall only endeavour to analyze the idea which I suppose already to exist in the reader's mind. We all have some notion, most of us a very determined one, of the meaning of the term Gothic; but I know that many persons have this idea in their minds without being able to define it: that is to say, understanding generally that Westminster Abbey is Gothic, and St. Paul's is not, that Strasburg Cathedral is Gothic, and St. Peter's[2] is not, they have, nevertheless, no clear notion of what it is that they recognize in the one or miss in the other such as would enable them to say how far the work at Westminster or Strasburg is good and pure of its kind; still less to say of any nondescript building, like St. James's Palace or Windsor Castle,[3] how much right Gothic element there is in it, and how much wanting. And I believe this inquiry to be a pleasant and profitable one; and that there will be found something more than usually interesting in tracing out this grey,

---

1 Arched supports.
2 Westminster Abbey, London; St. Paul's Cathedral, London; Strasbourg Cathedral, Strasbourg, France; St. Peter's Basilica, Vatican City, Rome, Italy.
3 St. James's Palace, London; Windsor Castle, Windsor.

shadowy, many-pinnacled image of the Gothic spirit within us; and discerning what fellowship there is between it and our Northern hearts....

We have, then, the Gothic character submitted to our analysis, just as the rough mineral is submitted to that of the chemist, entangled with many other foreign substances, itself perhaps in no place pure, or ever to be obtained or seen in purity for more than an instant; but nevertheless a thing of definite and separate nature, however inextricable or confused in appearance. Now observe: the chemist defines his mineral by two separate kinds of character; one external, its crystalline form, hardness, lustre, &c.; the other internal, the proportions and nature of its constituent atoms. Exactly in the same manner, we shall find that Gothic architecture has external forms and internal elements. Its elements are certain mental tendencies of the builders, legibly expressed in it; as fancifulness, love of variety, love of richness, and such others. Its external forms are pointed arches, vaulted roofs, &c. And unless both the elements and the forms are there, we have no right to call the style Gothic. It is not enough that it has the Form, if it have not also the power and life. It is not enough that it has the Power, if it have not the form. We must therefore inquire into each of these characters successively; and determine first, what is the Mental Expression, and secondly, what the Material Form, of Gothic architecture, properly so called.

1st. Mental Power or Expression. What characters, we have to discover, did the Gothic builders love, or instinctively express in their work, as distinguished from all other builders?

Let us go back for a moment to our chemistry, and note that, in defining a mineral by its constituent parts, it is not one nor another of them, that can make up the mineral, but the union of all: for instance, it is neither in charcoal, nor in oxygen, nor in lime, that there is the making of chalk, but in the combination of all three in certain measures; they are all found in very different things from chalk, and there is nothing like chalk either in charcoal or in oxygen, but they are nevertheless necessary to its existence.

So in the various mental characters which make up the soul of Gothic. It is not one nor another that produces it; but their union in certain measures. Each one of them is found in many other architectures besides Gothic; but Gothic cannot exist where they are not found, or, at least, where their place is not in some way supplied....

I believe, then, that the characteristic or moral elements of Gothic are the following, placed in the order of their importance:

1. Savageness.
2. Changefulness.
3. Naturalism.
4. Grotesqueness.
5. Rigidity.
6. Redundance.

These characters are here expressed as belonging to the building; as belonging to the builder, they would be expressed thus:—1. Savageness, or Rudeness. 2. Love of Change. 3. Love of Nature. 4. Disturbed Imagination. 5. Obstinacy. 6. Generosity. And I repeat, that the withdrawal of any one, or any two, will not at once destroy the Gothic character of a building, but the removal of a majority of them will. I shall proceed to examine them in their order.

SAVAGENESS. I am not sure when the word "Gothic" was first generically applied to the architecture of the North; but I presume that, whatever the date of its original usage, it was intended to imply reproach, and express the barbaric character of the nations among whom that architecture arose.... [It implied] that they and their buildings together exhibited a degree of sternness and rudeness, which, in contradistinction to the character of Southern and Eastern nations, appeared like a perpetual reflection of the contrast between the Goth and the Roman in their first encounter.[4] And when that fallen Roman, in the utmost impotence of his luxury, and insolence of his guilt, became the model for the imitation of civilized Europe, at the close of the so-called Dark ages,[5] the word Gothic became a term of unmitigated contempt, not unmixed with aversion. From that contempt, by the exertion of the antiquaries and architects of this century, Gothic architecture has been sufficiently vindicated; and perhaps some among us, in our admiration of the magnificent science of its structure, and sacredness of its expression, might desire that the term of ancient reproach should be withdrawn, and some other, of more apparent honourableness, adopted in its place. There is no chance, as there is no need, of such a substitution. As far as the epithet was used scornfully, it was used falsely; but there is no reproach in the word, rightly understood; on the contrary, there is a profound truth, which the instinct of mankind almost unconsciously recognizes. It is true, greatly and deeply true, that the architecture of the North is rude and wild; but it is not true, that, for this reason, we are to condemn it, or despise. Far otherwise: I believe it is in this very character that it deserves our profoundest reverence....

There is, I repeat, no degradation, no reproach in this, but all dignity and honourableness: and we should err grievously in refusing either to recognize as an essential character of the existing architecture of the North, or to admit as a desirable character in that which it yet may be, this wildness of thought, and roughness of work; this look of mountain brotherhood between the cathedral and the Alp; this magnificence of sturdy power, put forth only the more energetically because the fine finger-touch was chilled away by the frosty wind, and the eye dimmed by the moor-mist, or blinded by the hail; this outspeaking of the strong spirit of men who may not gather redundant fruitage from the earth, nor bask in dreamy benignity of sunshine, but must break the rock for bread, and cleave the forest for fire, and show, even in what they did for their delight, some of the hard habits of the arm and heart that grew on them as they swung the axe or pressed the plough....

The second mental element above named was CHANGEFULNESS, or Variety....

Wherever the workman is utterly enslaved, the parts of the building must of course be absolutely like each other; for the perfection of his execution can only be reached by exercising him in doing one thing, and giving him nothing else to do. The degree in which the workman is degraded may be thus known at a glance, by observing whether the several parts of the building are similar or not; and if, as in Greek work, all the capitals[6] are alike, and all the mouldings unvaried, then the degradation is complete; if, as in Egyptian or Ninevite[7] work, though the manner of executing certain figures is always the same, the order of design is perpetually varied, the degradation is less total; if, as in Gothic

---

4   The Goths were a group of Germanic tribes that originated in Scandinavia and raided Roman territories in the late second and third centuries.
5   The so-called Dark Ages ended around 1000.
6   The tops of architectural columns.
7   Of Nineveh, an ancient Assyrian city destroyed in 612 BCE.

work, there is perpetual change both in design and execution, the workman must have been altogether set free.

How much the beholder gains from the liberty of the labourer may perhaps be questioned in England, where one of the strongest instincts in nearly every mind is that Love of Order which makes us desire that our house windows should pair like our carriage horses.... I would not impeach love of order: it is one of the most useful elements of the English mind.... Only do not let us suppose that love of order is love of art. It is true that order, in its highest sense, is one of the necessities of art, just as time is a necessity of music; but love of order has no more to do with our right enjoyment of architecture or painting, than love of punctuality with the appreciation of an opera.... Our architects gravely inform us that, as there are four rules of arithmetic, there are five orders of architecture;[8] we, in our simplicity, think that this sounds consistent, and believe them. They inform us also that there is one proper form for Corinthian capitals, another for Doric, and another for Ionic. We, considering that there is also a proper form for the letters A, B, and C, think that this also sounds consistent, and accept the proposition. Understanding, therefore, that one form of the said capitals is proper, and no other, and having a conscientious horror of all impropriety, we allow the architect to provide us with the said capitals, of the proper form, in such and such a quantity, and in all other points to take care that the legal forms are observed; which having done, we rest in forced confidence that we are well housed.

But our higher instincts are not deceived. We take no pleasure in the building provided for us, resembling that which we take in a new book or a new picture. We may be proud of its size, complacent in its correctness, and happy in its convenience. We may take the same pleasure in its symmetry and workmanship as in a well-ordered room, or a skilful piece of manufacture. And this we suppose to be all the pleasure that architecture was ever intended to give us. The idea of reading a building as we would read Milton or Dante,[9] and getting the same kind of delight out of the stones as out of the stanzas, never enters our mind for a moment.... [I]t requires a strong effort of common sense to shake ourselves quit of all that we have been taught for the last two centuries, and wake to the perception of a truth just as simple and certain as it is new: that great art, whether expressing itself in words, colours, or stones, does *not* say the same thing over and over again; that the merit of architectural, as of every other art, consists in its saying new and different things; that to repeat itself is no more a characteristic of genius in marble than it is of genius in print; and that we may, without offending any laws of good taste, require of an architect, as we do of a novelist, that he should be not only correct, but entertaining....

Let us then understand at once, that change or variety is as much a necessity to the human heart and brain in buildings as in books; that there is no merit, though there is some occasional use, in monotony; and that we must no more expect to derive either pleasure or profit from an architecture whose ornaments are of one pattern, and whose pillars are of one proportion, than we should out of a universe in which the clouds were all of one shape, and the trees all of one size.

All this we confess in deeds, though not in words. All the pleasure which the people of the nineteenth century take in art, is in pictures, sculpture, minor objects of virtù,[10] or mediæval architecture, which we enjoy under the term picturesque: no pleasure is taken anywhere in modern buildings, and we find

---

8   The four rules of arithmetic are addition, subtraction, multiplication, and division; the five orders of architecture are Tuscan, Doric, Ionic, Corinthian, and Composite.
9   John Milton (1608–74), poet; Dante Alighieri (1265–1321), Italian poet.
10 Curios or fine art objects.

all men of true feeling delighting to escape out of modern cities into natural scenery: hence, as I shall hereafter show, that peculiar love of landscape which is characteristic of the age. It would be well, if, in all other matters, we were as ready to put up with what we dislike, for the sake of compliance with established law, as we are in architecture.

How so debased a law ever came to be established, we shall see when we come to describe the Renaissance schools:[11] here we have only to note, as the second most essential element of the Gothic spirit, that it broke through that law wherever it found it in existence; it not only dared, but delighted in, the infringement of every servile principle; and invented a series of forms of which the merit was, not merely that they were new, but that they were *capable of perpetual novelty*. The pointed arch was not merely a bold variation from the round, but it admitted of millions of variations in itself; for the proportions of a pointed arch are changeable to infinity, while a circular arch is always the same. The grouped shaft was not merely a bold variation from the single one, but it admitted of millions of variations in its grouping, and in the proportions resultant from its grouping. The introduction of tracery[12] was not only a startling change in the treatment of window lights, but admitted endless changes in the interlacement of the tracery bars themselves. So that, while in all living Christian architecture the love of variety exists, the Gothic schools exhibited that love in culminating energy; and their influence, wherever it extended itself, may be sooner and farther traced by this character than by any other; the tendency to the adoption of Gothic types being always first shown by greater irregularity and richer variation in the forms of the architecture it is about to supersede, long before the appearance of the pointed arch or of any other recognizable *outward* sign of the Gothic mind....

The variety of the Gothic schools is the more healthy and beautiful, because in many cases it is entirely unstudied, and results, not from mere love of change, but from practical necessities.... Undefined in its slope of roof, height of shaft, breadth of arch, or disposition of ground plan, [Gothic architecture] can shrink into a turret, expand into a hall, coil into a staircase, or spring into a spire, with undegraded grace and unexhausted energy.... [I]t is one of the chief virtues of the Gothic builders, that they never suffered ideas of outside symmetries and consistencies to interfere with the real use and value of what they did. If they wanted a window, they opened one; a room, they added one; a buttress, they built one; utterly regardless of any established conventionalities of external appearance, knowing (as indeed it always happened) that such daring interruptions of the formal plan would rather give additional interest to its symmetry than injure it....

The third constituent element of the Gothic mind was stated to be NATURALISM; that is to say, the love of natural objects for their own sake, and the effort to represent them frankly, unconstrained by artistical laws.

This characteristic of the style partly follows in necessary connexion with those named above. For, so soon as the workman is left free to represent what subjects he chooses, he must look to the nature that is round him for material, and will endeavour to represent it as he sees it, with more or less accuracy according to the skill he possesses, and with much play of fancy, but with small respect for law....

There is ... one direction in which the Naturalism of the Gothic workmen is peculiarly manifested; and this direction is even more characteristic of the school than the Naturalism itself; I mean their peculiar

---

11   European styles of art that flourished in the fourteenth through sixteenth centuries.
12   Elaborate stonework.

fondness for the forms of Vegetation.... [T]o the Gothic workman the living foliage became a subject of intense affection, and he struggled to render all its characters with as much accuracy as was compatible with the laws of his design and the nature of his material, not unfrequently tempted in his enthusiasm to transgress the one and disguise the other.

There is a peculiar significance in this, indicative both of higher civilization and gentler temperament, than had before been manifested in architecture. Rudeness,[13] and the love of change, which we have insisted upon as the first elements of Gothic, are also elements common to all healthy schools. But here is a softer element mingled with them, peculiar to the Gothic itself. The rudeness or ignorance which would have been painfully exposed in the treatment of the human form, are still not so great as to prevent the successful rendering of the wayside herbage; and the love of change, which becomes morbid and feverish in following the haste of the hunter, and the rage of the combatant, is at once soothed and satisfied as it watches the wandering of the tendril, and the budding of the flower. Nor is this all: the new direction of mental interest marks an infinite change in the means and the habits of life. The nations whose chief support was in the chase, whose chief interest was in the battle, whose chief pleasure was in the banquet, would take small care respecting the shapes of leaves and flowers; and notice little in the forms of the forest trees which sheltered them, except the signs indicative of the wood which would make the toughest lance, the closest roof, or the clearest fire. The affectionate observation of the grace and outward character of vegetation is the sure sign of a more tranquil and gentle existence, sustained by the gifts, and gladdened by the splendour, of the earth. In that careful distinction of species, and richness of delicate and undisturbed organization, which characterize the Gothic design, there is the history of rural and thoughtful life, influenced by habitual tenderness, and devoted to subtle inquiry; and every discriminating and delicate touch of the chisel, as it rounds the petal or guides the branch, is a prophecy of the development of the entire body of the natural sciences, beginning with that of medicine, of the recovery of literature, and the establishment of the most necessary principles of domestic wisdom and national peace....

The fourth essential element of the Gothic mind was above stated to be the sense of the GROTESQUE; but I shall defer the endeavour to define this most curious and subtle character until we have occasion to examine one of the divisions of the Renaissance schools, which was morbidly influenced by it.... It is the less necessary to insist upon it here, because every reader familiar with Gothic architecture must understand what I mean, and will, I believe, have no hesitation in admitting that the tendency to delight in fantastic and ludicrous, as well as in sublime, images, is a universal instinct of the Gothic imagination.

The fifth element above named was RIGIDITY; and this character I must endeavour carefully to define, for neither the word I have used, nor any other that I can think of, will express it accurately. For I mean, not merely stable, but *active* rigidity; the peculiar energy which gives tension to movement, and stiffness to resistance, which makes the fiercest lightning forked rather than curved, and the stoutest oak-branch angular rather than bending, and is as much seen in the quivering of the lance as in the glittering of the icicle....

Last, because the least essential, of the constituent elements of this noble school, was placed that of REDUNDANCE,—the uncalculating bestowal of the wealth of its labour.... That humility, which is the very life of the Gothic school, is shown not only in the imperfection, but in the accumulation, of ornament. The inferior rank of the workman is often shown as much in the richness, as the roughness, of his work; and if

---

13 Rough-hewn style.

the co-operation of every hand, and the sympathy of every heart, are to be received, we must be content to allow the redundance which disguises the failure of the feeble, and wins the regard of the inattentive. There are, however, far nobler interests mingling, in the Gothic heart, with the rude love of decorative accumulation: a magnificent enthusiasm, which feels as if it never could do enough to reach the fulness of its ideal; an unselfishness of sacrifice, which would rather cast fruitless labour before the altar than stand idle in the market; and, finally, a profound sympathy with the fulness and wealth of the material universe, rising out of that Naturalism whose operation we have already endeavoured to define. The sculptor who sought for his models among the forest leaves, could not but quickly and deeply feel that complexity need not involve the loss of grace, nor richness that of repose; and every hour which he spent in the study of the minute and various work of Nature, made him feel more forcibly the barrenness of what was best in that of man: nor is it to be wondered at, that, seeing her perfect and exquisite creations poured forth in a profusion which conception could not grasp nor calculation sum, he should think that it ill became him to be niggardly[14] of his own rude craftsmanship; and where he saw throughout the universe a faultless beauty lavished on measureless spaces of broidered field and blooming mountain, to grudge his poor and imperfect labour to the few stones that he had raised one upon another, for habitation or memorial. The years of his life passed away before his task was accomplished; but generation succeeded generation with unwearied enthusiasm, and the cathedral front was at last lost in the tapestry of its traceries, like a rock among the thickets and herbage of spring....

We have now, I believe, obtained a sufficiently accurate knowledge both of the spirit and form of Gothic architecture; but it may, perhaps, be useful to the general reader, if, in conclusion, I set down a few plain and practical rules for determining, in every instance, whether a given building be good Gothic or not, and, if not Gothic, whether its architecture is of a kind which will probably reward the pains of careful examination.

First. Look if the roof rises in a steep gable, high above the walls. If it does not do this, there is something wrong; the building is not quite pure Gothic, or has been altered.

Secondly. Look if the principal windows and doors have pointed arches with gables over them. If not pointed arches, the building is not Gothic; if they have not any gables over them, it is either not pure, or not first-rate.

If, however, it has the steep roof, the pointed arch, and gable all united, it is nearly certain to be a Gothic building of a very fine time.

Thirdly. Look if the arches are cusped, or apertures foliated.[15] If the building has met the first two conditions, it is sure to be foliated somewhere; but, if not everywhere, the parts which are unfoliated are imperfect, unless they are large bearing arches, or small and sharp arches in groups, forming a kind of foliation by their own multiplicity, and relieved by sculpture and rich mouldings. The upper windows, for instance, in the east end of Westminster Abbey are imperfect for want of foliation. If there be no foliation anywhere, the building is assuredly imperfect Gothic.

Fourthly. If the building meets all the first three conditions, look if its arches in general, whether of windows and doors, or of minor ornamentation, are carried on *true shafts with bases and capitals*. If they are, then the building is assuredly of the finest Gothic style. It may still, perhaps, be an imitation, a

---

14   Stingy or sparing.
15   Cusped arches are pointed arches; foliated apertures are wall openings decorated with leaves.

feeble copy, or a bad example, of a noble style; but the manner of it, having met all these four conditions, is assuredly first-rate....

This is all that is necessary to determine whether the building be of a fine Gothic style. The next tests to be applied are in order to discover whether it be good architecture or not; for it may be very impure Gothic, and yet very noble architecture; or it may be very pure Gothic, and yet, if a copy, or originally raised by an ungifted builder, very bad architecture....

First. See if it looks as if it had been built by strong men; if it has the sort of roughness, and largeness, and nonchalance, mixed in places with the exquisite tenderness which seems always to be the sign-manual of the broad vision, and massy power of men who can see *past* the work they are doing, and betray here and there something like disdain for it. If the building has this character, it is much already in its favour; it will go hard but it proves a noble one. If it has not this, but is altogether accurate, minute, and scrupulous in its workmanship, it must belong to either the very best or the very worst of schools: the very best, in which exquisite design is wrought out with untiring and conscientious care, as in the Giottesque Gothic;[16] or the very worst, in which mechanism has taken the place of design. It is more likely, in general, that it should belong to the worst than the best: so that, on the whole, very accurate workmanship is to be esteemed a bad sign; and if there is nothing remarkable about the building but its precision, it may be passed at once with contempt.

Secondly. Observe if it be irregular, its different parts fitting themselves to different purposes, no one caring what becomes of them, so that they do their work. If one part always answers accurately to another part, it is sure to be a bad building; and the greater and more conspicuous the irregularities, the greater the chances are that it is a good one....

Thirdly. Observe if all the traceries, capitals, and other ornaments are of perpetually varied design. If not, the work is assuredly bad.

Lastly. *Read* the sculpture.... On a good building, the sculpture is *always* so set, and on such a scale, that at the ordinary distance from which the edifice is seen, the sculpture shall be thoroughly intelligible and interesting....

And, having ascertained this, let him set himself to read them. Thenceforward the criticism of the building is to be conducted precisely on the same principles as that of a book; and it must depend on the knowledge, feeling, and not a little on the industry and perseverance of the reader, whether, even in the case of the best works, he either perceive them to be great, or feel them to be entertaining.

---

16 Reference to Giotto di Bondone (1266–1337), Italian painter.

"Stabat Mater." Anna Jameson, *Legends of the Madonna*. London: Longman, Brown, Green, and Longmans, 1852. Facing page 37.

Anna Jameson

from *Legends of the Madonna, as Represented in the Fine Arts* (1852)

Essayist and art critic Anna Brownell Jameson (1794–1860) worked as a governess before her marriage in 1825. After the marriage broke down in the mid-1830s, her writing income helped support her parents, sisters, and (later) her niece. Over her 30-year writing career, Jameson published essays and books on Shakespeare's heroines, her travels in Upper Canada and elsewhere, and art collections and legends. Notable as the first woman to write art criticism professionally, Jameson enjoyed friendships with a number of influential women artists and writers, including Elizabeth Barrett Browning, George Eliot (see Aesthetics and Culture), Elizabeth Gaskell, Fanny Kemble, and Harriet Martineau (see Life Writing, Condition of England, Education). She also supported a younger generation of first-wave feminists, including Barbara Leigh Smith Bodichon (see Gender and Sexuality) and Bessie Rayner Parkes, with whom she helped to found the *English Woman's Journal*.

In this excerpt from *Legends of the Madonna, as Represented in the Fine Arts* (1852), Jameson instructs her largely middle-class British Protestant readership on how to comprehend the Catholic tradition of the Madonna in European art.

The Mater Dolorosa

"Pietà (Raphael)." Anna Jameson, *Legends of the Madonna* (London: Longman, Brown, Green, and Longmans, 1852). 37.

... One of the most important of [the] devotional subjects proper to the Madonna is the "Mourning Mother," the *Mater Dolorosa*, in which her character is that of the mother of the crucified Redeemer; the mother of the atoning Sacrifice; the queen of martyrs; the woman whose bosom was pierced with a sharp sword;[17] through whose sorrow the world was saved, whose anguish was our joy, and to whom the Catholic Christians address their prayers as consoler of the afflicted,[18] because she had herself tasted of the bitterest of all earthly sorrow, the pang of the agonised mother for the loss of her child.

In this character we have three distinct representations of the Madonna.

In the first she appears alone, a seated or standing figure, often the head or half length only; the hands clasped, the head bowed in sorrow, tears streaming from the heavy eyes, and the whole expression intensely mournful. The features are properly those of a woman in middle age; but in later times the sentiment of beauty predominated over that of the mother's agony; and I have seen the sublime Mater

"Mater Dolorosa (Murillo)." Anna Jameson, *Legends of the Madonna* (London: Longman, Brown, Green, and Longmans, 1852). 38.

17 The Mater Dolorosa often represents Mary with seven swords in her heart, an allusion to Simeon's prophecy that the infant Jesus would eventually be crucified and a sword would pierce through Mary's soul (Luke 2:25–35).
18 As a daily devotion, Catholics repeat the Angelic Salutation ("Hail Mary, full of grace ...") seven times for each of Mary's seven sorrows.

Dolorosa transformed into a merely beautiful and youthful maiden, with such an air of sentimental grief as might serve for the loss of a sparrow.

Not so with the older heads; even those of the Carracci and the Spanish school[19] have often a wonderful depth of feeling....

It is common in such representations to represent the Virgin with a sword in her bosom, and even with *seven* swords, in allusion to the *seven* sorrows.[20] This very material and palpable version of the allegorical prophecy has been found extremely effective as an appeal to the popular feelings, so that there are few Roman Catholic churches without such a painful and literal interpretation of the text. It occurs perpetually in prints, and there is a fine example after Vandyck;[21] sometimes the swords are placed round her head;—but there is no instance from the best period of religious art, and it must be considered as any thing but artistic: in this case, the more materialised and the more matter of fact, the more *unreal*.

"Mater Dolorosa." Anna Jameson, *Legends of the Madonna* (London: Longman, Brown, Green, and Longmans, 1852). 39.

---

19 Annibale Carracci (1560–1609), the most influential of the Carracci family of Renaissance painters, emphasized classicism and painted many religious scenes; Spanish painters Diego Velázquez (1599–1660) and Bartolomé Esteban Murillo (1617–82) both painted religious subjects.

20 Simeon's prophecy that the infant Jesus would eventually be crucified; the holy family's flight into Egypt; the three-day loss of Jesus as a child; Jesus' and Mary's meeting along the Way of the Cross; the crucifixion; Jesus' descent from the cross; and Jesus' burial.

21 Anthony van Dyck (1599–1641), Flemish painter.

"Notre Dame des Sept Douleurs." Anna Jameson, *Legends of the Madonna* (London: Longman, Brown, Green, and Longmans, 1852). 39.

    A second representation of the *Madre di Dolore*[22] is that figure of the Virgin which, from the very earliest times, was placed on the right of the crucifix, St. John the Evangelist[23] being invariably on the left. I am speaking here of the *crucifix* as a wholly ideal and mystical emblem of our faith in a crucified Saviour; not of the *crucifixion* as an event, in which the Virgin is an actor and spectator, and is usually fainting in the arms of her attendants. In the ideal subject she is merely an ideal figure, at once the mother of Christ, and the personified Church. This, I think, is evident from those very ancient carvings, and examples in stained glass, in which the Virgin, as the Church, stands on one side of the cross, trampling on a female figure which personifies Judaism or the synagogue. Even when the allegory is less palpable, we feel that the treatment is wholly religious and poetical.

---

22   Italian: grieving mother.
23   One of Jesus' disciples, author of the Gospel of John.

The usual attitude of the *Mater Dolorosa* by the crucifix is that of intense but resigned sorrow; the hands clasped, the head declined and shaded by a veil, the figure closely wrapped in a dark blue or violet mantle. In some instances a more generally religious and ideal cast is given to the figure; she stands with outspread arms, and looking up; not weeping, but in her still beautiful face a mingled expression of faith and anguish. This is the true conception of the sublime hymn,

> "Stabat Mater Dolorosa
> Juxta crucem lachrymosa
> Dum pendebat filius."[24] ...

"Mater Dolorosa (P. de Champagne)." Anna Jameson, *Legends of the Madonna* (London: Longman, Brown, Green, and Longmans, 1852). 40.

---

24 Latin: "The sorrowful mother stood / weeping beside the Cross / where her Son was hanging": *Stabat Mater* (c. 1300); this poem focuses on Mary's suffering during Jesus' crucifixion.

The third, and it is the most important and most beautiful of all as far as the Virgin is concerned, is the group called the Pietà, which, when strictly devotional, consists only of the Virgin with her dead Son in her arms, or on her lap, or lying at her feet; in some instances with lamenting angels, but no other personages. This group has been varied in a thousand ways: no doubt the two most perfect conceptions are those of Michael Angelo and Raphael;[25] the first excelling in sublimity, the latter in pathos. The celebrated marble group by Michael Angelo stands in the Vatican[26] in a chapel to the right as we enter. The Virgin is seated; the dead Saviour lies across the knees of his mother: she looks down on him in mingled sorrow and resignation, but the majestic resignation predominates. The composition of Raphael exists only as a print; but the flimsy paper, consecrated through its unspeakable beauty, is likely to be as lasting as the marble. It represents the Virgin standing with outstretched arms, and looking up with an appealing agonized expression towards heaven; before her, on the earth, lies extended the form of the Saviour. In tenderness, dignity, simplicity, and tragic pathos, nothing can exceed this production; the head of the Virgin in particular is regarded as a masterpiece, so far exceeding in depth of sentiment and delicacy of execution every other work of Marc Antonio,[27] that some have thought that Raphael himself took the burin[28] from his hand, and touched himself that face of woe.

Another example of wonderful beauty is the Pietà by Francia,[29] in our National Gallery.[30] The form of Christ lies extended before his mother; a lamenting angel sustains the head, another is at the feet; the Virgin, with eyes red and heavy with weeping, looks out of the picture. There needs no visible sword in her bosom to tell what anguish has pierced that maternal heart.

There is another Pietà, by Michael Angelo, quite a different conception. The Virgin sits at the foot of the cross; before her, and half-sustained by her knees, lies the form of the dead Saviour, seen in front; his arms are held up by two angels (unwinged, as is usual with Michael Angelo). The Virgin looks up to heaven with an appealing expression; and in one engraving of this composition the cross is inscribed with the words, "Tu non pensi quanto sangue costa."[31] There is no painting by Michael Angelo himself, but many copies and engravings of the drawing. A beautiful small copy, by Marcello Venusti,[32] is in the Queen's Gallery.

There is yet another version of the Pietà, quite mystical and devotional in its significance,—but, to my feeling, more painful and material than poetical. It is variously treated; for example:—1. The dead Redeemer is seen half-length within the tomb; his hands are extended to show his wounds; his eyes are closed, his head declined, his bleeding brow encircled by thorns. On one side is the Virgin, on the other ... St. John the Evangelist, in attitudes of profound grief and commiseration. 2. The dead form, half emerging from the tomb, is sustained in the arms of the Mater Dolorosa. St. John the Evangelist on the other side. There are sometimes angels.

---

25 Michelangelo (1475–1564) and Raphael (1483–1520), Italian Renaissance artists.
26 The pope's palace in Rome.
27 Marcantonio Raimondi (c. 1480–c. 1534), Italian Renaissance engraver, especially of Raphael's work.
28 Engraving tool for use on copper.
29 Francia (c. 1450–1517), Italian Renaissance artist.
30 Art museum in London (founded 1824) that houses England's national collection of European paintings.
31 Italian: "You don't think about how much blood it costs."
32 Marcello Venusti (c. 1512–79), Italian painter.

"Pietà (B. Angelico)." Anna Jameson, *Legends of the Madonna* (London: Longman, Brown, Green, and Longmans, 1852). 42.

The Pietà thus conceived as a purely religious and ideal impersonation of the atoning Sacrifice is commonly placed over the altar of the sacrament; and in many altar-pieces it forms the centre of the predella, just in front where the mass is celebrated, or on the door of the tabernacle, where the Host is deposited.[33]

When, with the Mater Dolorosa and St. John, Mary Magdalene[34] is introduced with her dishevelled hair, the group ceases to be properly a Pietà, and becomes a representation rather than a symbol.

There are also examples of a yet more complex but still perfectly ideal and devotional treatment, in which the Mourning Mother is attended by saints.

A most celebrated instance of this treatment is the Pietà by Guido.[35] In the upper part of the composition, the figure of the dead Redeemer lies extended on a white shroud; behind him stands

---

33 A predella is the base of an altar or the shelf at the rear of an altar, often painted; a tabernacle is a decorated container that holds the box of consecrated bread (the Host) distributed during mass.
34 One of Jesus' followers, Mary Magdalene witnessed his crucifixion and burial.
35 Guido Reni (1575–1642), Italian painter.

the Virgin mother, with her eyes raised to heaven, and sad appealing face, touched with so divine a sorrow—so much of dignity in the midst of infinite anguish, that I know nothing finer in its way. Her hands are resignedly folded in each other, not raised, not clasped, but languidly drooping. An angel stands at the feet of Christ looking on with a tender adoring commiseration; another, at his head, turns away weeping. A kind of curtain divides this group from the lower part of the picture, where, assembled on a platform, stand or kneel the guardian saints of Bologna: in the centre, the benevolent St. Charles Borromeo, who just about that time had been canonised[36] and added to the list of the patrons of Bologna by a decree of the senate; on the right, St. Dominick and St. Petronius; on the left, St. Proculus and St. Francis.[37] These sainted personages look up as if adjuring the Virgin, even by her own deep anguish, to intercede for the city; she is here at once our Lady of Pity, of Succour, and of Sorrow. This wonderful picture was dedicated, as an act of penance and piety, by the magistrates of Bologna, in 1616, and placed in their chapel in the church of the "Mendicanti,"[38] otherwise S. Maria-della-Pietà. It hung there for two centuries, for the consolation of the afflicted; it is now placed in the academy of Bologna for the admiration of connoisseurs....

"Lamenting Angel, from an ancient Greek Pietà." Anna Jameson, *Legends of the Madonna* (London: Longman, Brown, Green, and Longmans, 1852). 44.

---

36 Made a saint.
37 Patron saints of the city of Bologna.
38 Italian: beggars.

George Eliot
from *Adam Bede* (1859)

Essayist, translator, and novelist George Eliot (born Mary Anne Evans) (1819–80) converted to evangelicalism in her teens but soon lost her faith under the influence of freethinkers. Through them, she met many leading liberals, including Herbert Spencer (see Science), Harriet Martineau (see Life Writing, Condition of England, Education), and John Chapman, editor of the radical *Westminster Review* (which she wrote for and briefly helped edit). Eliot translated from German two controversial works of nineteenth-century Biblical scholarship: David Friedrich Strauss's *The Life of Jesus* (1846) and Ludwig von Feuerbach's *The Essence of Christianity* (1854). In 1854, she made public her relationship with writer George Henry Lewes, a married man unable to obtain a divorce. In 1857, Eliot began writing meticulously researched realist fiction, including *Adam Bede* (1859), *The Mill on the Floss* (1860), and *Middlemarch* (1871–72).

While this excerpt from *Adam Bede* is taken from Eliot's fiction, it functions as a manifesto for the moral value of realism. Here Eliot argues that the "faithful" representation "of commonplace things" leads to "human sympathy."

Vol. 2, Chapter 17: In which the Story Pauses a Little

"THIS Rector of Broxton is little better than a pagan!" I hear one of my lady readers exclaim. "How much more edifying it would have been if you had made him give Arthur some truly spiritual advice. You might have put into his mouth the most beautiful things—quite as good as reading a sermon."

Certainly I could, my fair critic, if I were a clever novelist, not obliged to creep servilely after nature and fact, but able to represent things as they never have been and never will be. Then, of course, my characters would be entirely of my own choosing, and I could select the most unexceptionable type of clergyman, and put my own admirable opinions into his mouth on all occasions. But you must have perceived long ago that I have no such lofty vocation, and that I aspire to give no more than a faithful account of men and things as they have mirrored themselves in my mind. The mirror is doubtless defective; the outlines will sometimes be disturbed; the reflection faint or confused; but I feel as much bound to tell you, as precisely as I can, what that reflection is, as if I were in the witness-box narrating my experience on oath.

Sixty years ago—it is a long time, so no wonder things have changed—all clergymen were not zealous; indeed, there is reason to believe that the number of zealous clergymen was small, and it is probable that if one among the small minority had owned the livings of Broxton and Hayslope in the year 1799, you would have liked him no better than you like Mr Irwine. Ten to one, you would have thought him a tasteless, indiscreet, methodistical[39] man. It is so very rarely that facts hit that nice medium required by

---

39 Methodism was a reformist movement within the Anglican Church founded by John Wesley in the eighteenth century.

our own enlightened opinions and refined taste! Perhaps you will say, "Do improve the facts a little, then; make them more accordant with those correct views which it is our privilege to possess. The world is not just what we like; do touch it up with a tasteful pencil, and make believe it is not quite such a mixed, entangled affair. Let all people who hold unexceptionable opinions act unexceptionably. Let your most faulty characters always be on the wrong side, and your virtuous ones on the right. Then we shall see at a glance whom we are to condemn, and whom we are to approve. Then we shall be able to admire, without the slightest disturbance of our prepossessions: we shall hate and despise with that true ruminant relish which belongs to undoubting confidence."

But, my good friend, what will you do then with your fellow-parishioner who opposes your husband in the vestry?—with your newly appointed vicar, whose style of preaching you find painfully below that of his regretted predecessor?—with the honest servant, who worries your soul with her one failing?—with your neighbour, Mrs Green, who was really kind to you in your last illness, but has said several ill-natured things about you since your convalescence?—nay, with your excellent husband himself, who has other irritating habits besides that of not wiping his shoes? These fellow-mortals, every one, must be accepted as they are: you can neither straighten their noses, nor brighten their wit, nor rectify their dispositions; and it is these people—amongst whom your life is passed—that it is needful you should tolerate, pity, and love: it is these more or less ugly, stupid, inconsistent people, whose movements of goodness you should be able to admire—for whom you should cherish all possible hopes, all possible patience. And I would not, even if I had the choice, be the clever novelist who could create a world so much better than this, in which we get up in the morning to do our daily work, that you would be likely to turn a harder, colder eye on the dusty streets and the common green fields—on the real breathing men and women, who can be chilled by your indifference or injured by your prejudice; who can be cheered and helped onward by your fellow-feeling, your forbearance, your outspoken, brave justice.

So I am content to tell my simple story, without trying to make things seem better than they were; dreading nothing, indeed, but falsity, which, in spite of one's best efforts, there is reason to dread. Falsehood is so easy, truth so difficult. The pencil is conscious of a delightful facility in drawing a griffin—the longer the claws, and the larger the wings, the better; but that marvellous facility which we mistook for genius, is apt to forsake us when we want to draw a real unexaggerated lion. Examine your words well, and you will find that even when you have no motive to be false, it is a very hard thing to say the exact truth, even about your own immediate feelings—much harder than to say something fine about them which is *not* the exact truth.

It is for this rare, precious quality of truthfulness that I delight in many Dutch paintings,[40] which lofty-minded people despise. I find a source of delicious sympathy in these faithful pictures of a monotonous homely existence, which has been the fate of so many more among my fellow-mortals than a life of pomp or of absolute indigence, of tragic suffering or of world-stirring actions. I turn without shrinking, from cloud-borne angels, from prophets, sibyls, and heroic warriors, to an old woman bending over her flower-pot, or eating her solitary dinner, while the noonday light, softened perhaps by a screen of leaves, falls on her mob-cap,[41] and just touches the rim of her spinning-wheel, and her stone jug, and all those cheap common things which are the precious necessaries of life to her;—or I turn to that village wedding,

---

40 Seventeenth-century Dutch painters were known for their attention to everyday detail.
41 Bonnet.

kept between four brown walls, where an awkward bridegroom opens the dance with a high-shouldered, broad-faced bride, while elderly and middle-aged friends look on, with very irregular noses and lips, and probably with quart pots in their hands, but with an expression of unmistakable contentment and good-will. "Foh!" says my idealistic friend, "what vulgar details! What good is there in taking all these pains to give an exact likeness of old women and clowns? What a low phase of life!—what clumsy, ugly people!"

But, bless us, things may be lovable that are not altogether handsome, I hope? I am not at all sure that the majority of the human race have not been ugly, and even among those "lords of their kind," the British, squat figures, ill-shapen nostrils, and dingy complexions are not startling exceptions. Yet there is a great deal of family love amongst us. I have a friend or two whose class of features is such that the Apollo[42] curl on the summit of their brows would be decidedly trying; yet to my certain knowledge tender hearts have beaten for them, and their miniatures—flattering, but still not lovely—are kissed in secret by motherly lips. I have seen many an excellent matron, who could never in her best days have been handsome, and yet she had a packet of yellow love-letters in a private drawer, and sweet children showered kisses on her sallow cheeks. And I believe there have been plenty of young heroes, of middle stature and feeble beards, who have felt quite sure they could never love anything more insignificant than a Diana,[43] and yet have found themselves in middle life happily settled with a wife who waddles. Yes! thank God; human feeling is like the mighty rivers that bless the earth: it does not wait for beauty—it flows with resistless force and brings beauty with it.

All honour and reverence to the divine beauty of form! Let us cultivate it to the utmost in men, women, and children—in our gardens and in our houses. But let us love that other beauty too, which lies in no secret of proportion, but in the secret of deep human sympathy. Paint us an angel, if you can, with a floating violet robe, and a face paled by the celestial light; paint us yet oftener a Madonna, turning her mild face upward and opening her arms to welcome the divine glory; but do not impose on us any æsthetic rules which shall banish from the region of Art those old women scraping carrots with their work-worn hands, those heavy clowns taking holiday in a dingy pot-house,[44] those rounded backs and stupid weather-beaten faces that have bent over the spade and done the rough work of the world—those homes with their tin pans, their brown pitchers, their rough curs, and their clusters of onions. In this world there are so many of these common, coarse people, who have no picturesque sentimental wretchedness! It is so needful we should remember their existence, else we may happen to leave them quite out of our religion and philosophy, and frame lofty theories which only fit a world of extremes. Therefore let Art always remind us of them; therefore let us always have men ready to give the loving pains of a life to the faithful representing of commonplace things—men who see beauty in these commonplace things, and delight in showing how kindly the light of heaven falls on them. There are few prophets in the world; few sublimely beautiful women; few heroes. I can't afford to give all my love and reverence to such rarities: I want a great deal of those feelings for my everyday fellow-men, especially for the few in the foreground of the great multitude, whose faces I know, whose hands I touch, for whom I have to make way with kindly courtesy. Neither are picturesque lazzaroni[45] or romantic criminals half so frequent as your common labourer, who gets his own bread, and eats it vulgarly but creditably with his own pocket-knife. It is

---

42 Greek god of music, poetry, and dance.
43 Roman goddess of hunting, marked by her beauty and chastity.
44 Tavern.
45 The poor class of Naples.

more needful that I should have a fibre of sympathy connecting me with that vulgar citizen who weighs out my sugar in a vilely assorted cravat and waistcoat, than with the handsomest rascal in red scarf and green feathers;—more needful that my heart should swell with loving admiration at some trait of gentle goodness in the faulty people who sit at the same hearth with me, or in the clergyman of my own parish, who is perhaps rather too corpulent, and in other respects is not an Oberlin or a Tillotson,[46] than at the deeds of heroes whom I shall never know except by hearsay, or at the sublimest abstract of all clerical graces that was ever conceived by an able novelist....

Matthew Arnold
from "Culture and Its Enemies" (1867)

Initially known for his poetry, in the 1860s and 1870s Matthew Arnold (1822–88) became England's leading critic with essays on literary, religious, social, and educational issues. The son of Thomas Arnold (see Education), he was educated at Winchester, Rugby, and Oxford. Beginning in 1851, Arnold worked as a school inspector for 35 years, observing the social conditions of education. In his criticism, Arnold denounced "Philistinism," his term for middle-class people's lack of liberal culture; he argued for intellectual curiosity and openness, qualities he lauded in European educational models.

Initially published in 1867 in the *Cornhill Magazine* (the version excerpted here) and revised for *Culture and Anarchy* (1869), "Culture and Its Enemies" responded to the Reform Bill of 1867, which expanded the franchise to include all male householders. Arnold argued, however, that the franchise alone was insufficient—culture would be needed to promote the ideals that England required in its "new democracy."

... The disparagers of culture make its motive curiosity; sometimes, indeed, they make its motive mere exclusiveness and vanity. The culture which is supposed to plume itself on a smattering of Greek and Latin is a culture which is begotten by nothing so intellectual as curiosity; it is valued either out of sheer vanity and ignorance, or else as an engine of social and class distinction.... No serious man would call this *culture*, or attach any value to it, as culture, at all. To find the real ground for the very differing estimate which serious people will set upon culture, we must find some motive for culture in the terms of which may lie a real ambiguity; and such a motive the word *curiosity* gives us. I have before now pointed out that in English we do not, like the foreigners, use this word in a good sense as well as in a bad sense; with us the word is always used in a somewhat disapproving sense; a liberal and intelligent eagerness about the things of the mind may be meant by a foreigner when he speaks of curiosity, but with us the word always conveys a certain notion of frivolous and unedifying activity.... For as there is a curiosity about intellectual matters which is futile, and merely a disease, so there is certainly a curiosity,—a desire for the things of

---

46 Johann Friedrich Oberlin (1740–1826), French clergyman; John Tillotson (1630–94), archbishop of Canterbury.

the mind simply for their own sakes and for the pleasure of seeing them as they are,—which is, in an intelligent being, natural and laudable. Nay, and the very desire to see things as they are implies a balance and regulation of mind which is not often attained without fruitful effort, and which is the very opposite of the blind and diseased impulse of mind which is what we mean to blame when we blame curiosity.

Montesquieu says:—"The first motive which ought to impel us to study is the desire to augment the excellence of our nature, and to render an intelligent being yet more intelligent."[47] This is the true ground to assign for the genuine scientific passion, however manifested, and for culture, viewed simply as a fruit of this passion; and it is a worthy ground, even though we let the term *curiosity* stand to describe it. But there is of culture another view, in which not solely the scientific passion, the sheer desire to see things as they are, natural and proper in an intelligent being, appears as the ground of it; a view in which all the love of our neighbour, the impulses towards action, help, and beneficence, the desire for stopping human error, clearing human confusion, and diminishing the sum of human misery, the noble aspiration to leave the world better and happier than we found it—motives eminently such as are called social—come in as part of the grounds of culture, and the main and primary part. Culture is then properly described not as having its origin in curiosity, but as having its origin in the love of perfection; it is a study of perfection. It moves by the force, not merely or primarily of the scientific passion for pure knowledge, but also of the moral and social passion for doing good. As, in the first view of it, we took for its worthy motto Montesquieu's words: "To render an intelligent being yet more intelligent!" so, in the second view of it, there is no better motto which it can take than these words of Bishop Wilson: "To make reason and the will of God prevail!"[48] Only, whereas the passion for doing good is apt to be overhasty in determining what reason and the will of God say, because its turn is for acting rather than thinking, and it wants to be beginning to act; and whereas it is apt to take its own conceptions, proceeding from its own state of development and sharing in all the imperfections and immaturities of this, for a basis of action; what distinguishes culture is that it is possessed by the scientific passion, as well as by the passion of doing good; that it has worthy notions of reason and the will of God, and does not readily suffer its own crude conceptions to substitute themselves for them; and that, knowing that no action or institution can be salutary and stable which are not based on reason and the will of God, it is not so bent on acting and instituting, even with the great aim of diminishing human error and misery ever before its thoughts, but that it can remember that acting and instituting are of little use, unless we know how and what we ought to act and to institute.

This culture is more interesting and more far-reaching than that other, which is founded solely on the scientific passion for knowing. But it needs times of faith and ardour, times when the intellectual horizon is opening and widening all round us, to flourish in. And is not the close and bounded intellectual horizon within which we have long lived and moved now lifting up, and are not new lights finding free passage to shine in upon us? ... [N]ow the iron force of adhesion to the old routine—social, political, religious—has wonderfully yielded; the iron force of exclusion of all which is new has wonderfully yielded; the danger now is, not that people should obstinately refuse to allow anything but their old routine to pass for reason and the will of God, but either that they should allow some novelty or other to pass for these too easily, or else that they should underrate the importance of them altogether, and think it enough to follow action for its own sake, without troubling themselves to make reason and the will of God prevail in it. Now, then,

---

47   Charles-Louis de Secondat Montesquieu, *Discours sur les motifs qui doivent nous encourager aux sciences* (1725).
48   Bishop Thomas Wilson, *Sacra Privata* (1781).

is the moment for culture to be of service, culture which believes in making reason and the will of God prevail, believes in perfection, is the study and pursuit of perfection, and is no longer debarred, by a rigid invincible exclusion of whatever is new, from getting acceptance for its ideas, simply because they are new.

The moment this view of culture is seized, the moment it is regarded not solely as the endeavour to see things as they are, to draw towards a knowledge of the universal order which seems to be intended and aimed at in the world, and which it is a man's happiness to go along with or his misery to go counter to, to learn, in short, the will of God,—the moment, I say, culture is considered not as the endeavour to merely *see* and *learn* this, but as the endeavour, also, to make it *prevail*, the moral, social, and beneficent character of culture becomes manifest. The mere endeavour to see and learn it for our own personal satisfaction is indeed a commencement for making it prevail, a preparing the way for it, which always serves this, and is wrongly, therefore, stamped with blame absolutely in itself, and not only in its caricature and degeneration; but perhaps it has got stamped with blame, and disparaged with the dubious title of curiosity, because in comparison with this wider endeavour of such great and plain utility it looks selfish, petty, and unprofitable.

And religion, the greatest and most important of the efforts by which the human race has manifested its impulse to perfect itself—religion, that voice of the deepest human experience, does not only enjoin and sanction the aim which is the great aim of culture, the aim of setting ourselves to ascertain what perfection is and to make it prevail, but also, in determining generally in what human perfection consists, religion comes to a conclusion identical with that which culture—seeking the determination of this question through all the voices of human experience which have been heard upon it, art, science, poetry, philosophy, history, as well as religion, in order to give a greater fulness and certainty to its solution—likewise reaches. Religion says: *The kingdom of God is within you*;[49] and culture, in like manner, places human perfection in an internal condition, in the growth and predominance of our humanity proper, as distinguished from our animality, in the ever-increasing efficaciousness and in the general harmonious expansion of those gifts of thought and feeling which make the peculiar dignity, wealth, and happiness of human nature. As I have said on a former occasion: "It is in making endless additions to itself, in the endless expansion of its powers, in endless growth in wisdom and beauty, that the spirit of the human race finds its ideal. To reach this ideal culture is an indispensable aid, and that is the true value of culture."[50] Not a having and a resting, but a growing and a becoming, is the character of perfection as culture conceives it; and here, too, it coincides with religion. And because men are all members of one great whole, and the sympathy which is in human nature will not allow one member to be indifferent to the rest, or to have a perfect welfare independent of the rest, the expansion of our humanity, to suit the idea of perfection which culture forms, must be a general expansion. Perfection, as culture conceives it, is not possible while the individual remains isolated: the individual is obliged, under pain of being stunted and enfeebled in his own development if he disobeys, to carry others along with him in his march towards perfection, to be continually doing all he can to enlarge and increase the volume of the human stream sweeping thitherward; and here, once more, it lays on us the same obligation as religion. Finally, perfection—as culture, from a thorough disinterested study of human nature and human experience, learns to conceive it—is an harmonious expansion of *all* the powers which make the beauty and worth of human nature,

---

49 Luke 17:21.
50 Matthew Arnold, *A French Eton, Or, Middle-Class Education and the State* (1864).

and is not consistent with the over-development of any one power at the expense of the rest. Here it goes beyond religion, as religion is generally conceived by us.

If culture, then, is a study of perfection, and of harmonious perfection, general perfection, and perfection which consists in becoming something rather than in having something, in an inward condition of the mind and spirit, not in an outward set of circumstances,—it is clear that culture ... has a very important function to fulfil for mankind. And this function is particularly important in our modern world, of which the whole civilization is, to a much greater degree than the civilization of Greece and Rome, mechanical and external, and tends constantly to become more so. But above all in our own country has culture a weighty part to perform, because here that mechanical character, which civilization tends to take everywhere, is shown in the most eminent degree. Indeed nearly all the characters of perfection, as culture teaches us to fix them, meet in this country with some powerful tendency which thwarts them and sets them at defiance.... The idea of perfection as a *general* expansion of the human family is at variance with our strong individualism, our hatred of all limits to the unrestrained swing of the individual's personality, our maxim of "every man for himself." The idea of perfection as an harmonious expansion of human nature is at variance with our want of flexibility, with our inaptitude for seeing more than one side of a thing, with our intense energetic absorption in the particular pursuit we happen to be following. So culture has a rough task to do in this country; and its preachers have, and are likely long to have, a hard time of it, and they will much oftener be regarded, for a great while to come, as elegant or spurious Jeremiahs,[51] than as friends and benefactors. That, however, will not prevent their doing in the end good service if they persevere; and meanwhile, the mode of action they have to pursue, and the sort of habits they must fight against, may be made quite clear to any one who will look at the matter attentively and dispassionately.

Faith in machinery is, I said, our besetting danger; often in machinery most absurdly disproportioned to the end which this machinery, if it is to do any good at all, is to serve; but always in machinery, as if it had a value in and for itself. What is freedom but machinery? what is population but machinery? what is coal but machinery? what are railroads but machinery? what is wealth but machinery? what are religious organizations but machinery? Now almost every voice in England is accustomed to speak of these things as if they were precious ends in themselves, and therefore had some of the characters of perfection indisputably joined to them.... But the aspirations of culture, which is the study of perfection, are not satisfied, unless what men say, when they may say what they like, is worth saying,—has good in it, and more good than bad. In the same way *The Times*, replying to some foreign strictures on the dress, looks, and behaviour of the English abroad, urges that the English ideal is that every one should be free to do and to look just as he likes. But culture indefatigably tries, not to make what each raw person may like the rule by which he fashions himself; but to draw ever nearer to a sense of what is indeed beautiful, graceful, and becoming, and to get the raw person to like that.

In the same way with respect to railroads and coal. Every one must have observed the strange language current during the late discussions as to the possible failure of our supplies of coal. Our coal, thousands of people were saying, is the real basis of our national greatness; if our coal runs short, there is an end of the greatness of England.[52] But what *is* greatness?—culture makes us ask. Greatness is a spiritual condition

---

51 Biblical prophet who urged the Israelites to return to God to avoid impending doom.
52 The late eighteenth- and early nineteenth-century Industrial Revolution was largely fuelled by coal, one of England's major resources.

worthy to excite love, interest, and admiration; and the outward proof of possessing greatness is that we excite love, interest, and admiration. If England were swallowed up by the sea to-morrow, which, a hundred years hence, would most excite the love, interest, and admiration of mankind,—would most, therefore, shew the evidences of having possessed greatness,—the England of the last twenty years, or the England of Elizabeth, of a time of splendid spiritual effort, but when our coal, and our industrial operations depending on coal, were very little developed? ...

Wealth, again, that end to which our prodigious works for material advantage are directed,—the commonest of commonplaces tells us how men are always apt to regard wealth as a precious end in itself; and certainly they have never been so apt thus to regard it as they are in England at the present time. Never did people believe anything more firmly than nine Englishmen out of ten at the present day believe that our greatness and welfare are proved by our being so very rich. Now, the use of culture is that it helps us, by means of its spiritual standard of perfection, to regard wealth as but machinery, and not only to say as a matter of words that we regard wealth as but machinery, but really to perceive and feel that it is so. If it were not for this purging effect wrought upon our minds by culture, the whole world, the future as well as the present, would inevitably belong to the Philistines.[53] The people who believe most that our greatness and welfare are proved by our being very rich, and who most give their lives and thoughts to becoming rich, are just the very people whom we call the Philistines. Culture says: "Consider these people, then, their way of life, their habits, their manners, the very tones of their voice; look at them attentively; observe the literature they read, the things which give them pleasure, the words which come forth out of their mouths, the thoughts which make the furniture of their minds; would any amount of wealth be worth having with the condition that one was to become just like these people by having it?" And thus culture begets a dissatisfaction which is of the highest possible value in stemming the common tide of men's thoughts in a wealthy and industrial community, and which saves the future, as one may hope, from being vulgarized, even if it cannot save the present.

Population, again, and bodily health and vigour, are things which are nowhere treated in such an unintelligent, misleading, exaggerated way as in England. Both are really machinery; yet how many people all around us do we see rest in them and fail to look beyond them! Why, I have heard people, fresh from reading certain articles of *The Times* on the Registrar-General's returns of marriages and births in this country,[54] who would talk of large families in quite a solemn strain, as if they had something in itself beautiful, elevating, and meritorious in them.... Bodily health and vigour, it may be said, are not to be classed with wealth and population as mere machinery; they have a more real and essential value. True; but only as they are more intimately connected with a perfect spiritual condition than wealth or population are. The moment we disjoin them from the idea of a perfect spiritual condition, and pursue them, as we do pursue them, for their own sake and as ends in themselves, our worship of them becomes as mere worship of machinery, as our worship of wealth or population, and as unintelligent and vulgarizing a worship as that is.... "Bodily exercise profiteth little; but godliness is profitable unto all things,"[55] says the author of the Epistle to Timothy.... But the point of view of culture, keeping the mark of human perfection simply and broadly in view, and not assigning to this perfection, as religion or utilitarianism assign to it, a special

---

53 Enemies of the Israelites in the Old Testament; a term used in the nineteenth century to refer to someone ignorant or uncultured.
54 From 1836, the Registrar General oversaw the registration of births, marriages, and deaths.
55 Timothy 4:8.

and limited character,—this point of view, I say, of culture, is best given by these words of Epictetus:—"It is a sign of αφυια," says he,—that is, of a nature not finely tempered,—"to give yourselves up to things which relate to the body; to make, for instance, a great fuss about exercise, a great fuss about eating, a great fuss about drinking, a great fuss about walking, a great fuss about riding. All these things ought to be done merely *by the way*: the formation of the spirit and character must be our real concern."[56] This is admirable; and, indeed, the Greek words αφυια, ευφυια, a finely tempered nature, a coarsely tempered nature, give exactly the notion of perfection as culture brings us to conceive of it: a perfection in which the characters of beauty and intelligence are both present, which unites "the two noblest of things,"—as Swift who of one of the two at any rate, had himself all too little, most happily calls them in his *Battle of the Books*,—"the two noblest of things, *sweetness and light*."[57] The ευφυης is the man who tends towards sweetness and light; the αφυης is precisely our Philistine....

It is by thus making sweetness and light to be characters of perfection, that culture is of like spirit with poetry, follows one law with poetry. I have called religion a more important manifestation of human nature than poetry, because it has worked on a broader scale for perfection, and with greater masses of men. But the idea of beauty and of a human nature perfect on all its sides, which is the dominant idea of poetry, is a true and invaluable idea, though it has not yet had the success that the idea of conquering the obvious faults of our animality, and of a human nature perfect on the moral side, which is the dominant idea of religion, has been enabled to have; and it is destined, adding to itself the religious idea of a devout energy, to transform and govern the other. The best art and poetry of the Greeks, in which religion and poetry are one, in which the idea of beauty and of a human nature perfect on all sides adds to itself a religious and devout energy, and works in the strength of that, is on this account of such surpassing interest and instructiveness for us, though it was,—as, having regard to the human race in general, and, indeed, having regard to the Greeks themselves, we must own,—a premature attempt, an attempt which for success needed the moral and religious fibre in humanity to be more braced and developed than it had yet been. But Greece did not err in having the idea of beauty, harmony, and complete human perfection so present and paramount; it is impossible to have this idea too present and paramount; only the moral fibre must be braced too. And we, because we have braced the moral fibre, are not on that account in the right way, if at the same time the idea of beauty, harmony, and complete human perfection, is wanting or misapprehended amongst us, and evidently it *is* wanting or misapprehended at present. And when we rely as we do on our religious organizations, which in themselves do not and cannot give us this idea, and think we have done enough if we make them spread and prevail, then, I say, we fall into our common fault of overvaluing machinery.

Nothing is more common than for people to confound the inward peace and satisfaction which follows the subduing of the obvious faults of our animality with what I may call absolute inward peace and satisfaction—the peace and satisfaction which are reached as we draw near to complete spiritual perfection, and not merely to moral perfection, or rather to relative moral perfection.... And we have had our reward, not only in the great worldly prosperity which our obedience to this command has brought us, but also, and far more, in great inward peace and satisfaction. But to me nothing is more pathetic than to see people, on the strength of the inward peace and satisfaction which their rudimentary efforts towards perfection

---

56 Epictetus, *Encheiridion* (135).
57 Jonathan Swift, *Battle of the Books* (1697).

have brought them, use concerning their incomplete perfection and the religious organizations within which they have found it, language which properly applies only to complete perfection, and is a far-off echo of the human soul's prophecy of it. Religion itself supplies in abundance this grand language which is really the severest criticism of such an incomplete perfection as alone we have yet reached through our religious organizations.

    The impulse of the English race towards moral development and self-conquest has nowhere so powerfully manifested itself as in Puritanism; nowhere has Puritanism found so adequate an expression as in the religious organization of the Independents.[58] The modern Independents have a newspaper, the *Nonconformist*,[59] written with great sincerity and ability, which serves as their organ. The motto, the standard, the profession of faith which this organ of theirs carries aloft, is: "The dissidence of Dissent and the Protestantism of the Protestant religion." There is sweetness and light, and an ideal of complete harmonious human perfection! One need not go to culture and poetry to find language to judge it. Religion, with its instinct for perfection, supplies language to judge it: "Finally, be of one mind, united in feeling," says St. Peter.[60] There is an ideal which judges the Puritan ideal!—"The dissidence of Dissent and the Protestantism of the Protestant religion." And religious organizations like this are what people believe in, rest in, would give their lives for! Such, I say, is the wonderful virtue of even the beginnings of perfection, of having conquered even the first faults of our animality, that the religious organization which has helped us to do it can seem to us something precious, salutary, and to be propagated, even when it wears such a brand of imperfection on its forehead as this. And men have got such a habit of giving to the language of religion a special application, of making it a mere jargon, that for the condemnation which religion itself passes on the shortcomings of their religious organizations they have no ear; they are sure to cheat themselves and to explain this condemnation away. They can only be reached by the criticism which culture, like poetry, speaking a language not to be sophisticated, and resolutely testing these organizations by the ideal of a human perfection complete on all sides, applies to them.

    But men of culture and poetry, it will be said, are again and again failing, and failing conspicuously, in the necessary first stage to perfection, in the subduing of the great obvious faults of our animality, which it is the glory of these religious organizations to have helped us to subdue. True, they do often so fail: they have often had neither the virtues nor the faults of the Puritan; it has been one of their dangers that they so felt the Puritan's faults that they too much neglected the practice of his virtues. I will not, however, exculpate them at the Puritan's expense; they have often failed in morality, and morality is indispensable; they have been punished for their failure, as the Puritan has been rewarded for his performance. They have been punished wherein they erred; but their ideal of beauty and sweetness and light, and a human nature complete on all its sides, remains the true ideal of perfection still; just as the Puritan's ideal of perfection remains narrow and inadequate, although for what he did well he has been abundantly rewarded. Notwithstanding the mighty results of the Pilgrim Fathers'[61] voyage, they and

---

58 Puritanism was a sixteenth-century Protestant religious movement whose followers wished to purge the Church of England of Catholic tendencies; Independents (or Congregationalists) believed that church congregations should be independent from a larger institutional body such as the Church of England.
59 A newspaper (begun in 1841) that decried the Church of England.
60 Peter 3:8.
61 English Puritans who fled to America in 1620 to avoid religious persecution.

their standard of perfection are rightly judged when we figure to ourselves Shakspeare or Virgil[62]—souls in whom sweetness and light, and all that in human nature is most humane, were eminent—accompanying them on their voyage, and think what intolerable company Shakspeare and Virgil would have found them! In the same way let us judge the religious organizations which we see all round us. Do not let us deny the good and the happiness which they have accomplished; but do not let us fail to see clearly that their idea of human perfection is narrow and inadequate, and that the dissidence of Dissent and the Protestantism of the Protestant religion will never bring humanity to its true goal. As I said with regard to wealth,—let us look at the life of those who live in and for it;—so I say with regard to the religious organizations. Look at the life imaged in such a newspaper as the *Nonconformist*;—a life of jealousy of the Establishment, disputes, tea-meetings, openings of chapels, sermons; and then think of it as an ideal of a human life completing itself on all sides, and aspiring with all its organs after sweetness, light, and perfection!

Another newspaper, representing, like the *Nonconformist*, one of the religious organizations of this country, was, a few days ago, giving an account of the crowd at Epsom on the Derby day,[63] and of all the vice and hideousness which was to be seen in that crowd; and then the writer turned suddenly round upon Professor Huxley,[64] and asked him how he proposed to cure all this vice and hideousness without religion. I confess I felt disposed to ask the asker this question: And how do you propose to cure it, with such a religion as yours? How is the ideal of a life so unlovely, so unattractive, so narrow, so far removed from a true and satisfying ideal of human perfection, as is the life of your religious organization as you yourself image it, to conquer and transform all this vice and hideousness? ... We are all of us enrolled in some religious organization or other; we all call ourselves, in the sublime and aspiring language of religion which I have before noticed, *children of God*.[65] Children of God—it is an immense pretension!—and how are we to justify it? By the works which we do, and the words which we speak? And the work which we collective children of God do, our grand centre of life, our *city*, is London! London, with its unutterable external hideousness, and with its internal canker of *publicé egestas, privatim opulentia,*—to use the words which Sallust puts into Cato's mouth about Rome,[66]—unequalled in the world! The word which we children of God speak, the voice which most hits our collective thought, the newspaper with the largest circulation in England, nay, with the largest circulation in the whole world, is the *Daily Telegraph*![67] I say, that when our religious organizations,—which I admit to express the most considerable effort after perfection that our race has yet made—land us in no better result than this, it is high time to examine carefully their idea of perfection, to see whether it does not leave out of account sides and forces of human nature which we might turn to great use; whether it would not be more operative if it were more complete. And I say that the English reliance on our religious organizations and on their ideas of human perfection just as they stand, is like our reliance on freedom, on muscular Christianity, on population, on coal, on wealth,—mere belief in machinery and unfruitful; and is wholesomely

---

62 Virgil (70–19 BCE), Roman poet and philosopher.
63 Annual summer horse race at Epsom.
64 Thomas Henry Huxley (1825–95), professor and biologist. See Science.
65 Romans 8:16; Galatians 3:26.
66 Latin: "Public poverty, private opulence": Sallust, *Bellum Catilinae* (42–1 BCE); Sallust (86–35 BCE), Roman historian; Marcus Porcius Cato (234–149 BCE), Roman censor, orator, and author.
67 Cheap London daily paper, begun in 1855.

counteracted by culture bent on seeing things as they are, and on drawing the human race onwards to a more complete perfection.

Culture, however, shows its single-minded love of perfection, its desire simply to make reason and the will of God prevail, its freedom from fanaticism, by its attitude towards all this machinery, even while it insists that it *is* machinery. Fanatics, seeing the mischief men do themselves by their blind belief in some machinery or other,—whether it is wealth and industrialism, or whether it is the cultivation of bodily strength and activity, or whether it is a political organization, or whether it is a religious organization,—oppose with might and main the tendency to this or that political and religious organization, or to games and athletic exercises, or to wealth and industrialism, and try violently to stop it. But the flexibility which sweetness and light give, and which is one of the rewards of culture pursued in good faith, enables a man to see that a tendency may be necessary, and as a preparation for something in the future, salutary, and yet that the generations or individuals who obey this tendency are sacrificed to it, that they fall short of the hope of perfection by following it; and that its mischiefs are to be criticised, lest it should take too firm a hold and last after it has served its purpose. Mr. Gladstone well pointed out, in a speech at Paris,[68] and others have pointed out the same thing, how necessary is the present great movement towards wealth and industrialism, in order to lay broad foundations of material well-being for the society of the future. The worst of these justifications is, that they are generally addressed to the very people engaged, body and soul, in the movement in question; at all events, that they are always seized with the greatest avidity by these people, and taken by them as quite justifying their life, and that thus they tend to harden them in their sins. Culture admits the necessity of the movement towards fortune-making and exaggerated industrialism, readily allows that the future may derive benefit from it; but insists, at the same time, that the passing generations of industrialists—forming, for the most part, the stout main body of Philistinism—are sacrificed to it. In the same way, the result of all the games and sports which occupy the passing generation of boys and young men may be the establishment of a better and sounder physical type for the future to work with. Culture does not set itself against the games and sports; it congratulates the future, and hopes it will make a good use of its improved physical basis; but it points out that our passing generation of boys and young men are sacrificed. Puritanism was necessary to develop the moral fibre of the English race, Nonconformity to break the yoke of ecclesiastical domination over men's minds and to prepare the way for freedom of thought in the distant future; still, culture points out that the harmonious perfection of generations of Puritans and Nonconformists have been in consequence sacrificed. Freedom of speech is necessary for the society of the future, but the young lions of the *Daily Telegraph* in the meanwhile are sacrificed. A voice for every man in his country's government is necessary for the society of the future, but meanwhile Mr. Beales and Mr. Bradlaugh[69] are sacrificed.

We in Oxford, brought up amidst beauty and sweetness, have not failed to seize the truth that beauty and sweetness are essential characters of a complete human perfection.... And the sentiment is true, and has never been wholly defeated, and has shown its power even in its defeat. We have not won our

---

68 William Ewart Gladstone (1809–98), then prime minister, as reported in the *Times* on 1 February 1867.
69 Edmond Beales (1803–81), political radical and president of the Reform League, which organized mass public demonstrations after the initial defeat of the Reform Bill in 1866; Beales was forced to cancel such demonstrations when a mass meeting in Hyde Park on 23 July 1866 turned violent. Charles Bradlaugh (1833–91), politician and editor of the *National Reformer*, also helped to organize the Hyde Park meeting.

political battles, we have not carried our main points, we have not stopped our adversaries' advance; but we have told silently upon the mind of the country, we have prepared currents of feeling which sap our adversaries' position when it seems gained, we have kept up our own communications with the future. Look at the course of the great movement which shook this place to its centre some thirty years ago![70] It was directed, as any one who reads Dr. Newman's *Apology*[71] may see, against what in one word may be called "liberalism." Liberalism prevailed; it was the appointed force to do the work of the hour; it was necessary, it was inevitable that it should prevail. The Oxford movement was broken, it failed; our wrecks are scattered on every shore:—

Quæ regio in terris nostri non plena laboris?[72]

And what was this liberalism, as Dr. Newman saw it, and as it really broke the Oxford movement? It was the great middle-class liberalism, which had for the cardinal points of its belief the Reform Bill of 1832,[73] and local self-government, in politics; in the social sphere, free-trade, unrestricted competition, and the making of large industrial fortunes; in the religious sphere, the dissidence of Dissent and the Protestantism of the Protestant religion.... And where is this great force of Philistinism now? It is thrust into the second rank, it is become a power of yesterday, it has lost the future. A new power has suddenly appeared, a power which it is impossible yet to judge fully, but which is certainly a wholly different force from middle-class liberalism; different in its cardinal points of belief, different in its tendencies in every sphere. It loves and admires neither the legislation of middle-class Parliaments, nor the local self-government of middle-class vestries,[74] nor the unrestricted competition of middle-class industrialists, nor the dissidence of middle-class dissent and the Protestantism of middle-class Protestant religion. I am not now praising this new force, or saying that its own ideals are better; all I say is, that they are wholly different. And who will estimate how much the currents of feeling created by Dr. Newman's movement, the keen desire for beauty and sweetness which it nourished, the deep aversion it manifested to the hardness and vulgarity of middle-class liberalism, the strong light it turned on the hideous and grotesque illusions of middle-class Protestantism,—who will estimate how much all these contributed to swell the tide of secret dissatisfaction which has mined the ground under the self-confident liberalism of the last thirty years, and has prepared the way for its sudden collapse and supersession? It is in this manner that the sentiment of Oxford for beauty and sweetness conquers, and in this manner long may it continue to conquer!

In this manner it works to the same end as culture, and there is plenty of work for it yet to do. I have said that the new and more democratic force which is now superseding our old middle-class liberalism cannot yet be rightly judged. It has its main tendencies still to form: we hear promises of its giving us administrative reform, law reform, reform of education, and I know not what; but those promises come rather from its advocates, wishing to make a good plea for it and to justify it for superseding

---

70 The Oxford Movement, which sought to restore traditional Catholicism to the Church of England.
71 John Henry Newman, *Apologia pro Vita Sua* (1864). See Faith and Doubt. Newman was one of the founders of the Oxford Movement.
72 Latin: "What region in the world is not full of suffering?": Virgil, *Aeneid* (29–19 BCE).
73 The bill extended suffrage to male middle-class voters and redistributed parliamentary regions for fairer representation.
74 A meeting of parishioners representing a council of church management named for the vestry area where such meetings were originally held.

middle-class liberalism, than from clear tendencies which it has itself yet developed. But meanwhile it has plenty of well-intentioned friends against whom culture may with advantage continue to uphold steadily its ideal of human perfection; that it is an inward spiritual activity, having for its characters increased sweetness, increased light, increased life, increased sympathy. Mr. Bright,[75] who has a foot in both worlds, the world of middle-class liberalism and the world of democracy, but who brings most of his ideas from the world of middle-class liberalism in which he was bred, always inclines to inculcate that faith in machinery to which, as we have seen, Englishmen are so prone, and which has been the bane of middle-class liberalism. He complains with a sorrowful indignation of people who "appear to have no proper estimate of the value of the franchise;" he leads his disciples to believe,—what the Englishman is always too ready to believe,—that the having a vote, like the having a large family, or a large business, or large muscles, has in itself some edifying and perfecting effect upon human nature. Or else he cries out to the democracy,—"the men," as he calls them, "upon whose shoulders the greatness of England rests"—he cries out to them: "See what you have done! I look over this country and see the cities you have built, the railroads you have made, the manufactures you have produced, the cargoes which freight the ships of the greatest mercantile navy the world has ever seen!... I know that you have created this wealth, and are a nation whose name is a word of power throughout all the world." Why, this is just the very style of laudation with which Mr. Roebuck or Mr. Lowe[76] debauch the minds of the middle classes, and make such Philistines of them. It is the same fashion of teaching a man to value himself not on what he *is*, not on his progress in sweetness and light, but on the number of the railroads he has constructed, or the bigness of the tabernacle[77] he has built. Only the middle classes are told they have done it all with their energy, self-reliance, and capital, and the democracy are told they have done it all with their hands and sinews. But teaching the democracy to put its trust in achievements of this kind is merely training them to be Philistines to take the place of the Philistines whom they are superseding; and they too, like the middle class, will be encouraged to sit down at the banquet of the future without having on a wedding garment,[78] and nothing excellent can come from them. Those who know their besetting faults, those who have watched them and listened to them, or those who will read the excellent account recently given of them by one of themselves, the *Journeyman Engineer*,[79] will agree that the idea which culture sets before us of perfection—an increased spiritual activity, having for its characters increased sweetness, increased light, increased life, increased sympathy—is an idea which the new democracy needs far more than the idea of the blessedness of the franchise or the wonderfulness of their own industrial performances....

... The pursuit of perfection is the pursuit of sweetness and light.... [H]e who works for sweetness works in the end for light also; he who works for light works in the end for sweetness also. He who works for sweetness and light works to make reason and the will of God prevail. He who works for machinery, he who works for hatred, works only for confusion. Culture looks beyond machinery, culture hates hatred; culture has but one great passion, the passion for sweetness and light. Yes, it has one

---

75 John Bright (1811–89), Quaker manufacturer and pro-reform Liberal politician.
76 John Arthur Roebuck (1802–79), radical politician; Robert Lowe, Viscount Sherbrooke (1811–92), Liberal politician.
77 A place of worship of Protestant non-conformists.
78 Matthew 22:1–14.
79 Pseudonym of Thomas Wright, author of *Some Habits and Customs of the Working Classes, by a Journeyman Engineer* (1867).

yet greater—the passion for making them *prevail*. It is not satisfied till we *all* come to a perfect man; it knows that the sweetness and light of the few must be imperfect until the raw and unkindled masses of humanity are touched with sweetness and light. If I have not shrunk from saying that we must work for sweetness and light, so neither have I shrunk from saying that we must have a broad basis, must have sweetness and light for as many as possible. I have again and again insisted how those are the happy moments of humanity, how those are the marking epochs of a people's life, how those are the flowering times for literature and art and all the creative power of genius, when there is a *national* glow of life and thought, when the whole of society is in the fullest measure permeated by thought, sensible to beauty, intelligent and alive....

Walter Pater
from *Studies in the History of the Renaissance* (1873)

Walter Pater (1839–94) was a leader in the fin-de-siècle Aesthetic movement. Educated at Oxford, Pater became a fellow of Brasenose College (in Classics), where he tutored Gerard Manley Hopkins. Influenced by the Pre-Raphaelites, he later advocated "aesthetic poetry." Pater's earliest periodical publications focused on Samuel Taylor Coleridge (1866), Johann Winckelmann (1867), and William Morris (see Education, Aesthetics and Culture) (1868); he drew upon these in *Studies in the History of the Renaissance* (1873). This controversial volume redirected attention away from the object per se (see Matthew Arnold, Education) and toward personal impressions of art, cultivated in seemingly hedonistic spirit. This approach inspired Oxford undergraduates and aesthetes, including Oscar Wilde (see Life Writing, Aesthetics and Culture), who adopted Pater's injunction to "burn always with this hard gem-like flame."

Studies was attacked from the pulpit and in the press for its hedonism and anti-historical bent. Its famous conclusion (printed here) attracted the greatest controversy. Pater withdrew it in 1877, reinstating it in 1888 and subsequent editions.

Conclusion[80]

To regard all things and principles of things as inconstant modes or fashions has more and more become the tendency of modern thought. Let us begin with that which is without—our physical life. Fix upon it in one of its more exquisite intervals, the moment, for instance, of delicious recoil from the flood of water in summer heat. What is the whole physical life in that moment but a combination of natural elements to which science gives their names? ... Our physical life is a perpetual motion of them—the passage of the

---

80 The Greek epigraph to the conclusion, as translated by Pater in 1893, reads, "Heraclitus says, All things give way: nothing remaineth": Plato, *Cratylus* (c. 384 BCE).

blood, the wasting and repairing of the lenses of the eye, the modification of the tissues of the brain by every ray of light and sound—processes which science reduces to simpler and more elementary forces. Like the elements of which we are composed, the action of these forces extends beyond us; it rusts iron and ripens corn. Far out on every side of us these elements are broadcast, driven by many forces; and birth and gesture and death and the springing of violets from the grave are but a few out of ten thousand resulting combinations. That clear perpetual outline of face and limb is but an image of ours under which we group them—a design in a web, the actual threads of which pass out beyond it. This at least of flame-like our life has, that it is but the concurrence, renewed from moment to moment, of forces parting sooner or later on their ways.

Or if we begin with the inward world of thought and feeling, the whirlpool is still more rapid, the flame more eager and devouring. There it is no longer the gradual darkening of the eye and fading of colour from the wall,—the movement of the shore side, where the water flows down indeed, though in apparent rest,—but the race of the midstream, a drift of momentary acts of sight and passion and thought. At first sight experience seems to bury us under a flood of external objects, pressing upon us with a sharp importunate reality, calling us out of ourselves in a thousand forms of action. But when reflection begins to act upon those objects they are dissipated under its influence; the cohesive force is suspended like a trick of magic; each object is loosed into a group of impressions,—colour, odour, texture,—in the mind of the observer. And if we continue to dwell on this world, not of objects in the solidity with which language invests them, but of impressions unstable, flickering, inconsistent, which burn and are extinguished with our consciousness of them, it contracts still further; the whole scope of observation is dwarfed into the narrow chamber of the individual mind. Experience, already reduced to a swarm of impressions, is ringed round for each one of us by that thick wall of personality through which no real voice has ever pierced on its way to us, or from us to that which we can only conjecture to be without. Every one of those impressions is the impression of the individual in his isolation, each mind keeping as a solitary prisoner its own dream of a world.

Analysis goes a step further still, and tells us that those impressions of the individual to which, for each one of us, experience dwindles down, are in perpetual flight; that each of them is limited by time, and that as time is infinitely divisible, each of them is infinitely divisible also; all that is actual in it being a single moment, gone while we try to apprehend it, of which it may ever be more truly said that it has ceased to be than that it is. To such a tremulous wisp constantly reforming itself on the stream, to a single sharp impression, with a sense in it, a relic more or less fleeting, of such moments gone by, what is *real* in our life fines[81] itself down. It is with the movement, the passage and dissolution of impressions, images, sensations, that analysis leaves off,—that continual vanishing away, that strange perpetual weaving and unweaving of ourselves.

... The service of philosophy, and of religion and culture as well, to the human spirit, is to startle it into a sharp and eager observation. Every moment some form grows perfect in hand or face; some tone on the hills or sea is choicer than the rest; some mood of passion or insight or intellectual excitement is irresistibly real and attractive for us,—for that moment only. Not the fruit of experience, but experience itself is the end. A counted number of pulses only is given to us of a variegated, dramatic life. How may we see in them all that is to be seen in them by the finest senses? How can we pass most swiftly from

---

81 Comes to an end; passes away.

point to point, and be present always at the focus where the greatest number of vital forces unite in their purest energy?

To burn always with this hard gem-like flame, to maintain this ecstasy, is success in life. Failure is to form habits; for habit is relative to a stereotyped[82] world; meantime it is only the roughness of the eye that makes any two persons, things, situations, seem alike. While all melts under our feet, we may well catch at any exquisite passion, or any contribution to knowledge that seems, by a lifted horizon, to set the spirit free for a moment, or any stirring of the senses, strange dyes, strange flowers, and curious odours, or work of the artist's hands, or the face of one's friend. Not to discriminate every moment some passionate attitude in those about us, and in the brilliance of their gifts some tragic dividing of forces on their ways is, on this short day of frost and sun, to sleep before evening. With this sense of the splendor of our experience and of its awful brevity, gathering all we are into one desperate effort to see and touch, we shall hardly have time to make theories about the things we see and touch. What we have to do is to be for ever curiously testing new opinions and courting new impressions, never acquiescing in a facile orthodoxy of Comte or of Hegel,[83] or of our own.... The theory, or idea, or system, which requires of us the sacrifice of any part of this experience, in consideration of some interest into which we cannot enter, or some abstract morality we have not identified with ourselves, or what is only conventional, has no real claim upon us.

One of the most beautiful places in the writings of Rousseau is that in the sixth book of the "Confessions,"[84] where he describes the awakening in him of the literary sense. An undefinable taint of death had clung always about him, and now in early manhood he believed himself stricken by mortal disease. He asked himself how he might make as much as possible of the interval that remained; and he was not biassed by anything in his previous life when he decided that it must be by intellectual excitement, which he found in the clear, fresh writings of Voltaire.[85] Well, we are all *condamnés*, as Victor Hugo says: *les hommes sont tous condamnés a morte* [sic] *avec des sursis indéfinis*:[86] we have an interval, and then our place knows us no more. Some spend this interval in listlessness, some in high passions, the wisest in art and song. For our one chance is in expanding that interval, in getting as many pulsations as possible into the given time. High passions give one this quickened sense of life, ecstasy and sorrow of love, political or religious enthusiasm, or the "enthusiasm of humanity."[87] Only, be sure it is passion, that it does yield you this fruit of a quickened, multiplied consciousness. Of this wisdom, the poetic passion, the desire of beauty, the love of art for art's sake has most; for art comes to you professing frankly to give nothing but the highest quality to your moments as they pass, and simply for those moments' sake.

---

82 Reference to Victorian printing technology: stereotyped plates were cast from set type and allowed for the mass reproduction of the same text numerous times.
83 Auguste Comte (1798–1857), French philosopher; Georg Wilhelm Friedrich Hegel (1770–1831), German philosopher.
84 Jean-Jacques Rousseau (Swiss philosopher), *Confessions* (1782–89).
85 Voltaire [François-Marie Arouet] (1694–1778), French writer and philosopher.
86 French: "Men are all condemned to death with an indefinite reprieve": Victor Hugo, *Le dernier jour d'un condamné* (1829).
87 Sir John Robert Seeley, *Ecce Homo: A Survey of the Life and Work of Jesus Christ* (1865).

William Morris
from *Hopes and Fears for Art* (1882)

William Morris (1834–96) rose to prominence as a poet, artist, and designer of home furnishings. Having encountered reformist politics—especially the writings of John Ruskin (see Life Writing, Condition of England, Aesthetics and Culture, Gender and Sexuality) and Thomas Carlyle (see Condition of England, Faith and Doubt)—at Oxford University, Morris affirmed the joy of labour in artistic production. In 1861, he founded his influential design company (later called Morris and Co.) and, in 1891, the Kelmscott Press, which produced high-quality illustrated books. Morris's philosophy ("Have nothing in your houses that you do not know to be useful or believe to be beautiful") inspired the Arts and Crafts movement. Despite the critical failure of *The Defence of Guinevere, and Other Poems* (1858), in the mid-1860s Morris was as popular as Browning, Tennyson, and Swinburne. A socialist, Morris wrote the utopian *News from Nowhere* (1890) and edited the Socialist League's *The Commonweal*.

In this essay on the decorative arts, Morris argues that they express "man's delight in beauty." Here he extends the utopian hope that art will someday take its place beside equality, liberty, and fraternity as one of the highest democratic values.

Chapter 1: The Lesser Arts

... Our subject is that great body of art, by means of which men have at all times more or less striven to beautify the familiar matters of everyday life: a wide subject, a great industry; both a great part of the history of the world, and a most helpful instrument to the study of that history.

A very great industry indeed, comprising the crafts of house-building, painting, joinery[88] and carpentry, smiths' work, pottery and glass-making, weaving, and many others.... True it is that in many or most cases we have got so used to ... ornament, that we look upon it as if it had grown of itself, and note it no more than the mosses on the dry sticks with which we light our fires. So much the worse! for there *is* the decoration, or some pretence of it, and it has, or ought to have, a use and a meaning. For, and this is at the root of the whole matter, everything made by man's hands has a form, which must be either beautiful or ugly; beautiful if it is in accord with Nature, and helps her; ugly if it is discordant with Nature, and thwarts her; it cannot be indifferent: we, for our parts, are busy or sluggish, eager or unhappy, and our eyes are apt to get dulled to this eventfulness of form in those things which we are always looking at. Now it is one of the chief uses of decoration, the chief part of its alliance with nature, that it has to sharpen our dulled senses in this matter: for this end are those wonders of intricate patterns interwoven, those strange forms invented, which men have so long delighted in: forms and intricacies that do not necessarily imitate nature, but in which the hand of the craftsman is guided to

---

88 Furniture or small-scale construction.

work in the way that she does; till the web, the cup, or the knife, look as natural, nay as lovely, as the green field, the river bank, or the mountain flint.

To give people pleasure in the things they must perforce *use*, that is one great office of decoration; to give people pleasure in the things they must perforce *make*, that is the other use of it.

Does not our subject look important enough now? I say that without these arts, our rest would be vacant and uninteresting, our labour mere endurance, mere wearing away of body and mind.

As for that last use of these arts, the giving us pleasure in our work, I scarcely know how to speak strongly enough of it; and yet if I did not know the value of repeating a truth again and again, I should have to excuse myself to you for saying any more about this, when I remember how a great man now living has spoken of it: I mean my friend Professor John Ruskin:[89] if you read the chapter in the 2nd vol. of his *Stones of Venice* entitled, "On the Nature of Gothic, and the Office of the Workman therein,"[90] you will read at once the truest and the most eloquent words that can possibly be said on the subject....

Now if the objection be made, that these arts have been the handmaids of luxury, of tyranny, and of superstition, I must needs say that it is true in a sense; they have been so used, as many other excellent things have been. But it is also true that, among some nations, their most vigorous and freest times have been the very blossoming times of art: while at the same time, I must allow that these decorative arts have flourished among oppressed peoples, who have seemed to have no hope of freedom: yet I do not think that we shall be wrong in thinking that at such times, among such peoples, art, at least, was free; when it has not been, when it has really been gripped by superstition, or by luxury, it has straightway begun to sicken under that grip. Nor must you forget that when men say popes, kings, and emperors built such and such buildings, it is a mere way of speaking. You look in your history-books to see who built Westminster Abbey, who built St. Sophia at Constantinople,[91] and they tell you Henry III., Justinian the Emperor.[92] Did they? or, rather, men like you and me, handicraftsmen, who have left no names behind them, nothing but their work?

Now as these arts call people's attention and interest to the matters of every-day life in the present, so also, and that I think is no little matter, they call our attention at every step to that history, of which, I said before, they are so great a part; for no nation, no state of society, however rude, has been wholly without them: nay, there are peoples not a few, of whom we know scarce anything, save that they thought such and such forms beautiful. So strong is the bond between history and decoration, that in the practice of the latter we cannot, if we would, wholly shake off the influence of past times over what we do at present. I do not think it is too much to say that no man, however original he may be, can sit down to-day and draw the ornament of a cloth, or the form of an ordinary vessel or piece of furniture, that will be other than a development or a degradation of forms used hundreds of years ago; and these, too, very often, forms that once had a serious meaning, though they are now become little more than a habit of the hand.... Those who have diligently followed the delightful study of these arts are able as if through windows to look upon the life of the past:—the very first beginnings of thought among nations whom we cannot

---

89 John Ruskin (1819–1900), writer and art critic. See Life Writing, Condition of England, Aesthetics and Culture, Gender and Sexuality.
90 John Ruskin, *The Stones of Venice* (1851–53). See Aesthetics and Culture.
91 Westminster Abbey, London, is a Gothic style church; Hagia Sophia in Istanbul, Turkey, was a Byzantine church that was converted to a mosque in 1453.
92 King Henry III (1207–72); Justinian I (483–565), Byzantine emperor.

even name; the terrible empires of the ancient East; the free vigour and glory of Greece; the heavy weight, the firm grasp of Rome; the fall of her temporal Empire which spread so wide about the world all that good and evil which men can never forget, and never cease to feel; the clashing of East and West, South and North, about her rich and fruitful daughter Byzantium; the rise, the dissensions, and the waning of Islam; the wanderings of Scandinavia; the Crusades;[93] the foundation of the States of modern Europe; the struggles of free thought with ancient dying system—with all these events and their meaning is the history of popular art interwoven; with all this, I say, the careful student of decoration as an historical industry must be familiar. When I think of this, and the usefulness of all this knowledge, at a time when history has become so earnest a study amongst us as to have given us, as it were, a new sense: at a time when we so long to know the reality of all that has happened, and are to be put off no longer with the dull records of the battles and intrigues of kings and scoundrels,—I say when I think of all this, I hardly know how to say that this interweaving of the Decorative Arts with the history of the past is of less importance than their dealings with the life of the present: for should not these memories also be a part of our daily life?

And now let me recapitulate a little before I go further, before we begin to look into the condition of the arts at the present day. These arts, I have said, are part of a great system invented for the expression of a man's delight in beauty: all peoples and times have used them; they have been the joy of free nations, and the solace of oppressed nations; religion has used and elevated them, has abused and degraded them; they are connected with all history, and are clear teachers of it; and, best of all, they are the sweeteners of human labour, both to the handicraftsman, whose life is spent in working in them, and to people in general who are influenced by the sight of them at every turn of the day's work: they make our toil happy, our rest fruitful.

And now if all I have said seems to you but mere open-mouthed praise of these arts, I must say that it is not for nothing that what I have hitherto put before you has taken that form.

It is because I must now ask you this question: All these good things—will you have them? will you cast them from you?

Are you surprised at my question—you, most of whom, like myself, are engaged in the actual practice of the arts that are, or ought to be, popular?

In explanation, I must somewhat repeat what I have already said. Time was when the mystery and wonder of handicrafts were well acknowledged by the world, when imagination and fancy mingled with all things made by man; and in those days all handicraftsmen were *artists*, as we should now call them. But the thought of man became more intricate, more difficult to express; art grew a heavier thing to deal with, and its labour was more divided among great men, lesser men, and little men; till that art, which was once scarce more than a rest of body and soul, as the hand cast the shuttle[94] or swung the hammer, became to some men so serious a labour, that their working lives have been one long tragedy of hope and fear, joy and trouble....

We who believe in the continuous life of the world, surely we are bound to hope that the change will bring us gain and not loss, and to strive to bring that gain about.

Yet how the world may answer my question, who can say? A man in his short life can see but a little way ahead, and even in mine wonderful and unexpected things have come to pass. I must needs say

---

93   The Byzantine Empire grew from the city of Byzantium (itself an ancient Greek colony), but succumbed to the Ottoman Turks in 1453; Islam refers to the Persian Empire (550 BCE–640 CE); Scandinavian Vikings invaded Europe from about 800 to 1000; Western Christians dispatched armies to reconquer the Holy Land and halt the growth of Islam in the eleventh century.
94   A tool used by weavers to pass the weft (horizontal) thread through the warp (vertical) thread on a loom.

that therein lies my hope rather than in all I see going on round about us. Without disputing that if the imaginative arts perish, some new thing, at present unguessed of, *may* be put forward to supply their loss in men's lives, I cannot feel happy in that prospect, nor can I believe that mankind will endure such a loss for ever: but in the meantime the present state of the arts and their dealings with modern life and progress seem to me to point in appearance at least to this immediate future; that the world, which has for a long time busied itself about other matters than the arts, and has carelessly let them sink lower and lower, till many not uncultivated men ... look upon them with mere contempt; that the world ... will one day wipe the slate, and be clean rid in her impatience of the whole matter with all its tangle and trouble.

And then—what then?

Even now amid the squalor of London it is hard to imagine what it will be. Architecture, Sculpture, Painting, with the crowd of lesser arts that belong to them, these, together with Music and Poetry, will be dead and forgotten, will no longer excite or amuse people in the least: for, once more, we must not deceive ourselves; the death of one art means the death of all; the only difference in their fate will be that the luckiest will be eaten the last—the luckiest, or the unluckiest: in all that has to do with beauty the invention and ingenuity of man will have come to a dead stop; and all the while Nature will go on with her eternal recurrence of lovely changes: spring, summer, autumn, and winter; sunshine, rain, and snow, storm and fair weather; dawn, noon, and sunset, day and night—ever bearing witness against man that he has deliberately chosen ugliness instead of beauty, and to live where he is strongest amidst squalor or blank emptiness.

You see, sirs, we cannot quite imagine it; any more, perhaps, than our forefathers of ancient London, living in the pretty carefully whitened houses, with the famous church and its huge spire rising above them,—than they, passing about the fair gardens running down to the broad river, could have imagined a whole county or more covered over with hideous hovels, big, middle-sized, and little, which should one day be called London....

The remedy ... is plain if it can be applied; the handicraftsman, left behind by the artist when the arts sundered, must come up with him, must work side by side with him: apart from the difference between a great master and a scholar, apart from the differences of the natural bent of men's minds, which would make one man an imitative, and another an architectural or decorative artist, there should be no difference between those employed on strictly ornamental work; and the body of artists dealing with this should quicken with their art all makers of things into artists also, in proportion to the necessities and uses of the things they would make....

There is a great deal of sham work in the world, hurtful to the buyer, more hurtful to the seller, if he only knew it, most hurtful to the maker: how good a foundation it would be towards getting good Decorative Art, that is ornamental workmanship, if we craftsmen were to resolve to turn out nothing but excellent workmanship in all things, instead of having, as we too often have now, a very low average standard of work, which we often fall below....

Simplicity of life, begetting simplicity of taste, that is, a love for sweet and lofty things, is of all matters most necessary for the birth of the new and better art we crave for; simplicity everywhere, in the palace as well as in the cottage....

I do not want art for a few, any more than education for a few, or freedom for a few.

No, rather than art should live this poor thin life among a few exceptional men, despising those beneath them for an ignorance for which they themselves are responsible, for a brutality that they will not struggle with,—rather than this, I would that the world should indeed sweep away all art for a while, as I said before I thought it possible she might do; rather than the wheat should rot in the miser's granary, I would that the earth had it, that it might yet have a chance to quicken in the dark.

I have a sort of faith, though, that this clearing away of all art will not happen, that men will get wiser, as well as more learned; that many of the intricacies of life, on which we now pride ourselves more than enough, partly because they are new, partly because they have come with the gain of better things, will be cast aside as having played their part, and being useful no longer. I hope that we shall have leisure from war,—war commercial, as well as war of the bullet and the bayonet; leisure from the knowledge that darkens counsel; leisure above all from the greed of money, and the craving for that overwhelming distinction that money now brings: I believe that as we have even now partly achieved LIBERTY, so we shall one day achieve EQUALITY, which, and which only, means FRATERNITY,[95] and so have leisure from poverty and all its griping, sordid cares.

Then, having leisure from all these things, amidst renewed simplicity of life we shall have leisure to think about our work, that faithful daily companion, which no man any longer will venture to call the Curse of labour: for surely then we shall be happy in it, each in his place, no man grudging at another; no one bidden to be any man's *servant*, everyone scorning to be any man's *master*: men will then assuredly be happy in their work, and that happiness will assuredly bring forth decorative, noble, *popular* art.

That art will make our streets as beautiful as the woods, as elevating as the mountain-sides: it will be a pleasure and a rest, and not a weight upon the spirits to come from the open country into a town; every man's house will be fair and decent, soothing to his mind and helpful to his work: all the works of man that we live amongst and handle will be in harmony with nature, will be reasonable and beautiful: yet all will be simple and inspiring, not childish nor enervating;[96] for as nothing of beauty and splendour that man's mind and hand may compass shall be wanted from our public buildings, so in no private dwelling will there be any signs of waste, pomp, or insolence, and every man will have his share of the *best*.

It is a dream, you may say, of what has never been and never will be: true, it has never been, and therefore, since the world is alive and moving yet, my hope is the greater that it one day will be: true, it is a dream; but dreams have before now come about of things so good and necessary to us, that we scarcely think of them more than of the daylight, though once people had to live without them, without even the hope of them.

Anyhow, dream as it is, I pray you to pardon my setting it before you, for it lies at the bottom of all my work in the Decorative Arts, nor will it ever be out of my thoughts: and I am here with you to-night to ask you to help me in realising this dream, this *hope*.

---

95   A reference to "Liberté, Egalité, Fraternité," the motto of the French Revolution.
96   Weakening.

James McNeill Whistler
from *Mr. Whistler's "Ten O'Clock"* (1885)

James McNeill Whistler (1834–1903), American artist and critic, trained in Paris before playing a key role in the late-Victorian Aesthetic movement. Influenced by Japanese art and by Algernon Charles Swinburne's and Charles Baudelaire's aesthetic theories, Whistler in turn influenced Oscar Wilde (see Life Writing, Aesthetics and Culture). In 1877, John Ruskin (see Life Writing, Condition of England, Aesthetics and Culture, Gender and Sexuality) published a hostile review of Whistler's painting *Nocturne in Black and Gold: The Falling Rocket*, in which he accused the artist of "flinging a pot of paint in the public's face." Whistler won a farthing (a quarter of a penny) in damages when he sued Ruskin for libel.

On 20 February 1885, Whistler delivered his "Ten O'Clock" lecture in London, later repeating it in Cambridge and Oxford. In the lecture, excerpted here, Whistler condemns popular art and insists that "Nature ... sings her exquisite song to the artist alone," who "does not confine himself to purposeless copying."

Ladies and Gentlemen,

It is with great hesitation and much misgiving that I appear before you, in the character of The Preacher....

... For I will not conceal from you that I mean to talk about Art. Yes, Art—that has of late become, as far as much discussion and writing can make it, a sort of common topic for the tea-table.

Art is upon the Town!—to be chucked under the chin by the passing gallant—to be enticed within the gates of the householder—to be coaxed into company, as a proof of culture and refinement.

If familiarity can breed contempt, certainly Art—or what is currently taken for it—has been brought to its lowest stage of intimacy.

The people have been harassed with Art in every guise, and vexed with many methods as to its endurance. They have been told how they shall love Art, and live with it. Their homes have been invaded, their walls covered with paper, their very dress taken to task—until, roused at last, bewildered and filled with the doubts and discomforts of senseless suggestion, they resent such intrusion, and cast forth the false prophets,[97] who have brought the very name of the beautiful into disrepute, and derision upon themselves.

Alas! ladies and gentlemen, Art has been maligned. She has naught in common with such practices. She is a goddess of dainty thought—reticent of habit, abjuring all obtrusiveness, purposing in no way to better others.

She is, withal, selfishly occupied with her own perfection only—having no desire to teach—seeking and finding the beautiful in all conditions and in all times, as did her high priest Rembrandt, when he saw picturesque grandeur and noble dignity in the Jews' quarter of Amsterdam,[98] and lamented not that its inhabitants were not Greeks....

---

97 Matthew 7:15.
98 Rembrandt van Rijn (1606–69), Dutch painter and printmaker who often used as models his Jewish neighbours in Amsterdam.

As did, at the Court of Philip, Velasquez, whose Infantas, clad in inæsthetic hoops,[99] are, as works of Art, of the same quality as the Elgin marbles.[100]

No reformers were these great men—no improvers of the way of others! Their productions alone were their occupation, and, filled with the poetry of their science, they required not to alter their surroundings—for, as the laws of their Art were revealed to them, they saw, in the development of their work, that real beauty which, to them, was as much a matter of certainty and triumph as is to the astronomer the verification of the result, foreseen with the light given to him alone. In all this, their world was completely severed from that of their fellow-creatures with whom sentiment is mistaken for poetry; and for whom there is no perfect work that shall not be explained by the benefit conferred upon themselves.

Humanity takes the place of Art, and God's creations are excused by their usefulness. Beauty is confounded with virtue, and, before a work of Art, it is asked: "What good shall it do?"

Hence it is that nobility of action, in this life, is hopelessly linked with the merit of the work that portrays it; and thus the people have acquired the habit of looking, as who should say, not *at* a picture, but *through* it, at some human fact, that shall, or shall not, from a social point of view, better their mental or moral state. So we have come to hear of the painting that elevates, and of the duty of the painter—of the picture that is full of thought, and of the panel that merely decorates.

A favourite faith, dear to those who teach, is that certain periods were especially artistic, and that nations, readily named, were notably lovers of Art.

So we are told that the Greeks were, as a people, worshippers of the beautiful, and that in the fifteenth century Art was engrained in the multitude....

That we, of to-day, in gross contrast to this Arcadian[101] purity, call for the ungainly, and obtain the ugly.

That, could we but change our habits and climate—were we willing to wander in groves—could we be roasted out of broadcloth[102]—were we to do without haste, and journey without speed, we should again *require* the spoon of Queen Anne, and pick at our peas with the fork of two prongs....[103]

Useless! quite hopeless and false is the effort!...

Listen! There never was an artistic period.

There never was an Art-loving nation.

In the beginning, man went forth each day—some to do battle, some to the chase; others, again, to dig and to delve in the field—all that they might gain and live, or lose and die. Until there was found among them one, differing from the rest, whose pursuits attracted him not, and so he stayed by the tents with the women, and traced strange devices with a burnt stick upon a gourd.

This man ... this deviser of the beautiful—who perceived in Nature about him curious curvings, as faces are seen in the fire—this dreamer apart, was the first artist.

---

99 Diego Velázquez (1599–1660), Spanish painter who made several paintings of the Infanta Margarita of the Spanish court.
100 A collection of marble sculptures taken from the Parthenon and shipped to the British Museum by Thomas Bruce, seventh Lord Elgin.
101 Arcadia is a region of Greece represented as a paradise in classical Greek and Roman poetry and Renaissance literature.
102 A densely woven fabric traditionally made from wool.
103 Queen Anne spoons were flat, had thin handles, and were not sufficiently durable for cooking; they were replaced by Hanoverian-style spoons with rat-tail handles. Dinner forks were originally made with two flat prongs, making them ineffectual for eating small food items such as grains or peas.

And when, from the field and from afar, there came back the people, they took the gourd—and drank from out of it.

And presently there came to this man another—and, in time, others—of like nature, chosen by the Gods—and so they worked together; and soon they fashioned, from the moistened earth, forms resembling the gourd. And with the power of creation, the heirloom of the artist, presently they went beyond the slovenly suggestion of Nature, and the first vase was born, in beautiful proportion.

And the toilers tilled, and were athirst; and the heroes returned from fresh victories, to rejoice and to feast; and all drank alike from the artists' goblets, fashioned cunningly, taking no note the while of the craftsman's pride, and understanding not his glory in his work; drinking at the cup, not from choice, not from a consciousness that it was beautiful, but because, forsooth, there was none other!...

And the people lived in marvels of art—and ate and drank out of masterpieces—for there was nothing else to eat and to drink out of, and no bad building to live in; no article of daily life, of luxury, or of necessity, that had not been handed down from the design of the master, and made by his workmen.

And the people questioned not, *and had nothing to say in the matter*.

So Greece was in its splendour, and Art reigned supreme—by force of fact, not by election—and there was no meddling from the outsider....

... And the customs of cultivation covered the face of the earth, so that all peoples continued to use what *the artist alone produced*.

And centuries passed in this using, and the world was flooded with all that was beautiful, until there arose a new class, who discovered the cheap, and foresaw fortune in the facture of the sham.

Then sprang into existence the tawdry, the common, the gewgaw.[104]

The taste of the tradesman supplanted the science of the artist....

And the artist's occupation was gone, and the manufacturer and the huckster[105] took his place.

And now the heroes filled from the jugs and drank from the bowls—with understanding—noting the glare of their new bravery, and taking pride in its worth.

And the people—this time—had much to say in the matter—and all were satisfied. And Birmingham and Manchester arose in their might—and Art was relegated to the curiosity shop.[106]

Nature contains the elements, in colour and form, of all pictures, as the keyboard contains the notes of all music.

But the artist is born to pick, and choose, and group with science, these elements, that the result may be beautiful—as the musician gathers his notes, and forms his chords, until he bring forth from chaos glorious harmony.

To say to the painter, that Nature is to be taken as she is, is to say to the player, that he may sit on the piano.

That Nature is always right, is an assertion, artistically, as untrue, as it is one whose truth is universally taken for granted. Nature is very rarely right, to such an extent even, that it might almost be said that Nature is usually wrong....

---

104 Bauble or trifle.
105 Peddler or hawker.
106 Shop selling antiques or rare objects.

The sun blares, the wind blows from the east, the sky is bereft of cloud, and without, all is of iron. The windows of the Crystal Palace[107] are seen from all points of London. The holiday-maker rejoices in the glorious day, and the painter turns aside to shut his eyes.

How little this is understood, and how dutifully the casual in Nature is accepted as sublime, may be gathered from the unlimited admiration daily produced by a very foolish sunset.

The dignity of the snow-capped mountain is lost in distinctness, but the joy of the tourist is to recognise the traveller on the top. The desire to see, for the sake of seeing, is, with the mass, alone the one to be gratified, hence the delight in detail.

And when the evening mist clothes the riverside with poetry, as with a veil, and the poor buildings lose themselves in the dim sky, and the tall chimneys become campanili,[108] and the warehouses are palaces in the night, and the whole city hangs in the heavens, and fairyland is before us—then the wayfarer hastens home; the working man and the cultured one, the wise man and the one of pleasure, cease to understand, as they have ceased to see, and Nature, who, for once, has sung in tune, sings her exquisite song to the artist alone, her son and her master—her son in that he loves her, her master in that he knows her.

To him her secrets are unfolded, to him her lessons have become gradually clear. He looks at her flower, not with the enlarging lens, that he may gather facts for the botanist, but with the light of the one who sees in her choice selection of brilliant tones and delicate tints, suggestions of future harmonies.

He does not confine himself to purposeless copying, without thought, each blade of grass, as commended by the inconsequent, but, in the long curve of the narrow leaf, corrected by the straight tall stem, he learns how grace is wedded to dignity, how strength enhances sweetness, that elegance shall be the result....

In all that is dainty and lovable he finds hints for his own combinations, and *thus* is Nature ever his resource and always at his service, and to him is naught refused.

Through his brain, as through the last alembic,[109] is distilled the refined essence of that thought which began with the Gods, and which they left him to carry out.

Set apart by them to complete their works, he produces that wondrous thing called the masterpiece, which surpasses in perfection all that they have contrived in what is called Nature; and the Gods stand by and marvel, and perceive how far away more beautiful is the Venus of Melos[110] than was their own Eve.

For some time past, the unattached writer has become the middleman in this matter of Art, and his influence, while it has widened the gulf between the people and the painter, has brought about the most complete misunderstanding as to the aim of the picture.

For him a picture is more or less a hieroglyph or symbol of story. Apart from a few technical terms, for the display of which he finds an occasion, the work is considered absolutely from a literary point of view; indeed, from what other can he consider it? And in his essays he deals with it as with a novel—a history—or an anecdote. He fails entirely and most naturally to see its excellences, or demerits—artistic—and so degrades Art, by supposing it a method of bringing about a literary climax....

---

107 A cast iron and glass building built to house the Great Exhibition of 1851 and subsequently moved to Penge Common, where it stood at the time of this lecture.
108 Italian: bell towers.
109 A three-part distilling apparatus, the last part of which is the receiver, in which the substance is condensed.
110 *Venus de Milo*, famous statue of Aphrodite, discovered in modern times on the Greek island of Melos.

Meanwhile, the *painter's* poetry is quite lost to him—the amazing invention, that shall have put form and colour into such perfect harmony, that exquisiteness is the result, he is without understanding—the nobility of thought, that shall have given the artist's dignity to the whole, says to him absolutely nothing....

A curious matter, in its effect upon the judgment of these gentlemen, is the accepted vocabulary, of poetic symbolism, that helps them, by habit, in dealing with Nature: a mountain, to them, is synonymous with height—a lake, with depth—the ocean, with vastness—the sun, with glory.

So that a picture with a mountain, a lake, and an ocean—however poor in paint—is inevitably "lofty," "vast," "infinite," and "glorious"—on paper.

There are those also, sombre of mien, and wise with the wisdom of books, who frequent museums and burrow in crypts; collecting—comparing—compiling—classifying—contradicting.

Experts these—for whom a date is an accomplishment—a hall mark, success!

Careful in scrutiny are they, and conscientious of judgment—establishing, with due weight, unimportant reputations—discovering the picture, by the stain on the back—testing the torso, by the leg that is missing ... disputatious and dictatorial, concerning the birthplace of inferior persons—speculating, in much writing, upon the great worth of bad work.

True clerks of the collection, they mix memoranda with ambition, and, reducing Art to statistics, they "file" the fifteenth century, and "pigeon-hole" the antique!

Then the Preacher "appointed"!

He stands in high places—harangues and holds forth.

Sage of the Universities—learned in many matters, and of much experience in all, save his subject.

Exhorting—denouncing—directing.

Filled with wrath and earnestness....

Crying out, and cutting himself—while the gods hear not.

Gentle priest of the Philistine[111] withal, again he ambles pleasantly from all point, and through many volumes, escaping scientific assertion—"babbles of green fields."[112]

So Art has become foolishly confounded with education—that all should be equally qualified.

Whereas, while polish, refinement, culture, and breeding, are in no way arguments for artistic result, it is also no reproach to the most finished scholar or greatest gentleman in the land that he be absolutely without eye for painting or ear for music—that in his heart he prefer the popular print to the scratch of Rembrandt's needle,[113] or the songs of the hall[114] to Beethoven's "C minor Symphony."[115] ...

Art happens—no hovel is safe from it, no Prince may depend upon it, the vastest intelligence cannot bring it about, and puny efforts to make it universal end in quaint comedy, and coarse farce.

This is as it should be—and all attempts to make it otherwise, are due to the eloquence of the ignorant, the zeal of the conceited.

---

111 Enemies of the Israelites in the Old Testament; a term used in the nineteenth century to refer to someone ignorant or uncultured.
112 Shakespeare, *Henry V* (II.iii.18).
113 Tool for engraving.
114 Music halls were venues of popular musical and theatrical entertainment.
115 The famous fifth symphony by Ludwig van Beethoven (1770–1827), German composer.

The boundary line is clear. Far from me to propose to bridge it over—that the pestered people be pushed across. No! I would save them from further fatigue. I would come to their relief, and would lift from their shoulders this incubus[116] of Art.

Why, after centuries of freedom from it, and indifference to it, should it now be thrust upon them by the blind—until, wearied and puzzled, they know no longer how they shall eat or drink—how they shall sit or stand—or wherewithal they shall clothe themselves—without afflicting Art?

But, lo! there is much talk without!

Triumphantly they cry, "Beware! This matter does indeed concern us. We also have our part in all true Art!—for, remember the 'one touch of Nature' that 'makes the whole world kin.'"[117]

True, indeed. But let not the unwary jauntily suppose that Shakespeare herewith hands him his passport to Paradise, and thus permits him speech among the chosen. Rather, learn that, in this very sentence, he is condemned to remain without—to continue with the common.

This one chord that vibrates with all—this "one touch of Nature" ... this one unspoken sympathy that pervades humanity, is—Vulgarity!

Vulgarity—under whose fascinating influence "the many" have elbowed "the few," and the gentle circle of Art swarms with the intoxicated mob of mediocrity, whose leaders prate and counsel, and call aloud, where the Gods once spoke in whisper!

And now from their midst the Dilettante stalks abroad. The amateur is loosed. The voice of the æsthete is heard in the land, and catastrophe is upon us....

... Here are no connections of ours.

We will have nothing to do with them.

Forced to seriousness, that emptiness may be hidden, they dare not smile—

While the artist, in fulness of heart and head, is glad, and laughs aloud, and is happy in his strength, and is merry at the pompous pretension—the solemn silliness that surrounds him.

For Art and Joy go together, with bold openness, and high head, and ready hand—fearing naught, and dreading no exposure.

Know, then, all beautiful women, that we are with you. Pay no heed, we pray you, to this outcry of the unbecoming—this last plea for the plain.

It concerns you not.

Your own instinct is near the truth—your own wit far surer guide than the untaught ventures of thick-heeled Apollos.[118]

What! will you up and follow the first piper that leads you down Petticoat Lane,[119] there, on a Sabbath, to gather, for the week, from the dull rags of ages, wherewith to bedeck yourselves? that, beneath your travestied awkwardness, we have trouble to find your own dainty selves? Oh, fie! Is the world, then, exhausted? and must we go back because the thumb of the mountebank[120] jerks the other way?

Costume is not dress.

---

116 An evil male spirit that descends on women in their sleep, seeking intercourse.
117 Shakespeare, *Troilus and Cressida* (III.iii.175).
118 Apollo, Greek god of music, poetry, and dance.
119 Clothing market in East London.
120 Itinerant entertainer; charlatan.

And the wearers of wardrobes may not be doctors of taste!

For by what authority shall these be pretty masters? Look well, and nothing have they invented—nothing put together for comeliness' sake.

Haphazard from their shoulders hang the garments of the hawker—combining in their person the motley of many manners with the medley of the mummers' closet.

Set up as a warning, and a finger-post of danger, they point to the disastrous effect of Art upon the middle classes.

Why this lifting of the brow in deprecation of the present—this pathos in reference to the past?

If Art be rare to-day, it was seldom heretofore.

It is false, this teaching of decay.

The master stands in no relation to the moment at which he occurs—a monument of isolation—hinting at sadness—having no part in the progress of his fellow men.

He is also no more the product of civilisation than is the scientific truth asserted, dependent upon the wisdom of a period. The assertion itself requires the *man* to make it. The truth was from the beginning.

So Art is limited to the infinite, and beginning there cannot progress.

A silent indication of its wayward independence from all extraneous advance, is in the absolutely unchanged condition and form of implement since the beginning of things.

The painter has but the same pencil—the sculptor the chisel of centuries.

Colours are not more since the heavy hangings of night were first drawn aside, and the loveliness of light revealed.

Neither chemist nor engineer can offer new elements of the masterpiece.

False again, the fabled link between the grandeur of Art and the glories and virtues of the State, for Art feeds not upon nations, and peoples may be wiped from the face of the earth, but Art *is*.

It is indeed high time that we cast aside the weary weight of responsibility and copartnership, and know that, in no way, do our virtues minister to its worth, in no way do our vices impede its triumph!

How irksome! how hopeless! how superhuman the self-imposed task of the nation! How sublimely vain the belief that it shall live nobly or art perish!...

... Art we in no way affect.

A whimsical goddess, and a capricious, her strong sense of joy tolerates no dulness, and, live we never so spotlessly, still may she turn her back upon us.

As, from time immemorial, she has done upon the Swiss in their mountains.

What more worthy people! Whose every Alpine gap yawns with tradition, and is stocked with noble story; yet, the perverse and scornful one will none of it, and the sons of patriots are left with the clock that turns the mill, and the sudden cuckoo, with difficulty restrained in its box!

For this was Tell a hero! For this did Gessler die![121]

Art, the cruel jade, cares not, and hardens her heart, and hies her off to the East, to find, among the opium-eaters of Nankin,[122] a favourite with whom she lingers fondly—caressing his blue porcelain,

---

[121] William Tell (c. fourteenth century), legendary Swiss hero arrested for insubordination by the tyrant Albrecht Gessler, who ordered Tell to shoot an apple off his son's head. Tell succeeded and later assassinated Gessler.
[122] Nanjing (Nanking), a city in China captured by Britain in 1842 during the Opium Wars.

and painting his coy maidens, and marking his plates with her six marks of choice—indifferent, in her companionship with him, to all save the virtue of his refinement!

He it is who calls her—he who holds her!

And again to the West, that her next lover may bring together the Gallery at Madrid, and show to the world how the Master towers above all;[123] and in their intimacy they revel, he and she, in this knowledge; and he knows the happiness untasted by other mortal.

She is proud of her comrade, and promises that, in after years, others shall pass that way, and understand.

So in all time does this superb one cast about for the man worthy her love—and Art seeks the Artist alone.

Where he is, there she appears, and remains with him—loving and fruitful—turning never aside in moments of hope deferred—of insult—and of ribald misunderstanding; and when he dies she sadly takes her flight, though loitering yet in the land, from fond association, but refusing to be consoled.[124]

With the man, then, and not with the multitude, are her intimacies; and in the book of her life the names inscribed are few—scant, indeed, the list of those who have helped to write her story of love and beauty.

From the sunny morning, when, with her glorious Greek relenting, she yielded up the secret of repeated line, as, with his hand in hers, together they marked, in marble, the measured rhyme of lovely limb and draperies flowing in unison, to the day when she dipped the Spaniard's brush in light and air, and made his people live within their frames, and *stand upon their legs*, that all nobility and sweetness, and tenderness, and magnificence should be theirs by right, ages had gone by, and few had been her choice.

Countless, indeed, the horde of pretenders! But she knew them not.

A teeming, seething, busy mass, whose virtue was industry, and whose industry was vice!

Their names go to fill the catalogue of the collection at home, of the gallery abroad, for the delectation of the bagman and the critic.

Therefore have we cause to be merry!—and to cast away all care—resolved that all is well—as it ever was—and that it is not meet that we should be cried at, and urged to take measures!

Enough have we endured of dulness! Surely are we weary of weeping, and our tears have been cozened from us falsely, for they have called out woe! when there was no grief—and, alas! where all is fair!

We have then but to wait—until, with the mark of the gods upon him—there come among us again the chosen—who shall continue what has gone before. Satisfied that, even were he never to appear, the story of the beautiful is already complete—hewn in the marbles of the Parthenon—and broidered, with the birds, upon the fan of Hokusai—at the foot of Fusi-yama.[125]

---

123 The Museo del Prado at Madrid holds the world's largest collection of the works of Diego Velázquez, whom Whistler revered as a great master of art.
124 Author's note: And so have we the ephemeral influence of the Master's memory—the afterglow, in which are warmed, for a while, the worker and disciple.
125 Hokusai (1760–1849), Japanese artist and printmaker; Mount Fuji (Fusiyama or Fujiyama) is a volcanic mountain in Japan, held in religious veneration and frequently represented in Japanese art.

Oscar Wilde
from "The Critic as Artist" (1891)

Prolific essayist, novelist, playwright, poet, editor, and lecturer Oscar Wilde (1854–1900) advocated art's importance for the sake of beauty rather than social or moral engagement. His views were influenced by John Ruskin (see Life Writing, Condition of England, Aesthetics and Culture, Gender and Sexuality) and Walter Pater (see Education, Aesthetics and Culture). Prominent in the Aesthetic movement, Wilde was satirized for his flamboyant dress and mannerisms—a criticism he embraced. His works include poetry, a novel, stories, plays, prose treaties and dialogues on aesthetic and political theory, and a term as editor of *Woman's World*. In a series of highly publicized 1895 trials, Wilde was convicted of gross indecency and sentenced to two years in prison with hard labour for homosexual acts.

Published in *Intentions* (1891), "The Critic as Artist" takes the form of a dialogue between two friends on the value of the "critical spirit." Here, Wilde proposes that "criticism of the highest kind ... treats the work of art simply as a starting-point for a new creation."

A DIALOGUE Part 1. Persons: Gilbert and Ernest. Scene: the library of a house in Piccadilly, overlooking the Green Park.

Gilbert (at the Piano). My dear Ernest, what are you laughing at?

Ernest (looking up). At a capital story that I have just come across in this volume of Reminiscences[126] that I have found on your table.

Gilbert. What is the book? Ah! I see. I have not read it yet. Is it good?

Ernest. Well, while you have been playing, I have been turning over the pages with some amusement, though, as a rule, I dislike modern memoirs. They are generally written by people who have either entirely lost their memories, or have never done anything worth remembering; which, however, is, no doubt, the true explanation of their popularity, as the English public always feels perfectly at its ease when a mediocrity is talking to it.

Gilbert. Yes: the public is wonderfully tolerant. It forgives everything except genius. But I must confess that I like all memoirs. I like them for their form, just as much as for their matter. In literature mere egotism is delightful. It is what fascinates us in the letters of personalities so different as Cicero and Balzac, Flaubert and Berlioz, Byron and Madame de Sévigné.[127] Whenever we come across it, and, strangely

---

126 William Powell Frith, *My Autobiography and Reminiscences* (1887) and *Further Reminiscences* (1888).

127 See Cicero's correspondence between 67 and 43 BCE, of which more than 900 letters have been preserved; Honoré de Balzac's *Lettres à l'étrangère* (4 vols., 1889–1950); Gustave Flaubert's letters, published by his niece Caroline (4 vols., 1887–93); Louis-Hector Berlioz's *Correspondance inédite de Hector Berlioz, 1819–1868* (1879) and *Lettres intimes* (1882); George Gordon Byron's letters, published in Thomas Moore's *Letters and Journals of Lord Byron, with Notices of his Life* (1830); Madame de Sévigné's letters to her daughter, written after their separation in 1671.

enough, it is rather rare, we cannot but welcome it, and do not easily forget it. Humanity will always love Rousseau for having confessed his sins, not to a priest, but to the world.[128] ... Yes; autobiography is irresistible.... When people talk to us about others they are usually dull. When they talk to us about themselves they are nearly always interesting, and if one could shut them up, when they become wearisome, as easily as one can shut up a book of which one has grown wearied, they would be perfect absolutely.

Ernest. There is much virtue in that If, as Touchstone[129] would say. But do you seriously propose that every man should become his own Boswell?[130] What would become of our industrious compilers of Lives and Recollections in that case?

Gilbert. What has become of them? They are the pest of the age, nothing more and nothing less. Every great man nowadays has his disciples, and it is always Judas[131] who writes the biography.

Ernest. My dear fellow!...

Gilbert. ... What was the story in the confessions of the remorseful Academician[132] that made you laugh? Tell it to me....

Ernest. Oh! I don't know that it is of any importance. But I thought it a really admirable illustration of the true value of ordinary art-criticism. It seems that a lady once gravely asked the remorseful Academician, as you call him, if his celebrated picture of "A Spring-Day at Whiteley's," or "Waiting for the Last Omnibus," or some subject of that kind, was all painted by hand?[133]

Gilbert. And was it?

Ernest. You are quite incorrigible. But, seriously speaking, what is the use of art-criticism? Why cannot the artist be left alone, to create a new world if he wishes it, or, if not, to shadow forth the world which we already know, and of which, I fancy, we would each one of us be wearied if Art, with her fine spirit of choice and delicate instinct of selection, did not, as it were, purify it for us, and give to it a momentary perfection.... Why should the artist be troubled by the shrill clamour of criticism? Why should those who cannot create take upon themselves to estimate the value of creative work? What can they know about it? If a man's work is easy to understand, an explanation is unnecessary....

Gilbert. And if his work is incomprehensible, an explanation is wicked....

Ernest. ... In the best days of art there were no art-critics. The sculptor hewed from the marble block the great white-limbed Hermes[134] that slept within it. The waxers and gilders of images gave tone and texture to the statue, and the world, when it saw it, worshipped and was dumb. He poured the glowing bronze into the mould of sand, and the river of red metal cooled into noble curves and took the impress of the body of a god. With enamel or polished jewels he gave sight to the sightless eyes. The hyacinth-like curls[135] grew crisp beneath his graver.... In those days the artist was free. From the river valley he took the fine clay in his fingers, and with a little tool of wood or bone, fashioned it into forms so exquisite that

---

128 Jean-Jacques Rousseau, *Les Confessions* (1782–89).
129 Shakespeare, *As You Like It* (V.iv.101).
130 James Boswell (1740–95), author of the *Life of Johnson* (1791).
131 Judas Iscariot (d. 30 CE), one of Jesus' disciples and his betrayer.
132 A member of the Royal Academy of Arts (est. 1768), the leading British artists' society and school.
133 Wilde had earlier criticized William Powell Frith's realist paintings for bringing painting too close to photography; see "The Rout of the R.A.," *Court and Society Review* (April 1887).
134 Messenger of the Greek gods.
135 According to Greek legend, Apollo fell in love with Hyacinthus because of his beauty. After Hyacinthus' death, Apollo used his lover's blood to create the hyacinth plant.

the people gave them to the dead as their playthings, and we find them still in the dusty tombs on the yellow hillside by Tanagra,[136] with the faint gold and the fading crimson still lingering about hair and lips and raiment.... All life, indeed, was his, from the merchants seated in the market-place to the cloaked shepherd lying on the hill; from the nymph hidden in the laurels and the faun that pipes at noon, to the king whom, in long green-curtained litter, slaves bore upon oil-bright shoulders, and fanned with peacock fans. Men and women, with pleasure or sorrow in their faces, passed before him. He watched them, and their secret became his. Through form and colour he recreated a world.

... And no one came to trouble the artist at his work. No irresponsible chatter disturbed him. He was not worried by opinions. By the Ilyssus, says Arnold somewhere, there was no Higginbotham.[137] By the Ilyssus, my dear Gilbert, there were no silly art-congresses, bringing provincialism to the provinces and teaching the mediocrity how to mouth.... The Greeks had no art-critics.

Gilbert. Ernest, you are quite delightful, but your views are terribly unsound.... It would be more just to say that the Greeks were a nation of art-critics.

Ernest. Really?

Gilbert. Yes, a nation of art-critics. But I don't wish to destroy the delightfully unreal picture that you have drawn of the relation of the Hellenic[138] artist to the intellectual spirit of his age.... Still less do I desire to talk learnedly....

Ernest. You are horribly wilful. I insist on your discussing this matter with me. You have said that the Greeks were a nation of art-critics. What art-criticism have they left us?

Gilbert. My dear Ernest, even if not a single fragment of art-criticism had come down to us from Hellenic or Hellenistic days, it would be none the less true that the Greeks were a nation of art-critics, and that they invented the criticism of art just as they invented the criticism of everything else. For, after all, what is our primary debt to the Greeks? Simply the critical spirit....

... An age that has no criticism is either an age in which art is immobile, hieratic,[139] and confined to the reproduction of formal types, or an age that possesses no art at all. There have been critical ages that have not been creative, in the ordinary sense of the word, ages in which the spirit of man has sought to set in order the treasures of his treasure-house, to separate the gold from the silver, and the silver from the lead, to count over the jewels, and to give names to the pearls. But there has never been a creative age that has not been critical also....

... As a rule, the critics—I speak, of course, of the higher class, of those in fact who write for the six-penny papers[140]—are far more cultured than the people whose work they are called upon to review. This is, indeed, only what one would expect, for criticism demands infinitely more cultivation than creation does.

Ernest. Really?

Gilbert. Certainly. Anybody can write a three-volumed novel.[141] It merely requires a complete ignorance of both life and literature. The difficulty that I should fancy the reviewer feels is the difficulty of

---

136 City of ancient Boeotia, Greece, famous for a trove of terra-cotta figurines discovered in 1874.
137 Slightly inaccurate: in "The Functions of Criticism at the Present Time" (1864), Matthew Arnold refers to "hideous" modern British names such as Higginbottom and Wragg, writing, "[B]y the Ilissus there was no Wragg." See Education.
138 Greek.
139 Priestly.
140 Gilbert differentiates between the penny press (cheap newspapers for the masses) and slightly more expensive periodicals.
141 A common mid-Victorian novel format, popular with the circulating libraries, that had become outdated by late century.

sustaining any standard.... It is sometimes said of them that they do not read all through the works they are called upon to criticise. They do not. Or at least they should not.... To know the vintage and quality of a wine one need not drink the whole cask. It must be perfectly easy in half an hour to say whether a book is worth anything or worth nothing.... I am aware that there are many honest workers in painting as well as in literature who object to criticism entirely. They are quite right. Their work stands in no intellectual relation to their age. It brings us no new element of pleasure. It suggests no fresh departure of thought, or passion, or beauty. It should not be spoken of. It should be left to the oblivion that it deserves.

Ernest. But, my dear fellow—excuse me for interrupting you—you seem to me to be allowing your passion for criticism to lead you a great deal too far. For, after all, even you must admit that it is much more difficult to do a thing than to talk about it.

Gilbert. More difficult to do a thing than to talk about it? Not at all. That is a gross popular error. It is very much more difficult to talk about a thing than to do it....

... When man acts he is a puppet. When he describes he is a poet. The whole secret lies in that. It was easy enough on the sandy plains by windy Ilion[142] to send the notched arrow from the painted bow, or to hurl against the shield of hide and flame-like brass the long ash-handled spear. It was easy for the adulterous queen[143] to spread the Tyrian[144] carpets for her lord, and then, as he lay couched in the marble bath,[145] to throw over his head the purple net, and call to her smooth-faced lover[146] to stab through the meshes at the heart that should have broken at Aulis....[147] But what of those who wrote about these things? What of those who gave them reality, and made them live for ever? Are they not greater than the men and women they sing of? ...

Ernest. Yes; I see now what you mean. But, surely, the higher you place the creative artist, the lower must the critic rank.

Gilbert. Why so?

Ernest. Because the best that he can give us will be but an echo of rich music, a dim shadow of clear-outlined form. It may, indeed, be that life is chaos, as you tell me that it is; that its martyrdoms are mean and its heroisms ignoble; and that it is the function of Literature to create, from the rough material of actual existence, a new world that will be more marvellous, more enduring, and more true than the world that common eyes look upon, and through which common natures seek to realize their perfection. But surely, if this new world has been made by the spirit and touch of a great artist, it will be a thing so complete and perfect that there will be nothing left for the critic to do....

Gilbert. But, surely, Criticism is itself an art. And just as artistic creation implies the working of the critical faculty, and, indeed, without it cannot be said to exist at all, so Criticism is really creative in the highest sense of the word. Criticism is, in fact, both creative and independent.

Ernest. Independent?

Gilbert. Yes; independent. Criticism is no more to be judged by any low standard of imitation or resemblance than is the work of poet or sculptor. The critic occupies the same relation to the work of art

---

142 Troy.
143 Clytemnestra, wife of Agamemnon, leader of the Greeks at Troy.
144 Refers to the purple colouring from the famous mollusc-derived dye made in Tyre, a Phoenician city.
145 Traditional bath of welcoming for a guest or relative after a journey.
146 Aegisthus, Agamemnon's cousin and worst enemy, began an affair with Clytemnestra in Agamemnon's absence.
147 Gilbert suggests that Agamemnon's heart should have broken at Aulis, where he sacrificed his eldest daughter, Iphigenia, to Artemis in exchange for fair winds to Troy. This sacrifice prompted Clytemnestra's affair and Agamemnon's murder.

that he criticises as the artist does to the visible world of form and colour, or the unseen world of passion and of thought. He does not even require for the perfection of his art the finest materials. Anything will serve his purpose. And just as out of the sordid and sentimental amours of the silly wife of a small country doctor in the squalid village of Yonville-l'Abbaye, near Rouen, Gustave Flaubert was able to create a classic, and make a masterpiece of style,[148] so, from subjects of little or of no importance, such as the pictures in this year's Royal Academy,[149] or in any year's Royal Academy for that matter, Mr. Lewis Morris's poems, M. Ohnet's novels, or the plays of Mr. Henry Arthur Jones,[150] the true critic can, if it be his pleasure so to direct or waste his faculty of contemplation, produce work that will be flawless in beauty and instinct with intellectual subtlety....

Ernest. But is Criticism really a creative art?

Gilbert. Why should it not be? It works with materials, and puts them into a form that is at once new and delightful. What more can one say of poetry? Indeed, I would call criticism a creation within a creation.... No ignoble considerations of probability, that cowardly concession to the tedious repetitions of domestic or public life, affect it ever. One may appeal from fiction unto fact. But from the soul there is no appeal.

Ernest. From the soul?

Gilbert. Yes, from the soul. That is what the highest criticism really is, the record of one's own soul. It is more fascinating than history, as it is concerned simply with oneself. It is more delightful than philosophy, as its subject is concrete and not abstract, real and not vague. It is the only civilized form of autobiography, as it deals not with the events, but with the thoughts of one's life; not with life's physical accidents of deed or circumstance, but with the spiritual moods and imaginative passions of the mind.... The best that one can say of most modern creative art is that it is just a little less vulgar than reality, and so the critic, with his fine sense of distinction and sure instinct of delicate refinement, will prefer to look into the silver mirror or through the woven veil, and will turn his eyes away from the chaos and clamour of actual existence, though the mirror be tarnished and the veil be torn. His sole aim is to chronicle his own impressions. It is for him that pictures are painted, books written, and marble hewn into form.

Ernest. I seem to have heard another theory of Criticism.

Gilbert. Yes: it has been said by one whose gracious memory we all revere, and the music of whose pipe once lured Proserpina[151] from her Sicilian fields, and made those white feet stir, and not in vain, the Cumnor[152] cowslips, that the proper aim of Criticism is to see the object as in itself it really is.[153] But this is a very serious error, and takes no cognizance of Criticism's most perfect form, which is in its essence purely subjective, and seeks to reveal its own secret and not the secret of another. For the highest Criticism deals with art not as expressive but as impressive purely.

Ernest. But is that really so?

---

148 Gustave Flaubert, *Madame Bovary* (1856).
149 The Royal Academy held an annual lecture series on and exhibit of art and architecture.
150 Lewis Morris (1833–1907), poet; Georges Ohnet (1848–1918), French novelist; Henry Arthur Jones (1851–1929), playwright.
151 Roman version of the Greek goddess Persephone, who was abducted and taken to the underworld.
152 Village in Oxfordshire, near Oxford.
153 Matthew Arnold, "The Functions of Criticism at the Present Time" (1864). See Education.

Gilbert. Of course it is. Who cares whether Mr. Ruskin's views on Turner[154] are sound or not? What does it matter? That mighty and majestic prose of his, so fervid and so fiery-coloured in its noble eloquence, so rich in its elaborate symphonic music, so sure and certain, at its best, in subtle choice of word and epithet, is at least as great a work of art as any of those wonderful sunsets that bleach or rot on their corrupted canvases in England's Gallery....[155] Who, again, cares whether Mr. Pater has put into the portrait of Monna Lisa something that Lionardo never dreamed of? ...[156]

... Do you ask me what Lionardo would have said had any one told him of this picture that "all the thoughts and experience of the world had etched and moulded there in that which they had of power to refine and make expressive the outward form, the animalism of Greece, the lust of Rome, the reverie of the Middle Age with its spiritual ambition and imaginative loves, the return of the Pagan world, the sins of the Borgias?"[157] He would probably have answered that he had contemplated none of these things, but had concerned himself simply with certain arrangements of lines and masses, and with new and curious colour-harmonies of blue and green. And it is for this very reason that the criticism which I have quoted is criticism of the highest kind. It treats the work of art simply as a starting-point for a new creation.... For when the work is finished it has, as it were, an independent life of its own, and may deliver a message far other than that which was put into its lips to say....

Ernest. The highest Criticism, then, is more creative than creation, and the primary aim of the critic is to see the object as in itself it really is not; that is your theory, I believe?

Gilbert. Yes, that is my theory. To the critic the work of art is simply a suggestion for a new work of his own, that need not necessarily bear any obvious resemblance to the thing it criticises. The one characteristic of a beautiful form is that one can put into it whatever one wishes, and see in it whatever one chooses to see; and the Beauty, that gives to creation its universal and æsthetic element, makes the critic a creator in his turn, and whispers of a thousand different things which were not present in the mind of him who carved the statue or painted the panel or graved the gem....

A DIALOGUE. Part 2. Persons: the same. Scene: the same.

Ernest. ... I want to discuss the critic and criticism. You have told me that the highest criticism deals with art, not as expressive, but as impressive purely, and is consequently both creative and independent, is in fact an art by itself, occupying the same relation to creative work that creative work does to the visible world of form and colour, or the unseen world of passion and of thought. Well, now tell me, will not the critic be sometimes a real interpreter?

Gilbert. Yes; the critic will be an interpreter, if he chooses. He can pass from his synthetic[158] impression of the work of art as a whole, to an analysis or exposition of the work itself, and in this lower sphere, as I hold it to be, there are many delightful things to be said and done. Yet his object will not always be to

---

154 John Ruskin's first book, *Modern Painters Vol. 1* (1843), was a defence of painter J.M.W. Turner.
155 The National Gallery, founded 1824 in London, relocated to its present location in 1838.
156 Walter Pater, *Studies in the History of the Renaissance* (1873). See Aesthetics and Culture.
157 Original: "All the thoughts and experience of the world have etched and moulded there, in that which they have of power to refine and make expressive the outward form, the animalism of Greece, the lust of Rome, the mysticism of the Middle Age with its spiritual ambition and imaginative loves, the return of the Pagan world, the sins of the Borgias?" From Pater, *Studies in the History of the Renaissance* (1873).
158 Constructed through synthesis, building upon the original piece of art.

explain the work of art. He may seek rather to deepen its mystery, to raise round it, and round its maker, that mist of wonder which is dear to both gods and worshippers alike. Ordinary people are "terribly at ease in Zion."[159] They propose to walk arm in arm with the poets, and have a glib ignorant way of saying "Why should we read what is written about Shakespeare and Milton? We can read the plays and the poems. That is enough." But an appreciation of Milton is, as the late Rector of Lincoln remarked once, the reward of consummate scholarship.[160] And he who desires to understand Shakespeare truly must understand the relations in which Shakespeare stood to the Renaissance and the Reformation,[161] to the age of Elizabeth and the age of James;[162] he must be familiar with the history of the struggle for supremacy between the old classical forms and the new spirit of romance, between the school of Sidney, and Daniel, and Jonson, and the school of Marlowe and Marlowe's greater son;[163] he must know the materials that were at Shakespeare's disposal, and the method in which he used them, and the conditions of theatric presentation in the sixteenth and seventeenth century, their limitations and their opportunities for freedom, and the literary criticism of Shakespeare's day, its aims and modes and canons; he must study the English language in its progress, and blank or rhymed verse in its various developments; he must study the Greek drama, and the connection between the art of the creator of the Agamemnon and the art of the creator of Macbeth;[164] in a word, he must be able to bind Elizabethan London to the Athens of Pericles,[165] and to learn Shakespeare's true position in the history of European drama and the drama of the world. The critic will certainly be an interpreter, but he will not treat Art as a riddling Sphinx,[166] whose shallow secret may be guessed and revealed by one whose feet are wounded and who knows not his name.[167] Rather, he will look upon Art as a goddess whose mystery it is his province to intensi[f]y, and whose majesty his privilege to make more marvellous in the eyes of men.

And here, Ernest, this strange thing happens. The critic will indeed be an interpreter, but he will not be an interpreter in the sense of one who simply repeats in another form a message that has been put into his lips to say. For, just as it is only by contact with the art of foreign nations that the art of a country gains that individual and separate life that we call nationality, so, by curious inversion, it is only by intensifying his own personality that the critic can interpret the personality and work of others, and the more strongly this personality enters into the interpretation the more real the interpretation becomes, the more satisfying, the more convincing, and the more true....

... [The critic] shows the poet's work under new conditions, and by a method special to himself. He takes the written word, and action, gesture, and voice become the media of revelation. The singer, or the

---

159 Amos 6:1 ("at ease in Zion").
160 Mark Pattison, *Milton* (1879).
161 The English Renaissance of the fifteenth and sixteenth centuries represented a burst of artistic production inspired by Roman and Greek models; the English Reformation of the sixteenth century saw agitation for the reform of the Catholic Church and the formation of various reformed and Protestant churches.
162 Queen Elizabeth I (1533–1603); King James I (1566–1625).
163 Philip Sidney (1554–86), poet; Samuel Daniel (c. 1562–1619), poet; Ben Jonson (1572–1637), poet and playwright; Christopher Marlowe (c. 1564–93), playwright and poet; "the school of Marlowe" refers to playwrights who wrote in Marlowe's blank-verse style. "Marlowe's greater son" is Shakespeare.
164 Aeschylus (c. 525–c. 456 BCE), Greek playwright; Shakespeare.
165 Elizabethan London: 1558–1603; Athens of Pericles: c. 495–429 BCE.
166 In Greek mythology, the Sphinx is a creature with wings, a woman's head, and a lion's body. It guards the entrance to the city of Thebes with a riddle and eats those who cannot answer.
167 Oedipus (which translates as swollen-footed), Greek mythological character who answered the Sphinx's riddle.

player on lute and viol, is the critic of music. The etcher of a picture robs the painting of its fair colours, but shows us by the use of a new material its true colour-quality, its tones and values, and the relations of its masses, and so is, in his way, a critic of it, for the critic is he who exhibits to us a work of art in a form different from that of the work itself, and the employment of a new material is a critical as well as a creative element.... [I]n the case of all these creative critics of art it is evident that personality is an absolute essential for any real interpretation. When Rubinstein plays to us the *Sonata Appassionata* of Beethoven,[168] he gives us not merely Beethoven, but also himself, and so gives us Beethoven absolutely—Beethoven reinterpreted through a rich artistic nature, and made vivid and wonderful to us by a new and intense personality. When a great actor plays Shakespeare we have the same experience. His own individuality becomes a vital part of the interpretation....

Ernest. The critic, then, considered as the interpreter, will give no less than he receives, and lend as much as he borrows?

Gilbert. He will be always showing us the work of art in some new relation to our age. He will always be reminding us that great works of art are living things—are, in fact, the only things that live....

Ernest. Must we go, then, to Art for everything?

Gilbert. For everything. Because Art does not hurt us. The tears that we shed at a play are a type of the exquisite sterile emotions that it is the function of Art to awaken. We weep, but we are not wounded. We grieve, but our grief is not bitter. In the actual life of man, sorrow, as Spinoza says somewhere, is a passage to a lesser perfection.[169] But the sorrow with which Art fills us both purifies and initiates, if I may quote once more from the great art-critic of the Greeks.[170] It is through Art, and through Art only, that we can realize our perfection; through Art, and through Art only, that we can shield ourselves from the sordid perils of actual existence....

Ernest. Stop a moment. It seems to me that in everything that you have said there is something radically immoral.

Gilbert. All art is immoral.

Ernest. All art?

Gilbert. Yes. For emotion for the sake of emotion is the aim of art, and emotion for the sake of action is the aim of life, and of that practical organization of life that we call society. Society, which is the beginning and basis of morals, exists simply for the concentration of human energy, and in order to ensure its own continuance and healthy stability it demands, and no doubt rightly demands, of each of its citizens that he should contribute some form of productive labour to the common weal, and toil and travail that the day's work may be done. Society often forgives the criminal; it never forgives the dreamer. The beautiful sterile emotions that art excites in us are hateful in its eyes, and so completely are people dominated by the tyranny of this dreadful social ideal that they are always coming shamelessly up to one at Private Views[171] and other places that are open to the general public, and saying in a loud stentorian voice, "What are you doing?" whereas "What are you thinking?" is the only question that any single civilized being should ever be allowed to whisper to another. They mean well, no doubt, these honest beaming folk. Perhaps

---

168 Anton Rubinstein (1829–94), Russian composer and pianist; Ludwig van Beethoven, Piano Sonata No. 23 in F-minor (c. 1804-06).
169 Benedict de Spinoza, *Ethics*, Part 3: "Origin and Nature of the Affects" (1677).
170 Refers to the Aristotelian idea that tragedy purifies and elevates the viewer through catharsis.
171 Private art gallery openings.

that is the reason why they are so excessively tedious. But some one should teach them that while, in the opinion of society, Contemplation is the gravest sin of which any citizen can be guilty, in the opinion of the highest culture it is the proper occupation of man.

Ernest. Contemplation?

Gilbert. Contemplation. I said to you some time ago that it was far more difficult to talk about a thing than to do it. Let me say to you now that to do nothing at all is the most difficult thing in the world, the most difficult and the most intellectual. To Plato, with his passion for wisdom, this was the noblest form of energy. To Aristotle, with his passion for knowledge, this was the noblest form of energy also.[172] It was to this that the passion for holiness led the saint and the mystic of mediæval days.

Ernest. We exist, then, to do nothing?

Gilbert. It is to do nothing that the elect exist. Action is limited and relative. Unlimited and absolute is the vision of him who sits at ease and watches, who walks in loneliness and dreams....

Ernest. What then do you propose?

Gilbert. It seems to me that with the development of the critical spirit we shall be able to realize, not merely our own lives, but the collective life of the race, and so to make ourselves absolutely modern, in the true meaning of the word modernity. For he to whom the present is the only thing that is present, knows nothing of the age in which he lives. To realize the nineteenth century, one must realize every century that has preceded it and that has contributed to its making. To know anything about oneself, one must know all about others. There must be no mood with which one cannot sympathize, no dead mode of life that one cannot make alive....

Ernest. But where in this is the function of the critical spirit?

Gilbert. The culture that this transmission of racial experiences makes possible can be made perfect by the critical spirit alone, and indeed may be said to be one with it. For who is the true critic but he who bears within himself the dreams, and ideas, and feelings of myriad generations, and to whom no form of thought is alien, no emotional impulse obscure? And who the true man of culture, if not he who by fine scholarship and fastidious rejection has made instinct self-conscious and intelligent, and can separate the work that has distinction from the work that has it not, and so by contact and comparison makes himself master of the secrets of style and school, and understands their meanings, and listens to their voices, and develops that spirit of disinterested curiosity which is the real root, as it is the real flower, of the intellectual life, and thus attains to intellectual clarity, and, having learned "the best that is known and thought in the world,"[173] lives—it is not fanciful to say so—with those who are the Immortals....

Is such a mode of life immoral? Yes: all the arts are immoral, except those baser forms of sensual or didactic art that seek to excite to action of evil or of good. For action of every kind belongs to the sphere of ethics. The aim of art is simply to create a mood. Is such a mode of life unpractical? Ah! it is not so easy to be unpractical as the ignorant Philistine[174] imagines. It were well for England if it were so. There is no country in the world so much in need of unpractical people as this country of ours. With us, Thought

---

172 In section 189 of his Commonplace Book, Wilde quotes Aristotle's views on contemplation: "for wisdom does not consider because of what things a man will be happy" (*Ethics* 6.13). Wilde changes the verb tense to the present ("does not") from Aristotle's future tense ("will not").

173 Matthew Arnold, "The Functions of Criticism at the Present Time" (1864). See Education.

174 Enemies of the Israelites in the Old Testament; used in the nineteenth century to refer to someone ignorant or uncultured.

is degraded by its constant association with practice.... The sure way of knowing nothing about life is to try to make oneself useful.

Ernest. A charming doctrine, Gilbert.

Gilbert. I am not sure about that, but it has at least the minor merit of being true. That the desire to do good to others produces a plentiful crop of prigs[175] is the least of the evils of which it is the cause. The prig is a very interesting psychological study, and though of all poses a moral pose is the most offensive, still to have a pose at all is something. It is a formal recognition of the importance of treating life from a definite and reasoned standpoint. That Humanitarian Sympathy wars against Nature, by securing the survival of the failure, may make the man of science loathe its facile virtues. The political economist may cry out against it for putting the improvident on the same level as the provident, and so robbing life of the strongest, because most sordid, incentive to industry. But, in the eyes of the thinker, the real harm that emotional sympathy does is that it limits knowledge, and so prevents us from solving any single social problem. We are trying at present to stave off the coming crisis, the coming revolution as my friends the Fabianists[176] call it, by means of doles and alms. Well, when the revolution or crisis arrives, we shall be powerless because we shall know nothing. And so, Ernest, let us not be deceived. England will never be civilized till she has added Utopia to her dominions. There is more than one of her colonies that she might with advantage surrender for so fair a land. What we want are unpractical people who see beyond the moment, and think beyond the day. Those who try to lead the people can only do so by following the mob. It is through the voice of one crying in the wilderness that the ways of the gods must be prepared....[177]

Ernest. ... I wish you would tell me what are the qualities that should characterize the true critic.

Gilbert. What would you say they were?

Ernest. Well, I should say that a critic should above all things be fair.

Gilbert. Ah! not fair. A critic cannot be fair in the ordinary sense of the word. It is only about things that do not interest one that one can give a really unbiassed opinion, which is no doubt the reason why an unbiassed opinion is always absolutely valueless. The man who sees both sides of a question, is a man who sees absolutely nothing at all. Art is a passion, and, in matters of art, Thought is inevitably coloured by emotion, and so is fluid rather than fixed, and, depending upon fine moods and exquisite moments, cannot be narrowed into the rigidity of a scientific formula or a theological dogma. It is to the soul that Art speaks, and the soul may be made the prisoner of the mind as well as of the body.... No: fairness is not one of the qualities of the true critic. It is not even a condition of criticism. Each form of Art with which we come in contact dominates us for the moment to the exclusion of every other form. We must surrender ourselves absolutely to the work in question, whatever it may be, if we wish to gain its secret....

Ernest. The true critic will be rational, at any rate, will he not?

Gilbert. Rational? There are two ways of disliking art, Ernest. One is to dislike it. The other, to like it rationally. For Art, as Plato saw, and not without regret, creates in listener and spectator a form of divine madness.[178] It does not spring from inspiration, but it makes others inspired. Reason is not the faculty to which it appeals. If one loves Art at all, one must love it beyond all other things in the world, and against such love, the reason, if one listened to it, would cry out....

---

175 A self-important and didactic person.
176 Members of the Fabian Society, a socialist political group that believed in gradual political change.
177 The voice of John the Baptist, who announced the coming of Christ: Matthew 3:3, Mark 1:3, Luke 3:4, John 1:23.
178 Plato, *Phaedrus* (c. 360 BCE).

Ernest. Well, at least, the critic will be sincere.

Gilbert. A little sincerity is a dangerous thing, and a great deal of it is absolutely fatal. The true critic will, indeed, always be sincere in his devotion to the principle of beauty, but he will seek for beauty in every age and in each school, and will never suffer himself to be limited to any settled custom of thought, or stereotyped mode of looking at things. He will realize himself in many forms, and by a thousand different ways, and will ever be curious of new sensations and fresh points of view. Through constant change, and through constant change alone, he will find his true unity.... The essence of thought, as the essence of life, is growth. You must not be frightened by words, Ernest. What people call insincerity is simply a method by which we can multiply our personalities.

Ernest. I am afraid I have not been fortunate in my suggestions.

Gilbert. Of the three qualifications you mentioned, two, sincerity and fairness, were, if not actually moral, at least on the border-land of morals, and the first condition of criticism is that the critic should be able to recognize that the sphere of Art and the sphere of Ethics are absolutely distinct and separate.... Art is out of the reach of morals, for her eyes are fixed upon things beautiful and immortal and ever-changing. To morals belong the lower and less intellectual spheres....

... Temperament is the primary requisite for the critic—a temperament exquisitely susceptible to beauty, and to the various impressions that beauty gives us. Under what conditions, and by what means, this temperament is engendered in race or individual, we will not discuss at present. It is sufficient to note that it exists, and that there is in us a beauty-sense, separate from the other senses and above them, separate from the reason and of nobler import, separate from the soul and of equal value—a sense that leads some to create, and others, the finer spirits as I think, to contemplate merely. But to be purified and made perfect, this sense requires some form of exquisite environment. Without this it starves, or is dulled. You remember that lovely passage in which Plato describes how a young Greek should be educated, and with what insistence he dwells upon the importance of surroundings, telling us how the lad is to be brought up in the midst of fair sights and sounds, so that the beauty of material things may prepare his soul for the reception of the beauty that is spiritual....[179] I need hardly say, Ernest, how far we in England have fallen short of this ideal, and I can imagine the smile that would illuminate the glossy face of the Philistine if one ventured to [suggest to] him that the true aim of education was the love of beauty, and that the methods by which education should work were the development of temperament, the cultivation of taste, and the creation of the critical spirit.

Yet, even for us, there is left some loveliness of environment, and the dulness of tutors and professors matters very little when one can loiter in the grey cloisters at Magdalen, and listen to some flute-like voice singing in Waynfleete's chapel,[180] or lie in the green meadow, among the strange snake-spotted fritillaries,[181] and watch the sunburnt noon smite to a finer gold the tower's gilded vanes, or wander up the Christ Church staircase beneath the vaulted ceiling's shadowy fans,[182] or pass through the sculptured gateway of Laud's building in the College of St. John....[183]

---

179 Plato, *Symposium* (c. 360 BCE).
180 Magdalen College, Oxford, which Wilde attended; the college was founded by Bishop William Waynflete (c. 1395–1486), after whom the chapel is named.
181 Type of lily; the Snake's Head variety (purple with white spots) is common in Oxfordshire.
182 The stairway to the dining hall, Christ Church, Oxford.
183 The entrance to the Canterbury Quadrangle, St. John's College, Oxford, commissioned by William Laud.

... The harmony that resides in the delicate proportions of lines and masses becomes mirrored in the mind. The repetitions of pattern give us rest. The marvels of design stir the imagination. In the mere loveliness of the materials employed there are latent elements of culture....

... And so, to return to the sphere of Art, it is Form that creates not merely the critical temperament, but also the æsthetic instinct, that unerring instinct that reveals to one all things under their conditions of beauty. Start with the worship of form, and there is no secret in art that will not be revealed to you, and remember that in criticism, as in creation, temperament is everything, and that it is, not by the time of their production, but by the temperaments to which they appeal, that the schools of art should be historically grouped.

Ernest. Your theory of education is delightful. But what influence will your critic, brought up in these exquisite surroundings, possess? Do you really think that any artist is ever affected by criticism?

Gilbert. The influence of the critic will be the mere fact of his own existence. He will represent the flawless type. In him the culture of the century will see itself realized. You must not ask of him to have any aim other than the perfecting of himself. The demand of the intellect, as has been well said, is simply to feel itself alive. The critic may, indeed, desire to exercise influence; but, if so, he will concern himself not with the individual, but with the age, which he will seek to wake into consciousness, and to make responsive, creating in it new desires and appetites, and lending it his larger vision and his nobler moods....

... You have spoken against Criticism as being a sterile thing. The nineteenth century is a turning point in history simply on account of the work of two men, Darwin and Renan,[184] the one the critic of the Book of Nature, the other the critic of the books of God. Not to recognize this is to miss the meaning of one of the most important eras in the progress of the world. Creation is always behind the age. It is Criticism that leads us. The Critical Spirit and the World-Spirit are one.

Ernest. And he who is in possession of this spirit or whom this spirit possesses, will, I suppose, do nothing?

Gilbert. Like the Persephone of whom Landor tells us, the sweet pensive Persephone around whose white feet the asphodel and amaranth are blooming, he will sit contented "in that deep, motionless, quiet which mortals pity, and which the gods enjoy."[185] He will look out upon the world and know its secret. By contact with divine things, he will become divine. His will be the perfect life, and his only.

Ernest. You have told me many strange things tonight, Gilbert. You have told me that it is more difficult to talk about a thing than to do it, and that to do nothing at all is the most difficult thing in the world; you have told me that all Art is immoral, and all thought dangerous; that criticism is more creative than creation, and that the highest criticism is that which reveals in the work of Art what the artist had not put there; that it is exactly because a man cannot do a thing that he is the proper judge of it; and that the true critic is unfair, insincere, and not rational. My friend, you are a dreamer.

Gilbert. Yes: I am a dreamer. For a dreamer is one who can only find his way by moonlight, and his punishment is that he sees the dawn before the rest of the world.

Ernest. His punishment?

---

184 Charles Darwin (1809–82), scientist famous for evolutionary theories. See Science, Travel and Exploration. Joseph Ernest Renan (1823–92), French theologian and philosopher, author of the controversial *Vie de Jésus* (1863).

185 Walter Savage Landor, "Alfieri and Salomon the Fortunate Jew," *Imaginary Conversations of Literary Men and Statesmen* (1824–28).

Gilbert. And his reward. But see, it is dawn already. Draw back the curtains and open the windows wide. How cool the morning air is! Piccadilly lies at our feet like a long riband of silver. A faint purple mist hangs over the Park, and the shadows of the white houses are purple. It is too late to sleep. Let us go down to Covent Garden and look at the roses.[186] Come! I am tired of thought.

Vernon Lee and Clementina Anstruther-Thomson
from "Beauty and Ugliness" (1897)

Writer and critic Violet Paget (1856–1935) wrote under the pseudonym Vernon Lee. As a child, Lee moved with her family around Europe, gaining an international viewpoint and fluency in four languages. Her critically acclaimed *Studies of the Eighteenth Century in Italy* (1880) secured her entrance into London's literary and artistic networks. During the 1880s and 1890s, Lee cultivated her literary reputation as she published fiction, personal essays, travel writing, and essays on religion, aesthetics, and literature. Beginning in the early 1890s, Lee often collaborated with painter and close friend Clementina (Kit) Anstruther-Thomson (1857–1921).

Together the two artists staged experiments to observe physiological reactions to art in an attempt to answer the questions, "What is the process of perceiving Form?" and "What portions of our organism participate therein?" Their study on beauty and ugliness was published in the *Contemporary Review* (1897).

Part 1

The facts and theories we are about to exhibit constitute an attempt at giving to the phenomena of æsthetics an explanation different from that furnished by recent mental science, but an explanation more really consonant with the psychological thought of our day.

These facts and theories will allow us to discard, as mere side issues, the doubtful assumptions concerning association of ideas and the play instinct, as well as the various attempts to account for notions of beauty and ugliness by reference to transmuted recognition of utility and inutility, to sexual selection, and to the survival of obsolete primeval[187] activities, and they will also render superfluous all recourse to a mysterious ultimate principle of supersensuous,[188] not to say supernatural, origin.

For our facts and theories, if at all correct, would establish that the æsthetic phenomenon as a whole is the function which regulates the perception of Form, and that the perception of Form, in visual cases certainly, and with reference to hearing presumably, implies an active participation of the most important

---

186 Covent Garden in London boasted two conservatories.
187 Primitive.
188 Spiritual.

organs of animal life, a constant alteration in vital processes requiring stringent regulation for the benefit of the total organism....

... [Our] method consists, even like the method evidently employed by Mr. James,[189] in bringing under observation, by means of isolation, diminution of rapidity and repeated repetition and comparison, processes in ourselves which constant repetition and constant connection with other processes have made so swift, so blurred and above all so subordinate to an objective synthesis, that we have in our normal condition no clear notion of their nature or even of their existence. For it must be remembered that the practical necessities of life tend constantly not merely to shorten every conscious process, but also to direct our attention away from our subjective phenomena to the externalised summing up of our conditions which we conceive as the objective cause of those phenomena. Instead of being conscious as such of changes of condition in our eye and ear, we have long since become incapable—probably utterly incapable—of knowing them otherwise than as objective qualities, colour or pitch, of the non-ego;[190] and similarly, though to a less degree, our attention has become engaged not with the change in ourselves productive of the sense of height, or roundness or symmetry, but with the objective external causes of these changes; and the formula of perception has become not "I *feel* roundness, or height, or symmetry," but "this or that object *is* round, or high or symmetrical."

It is only the rarer and more sudden alterations of our condition summed up as *emotions*, which on account of this rarity and violence, have preserved obvious traces of their real nature.... Practical or thoughtful habits have diminished, to an extraordinary extent, that full perception of Form which alone can enter into the æsthetic experience, and most of the business of life, and the work of reasoning, is carried on through the mere recognition of a few qualities in objects and the labelling them accordingly for use, so that the majority of persons go through existence with comparatively few thorough realisations of Form, and few occasions for the æsthetic pleasure and displeasure by which such realisation is attended; while, on the other hand, highly æsthetic natures, and artists more particularly, are undergoing a constant training which makes the phenomena of perception so rapid, contemporaneous,[191] and homogeneous[192] as to defy all analysis. Such specially developed persons are in the position of a fencer or pianist of whom we should ask for detailed description of the minute adjustments constituting some perpetually repeated series of movements. Students of psychology may judge of the difficulty of obtaining these data of æsthetics by asking themselves how many men of science and of letters could probably confirm, from their own experience, the details which Fechner[193] and Mr. William James have given us of the psychical sensations accompanying or underlying certain of their intellectual cognitions.

So much for our method. It is necessary, moreover, to limit our subject. The explanation we hope to give refers to the question: *Why should a specific kind of condition, either agreeable or disagreeable, accompany the recognition of those co-related qualities of form called respectively Beauty and Ugliness*; and

---

189 William James (1842–1910), American psychologist and brother of novelist Henry James.
190 The object under scrutiny by the senses.
191 Simultaneous.
192 Uniform.
193 Gustav Theodor Fechner (1801–87), German philosopher and physicist who studied the relationship between physical stimulation and sensation.

this explanation itself rests upon the explanation of a previous question: *What is the process of perceiving Form, and what portions of our organism participate therein?*

Now, we all know that visible and audible Form is a grouping of elementary impressions furnished by the senses of sight and hearing; and we all recognise that these sense impressions are themselves liable to the distinction of agreeable and disagreeable, in common parlance, beautiful and ugly. In so far, therefore, as these sense impressions enter into the perception of Form, there is given to Form a quality of agreeableness or disagreeableness due to its elementary constituents; and this emotional quality of sense impression has often been made to explain in large measure the agreeable or disagreeable quality of our æsthetic experiences. But this explanation has invariably broken down (many far-fetched items being used to fill up the gap) because it is a matter of universal experience that a sense impression, the quality, for instance, of a colour or of a sound, exists quite separately from that of the Form into which it enters; and that elementary visual or audible qualities of undoubted beauty may enter into a Form which is nevertheless admitted to be ugly, and even *vice-versâ*; nay, that the chief qualities of the Form, its beauty or ugliness, may remain unaltered despite a change in its constituent sense elements, provided the relations of those constituent sense elements remain unaltered; for instance, that the same pattern may exist in red, orange and white, or in blue, violet and white; or the same musical phrase preserve its identity despite a change in pitch, let alone a change in *timbre*,[194] so that we recognise it and are pleased or displeased by what we call its beauty or ugliness. *There is, therefore, a specific quality which may be agreeable or disagreeable in certain facts of relation which, united, constitute Form.* And it is into the reason for the various qualities of Form, or, in other words, for the various conditions produced in us by various arrangements of the possible relations of sense impressions, that we are about to explore....

Part 2

And now let us proceed to examine what happens, apart from the stimulation of the special sense organ, when we perceive visual Form—that is to say, what phenomena, besides the mere sense impressions, can be detected in ourselves as the raw materials of an æsthetic cognition.

The object of perception shall be this chair. It is about four feet six inches high, an oblong about half as wide as its height. It has curved arms, rather a high square seat and a square panel on the back. The two top corners reach some inches higher than the panel and are terminated by carved foliated[195] clumps. While seeing this chair, there happen movements of the two eyes, of the head, and of the thorax,[196] and balancing movements in the back, all of which we proceed to detail, following the attention (whatever the attention may be) which accompanies these movements. The chair is a bilateral object, so the two eyes are equally active. They meet the two legs of the chair at the ground and run up both sides simultaneously. There is a feeling as if the width of the chair were pulling the two eyes wide apart during this process of following the upward line of the chair. Arrived at the top the eyes seem no longer pulled apart; on the contrary, they converge inward along the top of the chair, until, having arrived at the middle thereof, they cease focussing the chair. Meanwhile the movements of the eyes seem to have been followed by the

---

194 The particular quality of musical sounds (such as tenor vs. soprano).
195 In the shape of leaves.
196 Upper torso.

breath. The bilateralness of the object seems to have put both lungs into play. There has been a feeling of the two sides of the chest making a sort of pull apart; the breath has been begun low down and raised on both sides of the chest; a slight contraction of the chest seems to accompany the eyes as they move along the top of the chair till they got to the middle; then, when the eyes ceased focussing the chair, the breath was exhaled.

These movements of the eye and of the breath were accompanied by alterations in the equilibrium of various parts of the body. At the beginning the feet were pressed hard on the ground in involuntary imitation of the front legs of the chair, and the body was stretched upwards. At the moment that the eyes reached the top of the chair and moved inwards along the line of the top, the tension of the body ceased going upwards and the balance seemed swung along the top of the chair towards the right. At this point the movements of balance seemed to help out those of the eyes and the breath; for, during the time of expiration, the eyes do not focus the chair so completely. During this partial interruption in the form-perceiving movements of the eyes and the breath, the balance seemed to alter, and the weight to swing across the top of the chair downwards to the right side till it seemed to land in the right foot. The weight seemed thus to have followed the oblong shape of the chair going up the *left* side, swinging across the top and then descending on the right side. All these changes have taken place during one breath, inspiration and expiration, and they have answered to a knowledge of the general shape of the chair.

With the next breath comes the recognition of the chair's details. Recognition of the height of the chair, begun with pressure of both feet on the ground, is accompanied by an upward stretch of the body. This stretch upwards seems suddenly checked by the sight of the heavy clump of ornament on the chair's two top corners; there is a sudden sense of the head being weighed downwards; and the size of the chair seems limited within this pressure and the previous stretch upwards; *the interest seems to concentrate itself within those limits and the height of the chair to be measured off on the body of the spectator....*

Meanwhile, in accompanying the movements connected with height, the breathing seems limited by the limitations of the height; the breath does not rise as high as it can, but follows the rise of the eye to the top of the chair and then changes direction.

There seems to be a pull sideways of the thorax, and the breath seems to stretch out in width as the balance swings across and the eyes alter their movement across the chair; then follows the expiration....

The movements of the eyes have been too rapid to be separately felt, and they do not seem to leave any traces behind, *whereas the movements of the breath seem to remain conscious*; and there is a double sensation in one breath of height and width going on in relation to one another....

This mass of details will show, we think, that the act of perception includes, besides the intellectual recognition which remains as mysterious as ever, elements of bodily alteration far beyond any chemical or muscular change in the eye. It is true that readers to whom the identification of emotional phenomena and of certain senses of relation with bodily phenomena is either unfamiliar or repugnant will object in this case also that the altered breathing, senses of tension, and altered balance enumerated in the foregoing experiment, are not a part of the perception of Form, but a reaction (on the same principle as the thoracic changes said to result from grief) produced by the perception itself. To this we would answer that the objection takes perception of Form for granted, either as explicable by ocular changes which are insufficient and cerebral changes of which there is no evidence, or as a generally inexplicable process....

Part 7

Before concluding these notes, we desire to remind the reader that we are fully prepared to find that our observations have been extremely rudimentary, imperfect, and partial. Moreover, that personal idiosyncrasies may have passed in our eyes as universally obtaining processes, and that our object in the present paper has been mainly not to establish facts, but to suggest a method.

More serious opposition, and far wider spread, will meet us in the shape of absolute disbelief in the existence of such half-hidden motor adjustments and the dependence thereon of a process so important, and hitherto so unexplained, as the Perception of Form. There is undoubtedly, at first sight, something startling in the notion that it is we, the beholders, who, so to speak, *make form exist* in ourselves by alteration in our respiratory and equilibratory processes, and by initiated movements of various parts of the body. But there is nothing at variance with the trend of philosophy since Kant,[197] in thus adding *Form* to the daily increasing list of apparently objective existences which we must recognise as modes of function of our mind; still less at variance with the tendencies of the most recent psychology, in adding another of the functions of what we call *mind*, to the processes of what we rather arbitrarily distinguish from it as *body*. We must point out, also, that grotesque as may appear at first sight the notion of external form being in a way executed, or, to use a convenient word, *mimed*, by the beholder, we are daily postulating, though without perceiving it, some similar mimetic connection between perception and motion. We refer to the fact that we all of us reproduce through our gesture, not merely the gestures of other creatures, but the forms, the lines of directions, the pressures and upliftings of inanimate objects; that we can place the muscles of our face in the same position as those of the person whom we choose to mimic; and that we can nearly all of us, from our infancy and utterly untaught, reproduce more or less correctly on paper, or with movable objects, the shapes and positions of surrounding objects.... [I]t is patent[198] to all of us that the perception of various rhythmical relations in music is accompanied by very perceptible stimulation of movement, often externalised in movements of the head, the feet, and what is called beating time; and it must be a matter of experience to many that the hearing of musical phrases, and still more, the repetition of them in memory, is accompanied by faint sensations in the chest and larynx,[199] absolutely corresponding to the actual movements necessary for audible performance. Indeed, the fact that sequence of notes is so thoroughly remembered, while simultaneity of notes seems to escape actual vivid memory, seems to prove that while harmony is perceived only by the auditive apparatus, melody, which is essentially audible *form*, ... depends for perception on motor adjustments which are reproducible in the absence of an external stimulus.... Why such mimetic processes should exist is indeed a difficult question, but one which physiology[200] may some day answer. But, answered or unanswered, the difficulty of explaining the connection between retinal and muscular sensations in the eye and muscular adjustments of the chest, back, nape of the neck, and so forth, this difficulty is not any greater than explaining the connection between impressions on the ear and muscular adjustments of the throat, mouth, and limbs; or, perhaps, of explaining any of the numerous interworkings of apparently dissimilar and distant organs.

A more difficult question appears to be raised, yet one which psychology may perhaps some day solve, when we ask how it is possible that a combination of ocular sensations and sensations of motor

---

197 Immanuel Kant (1724–1804), German philosopher.
198 Obvious.
199 The part of the throat that houses the vocal cords.
200 The scientific study of living things and their bodily functions.

adjustment should be transmuted, in our normal experience, into ideas of qualities of form in external objects; how the subjective inside us can turn into the objective outside? Yet such a transformation is accepted without difficulty whenever we recognise the fact that alterations in the chemical and mechanical conditions of our eye are transmitted to consciousness in the utterly different state of qualities of colour, light, and rudimentary line and curve of external objects.

Indeed, it seems to the present writers that these mysteries at present besetting on all sides the most elementary facts of mental science, are not so much hindrances to the acceptance of the æsthetical hypothesis herein put forward as indications that the further progress of psychology depends in great measure upon the employment of just such hypotheses. Psychology has problems more important and more mysterious than the problem of æsthetics—memory, emotion, volition, logical connection, intellectual construction. Before relegating any of these to the limbo of the unintelligible, will it not be necessary to seek for whatever accompaniment of bodily sensations we may discover for them in the dim places of our consciousness?

And, this being the case, the authors of the present notes desire to call the attention of psychologists to whatever facts and suggestions may be contained in this hypothesis of the æsthetic perception of visible form.

GENDER AND SEXUALITY

Introduction
Susan Hamilton

In his seminal study *The History of Sexuality* (1973), Michel Foucault demonstrates that, contrary to popular stereotyping, the Victorians did not enforce silence on sexual matters. As the selections assembled here demonstrate, Victorians paid persistent attention to ideas of gender and sexuality. Gender roles and conceptions of sexuality were in flux. Both highly contentious and seemingly conservative ideas about acceptable sexual behaviour and the daily embodiment of gender could underwrite radically different political and social agendas.

The materials in this section represent some of the most critical forms of that attention and interrogation. The conduct book, a form of the female advice book, offered guidance on such topics as fashion, how to manage a nursery, and the proper duty owed to parents. One of its most influential practitioners, Sarah Stickney Ellis, wrote at a time of perceived national urgency, when the effects of industrialization on the middle classes were as yet unknown. Addressing middle-class women, those "restricted to the services of from one to four domestics,—who ... enjoy the advantages of a liberal education, and ... have no pretension to family rank" (21), Ellis asserted that "a nation's moral wealth is in your keeping" (16). These books demonstrate how women's domestic roles changed under industrialization and suggest how quickly prescriptive guides inscribed what has come to be known as the separate-spheres ideology.

The *separate-spheres ideology* defined middle-class women's arenas of action as private and domestic, broadly including the nursery, relations with servants, and those elements of public life that called upon women's supposedly natural interests: the education and care of children, animals, and lower-class people. Involvement in the village school, home nursing and visiting, charitable work with poor people or abused animals—such activities constituted acceptable, indeed welcome, components of middle-class women's daily lives. In contrast, separate-spheres prescriptions associated middle-class men's arenas of action with physical activity and public competition, such as business and commercial pursuits, government, law, and international relations. Under a separate-spheres ideology, Victorians lauded men as the protectors and beneficiaries of domesticity who found energy for public work in the tranquility of a well-run middle-class home and under the moral influence of a well-ordered middle-class woman. These social scripts for the appropriate performance of gender roles were supported by biological narratives of sexual difference; such narratives mapped sexual behaviours onto social codes, differentially assigning active sex drives and receptive or responsive sexual behaviours to men and women. The separate-spheres conception of gender roles represented an immensely powerful prescription in this period, as we see in John Ruskin's "Of Queen's Gardens" (1865), which argues that a woman's education should fit her duties as a noble influence in the home. For Ruskin, a woman's gentle persuasion and gracious example rested at the root of a well-ordered society.

Despite its power, the prescription of separate spheres was contested by men and women of all classes in this period. On the one hand, the concept of women's influence buttressed demands that, for many, threatened the domestic basis of femininity. Calling for improved employment and education for women as well as fairer laws concerning divorce, married women's property, and women's suffrage, many feminists argued that women's moral nature justified a wider sphere of action, equitable treatment under the law, and access to political power. In "Cassandra" (1860), Florence Nightingale called upon her fellow women to "Awake" from the stupor imposed by domesticity (407). At the same time, as Barbara Bodichon's pamphlet and John Stuart Mill's *The Subjection of Women* (1869) indicate, for other critics and political activists, the separate-spheres model neither reflected lived experience nor promised a model for future gender relations. For Mill, womanly influence constituted an inferior force exercised by an undeveloped being whose potential had been stunted by social codes designed to keep men in power. For the activist Bodichon, educating women and men about the social and legal codes surrounding gender roles lay at the heart of improving women's economic and social conditions, whether by legal reforms or through expanded employment and educational choices. Along with fellow feminist activists, Bodichon attempted to bring debates about law and other relevant social institutions to general readers.

"Mill's Logic; Or, Franchise for Females." *Punch* (30 March 1867): 129.

For both Mill and Bodichon, marriage represented an entrenched example of inequity between the sexes and the perniciousness of influence as a substitute for individual autonomy. Like Mona Caird, whose writing on marriage would re-galvanize public debate on marriage in the late 1880s, Mill and Bodichon viewed legal changes in marriage as critical to a broader cultural shift about gender and sex roles. In a period that saw liberalized divorce law, substantial gains for married women as property owners, and an expansion of women's suffrage at the local and municipal (though not national) level, reformers saw legal avenues as a significant force for social good.

Nevertheless, law reform had its limits as a mechanism for social change. As Caird's essays on marriage reveal, marriage law, as well as legislation defining such concepts as sexual consent and sexual deviance, underpinned discussions of gender and sexuality in this period. They also point to how social constructions of biological differences between the sexes helped naturalize gender and class differences. For example, the selections from W.T. Stead's *Maiden Tribute of Modern Babylon* (1885) show us how shifting definitions of sexual difference, here coded in the notion of sexual consent, prompted changes in gender roles and shaped ideas of appropriate sexual behaviour. Stead's crusading investigative journalism into child prostitution in London identifies young working-class prostitutes as either passive victims of dissolute families that failed to protect them or debased agents in the seduction of fellow victims. Stead portrays both as vulnerable to an aggressive male sex drive exploiting economic misery and class privilege in its search for sexual gratification and requiring national legislation to stop it. The narrative drive of

"Her Rights." *Punch* (9 Dec. 1882): 267.

his series stems from his self-presentation as the heroic embodiment of a regulated masculinity able to harness men's physical drives to a protective social task.

Like many such social purity movements in the last decades of the century, Stead's campaign against child prostitution generated new targets for sexual regulation by the state. Stead's lurid revelations concerning child prostitution prompted the passage of the Criminal Law Amendment Act of 1885, which raised the age of sexual consent for girls to 16 and tightened regulations and strengthened punishments for brothel keepers. Attached to that act, the Labouchère Amendment created a new category of offence by criminalizing acts of "gross indecency" between men, whether consensual or not, and specifying harsh new punishments. Under this amendment, which came to be known as the "Blackmailer's Charter," Oscar Wilde would be incarcerated for two years with hard labour. It was this law that John Addington Symonds opposed, arguing that the legislation was "interfering with the liberty of individuals, under a certain misconception regarding the nature of their offence" (132) and challenging those who supported the law "to prove that the coercions, punishment, and defamation of such persons are justified" (132).

At the beginning of Victoria's reign, Sarah Stickney Ellis's conduct books sought to prescribe new behaviours for middle-class women in a tumultuous, industrializing world. By the century's end, Havelock Ellis and Symonds demonstrated, and argued in defence of, an expanded repertoire of conduct and sexual desires for men and women. Like Havelock Ellis's exploration of the psychology of "deviant" sexuality, with its explicit evidence that "abnormal" inclinations are natural, congenital, and cannot be changed, Symonds's critique of the law's severe response to so-called unnatural offences was fundamental to the Victorians' continuing investigation of sex differences and gender roles, of what constituted proper sexual and gendered comportment, and of the state's role in patrolling and defining abnormal sexual behaviour.

Works Cited and Further Reading

Davidoff, Leonore, and Catherine Hall. *Family Fortunes: Men and Women of the English Middle Class, 1780–1850*. London: Hutchinson, 1987. Print.

Dellamora, Richard. *Masculine Desires: The Sexual Politics of Victorian Aestheticism*. Chapel Hill: U of North Carolina P, 1990. Print.

Ellis, Sarah Stickney. *The Women of England: Their Social Duties and Domestic Habits*. New York: Appleton, 1839. Print.

Foucault, Michel. *The History of Sexuality*. Trans. Robert Hurley. New York: Pantheon, 1978. Print.

Laqueur, Thomas. *Making Sex: Body and Gender from the Greeks to Freud*. Cambridge, MA: Harvard UP, 1990. Print.

Mangan, J.A., and James Walvin, eds. *Manliness and Morality: Middle-Class Masculinity in Britain and America, 1800–1940*. New York: St Martin's, 1987. Print.

Marcus, Sharon. *Between Women: Friendship, Desire and Marriage in Victorian England*. Princeton: Princeton UP, 2007. Print.

Nightingale, Florence. *Suggestions for Thought to the Searchers After Truth Among the Artizans of England*. London: George E. Eyre and William Spottiswoode, 1860. Print.

Roper, Michael, and John Tosh, eds. *Manful Assertions: Masculinities in Britain since 1800*. London: Routledge, 1991. Print.

"Ladies Not Admitted." *Punch* (21 March 1896): 134.

Sedgwick, Eve Kosofky. *Between Men: English Literature and Male Homosexual Desire*. New York: Columbia UP, 1985. Print.

Shanley, Mary Lyndon. *Feminism, Marriage and the Law in Victorian England, 1850–1895*. Princeton: Princeton UP, 1989. Print.

Symonds, John Addington. *A Problem in Modern Ethics*. London: N.p., 1896. Print.

Tosh, John. *A Man's Place: Masculinity and the Middle-Class Home in Victorian England*. New Haven: Yale UP, 1999. Print.

Vicinus, Martha. *Independent Women: Work and Community for Single Women, 1850–1920*. Chicago: U of Chicago P, 1985. Print.

——. *Intimate Friends: Women Who Loved Women, 1778–1928*. Chicago: U of Chicago P, 2004. Print.

Walkowitz, Judith. *City of Dreadful Delight: Narratives of Sexual Danger in Late-Victorian London*. Chicago: U of Chicago P, 1992. Print.

Sarah Stickney Ellis
from *The Women of England: Their Social Duties and Domestic Habits* (1839)

Sarah Stickney Ellis (1799–1872) was a successful writer of conduct books outlining women's domestic middle-class roles. Following the success of *The Women of England*, she published advice books for the daughters, wives, and mothers of England (1842–43). She also published poetry, fiction, and an 1830 anti-slavery narrative. She edited several periodicals (1840–52) and opened a school for girls. In 1837, she married Congregationalist minister and missionary William Ellis.

Her books promoted separate-spheres ideology, which championed women's domestic achievements and moral influence. Though she upheld women's subservience to men in her published material, a letter to her fiancé expressed an independence that apparently contradicted these views: "I often ask, but seldom take advice." Responding to her popular conduct books, *Punch* satirized her views in 1843–47 by suggesting that she encouraged women to manipulate their husbands.

Chapter 2: Influence of the Women of England

... [T]he immediate object of the present work is to show how intimate is the connexion which exists between the women of England, and the moral character maintained by their country in the scale of nations. For a woman to undertake such a task, may at first sight appear like an act of presumption; yet ... it may surely be deemed pardonable for a woman to solicit the serious attention of her own sex, while she endeavours to prove that it is the minor morals of domestic life which give the tone to English character, and that over this sphere of duty it is her peculiar province to preside....

... The sphere of woman's happiest and most beneficial influence is a domestic one, but it is not easy to award even to her quiet and unobtrusive virtues that meed[1] of approbation which they really deserve, without exciting a desire to forsake the homely household duties of the family circle, to practise such as are more conspicuous, and consequently more productive of an immediate harvest of applause.

I say this with all kindness, and I desire to say it with all gentleness, to the young, the amiable, and the—*vain*; at the same time that my perception of the temptation to which they are exposed, enhances my value for the principle that *is* able to withstand it, and increases my admiration of those noble-minded women who *are* able to carry forward, with exemplary patience and perseverance, the public offices of benevolence, without sacrificing their home-duties, and who thus prove to the world, that the perfection of female character is a combination of private and public virtue,—of domestic charity, and zeal for the temporal and eternal happiness of the whole human race....

It is a widely mistaken notion to suppose that the sphere of usefulness recommended here is a humiliating and degrading one. As if the earth that fosters and nourishes in its lovely bosom the roots of all the plants and trees which ornament the garden of the world, feeding them from her secret storehouse with supplies that never fail, were less important, in the economy of vegetation, than the sun that brings to light their verdure and their flowers, or the genial atmosphere that perfects their growth, and diffuses their perfume abroad upon the earth. To carry out the simile still farther, it is but just to give the preference to that element which, in the absence of all other favouring circumstances, withholds not its support; but when the sun is shrouded, and the showers forget to fall, and blighting winds go forth, and the hand of culture is withdrawn, still opens out its hidden fountains, and yields up its resources, to invigorate, to cherish, and sustain.

It would be an easy and a grateful task, thus, by metaphor and illustration, to prove the various excellencies and amiable peculiarities of woman, did not the utility of the present work demand a more minute and homely detail of that which constitutes her practical and individual duty. It is too much the custom with writers, to speak in these general terms of the *loveliness* of the female character; as if woman were some fragrant flower, created only to bloom, and exhale in sweets; when perhaps these very writers are themselves most strict in requiring that the domestic drudgery of their own households should each day be faithfully filled up. How much more generous, just, and noble it would be to deal fairly by woman in these matters, and to tell her that to be *individually*, what she is praised for being *in general*, it is necessary for her to lay aside all her natural caprice, her love of self-indulgence, her vanity, her indolence—in short, her very *self*—and assuming a new nature, which nothing less than watchfulness and prayer can enable her constantly to maintain, to spend her mental and moral capabilities in devising means for promoting the happiness of others, while her own derives a remote and secondary existence from theirs.

If an admiration almost unbounded for the perfection of female character, with a sisterly participation in all the errors and weaknesses to which she is liable, and a profound sympathy with all that she is necessarily compelled to feel and suffer, are qualifications for the task I have undertaken, these certainly are points on which I yield to none; but at the same time that I do my feeble best, I must deeply regret that so few are the voices lifted up in her defence against the dangerous influence of popular applause,

---

1   Deserved share.

and the still more dangerous tendency of modern habits, and modern education. Perhaps it is not to be expected that those who write most powerfully, should most clearly perceive the influence of the one, or the tendency of the other; because the very strength and consistency of their own minds must in some measure exempt them from participation in either. While, therefore, in the art of reasoning, a writer like myself must be painfully sensible of her own deficiency; in sympathy of feeling, she is perhaps the better qualified to address the weakest of her sex.

With such, it is a favourite plea, brought forward in extenuation of their own uselessness, that they have no influence—that they are not leading women—that society takes no note of them;—forgetting, while they shelter themselves beneath these indolent excuses, that the very feather on the stream may serve to warn the doubtful mariner of the rapid and fatal current by which his bark[2] might be hurried to destruction. It is, moreover, from amongst this class that wives are more frequently chosen; for there is a peculiarity in men—I would fain call it *benevolence*—which inclines them to offer the benefit of their protection to the most helpless and dependent of the female sex; and therefore it is upon this class that the duty of training up the young most frequently devolves; not certainly upon the naturally imbecile, but upon the uncalculating creatures whose non-exercise of their own mental and moral faculties renders them not only willing to be led through the experience of life, but thankful to be relieved from the responsibility of thinking and acting for themselves.

It is an important consideration, that from such women as these, myriads of immortal beings derive that early bias of character, which under Providence decides their fate, not only in this world, but in the world to come. And yet they flutter on, and say they have no influence—they do not aspire to be leading women—they are in society but as grains of sand on the sea-shore. Would they but pause one moment to ask how will this plea avail them, when, as daughters without gratitude, friends without good faith, wives without consideration, and mothers without piety, they stand before the bar of judgment, to render an account of the talents committed to their trust![3] Have they not parents, to whom they might study to repay the debt of care and kindness accumulated in their childhood? ... Have they not their young friendships, for those sunny hours when the heart expands itself in the genial atmosphere of mutual love, and shrinks not from revealing its very weaknesses and errors[?]... Have they not bound themselves by a sacred and enduring bond, to be to one fellow-traveller along the path of life, a companion on his journey, and, as far as ability might be granted them, a guide and a help in the doubts and the difficulties of his way? ... Above all, have they not, many of them, had the feeble steps of infancy committed to their care—the pure unsullied page of childhood presented to them for its first and most durable inscription?—and what have they written there? ... Experience will prove to them they have written; and the transcript of *what* they have written, will be treasured up, either for or against them, among the awful records of eternity.

It is therefore not only false in reasoning, but wrong in principle, for women to assert ... that they have no influence. An influence fraught either with good or evil, they must have; and though the one may be above their ambition, and the other beyond their fears, by neglecting to obtain an influence which shall be beneficial to society, they necessarily assume a bad one: just in the same proportion as their selfishness, indolence, or vacuity of mind, render them in youth an easy prey to every species of unamiable temper,

---

2   Boat.
3   See Matthew 25:14-30.

in middle age the melancholy victims of mental disease, and, long before the curtain of death conceals their follies from the world, a burden and a bane to society at large....

It is not to be presumed that women *possess* more moral power than men; but happily for them, such are their early impressions, associations, and general position in the world, that their moral feelings are less liable to be impaired by the pecuniary objects which too often constitute the chief end of man, and which, even under the limitations of better principle, necessarily engage a large portion of his thoughts. There are many humble-minded women, not remarkable for any particular intellectual endowments, who yet possess so clear a sense of the right and wrong of individual actions, as to be of essential service in aiding the judgments of their husbands, brothers, or sons, in those intricate affairs in which it is sometimes difficult to dissever worldly wisdom from religious duty.

To men belongs the potent—(I had almost said the *omnipotent*) consideration of worldly aggrandisement.... Long before the boy has learned to exult in the dignity of the man, his mind has become familiarized to the habit of investing with supreme importance, all considerations relating to the acquisition of wealth. He hears on the Sabbath, and on stated occasions, when men meet for that especial purpose, of a God to be worshipped, a Saviour to be trusted in, and a holy law to be observed; but he sees before him, every day and every hour, a strife, which is nothing less than deadly to the highest impulses of the soul, after another god—the mammon[4] of unrighteousness—the moloch[5] of this world; and believing rather what men do, than what they preach, he learns too soon to mingle with the living mass, and to unite his labours with theirs. To unite? Alas! there is no union in the great field of action in which he is engaged; but envy, and hatred, and opposition, to the close of the day—every man's hand against his brother....[6]

This ... is scarcely an exaggerated picture of the engagements of men of business in the present day. And surely they now need more than ever all the assistance which Providence has kindly provided, to win them away from this warfare, to remind them that they are hastening on towards a world into which none of the treasures they are amassing can be admitted;[7] and, next to those holier influences which operate through the medium of revelation, or through the mysterious instrumentality of Divine love, I have little hesitation in saying, that the society of woman in her highest moral capacity, is best calculated to effect this purpose.

How often has man returned to his home with a mind confused by the many voices, which in the mart,[8] the exchange, or the public assembly, have addressed themselves to his inborn selfishness, or his worldly pride; and while his integrity was shaken, and his resolution gave way beneath the pressure of apparent necessity, or the insidious pretences of expediency, he has stood corrected before the clear eye of woman, as it looked directly to the naked truth, and detected the lurking evil of the specious act he was about to commit. Nay, so potent may have become this secret influence, that he may have borne it about with him like a kind of second conscience, for mental reference, and spiritual counsel, in moments of trial; and when the snares of the world were around him, and temptations from within and without

---

4   Selfish greed, money: Matthew 6:24. See also Carlyle, "Gospel of Mammonism," Condition of England.
5   A false idol for whom children were burnt as offerings: Leviticus 18:21, 2 Kings 23:10; in John Milton's *Paradise Lost* (1667), Moloch is one of the rebel angels.
6   See Genesis 16:12.
7   1 Timothy 6:7.
8   Market or trading hall.

have bribed over the witness in his own bosom, he has thought of the humble monitress who sat alone, guarding the fireside comforts of his distant home; and the remembrance of her character, clothed in moral beauty, has scattered the clouds before his mental vision, and sent him back to that beloved home, a wiser and a better man.

The women of England, possessing the grand privilege of being better instructed than those of any other country, in the minutiæ of domestic comfort, have obtained a degree of importance in society far beyond what their unobtrusive virtues would appear to claim. The long-established customs of their country, have placed in their hands the high and holy duty of cherishing and protecting the minor morals of life, from whence springs all that is elevated in purpose, and glorious in action. The sphere of their direct personal influence is central, and consequently small; but its extreme operations are as widely extended as the range of human feeling. They may be less striking in society than some of the women of other countries, and may feel themselves, on brilliant and stirring occasions, as simple, rude, and unsophisticated in the popular science of excitement; but as far as the noble daring of Britain has sent forth her adventurous sons, and that is to every point of danger on the habitable globe, they have borne along with them a generosity, a disinterestedness, and a moral courage, derived in no small measure from the female influence of their native country.

Barbara Leigh Smith Bodichon

from *A Brief Summary, in Plain Language, of the Most Important Laws Concerning Women; Together with a Few Observations Thereon* (1854)

Barbara Leigh Smith Bodichon (1827–91), painter and feminist activist, was the daughter of radical MP Benjamin Smith, who saw marriage laws as unjust to women and hence did not marry her mother. Because she was illegitimate, Bodichon was shunned by some relatives, including the family of her cousin Florence Nightingale (see Gender and Sexuality). The private education and income Bodichon received from her father enabled her to become a professional artist and supporter of feminist causes (Girton College, the *English Woman's Journal*). As a founder of the Langham Place Group, she fought for women's suffrage, higher education, legal rights, and employment. Her 1857 marriage to Eugène Bodichon, French doctor and ethnographer, took her to Algiers for six months of every year.

Her *Brief Summary* of the most important laws concerning women was her first political action; her friend George Eliot (see Aesthetics and Culture) recognized Bodichon's campaign for women's equality as "one rung of a long ladder stretching far beyond our lives."

LAWS CONCERNING MARRIED WOMEN

Matrimony is a civil and indissoluble contract between a consenting man and woman of competent capacity.

These marriages are prohibited:—A widower with his deceased wife's sister; a widow with the brother of her deceased husband; a widower with his deceased wife's sister's daughter, for she is by affinity in the same degree as a niece to her uncle by consanguinity;[9] a widower with a daughter of his deceased wife by a former husband; and a widower with his deceased wife's mother's sister. Consanguinity or affinity, where the children are illegitimate, is equally an impediment.

A lunatic or idiot cannot lawfully contract a marriage, but insanity after marriage does not make the marriage null and void.

A lunatic may contract a marriage during a lucid interval. Deaf and dumb people may marry by signs.

The consent of the father or guardians is necessary to the marriage of an *infant* (*i.e.*, a person under twenty-one), unless the marriage takes place by banns.[10] The consent of the mother is not necessary if there be a father or a guardian appointed by him.

A second marriage while a husband or wife is living is felony, and punishable by transportation.

An agreement to marry made by a man and woman who do not come under any of these disabilities is a contract of betrothment,[11] and either party can bring an action upon a refusal to complete the contract in a superior court of Common Law.

Marriages may be celebrated as a religious ceremony after the requisite public proclamations or banns, or as a secular form.

The object of the Act ... for authorizing civil marriages was to relieve Dissenters[12] and those who could not conscientiously join in the formulary of the Church. Due provision is made for necessary publicity, and the marriage can be legally contracted in a Register Office....

Marriage with a deceased wife's sister is valid in England, if it has been celebrated in a country where such marriage is legal, provided the parties were at the time of the marriage domiciled in such country.

A man and wife are one person in law; the wife loses all her rights as a single woman, and her existence is entirely absorbed in that of her husband. He is civilly responsible for her acts; she lives under his protection or cover, and her condition is called coverture.

A woman's body belongs to her husband;[13] she is in his custody, and he can enforce his right by a writ of *habeas corpus*.[14]

What was her personal property[15] before marriage, such as money in hand, money at the bank, jewels, household goods, clothes, &c., becomes absolutely her husband's, and he may assign or dispose of them at his pleasure whether he and his wife live together or not.

---

9   Common blood.
10 Notice given in church on the three Sundays prior to the marriage so that objectors have ample time to register concerns.
11 Engagement.
12 Under the Civil Marriages Act of 1836, non-Anglicans were able to marry either in their own church or in a Registry Office (a civil office where births, deaths, and marriages are licensed and recorded).
13 A right to sexual intercourse.
14 Latin: "having a body"; in this instance, it refers to a husband's legal right to order his wife into his presence, even against her will.
15 As opposed to real property (land).

A wife's *chattels real* (*i.e.*, estates held during a term of years, or the next presentation to a church living,[16] &c.) become her husband's by his doing some act to appropriate them; but, if the wife survives, she resumes her property.

Equity is defined to be a correction or qualification of the law, generally made in the part wherein it faileth, or is too severe. In other words, the correction of that wherein the law, by reason of its universality, is deficient. While the Common Law gives the whole of a wife's personal property to her husband, the Courts of Equity, when he proceeds therein to recover property in right of his wife, oblige him to make a settlement of some portion of it upon her, if she be unprovided for and virtuous.

If her property be under 200*l.*, or 10*l.* a-year,[17] a Court of Equity will not interpose.

Neither the Courts of Common Law nor Equity have any direct power to oblige a man to support his wife,—the Ecclesiastical Courts (*i.e.* Courts held by the Queen's authority as governor of the Church, for matters which chiefly concern religion) and a Magistrate's court[18] at the instance of her parish alone can do this.

A husband has a freehold estate in his wife's lands during the joint existence of himself and his wife, that is to say, he has absolute possession of them as long as they both live. If the wife dies without children, the property goes to her heir, but if she has borne a child, her husband holds possession until his death.

Money earned by a married woman belongs absolutely to her husband; that and all sources of income, excepting those mentioned above, are included in the term personal property.

By the particular permission of her husband she can make a will of her personal property, for by such a permission he gives up his right. But he may revoke his permission at any time before *probate* (*i.e.* the exhibiting and proving a will before the Ecclesiastical Judge having jurisdiction over the place where the party died).

The legal custody of children belongs to the father. During the life-time of a sane father, the mother has no rights over her children, except a limited power over infants,[19] and the father may take them from her and dispose of them as he thinks fit.

If there be a legal separation of the parents, and there be neither agreement nor order of the Court, giving the custody of the children to either parent, then the *right to the custody of the children* (except for the nutriment of infants) belongs legally to the father.

A married woman cannot sue or be sued for contracts—nor can she enter into contracts except as the agent of her husband; that is to say, her word alone is not binding in law, and persons giving a wife credit have no remedy against her.[20] There are some exceptions, as where she contracts debts upon estates settled to her separate use, or where a wife carries on trade separately, according to the custom of London, &c.

A husband is liable for his wife's debts contracted before marriage, and also for her breaches of trust committed before marriage.

Neither a husband nor a wife can be witnesses against one another in criminal cases, not even after the death or divorce of either.

---

16   The right to designate a replacement to a vacant position in the Church of England.
17   £200 or £10 a year.
18   A court dealing with smaller, local criminal acts.
19   Under the Custody of Infants Act of 1839, a mother could petition for custody of her children up to the age of seven and for access to older children.
20   That is, a husband was legally responsible for his wife's debts.

A wife cannot bring actions[21] unless the husband's name is joined.

As the wife acts under the command and control of her husband, she is excused from punishment for certain offences, such as theft, burglary, housebreaking, &c., if committed in his presence and under his influence. A wife cannot be found guilty of concealing her felon husband or of concealing a felon jointly with her husband. She cannot be found guilty of stealing from her husband or of setting his house on fire, as they are one person in law. A husband and wife cannot be found guilty of conspiracy, as that offence cannot be committed unless there are two persons....

SEPARATION AND DIVORCE

A husband and wife can separate upon a deed containing terms for their immediate separation, but they cannot legally agree to separate at a *future* time. The trustees of the wife must be parties to the deed, and agree with the husband as to what property the wife is to take, for a husband and wife cannot covenant[22] together.

Divorce is of two kinds:—

1st. Divorce à mensâ et thoro,[23] being only a separation from bed and board.

2nd. Divorce à vinculo matrimonii,[24] being an entire dissolution of the bonds of matrimony.

The grounds for the first kind of divorce are, 1st. Adultery, 2nd. Intolerable Cruelty, and 3rd. Unnatural Practices.[25] The Ecclesiastical Courts can do no more than pronounce for this first kind of divorce, or rather separation, as the matrimonial tie is not severed, and there is always a possibility of reconciliation.

The law cannot dissolve a lawful marriage; it is only in the Legislature that this power is vested. It requires an act of Parliament to constitute a divorce à vinculo matrimonii, but the investigation rests by usage with the Lords alone, the House of Commons acting upon the faith that the House of Lords came to a just conclusion.

This divorce is pronounced on account of adultery in the wife, and in some cases of aggravated adultery on the part of the husband.

The expenses of only a common divorce bill are between six hundred and seven hundred pounds, which makes the possibility of release from the matrimonial bond a privilege of the rich.

A wife cannot be plaintiff, defendant, or witness in an important part of the proceeding for a divorce, which evidently must lead to much injustice....

LAWS CONCERNING ILLEGITIMATE CHILDREN AND THEIR MOTHERS

A single woman having a child may throw the maintenance upon the putative father, so called to distinguish him from a husband, until the age of thirteen.

---

21 Lawsuits.
22 Pledge to do something for one another.
23 Latin: "of bed and board": a separation through the ecclesiastical court that did not give the right to remarry.
24 Latin: "of the marriage bonds": a parliamentary divorce, allowing the parties to remarry.
25 Of the 184 private divorce acts passed by parliament from 1800 to 1856, four were passed upon the wife's request. In these cases, "unnatural acts" included incestuous adultery and bigamy.

The law only enforces the parents to maintain such child, and the sum the father is obliged to pay, after an order of affiliation is proved against him, never exceeds two shillings and sixpence a week.

The mother, as long as she is unmarried or a widow, is bound to maintain such child as a part of her family until such child attain the age of sixteen.

A man marrying a woman having a child or children at the time of such marriage is bound to support them, whether legitimate or not, until the age of sixteen.

The rights of an illegitimate child are only such as he can acquire; he can inherit nothing, being in the law looked upon as nobody's son, but he may acquire property by devise or bequest. He may acquire a surname by reputation, but does not inherit one.

The only incapacity under which he labours is that he cannot be heir-at-law nor next of kin to any person, nor can he have collateral heirs,[26] but only lineal descendants; if he acquire property and die without a will, such property will go to the crown unless he have lineal descendants.

Remarks.

These are the principal laws concerning women.

It is not now as it once was, when all existing institutions were considered sacred and unalterable; and the spirit which made Blackstone[27] an admirer of, rather than a critic on, every law because it was *law*, is exchanged for a bolder and more discriminating spirit, which seeks to judge calmly what is good and to amend what is bad.

Philosophical thinkers have generally come to the conclusion that the tendency of progress is gradually to dispense with law,—that is to say, as each individual man becomes unto himself a law, less external restraint is necessary. And certainly the most urgently needed reforms are simple erasures from the statute book. Women, more than any other members of the community, suffer from over-legislation.

A woman of twenty-one becomes an independent human creature,[28] capable of holding and administering property to any amount; or, if she can earn money, she may appropriate her earnings freely to any purpose she thinks good. Her father has no power over her or her property. But if she unites herself to a man, the law immediately steps in, and she finds herself legislated for, and her condition of life suddenly and entirely changed. Whatever age she may be of, she is again considered as an infant,—she is again under "*reasonable restraint*,"—she loses her separate existence, and is merged in that of her husband.

"In short," says Judge Hurlbut, "a woman is courted and wedded as an angel, and yet denied the dignity of a rational and moral being ever after."[29]

"The next thing that I will show you is this particularitie of law; in this consolidation which we call wedlock is a locking together; it is true that man and wife are one person, but understand in what

---

26 Appointed heirs; that is, someone who is not a relation but chosen to inherit.
27 William Blackstone (1723–80), jurist and author of *Commentaries on the Laws of England* (1765–69).
28 Author's note: With regard to the property of women, there is taxation without representation, for they pay taxes without having the liberty of voting for representatives, and indeed there seems at present no reason why single women should be denied this privilege....
29 Elisha P. Hurlbut, *Essays on Human Rights and Their Political Guaranties* (1845).

manner. When a small brooke or little river incorporateth with Rhodanus, Humber, or the Thames,[30] the poore rivulet loseth her name, it is carried and recarried with the new associate, it beareth no sway, it possesseth nothing during coverture. A woman as soone as she is married is called covert, in Latine nupta,[31] that is vailed, as it were clouded and overshadowed she hath lost her streame…. I may more truly farre away say to a married woman, her new selfe is her superior, her companion, her master. The mastership shee is fallen into may be called in a terme which civilians borrow from Esop's Fables, Leonina societate."[32] …

Truly "she hath lost her streame," she is absorbed, and can hold nothing of herself, she has no legal right to any property; not even her clothes, books, and household goods are her own, and any money which she earns can be robbed from her legally by her husband, nay, even after the commencement of a treaty of marriage she cannot dispose of her own property without the knowledge of her betrothed. If she should do so, it is deemed a fraud in law and can be set aside after marriage as an injury to her husband.

It is always said, even by those who support the existing law, that it is in fact never acted upon by men of good feeling. That is true; but the very admission condemns the law, and it is not right that the good feeling of men should be all that a woman can look to for simple justice.

There is now a large and increasing class of women who gain their own livelihood, and the abolition of the laws which give husbands this unjust power is most urgently needed.

Rich men and fathers might still make what settlements they pleased, and appoint trustees for the protection of minors and such women as needed protection; but we imagine it well proved that the principle of protection is wrong, and that the education of freedom and responsibility will enable women to take better care of themselves and others too than can be insured to them by any legal precautions.

Upon women of the labouring classes the difficulty of keeping and using their own earnings presses most hardly. In that rank of life where the support of the family depends often on the joint earnings of husband and wife, it is indeed cruel that the earnings of both should be in the hands of one, and not even in the hands of that one who has naturally the strongest desire to promote the welfare of the children….

… In the early times, when women were obliged by the violent state of society to be always under the guardianship of father, brother, or husband, these laws might be necessary; but in our peaceful times, such guardianship is proved to be superfluous by the fact of the secure, honourable, and independent position of single women who are sufficiently protected by the sanctuary of civilisation.

Since all the unmarried women in England are supported either by their own exertions or by the exertions or bequests of their fathers and relations, there is no reason why upon marriage they should be thrown upon the pecuniary resources of their husbands, except in so far as the claims of a third party—children—may lessen the wife's power of earning money, at the same time that it increases her

---

30   The Rhodanus is the Rhône, a river running from the Swiss Alps through France to the Mediterranean; the Humber is an estuary in northeastern England; the Thames is a major river in southern England.
31   Latin: a married woman.
32   Author's note: [John Dodderidge,] The Lawe's Resolution of Women's Rights, A.D. 1632; editors' note: Aesop (c. sixth century BCE), a Greek slave and storyteller to whom over 600 fables are attributed; *leonine societate* is Latin for leonine company, in which the stronger party takes all the benefits from the weaker and participates in none of the losses.

expenses. Of course a woman may, and often does, by acting as housekeeper and manager of her husband's concerns, earn a maintenance and a right to share in his property, independent of any children which may come of the marriage. But it is evident that daughters ought to have some sure provision—either a means of gaining their own bread, or property—as it is most undesirable that they should look upon marriage as a means of livelihood.

Fathers seldom feel inclined to trust their daughters' fortunes in the power of a husband, and, in the appointment of trustees, partially elude the law by a legal device. Also, the much abused Court of Chancery[33] tried to palliate the Common Law, and recognizes a separate interest between husband and wife, and allows the wife alone to file a bill to recover and protect her property, and trustees are not necessary if there has been an agreement.

Why should not these legal devices be done away with, by the simple abolition of a law which we have outgrown?

We do not say that these laws of property are the only unjust laws concerning women to be found in the short summary which we have given, but they form a simple, tangible, and not offensive point of attack.

Florence Nightingale
from *Suggestions for Thought to the Searchers after Truth among the Artizans of England* (1860)

Florence Nightingale (1820–1910), reformer and expert in nursing training, sanitation, and hospital management, captured Victorian imaginations by leading a nursing party to alleviate appalling conditions in Crimean military hospitals. As a girl, she received a liberal education but begged for instruction in mathematics, a masculine domain. At 16, she experienced a call to Christian service. Her parents initially disapproved of her nursing, but she obtained training in Germany (1850–51). After the Crimean War (1854–56), despite poor health, she used her fame to push for improved hospital conditions, military sanitation, and the founding of a London nursing school. She never married and lived on an allowance from her father, never accepting pay for her public service.

"Cassandra" (privately printed in 1860 in *Suggestions for Thought*) was drafted as part of a novel. Described by John Stuart Mill (see Life Writing, Condition of England, Gender and Sexuality) as a "cri du coeur," it criticizes women's lack of educational opportunities and worthwhile occupations.

---

[33] The court of equity, based on principles of equity and conscience, provided relief where there was no remedy in the common-law courts.

Volume 2, Section 5: Cassandra

"L'enthousiasme et la faiblesse d'un temps où l'intelligence monte très haut, entraînée par l'imagination, et tombe très bas, écrasée par une réalité, sans poésie et sans grandeur."[34]

Women dream till they have no longer the strength to dream; those dreams against which they so struggle, so honestly, vigorously, and conscientiously, and so in vain, yet which are their life, without which they could not have lived; those dreams go at last. All their plans and visions seem vanished, and they know not where; gone, and they cannot recall them. They do not even remember them. And they are left without the food either of reality or of hope.

Later in life, they neither desire nor dream, neither of activity, nor of love, nor of intellect.... They wish, if their experiences would benefit anybody, to give them to some one. But they never find an hour free in which to collect their thoughts, and so discouragement becomes ever deeper and deeper, and they less and less capable of undertaking anything.

It seems as if the female spirit of the world were mourning everlastingly over blessings, *not* lost, but which she has never had, and which, in her discouragement, she feels that she never will have, they are so far off.

The more complete a woman's organization, the more she will feel it, till at last there shall arise a woman, who will resume, in her own soul, all the sufferings of her race, and that woman will be the Saviour of her race.

Jesus Christ raised women above the condition of mere slaves, mere ministers to the passions of the man, raised them by his sympathy, to be ministers of God. He gave them moral activity.[35] But the Age, the World, Humanity, must give them the means to exercise this moral activity, must give them intellectual cultivation, spheres of action.

There is perhaps no century where the woman shows so meanly as in this.[36] Because her education seems entirely to have parted company with her vocation; there is no longer unity between the woman as inwardly developed, and as outwardly manifested.

In the last century it was not so. In the succeeding one let us hope that it will no longer be so.

But now she is like the Archangel Michael as he stands upon Saint Angelo at Rome.[37] She has an immense provision of wings, which seem as if they would bear her over earth and heaven; but when she tries to use them, she is petrified into stone, her feet are grown into the earth, chained to the bronze pedestal.

Nothing can well be imagined more painful than the present position of woman, unless, on the one hand, she renounces all outward activity and keeps herself within the magic sphere, the bubble of her

---

34 French: "The enthusiasm and the inadequacy of a time when intelligence climbs very high, trained by imagination, and falls very low, crushed by a reality without poetry or grandeur": George Sand, 1839 Preface to *Lélia* (1833).
35 Women were among Jesus' closest followers and were the first witnesses to his resurrection.
36 Author's note: At almost every period of social life, we find, as it were, two under currents running different ways. There is the noble woman who dreams the following out her useful vocation; but there is also the selfish dreamer now, who is ever turning to something new, regardless of the expectations she has voluntarily excited, who is ever talking about "making a life for herself," heedless that she is spoiling another life, undertaken, perhaps, at her own bidding. This is the ugly reverse of the medal.
37 Castel Sant'Angelo, built by the Roman Emperor Hadrian, has a statue of the Archangel Michael on the roof; the Archangel Michael was the head of the Heavenly Army, the force opposing Lucifer's rebel army in the battle that saw the latter's fall to Hell and transformation into Satan.

dreams; or, on the other, surrendering all aspiration, she gives herself to her real life, soul and body. For those to whom it is possible, the latter is best; for out of activity may come thought, out of mere aspiration can come nothing.

But now—when the young imagination is so high and so developed, and reality is so narrow and conventional—there is no more parallelism between life in the thought and life in the actual than between the corpse, which lies motionless in its narrow bed, and the spirit, which, in our imagination, is at large among the stars.

The ideal life is passed in noble schemes of good consecutively followed up, of devotion to a great object, of sympathy given and received for high ideas and generous feelings. The actual life is passed in sympathy given and received for a dinner, a party, a piece of furniture, a house built or a garden laid out well, in devotion to your guests—(a too real devotion, for it implies that of all your time)—in schemes of schooling for the poor, which you follow up perhaps in an odd quarter of an hour, between luncheon and driving out in the carriage—broth and dripping are included in the plan—and the rest of your time goes in ordering the dinner, hunting for a governess for your children, and sending pheasants and apples to your poorer relations. Is there anything in *this* life which can be called an Incarnation of the ideal life within? Is it a wonder that the unhappy woman should prefer to keep them entirely separate? not to take the bloom off her Ideal by mixing it up with her Actual; not to make her Actual still more unpalatable by trying to *inform* it with her Ideal? And then she is blamed, and her own sex unites against her, for not being content with the "day of small things."[38] She is told that "trifles make the sum of human things;"[39] they do indeed. She is contemptuously asked, "Would she abolish domestic life?" Men are afraid that their houses will not be so comfortable, that their wives will make themselves "remarkable"—women, that they will make themselves distasteful to men; they write books (and very wisely) to teach themselves to dramatize "little things," to persuade themselves that "domestic life is their sphere"[40] and to idealize the "sacred hearth."[41] Sacred it is indeed. Sacred from the touch of their sons almost as soon as they are out of childhood—from its dulness and its tyrannous trifling *these* recoil. Sacred from the grasp of their daughters' affections, upon which it has so light a hold that they seize the first opportunity of marriage, *their* only chance of emancipation. The "sacred hearth;" sacred to their husband's sleep, their sons' absence in the body and their daughters' in mind.

Oh! mothers, who talk about this hearth, how much do you know of your sons' real life, how much of your daughters' imaginary one? Awake, ye women, all ye that sleep, awake![42]

---

38 Zechariah 4:10.
39 Hannah More, *Sensibility* (1782).
40 Mrs. John Sandford (Elizabeth Poole Sandford), *Woman in Her Social and Domestic Character* (1831).
41 Vesta, the Roman goddess of the hearth, was worshipped at the hearth in Roman houses; by extension, the "sacred hearth" here refers to the Victorian idealization of the home.
42 Ephesians 5:14.

John Ruskin
from *Sesame and Lilies* (1865)

Writer and artist John Ruskin (1819–1900) was one of the most influential art and social critics of the Victorian period. Though confirmed as an Anglican while at Oxford, he was not swept up by the Oxford Movement. After Oxford, Ruskin abandoned poetry to write criticism of art and architecture. With his father's financial support, Ruskin launched his writing career by defending artist J.M.W. Turner in *Modern Painters* (1843–60), in which he argued for the apprehension of divinity via contemplation of the beautiful in art. His failed marriage prompted scandal just as he emerged as a public intellectual and proponent of the Pre-Raphaelites.

"Of Queens' Gardens" was delivered in 1864 as a lecture in Manchester. It stands as a classic Victorian statement of separate-spheres ideology: Ruskin elevates women as "queens" of the domestic domain, urging them to take up the cause of social service with their "[p]ower to heal, to redeem, to guide, and to guard."

~

Lecture 2: Lilies: Of Queens' Gardens

... It will, perhaps, be well, as this Lecture is the sequel of one previously given, that I should shortly state to you my general intention in both. The questions specially proposed to you in the first, namely, How and What to Read, rose out of a far deeper one, which it was my endeavour to make you propose earnestly to yourselves, namely, *Why* to Read. I want you to feel, with me, that whatever advantages we possess in the present day in the diffusion of education and of literature, can only be rightly used by any of us when we have apprehended clearly what education is to lead to, and literature to teach. I wish you to see that both well-directed moral training and well-chosen reading lead to the possession of a power over the ill-guided and illiterate, which is, according to the measure of it, in the truest sense, *kingly*; conferring indeed the purest kingship that can exist among men: too many other kingships, (however distinguished by visible insignia or material power) being either spectral, or tyrannous;—Spectral—that is to say, aspects and shadows only of royalty, hollow as death, and which only the "Likeness of a kingly crown have on;"[43] or else tyrannous—that is to say, substituting their own will for the law of justice and love by which all true kings rule.

There is, then, I repeat—and as I want to leave this idea with you, I begin with it, and shall end with it—only one pure kind of kingship; an inevitable and eternal kind, crowned or not: the kingship, namely, which consists in a stronger moral state, and a truer thoughtful state, than that of others; enabling you, therefore, to guide, or to raise them....

Believing that all literature and all education are only useful so far as they tend to confirm this calm, beneficent, and *therefore* kingly, power—first, over ourselves, and, through ourselves, over all around us, I

---

43   John Milton, *Paradise Lost* (1667).

am now going to ask you to consider with me farther, what special portion or kind of this royal authority, arising out of noble education, may rightly be possessed by women; and how far they also are called to a true queenly power. Not in their households merely, but over all within their sphere. And in what sense, if they rightly understood and exercised this royal or gracious influence, the order and beauty induced by such benignant power would justify us in speaking of the territories over which each of them reigned, as "Queens' Gardens."

And here, in the very outset, we are met by a far deeper question, which—strange though this may seem—remains among many of us yet quite undecided, in spite of its infinite importance.

We cannot determine what the queenly power of women should be, until we are agreed what their ordinary power should be. We cannot consider how education may fit them for any widely extending duty, until we are agreed what is their true constant duty. And there never was a time when wilder words were spoken, or more vain imagination permitted, respecting this question—quite vital to all social happiness. The relations of the womanly to the manly nature, their different capacities of intellect or of virtue, seem never to have been yet measured with entire consent. We hear of the mission and of the rights of Woman, as if these could ever be separate from the mission and the rights of Man;—as if she and her lord were creatures of independent kind and of irreconcileable claim. This, at least, is wrong. And not less wrong—perhaps even more foolishly wrong (for I will anticipate thus far what I hope to prove)—is the idea that woman is only the shadow and attendant image of her lord, owing him a thoughtless and servile obedience, and supported altogether in her weakness by the pre-eminence of his fortitude.

This, I say, is the most foolish of all errors respecting her who was made to be the helpmate of man.[44] As if he could be helped effectively by a shadow, or worthily by a slave!

Let us try, then, whether we cannot get at some clear and harmonious idea (it must be harmonious if it is true) of what womanly mind and virtue are in power and office, with respect to man's; and how their relations, rightly accepted, aid, and increase, the vigour, and honour, and authority of both....

We are foolish, and without excuse foolish, in speaking of the "superiority" of one sex to the other, as if they could be compared in similar things. Each has what the other has not: each completes the other, and is completed by the other: they are in nothing alike, and the happiness and perfection of both depends on each asking and receiving from the other what the other only can give.

Now their separate characters are briefly these. The man's power is active, progressive, defensive. He is eminently the doer, the creator, the discoverer, the defender. His intellect is for speculation and invention; his energy for adventure, for war, and for conquest, wherever war is just, wherever conquest necessary. But the woman's power is for rule, not for battle,—and her intellect is not for invention or creation, but for sweet ordering, arrangement, and decision. She sees the qualities of things, their claims, and their places. Her great function is Praise: she enters into no contest, but infallibly adjudges the crown of contest. By her office, and place, she is protected from all danger and temptation. The man, in his rough work in open world, must encounter all peril and trial.... But he guards the woman from all this; within his house, as ruled by her, unless she herself has sought it, need enter no danger, no temptation, no cause of error or offence. This is the true nature of home—it is the place of Peace; the shelter, not only from all injury, but from all terror, doubt, and division. In so far as it is not this, it is not home; so far as the anxieties of the outer life penetrate into it, and the inconsistently-minded, unknown, unloved, or hostile society of the

---

44 Genesis 2:18.

outer world is allowed by either husband or wife to cross the threshold, it ceases to be home; it is then only a part of that outer world which you have roofed over, and lighted fire in. But so far as it is a sacred place, a vestal[45] temple, a temple of the hearth watched over by Household Gods, before whose faces none may come but those whom they can receive with love,—so far as it is this, and roof and fire are types only of a nobler shade and light,—shade as of the rock in a weary land, and light as of the Pharos[46] in the stormy sea;—so far it vindicates the name, and fulfills the praise, of Home....

This, then, I believe to be,—will you not admit it to be,—the woman's true place and power? But do not you see that, to fulfil this, she must—as far as one can use such terms of a human creature—be incapable of error? So far as she rules, all must be right, or nothing is. She must be enduringly, incorruptibly good; instinctively, infallibly wise—wise, not for self-development, but for self-renunciation: wise, not that she may set herself above her husband, but that she may never fail from his side: wise, not with the narrowness of insolent and loveless pride, but with the passionate gentleness of an infinitely variable, because infinitely applicable, modesty of service—the true changefulness of woman....

II.
I have been trying, thus far, to show you what should be the place, and what the power of woman. Now, secondly, we ask, What kind of education is to fit her for these?

And if you indeed think this is a true conception of her office and dignity, it will not be difficult to trace the course of education which would fit her for the one, and raise her to the other....

All such knowledge should be given her as may enable her to understand, and even to aid, the work of men: and yet it should be given, not as knowledge,—not as if it were, or could be, for her an object to know; but only to feel, and to judge. It is of no moment, as a matter of pride or perfectness in herself, whether she knows many languages or one; but it is of the utmost, that she should be able to show kindness to a stranger, and to understand the sweetness of a stranger's tongue. It is of no moment to her own worth or dignity that she should be acquainted with this science or that; but it is of the highest that she should be trained in habits of accurate thought; that she should understand the meaning, the inevitableness, and the loveliness of natural laws, and follow at least some one path of scientific attainment, as far as to the threshold of that bitter Valley of Humiliation,[47] into which only the wisest and bravest of men can descend, owning themselves forever children, gathering pebbles on a boundless shore. It is of little consequence how many positions of cities she knows, or how many dates of events, or how many names of celebrated persons—it is not the object of education to turn a woman into a dictionary; but it is deeply necessary that she should be taught to enter with her whole personality into the history she reads; to picture the passages of it vitally in her own bright imagination; to apprehend, with her fine instincts, the pathetic circumstances and dramatic relations, which the historian too often only eclipses by his reasoning, and disconnects by his arrangement: it is for her to trace the hidden equities of divine reward, and catch sight, through the darkness, of the fateful threads of woven fire that connect error with its retribution. But, chiefly of all, she is to be taught to extend the limits of her sympathy with respect to that history which is being for ever determined, as the moments pass in which she draws her peaceful breath; and to the contemporary calamity which, were it but rightly

---

45 Of the goddess Vesta; pure; virginal.
46 Lighthouse on the Mediterranean island of Pharos (c. 280 BCE).
47 The place where Christian meets the Devil in John Bunyan's *Pilgrim's Progress* (1678, 1684).

mourned by her, would recur no more hereafter. She is to exercise herself in imagining what would be the effects upon her mind and conduct, if she were daily brought into the presence of the suffering which is not the less real because shut from her sight. She is to be taught somewhat to understand the nothingness of the proportion which that little world in which she lives and loves, bears to the world in which God lives and loves;—and solemnly she is to be taught to strive that her thoughts of piety may not be feeble in proportion to the number they embrace, nor her prayer more languid than it is for the momentary relief from pain of her husband or her child, when it is uttered for the multitudes of those who have none to love them,—and is "for all who are desolate and oppressed."[48] ...

I believe, then, ... that a girl's education should be nearly, in its course and material of study, the same as a boy's; but quite differently directed. A woman, in any rank of life, ought to know whatever her husband is likely to know, but to know it in a different way. His command of it should be foundational and progressive, hers, general and accomplished for daily and helpful use. Not but that it would often be wiser in men to learn things in a womanly sort of way, for present use, and to seek for the discipline and training of their mental powers in such branches of study as will be afterwards fittest for social service; but, speaking broadly, a man ought to know any language or science he learns, thoroughly while a woman ought to know the same language, or science, only so far as may enable her to sympathise in her husband's pleasures, and in those of his best friends....

... [T]here is just this difference between the making of a girl's character and a boy's—you may chisel a boy into shape, as you would a rock, or hammer him into it, if he be of a better kind, as you would a piece of bronze. But you cannot hammer a girl into anything. She grows as a flower does,—she will wither without sun; she will decay in her sheath, as the narcissus does, if you do not give her air enough; she may fall, and defile her head in dust, if you leave her without help at some moments of her life; but you cannot fetter her; she must take her own fair form and way, if she take any, and in mind as in body, must have always

> Her household motions light and free
> And steps of virgin liberty.[49] ...

And not only in the material and in the course, but yet more earnestly in the spirit of it, let a girl's education be as serious as a boy's. You bring up your girls as if they were meant for sideboard ornaments, and then complain of their frivolity. Give them the same advantages that you give their brothers—appeal to the same grand instincts of virtue in them; teach *them* also that courage and truth are the pillars of their being: do you think that they would not answer that appeal, brave and true as they are even now, when you know that there is hardly a girl's school in this Christian kingdom where the children's courage or sincerity would be thought of half so much importance as their way of coming in at a door....

And give them, lastly, not only noble teachings, but noble teachers. You consider somewhat, before you send your boy to school, what kind of a man the master is;—whatsoever kind of a man he is, you at least give him full authority over your son, and show some respect to him yourself: if he comes to dine with you, you do not put him at a side table; you know also that, at his college, your child's immediate

---

48 The Litany, *Book of Common Prayer*.
49 William Wordsworth, "She Was a Phantom of Delight" (1807).

tutor will be under the direction of some still higher tutor, for whom you have absolute reverence. You do not treat the Dean of Christ Church or the Master of Trinity[50] as your inferiors.

But what teachers do you give your girls, and what reverence do you show to the teachers you have chosen? Is a girl likely to think her own conduct, or her own intellect, of much importance, when you trust the entire formation of her character, moral and intellectual, to a person whom you let your servants treat with less respect than they do your housekeeper[51] (as if the soul of your child were a less charge than jams and groceries), and whom you yourself think you confer an honour upon by letting her sometimes sit in the drawing-room in the evening? ...[52]

... Suppose you had each, at the back of your houses, a garden, large enough for your children to play in, with just as much lawn as would give them room to run,—no more—and that you could not change your abode; but that, if you chose, you could double your income, or quadruple it, by digging a coal shaft in the middle of the lawn, and turning the flower-beds into heaps of coke.[53] Would you do it? I think not. I can tell you, you would be wrong if you did, though it gave you income sixty-fold instead of four-fold.

Yet this is what you are doing with all England. The whole country is but a little garden, not more than enough for your children to run on the lawns of, if you would let them *all* run there. And this little garden you will turn into furnace-ground, and fill with heaps of cinders, if you can; and those children of yours, not you, will suffer for it. For the fairies will not be all banished; there are fairies of the furnace as of the wood, and their first gifts seem to be "sharp arrows of the mighty;" but their last gifts are "coals of juniper."[54] ...

... Here is a little account of a Welsh school, from page 261 of the Report on Wales, published by the Committee of Council on Education. This is a school close to a town containing 5,000 persons:—

> I then called up a larger class, most of whom had recently come to the school. Three girls repeatedly declared that they had never heard of Christ, and two that they had never heard of God. Two out of six thought Christ was on earth now '(they might have had a worse thought, perhaps),' three knew nothing about the crucifixion. Four out of seven did not know the names of the months, nor the number of days in a year. They had no notion of addition beyond two and two, or three and three; their minds were perfect blanks.

Oh ye women of England! from the Princess of that Wales to the simplest of you, do not think your own children can be brought into their true fold of rest, while these are scattered on the hills, as sheep having no shepherd....

III.

Thus far, then, of the nature, thus far of the teaching, of woman, and thus of her household office, and queenliness. We come now to our last, our widest question,—What is her queenly office with respect to the state?

Generally, we are under an impression that a man's duties are public, and a woman's private. But this is not altogether so. A man has a personal work or duty, relating to his own home, and a public work or

---

50 Colleges at Oxford and Cambridge; the dean and master are the heads of these colleges.
51 A woman responsible for overseeing a household's female servants.
52 That is, a governess: a woman hired to instruct her charges at their family home.
53 Mineral coal that has been distilled to make charcoal.
54 Psalm 120:4.

duty, which is the expansion of the other, relating to the state. So a woman has a personal work or duty, relating to her own home, and a public work or duty, which is also the expansion of that.

Now the man's work for his own home is, as has been said, to secure its maintenance, progress, and defense; the woman's to secure its order, comfort, and loveliness.

Expand both these functions. The man's duty, as a member of a commonwealth,[55] is to assist in the maintenance, in the advance, in the defence of the state. The woman's duty, as a member of the commonwealth, is to assist in the ordering, in the comforting, and in the beautiful adornment of the state.

What the man is at his own gate, defending it, if need be, against insult and spoil, that also, not in a less, but in a more devoted measure, he is to be at the gate of his country, leaving his home, if need be, even to the spoiler, to do his more incumbent work there.

And, in like manner, what the woman is to be within her gates, as the centre of order, the balm of distress, and the mirror of beauty; that she is also to be without her gates, where order is more difficult, distress more imminent, loveliness more rare.

And as within the human heart there is always set an instinct for all its real duties,—an instinct which you cannot quench, but only warp and corrupt if you withdraw it from its true purpose;—as there is the intense instinct of love, which, rightly disciplined, maintains all the sanctities of life, and, misdirected, undermines them; and *must* do either the one or the other;—so there is in the human heart an inextinguishable instinct, the love of power, which, rightly directed, maintains all the majesty of law and life, and misdirected, wrecks them.

Deep rooted in the innermost life of the heart of man, and of the heart of woman, God set it there, and God keeps it there. Vainly, as falsely, you blame or rebuke the desire of power!—For Heaven's sake, and for Man's sake, desire it all you can. But *what* power? That is all the question. Power to destroy? ... Not so. Power to heal, to redeem, to guide, and to guard. Power of the sceptre and shield; the power of the royal hand that heals in touching,—that binds the fiend, and looses the captive; the throne that is founded on the rock of Justice, and descended from only by steps of mercy. Will you not covet such power as this, and seek such throne as this, and be no more housewives, but queens?

It is now long since the women of England arrogated, universally, a title which once belonged to nobility only; and, having once been in the habit of accepting the simple title of gentlewoman, as correspondent to that of gentleman, insisted on the privilege of assuming the title of "Lady," ... which properly corresponds only to the title of "Lord."

I do not blame them for this; but only for their narrow motive in this. I would have them desire and claim the title of Lady, provided they claim, not merely the title, but the office and duty signified by it. Lady means "bread-giver" or "loaf-giver," and Lord means "maintainer of laws,"[56] and both titles have reference, not to the law which is maintained in the house, nor to the bread which is given to the household; but to law maintained for the multitude, and to bread broken among the multitude....

And this beneficent and legal dominion, this power of the Dominus, or House-Lord, and of the Domina, or House-Lady, is great and venerable, not in the number of those through whom it has lineally descended, but in the number of those whom it grasps within its sway; it is always regarded with reverent worship wherever its dynasty is founded on its duty, and its ambition co-relative with its beneficence.

---

55 The body of people making up a democratic nation.
56 The *Oxford English Dictionary* provides similar Old English etymologies pertaining to bread for both words.

Your fancy is pleased with the thought of being noble ladies, with a train of vassals.[57] Be it so ... but see to it that your train is of vassals whom you serve and feed, not merely of slaves who serve and feed *you*; and that the multitude which obeys you is of those whom you have comforted, not oppressed,—whom you have redeemed, not led into captivity.

And this, which is true of the lower or household dominion, is equally true of the queenly dominion;—that highest dignity is open to you, if you will also accept that highest duty. Rex et Regina—Roi et Reine[58]—"*Right*-doers;" they differ but from the Lady and Lord, in that their power is supreme over the mind as over the person—that they not only feed and clothe, but direct and teach. And whether consciously or not, you must be, in many a heart, enthroned: there is no putting by that crown; queens you must always be; queens to your lovers; queens to your husbands and your sons; queens of higher mystery to the world beyond, which bows itself, and will forever bow, before the myrtle crown,[59] and the stainless sceptre, of womanhood. But, alas! you are too often idle and careless queens, grasping at majesty in the least things, while you abdicate it in the greatest; and leaving misrule and violence to work their will among men, in defiance of the power, which, holding straight in gift from the Prince of all Peace,[60] the wicked among you betray, and the good forget.

"Prince of Peace." Note that name. When kings rule in that name, and nobles, and the judges of the earth, they also, in their narrow place, and mortal measure, receive the power of it. There are no other rulers than they: other rule than theirs is but *mis*rule; they who govern verily "Dei gratià"[61] are all princes, yes, or princesses, of peace. There is not a war in the world, no, nor an injustice, but you women are answerable for it; not in that you have provoked, but in that you have not hindered. Men, by their nature, are prone to fight.... It is for you to choose their cause for them, and to forbid them when there is no cause. There is no suffering, no injustice, no misery in the earth, but the guilt of it lies lastly with you. Men can bear the sight of it, but you should not be able to bear it.... [I]t is you only who can feel the depths of pain; and conceive the way of its healing. Instead of trying to do this, you turn away from it; you shut yourselves within your park walls and garden gates; and you are content to know that there is beyond them a whole world in wilderness—a world of secrets which you dare not penetrate; and of suffering which you dare not conceive....

... You have heard it said—(and I believe there is more than fancy even in that saying, but let it pass for a fanciful one)—that flowers only flourish rightly in the garden of some one who loves them. I know you would like that to be true; you would think it a pleasant magic if you could flush your flowers into brighter bloom by a kind look upon them ... —if you could bid the dew fall upon them in the drought, and say to the south wind, in frost—"Come, thou south, and breathe upon my garden, that the spices of it may flow out."[62] This you would think a great thing? And do you think it not a greater thing, that all this, (and how much more than this!) you *can* do, for fairer flowers than these ... —flowers that have eyes like yours, and thoughts like yours, and lives like yours; which, once saved, you save for ever? Is this only a

---

57 Servants.
58 Latin and French: King and Queen.
59 A lesser crown than the crown of laurels that was given to those who secured a victory without battle or injury.
60 Christ; Isaiah 9:6.
61 Latin: by God's grace.
62 Song of Solomon 4:16.

little power? Far among the moorlands[63] and the rocks,—far in the darkness of the terrible streets,—these feeble florets are lying, with all their fresh leaves torn, and their stems broken—will you never go down to them, nor set them in order in their little fragrant beds, nor fence them in their shuddering from the fierce wind? Shall morning follow morning, for you, but not for them; and the dawn rise to watch, far away, those frantic Dances of Death; ... but no dawn rise to breathe upon these living banks of wild violet, and woodbine, and rose; nor call to you, through your casement,—call, (not giving you the name of the English poet's lady, but the name of Dante's great Matilda, who, on the edge of happy Lethe, stood, wreathing flowers with flowers),[64] saying:—

> Come into the garden, Maud,
> For the black bat, night, has flown,
> And the woodbine spices are wafted abroad
> And the musk of the roses blown?[65]

Will you not go down among them?—among those sweet living things, whose new courage, sprung from the earth with the deep colour of heaven upon it, is starting up in strength of goodly spire; and whose purity, washed from the dust, is opening, bud by bud, into the flower of promise;—and still they turn to you, and for you, "The Larkspur listens—I hear, I hear! And the Lily whispers—I wait."[66]

Did you notice that I missed two lines when I read you that first stanza; and think that I had forgotten them? Hear them now:—

> Come into the garden, Maud,
> For the black bat, night, has flown;
> Come into the garden, Maud,
> I am here at the gate, alone.

Who is it, think you, who stands at the gate of this sweeter garden, alone, waiting for you? Did you ever hear, not of a Maude, but a Madeleine, who went down to her garden in the dawn, and found One waiting at the gate, whom she supposed to be the gardener?[67] Have you not sought Him often;—sought Him in vain, all through the night;—sought Him in vain at the gate of that old garden where the fiery sword is set?[68] He is never there; but at the gate of *this* garden He is waiting always— ... ready to go down to see the fruits of the valley, to see whether the vine has flourished, and the pomegranate budded.[69] There you shall see with Him the little tendrils of the vines that His hand is guiding—there you shall see the pomegranate springing where His hand cast the sanguine seed;—more: you shall see the troops of the angel keepers that, with their wings, wave away the hungry birds from the pathsides where He has sown, and call to each other between the vineyard rows, "Take us the foxes, the little foxes, that spoil the vines,

---

63 Open, unfarmed land.
64 Dante Alighieri, *La Divina Commedia* (c. 1308–21): Dante stands on one side of the River Lethe and Matilda resides on the other bank, where she sings and picks flowers. She lives alone in an Edenic landscape, a place lost to humanity after the fall.
65 Alfred Tennyson, *Maud* (1855).
66 Tennyson, *Maud* (1855).
67 John 20:15.
68 That is, Eden; Genesis 3:24.
69 Song of Solomon 6:11.

for our vines have tender grapes."[70] Oh—you queens—you queens! among the hills and happy greenwood of this land of yours, shall the foxes have holes, and the birds of the air have nests; and, in your cities, shall the stones cry out against you, that they are the only pillows where the Son of Man[71] can lay His head?[72]

John Stuart Mill
from *The Subjection of Women* (1869)

A progressive philosopher, economist, and women's rights advocate, John Stuart Mill (1806–73) became one of the nineteenth century's most influential public intellectuals. Rigorously educated from age three by his father, the young Mill mixed with his father's radical associates. Reading Jeremy Bentham converted him to utilitarianism, but a mental crisis in 1826–27 prompted dissent from Benthamism. Striving for practical reform, Mill spent his professional career at the India Office while editing and writing for periodicals. He also authored works on philosophy and political, economic, and social theory, including *On Liberty* (1859) and *The Subjection of Women* (1869). Mill first encountered the married Harriet Taylor in 1830; they married in 1851 after her first husband died, and Mill credited her collaboration on almost all his mature work.

In *The Subjection of Women* (1869), Mill argues that "the legal subordination of one sex to the other ... [is] now one of the chief hindrances to human improvement." The work proved unpopular and unprofitable, but it galvanized the emergent women's movement.

Chapter 1

The object of this Essay is to explain as clearly as I am able, the grounds of an opinion which I have held from the very earliest period when I had formed any opinions at all on social or political matters, and which, instead of being weakened or modified, has been constantly growing stronger by the progress of reflection and the experience of life: That the principle which regulates the existing social relations between the two sexes—the legal subordination of one sex to the other—is wrong itself, and now one of the chief hindrances to human improvement; and that it ought to be replaced by a principle of perfect equality, admitting no power or privilege on the one side, nor disability on the other....

... If the authority of men over women, when first established, had been the result of a conscientious comparison between different modes of constituting the government of society; if, after trying various other modes of social organisation[,] ... it had been decided, on the testimony of experience, that the mode in which women are wholly under the rule of men, having no share at all in public concerns, and

---

70 Song of Solomon 2:15.
71 Christ.
72 Luke 9:58.

each in private being under the legal obligation of obedience to the man with whom she has associated her destiny,[73] was the arrangement most conducive to the happiness and well being of both; its general adoption might then be fairly thought to be some evidence that, at the time when it was adopted, it was the best: though even then the considerations which recommended it may, like so many other primeval social facts of the greatest importance, have subsequently, in the course of ages, ceased to exist. But the state of the case is in every respect the reverse of this. In the first place, the opinion in favour of the present system, which entirely subordinates the weaker sex to the stronger, rests upon theory only; for there never has been trial made of any other: so that experience, in the sense in which it is vulgarly opposed to theory, cannot be pretended to have pronounced any verdict. And in the second place, the adoption of this system of inequality never was the result of deliberation, or forethought, or any social ideas, or any notion whatever of what conduced to the benefit of humanity or the good order of society. It arose simply from the fact that from the very earliest twilight of human society, every woman (owing to the value attached to her by men, combined with her inferiority in muscular strength) was found in a state of bondage to some man. Laws and systems of polity always begin by recognising the relations they find already existing between individuals. They convert what was a mere physical fact into a legal right, give it the sanction of society, and principally aim at the substitution of public and organised means of asserting and protecting these rights, instead of the irregular and lawless conflict of physical strength. Those who had already been compelled to obedience became in this manner legally bound to it. Slavery, from being a mere affair of force between the master and the slave, became regularized and a matter of compact among the masters, who, binding themselves to one another for common protection, guaranteed by their collective strength the private possessions of each, including his slaves. In early times, the great majority of the male sex were slaves, as well as the whole of the female. And many ages elapsed, some of them ages of high cultivation, before any thinker was bold enough to question the rightfulness, and the absolute social necessity, either of the one slavery or of the other. By degrees such thinkers did arise; and (the general progress of society assisting) the slavery of the male sex has, in all the countries of Christian Europe at least (though, in one of them, only within the last few years)[74] been at length abolished, and that of the female sex has been gradually changed into a milder form of dependence. But this dependence, as it exists at present, is not an original institution, taking a fresh start from considerations of justice and social expediency—it is the primitive state of slavery lasting on, through successive mitigations and modifications occasioned by the same causes which have softened the general manners, and brought all human relations more under the control of justice and the influence of humanity. It has not lost the taint of its brutal origin. No presumption in its favour, therefore, can be drawn from the fact of its existence. The only such presumption which it could be supposed to have, must be grounded on its having lasted till now, when so many other things which came down from the same odious source have been done away with. And this, indeed, is what makes it strange to ordinary ears, to hear it asserted that the inequality of rights between men and women has no other source than the law of the strongest.

---

73 Under the Victorian marriage vows of the Church of England, wives promised to obey their husbands.
74 Britain abolished the slave trade in 1807; slavery was thereafter abolished in British colonies in 1833; in French colonies in 1848; in Dutch colonies in 1863; in the United States in 1865; and in Portuguese colonies in 1869.

That this statement should have the effect of a paradox, is in some respects creditable to the progress of civilization, and the improvement of the moral sentiments of mankind. We now live ... in a state in which the law of the strongest seems to be entirely abandoned as the regulating principle of the world's affairs: nobody professes it, and, as regards most of the relations between human beings, nobody is permitted to practise it.... This being the ostensible state of things, people flatter themselves that the rule of mere force is ended; that the law of the strongest cannot be the reason of existence of anything which has remained in full operation down to the present time. However any of our present institutions may have begun, it can only, they think, have been preserved to this period of advanced civilization by a well-grounded feeling of its adaptation to human nature, and conduciveness to the general good. They do not understand the great vitality and durability of institutions which place right on the side of might; ... how very rarely those who have obtained legal power because they first had physical, have ever lost their hold of it until the physical power had passed over to the other side. Such shifting of the physical force not having taken place in the case of women; this fact, combined with all the peculiar and characteristic features of the particular case, made it certain from the first that this branch of the system of right founded on might, though softened in its most atrocious features at an earlier period than several of the others, would be the very last to disappear. It was inevitable that this one case of a social relation grounded on force, would survive through generations of institutions grounded on equal justice, an almost solitary exception to the general character of their laws and customs; but which, so long as it does not proclaim its own origin, and as discussion has not brought out its true character, is not felt to jar with modern civilization, any more than domestic slavery among the Greeks jarred with their notion of themselves as a free people.

The truth is, that people of the present and the last two or three generations have lost all practical sense of the primitive condition of humanity.... People are not aware how entirely, in former ages, the law of superior strength was the rule of life; how publicly and openly it was avowed....

... People are mostly so little aware how completely, during the greater part of the duration of our species, the law of force was the avowed rule of general conduct ... as little do people remember or consider, how institutions and customs which never had any ground but the law of force, last on into ages and states of general opinion which never would have permitted their first establishment. Less than forty years ago, Englishmen might still by law hold human beings in bondage as saleable property: within the present century they might kidnap them and carry them off, and work them literally to death. This absolutely extreme case of the law of force, condemned by those who can tolerate almost every other form of arbitrary power, and which, of all others, presents features the most revolting to the feelings of all who look at it from an impartial position, was the law of civilized and Christian England within the memory of persons now living: and in one half of Anglo-Saxon America three or four years ago, not only did slavery exist, but the slave trade, and the breeding of slaves expressly for it, was a general practice between slave states. Yet not only was there a greater strength of sentiment against it, but, in England at least, a less amount either of feeling or of interest in favour of it, than of any other of the customary abuses of force: for its motive was the love of gain, unmixed and undisguised; and those who profited by it were a very small numerical fraction of the country, while the natural feeling of all who were not personally interested in it, was unmitigated abhorrence.... How different are these cases from that of the power of men over women! I am not now prejudging the question of its justifiableness. I am showing how vastly more permanent it could not but be, even if not justifiable, than these other dominations which have nevertheless lasted down to our own time. Whatever gratification of pride there is in the possession of power, and whatever personal interest in its exercise, is in this case not confined to a limited class, but common to the whole male sex. Instead of being, to most of its supporters, a thing desirable chiefly in the abstract, or, like the political ends usually contended for by factions, of little private importance to any but the leaders; it comes home to the person and hearth of every male head of a family, and of everyone who looks forward to being so.... We must consider, too, that the possessors of the power have facilities in this case, greater than in any other, to prevent any uprising against it. Every one of the subjects lives under the very eye, and almost, it may be said, in the hands, of one of the masters—in closer intimacy with him than with any of her fellow-subjects; with no means of combining against him, no power of even locally overmastering him, and, on the other hand, with the strongest motives for seeking his favour and avoiding to give him offence. In struggles for political emancipation, everybody knows how often its champions are bought off by bribes, or daunted by terrors. In the case of women, each individual of the subject-class is in a chronic state of bribery and intimidation combined....

Some will object, that a comparison cannot fairly be made between the government of the male sex and the forms of unjust power which I have adduced in illustration of it, since these are arbitrary, and the effect of mere usurpation, while it on the contrary is natural. But was there ever any domination which did not appear natural to those who possessed it? There was a time when the division of mankind into two classes, a small one of masters and a numerous one of slaves, appeared, even to the most cultivated minds, to be natural, and the only natural, condition of the human race.... Did not the slaveowners of the Southern United States maintain the same doctrine, with all the fanaticism with which men cling to the theories that justify their passions and legitimate their personal interests? Did they not call heaven and earth to witness that the dominion of the white man over the black is natural, that the black race is by nature incapable of freedom, and marked out for slavery? some even going so far as to say that the freedom of manual labourers is an unnatural order of things anywhere. Again, the theorists of absolute monarchy have always affirmed it to be the only natural form of government; issuing from the patriarchal, which was the primitive and spontaneous form of society, framed on the model of the paternal, which is anterior to society itself, and, as they contend, the most natural authority of all.... So true is it that unnatural generally means only uncustomary, and that everything which is usual appears natural. The subjection of women to men being a universal custom, any departure from it quite naturally appears unnatural. But how entirely, even in this case, the feeling is dependent on custom, appears by ample experience. Nothing so much astonishes the people of distant parts of the world, when they first learn anything about England, as to be told that it is under a queen; the thing seems to them so unnatural as to be almost incredible. To Englishmen this does not seem in the least degree unnatural, because they are used to it; but they do feel it unnatural that women should be soldiers or members of parliament. In the feudal ages, on the contrary, war and politics were not thought unnatural to women, because not unusual; it seemed natural that women of the privileged classes should be of manly character, inferior in nothing but bodily strength to their husbands and fathers. The independence of women seemed rather less unnatural to the Greeks than to other ancients, on account of the fabulous Amazons[75] (whom they believed to be historical), and the

---

75 A race of warrior women in Greek mythology.

partial example afforded by the Spartan women; who, though no less subordinate by law than in other Greek states, were more free in fact, and being trained to bodily exercises in the same manner with men, gave ample proof that they were not naturally disqualified for them.[76] There can be little doubt that Spartan experience suggested to Plato, among many other of his doctrines, that of the social and political equality of the two sexes.[77]

But, it will be said, the rule of men over women differs from all these others in not being a rule of force: it is accepted voluntarily; women make no complaint, and are consenting parties to it. In the first place, a great number of women do not accept it. Ever since there have been women able to make their sentiments known by their writings (the only mode of publicity which society permits to them), an increasing number of them have recorded protests against their present social condition: and recently many thousands of them, headed by the most eminent women known to the public, have petitioned Parliament for their admission to the Parliamentary Suffrage.[78] The claim of women to be educated as solidly, and in the same branches of knowledge, as men, is urged with growing intensity, and with a great prospect of success; while the demand for their admission into professions and occupations hitherto closed against them, becomes every year more urgent.[79] Though there are not in this country, as there are in the United States, periodical Conventions and an organized party to agitate for the Rights of Women, there is a numerous and active society organized and managed by women, for the more limited object of obtaining the political franchise.[80] Nor is it only in our own country and in America that women are beginning to protest, more or less collectively, against the disabilities under which they labour. France, and Italy, and Switzerland, and Russia now afford examples of the same thing.[81] How many more women there are who silently cherish similar aspirations, no one can possibly know; but there are abundant tokens how many *would* cherish them, were they not so strenuously taught to repress them as contrary to the proprieties of their sex. It must be remembered, also, that no enslaved class ever asked for complete liberty at once. When Simon de Montfort called the deputies of the commons to sit for the first time in Parliament,[82] did any of them dream of demanding that an assembly, elected by their constituents, should make and destroy ministries, and dictate to the king in affairs of state? No such thought entered into the imagination of the most ambitious of them.... It is a political law of nature that those who are under any power of ancient origin, never begin by complaining of the power itself, but only of its oppressive exercise.

---

76 Spartan women were intensely involved in athletic exercises such as running, wrestling, and javelin throwing.

77 Plato, *Republic*, Book 5 (c. 360 BCE).

78 The petition was submitted in 1866 by John Stuart Mill on behalf of a group of women that included Emily Davies (see Education), Elizabeth Garrett Anderson (see Education), and Barbara Leigh Smith Bodichon (see Gender and Sexuality).

79 See, for example, Bessie Rayner Parkes, "What Can Educated Women Do?" (1859, 1860); Elizabeth Blackwell, "Medicine as a Profession for Women" (1860); Emily Davies, "Female Physicians" (1862) and *The Higher Education of Women* (1866; see Education).

80 In the US, conventions such as the Seneca Falls Convention and the National Women's Rights Convention had been taking place since the late 1840s and the American Woman Suffrage Association (earlier the National Woman Suffrage Association) pushed for an amendment to allow women to vote; in the UK, the Langham Place Group and the Ladies' Institute provided spaces for social and political activism.

81 French women began to push for women's suffrage in the late eighteenth century; the unified Italian state (1861) entrenched women's inequality, but a feminist movement started in the 1860s despite this; Swiss women petitioned for suffrage in 1886; Russian women were subordinate under family, civil, and criminal law from the mid-eighteenth century onward, but a Russian feminist movement emerged after the Crimean War (1853–56).

82 Simon de Montfort (c. 1208–65), Norman and English soldier who led a rebellion against Henry III and briefly held power, establishing an elected parliament in 1265; Edward I, Henry's heir, who defeated Montfort later that year.

There is never any want of women who complain of ill usage by their husbands. There would be infinitely more, if complaint were not the greatest of all provocatives to a repetition and increase of the ill usage. It is this which frustrates all attempts to maintain the power but protect the woman against its abuses. In no other case (except that of a child) is the person who has been proved judicially to have suffered an injury, replaced under the physical power of the culprit who inflicted it.[83] Accordingly wives, even in the most extreme and protracted cases of bodily ill usage, hardly ever dare avail themselves of the laws made for their protection: and if, in a moment of irrepressible indignation, or by the interference of neighbours, they are induced to do so, their whole effort afterwards is to disclose as little as they can, and to beg off their tyrant from his merited chastisement.

All causes, social and natural, combine to make it unlikely that women should be collectively rebellious to the power of men. They are so far in a position different from all other subject classes, that their masters require something more from them than actual service. Men do not want solely the obedience of women, they want their sentiments. All men, except the most brutish, desire to have, in the woman most nearly connected with them, not a forced slave but a willing one, not a slave merely, but a favourite. They have therefore put everything in practice to enslave their minds. The masters of all other slaves rely, for maintaining obedience, on fear; either fear of themselves, or religious fears. The masters of women wanted more than simple obedience, and they turned the whole force of education to effect their purpose. All women are brought up from the very earliest years in the belief that their ideal of character is the very opposite to that of men; not self-will, and government by self-control, but submission, and yielding to the control of others. All the moralities tell them that it is the duty of women, and all the current sentimentalities that it is their nature, to live for others; to make complete abnegation of themselves, and to have no life but in their affections. And by their affections are meant the only ones they are allowed to have—those to the men with whom they are connected, or to the children who constitute an additional and indefeasible tie between them and a man. When we put together three things—first, the natural attraction between opposite sexes; secondly, the wife's entire dependence on the husband, every privilege or pleasure she has being either his gift, or depending entirely on his will; and lastly, that the principal object of human pursuit, consideration, and all objects of social ambition, can in general be sought or obtained by her only through him, it would be a miracle if the object of being attractive to men had not become the polar star of feminine education and formation of character. And, this great means of influence over the minds of women having been acquired, an instinct of selfishness made men avail themselves of it to the utmost as a means of holding women in subjection, by representing to them meekness, submissiveness, and resignation of all individual will into the hands of a man, as an essential part of sexual attractiveness. Can it be doubted that any of the other yokes which mankind have succeeded in breaking, would have subsisted till now if the same means had existed, and had been as sedulously used, to bow down their minds to it? ...

The preceding considerations are amply sufficient to show that custom, however universal it may be, affords in this case no presumption, and ought not to create any prejudice, in favour of the arrangements which place women in social and political subjection to men. But I may go farther, and maintain that the course of history, and the tendencies of progressive human society, afford not only no presumption in favour of this system of inequality of rights, but a strong one against it; and that, so far

---

83 Under the Matrimonial Causes Act (1857), a woman could divorce her abusive husband only if she could prove he was also adulterous; therefore, many women were still subject to their husbands' power after an assault conviction.

as the whole course of human improvement up to the time, the whole stream of modern tendencies, warrants any inference on the subject, it is, that this relic of the past is discordant with the future, and must necessarily disappear.

For, what is the peculiar character of the modern world—the difference which chiefly distinguishes modern institutions, modern social ideas, modern life itself, from those of times long past? It is, that human beings are no longer born to their place in life, and chained down by an inexorable bond to the place they are born to, but are free to employ their faculties, and such favourable chances as offer, to achieve the lot which may appear to them most desirable....

At present, in the more improved countries, the disabilities of women are the only case, save one, in which laws and institutions take persons at their birth, and ordain that they shall never in all their lives be allowed to compete for certain things. The one exception is that of royalty. Persons still are born to the throne.... All other dignities and social advantages are open to the whole male sex: many indeed are only attainable by wealth, but wealth may be striven for by any one, and is actually obtained by many men of the very humblest origin. The difficulties, to the majority, are indeed insuperable without the aid of fortunate accidents; but no male human being is under any legal ban: neither law nor opinion superadd artificial obstacles to the natural ones.... The disabilities, therefore, to which women are subject from the mere fact of their birth, are the solitary examples of the kind in modern legislation. In no instance except this, which comprehends half the human race, are the higher social functions closed against any one by a fatality of birth which no exertions, and no change of circumstances, can overcome; for even religious disabilities (besides that in England and in Europe they have practically almost ceased to exist) do not close any career to the disqualified person in case of conversion.[84]

The social subordination of women thus stands out an isolated fact in modern social institutions; a solitary breach of what has become their fundamental law; a single relic of an old world of thought and practice exploded in everything else, but retained in the one thing of most universal interest; as if a gigantic dolmen, or a vast temple of Jupiter Olympius, occupied the site of St. Paul's[85] and received daily worship, while the surrounding Christian churches were only resorted to on fasts and festivals. This entire discrepancy between one social fact and all those which accompany it ... surely affords, to a conscientious observer of human tendencies, serious matter for reflection. It raises a primâ facie[86] presumption on the unfavourable side, far outweighing any which custom and usage could in such circumstances create on the favourable; and should at least suffice to make this, like the choice between republicanism and royalty,[87] a balanced question.

The least that can be demanded is, that the question should not be considered as prejudged by existing fact and existing opinion, but open to discussion on its merits, as a question of justice and expediency:

---

84 Following the Reformation, Roman Catholic Britons could not purchase land, vote, sit in Parliament, hold civil or military offices, inherit property, or attend Oxford or Cambridge. In 1829, the Catholic Emancipation Act removed most of these restrictions (except the ban on a few public offices). The University Tests Act of 1871 lifted the restrictions on attendance at Oxford and Cambridge. Jews who refused to take a Christian oath were effectively barred from holding public office (including in Parliament) before the Oath Act of 1858.
85 "Dolmen" are Celtic monuments or tombs made of large stones; Jupiter Olympius, or Zeus, was the supreme deity of the ancient Greeks and Romans; St. Paul's Cathedral is the cathedral of the diocese of London and here symbolizes the centre of Christian worship in England.
86 Latin: at first sight; such a presumption prevails failing evidence to the contrary.
87 The choice between a democratic political structure (a republic) and a monarchical one (headed by royalty).

the decision on this, as on any of the other social arrangements of mankind, depending on what an enlightened estimate of tendencies and consequences may show to be most advantageous to humanity in general, without distinction of sex. And the discussion must be a real discussion, descending to foundations, and not resting satisfied with vague and general assertions. It will not do, for instance to assert in general terms, that the experience of mankind has pronounced in favour of the existing system. Experience cannot possibly have decided between two courses, so long as there has only been experience of one. If it be said that the doctrine of the equality of the sexes rests only on theory, it must be remembered that the contrary doctrine also has only theory to rest upon. All that is proved in its favour by direct experience, is that mankind have been able to exist under it, and to attain the degree of improvement and prosperity which we now see; but whether that prosperity has been attained sooner, or is now greater, than it would have been under the other system, experience does not say. On the other hand, experience does say, that every step in improvement has been so invariably accompanied by a step made in raising the social position of women, that historians and philosophers have been led to adopt their elevation or debasement as on the whole the surest test and most correct measure of the civilization of a people or an age. Through all the progressive period of human history, the condition of women has been approaching nearer to equality with men. This does not of itself prove that the assimilation must go on to complete equality; but it assuredly affords some presumption that such is the case.

Neither does it avail anything to say that the *nature* of the two sexes adapts them to their present functions and position, and renders these appropriate to them. Standing on the ground of common sense and the constitution of the human mind, I deny that any one knows, or can know, the nature of the two sexes, as long as they have only been seen in their present relation to one another. If men had ever been found in society without women, or women without men, or if there had been a society of men and women in which the women were not under the control of the men, something might have been positively known about the mental and moral differences which may be inherent in the nature of each. What is now called the nature of women is an eminently artificial thing—the result of forced repression in some directions, unnatural stimulation in others. It may be asserted without scruple, that no other class of dependents have had their character so entirely distorted from its natural proportions by their relation with their masters; for, if conquered and slave races have been, in some respects, more forcibly repressed, whatever in them has not been crushed down by an iron heel has generally been let alone, and if left with any liberty of development, it has developed itself according to its own laws; but in the case of women, a hot-house and stove cultivation[88] has always been carried on of some of the capabilities of their nature, for the benefit and pleasure of their masters. Then, because certain products of the general vital force sprout luxuriantly and reach a great development in this heated atmosphere and under this active nurture and watering, while other shoots from the same root, which are left outside in the wintry air, with ice purposely heaped all round them, have a stunted growth, and some are burnt off with fire and disappear; men, with that inability to recognise their own work which distinguishes the unanalytic mind, indolently believe that the tree grows of itself in the way they have made it grow, and that it would die if one half of it were not kept in a vapour bath and the other half in the snow....

---

88 The Victorian "hot house" or "stove house" was a greenhouse for exotic plants, warmed by piped-in heat during the cold winter months.

Even the preliminary knowledge, what the differences between the sexes now are, apart from all question as to how they are made what they are, is still in the crudest and most incomplete state. Medical practitioners and physiologists have ascertained, to some extent, the differences in bodily constitution; and this is an important element to the psychologist: but hardly any medical practitioner is a psychologist. Respecting the mental characteristics of women; their observations are of no more worth than those of common men. It is a subject on which nothing final can be known, so long as those who alone can really know it, women themselves, have given but little testimony, and that little, mostly suborned....[89] It is only a man here and there who has any tolerable knowledge of the character even of the women of his own family. I do not mean, of their capabilities; these nobody knows, not even themselves, because most of them have never been called out. I mean their actually existing thoughts and feelings. Many a man thinks he perfectly understands women, because he has had amatory relations with several, perhaps with many of them. If he is a good observer, and his experience extends to quality as well as quantity, he may have learnt something of one narrow department of their nature—an important department, no doubt. But of all the rest of it, few persons are generally more ignorant, because there are few from whom it is so carefully hidden. The most favourable case which a man can generally have for studying the character of a woman, is that of his own wife: for the opportunities are greater, and the cases of complete sympathy not so unspeakably rare. And in fact, this is the source from which any knowledge worth having on the subject has, I believe, generally come. But most men have not had the opportunity of studying in this way more than a single case: accordingly one can, to an almost laughable degree, infer what a man's wife is like, from his opinions about women in general. To make even this one case yield any result, the woman must be worth knowing, and the man not only a competent judge, but of a character so sympathetic in itself, and so well adapted to hers, that he can either read her mind by sympathetic intuition, or has nothing in himself which makes her shy of disclosing it. Hardly anything, I believe, can be more rare than this conjunction. It often happens that there is the most complete unity of feeling and community of interests as to all external things, yet the one has as little admission into the internal life of the other as if they were common acquaintance. Even with true affection, authority on the one side and subordination on the other prevent perfect confidence. Though nothing may be intentionally withheld, much is not shown. In the analogous relation of parent and child, the corresponding phenomenon must have been in the observation of every one. As between father and son, how many are the cases in which the father, in spite of real affection on both sides, obviously to all the world does not know, nor suspect, parts of the son's character familiar to his companions and equals. The truth is, that the position of looking up to another is extremely unpropitious to complete sincerity and openness with him.... How much more true, then, must all this be, when the one is not only under the authority of the other, but has it inculcated on her as a duty to reckon everything else subordinate to his comfort and pleasure, and to let him neither see nor feel anything coming from her, except what is agreeable to him. All these difficulties stand in the way of a man's obtaining any thorough knowledge even of the one woman whom alone, in general, he has sufficient opportunity of studying. When we further consider that to understand one woman is not necessarily to understand any other woman; that even if he could study many women of one rank, or of one country, he would not thereby understand women of other ranks or countries; and even if he did, they are still only the women of a single period of history; we may safely assert that the knowledge

---

89 Falsely or deceptively procured.

which men can acquire of women, even as they have been and are, without reference to what they might be, is wretchedly imperfect and superficial, and always will be so, until women themselves have told all that they have to tell.

And this time has not come; nor will it come otherwise than gradually. It is but of yesterday that women have either been qualified by literary accomplishments or permitted by society, to tell anything to the general public. As yet very few of them dare tell anything, which men, on whom their literary success depends, are unwilling to hear. Let us remember in what manner, up to a very recent time, the expression, even by a male author, of uncustomary opinions, or what are deemed eccentric feelings, usually was, and in some degree still is, received; and we may form some faint conception under what impediments a woman, who is brought up to think custom and opinion her sovereign rule, attempts to express in books anything drawn from the depths of her own nature. The greatest woman who has left writings behind her sufficient to give her an eminent rank in the literature of her country, thought it necessary to prefix as a motto to her boldest work, "Un homme peut braver l'opinion; une femme doit s'y soumettre."[90] The greater part of what women write about women is mere sycophancy[91] to men. In the case of unmarried women, much of it seems only intended to increase their chance of a husband. Many, both married and unmarried, overstep the mark, and inculcate a servility beyond what is desired or relished by any man, except the very vulgarest. But this is not so often the case as, even at a quite late period, it still was. Literary women are becoming more freespoken, and more willing to express their real sentiments. Unfortunately, in this country especially, they are themselves such artificial products, that their sentiments are compounded of a small element of individual observation and consciousness, and a very large one of acquired associations. This will be less and less the case, but it will remain true to a great extent, as long as social institutions do not admit the same free development of originality in women which is possible to men. When that time comes, and not before, we shall see, and not merely hear, as much as it is necessary to know of the nature of women, and the adaptation of other things to it....

One thing we may be certain of—that what is contrary to women's nature to do, they never will be made to do by simply giving their nature free play. The anxiety of mankind to interfere in behalf of nature, for fear lest nature should not succeed in effecting its purpose, is an altogether unnecessary solicitude. What women by nature cannot do, it is quite superfluous to forbid them from doing. What they can do, but not so well as the men who are their competitors, competition suffices to exclude them from.... If women have a greater natural inclination for some things than for others, there is no need of laws or social inculcation to make the majority of them do the former in preference to the latter. Whatever women's services are most wanted for, the free play of competition will hold out the strongest inducements to them to undertake. And, as the words imply, they are most wanted for the things for which they are most fit; by the apportionment of which to them, the collective faculties of the two sexes can be applied on the whole with the greatest sum of valuable result.

The general opinion of men is supposed to be, that the natural vocation of a woman is that of a wife and mother. I say, is supposed to be, because, judging from acts—from the whole of the present constitution of society—one might infer that their opinion was the direct contrary. They might be supposed to think that the alleged natural vocation of women was of all things the most repugnant to their

---

90 French: "A man can brave public opinion; a woman must submit to it": Germaine de Staël, *Delphine* (1802).
91 Servility.

nature; insomuch that if they are free to do anything else[,] ... there will not be enough of them who will be willing to accept the condition said to be natural to them. If this is the real opinion of men in general, it would be well that it should be spoken out. I should like to hear somebody openly enunciating the doctrine (it is already implied in much that is written on the subject)—"It is necessary to society that women should marry and produce children. They will not do so unless they are compelled. Therefore it is necessary to compel them." The merits of the case would then be clearly defined. It would be exactly that of the slaveholders of South Carolina and Louisiana. "It is necessary that cotton and sugar should be grown. White men cannot produce them. Negroes will not, for any wages which we choose to give. *Ergo*[92] they must be compelled." An illustration still closer to the point is that of impressment.[93] Sailors must absolutely be had to defend the country. It often happens that they will not voluntarily enlist. Therefore there must be the power of forcing them. How often has this logic been used! and, but for one flaw in it, without doubt it would have been successful up to this day. But it is open to the retort—First pay the sailors the honest value of their labour. When you have made it as well worth their while to serve you, as to work for other employers, you will have no more difficulty than others have in obtaining their services. To this there is no logical answer except "I will not:" and as people are now not only ashamed, but are not desirous, to rob the labourer of his hire, impressment is no longer advocated. Those who attempt to force women into marriage by closing all other doors against them, lay themselves open to a similar retort. If they mean what they say, their opinion must evidently be, that men do not render the married condition so desirable to women, as to induce them to accept it for its own recommendations.... And here, I believe, is the clue to the feelings of those men, who have a real antipathy to the equal freedom of women. I believe they are afraid, not lest women should be unwilling to marry, for I do not think that anyone in reality has that apprehension; but lest they should insist that marriage should be on equal conditions.... And truly, if this consequence were necessarily incident to marriage, I think that the apprehension would be very well founded. I agree in thinking it probable that few women, capable of anything else, would, unless under an irresistible *entrainement*,[94] rendering them for the time insensible to anything but itself, choose such a lot, when any other means were open to them of filling a conventionally honourable place in life: and if men are determined that the law of marriage shall be a law of despotism, they are quite right, in point of mere policy, in leaving to women only Hobson's choice.[95] But, in that case, all that has been done in the modern world to relax the chain on the minds of women, has been a mistake. They never should have been allowed to receive a literary education. Women who read, much more women who write, are, in the existing constitution of things, a contradiction and a disturbing element: and it was wrong to bring women up with any acquirements but those of an odalisque,[96] or of a domestic servant.

---

92 Latin: therefore.
93 Forced conscription to the British navy.
94 French: training.
95 A "choice" with only one option; named after Thomas Hobson (1545–1631), renowned for his "take it or leave it" attitude.
96 Concubine or female sex slave; a member of a harem.

Thomas Hughes
from *The Manliness of Christ* (1879)

Social reformer and Christian socialist Thomas Hughes (1822–96) authored the popular *Tom Brown's Schooldays* (1857). Educated at Rugby under Thomas Arnold (see Education) and at Oxford, he idealized a public-school education in which older boys modelled sportsmanship and "manliness" to younger students. A barrister and politician, he was called to the bar in 1847 and served as MP for Lambeth and Frome. In 1848, he joined the Christian Socialists, a movement sympathetic to workers, though he had served as a special constable to patrol the Chartist rally on Kennington Common earlier that same year. With Frederick Denison Maurice (see Education) and other Christian Socialists, he co-founded London's Working Men's College (1854) and taught law, boxing, and Bible classes before serving as principal (1872–83).

In *The Manliness of Christ* (1879), Hughes extols Christian manliness by asserting that "Christ's whole life on earth was the ... example of true manliness—the setting forth in living act and word what man is meant to be."

Part 4: The Call of Christ

"Sound, thou trumpet of God! come forth, great cause, to array us!
King and leader, appear! thy soldiers sorrowing seek thee."
A. Clough.[97]

At last the good news for which they had been longing comes to the expecting nation. A voice is heard in the lonely tracts beyond Jordan[98]—the route along which the caravans of pilgrims from Galilee passed so often, to and from the feasts at Jerusalem—proclaiming that the kingdom of heaven is at hand.[99] The news is soon carried to the capital, and from Jerusalem and all Judæa, and all the region round about Jordan, the people go out to hear it; and, when they have heard it, are baptized in crowds, eagerly claiming each for himself a place in this kingdom....[100] It spreads northward also, and the despised Galileans from lake shore and half pagan cities flock down to hear it for themselves, and the simplest and bravest souls amongst them, such as Andrew and Simon Peter, to attach themselves to the preacher.[101] From the highways and lake cities it pierces the Galilean valleys, and comes to the ears of Jesus, in the carpenter's cottage at Nazareth.

---

97 Arthur Hugh Clough, *The Bothie of Tober-na-Vuolich* (1848).
98 The voice of John the Baptist: John 1:28.
99 Matthew 3:2.
100 Matthew 3:5–6.
101 John 1:40–41.

He, too, is moved by the call, and starts for the Jordan.... May we not also fairly conjecture that, on his way to Bethabara,[102] to claim his place in the national confession and uprising,[103] He must have had moments of rejoicing that the chief part in the great drama seemed likely after all to be laid on another? As a rule, the more thoroughly disciplined and fit a man may be for any really great work, the more conscious will he be of his own unfitness for it.... It is only the zeal of the half-instructed when the hour of a great deliverance has come at last—of those who have had a glimpse of the glory of the goal, but have never known or counted the perils of the path which leads to it—which is ready with the prompt response, "Yes—we can drink of the cup; we can be baptized with the baptism."[104]

But in Christ, after the discipline of those long waiting years, there was no ambition, no self-delusion. He had measured the way, and counted the cost, of lifting his own people and the world out of bondage to visible things and false gods, and bringing them to the only Father of their spirits, into the true kingdom of their God. He must, indeed, have been well enough aware how infinitely more fit for the task He Himself was than any of his own brethren in the flesh, with whom He was living day by day, or of the men of Nazareth with whom He had been brought up. But He knew also that the same voice which had been speaking to him, the same wisdom which had been training him, must have been speaking to and training other humble and brave souls, wherever there were open hearts and ears, in the whole Jewish nation. As the humblest and most guileless of men He could not have assumed that no other Israelite had been able to render that perfect obedience of which He was Himself conscious. And so He may well have hurried to the Jordan in the hope of finding there ... the Messiah, the great deliverer—and of enlisting under his banner, and rendering Him true and loyal service....[105] For, we must remember that Christ could not have heard before He came to Bethabara that John had disclaimed the great title. It was not till the very day before his own arrival that the Baptist had told the questioners from Jerusalem, "I am not He."[106]

But if any such thought had crossed his mind, or hope filled his heart, on the way to the Baptist, it was soon dispelled, and He, left again in his own loneliness, now more clearly than ever before, face to face with the task, before which even the Son of God, appointed to it before the world was, might well quail, as it confronted Him in his frail human body. For John recognizes Him, singles Him out at once, proclaims to the bystanders, "This is He! Behold the Lamb of God! This is He who shall baptize with the fire of God's own Spirit. Here is the deliverer whom all our prophets have foretold.["][107] And by a mysterious outward sign, as well as by the witness in his own heart and conscience, Christ is at once assured of the truth of the Baptist's words—that it is indeed He Himself and no other, and that his time has surely come.[108]

That He now thoroughly realized the fact for the first time, and was startled and severely tried by the confirmation of what He must have felt for years to be probable ... seems the true inference from the gospel narratives. For, although as soon as the full truth breaks upon Him He accepts the mission and work to which God is calling Him, and speaks with authority to the Baptist, "Suffer it to be so now,"[109] yet the im-

---

102 John the Baptist baptized Jesus beyond the Jordan at Bethabara: John 1:28.
103 Lifting up.
104 Matthew 20:22–23; Mark 10:38–39.
105 The messiah, or "anointed one," was the prophesied rescuer and redeemer of the Jews; Christians believe that Jesus is the messiah.
106 John 1:19–20.
107 Matthew 3:11; John 1:29.
108 John 1–2; the sign is "the Spirit descending from heaven like a dove."
109 Matthew 3:15.

mediate effect of the call is to drive Him away into the wilderness, there in the deepest solitude to think over once again, and for the last time to wrestle with and master, the tremendous disclosure.[110] And the story of the temptation which immediately follows ... is invaluable for the light which it casts, not only on this crisis of his life, but before and after—on the history of the world's redemption, and the method by which that redemption is to be accomplished, the part which each individual man and woman is called to play in it.

For Christ's whole life on earth was the assertion and example of true manliness—the setting forth in living act and word what man is meant to be, and how he should carry himself in this world of God's,—one long campaign, in which "the temptation"[111] stands out as the first great battle and victory. The story has depths in it which we can never fathom, but also clear, sharp lessons which he who runs may read, and no man can master too thoroughly. We must follow Him reverently into the wilderness, where He flies from the crowds who are pressing to the Baptist, and who to-morrow will be thronging around Him, if He goes back amongst them, after what the Baptist has said about Him to-day.

Day after day in the wilderness the struggle goes on in his heart. He is faint from insufficient food in those solitudes, and with bodily weakness the doubts grow in strength and persistence, and the tempter is always at his side, soliciting Him to end them once for all, by one act of self-assertion.... There are mocking voices whispering again as of old, but more scornfully and keenly, in his ear, "Are you really the Messiah, the Son of God, so long looked for? What more proof have you to go upon than you have had for these many years, during which you have been living as a poor peasant in a Galilean village? ... This sign of a descending dove, and a voice which no one has heard but yourself? ... [A]t least for the sake of others if not for your own sake, put this conviction to the proof, here, at once.... Command these stones to become bread, and see whether they will obey you. Cast yourself down from this height. If you are what you think, your Father's angels will bear you up. Then, after they have borne you up, you may go on with some reasonable assurance that your claim is not a mere delusion, and that you will not be leading these poor men whom you call your brethren to misery and destruction."[112]

And when neither long fasting and weakness, or natural doubt, distrust, impatience, or the most subtle suggestions of the tempter, can move his simple trust in his Father, or wring from Him one act of self-assertion, the enemy changes front and the assault comes from another quarter. "You may be right," the voices seem now to be saying; "you may not be deceived, or dreaming, when you claim to be the Son of God, sent to redeem this fair world.... That may be your origin, and that your work. But ... you have no experience or knowledge of the methods or powers which sway men, and establish and maintain these kingdoms of the world, the glory of which you are beholding.... You have only to say the word, and you may use and control these methods and powers as you please.... Your time is short, and you have already wasted much of it, standing shivering on the brink, and letting the years slip by in that cottage at Nazareth. The wisest of your ancestors acknowledged and used them, and spread his kingdom from the river to the Great Sea. Why should you reject them?"[113]

---

110 Matthew 3:14–17, 4.
111 The temptation of Jesus in the wilderness: Matthew 4:1–11; Mark 1:12–13; Luke 4:1–13.
112 The Devil's first suggestion is that Jesus turn stones into bread, for he had been fasting (Matthew 4:3–4; Luke 4:3–4); the Devil also suggests that Jesus cast himself from a great height to see whether he is rescued by angels (Matthew 4:5–7; Luke 4:9–12).
113 The additional temptation is that Jesus become the earthly king of all men (Matthew 4:8–10; Luke 4:5–8).

This, very roughly and inadequately stated, is some shadow of the utmost part or skirt, as it were, of the trial-crisis, lasting forty days, through which Christ passed from his private to his public career.... At the end of that time He has fairly mastered and beaten down every doubt as to his call, every tempting suggestion to assert Himself, or to accept or use any aid in establishing his Father's kingdom which does not clearly bear his Father's stamp and seal on the face of it. In the strength of this victory He returns from the desert, to take up the burden which has been laid on Him, and to set up God's kingdom in the world by the methods which He has learned of God Himself—and by no other.

Thus in following the life of Christ up to this point, so far as we have any materials, we have found its main characteristic to be patience—a resolute waiting on God's mind. I have asked you to test in every way you can, whether this kind of patience does not constitute the highest ideal we can form of human conduct, is not in fact the noblest type of true manliness. Pursue the same method as to this isolated section of that life, the temptation, which I readily admit has much in it that we cannot understand. But take the story simply as you find it ... and see whether you can detect any weakness, any flaw, in the perfect manliness of Christ under the strain of which it speaks—whether He does not here also realize for us the most perfect type of manliness in times of solitary and critical trial....

There is scarcely any life of first-rate importance to the world in which we do not find a crisis corresponding to this, but the nearest parallel must be sought amongst those men, the greatest of their kind, who have founded or recast one of the great religions of the world. Of these (if we except the greatest of all, Moses) Mohammed is the only one of whose call we know enough to speak.[114] Whatever we may think of him and the religion he founded, we shall all probably admit that he was at any rate a man of the rarest courage. In his case, too, it is only at the end of long and solitary vigils in the desert that the vision comes which seals him for his work. The silver roll is unfolded before his eyes, and he who holds it bids him read therein the decrees of God, and tells him, "Thou art the prophet of God, and I his angel."[115]

He is unmanned by the vision, and flies trembling to his wife, whose brave and loving counsel, and those of his friends and first disciples, scarcely keep him from despair and suicide.

I would not press the parallel further than to remark that Christ came out of the temptation with no human aid ... serene and resolute from that moment for the work to which God had called Him.

It remains to follow his life in action, and to scrutinize its special characteristics there. And again I would ask you to sift every step thoroughly for yourselves, and see whether it will not bear the supreme crucial test from first to last. Apply that test, therefore, without scruple or limitation in respect of this special quality of manliness, from which we started on our inquiry. I have admitted, and admit again, frankly and at once, that if the life will not stand the test throughout, in every separate action and detail, the Christian hypothesis breaks down. For we may make allowances for the noblest and bravest men, for Moses and Elijah and St. Paul, for Socrates and Luther and Mohammed,[116] and every other great prophet, but we can make none for the perfect Son of man and Son of God. His life must stand the test under all circumstances, and at every moment, or the ground breaks through under our feet, and God

---

114 Moses, Old Testament prophet who frees the Israelites from Egypt and leads them to the promised land; Muhammad (c. 570–632), prophet and founder of Islam.
115 For an account of the Prophet Muhammad's call, see Ishaq's *Sirat Rasul Allah*.
116 Elijah, Old Testament prophet; St. Paul (d. c. 64) or Paul the Apostle, Christian missionary; Socrates (469–399 BCE), Greek philosopher; Martin Luther (1483–1546), German founder of Protestantism.

has not revealed Himself in man to men, or redeemed the world by the methods in which Christendom has believed for nineteen hundred years.

William Thomas Stead
from "The Maiden Tribute of Modern Babylon"[117] (1885)

Social-purity activist William Thomas Stead (1849–1912) edited the *Pall Mall Gazette* (1883–90), inaugurating the "new journalism," which emphasized interviews, bold headlines, tantalizing leading articles, and "government by journalism." Previously, as editor of the *Northern Echo* (1871–80), he had embraced Liberal causes, including universal suffrage, education, collective bargaining, an eight-hour day for coal miners, and the repealing of the Contagious Diseases Acts. Also a spiritualist, peace activist, and Salvation Army supporter, Stead ghost-wrote William Booth's *In Darkest England and the Way Out* (1890; see Condition of England). He died on the *Titanic* en route to an American peace conference.

For the "Maiden Tribute," his exposé of London child prostitution, Stead went undercover to prove the ease of procuring a 13-year-old virgin prostitute. The series secured passage of the 1885 Criminal Law Amendment Act, raising girls' age of consent from 13 to 16; however, Stead was convicted of abduction and served three months in prison. He accepted this penalty but defied any shameful implications by wearing his prison uniform on each anniversary of his imprisonment.

A Child of Thirteen Bought for £5[118]

Let me conclude the chapter of horrors by one incident, and only one of those which are constantly occurring in those dread regions of subterranean vice in which sexual crime flourishes almost unchecked. I can personally vouch for the absolute accuracy of every fact in the narrative.

At the beginning of this Derby week,[119] a woman, an old hand in the work of procuration, entered a brothel in —— st. M——, kept by an old acquaintance, and opened negotiations for the purchase of a

---

117 In Part 1, Stead explains this reference to the Maiden Tribute: "In ancient times, if we may believe the myths of Hellas, Athens, after a disastrous campaign, was compelled by her conqueror to send once every nine years a tribute to Crete of seven youths and seven maidens. The doomed fourteen, who were selected by lot amid the lamentations of the citizens, returned no more. The vessel that bore them to Crete unfurled black sails as the symbol of despair, and on arrival her passengers were flung into the famous Labyrinth of Daedalus, there to wander about blindly until such time as they were devoured by the Minotaur, a frightful monster, half man, half bull, the foul product of an unnatural lust." The "Modern Babylon" of the title is London.
118 This section of "The Maiden Tribute" appeared in the *Pall Mall Gazette*, 6 July 1885: 6.
119 The week of the Epsom Derby, an annual horse race, which occurs in June every year.

maid.[120] One of the women who lodged in the house had a sister as yet untouched. Her mother was far away, her father was dead.... The child was between thirteen and fourteen, and after some bargaining it was agreed that she should be handed over to the procuress for the sum of £5. The maid was wanted, it was said, to start a house with, and there was no disguise on either side that the sale was to be effected for immoral purposes. While the negotiations were going on, a drunken neighbour came into the house, and so little concealment was then used, that she speedily became aware of the nature of the transaction. So far from being horrified at the proposed sale of the girl, she whispered eagerly to the seller, "Don't you think she would take our Lily? I think she would suit." Lily was her own daughter, a bright, fresh-looking little girl, who was thirteen years old last Christmas. The bargain, however, was made for the other child, and Lily's mother felt she had lost her market.

The next day, Derby Day as it happened, was fixed for the delivery of this human chattel. But as luck would have it, another sister of the child who was to be made over to the procuress heard of the proposed sale. She was living respectably in a situation, and on hearing of the fate reserved for the little one she lost no time in persuading her dissolute sister to break off the bargain. When the woman came for her prey the bird had flown. Then came the chance of Lily's mother. The brothel-keeper sent for her, and offered her a sovereign for her daughter. The woman was poor, dissolute, and indifferent to everything but drink. The father, who was also a drunken man, was told his daughter was going to a situation. He received the news with indifference, without even inquiring where she was going to. The brothel-keeper having thus secured possession of the child, then sold her to the procuress in place of the child whose sister had rescued her from her destined doom for £5—£3 paid down and the remaining £2 after her virginity had been professionally certified. The little girl, all unsuspecting the purpose for which she was destined, was told that she must go with this strange woman to a situation.[121] The procuress, who was well up to her work, took her away, washed her, dressed her up neatly, and sent her to bid her parents good-bye. The mother was so drunk she hardly recognized her daughter. The father was hardly less indifferent. The child left her home, and was taken to the woman's lodging in A—— street.

The first step had thus been taken. But it was necessary to procure the certification of her virginity—a somewhat difficult task, as the child was absolutely ignorant of the nature of the transaction which had transferred her from home to the keeping of this strange, but apparently kind-hearted woman. Lily was a little cockney[122] child, one of those who by the thousand annually develop into the servants of the poorer middle-class. She had been at school, could read and write, and although her spelling was extraordinary, she was able to express herself with much force and decision. Her experience of the world was limited to the London quarter in which she had been born.... The poor child was full of delight at going to her new situation, and clung affectionately to the keeper who was taking her away—where, she knew not.

The first thing to be done after the child was fairly severed from home was to secure the certificate of virginity without which the rest of the purchase-money would not be forthcoming. In order to avoid trouble she was taken in a cab to the house of a midwife, whose skill in pronouncing upon the physical evidences of virginity is generally recognized in the profession. The examination was very brief and completely satisfactory. But the youth, the complete innocence of the girl, extorted pity even from the

---

120 A virgin.
121 A job for wages.
122 A born Londoner.

hardened heart of the old abortionist. "The poor little thing," she exclaimed. "She is so small, her pain will be extreme. I hope you will not be too cruel with her"—as if to lust when fully roused the very acme[123] of agony on the part of the victim has not a fierce delight. To quiet the old lady the agent of the purchaser asked if she could supply anything to dull the pain. She produced a small phial of chloroform. "This," she said, "is the best. My clients find this much the most effective." The keeper took the bottle, but unaccustomed to anything but drugging by the administration of sleeping potions, she would infallibly have poisoned the child had she not discovered by experiment that the liquid burned the mouth when an attempt was made to swallow it. £1 1s. was paid for the certificate of virginity—which was verbal and not written—while £1 10s. more was charged for the chloroform, the net value of which was probably less than a shilling. An arrangement was made that if the child was badly injured Madame would patch it up to the best of her ability, and then the party left the house.

From the midwife's the innocent girl was taken to a house of ill fame, No. —, P—— street, Regent-street, where, notwithstanding her extreme youth, she was admitted without question. She was taken up stairs, undressed, and put to bed, the woman who bought her putting her to sleep. She was rather restless, but under the influence of chloroform she soon went over. Then the woman withdrew. All was quiet and still. A few moments later the door opened, and the purchaser entered the bedroom. He closed and locked the door. There was a brief silence. And then there rose a wild and piteous cry—not a loud shriek, but a helpless, startled scream like the bleat of a frightened lamb. And the child's voice was heard crying, in accents of terror, "There's a man in the room! Take me home; oh, take me home!"

* * * * * *

And then all once more was still.

That was but one case among many, and by no means the worst. It only differs from the rest because I have been able to verify the facts. Many a similar cry will be raised this very night in the brothels of London, unheeded by man, but not unheard by the pitying ear of Heaven—

> For the child's sob in the darkness curseth deeper
> Than the strong man in his wrath.[124]

Two Stories from Life[125]

In melancholy contrast to the story of Annie —— is the story of another Annie, a London girl of singularly interesting countenance and pleasing manner.... She was about fifteen years of age, and at the time when I saw her had only been on the streets for a few weeks. Her story, as she told it me with the utmost simplicity and unreserve, was as follows:—

> It was about two months since I was seduced. A friend of mine, Jane B——, met me one evening
> in the street near our house, and asked me if I would go for a walk with her. I said yes, and she

---

123 Height.
124 Elizabeth Barrett Browning, "The Cry of the Children" (1843).
125 The following three sections of "The Maiden Tribute" appeared in the *Pall Mall Gazette*, 7 July 1885: 2–5.

proposed to come and have an ice at the very restaurant in which we are now sitting. "It is such a famous shop for ices," she said, "and perhaps we shall see my uncle." I did not know her uncle, nor did I think anything about it, but I walked down to Leicester-square to the restaurant. She asked me to come upstairs to a sitting-room, where we had some ices and some cake. After a time a gentleman came in, whom she said was her uncle; but I found out afterwards he was no more her uncle than I was. He asked us to have some wine and something to eat, and we sat eating and drinking. I had never tasted wine before, but he pressed it on me, and I took one glass and then another, until I think I had four glasses. My head got very queer, and I hardly knew what I did. Then my friend said, "Annie, you must come upstairs now." "What for?" I said. "Never mind what for," she said; "you will get lots of money." My head was queer; I did not care what I did, but I remember thinking that it was after no good this going upstairs. She insisted, however, and I went upstairs. The man she called her uncle followed us. She began to undress me. "What are you doing that for?" I said. "You shan't undress me. I don't want to be undressed here." I struggled, and then everything went dizzy. I remember nothing more till I woke and found that I had been undressed and put in bed. The man was in bed with me. I screamed, and begged him to go away. He paid no heed to me, and began to hurt me dreadfully. "Keep quiet, you silly girl," said ——, who stood by the bed; "you will get lots of money." Oh, I was frightened, and the man hurt me so much! But I could do nothing. When it was all over the man gave her £4. She gave me half and kept the other half for herself, as her pay for getting me seduced. I do not know who the man was, and I have never seen him since.

Of course it is obvious that this story rests solely on the authority of the child herself. But there was no reason to question its accuracy. She told me her story very simply in the presence of a friend. It was perfectly natural, and the girl's remembrance of the way in which she had been ruined was very clear. She seemed a girl of excellent disposition, a Sunday scholar,[126] and of refined manners, and with a sweetness of expression unusual in her class.

Her companion, a young girl of thirteen, was a child of much greater character and resolution, who, I am glad to say, is now in good hands in the country. Her story was as follows:—

One night a girl I knew came and spoke to me. "Will you come and see a gentleman?" she said. "Me see a gentleman—what do you mean?" said I. "Oh, I forgot," she says; "will you come and take a walk?" I had no objection, so we went for a walk. After a while, she proposed we should go into a house in P—— street and get something to eat. We went in, and after we had been there a little time in came a gentleman. He sat down and talked a bit, and then my friend says, "Take off your things, Lizzie." "No, I won't," I said. "Why should I take off my things?" "Don't be a fool," says she, "and do as I tell you, you will get lots of money;" and she began to undress me. I objected, but she was older than I, and stronger, and the man took her side. "Now," she said after she had undressed me, "get into bed with you." "What for?" says I, for I had no idea what she meant. "Do as I tell you, you little fool, or I will knock you[r] head off you. This gentleman will give you lots of money, pounds and pounds, if you are good; but he won't give you a penny if you are stupid." And she half forced

---

126 A child who could not attend school during the week, but who took advantage of free Sunday schools at the local church to become literate.

me, half persuaded me, to get into bed. Then the gentleman got into bed. I did not know what he wanted. I was very frightened, and was crying bitterly. Then he began to hurt me, and I yelled at the top of my voice. Madame who kept the house heard me scream, and she came running up. "Vot is you a doin to that von leetle girl?" she asked. "Nothing," said the man; "she has only run a pin into her foot;" and my friend whispered, "Only keep quiet and you shall have it all. I will give you all the money. But mind you won't get off, no matter how you scream." Madame went away, and the man finished me. He gave me £3. My friend took half and gave me £1 10s.

Lizzie, who told me the above story, is a mere child, thirteen years old last June. Her mother was dead. Her father was a foreman in a City warehouse. She is a girl of great energy and restlessness, affectionate, and I believe she is now doing well. Both of these girls, after being seduced, went on the streets occasionally. It is the first step which costs, and after having lost their virtue, they argued that they might now and then add to their scanty earnings by the easily acquired gold to be earned in the brothel.

A Firm of Procuresses

The recruiting for the brothel is by no means left to occasional and irregular agents. It is a systematized business. Mesdames X. and Z., procuresses, London, is a firm whose address is not to be found in "The Post Office Directory." It exists, however, and its operations are in full swing at this moment. Its members have made the procuration of virgins their speciality. The ordinary house of ill-fame recruits its inmates occasionally by purchase, by contract, by force, or by fraud, but as a rule the ordinary brothel keeper relies for the staple of her commodities upon those who have already been seduced. To oblige a customer they will procure a maid, in many cases passing off as virgins those who had long before bade farewell to the estate of maidenhood.... These are, however, but the tricks of the trade, which in no way concern the object of the present inquiry. The difference between the firm of Mesdames X. and Z. and the ordinary keeper of an introducing house is that the procuring of maids (which in the case of the latter is occasional) is the constant occupation of their lives. They do nothing else. They keep no house of ill-fame. One of the members of this remarkable firm lives in all the odour of propriety if not of sanctity with her parents; the other, who has her own lodgings, nominally holds a position of trust and of influence in the establishment of a well-known firm in Oxford-street. These things, however, are but as blinds. Their real work, to which they devote every day in the week, is the purveying of maidens to an extensive and ever-widening circle of customers. The office of the firm is at ——, ——place, the lodgings of the junior partner, where letters and telegrams are sent and orders received, and the necessary correspondence conducted.... I am thus precise in giving details not only because the firm is only one of several which have hitherto escaped the attention of the social observer, but because the very existence of such an organized business for the procuration of virgins has been stoutly denied by those who are believed to know what is going on....

An Interview with the Firm

I had a long conversation with Mesdames X. and Z. on a subsequent day, as to their business—the way in which it was carried on, and the facility with which they were able to procure subjects. The members of the firm were very sociable and communicative, and in the course of the evening they gave me a good idea of the whole art and mystery of procuration....

"I was told the other day," said I, by way of opening the conversation, "that the demand for maidenheads[127] has rather fallen away of late, owing to the frauds of the procurers. The market has been glutted with vamped-up virgins,[128] of which the supply is always in excess of the demand, and there are fewer inquiries for the genuine article."

"That is not our experience," said the senior partner, a remarkable woman, attractive by the force of her character in spite of the ghastliness of her calling, compared to which that of the common hangman is more honourable. "We do not know anything about vamped virgins. Nor, with so many genuine maids to be had for the taking, do I think it worth while to manufacture virgins. I should say the market was looking up and the demand increasing. Prices may perhaps have fallen, but that is because our customers give larger orders. For instance, Dr. ——, one of my friends who used to take a maid a week at £10, now takes three a fortnight at from £5, to £7 each."

"What!" I exclaimed; "do you actually supply one gentleman with seventy fresh maids every year?"

"Certainly," said she; "and he would take a hundred if we could get them. But he is so very particular. He will not take a shop-girl, and he always must have a maid over sixteen."

"A Flame Which Shall Never Be Extinguished"[129]

The report of our Secret Commission, it is now evident, has produced an effect unparalleled in the history of journalism.... We knew that we had forged a thunderbolt; but even we were hardly prepared for the overwhelming impression which it has produced on the public mind. The great monopoly of railway bookstalls that bears the name of one of the members of an Administration which has just declared in favour of amending the law to deal with the criminals we have exposed, forbade the sale of the most convincing demonstration of the necessity for such legislation.[130] This helped us somewhat by reducing a demand which we were still utterly unable to meet. In view of the enormous result that has followed the simple setting forth of a few of the indisputable facts which the public has hitherto been afraid to face, we are filled with a new confidence and a greater hope. With all humility we feel tempted to exclaim with the martyr RIDLEY, "Be of good cheer, for we have this day lighted up such a flame in England as I trust in GOD shall never be extinguished."[131]

---

127 Virgins.
128 False virgins: to vamp is to serve up something old as new.
129 This section of "The Maiden Tribute" appeared in the *Pall Mall Gazette*, 8 July 1885: 1; the quotation refers to Philip Schaff, *The Person of Christ: The Miracle of History. With a Reply to Strauss and Renan, and A Collection of Testimonies of Unbelievers* (1865).
130 William Henry Smith (1825–91), founder of the still-extant W.H. Smith stationers and Conservative MP. The *Pall Mall Gazette* was not sold at W.H. Smith stands while "The Maiden Tribute" was being published, as Smith thought the content too lurid. The Criminal Law Amendment Act of 1885 raised the age of consent to 16 from 13, regulated brothels, and made it an offence to abduct girls under 18 for sexual acts, to allow underage sex, and to prostitute girls through use of force, fraud, or drugs.
131 John Foxe, *Acts and Monuments* (1563), which depicts the burning of Protestant martyrs Bishop Nicholas Ridley and Bishop Hugh Latimer.

We have been most fortunate, not only in our supporters, but even more so in our assailants. The evil seems to unite with the good in order to increase to the uttermost the dynamic effect of our revelation. When we learned by whom the attempt to hide these crimes from the eye of the public was headed in Parliament and in the press,[132] we took courage. Next to the honour of heading a cause in which we have the enthusiastic support of the best men, we covet nothing so much as that of having to face the strenuous opposition of the worst.... As for the threats of criminal prosecution in which some even more foolish than the rest of their fellows have thought fit to indulge, that is the one thing of all others which those who shriek for silence most dread. Surely those simpletons who send down every afternoon to ask if we have been arrested can hardly imagine that the conspirators of silence will create for us such an opportunity of publicity as would be afforded by a trial, in which, as a distinguished correspondent writes, we might subpœna[133] almost half the Legislature in order to prove the accuracy of our revelations. Mrs. JEFFERIES pleaded guilty in order to save her noble and Royal patrons from exposure.[134] There would be no such abrupt termination to any proceedings which might be commenced against us, and that is very well known to those who talk this nonsense about prosecuting as criminals those who have been reluctantly driven to expose crimes at which the nation stands aghast. We await the commencement of those talked of proceedings with a composure that most certainly is not shared by those whom in such an extremity we should be compelled to expose in the witness-box.

... It is the "men of the world" who cry out—the accomplices of the criminals and the apologists for the offences which we have exposed. If we had only committed these crimes instead of exposing them not one word would have been said. This is, perhaps, the most fatal sign of the corruption which has eaten into the heart of our luxurious society. In reading the report which we continue to-day, we feel as if our Commissioners "had stirred up Hell To heave its lowest dreg-fiends uppermost, In fiery whirls of slime;"[135] but not all the damnable crew on whose deeds they have shed so lurid a light—no, not even the great London Minotaur himself[136]—that portentous incarnation of lust and wealth—fill us with such sorrow and shame as are occasioned by the attitude of some decent people who, while admitting the truth of all these horrors, would have them continue for ever rather than that their ears should be shocked by hearing of the horrors which others have to endure. That surely is the lowest depth yet fathomed by human selfishness....

---

132 Possibly a reference to Charles Hopwood, an outspoken opponent of the amendment. More libertarian than Liberal, he believed in "freedom—freedom from being made good or better as well as freedom from worse oppression; freedom from state control; freedom from the tyranny of the multitude, as well as from fussy, meddlesome legislation" (The *Times*, 17 Oct. 1904: 4).

133 Issue a written order for a person to appear in court.

134 Mary Jefferies, child procuress who, in 1883, pleaded guilty to charges of keeping a disorderly house to avoid outing her powerful clients and being sentenced on worse charges; her clients included politicians and aristocrats, such as Belgium's King Leopold II.

135 Elizabeth Barrett Browning, *Aurora Leigh* (1856).

136 Stead had earlier used this term to describe wealthy brothel-goers: "The maw of the London Minotaur is insatiable, and none that go into the secret recesses of his lair return again."

Mona Caird
from "Marriage" (1888)

[Alice] Mona Caird (1854–1932), New Woman novelist and critic, caused an outcry in the press when she published a critique of marriage in the *Westminster Review* (August 1888). Other essays by Caird critiqued the patriarchal system and promoted women's education, suffrage, and equal access to divorce. Caird's fiction—including *The Wing of Azrael* (1889), *The Daughters of Danaus* (1894), and *The Stones of Sacrifice* (1915)—embraced feminist, pacifist, anti-vivisectionist, and anti-eugenic causes.

In "Marriage," published in the *Westminster Review*, Caird argues that "the present form of marriage ... is a vexatious failure." In a striking example of the "new journalism," the *Daily Telegraph* invited readers to weigh in on the question, "Is Marriage a Failure?" Between 9 August and 29 September 1888, 27,000 people responded, an indication of the subject's volatility and topicality. As Annie S. Swan wrote, Caird's article resembled "a flaming bomb"; the debate was eclipsed only by the Whitechapel ("Jack the Ripper") murders of 1888.

It is not difficult to find people mild and easy-going about religion, and even politics may be regarded with wide-minded tolerance; but broach social subjects, and English men and women at once become alarmed and talk about the foundations of society and the sacredness of the home! Yet the particular form of social life, or of marriage, to which they are so deeply attached, has by no means existed from time immemorial; in fact, modern marriage, with its satellite ideas, only dates as far back as the age of Luther.[137] Of course the institution existed long before, but our particular mode of regarding it can be traced to the era of the Reformation,[138] when commerce, competition, the great *bourgeois* class, and that remarkable thing called "Respectability," also began to arise.

Before entering upon the history of marriage, it is necessary to clear the ground for thought upon this subject by a protest against the careless use of the words "human nature," and especially "woman's nature." History will show us, if anything will, that human nature has an apparently limitless adaptability, and that therefore no conclusion can be built upon special manifestations which may at any time be developed. Such development must be referred to certain conditions, and not be mistaken for the eternal law of being. With regard to "woman's nature," concerning which innumerable contradictory dogmas are held, there is so little really known about it, and its power of development, that all social philosophies are more or less falsified by this universal though sublimely unconscious ignorance....

There is a strange irony in this binding of women to the evil results in their own natures of the restrictions and injustice which they have suffered for generations. We chain up a dog to keep watch over our

---

137 Martin Luther (1483–1546), German theological reformer whose influential writings prompted the Protestant Reformation.
138 The sixteenth-century Reformation, in which religious reformers such as Martin Luther and John Calvin (1509–64) repudiated late-medieval Roman Catholic practices to found Protestantism.

home; we deny him freedom, and in some cases, alas! even sufficient exercise to keep his limbs supple and his body in health. He becomes dull and spiritless, he is miserable and ill-looking, and if by any chance he is let loose, he gets into mischief and runs away. He has not been used to liberty or happiness, and he cannot stand it.

Humane people ask his master: "Why do you keep that dog always chained up?"

"Oh! he is accustomed to it; he is suited for the chain; when we let him loose he runs wild."

So the dog is punished by chaining for the misfortune of having been chained, till death releases him.... We chain, because we *have chained*. The dog must not be released, because his nature has adapted itself to the misfortune of captivity.

He has no revenge in his power; he must live and die, and no one knows his wretchedness. But the woman takes her unconscious vengeance, for she enters into the inmost life of society. *She* can pay back the injury with interest. And so she does, item by item. Through her, in a great measure, marriage becomes what Milton calls "a drooping and disconsolate household captivity,"[139] and through her influence over children she is able to keep going much physical weakness and disease which might, with a little knowledge, be readily stamped out; she is able to oppose new ideas by the early implanting of prejudice; and, in short, she can hold back the wheels of progress, and send into the world human beings likely to wreck every attempt at social reorganization that may be made, whether it be made by men or by gods.[140]

Seeing, then, that the nature of women is the result of their circumstances, ... no protest can be too strong against the unthinking use of the term "woman's nature." An unmanageable host of begged questions, crude assertions, and unsound habits of thought are packed into those two hackneyed words.

Having made this protest, we propose to take a brief glance at the history of marriage, then to consider marriage at the present day, and finally to discuss the marriage of the future.... The first era that bears closely upon our subject is the matriarchal age, to which myths and folk-lore, in almost all countries, definitely point. The mother was the head of the family, priestess, and instructress in the arts of husbandry. She was the first agriculturist, the first herbalist, the initiator (says Karl Pierson)[141] of all civilization.... The family knew only one parent: the mother; her name was transmitted, and property—when that began to exist—was inherited through her, and her only. A woman's indefeasible right to her own child of course remained unquestioned, and it was not until many centuries later that men resorted to all kinds of curious devices with a view of claiming authority over children, which was finally established by force, entirely irrespective of moral right....

During the mother-age, some men of the tribe became wandering hunters, while others remained at home to till the soil. The hunters, being unable to procure wives in the woods and solitudes, used to make raids upon the settlements and carry off some of the women. This was the origin of our modern idea of

---

139 John Milton, *The Doctrine and Discipline of Divorce, Restored to the Good of Both Sexes from the Bondage of Canon Law and Other Mistakes to Christian Freedom* (1643).

140 Author's note: With regard to the evil effects of ignorance in the management of young children, probably few people realize how much avoidable pain is endured, and how much weakness in after-life is traceable to the absurd traditional modes of treating infants and children.

The current ideas are incredibly stupid; one ignorant nurse hands them on to another, and the whole race is brought up in a manner that offends, not merely scientific acumen, but the simplest common-sense.

141 Statistician and eugenics proponent Karl Pearson (1857–1936) founded the Men's and Women's Club in 1885 as a place for open debate about sexual relations; for his views on matriarchy, see, for example, "Evidence of Mother-Right" (1890).

possession in marriage. The woman became the property of the man, his own by right of conquest. Now the wife is his own by right of law....[142]

The transition period from the mother-age to the father-age was long and painful. It took centuries to deprive the woman of her powerful position as head of the family.... Of this long struggle we find many traces in old legends, in folklore, and in the survival of customs older than history. Much later, in the witch-persecutions of the Middle Ages,[143] we come upon the remnants of belief in the woman's superior power and knowledge, and the determination of man to extinguish it.[144] The awe remained in the form of superstition, but the old reverence was changed to antagonism....

During the transition period, capture-marriages, of course, met with strenuous opposition from the mother of the bride, not only as regarded the high-handed act itself, but also in respect to the changes relating to property which the establishment of father-rule brought about....

On the spread of Christianity and the ascetic doctrines of its later teachers, feminine influence received another check. "Woman!" exclaims Tertullian with startling frankness, "thou art the gate of hell!"[145] This is the key-note of the monastic age. Woman was an ally of Satan, seeking to lead men away from the paths of righteousness.... We have a century of almost universal corruption, ushering in the period of the Minne-singers[146] and troubadours, or what is called the age of chivalry.[147] In spite of a licentious society, this age has given us the precious germ of a new idea with regard to sex-relationship, for art and poetry now began to soften and beautify the cruder passion, and we have the first hint of a distinction which can be quite clearly felt between love as represented by classical authors and what may be called modern, or romantic, love.... This nobler sentiment, when developed and still further inwoven with ideas of modern growth, forms the basis of the ideal marriage, which is founded upon a full attraction and expression of the whole nature.

But this development was checked, though the idea was not destroyed, by the Reformation. It is to Luther and his followers that we can immediately trace nearly all the notions that now govern the world with regard to marriage. Luther ... placed marriage on the lowest possible platform, and, as one need scarcely add, he did not take women into counsel in a matter so deeply concerning them. In the age of chivalry the marriage-tie was not at all strict, and our present ideas of "virtue" and "honour" were practically non-existent. Society was in what is called a chaotic state; there was extreme licence on all sides, and although the standard of morality was far severer for the woman than for the man, still she had more or less liberty to give herself as passion dictated, and society tacitly accorded her a right of choice in matters of love. But Luther ignored all the claims of passion in a woman; in fact, she had no

---

142 Under the English law of coverture, a married woman became subject to her husband's authority. In *Commentaries on the Laws of England* (1765–69), eighteenth-century legal scholar William Blackstone defined coverture as a position in which "the very being or legal existence of the woman is suspended upon marriage," when she and her husband become "one person in law." As a result, married women could not own property, sign contracts, make wills, or determine how or where their children would be raised.

143 Witch hunts to identify people (often women) who were supposedly witches emerged in the Middle Ages as part of the church's denunciation of heretics. Witch trials began around 1300 and continued for several hundred years, peaking from 1580 to 1630.

144 Author's note: *Sex-Relations in Germany*. By Karl Pierson.

145 Tertullian, *De Cultu Feminarum* (c. 200).

146 Twelfth- to fourteenth-century German lyrical poets and singers who wrote and sang about courtly love.

147 The European Middle Ages. The idea of chivalry as the honourable behaviour expected of knights peaked in the twelfth and thirteenth centuries.

recognized claims whatever; she was not permitted to object to any part in life that might be assigned her; ... —her *rôle* was one of duty and of service; she figured as the legal property of a man, the safeguard against sin, and the victim of that vampire "Respectability" which thenceforth was to fasten upon, and suck the life-blood of all womanhood.

... Hypocrisy became a household god; true passion was dethroned, and with it poetry and romance; the commercial spirit, staid and open-eyed, entered upon its long career, and began to regulate the relations of the sexes. We find a peculiar medley of sensuality and decorum: the mercenary spirit entering into the idea of marriage, women were bought and sold as if they were cattle, and were educated, at the same time, to strict ideas of "purity" and duty, to Griselda-like[148] patience under the severest provocation. Carried off by the highest bidder, they were gravely exhorted to be moral, to be chaste, and faithful and God-fearing, serving their lords in life and in death.... With the growth of the commercial system, of the rich burgher class,[149] and of all the ideas that thrive under the influence of wealth when divorced from mental cultivation, the status of women gradually established itself upon this degrading basis, and became fixed more and more firmly as the *bourgeois* increased in power and prosperity....

Luther in destroying the religious sanctity of marriage destroyed also the idea of spiritual union which the religious conception implied; he did his utmost to deprive it of the elements of real affection and sympathy, and to bring it to the very lowest form which it is capable of assuming. It was to be regarded merely as a means of avoiding general social chaos; as a "safeguard against sin;" and the wife's position—unless human laws have some supernatural power of sanctification—was the most completely abject and degraded position which it is possible for a human being to hold.

That Luther did not observe the insult to womanhood of such a creed is not to be wondered at, since the nineteenth century has scarcely yet discovered it. Of course from such ideas spring rigid ideas of wifehood. Woman's chastity becomes the watch-dog of man's possession. She has taken the sermon given to her at the time of her purchase deeply to heart, and chastity becomes her chief virtue. If we desire to face the matter honestly, we must not blink the fact that this virtue has originally no connection with the woman's own nature; it does *not* arise from the feelings which protect individual dignity. The quality, whatever be its intrinsic merits, has attained its present mysterious authority and rank through man's monopolizing jealousy, through the fact that he desired to "have and to hold"[150] one woman as his exclusive property, and that he regarded any other man who would dispute his monopoly as the unforgivable enemy. From this starting-point the idea of a man's "honour" grew up, creating the remarkable paradox of a moral possession or attribute, which could be injured by the action of some other person than the possessor. Thus also arose woman's "honour," which was lost if she did not keep herself solely for her lord, present or to come. Again, we see that *her* honour has reference to someone other than herself, though in course of time the idea was carried further, and has now acquired a relation with the woman's own moral nature, and a still firmer hold upon the conscience. However valuable the quality, it certainly did not take its rise from a sense of self-respect in woman, but from the fact of her subjection to man.

---

148 A medieval and Renaissance character noted for her patience and fidelity, Griselda first appeared in Giovanni Boccaccio's *Decameron* (c. 1348–53).
149 Those who lived in burghs, boroughs, or towns with municipal rights; similar to the French bourgeois.
150 Marriage service, *Book of Common Prayer*.

While considering the development of this burgher age, one must not forget to note the concurrence of strict marriage and systematic or legalized prostitution. The social chaos of the age of chivalry was exchanged for comparative order, and there now arose a hard-and-fast line (far more absolute than had existed before in Germany) between two classes of women: those who submitted to the yoke of marriage on Luther's terms, and those who remained on the other side of the great social gulf, subject also to stringent laws, and treated also as the property of men (though not of *one* man). We now see completed our own way of settling the relations of the sexes. The factors of our system are: respectability, prostitution, strict marriage, commercialism, unequal moral standard for the two sexes, and the subjection of women.

In this brief sketch we have not dwelt upon the terrible sufferings of the subject sex through all the changes of their estate; to do so in a manner to produce realization would lead us too far afield and would involve too many details. Suffice it to say that the cruelties, indignities, and insults to which women were exposed are (as every student of history knows) hideous beyond description. In Mongolia there are large cages in the market-place wherein condemned prisoners are kept and starved to death. The people collect in front of these cages to taunt and insult the victims as they die slowly day by day before their eyes. In reading the history of the past, and even the literature of our own day, it is difficult to avoid seeing in that Mongolian market-place a symbol of our own society, with its iron cage, wherein women are held in bondage, suffering moral starvation, while the thoughtless gather round to taunt and to insult their lingering misery.... The pitiful cry of Elsie in *The Golden Legend* has had many a repetition in the hearts of women age after age—

> Why should I live? Do I not know
> The life of woman is full of woe!
> Toiling on, and on, and on,
> With breaking heart, and tearful eyes,
> And silent lips, and in the soul
> The secret longings that arise
> Which this world never satisfies![151]

So much for the past and its relation to the present. Now we come to the problem of to-day. This is extremely complex. We have a society ruled by Luther's views on marriage; we have girls brought up to regard it as their destiny; and we have, at the same time, such a large majority of women that they cannot all marry, even (as I think Miss Clapperton[152] puts it) if they had the fascinations of Helen of Troy and Cleopatra[153] rolled into one. We find, therefore, a number of women thrown on the world to earn their own living in the face of every sort of discouragement.... It is folly to inveigh against mercenary marriages, however degrading they may be, for a glance at the position of affairs shows that there is no reasonable alternative. We cannot ask every woman to be a heroine and choose a hard and thorny path when a

---

151 From Arthur Sullivan's 1886 cantata (with lyrics by Joseph Bennett), based on Henry Wadsworth Longfellow's 1851 poem.
152 Author's note: *Scientific Meliorism*. By Jane Hume Clapperton.
153 According to Greek legend, Helen's beauty prompted the Trojan War: when she abandoned her Greek husband (Menelaus) for her Trojan lover (Paris), Menelaus rallied support for war on Troy; immortalized by Shakespeare, Egyptian queen Cleopatra achieved fame as Julius Caesar's lover and Mark Antony's wife.

comparatively smooth one, (as it seems), offers itself, and when the pressure of public opinion urges strongly in that direction. A few higher natures will resist and swell the crowds of worn-out, underpaid workers, but the majority will take the voice of society for the voice of God, or at any rate of wisdom, and our common respectable marriage— ... will remain, as it is now, the worst, because the most hypocritical, form of woman-purchase....

Bebel[154] is very eloquent upon the sufferings of unmarried women, which must be keen indeed for those who have been prepared for marriage and for nothing else, whose emotions have been stimulated and whose ideas have been coloured by the imagination of domestic cares and happiness. Society, having forbidden or discouraged other ambitions for women, flings them scornfully aside as failures when through its own organization they are unable to secure a fireside and a proper "sphere" in which to practise the womanly virtues. Insult and injury to women is literally the key-note and the foundation of society.

Mrs. Augusta Webster amusingly points out the inconsistencies of popular notions on this subject. She says:—"People think women who do not want to marry unfeminine; people think women who do want to marry immodest; people combine both opinions by regarding it as unfeminine for women not to look forward longingly to wifehood as the hope and purpose of their lives, and ridiculing and contemning any individual woman of their acquaintance whom they suspect of entertaining such a longing. They must wish and not wish; they must by no means give, and they must certainly not withhold, encouragement—and so it goes on, each precept cancelling the last, and most of them negative."[155] There are, doubtless, equally absurd social prejudices which hamper a man's freedom, by teaching girls and their friends to look for proposals, instead of regarding signs of interest and liking in a more wholesome spirit. We shall never have a world really worth living in until men and women can show interest in one another, without being driven either to marry or to forego altogether the pleasure and profit of frequent meeting. Nor will the world be really a pleasant world while it continues to make friendship between persons of opposite sexes well-nigh impossible.... All this false sentiment and shallow shrewdness, with the restrictions they imply, make the ideal marriage—that is, a union prompted by love, by affinity or attraction of nature and by friendship—almost beyond the reach of this generation. While we are on this part of the subject it may be worth while to quote a typical example of some letters written to Max O'Rell on the publication of *The Daughters of John Bull*.[156] One lady of direct language ... explain[s] in gleeful strains that, having been left a small fortune by a relative, she is able to dispense with the society of "the odious creature." ... "At last," another lady bursts forth, "we have some one among us with wit to perceive that the life which a woman leads with the ordinary sherry-drinking, cigar-smoking husband is no better than that of an Eastern slave. Take my own case, which is that of thousands of others in our land. I belong to my lord and master, body and soul; the duties of a housekeeper, upper nurse, and governess are required of me; I am expected to be always at home, at my husband's beck and call. It is true that he feeds me, and that for his own glorification he gives me handsome clothing. It is also true that he does not beat me. For this I ought, of course, to be duly grateful; but I often think what you say on the wife and servant question, and wonder how many of us would like to have the cook's privilege of being able to give warning to leave."

---

154 August Bebel (1840–1913), influential German Socialist leader and author of *Die Frau und der Sozialismus* (1883).
155 Augusta Webster, *A Housewife's Opinions* (1879).
156 Translation of Max O'Rell [Léon Paul Blouet], *Les filles de John Bull* (1884).

If the wife feels thus we may be sure the husband thinks he has his grievances also, and when we place this not exaggerated description side by side with that of the unhappy plight of bored husbands commiserated by Mrs. Lynn Linton,[157] there is no escaping the impression that there is something very "rotten in the state of Denmark."[158] Amongst other absurdities, we have well-meaning husbands and wives harassing one another to death for no reason in the world but the desire of conforming to current notions regarding the proper conduct of married people. These victims are expected to go about perpetually together, as if they were a pair of carriage-horses; to be for ever holding claims over one another, exacting or making useless sacrifices, and generally getting in one another's way. The man who marries finds that his liberty has gone, and the woman exchanges one set of restrictions for another. She thinks herself neglected if the husband does not always return to her in the evenings, and the husband and society think her undutiful, frivolous, and so forth if she does not stay at home alone, trying to sigh him back again.... No wonder that while all this is forbidden we have so many unhappy wives and bored husbands....

Of course there are bright exceptions to this picture of married life, but we are not dealing with exceptions. In most cases, the chain of marriage chafes the flesh, if it does not make a serious wound; and where there is happiness the happiness is dearly bought and is not on a very high plane. For husband and wife are then apt to forget everything in the absorbing but narrow interests of their home, to depend entirely upon one another, to steep themselves in the same ideas, till they become mere echoes, half creatures, useless to the world, because they have run into a groove and have let individuality die. There are few things more stolidly irritating than a very "united" couple. The likeness that may often be remarked between married people is a melancholy index of this united degeneration.

We come then to the conclusion that the present form of marriage—exactly in proportion to its conformity with orthodox ideas—is a vexatious failure.... We are also led to conclude that modern "Respectability" draws its life-blood from the degradation of womanhood in marriage and in prostitution. But what is to be done to remedy these manifold evils? how is marriage to be rescued from a mercenary society, torn from the arms of "Respectability," and established on a footing which will make it no longer an insult to human dignity?

First of all we must set up an ideal, undismayed by what will seem its Utopian impossibility.... The ideal marriage then, despite all dangers and difficulties, should be *free*. So long as love and trust and friendship remain, no bonds are necessary to bind two people together; life apart will be empty and colourless; but whenever these cease the tie becomes false and iniquitous, and no one ought to have power to enforce it.... Even the idea of "duty" ought to be excluded from the most perfect marriage, because the intense attraction of one being for another, the intense desire for one another's happiness, would make interchanges of whatever kind the outcome of a feeling far more passionate than that of duty. It need scarcely be said that there must be a full understanding and acknowledgment of the obvious right of the woman to *possess herself* body and soul, to give or withhold herself body and soul exactly as she wills. The moral right here is so palpable, and its denial implies ideas so low and offensive to human dignity, that no fear of consequences ought to deter us from making this liberty an element

---

157 Novelist and journalist Eliza Lynn Linton (1822–98) wrote on women's issues in the periodical press, often from a conservative standpoint.
158 Shakespeare, *Hamlet* (I.iv.90).

of our ideal, in fact its fundamental principle. Without it, no ideal could hold up its head. Moreover, "consequences" in the long run are never beneficent, where obvious moral rights are disregarded. The idea of a perfectly free marriage would imply the possibility of any form of contract being entered into between the two persons, the State and society standing aside, and recognizing the entirely private character of the transaction.

The economical independence of woman is the first condition of free marriage. She ought not to be tempted to marry, or to remain married, for the sake of bread and butter. But the condition is a very hard one to secure. Our present competitive system, with the daily increasing ferocity of the struggle for existence, is fast reducing itself to an absurdity, woman's labour helping to make the struggle only the fiercer. The problem now offered to the mind and conscience of humanity is to readjust its industrial organization in such a way as to gradually reduce this absurd and useless competition within reasonable limits, and to bring about in its place some form of cooperation, in which no man's interest will depend on the misfortune of his neighbour, but rather on his neighbour's happiness and welfare.... Under improved economical conditions the difficult problem of securing the real independence of women, and thence of the readjustment of their position in relation to men and to society would find easy solution....

The proposed freedom in marriage would of course have to go hand-in-hand with the co-education of the sexes.... Already the good results of this method of co-education have been proved by experiment in America, but we ought to go farther in this direction than our go-ahead cousins have yet gone. Meeting freely in their working-hours as well as at times of recreation, men and women would have opportunity for forming reasonable judgments of character, for making friendships irrespective of sex, and for giving and receiving that inspiring influence which apparently can only be given by one sex to the other.[159] There would also be a chance of forming genuine attachments founded on friendship; ... girls would no longer fancy themselves in love with a man because they had met none other on terms equally intimate, and they would not be tempted to marry for the sake of freedom and a place in life, for existence would be free and full from the beginning.

The general rise in health, physical and moral, following the improvement in birth, surroundings, and training, would rapidly tell upon the whole state of society. Any one who has observed carefully knows how grateful a response the human organism gives to improved conditions, if only these remain constant. We should have to deal with healthier, better equipped, more reasonable men and women, possessing well-developed minds, and hearts kindly disposed towards their fellow-creatures.... With the social changes which would go hand in hand with changes in the status of marriage, would come inevitably many fresh forms of human power, and thus all sorts of new and stimulating influences would be brought to bear upon society.... The action of the man's nature upon the woman's and of the woman's upon the man's, is now only known in a few instances; there is a whole world yet to explore in this direction, and it is more than probable that the future holds a discovery in the domain of spirit as great as that of Columbus[160] in the domain of matter.

---

159 Author's note: Mr. Henry Stanton, in his work on *The Woman Question in Europe*, speaks of the main idea conveyed in Legouvé's *Histoire des Femmes* as follows:—"Equality in difference is its key-note. The question is not to make woman a man, but to complete man by woman."

160 Christopher Columbus (1451–1506), Italian-born Spanish explorer.

With regard to the dangers attending these readjustments, there is no doubt much to be said. The evils that hedge around marriage are linked with other evils, so that movement is difficult and perilous indeed. Nevertheless, we have to remember that we now live in the midst of dangers, and that human happiness is cruelly murdered by our systems of legalized injustice. By sitting still circumspectly and treating our social system as if it were a card-house which would tumble down at a breath, we merely wait to see it fall from its own internal rottenness, and *then* we shall have dangers to encounter indeed! The time has come, not for violent overturning of established institutions before people admit that they are evil, but for a gradual alteration of opinion which will rebuild them from the very foundation. The method of the most enlightened reformer is to crowd out old evil by new good, and to seek to sow the seed of the nobler future where alone it can take root and grow to its full height: in the souls of men and women. Far-seeing we ought to be, but we know in our hearts right well that fear will never lead us to the height of our ever-growing possibility. Evolution has ceased to be a power driving us like dead leaves on a gale; thanks to science, we are no longer entirely blind, and we aspire to direct that mighty force for the good of humanity. We see a limitless field of possibility opening out before us; the adventurous spirit in us might leap up at the wonderful romance of life! We recognize that no power, however trivial, fails to count in the general sum of things which moves this way or that—towards heaven or hell, according to the preponderating motives of individual units. We shall begin, slowly but surely, to see the folly of permitting the forces of one sex to pull against and neutralize the workings of the other, to the confusion of our efforts and the checking of our progress. We shall see, in the relations of men and women to one another, the source of all good or of all evil, precisely as those relations are true and noble and equal, or false and low and unjust. With this belief we shall seek to move opinion in all the directions that may bring us to this "consummation devoutly to be wished,"[161] and we look forward steadily, hoping and working for the day when men and women shall be comrades and fellow-workers as well as lovers and husbands and wives, when the rich and many-sided happiness which they have the power to bestow one on another shall no longer be enjoyed in tantalizing snatches, but shall gladden and give new life to all humanity. That will be the day prophesied by Lewis Morris in *The New Order*—

> When man and woman in an equal union
> Shall merge, and marriage be a true communion.[162]

---

161 Shakespeare, *Hamlet* (III.i.62–63).
162 Lewis Morris, "The New Order," *Songs of Two Worlds* (Second Series, 1874).

John Addington Symonds
from *A Problem in Modern Ethics* (1891)

Trained in classics at Oxford, John Addington Symonds (1840–93) became an author and an early proponent of sexual reform. He wrote almost 40 books, including the *Renaissance in Italy* (seven volumes, 1875–86), his own poetry as well as translations from Greek and Italian, and collections of travel essays. Married in 1864, he nevertheless acknowledged his homosexuality, advocating legal reform and recognition of homosexuality as innate. His death in 1893 ended his early collaboration with Havelock Ellis (see Gender and Sexuality) on *Sexual Inversion* (1897), which includes a case study of Symonds and two privately printed pamphlets on homosexuality that Ellis partly reproduced. Symonds's fragile health, including his tuberculosis, prompted long stays in alpine climates.

His "Suggestions" (from *A Problem in Modern Ethics*) protested against the criminalization of homosexual acts in England, questioning "whether England is still justified in restricting the freedom of adult persons, and rendering certain abnormal forms of sexuality criminal, by any real dangers to society."

~

Chapter 10: Suggestions on the Subject of Sexual Inversion in Relation to Law and Education

1

The laws in force against what are called unnatural offences derive from an edict of Justinian, A.D. 538.[163] The Emperor treated these offences as criminal, on the ground that they brought plagues, famines, earthquakes, and the destruction of whole cities, together with their inhabitants, upon the nations who tolerated them.

2

A belief that sexual inversion is a crime against God, nature, and the State pervades all subsequent legislation on the subject. This belief rests on (1) theological conceptions derived from the Scriptures;[164] (2) a dread of decreasing the population; (3) the antipathy of the majority for the tastes of the minority; (4) the vulgar error that antiphysical[165] desires are invariably voluntary, and the result either of inordinate lust or of satiated appetites.

---

163 In *Novel 77* (538), Justinian I condemns homosexual acts.
164 Leviticus 18:22 and 20:13; Deuteronomy 23:17.
165 Contrary to nature; in this context, homosexual.

3

Scientific investigation has proved in recent years that a very large proportion of persons in whom abnormal sexual inclinations are manifested possess them from their earliest childhood, that they cannot divert them into normal channels, and that they are powerless to get rid of them. In these cases, then, legislation[166] is interfering with the liberty of individuals, under a certain misconception regarding the nature of their offense.

4

Those who support the present laws are therefore bound to prove that the coercion, punishment, and defamation of such persons are justified either (1) by any injury which these persons suffer in health of body or mind, or (2) by any serious danger arising from them to the social organism.

5

Experience, confirmed by scientific observation, proves that the temperate indulgence of abnormal sexuality is no more injurious to the individual than a similar indulgence of normal sexuality.

6

In the present state of over-population, it is not to be apprehended that a small minority of men exercising sterile and abnormal sexual inclinations should seriously injure society by limiting the increase of the human race.

7

Legislation does not interfere with various forms of sterile intercourse between men and women: (1) prostitution, (2) cohabitation in marriage during the period of pregnancy, (3) artificial precautions against impregnation,[167] and (4) some abnormal modes of congress[168] with the consent of the female. It is therefore in an illogical position, when it interferes with the action of those who are naturally sterile, on the ground of maintaining the numerical standard of the population.

8

The danger that unnatural vices, if tolerated by the law, would increase until whole nations acquired them, does not seem to be formidable. The position of women in our civilisation renders sexual relations among us occidentals[169] different from those of any country—ancient Greece and Rome, modern Turkey and Persia—where antiphysical habits have hitherto become endemic.

---

166 Contemporary British law criminalized all homosexual acts: the Buggery Act of 1533 made sodomy punishable by death; the Offences Against the Person Act of 1861 repealed the death sentence in favour of imprisonment for a minimum of ten years; the Labouchere Amendment, part of the Criminal Law Amendment Act of 1885, criminalized all acts of "gross indecency" between men.
167 Birth control.
168 Sexual intercourse.
169 Inhabitants of the Occident, or the West.

9

In modern France, since the promulgation of the Code Napoleon,[170] sexual inversion has been tolerated under the same restrictions as normal sexuality. That is to say, violence and outrages to public decency are punished, and minors are protected, but adults are allowed to dispose as they like of their own persons. The experience of nearly a century shows that in France, where sexual inversion is not criminal *per se*, there has been no extension of it through society. Competent observers, like agents of police, declare that London, in spite of our penal legislation, is no less notorious for abnormal vice than Paris.

10

Italy, by the Penal Code of 1889,[171] adopted the principles of the Code Napoleon on this point. It would be interesting to know what led to this alteration of the Italian law. But it cannot be supposed that the results of the Code Napoleon in France were not fully considered.

11

The severity of the English statutes render them almost incapable of being put in force. In consequence of this the law is not unfrequently evaded, and crimes are winked at.

12

At the same time our laws encourage blackmailing upon false accusation;[172] and the presumed evasion of their execution places from time to time a vile weapon in the hands of unscrupulous politicians, to attack the Government in office. Examples: the Dublin Castle Scandals of 1884, the Cleveland Street Scandals of 1889.[173]

13

Those who hold that our penal laws are required by the interests of society must turn their attention to the higher education. This still rests on the study of the Greek and Latin classics, a literature impregnated with pæderastia.[174] It is carried on at public schools, where young men are kept apart from females, and where homo-sexual vices are frequent. The best minds of our youth are therefore exposed to the influences of a pæderastic literature[175] at the same time that they acquire the knowledge and experience of unnatural practices. Nor is any trouble taken to correct these adverse influences by physiological instruction in the laws of sex.

---

170 The French civil and penal codes introduced by Napoleon between 1804 and 1810 purposefully omitted laws against sodomy.
171 The Italian penal code of 1889 purposefully omitted laws against sodomy.
172 The 1885 Labouchere Amendment was known as the "Blackmailers' Charter."
173 Dublin Castle, the seat of British power in Ireland, was embroiled in scandal when several high-ranking officials and aristocrats were accused of homosexual acts and a male-male brothel's existence was hinted at in the ensuing court cases; Charles Hammond's male-male brothel on Cleveland Street in London was discovered and raided in 1889, but charges were dropped to protect the identity of some of the aristocratic clients, allegedly including Prince Albert Victor, next in line to the throne after his father, the Prince of Wales.
174 Greek: "love of boys"; pederasty refers to a relationship (usually sexual) between a boy and a man that was considered in ancient Greece to be a more spiritual love than that between a man and a woman.
175 Ancient Greek literature.

14

The points suggested for consideration are whether England is still justified in restricting the freedom of adult persons, and rendering certain abnormal forms of sexuality criminal, by any real dangers to society: after it has been shown (1) that abnormal inclinations are congenital,[176] natural, and ineradicable in a large percentage of individuals; (2) that we tolerate sterile intercourse of various types between the two sexes; (3) that our legislation has not suppressed the immorality in question; (4) that the operation of the Code Napoleon for nearly a century has not increased this immorality in France; (5) that Italy, with the experience of the Code Napoleon to guide her, adopted its principles in 1889; (6) that the English penalties are rarely inflicted to their full extent; (7) that their existence encourages blackmailing, and their non-enforcement gives occasion for base political agitation; (8) that our higher education is in open contradiction to the spirit of our laws.[177]

FINIS.

Havelock Ellis
from *Studies in the Psychology of Sex: Sexual Inversion* (1897)

Sexologist (Henry) Havelock Ellis (1859–1939) believed that both sexes could achieve happiness through sexual freedom. Trained in medicine at London's St. Thomas's Hospital, he was licensed by the Society of Apothecaries. A member of the Fellowship of New Life, he served as secretary of the Progressive Association and worked on *Today*, a radical journal. He enjoyed friendships with progressive intellectuals Olive Schreiner, George Bernard Shaw, Eleanor Marx, Edward Carpenter, and Arthur Symons. Ellis's marriage was unconventional: his wife, Edith, pursued lesbian affairs and Ellis himself had intense (though perhaps not sexual) extra-marital relationships with women.

Ellis's series, *Studies in the Psychology of Sex*, started with the 1897 publication of *Sexual Inversion* (a term used to describe homosexuality), a work he planned with poet and homosexual rights advocate John Addington Symonds (see Education, Gender and Sexuality). The work featured case studies of homosexuals and included thinly disguised portraits of Edith Ellis and Symonds.

---

176 Inborn.

177 Author's note: It may not be superfluous to recapitulate the main points of English legislation on this topic. (1) Sodomy is a felony, defined as the carnal knowledge (per anum) of any man or of any woman by a male person; punishable with penal servitude for life as a maximum, for ten years as a minimum. (2) The attempt to commit sodomy is punishable with ten years' penal servitude as a maximum. (3) The commission, in public or private, by any male person with another male person, of "any act of gross indecency," is punishable with two years' imprisonment and hard labour.

Chapter 3: Sexual Inversion in Men

... The next case is interesting as showing the mental and emotional development in a very radical case of sexual inversion.

History XX.—Englishman, of independent means, aged 49. His father and his father's family were robust, healthy, and prolific. On his mother's side, phthisis,[178] insanity, and eccentricity are traceable. He belongs to a large family, some of whom died in early childhood and at birth, while others are normal. He himself was a weakly and highly nervous child, subject to night-terrors and somnambulism, excessive shyness and religious disquietude.

Sexual consciousness awoke before the age of 8, when his attention was directed to his own penis. His nurse, while out walking with him one day, told him that when little boys grow up their penes fall off. The nursery-maid sniggered, and he felt that there must be something peculiar about the penis. He suffered from irritability of the prepuce,[179] and the nurse powdered it before he went to sleep. There was no transition from this to self-abuse.[180]

About the same time he became subject to curious half-waking dreams. In these he imagined himself the servant of several adult naked sailors; he crouched between their thighs and called himself their dirty pig, and by their orders he performed services for their genitals and buttocks, which he contemplated and handled with relish. At about the same period, when these visions began to come to him, he casually heard that a man used to come and expose his person before the window of a room where the maids sat; this troubled him vaguely. Between the age of 8 and 11 he twice took the penis of a cousin into his mouth, after they had slept together; the feeling of the penis pleased him. When sleeping with another cousin, they used to lie with hands outstretched to cover each other's penis or nates.[181] He preferred the nates, but his cousin the penis. Neither of these cousins was homosexual, and there was no attempt at mutual masturbation. He was in the habit of playing with five male cousins. One of these boys was unpopular with the others, and they invented a method of punishing him for supposed offenses. They sat around the room on chairs, each with his penis exposed, and the boy to be punished went around the room on his knees and took each penis into his mouth in turn. This was supposed to humiliate him. It did not lead to masturbation. On one occasion the child accidentally observed a boy who sat next to him in school playing with his penis and caressing it. This gave him a powerful, uneasy sensation. With regard to all these points the subject observes that none of the boys with whom he was connected at this period, and who were exposed to precisely the same influences, became homosexual.

He was himself, from the first, indifferent to the opposite sex. In early childhood, and up to the age of 13, he had frequent opportunities of closely inspecting the sexual organs of girls, his playfellows. These roused no sexual excitement. On the contrary, the smell of the female parts affected him disagreeably. When he once saw a schoolfellow copulating with a little girl, it gave him a sense of mystical horror. Nor did the sight of the male organs arouse any particular sensations. He is, however, of opinion that, living

---

178 Tuberculosis.
179 Foreskin.
180 Masturbation.
181 Buttocks.

with his sisters in childhood, he felt more curious about his own sex as being more remote from him. He showed no effeminacy in his preferences for games or work.

He went to a public school.[182] Here he was provoked by boy friends to masturbate, but, though he often saw the act in process, it only inspired him with a sense of indecency. In his fifteenth year puberty commenced with nocturnal emissions, and, at the same time, he began to masturbate, and continued to do so about once a week, or once a fortnight, during a period of eight months; always with a feeling that that was a poor satisfaction and repulsive. His thoughts were not directed either to males or females while masturbating. He spoke to his father about these signs of puberty, and by his father's advice he entirely abandoned onanism;[183] he only resumed the practice, to some extent, after the age of 30, when he was without male comradeship.

The nocturnal emissions, after he had abandoned self-abuse, became very frequent and exhausting. They were medically treated by tonics such as quinine and strychnine. He thinks this treatment exaggerated his neurosis.

All this time, no kind of sexual feeling for girls made itself felt. He could not understand what his schoolfellows found in women, or the stories they told about wantonness and delight of coitus.

His old dreams about the sailors had disappeared. But now he enjoyed visions of beautiful young men and exquisite statues; he often shed tears when he thought of them. These dreams persisted for years. But another kind gradually usurped their place to some extent. These second visions took the form of the large, erect organs of naked young grooms or peasants. These gross visions offended his taste and hurt him, though, at the same time, they evoked a strong, active desire for possession; he took a strange, poetic pleasure in the ideal form. But the seminal losses which accompanied both kinds of dreams were a perpetual source of misery to him.

There is no doubt that at this time—that is, between the fifteenth and seventeenth years—a homosexual diathesis[184] had become established. He never frequented loose women, though he sometimes thought that would be the best way of combating his growing inclination for males. And he thinks that he might have brought himself to indulge freely in purely sexual pleasure with women if he made their first acquaintance in a male costume, as *débardeuses*, *Cherubino*, court-pages, young halberdiers,[185] as it is only when so clothed that women on the stage or in the ball-room have excited him.

His ideal of morality and fear of venereal infection, more than physical incapacity, kept him what is called chaste. He never dreamed of women, never sought their society, never felt the slightest sexual excitement in their presence, never idealized them. Esthetically, he thought them far less beautiful than men. Statues and pictures of naked women had no attraction for him, while all objects of art which represented handsome males deeply stirred him.

It was in his eighteenth year that an event occurred which he regards as decisive in his development. He read Plato.[186] A new world opened, and he felt that his own nature had been revealed. Next year he

---

182 Originally founded to educate young men for church and public service positions, by the nineteenth century, public schools had become private boarding schools for boys.
183 Masturbation.
184 Susceptibility.
185 French: dock workers; Cherubino is a male page in Mozart's *Le nozze di Figaro* (1786); halberdiers are soldiers bearing halberds, weapons that incorporate both spear and battle-axe.
186 Plato (428/27–348/47 BCE), Greek philosopher.

formed a passionate, but pure, friendship with a boy of 15. Personal contact with the boy caused erection, extreme agitation, and aching pleasure, but not ejaculation. Through four years he never saw the boy naked or touched him pruriently.[187] Only twice he kissed him. He says that these two kisses were the most perfect joys he ever felt.

His father now became seriously anxious both about his health and his reputation. He warned him of the social and legal dangers attending his temperament.[188] But he did not encourage him to try coitus with women. He himself thinks that his own sense of danger might have made this method successful, or that, at all events, the habit of intercourse with women might have lessened neurosis and diverted his mind to some extent from homosexual thoughts.

A period of great pain and anxiety now opened for him. But his neurasthenia[189] increased; he suffered from insomnia, obscure cerebral discomfort, stammering, chronic conjunctivitis,[190] inability to concentrate his attention, and dejection. Meanwhile his homosexual emotions strengthened, and assumed a more sensual character. He abstained from indulging them, as also from onanism, but he was often forced, with shame and reluctance, to frequent places—baths, urinaries, and so forth—where there were opportunities of seeing naked men.

Having no passion for women, it was easy to avoid them. Yet they inspired him with no exact horror. He used to dream of finding an exit from his painful situation by cohabitation with some coarse, boyish girl of the people; but his dread of syphilis stood in the way. He felt, however, that he must conquer himself by efforts of will, and by a persistent direction of his thoughts to heterosexual images. He sought the society of distinguished women. Once he coaxed up a romantic affection for a young girl of 15, which came to nothing, probably because the girl felt the want of absolute passion in his wooing. She excited his imagination, and he really loved her; but she did not, even in the closest contact, stimulate his sexual appetite. Once, when he kissed her just after she had risen from bed in the morning, a curious physical repugnance came over him, attended with a sad feeling of disappointment.

He was strongly advised to marry by physicians. At last he did so. He found that he was potent, and begot several children, but he also found, to his disappointment, that the tyranny of the male genital organs on his fancy increased. Owing to this cause his physical, mental, and moral discomfort became acute. His health gave way.

At about the age of 30, unable to endure his position any longer, he at last yielded to his sexual inclinations. As he began to do this, he also began to regain calm and comparative health. He formed a close alliance with a youth of 19. This *liaison* was largely sentimental, and marked by a kind of etherealized[191] sensuality. It involved no sexual acts beyond kissing, naked contact, and rare involuntary emissions. About the age of 36 he began freely to follow homosexual inclinations. After this he rapidly recovered his health. The neurotic disturbances subsided.

He has always loved men younger than himself. At about the age of 27 he had begun to admire young soldiers. Since he yielded freely to his inclinations the men he has sought are invariably persons of a lower social rank than his own. He carried on one *liaison* continuously for twelve years; it began without

---

187 Sexually.
188 Under English law, sodomy was punishable by death until 1861.
189 Nervous exhaustion.
190 Pink-eye.
191 Spiritual rather than physical.

passion on the friend's side, but gradually grew to nearly equal strength on both sides. He is not attracted by uniforms, but seeks some uncontaminated child of nature.

The methods of satisfaction have varied with the phases of his passion. At first they were romantic and Platonic, when a hand-touch, a rare kiss, or mere presence sufficed. In the second period sleeping side by side, inspection of the naked body of the loved man, embraces, and occasional emissions after prolonged contact. In the third period the gratification became more frankly sensual. It took every shape: mutual masturbation, intercrural coitus, *fellatio, irrumatio*, and occasionally active *pedicatio*;[192] always according to the inclination or concession of the beloved male.

He himself always plays the active, masculine part. He never yields himself to the other, and he asserts that he never has the joy of finding himself desired with ardor equal to his own. He does not shrink from passive *pedicatio*; but it is never demanded of him. Coitus with males, as above described, always seems to him healthy and natural; it leaves a deep sense of well-being, and has cemented durable friendships. He has always sought to form permanent ties with the men whom he has adored so excessively.

He is of medium height, not robust, but with great nervous energy, with strong power of will and self-control, able to resist fatigue and changes of external circumstances.

In boyhood he had no liking for female occupations, or for the society of girls, preferring study and solitude. He avoided games and the noisy occupations of boys, but was only non-masculine in his indifference to sport, was never feminine in dress or habit. He never succeeded in his attempts to whistle. He is a great smoker, and has at times drunk much. He likes riding, skating, and climbing, but is a poor horseman, and is clumsy with his hands. He has no capacity for the fine arts and music, though much interested in them, and is a prolific author.

He has suffered extremely throughout life, owing to his sense of the difference between himself and normal human beings. No pleasure he has enjoyed, he declares, can equal a thousandth part of the pain caused by the internal consciousness of pariahdom.[193] The utmost he can plead in his own defense, he admits, is irresponsibility, for he acknowledges that his impulse may be morbid. But he feels absolutely certain that in early life his health was ruined and his moral repose destroyed owing to the perpetual conflict with his own inborn nature, and that relief and strength came with indulgence. Although he always has before him the terror of discovery, he is convinced that his sexual dealings with men have been thoroughly wholesome to himself, largely increasing his physical, moral, and intellectual energy, and not injurious to others. He has no sense whatever of moral wrong in his actions, and he regards the attitude of society toward those in his position as utterly unjust and founded on false principles.

The next case is, like the foregoing, that of a successful man of letters who also passed through a long period of mental conflict before he became reconciled to his homosexual instincts. He belongs to a family who are all healthy and have shown marked ability in different intellectual departments. He feels certain that one of his brothers is as absolute an invert[194] as himself and that another is attracted to both sexes. I am indebted to him for the following detailed narrative, describing his emotions and experiences in childhood, which I regard as of very great interest, not only as a contribution to the psychology of

---

192 Intercrural means between the legs; fellatio and irrumatio refer to oral sex: irrumatio is the act of the male inserting his penis into the mouth of his sexual partner, while fellatio is the act of taking a penis into the mouth; pedicatio is anal intercourse.
193 Being an outcast.
194 Ellis's term for homosexual.

inversion, but to the embryology[195] of the sexual emotions generally. We here see described, in an unduly precocious and hyperesthetic form, ideas and feelings which, in a slighter and more fragmentary shape, may be paralleled in the early experiences of many normal men and women. But it must be rare to find so many points in sexual psychology so definitely illustrated in a single child. It may be added that the narrative is also not without interest as a study in the evolution of a man of letters; a child whose imagination was thus early exercised and developed was predestined for a literary career.

---

195 Early development.

FAITH AND DOUBT

Introduction
Catherine Harland

Religion was a matter of primary and passionate concern for the Victorians. They energetically examined religious issues in sermons, tracts, spiritual autobiographies, letters, and critical monographs, as well as in their poetry, novels, and visual art. Yet while missionary work expanded and hundreds of new churches were built, religious beliefs were gradually transformed. The controversies that occupied the Victorians were complex and curious, but in their intense debates about such matters as the validity of the 39 Articles of the Church of England, the inspiration of scripture, or the divine nature of Christ, we see Victorian writers attempting both to interrogate the foundations of their faith and to confront the meaning of human life. The challenges to faith—and to a sense of meaning—came from the emerging sciences of geology, astronomy, archaeology, and biology, as well as from the growth of a historical consciousness. In the span of a few decades, people began to feel that their fundamental human identity was in peril, as well as their place in the cosmos.

The majority of Victorians assumed that theirs was a Christian culture. The Church of England was the established (state) church, encompassing a large spectrum of believers. On one end were the Evangelicals (or Low Church), who believed, as did the majority of Dissenters (other Nonconformist denominations such as the Baptists, Methodists, and Congregationalists), in a personal faith centred on the Bible and individual conscience. The Evangelicals led a number of humanitarian reforms such as the abolition of slavery in 1833 and the expansion of missionary work at home and abroad. The High Church wing remained closer to Catholicism, emphasizing ritual, tradition, and the importance of church authority as opposed to the individual conscience. In the middle, the Broad Church party was liberal, inclusive, and intellectually progressive.

Early in the century, many religious people found the Established Church increasingly moribund. Some academic clergy at Oxford responded to what they perceived as a growing theological "liberalism" with "Tracts for the Times," a series of 90 tracts written between 1833 and 1841. Led by John Henry Newman, these writers sought both to reassert the authority of the church in relation to the state and to reinvigorate the church by emphasizing its historical Catholic origins. The movement culminated in the publication of Newman's *Tract 90* in 1841, in which he analyzed some of the 39 Articles of the Church of England that articulate the differences between the Protestant and Catholic churches. His analysis, which was based on the historical context and language in which the articles were framed, shocked readers by showing that the articles could sustain a Roman Catholic interpretation. In his later spiritual autobiography, *Apologia pro Vita Sua* (1864), Newman defended himself by examining the spiritual and intellectual process that had led to his conclusions and ultimately to his conversion to Roman Catholicism in 1845. Although Newman's conversion effectively ended the Oxford Movement, the questions he had raised about how to interpret Protestantism's foundational texts continued to trouble Anglican believers.

Newman's conversion deeply alarmed most Anglicans. In 1829, Catholic emancipation removed political handicaps from non-Anglicans, but the long-standing antagonism between British Catholics and Protestants intensified in the nineteenth century as the numbers of Catholics rose (owing in part to the immigration of Irish labourers) and the Catholic community became revitalized. The distrust of Catholics peaked in 1850 when Pope Pius IX decided to establish Roman Catholic dioceses for the first time since the Reformation and appointed Cardinal Nicholas Wiseman Archbishop of Westminster. Fear of "papal aggression" was both theological and political: a strong Catholic influence threatened Anglican doctrine as well as England as a Protestant country.

While Newman was busy examining the history of the Church, scientific research investigating the history of the earth was well underway. In 1830, Sir Charles Lyell's *Principles of Geology* proved that geological change had happened gradually over eons, thus exploding the chronology of the Old Testament and the commonly held view that the earth was less than 6,000 years old. The public grew increasingly aware of "developmental" theories: Robert Chambers anonymously published his extremely popular *Vestiges of Creation* (1844); in the 1850s the unconventional naturalist Alfred Russel Wallace was at

"Conversions from Rome." *Punch* (13 Dec. 1856): 232.

work on the problem of the transmutation of species. Charles Darwin's *On the Origin of Species* (1859) built on Lyell's work and on the compelling evidence that Darwin had earlier accumulated as a naturalist on the voyage of the *Beagle*. The combined evidence of these sciences had a devastating impact on the faith of many Victorians. Thinking people could no longer imagine themselves at the centre of a stable universe, the happy result of intentional divine creation. Time now stretched back millions of years, and the hopeful belief that humanity represented an immutable species, made "in the image of God" (Genesis 1:27), seemed increasingly delusional. Humans now constituted merely an accidental part of a ruthless natural process. Alfred Tennyson, the poet laureate, read Lyell in 1837. Confronting the implications of these ideas, he voiced the grief, anguish, and fear of a whole generation in his poem "In Memoriam, A.H.H." (1850): "Are God and Nature then at strife, / That Nature lends such evil dreams?" (55.5–6). If whole species perish, might an extinct humanity become merely debris, "blown about the desert dust," or fossils, "seal'd within the iron hills?"(56.19–20).

Yet in spite of the blow that scientific discovery dealt to Victorian faith, over the next few decades liberal theologians and the general public absorbed both the concept and discourse of evolution. For some, it became possible to reconceive history as a providential evolution and Christian doctrine itself as a progressive revelation.

The greater threat to faith came from German historical criticism of the Bible. "The Higher Criticism" erupted into English culture through the 1846 translation by Mary Ann Evans (later to become the novelist George Eliot) of the difficult German of D.F. Strauss's *The Life of Jesus, Critically Examined* (1835). Heretofore, the supernatural dimension of the Bible had simply been assumed. Applying the evidence-based methodology of science, Strauss and other members of the Tübingen school approached each book of the Bible as a historical document by examining the social context in which it was written. Strauss represented Jesus as an ordinary man about whom Messianic stories and myths appropriate to a particular historical moment had developed. He argued that the Gospel stories of Jesus' "supernatural birth … miracles, … resurrection and ascension" contained "eternal truths," but he cast doubt on them as "historical facts" (xxx).

Over the next decades, several works continued the critical process begun by Strauss. In 1860, seven respected Anglicans published the enormously controversial *Essays and Reviews*. By subverting traditional biblical hermeneutics (ways of interpreting the Bible), and insisting on the validity of individual interpretations, the essayists questioned the authority of the Anglican Church. Benjamin Jowett, a distinguished Professor of Greek at Oxford, argued in his essay "On the Interpretation of Scripture" that one should "interpret the Scripture like any other book" (338), using the same inductive method appropriate to the study of Plato or Sophocles to recover the writer's original intentions through a reconstruction of his social context.

Two years later, claiming to have been influenced by the essayists, J.W. Colenso, the Bishop of Natal, in a bizarre application of mathematics to the first five books of the Bible, tried to prove that much of the Mosaic story of the Exodus was literally and statistically impossible. His book, *The Pentateuch and Book of Joshua Critically Examined* (1862), with its fixation on numbers, animal fodder, and sanitation in the desert, outraged both traditional and liberal readers. Here was a bishop on record as saying he did not believe in the literal truth of the Bible. The resulting clash between church and state over Colenso's continuing status in the Church of England was one of many conflicts generated by biblical criticism.

These debates were ferocious in part because the Bible lay at the foundation of Protestant doctrine. A rejection of orthodox belief in the Bible as the divinely inspired, infallible Word of God assaulted the very core of Protestant faith. The damage was cumulative. The scientists had undermined the story of the Creation; if there was no Garden of Eden and no Fall, the related doctrines of Original Sin and the atoning Sacrifice of Christ were also questionable. If Christ's promises might have been the invention of fallible writers, and if, as Matthew Arnold claimed in *Literature and Dogma*, "miracles do not happen" (6.146), what evidence was there for human immortality?

For some Victorians, "the parting with the Christian mythology" was a devastating loss, a "rending asunder of bones and marrow" (Ward 2.317); for others, however, the disintegration of the old faith was liberating. While Tennyson asserted in *In Memoriam* that "there lives more faith in honest doubt ... than in half the creeds" (96.11–12), many still felt a compelling need to find some other goal or purpose to replace their damaged beliefs. The interesting corollary to the disappearance of a miraculous and supernatural Christ—what one novelist called the "disappearance of Jesus into mythologic vapour" (White 54)—was a renewed interest in his human life. In theological circles, this fascination formed the focus of another divisive collection of essays, *Lux Mundi* (1889). In his provocative essay, "The Holy Spirit and Inspiration," the editor Charles Gore justified Christ's limited human knowledge by introducing the concept of *kenosis*, the "self-emptying" (359) of God in the incarnation. Predictable dismay ensued. Many biographies of Christ followed Strauss's *Life*, most notably Ernest Renan's *Vie de Jésus* in 1863, J.R. Seeley's *Ecce Homo* in 1865, F.W. Farrar's *Life of Christ* in 1874, and Thomas Hughes's *The Manliness of Christ* in 1879. All of these works focused on the humanity of Christ. If no longer the divine redeemer of revelation, he could still be retained as an ideal human example.

Among the responses to doubt was the reconstruction of new faiths. Earlier in the century, Thomas Carlyle had confronted the terror of a mechanistic universe controlled by the pleasure/pain calculus of a Utilitarian ethic (the philosophical radicalism of John Stuart Mill and Jeremy Bentham) by offering a paradigm for the personal transformation he believed must accompany social renewal. In his strange and original fiction *Sartor Resartus* (The Tailor Retailored) (1833–34, 1838), Carlyle employs the elaborate metaphor of the Clothes Philosophy to suggest that vital ideas and institutions, including the "mythus" of Christianity (103), were shrouded beneath the outworn garments which had originally manifested them. The visible symbol was now in desperate need of "retailoring"—reinterpretation or renewal—so that the invisible idea might again live.

Carlyle's impulse to penetrate through the hollow forms of religion to reach the original meaning characterizes that of many Victorians who retained a religious sensibility along with a skeptical intellect. Although alienated from Christian orthodoxy, most Victorians continued to believe absolutely in truth, social justice, morality, and progress. Among the alternatives to Christianity was agnosticism, a word coined by T.H. Huxley to describe his own position. Agnosticism took many forms—atheism, rationalism, secular humanism—but most agnostics agreed with Leslie Stephen that "man knows nothing of the Infinite and the Absolute" (860) and should not devise dogmas from hopes. The agnostics had to counter the pervasive fear that the loss of religious faith would mean the collapse of morality. They insisted that it was possible to be profoundly moral without religion; one of their major criticisms of Christian doctrine was that it seemed barbaric, immoral, and unjust. A tyrannical Deity who required a blood sacrifice to appease his wrath and was content to consign the souls he had created to everlasting torment—these were horrifying notions. George Eliot's repudiation of the "perverted moral judgment" of a well-known clergyman's fanatical Calvinism (184) was representative of this argument.

The attempt to preserve Christian ethics and dispense with Christian dogma caused controversy. Auguste Comte's positivism (or religion of humanity) replaced God with humanity as the focus of worship; his plan even included a rationalist "saints" calendar of great men. Matthew Arnold similarly defined religion as "morality touched by emotion" (6.176). But Frances Power Cobbe—one of several women who made major contributions to the religious debates of the century—disagreed with these attitudes, arguing that the agnostics had "failed to construct a morality on the ruins of religion." Responding to Vernon Lee's previously published "Responsibilities of Unbelief" (1883), Cobbe articulated the view of many Victorians confronting nineteenth-century rationalism by insisting that one should seek God not in external nature but in the internal realm of conscience and intuition. Her own life's work in humanitarian reform points to a general reorientation of belief: as Beatrice Webb remarked a generation later, "we all make the service of mankind the leading doctrine of our lives" (149). Vernon Lee's bold view was that educated agnostics had a further duty to share their reasons for unbelief with the working classes and to help them fashion a vital secular creed to replace the old one.

Carlyle's response to the anxiety and despair of a potentially godless universe was to endorse Goethe's dictum—"do the Duty which lies nearest"—and find what work you can do. George Eliot also considered it imperative to cultivate an ethics of sympathy that would encourage understanding and tolerance. The protagonist of Mary Ward's immensely popular and compelling novel, *Robert Elsmere* (1888), similarly abandons the pulpit for humanitarian work in the inner city. In this character, Ward traces the process of gradual erosion and subsequent reinterpretation of faith that had gone on throughout the century: the human community would become the source of meaning in an increasingly secular age.

Works Cited and Further Reading

Arnold, Matthew. *The Complete Prose Works of Matthew Arnold*. Ed. R.H. Super. 11 vols. Ann Arbor: U of Michigan P, 1960-77. Print.

Chadwick, Owen, ed. *The Victorian Church*. 2 vols. New York: Oxford UP, 1966, 1971. Print.

Cockshut, A.O.J. *The Unbelievers: English Agnostic Thought, 1840-1890*. London: Collins, 1964. Print.

Eliot, George. "Evangelical Teaching: Dr. Cumming." *Essays of George Eliot*. Ed. Thomas Pinney. New York: Columbia UP, 1963. Print.

Gore, Charles. *Lux Mundi: A Series of Studies in the Religion of the Incarnation*. London: John Murray, 1890. Print.

Jasper, David, and T.R. Wright, eds. *The Critical Spirit and the Will to Believe: Essays in Nineteenth-Century Literature and Religion*. London: Macmillan, 1989. Print.

Jowett, Benjamin. "On the Interpretation of Scripture." *Essays and Reviews*. London: John W. Parker and Son, 1860. Print.

Reardon, Bernard. *Religious Thought in the Nineteenth Century*. Cambridge: Cambridge UP, 1966. Print.

Shea, Victor, and William Whitla, eds. *Essays and Reviews: The 1860 Text and Its Reading*. Charlottesville: U of Virginia P, 2000. Print.

Stephen, Leslie. "An Agnostic's Apology." *The Fortnightly Review* (June 1876): 840-60. Print.

Strauss, David Friedrich. *The Life of Jesus, Critically Examined*. Trans. George Eliot. London: Swann Sonnenchein, 1906. Print.

Tennyson, Alfred. *The Poems of Tennyson*. Ed. Christopher Ricks. London: Longman, 1969. Print.

Ward, Mary Augusta. *Robert Elsmere*. 3 vols. London: Macmillan, 1888. Print.

Webb, Beatrice. *My Apprenticeship*. Cambridge: Cambridge UP, 1979. Print.

White, William Hale. *The Autobiography of Mark Rutherford and Mark Rutherford's Deliverance*. London: Libris, 1988. Print.

Thomas Carlyle
from *Sartor Resartus:*[1] *The Life and Opinions of Herr Teufelsdröckh*[2] (1833–34)

Thomas Carlyle (1795–1881), influential social critic, helped to introduce German literature and philosophy to England in the early to mid-nineteenth century. His debt to Germanic thought found expression in his translations of Goethe and in his Teutonic phrasings known as "Carlylese." *Sartor Resartus* (1833–34, 1838) and *The French Revolution: A History* (1837) established him as the "Sage of Chelsea," though he depended financially on lectures, including *On Heroes, Hero-Worship, and the Heroic in History* (1841). In *Chartism* (1841) and *Past and Present* (1843), Carlyle attacked laissez-faire policies and sympathized with the working poor. He rejected democracy for leadership by elites in *Latter-Day Pamphlets* (1850) and other works. His almost 40-year marriage to Jane Welsh Carlyle gained notoriety after his death, when J.A. Froude (see Education) published material suggesting their marital unhappiness.

In these semi-autobiographical selections from *Sartor Resartus*, Carlyle describes the progress of the protagonist, Professor Teufelsdröckh, as he moves through a spiritual crisis and "Fire-baptism" into moral resolution; the work was heavily influential among other Victorians who experienced similar crises of faith.

Chapter 7: The Everlasting No

Under the strange nebulous envelopment, wherein our Professor Teufelsdröckh has now shrouded himself, no doubt but his spiritual nature is nevertheless progressive, and growing: for how can the "Son of Time," in any case, stand still? We behold him, through those dim years, in a state of crisis, of transition: his mad Pilgrimings, and general solution into aimless Discontinuity, what is all this but a mad Fermentation; wherefrom the fiercer it is, the clearer product will one day evolve itself?

Such transitions are ever full of pain: thus the Eagle when he moults is sickly; and, to attain his new beak, must harshly dash off the old one upon rocks. What Stoicism soever our Wanderer, in his individual acts and motions, may affect, it is clear that there is a hot fever of anarchy and misery raging within; coruscations of which flash out: as, indeed, how could there be other? Have we not seen him disappointed, bemocked of Destiny, through long years? All that the young heart might desire and pray for has been denied.... Ever an "excellent Passivity"; but of useful, reasonable Activity, essential to the former as Food

---

1 Latin: the tailor retailored.
2 German: God-born devil's dung; the main character of *Sartor Resartus*.

to Hunger, nothing granted: till at length, in this wild Pilgrimage, he must forcibly seize for himself an Activity, though useless, unreasonable. Alas, his cup of bitterness, which had been filling drop by drop ... runs over,[3] and even hisses over in a deluge of foam.

He himself says once, with more justness than originality: "Man is, properly speaking, based upon Hope, he has no other possession but Hope; this world of his is emphatically the Place of Hope." What, then, was our Professor's possession? We see him, for the present, quite shut out from Hope; looking not into the golden orient, but vaguely all round into a dim copper firmament, pregnant with earthquake and tornado.

Alas, shut-out from Hope, in a deeper sense than we yet dream of! For, as he wanders wearisomely through this world, he has now lost all tidings of another and higher. Full of religion, or at least of religiosity ... he hides not that, in those days, he was wholly irreligious: "Doubt had darkened into Unbelief," says he; "shade after shade goes grimly over your soul, till you have the fixed, starless, Tartarean[4] black." To such readers as have reflected, what can be called reflecting, on man's life, and happily discovered, in contradiction to much Profit-and-Loss Philosophy,[5] speculative and practical, that Soul is *not* synonymous with Stomach; who understand, therefore, in our Friend's words, "that, for man's well-being, Faith is properly the one thing needful;[6] ... without it, worldlings puke-up their sick existence, by suicide, in the midst of luxury": to such it will be clear that, for a pure moral nature, the loss of his religious Belief was the loss of everything. Unhappy young man! All wounds, the crush of long-continued Destitution, the stab of false Friendship and of false Love, all wounds in thy so genial heart, would have healed again, had not its life-warmth been withdrawn. Well might he exclaim, in his wild way: "Is there no God, then; but at best an absentee God, sitting idle, ever since the first Sabbath, at the outside of his Universe, and *seeing* it go? Has the word Duty no meaning; is what we call Duty no divine Messenger and Guide, but a false earthly Phantasm, made up of Desire and Fear, of emanations from the Gallows and from Doctor Graham's Celestial-Bed?[7] Happiness of an approving Conscience! Did not Paul of Tarsus,[8] whom admiring men have since named Saint, feel that *he* was 'the chief of sinners';[9] and Nero of Rome,[10] jocund in spirit (*wohlgemuth*), spend much of his time in fiddling? Foolish Word-monger and Motive-grinder, who in thy Logic-mill hast an earthly mechanism for the Godlike itself, and wouldst fain grind me out Virtue from the husks of Pleasure,—I tell thee, Nay! To the unregenerate Prometheus Vinctus[11] of a man, it is ever the bitterest aggravation of his wretchedness that he is conscious of Virtue, that he feels himself the victim not of suffering only, but of injustice. What then? Is the heroic inspiration we name Virtue but some Passion; some bubble of the blood, bubbling in the direction others *profit* by? I know not: only this I know, If what thou namest Happiness be our true aim, then are we all astray....["]

---

3   Psalm 23:5: "My cup runneth over."
4   Belonging to Tartarus, the underworld in Greek mythology.
5   Theories of political economy invoked profit and loss, as in Adam Smith's *An Inquiry into the Nature and Causes of the Wealth of Nations* (1776).
6   Luke 10:42.
7   James Graham (1745–94), physician of dubious qualifications who promoted a bed that ostensibly cured infertility.
8   Saul of Tarsus (d. c. 62–4) converted to Christianity and took the name Paul after seeing a vision of Christ resurrected. His letters comprise much of the New Testament.
9   1 Timothy 1:15.
10 Nero Germanicus (37–68), Roman emperor notorious for his excesses.
11 *Prometheus Bound* (c. 470 BCE), a play commonly attributed to Aeschylus.

Thus has the bewildered Wanderer to stand, as so many have done, shouting question after question into the Sibyl-cave of Destiny,[12] and receive no Answer but an Echo. It is all a grim Desert, this once-fair world of his; wherein is heard only the howling of wild beasts, or the shrieks of despairing, hate-filled men; and no Pillar of Cloud by day, and no Pillar of Fire by night,[13] any longer guides the Pilgrim. To such length has the spirit of Inquiry carried him. "But what boots it (*was thut's*)?"[14] cries he: "it is but the common lot in this era.... The whole world is, like thee, sold to Unbelief; their old Temples of the Godhead, which for long have not been rainproof, crumble down; and men ask now: Where is the Godhead; our eyes never saw him?" ...

Meanwhile, under all these tribulations, and temporal and spiritual destitutions, what must the Wanderer, in his silent soul, have endured! "The painfullest feeling," writes he, "is that of your own Feebleness (*Unkraft*); ever, as the English Milton says, to be weak is the true misery.[15] And yet of your Strength there is and can be no clear feeling, save by what you have prospered in, by what you have done. Between vague wavering Capability and fixed indubitable Performance, what a difference! A certain inarticulate Self-consciousness dwells dimly in us; which only our Works can render articulate and decisively discernible. Our Works are the mirror wherein the spirit first sees its natural lineaments. Hence, too, the folly of that impossible Precept, *Know thyself*; till it be translated into this partially possible one, *Know what thou canst work at*.["]

"But for me, so strangely unprosperous had I been, the net-result of my Workings amounted as yet simply to—Nothing. How then could I believe in my Strength, when there was as yet no mirror to see it in? Ever did this agitating, yet, as I now perceive, quite frivolous question, remain to me insoluble: Hast thou a certain Faculty, a certain Worth, such even as the most have not; or art thou the completest Dullard of these modern times? Alas, the fearful Unbelief is unbelief in yourself; and how could I believe? Had not my first, last Faith in myself, when even to me the Heavens seemed laid open, and I dared to love, been all too cruelly belied? The speculative Mystery of Life grew ever more mysterious to me: neither in the practical Mystery had I made the slightest progress, but been everywhere buffeted, foiled, and contemptuously cast-out. A feeble unit in the middle of a threatening Infinitude, I seemed to have nothing given me but eyes, whereby to discern my own wretchedness. Invisible yet impenetrable walls, as of Enchantment, divided me from all living: was there, in the wide world, any true bosom I could press trustfully to mine? O Heaven, No, there was none! I kept a lock upon my lips: why should I speak much with that shifting variety of so-called Friends, in whose withered, vain and too-hungry souls Friendship was but an incredible tradition? ... Now when I look back, it was a strange isolation I then lived in. The men and women around me, even speaking with me, were but Figures.... In the midst of their crowded streets and assemblages, I walked solitary; and (except as it was my own heart, not another's, that I kept devouring) savage also, as the tiger in his jungle.... To me the Universe was all void of Life, of Purpose, of Volition, even of Hostility: it was one huge, dead, immeasurable Steam-engine, rolling on, in its dead indifference, to grind me limb from limb. Oh, the vast, gloomy, solitary Golgotha,[16] and Mill of Death!...["]

---

12 Sibyl of Cumae, female oracle in Greek mythology who lived in a cave.
13 Exodus 13:21.
14 German: what's the point?
15 John Milton, *Paradise Lost* (1667).
16 Aramaic: the skull; the location where Jesus was crucified.

A prey incessantly to such corrosions, might not, moreover, as the worst aggravation to them, the iron constitution even of a Teufelsdröckh threaten to fail? We conjecture that he has known sickness; and, in spite of his locomotive habits, perhaps sickness of the chronic sort. Hear this, for example: "How beautiful to die of broken-heart, on Paper! Quite another thing in practice; every window of your Feeling, even of your Intellect, as it were, begrimed and mud-bespattered, so that no pure ray can enter; a whole Drug shop in your inwards; the fordone soul drowning slowly in quagmires of Disgust!" …

"So had it lasted," concludes the Wanderer, "so had it lasted, as in bitter protracted Death-agony, through long years. The heart within me, unvisited by any heavenly dewdrop, was smouldering in sulphurous, slow-consuming fire…. [S]trangely enough, I lived in a continual, indefinite, pining fear; tremulous, pusillanimous,[17] apprehensive of I knew not what: it seemed as if all things in the Heavens above and the Earth beneath would hurt me; as if the Heavens and the Earth were but boundless jaws of a devouring monster, wherein I, palpitating, waited to be devoured.["]

"Full of such humour, and perhaps the miserablest man in the whole French Capital or Suburbs, was I, one sultry Dog-day,[18] after much perambulation, toiling along the dirty little *Rue Saint-Thomas de l'Enfer*,[19] among civic rubbish enough, in a close atmosphere, and over pavements hot as Nebuchadnezzar's Furnace;[20] whereby doubtless my spirits were little cheered; when, all at once, there rose a Thought in me, and I asked myself: 'What *art* thou afraid of? Wherefore, like a coward, dost thou forever pip[21] and whimper, and go cowering and trembling? Despicable biped! what is the sum-total of the worst that lies before thee? Death? Well, Death; and say the pangs of Tophet[22] too, and all that the Devil and Man may, will or can do against thee! Hast thou not a heart; canst thou not suffer whatsoever it be; and, as a Child of Freedom, though outcast, trample Tophet itself under thy feet, while it consumes thee? Let it come, then; I will meet it and defy it!' And as I so thought, there rushed like a stream of fire over my whole soul; and I shook base Fear away from me forever. I was strong, of unknown strength; a spirit, almost a god. Ever from that time, the temper of my misery was changed: not Fear or whining Sorrow was it, but Indignation and grim fire-eyed Defiance.["]

"Thus had the EVERLASTING NO (*das ewige Nein*) pealed authoritatively through all the recesses of my Being, of my ME; and then was it that my whole ME stood up, in native God-created majesty, and with emphasis recorded its Protest. Such a Protest, the most important transaction in Life, may that same Indignation and Defiance, in a psychological point of view, be fitly called. The Everlasting No had said: 'Behold, thou are fatherless, outcast, and the Universe is mine (the Devil's)'; to which my whole Me now made answer: '*I* am not thine, but Free, and forever hate thee!'["]

"It is from this hour that I incline to date my Spiritual New-birth, or Baphometic[23] Fire-baptism; perhaps I directly thereupon began to be a Man."

---

17 Lacking bravery.
18 The hottest days of late summer.
19 French: St. Thomas of Hell Street.
20 Daniel 3.
21 To make small noises, like those of a bird.
22 A place of torment and punishment; Jeremiah 19.
23 Refers to idols supposedly worshipped by the Knights Templar, a group formed during the Crusades to protect Christ's burial place.

Chapter 8: Centre of Indifference

Though, after this "Baphometic Fire-baptism" of his, our Wanderer signifies that his Unrest was but increased; as, indeed, "Indignation and Defiance," especially against things in general, are not the most peaceable inmates; yet can the Psychologist[24] surmise that it was no longer a quite hopeless Unrest; that henceforth it had at least a fixed centre to revolve round. For the fire-baptised soul, long so scathed and thunder-riven, here feels its own Freedom.... [W]e might say, if in that great moment, in the *Rue Saint-Thomas de l'Enfer*, the old inward Satanic School was not yet thrown out of doors, it received peremptory judicial notice to quit....

Accordingly, if we scrutinise these Pilgrimings well, there is perhaps discernible henceforth a certain incipient method in their madness. Not wholly as a Spectre does Teufelsdröckh now storm through the world; at worst as a spectre-fighting Man, nay who will one day be a Spectre-queller. If pilgriming restlessly to so many "Saints' Wells," and ever without quenching of his thirst, he nevertheless finds little secular wells, whereby from time to time some alleviation is ministered. In a word, he is now, if not ceasing, yet intermitting to "eat his own heart;" and clutches round him outwardly on the NOT-ME for wholesomer food. Does not the following glimpse exhibit him in a much more natural state?

"Towns also and Cities, especially the ancient, I failed not to look upon with interest. How beautiful to see thereby, as through a long vista, into the remote Time; to have, as it were, an actual section of almost the earliest Past brought safe into the Present, and set before your eyes! There, in that old City, was a live ember of Culinary Fire put down, say only two thousand years ago; and there, burning more or less triumphantly, with such fuel as the region yielded, it has burnt, and still burns, and thou thyself seest the very smoke thereof. Ah! and the far more mysterious live ember of Vital Fire was then also put down there; and still miraculously burns and spreads; and the smoke and ashes thereof (in these Judgment-Halls and Church-yards), and its bellows-engines (in these Churches), thou still seest; and its flame, looking out from every kind countenance, and every hateful one, still warms thee or scorches thee.["]

"Of Man's Activity and Attainment the chief results are aeriform,[25] mystic, and preserved in Tradition only: such are his Forms of Government, with the Authority they rest on; his Customs, or Fashions both of Cloth-habits and of Soul-habits; much more his collective stock of Handicrafts, the whole Faculty he has acquired of manipulating Nature: all these things, as indispensable and priceless as they are, cannot in any way be fixed under lock and key, but must flit, spirit-like, on impalpable vehicles, from Father to Son; if you demand sight of them, they are nowhere to be met with. Visible Ploughmen and Hammermen there have been, ever from Cain and Tubalcain downwards:[26] but where does your accumulated Agricultural, Metallurgic, and other Manufacturing SKILL lie warehoused? It transmits itself on the atmospheric air, on the sun's rays (by Hearing and by Vision); it is a thing aeriform, impalpable, of quite spiritual sort. In like manner, ask me not, Where are the LAWS; where is the GOVERNMENT? In vain wilt thou go to Schönbrunn, to Downing Street, to the Palais Bourbon;[27] thou findest nothing there but brick or stone

---

24   Someone who examines questions pertaining to the spirit.
25   Like air; that is, intangible.
26   Ploughmen and Hammermen are farmers and metalworkers respectively; Cain, son of Adam and Eve, was the first farmer; Tubalcain was the first metalworker. See Genesis 4:2, 22.
27   Schönbrunn Palace and Gardens are in Vienna, Austria; Downing Street is where the British prime minister, chief whip, and Chancellor of the Exchequer live; the Palais Bourbon became the meeting place of the French National Assembly

houses, and some bundles of Papers tied with tape. Where, then, is that same cunningly-devised almighty GOVERNMENT of theirs to be laid hands on? Everywhere, yet nowhere: seen only in its works, this too is a thing aeriform, invisible; or if you will, mystic and miraculous. So spiritual (*geistig*) is our whole daily Life: all that we do springs out of Mystery, Spirit, invisible Force; only like a little Cloud-image, or Armida's Palace,[28] air-built, does the Actual body itself forth from the great mystic Deep.["]

"Visible and tangible products of the Past, again, I reckon-up to the extent of three: Cities, with their Cabinets and Arsenals; then tilled Fields, to either or to both of which divisions Roads with their Bridges may belong; and thirdly—Books. In which third truly, the last invented, lies a worth far surpassing that of the two others. Wondrous indeed is the virtue of a true Book. Not like a dead city of stones, yearly crumbling, yearly needing repair; more like a tilled field, but then a spiritual field: like a spiritual tree, let me rather say, it stands from year to year, and from age to age (we have Books that already number some hundred-and-fifty human ages); and yearly comes its new produce of leaves ... every one of which is talismanic and thaumaturgic,[29] for it can persuade men. O thou who art able to write a Book, which once in the two centuries or oftener there is a man gifted to do, envy not him whom they name City-builder, and inexpressibly pity him whom they name Conqueror or City-burner! Thou too art a Conqueror and Victor: but of the true sort, namely over the Devil: thou too hast built what will outlast all marble and metal, and be a wonder-bringing City of the Mind, a Temple and Seminary and Prophetic Mount, whereto all kindreds of the Earth will pilgrim.—Fool! why journeyest thou wearisomely, in thy antiquarian fervor, to gaze on the stone pyramids of Geeza, or the clay ones of Sacchara?[30] These stand there, as I can tell thee, idle and inert, looking over the Desert, foolishly enough, for the last three-thousand years: but canst thou not open thy Hebrew BIBLE, then, or even Luther's Version[31] thereof?"

No less satisfactory is his sudden appearance not in Battle, yet on some Battle-field; which, we soon gather, must be that of Wagram;[32] so that here, for once, is a certain approximation to distinctness of date. Omitting much, let us impart what follows:

"Horrible enough! A whole Marchfeld[33] strewed with shell-splinters, cannon-shot, ruined tumbrils,[34] and dead men and horses; stragglers still remaining not so much as buried. And those red mould heaps: ay, there lie the Shells of Men, out of which all the Life and Virtue has been blown; and now are they swept together, and crammed-down out of sight, like blown Egg-shells!—Did Nature, when she bade the Donau bring down his mould-cargoes from the Carinthian and Carpathian Heights,[35] and spread them out here into the softest, richest level,—intend thee, O Marchfeld, for a corn-bearing Nursery,

---

(then the Council of the Five Hundred) in 1795.
28   The palace where Armida enchants Rinaldo in Torquato Tasso's *Jerusalem Delivered* (1581) became synonymous with an imaginary pleasure palace.
29   Able to perform miracles.
30   Giza is home to the Great Pyramid of Khufu (Cheops), the pyramids of Khafre and Menkaure, and the Sphinx; Sakkara is the location of Djoser's pyramid, the first known structure made solely from stone, and many other tombs from Egyptian history.
31   Martin Luther translated the Bible into German in an influential sixteenth-century edition.
32   In the Battle of Wagram (1809), during the Napoleonic Wars, France under Napoleon Bonaparte defeated Austria under Archduke Charles.
33   During the Battle of Marchfeld (Dürnkrut) (1278), German and Hungarian armies prevented Bohemian expansion.
34   Ammunition carts.
35   The Donau [Danube] River runs through the state of Carinthia's mountains, in Austria, and the Carpathian Mountains to the Black Sea.

whereon her children might be nursed; or for a Cockpit,[36] wherein they might the more commodiously be throttled and tattered? Were thy three broad Highways, meeting here from the ends of Europe, made for Ammunition-wagons, then? Were thy Wagrams and Stillfrieds but so many ready-built Casemates, wherein the house of Hapsburg might batter with artillery, and with artillery be battered? König Ottokar, amid yonder hillocks, dies under Rodolf's truncheon;[37] here Kaiser Franz falls a-swoon under Napoleon's: within which five centuries, to omit the others, how has thy breast, fair Plain, been defaced and defiled! The greensward is torn-up and trampled-down; man's fond care of it, his fruit-trees, hedge-rows, and pleasant dwellings blown-away with gun-powder; and the kind seedfield lies a desolate, hideous Place of Sculls.[38]—Nevertheless, Nature is at work; neither shall these Powder-Devilkins with their utmost devilry gainsay her: but all that gore and carnage will be shrouded in, absorbed into manure; and next year the Marchfeld will be green, nay greener. Thrifty unwearied Nature, ever out of our great waste educing some little profit of thy own,—how dost thou, from the very carcass of the Killer, bring Life for the Living!["]

"What, speaking in quite unofficial language, is the net-purport and upshot of war? To my own knowledge, for example, there dwell and toil, in the British village of Dumdrudge,[39] usually some five-hundred souls. From these, by certain 'Natural Enemies' of the French, there are successively selected, during the French war, say thirty able-bodied men; Dumdrudge, at her own expense, has suckled and nursed them: she has, not without difficulty and sorrow, fed them up to manhood, and even trained them to crafts, so that one can weave, another build, another hammer, and the weakest can stand under thirty stone avoirdupois.[40] Nevertheless, amid much weeping and swearing, they are selected; all dressed in red; and shipped away, at the public charges, some two-thousand miles, or say only to the south of Spain; and fed there till wanted. And now to that same spot, in the south of Spain, are thirty similar French artisans, from a French Dumdrudge, in like manner wending: till at length, after infinite effort, the two parties come into actual juxtaposition; and Thirty stands fronting Thirty, each with a gun in his hand. Straightway the word 'Fire!' is given; and they blow the souls out of one another; and in place of sixty brisk useful craftsmen, the world has sixty dead carcasses, which it must bury, and anew shed tears for. Had these men any quarrel? Busy as the Devil is, not the smallest! They lived far enough apart; were the entirest strangers; nay, in so wide a Universe, there was even, unconsciously, by Commerce, some mutual helpfulness between them. How then? Simpleton! their Governors had fallen-out; and, instead of shooting one another, had the cunning to make these poor blockheads shoot.... In that fiction of the English Smollet, it is true, the final Cessation of War is perhaps prophetically shadowed forth; where the two Natural Enemies, in person, take each a Tobacco-pipe, filled with Brimstone; light the same, and smoke in one another's faces, till the weaker gives in:[41] but from such predicted Peace-Era, what blood-filled trenches, and contentious centuries, may still divide us!"

Thus can the Professor, at least in lucid intervals, look away from his own sorrows, over the many-coloured world, and pertinently enough note what is passing there. We may remark, indeed, that for

---

36 A place where a contest is fought.
37 Stillfried is located near Marchfeld; casemates are protected spaces in a fortress's walls from which defenders can fight off invaders; when he invaded Austria, the Bohemian Ottokar stayed near Stillfried before being killed in the Battle of Marchfeld, where German King Rudolf Habsburg prevailed.
38 Matthew 27:33.
39 A fictional village of Carlyle's invention.
40 Merchandise that is sold by weight.
41 Tobias Smollett, *The Adventures of Ferdinand, Count Fathom* (1753).

the matter of spiritual culture, if for nothing else, perhaps few periods of his life were richer than this. Internally, there is the most momentous instructive Course of Practical Philosophy, with Experiments, going on; towards the right comprehension of which his Peripatetic habits, favorable to Meditation, might help him rather than hinder. Externally, again, as he wanders to and fro, there are, if for the longing heart little substance, yet for the seeing eye sights enough: in these so boundless Travels of his, granting that the Satanic School[42] was even partially kept down, what an incredible knowledge of our Planet, and its Inhabitants and their Works, that is to say, of all knowable things, might not Teufelsdröckh acquire!

"I have read in most Public Libraries," says he, "including those of Constantinople and Samarcand:[43] in most Colleges, except the Chinese Mandarin ones, I have studied, or seen that there was no studying. Unknown Languages have I oftenest gathered from their natural repertory, the Air, by my organ of Hearing; Statistics, Geographics, Topographics came, through the Eye, almost of their own accord. The ways of Man, how he seeks food, and warmth, and protection for himself, in most regions, are ocularly known to me. Like the great Hadrian,[44] I meted-out much of the terraqueous Globe with a pair of Compasses that belonged to myself only.["]

"Of great Scenes why speak? Three summer days, I lingered reflecting, and even composing (*dichtete*), by the Pinechasms of Vaucluse; and in that clear Lakelet moistened my bread. I have sat under the Palm-trees of Tadmor; smoked a pipe among the ruins of Babylon. The great Wall of China[45] I have seen; and can testify that it is of gray brick, coped and covered with granite, and shows only second-rate masonry.—Great Events, also, have not I witnessed? ... All kindreds and peoples and nations dashed together, and shifted and shovelled into heaps, that they might ferment there, and in time unite. The birth-pangs of Democracy, wherewith convulsed Europe was groaning in cries that reached Heaven, could not escape me.["]

"For great Men I have ever had the warmest predilection; and can perhaps boast that few such in this era have wholly escaped me. Great Men are the inspired (speaking and acting) Texts of that divine BOOK OF REVELATIONS, whereof a Chapter is completed from epoch to epoch, and by some named HISTORY; ... Thus did not I, in very early days, having disguised me as tavern-waiter, stand behind the field-chairs, under that shady Tree at Treisnitz by the Jena Highway;[46] waiting upon the great Schiller and greater Goethe;[47] and hearing what I have not forgotten. For——"

——But at this point the Editor recalls his principle of caution, some time ago laid down, and must suppress much. Let not the sacredness of Laurelled,[48] still more, of Crowned Heads, be tampered with. Should we, at a future day, find circumstances altered, and the time come for Publication, then may these glimpses into the privacy of the Illustrious be conceded; which for the present were little better than treacherous, perhaps traitorous Eavesdroppings. Of Lord Byron, therefore, of Pope Pius, Emperor

---

42 Derogatory term for English poets John Keats, Percy Bysshe Shelley, Leigh Hunt, and George Gordon Byron that implies immorality.
43 Constantinople's Imperial Library preserved ancient Greek and Roman texts for a thousand years until it was destroyed in 1204; Samarkand, in what is now Uzbekistan, was renowned for paper production and illustrated manuscripts.
44 Hadrian (76–138), Roman emperor who toured the empire, including Britain (where he built Hadrian's Wall).
45 Vaucluse is a region of France; Tadmor was an ancient Syrian city known for its palm trees; Babylon was the ancient capital of Babylonia; the Great Wall of China was begun in the third century BCE.
46 Trausnitz is a castle in Germany; Jena is a German city.
47 Johann Wolfgang von Goethe (1749–1832) and Johann Christoph Friedrich von Schiller (1759–1805), German poets, dramatists, and scholars.
48 In ancient Greece, laurel wreaths were worn for ceremonies and awarded for victories.

Tarakwang,[49] and the "White Water-roses" (Chinese Carbonari)[50] with their mysteries, no notice here! Of Napoleon[51] himself we shall only, glancing from afar, remark that Teufelsdröckh's relation to him seems to have been of very varied character. At first we find our poor Professor on the point of being shot as a spy; then taken into private conversation, even pinched on the ear, yet presented with no money; at last indignantly dismissed, almost thrown out of doors, as an "Ideologist." "He himself," says the Professor, "was among the completest Ideologists, at least Ideopraxists: in the Idea (*in der Idee*) he lived, moved and fought. The man was a Divine Missionary, though unconscious of it; and preached, through the cannon's throat, that great doctrine, *La carriere ouverte aux talens*[52] (The Tools to him that can handle them), which is our ultimate Political Evangel, wherein alone can liberty lie. Madly enough he preached, it is true, as Enthusiasts and first Missionaries are wont, with imperfect utterance, amid much frothy rant; yet as articulately perhaps as the case admitted. Or call him, if you will, an American Backwoodsman, who had to fell unpenetrated forests, and battle with innumerable wolves, and did not entirely forbear strong liquor, rioting, and even theft; whom, notwithstanding, the peaceful Sower will follow, and, as he cuts the boundless harvest, bless."

More legitimate and decisively authentic is Teufelsdröckh's appearance and emergence (we know not well whence) in the solitude of the North Cape,[53] on that June Midnight. He has "a light-blue Spanish cloak" hanging round him, as his "most commodious, principal, indeed sole uppergarment"; and stands there, on the World-promontory, looking over the infinite Brine, like a little blue Belfry (as we figure), now motionless indeed, yet ready, if stirred, to ring quaintest changes.

"Silence as of death," writes he; "for Midnight, even in the Arctic latitudes, has its character: nothing but the granite cliffs ruddy-tinged, the peaceable gurgle of that slow-heaving Polar Ocean, over which in the utmost North the great Sun hangs low and lazy, as if he too were slumbering. Yet is his cloud-couch wrought of crimson and cloth-of-gold; yet does his light stream over the mirror of waters, like a tremulous fire-pillar, shooting downwards to the abyss, and hide itself under my feet. In such moments, Solitude also is invaluable; for who would speak, or be looked on, when behind him lies all Europe and Africa, fast asleep, except the watchmen; and before him the silent Immensity, and Palace of the Eternal, whereof our Sun is but a porch-lamp?["]

... How prospered the inner man of Teufelsdröckh, under so much outward shifting? Does Legion[54] still lurk in him, though repressed; or has he exorcised that Devil's Brood? We can answer that the symptoms continue promising. Experience is the grand spiritual Doctor; and with him Teufelsdröckh has now been long a patient, swallowing many a bitter bolus. Unless our poor Friend belong to the numerous class of Incurables, which seems not likely, some cure will doubtless be effected....

"At length, after so much roasting," thus writes our Autobiographer, "I was what you might name calcined....[55] [B]y mere dint of practice, I had grown familiar with many things. Wretchedness was still

---

49 George Gordon Byron (1788–1824), poet; Pope Pius VII (1742–1823); Tao Kuang (1782–1850), Chinese emperor.
50 The White Lotus Society was a religious organization that rose against Emperor Chia Ch'ing (1796–1804); Carbonari (Italian for "charcoal burners") were members of an Italian secret religious/political organization.
51 Napoleon Bonaparte (1769–1821), French emperor.
52 Napoleon's slogan, meaning that careers are open based on merit, not rank.
53 A headland in Norway.
54 A demon; Mark 5:9 and Luke 8:30.
55 Burned into ash.

wretched; but I could now partly see through it, and despise it. Which highest mortal, in this inane Existence, had I not found a Shadow-hunter, or Shadow-hunted; and, when I looked through his brave garnitures, miserable enough? Thy wishes have all been sniffed aside, thought I: but what, had they even been all granted! Did not the Boy Alexander weep because he had not two Planets to conquer; or a whole Solar System; or after that, a whole Universe?[56] *Ach Gott*,[57] when I gazed into these Stars, have they not looked down on me as if with pity, from their serene spaces; like Eyes glistening with heavenly tears over the little lot of man! Thousands of human generations, all as noisy as our own, have been swallowed-up of Time, and there remains no wreck of them any more.... Pshaw! what is this paltry little Dog-cage of an Earth; what art thou that sittest whining there? Thou art still Nothing, Nobody: true; but who, then, is Something, Somebody? For thee the Family of Man has no use; it rejects thee; thou art wholly as a dissevered limb: so be it; perhaps it is better so!"

Too-heavy-laden Teufelsdröckh! Yet surely his bands are loosening; one day he will hurl the burden far from him, and bound forth free and with a second youth.

"This," says our Professor, "was the CENTRE OF INDIFFERENCE I had now reached; through which whoso travels from the Negative Pole to the Positive[58] must necessarily pass."

Chapter 9: The Everlasting Yea

"Temptations in the Wilderness!"[59] exclaims Teufelsdröckh: "Have we not all to be tried with such? Not so easily can the old Adam,[60] lodged in us by birth, be dispossessed. Our Life is compassed round with Necessity; yet is the meaning of Life itself no other than Freedom, than Voluntary Force: thus have we a warfare; in the beginning, especially, a hard-fought battle. For the God-given mandate, *Work thou in Welldoing*,[61] lies mysteriously written, in Promethean Prophetic Characters,[62] in our hearts; and leaves us no rest, night or day, till it be deciphered and obeyed; till it burn forth, in our conduct, a visible, acted Gospel of Freedom. And as the clay-given mandate, *Eat thou and be filled*, at the same time persuasively proclaims itself through every nerve,—must not there be a confusion, a contest, before the better Influence can become the upper?

"To me nothing seems more natural than that the Son of Man, when such God-given mandate first prophetically stirs within him, and the Clay must now be vanquished, or vanquish,[63]—should be carried of the spirit into grim Solitudes, and there fronting the Tempter do grimmest battle with him;[64] defiantly setting him at naught till he yield and fly. Name it as we choose: with or without visible Devil, whether in the natural Desert of rocks and sands, or in the populous moral Desert of selfishness and baseness,—to

---

56 Alexander the Great (356–23 BCE), king of Macedonia.
57 German: Oh God.
58 Alternate ends of a magnet, the halfway point between which is the centre of indifference, where neither pole exerts a greater pull than the other.
59 Matthew 4:1–11; Mark 1:12–13; Luke 4:1–13.
60 In Genesis 3, Adam succumbs to temptation, the Original Sin that all humans thereafter inherit.
61 Galatians 6:9; 2 Thessalonians 3:13.
62 In Greek mythology, Prometheus was a trickster and god of fire. His name means, literally, "forethinker."
63 The Son of Man is Jesus; the Clay is Adam (*adama* in Hebrew is mud or clay; Adam was made from clay).
64 After his baptism, Jesus fasted for forty days and nights in the desert, where he was tempted by the devil: see Matthew 4:1–11; Mark 1:12–13; and Luke 4:1–13.

such Temptation are we all called. Unhappy if we are not! Unhappy if we are but Half-men, in whom that divine handwriting has never blazed forth, all-subduing, in true sun-splendour; but quivers dubiously amid meaner lights: or smoulders, in dull pain, in darkness, under earthly vapors!—Our Wilderness is the wide World in an Atheistic Century; our Forty Days are long years of suffering and fasting: nevertheless, to these also comes an end. Yes, to me also was given, if not Victory, yet the consciousness of Battle, and the resolve to persevere therein while life or faculty is left....["]

He says elsewhere, under a less ambitious figure; as figures are, once for all, natural to him: "Has not thy Life been that of most sufficient men (*tüchtigen Männer*) thou hast known in this generation? An out-flush of foolish young Enthusiasm, like the first fallow-crop, wherein are as many weeds as valuable herbs: this all parched away, under the Droughts of practical and spiritual Unbelief, as Disappointment, in thought and act, often-repeated gave rise to Doubt, and Doubt gradually settled into Denial! If I have had a second-crop, and now see the perennial greensward, and sit under umbrageous cedars,[65] which defy all Drought (and Doubt); herein too, be the Heavens praised, I am not without examples, and even exemplars."

So that, for Teufelsdröckh, also, there has been a "glorious revolution"[66] these mad shadow-hunting and shadow-hunted Pilgrimings of his were but some purifying "Temptation in the Wilderness," before his apostolic work (such as it was) could begin; which Temptation is now happily over, and the Devil once more worsted! Was "that high moment in the *Rue de l'Enfer*," then, properly the turning-point of the battle; when the Fiend said, *Worship me, or be torn in shreds*; and was answered valiantly with an *Apage Satana?*[67]—Singular Teufelsdröckh, would thou hadst told thy singular story in plain words! But it is fruitless to look there, in those Paper-bags, for such. Nothing but innuendoes, figurative crotchets:[68] a typical Shadow, fitfully wavering, prophetico-satiric; no clear logical Picture. "How paint to the sensual eye," asks he once, "what passes in the Holy-of-Holies[69] of Man's Soul; in what words, known to these profane times, speak even afar-off of the unspeakable?" We ask in turn: Why perplex these times, profane as they are, with needless obscurity, by omission and by commission? Not mystical only is our Professor, but whimsical; and involves himself, now more than ever, in eye-bewildering *chiaroscuro*.[70] Successive glimpses, here faithfully imparted, our more gifted readers must endeavour to combine for their own behoof.

He says: "The hot Harmattan wind[71] had raged itself out; its howl went silent within me; and the long-deafened soul could now hear. I paused in my wild wanderings; and sat me down to wait, and consider; for it was as if the hour of change drew nigh. I seemed to surrender, to renounce utterly, and say: Fly, then, false shadows of Hope; I will chase you no more, I will believe you no more. And ye too, haggard spectres of Fear, I care not for you; ye too are all shadows and a lie. Let me rest here: for I am way-weary and life-weary; I will rest here, were it but to die: to die or to live is alike to me; alike insignificant."—And again: "Here, then, as I lay in that CENTRE OF INDIFFERENCE; cast, doubtless by benignant upper

---

65 Greensward is grassy ground; umbrageous cedars provide shade.
66 The Glorious Revolution (1688–89), in which Mary II and William III overthrew King James II of England without violence.
67 Latin: Get away, Satan; Matthew 4:10; Luke 4:8.
68 An imaginative literary device.
69 A sacred location in the temple of Jerusalem.
70 Use of light and shade in art.
71 Desert wind blowing from the Sahara to the west coast of Africa.

Influence, into a healing sleep, the heavy dreams rolled gradually away, and I awoke to a new Heaven and a new Earth.[72] The first preliminary moral Act, Annihilation of Self (*Selbst-tödtung*), had been happily accomplished; and my mind's eyes were now unsealed, and its hands ungyved."[73] ...

"Beautiful it was to sit there, as in my skyey Tent, musing and meditating; on the high table-land, in front of the Mountains; over me, as roof, the azure Dome, and around me, for walls, four azure-flowing curtains,—namely, of the Four azure Winds, on whose bottom-fringes also I have seen gilding. And then to fancy the fair Castles that stood sheltered in these Mountain hollows; with their green flower-lawns, and white dames and damosels, lovely enough: or better still, the straw-roofed Cottages, wherein stood many a Mother baking bread, with her children round her:—all hidden and protectingly folded-up in the valley-folds; yet there and alive, as sure as if I beheld them. Or to see, as well as fancy, the nine Towns and Villages, that lay round my mountain-seat, which, in still weather, were wont to speak to me (by their steeple-bells) with metal tongue; and, in almost all weather, proclaimed their vitality by repeated Smoke-clouds; whereon, as on a culinary horologe,[74] I might read the hour of the day. For it was the smoke of cookery, as kind housewives at morning, midday, eventide, were boiling their husbands' kettles; and ever a blue pillar rose up into the air, successively or simultaneously, from each of the nine, saying, as plainly as smoke could say: Such and such a meal is getting ready here.... If, in my wide Wayfarings, I had learned to look into the business of the World in its details, here perhaps was the place for combining it into general propositions, and deducing inferences therefrom.["]

"Often also could I see the black Tempest marching in anger through the Distance: round some Schreckhorn,[75] as yet grim-blue, would the eddying vapour gather, and there tumultuously eddy, and flow down like a mad witch's hair; till, after a space, it vanished, and, in the clear sunbeam, your Schreckhorn stood smiling grim-white, for the vapor had held snow. How thou fermentest and elaboratest, in thy great fermenting-vat and laboratory of an Atmosphere, of a World, O Nature!—Or what is Nature? Ha! why do I not name thee GOD? Art not thou the 'Living Garment of God'?[76] O Heavens, is it, in very deed, HE, then, that ever speaks through thee; that lives and loves in thee, that lives and loves in me?["]

"Fore-shadows, call them rather fore-splendours, of that Truth, and Beginning of Truths, fell mysteriously over my soul. Sweeter than Dayspring to the Shipwrecked in Nova Zembla;[77] ah, like the mother's voice to her little child that strays bewildered, weeping, in unknown tumults; like soft streamings of celestial music to my too-exasperated heart, came that Evangel. The Universe is not dead and demoniacal, a charnel-house[78] with spectres; but godlike, and my Father's!["]

"With other eyes, too, could I now look upon my fellow man; with an infinite Love, an infinite Pity. Poor, wandering, wayward man! Art thou not tired, and beaten with stripes, even as I am? Ever, whether thou bear the royal mantle or the beggar's gabardine,[79] art thou not so weary, so heavy-laden; and thy Bed of Rest is but a Grave. O my Brother, my Brother, why cannot I shelter thee in my bosom, and wipe away

---

72 Revelation 21:1.
73 Freed.
74 Timepiece.
75 Mountain in the Alps.
76 Johann Wolfgang von Goethe, *Faust* (1808–32).
77 Hendrik Tollens, "The Hollanders in Nova Zembla, 1596–1597: An Arctic Poem" (1819).
78 A building for corpses.
79 A loose smock made of coarse fabric.

all tears from thy eyes! Truly, the din of many-voiced Life, which, in this solitude, with the mind's organ, I could hear, was no longer a maddening discord, but a melting one; like inarticulate cries, and sobbings of a dumb creature, which in the ear of Heaven are prayers. The poor Earth, with her poor joys, was now my needy Mother, not my cruel Stepdame; Man, with his so mad Wants and so mean Endeavours, had become the dearer to me; and even for his sufferings and his sins, I now first named him Brother. Thus was I standing in the porch of that '*Sanctuary of Sorrow*;' by strange, steep ways had I too been guided thither; and ere long its sacred gates would open, and the '*Divine Depth of Sorrow*' lie disclosed to me."[80]

The Professor says, he here first got eye on the Knot that had been strangling him, and straightway could unfasten it, and was free. "A vain interminable controversy," writes he, "touching what is at present called Origin of Evil,[81] or some such thing, arises in every soul, since the beginning of the world; and in every soul, that would pass from idle Suffering into actual Endeavouring, must first be put an end to. The most, in our time, have to go content with a simple, incomplete enough Suppression of this controversy; to a few some Solution of it is indispensable. In every new era, too, such Solution comes-out in different terms; and ever the Solution of the last era has become obsolete, and is found unserviceable. For it is man's nature to change his Dialect from century to century; he cannot help it though he would. The authentic *Church-Catechism*[82] of our present century has not yet fallen into my hands: meanwhile, for my own private behoof, I attempt to elucidate the matter so. Man's Unhappiness, as I construe, comes of his Greatness; it is because there is an Infinite in him, which with all his cunning he cannot quite bury under the Finite. Will the whole Finance Ministers and Upholsterers and Confectioners of modern Europe undertake, in jointstock company,[83] to make one Shoeblack HAPPY? They cannot accomplish it, above an hour or two; for the Shoeblack also has a Soul quite other than his Stomach....["]

"But the whim we have of Happiness is somewhat thus. By certain valuations, and averages, of our own striking, we come upon some sort of average terrestrial lot; this we fancy belongs to us by nature, and of indefeasible right. It is simple payment of our wages, of our deserts; requires neither thanks nor complaint; only such *overplus* as there may be do we account Happiness; any *deficit* again is Misery. Now consider that we have the valuation of our own deserts ourselves, and what a fund of Self-conceit there is in each of us,—do you wonder that the balance should so often dip the wrong way, and many a Blockhead cry: See there, what a payment; was ever worthy gentleman so used!—I tell thee, Blockhead, it all comes of thy Vanity; of what thou *fanciest* those same deserts of thine to be. Fancy that thou deservest to be hanged (as is most likely), thou wilt feel it happiness to be only shot: fancy that thou deservest to be hanged in a hair-halter, it will be a luxury to die in hemp.["][84]

"So true is it, what I then say, that *the Fraction of Life can be increased in value not so much by increasing your Numerator as by lessening your Denominator*. Nay, unless my Algebra deceive me, *Unity* itself divided by *Zero* will give *Infinity*. Make thy claim of wages a zero, then; thou hast the world under thy feet. Well did the Wisest of our time write: 'It is only with Renunciation (*Entsagen*) that Life, properly speaking, can be said to begin.'["][85]

---

80 Johann Wolfgang von Goethe, *Wilhelm Meisters Lehrjahre* (1795–96).
81 Original Sin; see Genesis 3.
82 A form of Christian instruction involving question and answer.
83 A company that operates based on stock distribution among shareholders.
84 Hair-halter and hemp both refer to the hangman's rope.
85 Johann Wolfgang von Goethe, *Wilhelm Meisters Wanderjahre* (1821–29).

"I asked myself: What is this that, ever since earliest years, thou hast been fretting and fuming, and lamenting and self-tormenting, on account of? Say it in a word: is it not because thou art not HAPPY? Because the THOU (sweet gentleman) is not sufficiently honoured, nourished, soft-bedded, and lovingly cared for? Foolish soul! What Act of Legislature was there that *thou* shouldst be Happy? A little while ago thou hadst no right to *be* at all. What if thou wert born and predestined not to be Happy, but to be Unhappy! Art thou nothing other than a Vulture, then, that fliest through the Universe seeking after somewhat to *eat*; and shrieking dolefully because carrion enough is not given thee? Close thy *Byron*; open thy *Goethe*."

"*Es leuchtet mir ein*, I see a glimpse of it!"[86] cries he elsewhere: "there is in man a HIGHER than Love of Happiness: he can do without Happiness, and instead thereof find Blessedness! Was it not to preach-forth this same HIGHER that sages and martyrs, the Poet and the Priest, in all times, have spoken and suffered; bearing testimony, through life and through death, of the Godlike that is in Man, and how in the Godlike only has he Strength and Freedom? Which God-inspired Doctrine art thou also honoured to be taught; O Heavens! and broken with manifold merciful Afflictions, even till thou become contrite, and learn it! O, thank thy Destiny for these; thankfully bear what yet remain: thou hadst need of them; the Self in thee needed to be annihilated. By benignant fever-paroxysms is Life rooting out the deep-seated chronic Disease, and triumphs over Death. On the roaring billows of Time, thou art not engulfed, but borne aloft into the azure of Eternity. Love not Pleasure; love God. This is the EVERLASTING YEA, wherein all contradiction is solved: wherein whoso walks and works, it is well with him."

And again: "Small is it that thou canst trample the Earth with its injuries under thy feet, as old Greek Zeno[87] trained thee: thou canst love the Earth while it injures thee, and even because it injures thee; for this a Greater than Zeno was needed, and he too was sent. Knowest thou that '*Worship of Sorrow*'?[88] The Temple thereof, founded some eighteen centuries ago, now lies in ruins, overgrown with jungle, the habitation of doleful creatures: nevertheless, venture forward; in a low crypt, arched out of falling fragments, thou findest the Altar still there, and its sacred Lamp perennially burning."

Without pretending to comment on which strange utterances, the Editor will only remark, that there lies beside them much of a still more questionable character; unsuited to the general apprehension; nay wherein he himself does not see his way. Nebulous disquisitions on Religion, yet not without bursts of splendor; on the "perennial continuance of Inspiration;" on Prophecy; that there are "true Priests, as well as Baal-Priests,"[89] in our own day:" with more of the like sort. We select some fractions, by way of finish to this farrago.

"Cease, my much-respected Herr von Voltaire,"[90] thus apostrophises the Professor: "shut thy sweet voice; for the task appointed thee seems finished. Sufficiently hast thou demonstrated this proposition, considerable or otherwise: That the Mythus of the Christian Religion looks not in the eighteenth century as it did in the eighth. Alas, were thy six-and-thirty quartos, and the six-and-thirty thousand other quartos and folios, and flying sheets or reams, printed before and since on the same subject, all needed to convince us of so little! But what next? Wilt thou help us to embody the divine Spirit of that Religion

---

86 German: "It makes sense to me"; Johann Wolfgang von Goethe, *Wilhelm Meisters Wanderjahre* (1821–29).
87 Zeno (c. 335–263 BCE), Greek founder of Stoic philosophy.
88 Johann Wolfgang von Goethe, *Wilhelm Meisters Wanderjahre* (1821–29).
89 Priests of false gods.
90 Voltaire [François-Marie Arouet] (1694–1778), French writer and philosopher.

in a new Mythus, in a new vehicle and vesture, that our Souls, otherwise too like perishing, may live? What! thou hast no faculty in that kind? Only a torch for burning, no hammer for building? Take our thanks, then, and—thyself away.["]

"Meanwhile what are antiquated Mythuses to me? Or is the God present, felt in my own heart, a thing which Herr von Voltaire will dispute out of me; or dispute into me? To the '*Worship of Sorrow*' ascribe what origin and genesis thou pleasest, *has* not that Worship originated, and been generated; is it not *here*? Feel it in thy heart, and then say whether it is of God! This is Belief; all else is Opinion,—for which latter whoso will, let him worry and be worried."

"Neither," observes he elsewhere, "shall ye tear-out one another's eyes, struggling over 'Plenary Inspiration,'[91] and suchlike: try rather to get a little even Partial Inspiration, each of you for himself. One BIBLE I know, of whose Plenary Inspiration doubt is not so much as possible; nay with my own eyes I saw the God's-Hand writing it: thereof all other Bibles are but Leaves,—say, in Picture-Writing to assist the weaker faculty."

Or, to give the wearied reader relief, and bring it to an end, let him take the following perhaps more intelligible passage:—

"To me, in this our life," says the Professor, "which is an internecine warfare with the Time-spirit, other warfare seems questionable. Hast thou in any way a Contention with thy brother, I advise thee, think well what the meaning thereof is. If thou gauge it to the bottom, it is simply this: 'Fellow, see! thou art taking more than thy share of Happiness in the world, something from *my* share: which, by the Heavens, thou shalt not; nay I will fight thee rather.'—Alas, and the whole lot to be divided is such a beggarly matter, truly a 'feast of shells,'[92] for the substance has been spilled out: not enough to quench one Appetite; and the collective human species clutching at them!—Can we not, in all such cases, rather say: 'Take it, thou too-ravenous individual; take that pitiful additional fraction of a share, which I reckoned mine, but which thou so wantest; take it with a blessing: would to Heaven I had enough for thee!'—If Fichte's *Wissenschaftslehre*[93] be, 'to a certain extent, Applied Christianity,' surely to a still greater extent, so is this. We have here not a Whole Duty of Man,[94] yet a Half Duty, namely the Passive half: could we but do it, as we can demonstrate it!["]

"But indeed Conviction, were it never so excellent, is worthless till it convert itself into Conduct. Nay properly Conviction is not possible till then; inasmuch as all Speculation is by nature endless, formless, a vortex amid vortices, only by a felt indubitable certainty of Experience does it find any centre to revolve round, and so fashion itself into a system. Most true is it, as a wise man teaches us, that 'Doubt of any sort cannot be removed except by Action.' On which ground, too, let him who gropes painfully in darkness or uncertain light, and prays vehemently that the dawn may ripen into day, lay this other precept well to heart, which to me was of invaluable service: '*Do the Duty which lies nearest thee*,' which thou knowest to be a Duty! Thy second Duty will already have become clearer.["]

"May we not say, however, that the hour of Spiritual Enfranchisement is even this: When your Ideal World, wherein the whole man has been dimly struggling and inexpressibly languishing to work, becomes revealed, and thrown open; and you discover, with amazement enough, like the Lothario in *Wilhelm*

---

91 The belief that every word in the Bible comes directly from God.
92 James Macpherson, *Fingal* (1762) and *Temora* (1763).
93 German philosopher Johann Gottlieb Fichte (1762–1814), *Wissenschaftslehre* (1794).
94 Ecclesiastes 12:13.

Meister, that your 'America is here or nowhere'?[95] The Situation that has not its Duty, its Ideal, was never yet occupied by man. Yes here, in this poor, miserable, hampered, despicable Actual, wherein thou even now standest, here or nowhere is thy Ideal: work it out therefrom; and working, believe, live, be free. Fool! the Ideal is in thyself, the impediment too is in thyself: thy Condition is but the stuff thou art to shape that same Ideal out of: what matters whether such stuff be of this sort or that, so the Form thou give it be heroic, be poetic? O thou that pinest in the imprisonment of the Actual, and criest bitterly to the gods for a kingdom wherein to rule and create, know this of a truth: the thing thou seekest is already with thee, 'here or nowhere,' couldst thou only see![”]

"But it is with man's Soul as it was with Nature: the beginning of Creation is—Light. Till the eye have vision, the whole members are in bonds. Divine moment, when over the tempest-tost Soul, as once over the wild-weltering Chaos, it is spoken: Let there be Light![96] Ever to the greatest that has felt such moment, is it not miraculous and God-announcing; even as, under simpler figures, to the simplest and least. The mad primeval Discord is hushed; the rudely-jumbled conflicting elements bind themselves into separate Firmaments:[97] deep silent rock-foundations are built beneath; and the skyey vault with its everlasting Luminaries above: instead of a dark wasteful Chaos, we have a blooming, fertile, heaven-encompassed World.[”]

"I too could now say to myself: Be no longer a Chaos, but a World, or even Worldkin. Produce! Produce![98] Were it but the pitifullest infinitesimal fraction of a Product, produce it, in God's name! 'Tis the utmost thou hast in thee: out with it, then. Up, up! Whatsoever thy hand findeth to do, do it with thy whole might. Work while it is called Today; for the Night cometh, wherein no man can work."[99]

Benjamin Jowett
from "On the Interpretation of Scripture" (1860)

Educational reformer and influential Master of Balliol College at Oxford, Benjamin Jowett (1817–93) made the college a model of pluralism and internationalism. Coming from an evangelical background, he became increasingly liberal, promoting rational scriptural analysis and arguing that the New Testament should be studied "like any other book."

In 1860, Jowett's "On the Interpretation of Scripture" formed part of the controversial *Essays and Reviews,* a collection of essays by prominent Anglicans. Jowett suggested that Biblical exegesis should be freed from tradition: "It is better to close the book than to read it under conditions of thought which are imposed from without. Whether those conditions of thought are the traditions of the Church, or the opinions of the religious world ... makes no difference. They are inconsistent with the freedom of the truth and

---

95 Johann Wolfgang von Goethe, *Wilhelm Meisters Lehrjahre* (1795–96).
96 Genesis 1:3.
97 Genesis 1:6–8.
98 Genesis 1:22.
99 John 9:4.

the moral character of the Gospel." *Essays and Reviews* was attacked in the *Westminster Review* and the *Quarterly Review*.

~

It is a strange, though familiar fact, that great differences of opinion exist respecting the Interpretation of Scripture. All Christians receive the Old and New Testament as sacred writings, but they are not agreed about the meaning which they attribute to them.... Different individuals or bodies of Christians have a different point of view, to which their interpretation is narrowed or made to conform. It is assumed, as natural and necessary, that the same words will present one idea to the mind of the Protestant, another to the Roman Catholic; one meaning to the German, another to the English interpreter....

This effort to pull the authority of Scripture in different directions is not peculiar to our own day; the same phenomenon appears in the past history of the Church. At the Reformation, in the Nicene or Pelagian times,[100] the New Testament was the ground over which men fought; it might also be compared to the armoury which furnished them with weapons.... The difference of interpretation which prevails among ourselves is partly traditional, that is to say, inherited from the controversies of former ages. The use made of Scripture by Fathers of the Church, as well as by Luther and Calvin,[101] affects our idea of its meaning at the present hour.

Another cause of the multitude of interpretations is the growth or progress of the human mind itself. Modes of interpreting vary as time goes on; they partake of the general state of literature or knowledge.... Though roughly distinguishable by different ages, these modes or tendencies also exist together; the remains of all of them may be remarked in some of the popular commentaries of our own day.

More common than any of these methods, and not peculiar to any age, is that which may be called by way of distinction the rhetorical one. The tendency to exaggerate or amplify the meaning of simple words for the sake of edification may indeed have a practical use in sermons, the object of which is to awaken not so much the intellect as the heart and conscience. Spiritual food, like natural, may require to be of a certain bulk to nourish the human mind. But this "tendency to edification"[102] has had an unfortunate influence on the interpretation of Scripture. For the preacher almost necessarily oversteps the limits of actual knowledge, his feelings overflow with the subject; even if he have the power, he has seldom the time for accurate thought or inquiry.... Any one who has ever written sermons is aware how hard it is to apply Scripture to the wants of his hearers and at the same time to preserve its meaning.

... Let it be considered, then, that this extreme variety of interpretation is found to exist in the case of no other book, but of the Scriptures only. Other writings are preserved to us in dead languages—Greek, Latin, Oriental, some of them in fragments, all of them originally in manuscript....

To bring the parallel home, let us imagine the remains of some well-known Greek author, as Plato or Sophocles,[103] receiving the same treatment at the hands of the world which the Scriptures have

---

100 The Reformation was the sixteenth-century European movement to reform the Catholic Church that resulted in Protestantism; the Nicene Council met twice, once in the fourth century and once in the eighth; fifth-century followers of the monk Pelagius, Pelagians did not believe in the inheritance of original sin.
101 Martin Luther (1483–1546), German religious reformer; John Calvin (1509–64), French religious reformer.
102 John Calvin, *Commentary on the Epistles of Paul the Apostle to the Corinthians* (1546).
103 Plato (c. 428/7–348/7 BCE), Greek philosopher; Sophocles (496–406 BCE), Greek playwright.

experienced. The text of such an author, when first printed by Aldus or Stephens,[104] would be gathered from the imperfect or miswritten copies which fell in the way of the editors; after awhile older and better manuscripts come to light, and the power of using and estimating the value of manuscripts is greatly improved. We may suppose, further, that the readings of these older copies do not always conform to some received canons of criticism. Up to the year 1550, or 1624, alterations, often proceeding on no principle, have been introduced into the text; but now a stand is made—an edition which appeared at the latter of the two dates just mentioned is invested with authority; this authorized text is a *pièce de resistance* against innovation. Many reasons are given why it is better to have bad readings to which the world is accustomed than good ones which are novel and strange—why the later manuscripts of Plato or Sophocles are often to be preferred to earlier ones—why it is useless to remove imperfections where perfect accuracy is not to be attained. A fear of disturbing the critical canons which have come down from former ages is, however, suspected to be one reason for the opposition. And custom and prejudice, and the nicety of the subject, and all the arguments which are intelligible to the many against the truth, which is intelligible only to the few, are thrown into the scale to preserve the works of Plato or Sophocles as nearly as possible in the received text.

Leaving the text we proceed to interpret and translate. The meaning of Greek words is known with tolerable certainty; and the grammar of the Greek language has been minutely analyzed both in ancient and modern times. Yet the interpretation of Sophocles is tentative and uncertain; it seems to vary from age to age: to some the great tragedian has appeared to embody in his choruses certain theological or moral ideas of his own age or country; there are others who find there an allegory of the Christian religion or of the history of modern Europe. Several schools of critics have commented on his works; to the Englishman he has presented one meaning, to the Frenchman another, to the German a third; the interpretations have also differed with the philosophical systems which the interpreters espoused. To one the same words have appeared to bear a moral, to another a symbolical meaning; a third is determined wholly by the authority of old commentators; while there is a disposition to condemn the scholar who seeks to interpret Sophocles from himself only and with reference to the ideas and beliefs of the age in which he lived. And the error of such an one is attributed not only to some intellectual but even to a moral obliquity which prevents his seeing the true meaning....

No one who has a Christian feeling would place classical on a level with sacred literature; and there are other particulars in which the preceding comparison fails, as, for example, the style and subject. But, however different the subject, although the interpretation of Scripture requires "a vision and faculty divine,"[105] or at least a moral and religious interest which is not needed in the study of a Greek poet or philosopher, yet in what may be termed the externals of interpretation, that is to say, the meaning of words, the connexion of sentences, the settlement of the text, the evidence of facts, the same rules apply to the Old and New Testaments as to other books. And the figure is no exaggeration of the erring fancy of men in the use of Scripture, or of the tenacity with which they cling to the interpretations of other times, or of the arguments by which they maintain them. All the resources of knowledge may be turned into a means not of discovering the true rendering, but of upholding a received one. Grammar appears

---

104 Aldus Manutius (1449–1515), Italian publisher and printer; the Estienne [Stephenus] family, French scholars and printers (1502–1674).
105 William Wordsworth, *The Excursion* (1814).

to start from an independent point of view, yet inquiries into the use of the article or the preposition have been observed to wind round into a defence of some doctrine. Rhetoric often magnifies its own want of taste into the design of inspiration. Logic (that other mode of rhetoric) is apt to lend itself to the illusion, by stating erroneous explanations with a clearness which is mistaken for truth. "Metaphysical aid"[106] carries away the common understanding into a region where it must blindly follow. Learning obscures as well as illustrates; it heaps up chaff when there is no more wheat. These are some of the ways in which the sense of Scripture has become confused, by the help of tradition, in the course of ages, under a load of commentators.

The book itself remains as at the first unchanged amid the changing interpretations of it. The office of the interpreter is not to add another, but to recover the original one; the meaning, that is, of the words as they first struck on the ears or flashed before the eyes of those who heard and read them. He has to transfer himself to another age; to imagine that he is a disciple of Christ or Paul;[107] to disengage himself from all that follows. The history of Christendom is nothing to him; but only the scene at Galilee or Jerusalem, the handful of believers who gathered themselves together at Ephesus, or Corinth, or Rome. His eye is fixed on the form of one like the Son of man,[108] or of the Prophet who was girded with a garment of camel's hair,[109] or of the Apostle who had a thorn in the flesh.[110] The greatness of the Roman Empire is nothing to him; it is an inner not an outer world that he is striving to restore. All the after-thoughts of theology are nothing to him; they are not the true lights which light him in difficult places. His concern is with a book in which as in other ancient writings are some things of which we are ignorant; which defect of our knowledge cannot however be supplied by the conjectures of fathers or divines. The simple words of that book he tries to preserve absolutely pure from the refinements or distinctions of later times. He acknowledges that they are fragmentary, and would suspect himself, if out of fragments he were able to create a well-rounded system or a continuous history. The greater part of his learning is a knowledge of the text itself; he has no delight in the voluminous literature which has overgrown it. He has no theory of interpretation; a few rules guarding against common errors are enough for him. His object is to read Scripture like any other book, with a real interest and not merely a conventional one. He wants to be able to open his eyes and see or imagine things as they truly are.

Nothing would be more likely to restore a natural feeling on this subject than a history of the Interpretation of Scripture. It would take us back to the beginning; it would present in one view the causes which have darkened the meaning of words in the course of ages; it would clear away the remains of dogmas, systems, controversies, which are encrusted upon them. It would show us the "erring fancy" of interpreters assuming sometimes to have the Spirit of God Himself, yet unable to pass beyond the limits of their own age, and with a judgment often biassed by party. Great names there have been among them, names of men who may be reckoned also among the benefactors of the human race, yet comparatively few who have understood the thoughts of other times, or who have bent their minds to "interrogate" the meaning of words. Such a work would enable us to separate the elements of doctrine and tradition with which the meaning of Scripture is encumbered in our own day. It would mark the different epochs of interpretation

---

106 Shakespeare, *Macbeth* (I.v.29).
107 Paul (c. 4 BCE–62/4 CE), Christian apostle, missionary, and saint.
108 Jesus.
109 John; Matthew 3:4.
110 Paul; 2 Corinthians 12:7.

from the time when the living word was in process of becoming a book to Origen and Tertullian, from Origen to Jerome and Augustine, from Jerome and Augustine to Abelard and Aquinas;[111] again making a new beginning with the revival of literature, from Erasmus, the father of Biblical criticism in more recent times, with Calvin and Beza for his immediate successors, through Grotius and Hammond, down to De Wette and Meier,[112] our own contemporaries. We should see how the mystical interpretation of Scripture originated in the Alexandrian age; how it blended with the logical and rhetorical; how both received weight and currency from their use in support of the claims and teaching of the Church. We should notice how the "new learning" of the fifteenth and sixteenth centuries gradually awakened the critical faculty in the study of the sacred writings; how Biblical criticism has slowly but surely followed in the track of philological and historical (not without a remoter influence exercised upon it also by natural science); how, too, the form of the scholastic literature, and even of notes on the classics, insensibly communicated itself to commentaries on Scripture. We should see how the word inspiration, from being used in a general way to express what may be called the prophetic spirit of Scripture, has passed, within the last two centuries, into a sort of technical term; how, in other instances, the practice or feeling of earlier ages has been hollowed out into the theory or system of later ones. We should observe how the popular explanations of prophecy as in heathen (Thucyd. ii. 54),[113] so also in Christian times, had adapted themselves to the circumstances of mankind. We might remark that in our own country, and in the present generation especially, the interpretation of Scripture had assumed an apologetic character, as though making an effort to defend itself against some supposed inroad of science and criticism; while among German commentators there is, for the first time in the history of the world, an approach to agreement and certainty. For example, the diversity among German writers on prophecy is far less than among English ones. That is a new phenomenon which has to be acknowledged. More than any other subject of human knowledge, Biblical criticism has hung to the past; it has been hitherto found truer to the traditions of the Church than to the words of Christ. It has made, however, two great steps onward—at the time of the Reformation and in our day. The diffusion of a critical spirit in history and literature is affecting the criticism of the Bible in our own day in a manner not unlike the burst of intellectual life in the fifteenth or sixteenth centuries. Educated persons are beginning to ask, not what Scripture may be made to mean, but what it does. And it is no exaggeration to say that he who in the present state of knowledge will confine himself to the plain meaning of words and the study of their context may know more of the original spirit and intention of the authors of the New Testament than all the controversial writers of former ages put together.

Such a history would be of great value to philosophy as well as to theology. It would be the history of the human mind in one of its most remarkable manifestations. For ages which are not original show their character in the interpretation of ancient writings. Creating nothing, and incapable of that effort of imagination which is required in a true criticism of the past, they read and explain the thoughts of

---

111 Origen (c. 185–253), Alexandrian theologian; Tertullian (c. 155/60–c. 220), Carthaginian theologian; Jerome (c. 342–420), Dalmatian theologian and saint; Aurelius Augustine (354–430), Algerian theologian and saint; Peter Abelard (1079–1142), French theologian; Thomas Aquinas (c. 1225–74), Italian theologian and saint.
112 Desiderius Erasmus (c. 1467–1536), Dutch reformer and scholar; Theodore Beza (1519–1605), French theologian; Hugo Grotius (1583–1645), Dutch theologian and politician; Henry Hammond (1605–60), theologian; Wilhelm Martin Leberecht de Wette (1780–1849), German theologian; Heinrich August Wilhelm Meyer (Meier) (1800–73), German theologian.
113 Thucydides, *History of the Peloponnesian War* (c. 404 BCE).

former times by the conventional modes of their own. Such a history would form a kind of preface or prolegomena[114] to the study of Scripture. Like the history of science, it would save many a useless toil; it would indicate the uncertainties on which it is not worth while to speculate further; the byepaths or labyrinths in which men lose themselves; the mines that are already worked out. He who reflects on the multitude of explanations which already exist of the "number of the beast," "the two witnesses," "the little horn," "the man of sin,"[115] who observes the manner in which these explanations have varied with the political movements of our own time, will be unwilling to devote himself to a method of inquiry in which there is so little appearance of certainty or progress. These interpretations would destroy one another if they were all placed side by side in a tabular analysis. It is an instructive fact, which may be mentioned in passing, that Joseph Mede,[116] the greatest authority on this subject, twice fixed the end of the world in the last century and once during his own lifetime. In like manner, he who notices the circumstance that the explanations of the first chapter of Genesis have slowly changed, and, as it were, retreated before the advance of geology, will be unwilling to add another to the spurious reconcilements of science and revelation. Or to take an example of another kind, the Protestant divine who perceives that the types and figures of the Old Testament are employed by Roman Catholics in support of the tenets of their church, will be careful not to use weapons which it is impossible to guide, and which may with equal force be turned against himself. Those who have handled them on the Protestant side have before now fallen victims to them, not observing as they fell that it was by their own hand.

Much of the uncertainty which prevails in the interpretation of Scripture arises out of party efforts to wrest its meaning to different sides. There are, however, deeper reasons which have hindered the natural meaning of the text from immediately and universally prevailing. One of these is the unsettlement of many questions which have an important but indirect bearing on this subject. Some of these questions veil themselves in ambiguous terms; and no one likes to draw them out of their hiding-place into the light of day. In natural science it is felt to be useless to build on assumptions; in history we look with suspicion on *a priori*[117] ideas of what ought to have been; in mathematics, when a step is wrong, we pull the house down until we reach the point at which the error is discovered. But in theology it is otherwise; there the tendency has been to conceal the unsoundness of the foundation under the fairness and loftiness of the superstructure. It has been thought safer to allow arguments to stand which, although fallacious, have been on the right side, than to point out their defect. And thus many principles have imperceptibly grown up which have overridden facts. No one would interpret Scripture, as many do, but for certain previous suppositions with which we come to the perusal of it. "There can be no error in the Word of God," therefore the discrepancies in the books of Kings and Chronicles are only apparent, or may be attributed to differences in the copies. "It is a thousand times more likely that the interpreter should err, than the inspired writer." For a like reason the failure of a prophecy is never admitted, in spite of Scripture and of history (Jer. xxxvi. 30; Isai. xxiii.; Amos vii. 10–17);[118] the mention of a name later than the supposed age of the prophet is not allowed, as in other writings, to be taken in evidence of the date (Isaiah xlv. 1). The accuracy of the Old Testament is measured not by the standard of primeval history,

---

114 Preface to a book.
115 Revelation 13:17–18; Revelation 11; Daniel 7:8; 2 Thessalonians 2:3.
116 Joseph Mead [Mede] (1586–1638), theologian and Cambridge fellow.
117 Latin: assumed based on prior beliefs.
118 Jeremiah 36:30; Isaiah 23; Amos 7:10–17.

but of a modern critical one, which, contrary to all probability, is supposed to be attained; this arbitrary standard once assumed, it becomes a point of honour or of faith to defend every name, date, place, which occurs. Or to take another class of questions, it is said that "the various theories of the origin of the three first Gospels are all equally unknown to the Holy Catholic Church," or as another writer of a different school expresses himself, "they tend to sap the inspiration of the New Testament." Again, the language in which our Saviour speaks of his own union with the Father is interpreted by the language of the creeds. Those who remonstrate against double senses, allegorical interpretations, forced reconcilements, find themselves met by a sort of presupposition that "God speaks not as man speaks." The limitation of the human faculties is confusedly appealed to as a reason for abstaining from investigations which are quite within their limits. The suspicion of Deism,[119] or perhaps of Atheism, awaits inquiry. By such fears a good man refuses to be influenced, a philosophical mind is apt to cast them aside with too much bitterness. It is better to close the book than to read it under conditions of thought which are imposed from without. Whether those conditions of thought are the traditions of the Church, or the opinions of the religious world—Catholic or Protestant—makes no difference. They are inconsistent with the freedom of the truth and the moral character of the Gospel....

John William Colenso
from *The Pentateuch and Book of Joshua Critically Examined* (1862)

Anglican Bishop of Natal, John William Colenso (1814–83) abandoned evangelicalism, becoming an influential Broad Churchman and champion of the South African Zulu. Ordained in 1839 after studying mathematics at Cambridge, Colenso published two mathematics textbooks and *Ten Weeks in Natal* (1855) before assuming the Natal bishopric in 1855, establishing missions, and publishing a *Zulu-English Dictionary* (1861). Colenso attracted criticism for tolerating polygamy and supporting Zulu King Cetewayo during and after the Anglo-Zulu War of 1879.

Colenso's interest in Biblical criticism emerged from the practical difficulties of reconciling Old Testament violence with Christian morality for Zulu followers. His *The Pentateuch and Book of Joshua Critically Examined* (1862) offended many; he argued that if supposedly factual Biblical statements are untrue, then the principles founded upon these statements would also be invalid. Found guilty of heresy by a South African ecclesiastical court, Colenso contested his formal excommunication, preaching to crowds and finding support among liberals.

---

119 Deism developed in England and spread to France and Germany; Deists believed that God simply created the world and exerted no further influence.

Part 1: The Pentateuch Examined as an Historical Narrative

Chapter 1

Introductory Remarks

1. The first five books of the Bible,—commonly called the Pentateuch[120] ... —are supposed by most English readers of the Bible to have been written by Moses,[121] except the last chapter of Deuteronomy,[122] which records the death of Moses, and which, of course, it is generally allowed, must have been added by another hand, perhaps that of Joshua.[123] It is believed that Moses wrote under such special guidance and teaching of the Holy Spirit,[124] that he was preserved from making any error in recording those matters, which came within his own cognisance, and was instructed also in respect of events, which took place before he was born.... He was in this way, it is supposed, enabled to write a true account of the Creation. And, though the accounts of the Fall and of the Flood,[125] as well as of later events, which happened in the time of Abraham, Isaac, and Jacob,[126] may have been handed down by tradition from one generation to another, and even, some of them, perhaps, written down in words, or represented in hieroglyphics,[127] ... yet in all his statements, it is believed, he was under such constant control and superintendence of the Spirit of God, that he was kept from making any serious error, and certainly from writing anything altogether untrue. We may rely with undoubting confidence—such is the statement usually made—on the historical veracity, and infallible accuracy, of the Mosaic narrative[128] in all its main particulars....

2. But, among the many results of that remarkable activity in scientific enquiry of every kind, which, by God's own gift, distinguishes the present age, this also must be reckoned, that attention and labour are now being bestowed, more closely and earnestly than ever before, to search into the real foundations for such a belief as this. As the Rev. A.W. Haddan has well said, (*Replies to Essays and Reviews, p.*349,)[129]—

> It is a time when religious questions are being sifted with an apparatus of knowledge, and with faculties and a temper of mind, seldom, if ever, before brought to bear upon them. The entire creation of new departments of knowledge, such as philology,—the discovery, as of things before absolutely unknown, of the physical history of the globe,—the rising from the grave, as it were, of whole periods of history contemporary with the Bible, through newly found or newly interpreted monuments,—the science of manuscripts and of settling texts,—all these, and many more that might be named, embrace in themselves a whole universe of knowledge bearing upon

---

120 The first five books of the Old Testament.
121 Prophet in the Bible who leads the Israelites from Egypt and delivers the Ten Commandments; see Exodus, Deuteronomy, Leviticus, and Numbers.
122 Deuteronomy 34.
123 Leader of the Israelites after Moses' death.
124 Part of the Trinity (God, Christ, Holy Spirit).
125 Genesis 3; Genesis 6–9.
126 Genesis 17–49; Abraham is considered the father of Judaism, Christianity, and Islam; Isaac is Abraham's son; Jacob is Isaac's son.
127 Egypt was one of the main archaeological sites of Victorian times; the Rosetta Stone, which allowed the understanding of hieroglyphics, was deciphered in 1822.
128 That is, Moses' narrative.
129 Arthur West Haddan, *Replies to "Essays and Reviews"* (1862).

religion, and specially upon the Bible, to which our fathers were utter strangers. And beyond all these is the change in the very spirit of thought itself, equally great, and equally appropriate to the conditions of the present conflict,—the transformation of history by the critical weighing of evidence, by the separation from it of the subjective and the mythical, by the treatment of it in a living and real way,—*the advance in Biblical Criticism, which has undoubtedly arisen from the more thorough application to the Bible of the laws of human criticism.*

3. This must, in fact, be deemed, undoubtedly, *the* question of the present day, upon the reply to which depend vast and momentous interests. The time is come, as I believe, in the Providence of God, when this question can no longer be put by,—when it must be resolutely faced, and the whole matter fully and freely examined, if we would be faithful servants of the God of Truth....

4. For myself, I have become engaged in this enquiry, from no wish or purpose of my own, but from the plain necessities of my position as a Missionary Bishop.... What the end may be, God only, the God of Truth, can foresee. Meanwhile, believing and trusting in His guidance, I have launched my bark[130] upon the flood, and am carried along by the waters. Most gladly would I have turned away from all such investigations as these, if I *could* have done so,—as, in fact, I did, until I could do so no longer....

5. There was a time, indeed, in my life, before my attention had been drawn to the facts, which make such a view impossible for most reflecting and enquiring minds, when I could have heartily assented to such language as the following, which Burgon, *Inspiration and Interpretation*, p.89,[131] asserts to be the creed of orthodox believers, and which, probably, expresses the belief of many English Christians at the present day:—

> The Bible is none other than *the Voice of Him that sitteth upon the Throne!* Every book of it—every chapter of it—every verse of it—every word of it—every syllable of it—(where are we to stop?) every *letter* of it—is the direct utterance of the Most High! The Bible is none other than the Word of God....

Such was the creed of the School in which I was educated. God is my witness! what hours of wretchedness have I spent at times, while reading the Bible devoutly from day to day, and reverencing every word of it as the Word of God, when petty contradictions met me, which seemed to my reason to conflict with the notion of the absolute historical veracity of every part of Scripture, and which, as I felt, *in the study of any other book*, we should honestly treat as errors or misstatements, without in the least detracting from the real value of the book! But, in those days, I was taught that it was my duty to fling the suggestion from me at once.... And by many a painful effort I succeeded in doing so for a season....

7. But my labours, as a translator of the Bible, and a teacher of intelligent catechumens,[132] have brought me face to face with questions, from which I had hitherto shrunk, but from which, under the circumstances, I felt it would be a sinful abandonment of duty any longer to turn away. I have, therefore, as in the sight of God Most High, set myself deliberately to find the answer to such questions, with, I trust and believe, a sincere desire to know the Truth, as God wills us to know it, and with a humble dependence on that Divine Teacher, who alone can guide us into that knowledge, and help us to use the light of our

---

130 Boat.
131 John William Burgon, *Inspiration and Interpretation* (1861).
132 Lessons in religion.

minds aright. The result of my enquiry is this, that I have arrived at the conviction,—as painful to myself at first, as it may be to my reader, though painful now no longer under the clear shining of the Light of Truth,—that the Pentateuch, as a whole, cannot possibly have been written by Moses, or by any one acquainted personally with the facts which it professes to describe, and, further, that the (so-called) Mosaic narrative, by whomsoever written, and though imparting to us, as I fully believe it does, revelations of the Divine Will and Character, cannot be regarded as *historically true.*

8. Let it be observed that I am not here speaking of a number of petty variations and contradictions, such as, on closer examination, are found to exist throughout the books, but which may be in many cases sufficiently explained, by alleging our ignorance of all the circumstances of the case, or by supposing some misplacement, or loss, or corruption, of the original manuscript, or by suggesting that a later writer has inserted his own gloss here and there, or even whole passages, which may contain facts or expressions at variance with the true Mosaic Books, and throwing an unmerited suspicion upon them. However perplexing such contradictions are, when found in a book which is believed to be divinely infallible, yet a humble and pious faith will gladly welcome the aid of a friendly criticism, to relieve it in this way of its doubts. I can truly say that I would do so heartily myself. Nor are the difficulties, to which I am now referring, of the same kind as those, which arise from considering the accounts of the Creation and the Deluge,[133] (though these of themselves are very formidable,) or the stupendous character of certain miracles, as that of the sun and moon standing still,—or the waters of the river Jordan standing in heaps as solid walls, while the stream, we must suppose, was still running,—or the ass speaking with human voice,—or the miracles wrought by the magicians of Egypt, such as the conversion of a rod into a snake, and the latter being endowed with life.[134] They are not such, even, as are raised, when we regard the trivial nature of a vast number of conversations and commands, ascribed directly to Jehovah,[135] especially the multiplied ceremonial minutiæ, laid down in the Levitical Law.[136] They are not such, even, as must be started at once in most pious minds, when such words as these are read, professedly coming from the Holy and Blessed One, the Father and "Faithful Creator" of all mankind:—

"If the master (of a Hebrew servant) have given him a wife, and she have borne him sons or daughters, *the wife and her children shall be her master's*, and he shall go out free by himself," E.xxi.4:[137]

the wife and children in such a case being placed under the protection of such other words as these,—

"If a man smite his servant, or his maid, with a rod, and he die under his hand, he shall be surely punished. *Notwithstanding*, if he continue a day or two, he shall not be punished: for *he is his money*." E.xxi.20,21.[138]

---

133 Genesis 1, 5; Genesis 6–9.
134 Joshua 10:13–14; Joshua 3:13–17, 2 Kings 2:7–8; Numbers 22:28–33; Exodus 7:8–13.
135 God; Jehovah is used in some versions of the Bible in place of Lord.
136 Leviticus outlines the laws of religious ceremony and the laws of sexual conduct and marriage.
137 Exodus 21:4.
138 Exodus 21:20–21.

9. I shall never forget the revulsion of feeling, with which a very intelligent Christian native, with whose help I was translating these words into the Zulu tongue, first heard them as words said to be uttered by the same great and gracious Being, whom I was teaching him to trust in and adore. His whole soul revolted against the notion, that the Great and Blessed God, the Merciful Father of all mankind, would speak of a servant or maid as mere "money," and allow a horrible crime to go unpunished, because the victim of the brutal usage had survived a few hours. My own heart and conscience at the time fully sympathised with his. But I then clung to the notion, that the main substance of the narrative was historically true. And I relieved his difficulty and my own for the present by telling him, that I supposed that such words as these were written down by Moses, and believed by him to have been divinely given to him, because the thought of them arose in his heart, as he conceived, by the inspiration of God, and that hence to all such Laws he prefixed the formula, "Jehovah said unto Moses," without it being on that account necessary for us to suppose that they were actually spoken by the Almighty. This was, however, a very great strain upon the cord, which bound me to the ordinary belief in the historical veracity of the Pentateuch; and since then that cord has snapped in twain altogether.

10. But I wish to repeat here most distinctly that my reason, for no longer receiving the Pentateuch as historically true, is not that I find insuperable difficulties with regard to the *miracles*, or supernatural *revelations* of Almighty God, recorded in it, but solely that I cannot, as a true man, consent any longer to shut my eyes to the absolute, palpable, self-contradictions of the narrative. The notion of miraculous or supernatural interferences does not present to my own mind the difficulties which it seems to present to some. I could believe and receive the miracles of Scripture heartily, if only they were authenticated by a veracious history; though, if this is not the case with the Pentateuch, any miracles, which rest on such an unstable support, must necessarily fall to the ground with it....

... Our belief in the Living God remains as sure as ever, though not the Pentateuch only, but the whole Bible, were removed. It is written on our hearts by God's own Finger, as surely as by the hand of the Apostle in the Bible, that "GOD IS, and is a rewarder of them that diligently seek Him."[139] It is written there also, as plainly as in the Bible, that "God is not mocked,"—that, "whatsoever a man soweth, that shall he also reap,"—and that "he that soweth to the flesh, shall of the flesh reap corruption."[140] ...

14. In discharging, however, my present duty to God and to the Church, I trust that I shall be preserved from saying a single word that may cause *unnecessary* pain to those who now embrace with all their hearts, as a primary article of Faith, the ordinary view of Scripture Inspiration. *Pain*, I know, I must cause to some. But I feel very deeply that it behoves every one, who would write on such a subject as this, to remember how closely the belief in the historical truth of every portion of the Bible is interwoven, at the present time, in England, with the faith of many, whose piety and charity may far surpass his own.... We must be content to take the Bible as it is, and draw from it those Lessons which it really contains. Accordingly, that which I have done, or endeavoured to do, in this book, is to make out from the Bible—at least, from the first part of it—what account it gives of itself, what it really is, what, if we love the truth, we must understand and believe it to be, what, if we will speak the truth, we must represent it to be.

---

139 Hebrews 11:6; ascribed to Paul.
140 Galatians 6:7–8.

Chapter 5

Moses and Joshua Addressing All Israel

39. *These be the words which Moses spake unto all Israel. D.i.1.*[141]

> *And Moses called all Israel, and said unto them. D.v.1.*[142]
> *And afterward he read all the words of the Law, the blessings and the cursings, according to all that which is written in the Book of the Law. There was not a word of all that Moses commanded, which Joshua read not before all the Congregation of Israel, with the women, and the little ones, and the strangers that were conversant among them. Jo.viii.34,35.*[143]

We have just seen that the men in the prime of life, "above twenty years of age," N.i.3, were more than 600,000 in number[.][144] We may reckon that the women in the prime of life were about as many, the males under twenty years, 300,000, the females under twenty years, 300,000, and the old people, male and female together, 200,000, making the whole number about two millions. This number, which Kurtz adopts, iii.*p*.149,[145] is, indeed, a very moderate estimate. In Horne's *Introd*. iii.*p*.205, they are reckoned to have formed "an aggregate of upwards of three millions."[146]...

Kitto says, *Hist. of the Jews*, p.174:—

> As this prime class of the community (the able-bodied men) is usually in the proportion of one-fourth of the whole population, the result would give nearly two millions and a half as the number of the posterity of Jacob....[147]

... In short, for *general* purposes, we may fairly compare the whole body of Israelites, together with the "mixed multitude," E.xii.38,[148] to the entire population of the city of London, which was 2,362,236, by the census of 1851, increased to 2,803,035, by that of 1861.

41. How, then, is it conceivable that a man should do what Joshua is here said to have done, unless, indeed, the reading every "word of all that Moses commanded," with "the blessings and cursings, according to all that is written in the book of the Law,"[149] was a mere dumb show, without the least idea of those most solemn words being *heard* by those to whom they were addressed? For, surely, no human voice, unless strengthened by a miracle of which the Scripture tells us nothing, could have reached the ears of a crowded mass of people, as large as the whole population of London. The very crying of the "little ones,"[150] who are expressly stated to have been present, must have sufficed to drown the sounds at a few yards' distance.

---

141 Deuteronomy 1:1.
142 Deuteronomy 5:1.
143 Joshua 8:34–35.
144 Numbers 1:3, 46.
145 Johan Heinrich Kurtz, *Lehrbuch der Heiligen Geschichte* (1849).
146 Thomas Hartwell Horne, *Introduction to the Critical Study and Knowledge of the Holy Scriptures* (1818).
147 John Kitto, *Pictorial History of Palestine and the Holy Land, Including a Complete History of the Jews* (1840).
148 Exodus 12:38.
149 Joshua 8:34–35.
150 Joshua 8:35.

John Henry Newman
from *Apologia pro Vita Sua* (1864)

Catholic intellectual John Henry Newman (1801–90) was an important Anglican theologian before he converted to Catholicism in 1845. Educated at Trinity College, Oxford, he became a fellow of Oriel College and vicar of St. Mary's, Oxford, where his Anglican sermons enraptured audiences. In 1833, Newman (along with clergymen John Keble, Edward Bouverie Pusey, Richard Hurrell Froude, and others) founded the Oxford (Tractarian) Movement, which promoted seventeenth-century High-Church tradition in opposition to Broad-Church liberalism and state involvement in the church. *Tracts for the Times* (1833–41), the movement's pamphlet series, aroused controversy with the publication of Newman's *Tract 90* (1841), which proposed that the Church of England's 39 Articles were compatible with Catholicism. Oxford authorities subsequently banned the tracts and Newman resigned from St. Mary's in 1843. In 1845, he converted to Catholicism, eventually becoming a priest in 1847 and a cardinal in 1879.

His *Apologia pro Vita Sua* (1864) gives an account of his spiritual struggle. First published serially in weekly pamphlets, it became a bestseller and secured Newman financially.

∼

Part 5: History of My Religious Opinions

And now that I am about to trace, as far as I can, the course of that great revolution of mind, which led me to leave my own home, to which I was bound by so many strong and tender ties, I feel overcome with the difficulty of satisfying myself in my account of it, and have recoiled from doing so, till the near approach of the day, on which these lines must be given to the world, forces me to set about the task. For who can know himself, and the multitude of subtle influences which act upon him? and who can recollect, at the distance of twenty-five years, all that he once knew about his thoughts and his deeds, and that, during a portion of his life, when even at the time his observation, whether of himself or of the external world, was less than before or after, by very reason of the perplexity and dismay which weighed upon him,—when, though it would be most unthankful to seem to imply that he had not all-sufficient light amid his darkness, yet a darkness it emphatically was? ... I could not in cool blood, nor except upon the imperious call of duty, attempt what I have set myself to do. It is both to head and heart an extreme trial, thus to analyze what has so long gone by, and to bring out the results of that examination. I have done various bold things in my life: this is the boldest: and, were I not sure I should after all succeed in my object, it would be madness to set about it.

In the spring of 1839 my position in the Anglican Church was at its height. I had supreme confidence in my controversial *status*, and I had a great and still growing success, in recommending it to others.... In January, if I recollect aright, in order to meet the popular clamour against myself and others, and to satisfy the Bishop, I had collected into one all the strong things which they, and especially I, had said against the

Church of Rome, in order to their insertion among the advertisements appended to our publications. Conscious as I was that my opinions in religion were not gained, as the world said, from Roman sources, but were, on the contrary, the birth of my own mind and of the circumstances in which I had been placed, I had a scorn of the imputations which were heaped upon me. It was true that I held a large bold system of religion, very unlike the Protestantism of the day, but it was the concentration and adjustment of the statements of great Anglican authorities, and I had as much right to do so, as the Evangelical party had, and more right than the Liberal,[151] to hold their own respective doctrines....

What will best describe my state of mind at the early part of 1839, is an Article in the British Critic[152] for that April. I have looked over it now, for the first time since it was published; and have been struck by it for this reason:—it contains the last words which I ever spoke as an Anglican to Anglicans. It may now be read as my parting address and valediction, made to my friends. I little knew it at the time. It reviews the actual state of things, and it ends by looking towards the future.... It was published two years before the affair of Tract 90,[153] and was entitled "The State of Religious Parties."

In this Article, I begin by bringing together testimonies from our enemies to the remarkable success of our exertions. One writer said: "Opinions and views of a theology of a very marked and peculiar kind have been extensively adopted and strenuously upheld, and are daily gaining ground among a considerable and influential portion of the members, as well as ministers of the Established Church."[154] ... Another: "The time has gone by, when those unfortunate and deeply regretted publications can be passed over without notice, and the hope that their influence would fail is now dead." ... And, lastly, a bishop in a Charge:—It "is daily assuming a more serious and alarming aspect. Under the specious pretence of deference to Antiquity and respect for primitive models, the foundations of the Protestant Church are undermined by men, who dwell within her walls, and those who sit in the Reformers' seat are traducing the Reformation."[155]

After thus stating the phenomenon of the time, as it presented itself to those who did not sympathize in it, the Article proceeds to account for it; and this it does by considering it as a re-action from the dry and superficial character of the religious teaching and the literature of the last generation, or century, and as a result of the need which was felt both by the hearts and the intellects of the nation for a deeper philosophy, and as the evidence and as the partial fulfilment of that need, to which even the chief authors of the then generation had borne witness. First, I mentioned the literary influence of Walter Scott,[156] who turned men's minds to the direction of the middle ages. "The general need," I said, "of something deeper and more attractive, than what had offered itself elsewhere, may be considered to have led to his popularity; and by means of his popularity he re-acted on his readers, stimulating their mental thirst, feeding their hopes, setting before them visions, which, when once seen, are not easily forgotten, and silently indoctrinating them with nobler ideas, which might afterwards be appealed to as first principles."

---

151 Evangelicalism was a movement within the Church of England (Anglicanism) that emphasized individual connection with God and the aid of others; the Liberals had been in power for five years at the time of Newman's writing.
152 *The British Critic, and Quarterly Theological Review*, an Anglican magazine.
153 Newman's controversial tract suggested that the Church of England's 39 Articles, which articulate the differences between the Protestant and Catholic churches, could sustain a Roman Catholic interpretation.
154 The Anglican Church.
155 The Bishop suggests that Tractarians such as Newman, who purport to reform the Anglican Church, are actually betraying the religious Reformation of the sixteenth century.
156 Walter Scott (1771–1832), writer.

Then I spoke of Coleridge,[157] thus: "While history in prose and verse was thus made the instrument of Church feelings and opinions, a philosophical basis for the same was laid in England by a very original thinker, who, while he indulged a liberty of speculation, which no Christian can tolerate, and advocated conclusions which were often heathen rather than Christian, yet after all instilled a higher philosophy into inquiring minds, than they had hitherto been accustomed to accept. In this way he made trial of his age, and succeeded in interesting its genius in the cause of Catholic truth."

Then come Southey and Wordsworth,[158] "two living poets, one of whom in the department of fantastic fiction, the other in that of philosophical meditation, have addressed themselves to the same high principles and feelings, and carried forward their readers in the same direction."

Then comes the prediction of this re-action hazarded by "a sagacious observer withdrawn from the world, and surveying its movements from a distance," Mr. Alexander Knox.[159] He had said twenty years before the date of my writing: "No Church on earth has more intrinsic excellence than the English Church, yet no Church probably has less practical influence.... The rich provision, made by the grace and providence of God, for habits of a noble kind, is evidence that men shall arise, fitted both by nature and ability, to discover for themselves, and to display to others, whatever yet remains undiscovered, whether in the words or works of God." Also I referred to "a much venerated clergyman of the last generation," who said shortly before his death, "Depend on it, the day will come, when those great doctrines, now buried, will be brought out to the light of day, and then the effect will be fearful." I remarked upon this, that they who "now blame the impetuosity of the current, should rather turn their animadversions upon those who have dammed up a majestic river, till it had become a flood."

These being the circumstances under which the Movement[160] began and progressed, it was absurd to refer it to the act of two or three individuals. It was not so much a movement as a "spirit afloat;" it was within us, "rising up in hearts where it was least suspected, and working itself, though not in secret, yet so subtly and impalpably, as hardly to admit of precaution or encounter on any ordinary human rules of opposition. It is," I continued, "an adversary in the air, a something one and entire, a whole wherever it is, unapproachable and incapable of being grasped, as being the result of causes far deeper than political or other visible agencies, the spiritual awakening of spiritual wants." ...

While I thus republish what I then said about such extravagances as occurred in these years, at the same time I have a very strong conviction that they furnished quite as much the welcome excuse for those who were jealous or shy of us, as the stumbling-blocks of those who were well inclined to our doctrines. This too we felt at the time; but it was our duty to see that our good should not be evil-spoken of; and accordingly, two or three of the writers of the Tracts for the Times[161] had commenced a Series of what they called "Plain Sermons"[162] with the avowed purpose of discouraging and correcting whatever was uppish or extreme in our followers: to this Series I contributed a volume myself.

---

157 Samuel Taylor Coleridge (1772–1834), poet.
158 Robert Southey (1774–1843), poet; William Wordsworth (1770–1850), poet.
159 Alexander Knox (1757–1831), theologian.
160 The Oxford Movement, also known as Tractarianism.
161 Newman and other leaders of the Oxford Movement published most of these tracts anonymously with the goal of promoting the movement.
162 John and Thomas Keble, John Henry Newman, George Prevost, Edward Bouverie Pusey, Isaac Williams, and Robert Francis Wilson, *Plain Sermons* (1839).

Its conductors say in their Preface: "If ... there shall be any, who, in the silent humility of their lives, and in their unaffected reverence for holy things, show that they in truth accept these principles as real and substantial, and by habitual purity of heart and serenity of temper, give proof of their deep veneration for sacraments and sacramental ordinances, those persons, *whether our professed adherents or not*, best exemplify the kind of character which the writers of the Tracts for the Times have wished to form." ...

This state of things, however, I said, could not last, if men were to read and think. They "will not keep standing in that very attitude which you call sound Church-of-Englandism or orthodox Protestantism. They cannot go on for ever standing on one leg, or sitting without a chair, or walking with their feet tied, or grazing like Tityrus's stags in the air.[163] They will take one view or another, but it will be a consistent view. It may be Liberalism, or Erastianism, or Popery, or Catholicity;[164] but it will be real." ...

And thus I left the matter. But, while I was thus speaking of the future of the Movement, I was in truth winding up my accounts with it, little dreaming that it was so to be;—while I was still, in some way or other, feeling about for an available *Via Media*,[165] I was soon to receive a shock which was to cast out of my imagination all middle courses and compromises for ever....

The Long Vacation[166] of 1839 began early. There had been a great many visitors to Oxford from Easter to Commemoration;[167] and Dr. Pusey[168] and myself had attracted attention, more, I think, than any former year. I had put away from me the controversy with Rome for more than two years. In my Parochial Sermons[169] the subject had never been introduced: there had been nothing for two years, either in my Tracts or in the British Critic, of a polemical character. I was returning, for the Vacation, to the course of reading which I had many years before chosen as especially my own. I have no reason to suppose that the thoughts of Rome came across my mind at all. About the middle of June I began to study and master the history of the Monophysites....[170] It was during this course of reading that for the first time a doubt came upon me of the tenableness of Anglicanism....

I have described in a former work, how the history affected me. My stronghold was Antiquity; now here, in the middle of the fifth century, I found, as it seemed to me, Christendom of the sixteenth and the nineteenth centuries reflected. I saw my face in that mirror, and I was a Monophysite. The Church of the *Via Media* was in the position of the Oriental communion, Rome was, where she now is; and the Protestants were the Eutychians.[171] Of all passages of history, since history has been, who would have

---

163 Virgil, *Eclogues* (c. 37 BCE).
164 Liberalism posits that individuals have the right to determine their own political and religious opinions; Erastianism posits that the state has ultimate authority over the church; Popery posits that the Pope holds ultimate authority; Catholicity posits that Catholic doctrines hold ultimate authority.
165 Latin: middle way.
166 Summer vacation.
167 Commemoration week, which honours the university's forebears and supporters, is the last week of the academic year.
168 Edward Bouverie Pusey (1800–82), theologian.
169 Published between 1834 and 1842.
170 A Christian sect that believed Christ to possess a single divine nature rather than both divine and human natures.
171 Eutychians, after Eutyches (c. 375–454), orthodox abbot; an extremist monophysite church faction.

thought of going to the sayings and doings of old Eutyches, that *delirus senex*,[172] as (I think) Petavius[173] calls him, and to the enormities of the unprincipled Dioscorus,[174] in order to be converted to Rome!...

Hardly had I brought my course of reading to a close, when the Dublin Review of that same August was put into my hands,[175] by friends who were more favourable to the cause of Rome than I was myself. There was an Article in it on the "Anglican Claim" by Bishop Wiseman....[176] It was on the Donatists,[177] with an application to Anglicanism. I read it, and did not see much in it.... But my friend, an anxiously religious man, now, as then, very dear to me, a Protestant still, pointed out the palmary[178] words of St. Augustine,[179] which were contained in one of the extracts made in the Review, and which had escaped my observation. "Securus judicat orbis terrarum."[180] He repeated these words again and again, and, when he was gone, they kept ringing in my ears. "Securus judicat orbis terrarum;" they were words which went beyond the occasion of the Donatists: they applied to that of the Monophysites. They gave a cogency to the Article, which had escaped me at first. They decided ecclesiastical questions on a simpler rule than that of Antiquity; nay, St. Augustine was one of the prime oracles of Antiquity; here then Antiquity was deciding against itself.... Who can account for the impressions which are made on him? For a mere sentence, the words of St. Augustine, struck me with a power which I never had felt from any words before. To take a familiar instance, they were like the "Turn again Whittington" of the chime;[181] or, to take a more serious one, they were like the "Tolle, lege,—Tolle, lege,"[182] of the child, which converted St. Augustine himself. "Securus judicat orbis terrarum!" By those great words of the ancient Father, the theory of the *Via Media* was absolutely pulverized.

... He who has seen a ghost, cannot be as if he had never seen it. The heavens had opened and closed again. The thought for the moment had been, "The Church of Rome will be found right after all;" and then it had vanished. My old convictions remained as before....

Now to trace the succession of thoughts, and the conclusions, and the consequent innovations on my previous belief, and the general conduct, to which I was led, upon this sudden visitation....

When I got back to Oxford in October, 1839, after the visits which I had been paying, it so happened, there had been, in my absence, occurrences of an awkward character, bringing me into collision both with my Bishop and also with the University authorities; and this drew my attention at once to the state of what would be considered the Movement party there, and made me very anxious for the future. In the spring of the year, as has been seen in the Article analyzed above, I had spoken of the excesses which were to be found among persons commonly included in it; at that time I thought little of such an evil, but the new

---

172 Latin: silly old person.
173 Dionysius Petavius (1583–1652), French theologian.
174 Dioscorus (d. 454), Alexandrian bishop and supporter of Eutyches.
175 *Dublin Review*, a quarterly magazine and an important venue for Catholic debate.
176 Nicholas Patrick Stephen Wiseman (1802–65), archbishop of Westminster.
177 A North African religious sect existing from the fourth to the seventh centuries.
178 Estimable.
179 Aurelius Augustine (354–430), Algerian theologian and saint.
180 Latin: The whole world judges correctly: Augustine, *Contra epistolam Parmeniani* (400).
181 In pantomimes, the character Dick Whittington hears a message in the chime of London bells telling him to return to London.
182 Latin: Take up and read: Augustine, *Confessions* (c. 400).

thoughts, which had come on me during the Long Vacation, on the one hand made me comprehend it, and on the other took away my power of effectually meeting it. A firm and powerful control was necessary to keep men straight; I never had a strong wrist, but at the very time, when it was most needed, the reins had broken in my hands. With an anxious presentiment on my mind of the upshot of the whole inquiry, which it was almost impossible for me to conceal from men who saw me day by day, who heard my familiar conversation, who came perhaps for the express purpose of pumping me, and having a categorical *yes* or *no* to their questions,—how could I expect to say any thing about my actual, positive, present belief, which would be sustaining or consoling to such persons as were haunted already by doubts of their own? Nay, how could I, with satisfaction to myself, analyze my own mind, and say what I held and what I did not? or say with what limitations, shades of difference, or degrees of belief, I held that body of opinions which I had openly professed and taught? how could I deny or assert this point or that, without injustice to the new view, in which the whole evidence for those old opinions presented itself to my mind?

... My first business then, was to examine this question carefully, and see, if a great deal could not be said after all for the Anglican Church, in spite of its acknowledged short-comings. This I did in an Article "on the Catholicity of the English Church," which appeared in the British Critic of January, 1840....

But, secondly, the great stumbling-block lay in the 39 Articles.[183] It was urged that here was a positive Note *against* Anglicanism:—Anglicanism claimed to hold that the Church of England was nothing else than a continuation in this country, (as the Church of Rome might be in France or Spain,) of that one Church of which in old times Athanasius[184] and Augustine were members. But, if so, the doctrine must be the same; the doctrine of the Old Church must live and speak in Anglican formularies, in the 39 Articles. Did it? Yes, it did; that is what I maintained; it did in substance, in a true sense. Man had done his worst to disfigure, to mutilate, the old Catholic Truth, but there it was, in spite of them, in the Articles still. It was there, but this must be shown. It was a matter of life and death to us to show it. And I believed that it could be shown; I considered that those grounds of justification, which I gave above, when I was speaking of Tract 90, were sufficient for the purpose; and therefore I set about showing it at once. This was in March, 1840, when I went up to Littlemore.[185] And, as it was a matter of life and death with us, all risks must be run to show it. When the attempt was actually made, I had got reconciled to the prospect of it, and had no apprehensions as to the experiment; but in 1840, while my purpose was honest, and my grounds of reason satisfactory, I did nevertheless recognize that I was engaged in an *experimentum crucis*.[186] I have no doubt that then I acknowledged to myself that it would be a trial of the Anglican Church, which it had never undergone before,—not that the Catholic sense of the Articles had not been held or at least suffered by their framers and promulgators, and was not implied in the teaching of Andrewes or Beveridge,[187] but that it had never been publicly recognized, while the interpretation of the day was Protestant and exclusive. I observe also, that, though my Tract was an experiment, it was, as I said at the time, "no *feeler*," the event showed it; for, when my principle was not granted, I did not draw back, but gave up. I would not hold office in a Church which would not allow my sense of the Articles....

---

183 Statements of Anglican doctrine to which ordained ministers must subscribe.
184 Athanasius (c. 293–373), Alexandrian theologian and saint.
185 A village near Oxford.
186 Latin: crucial test.
187 Lancelot Andrewes (1555–1626), bishop of Winchester; William Beveridge (c. 1637–1708), bishop of St. Asaph.

This then was the second work to which I set myself; though when I got to Littlemore, other things came in the way of accomplishing it at the moment. I had in mind to remove all such obstacles as were in the way of holding the Apostolic and Catholic character of the Anglican teaching; to assert the right of all who chose to say in the face of day, "Our Church teaches the Primitive Ancient faith." I did not conceal this: in Tract 90, it is put forward as the first principle of all, "It is a duty which we owe both to the Catholic Church, and to our own, to take our reformed confessions in the most Catholic sense they will admit: we have no duties towards their framers." ...

A third measure which I distinctly contemplated, was the resignation of St. Mary's,[188] whatever became of the question of the Articles.... That I also contemplated even the further step of giving up St. Mary's itself as early as 1839, appears from a letter which I wrote in October, 1840, to the friend whom it was most natural for me to consult on such a point. It ran as follows:— ...

"... I cannot disguise from myself that my preaching is not calculated to defend that system of religion which has been received for 300 years, and of which the Heads of Houses[189] are the legitimate maintainers in this place....["]

"... I fear I must allow that, whether I will or no, I am disposing them towards Rome. First, because Rome is the only representative of the Primitive Church besides ourselves; in proportion then as they are loosened from the one, they will go to the other. Next, because many doctrines which I have held, have far greater, or their only scope, in the Roman system. And, moreover, if, as is not unlikely, we have in process of time heretical Bishops or teachers among us, an evil which *ipso facto*[190] infects the whole community to which they belong, and if, again (what there are at this moment symptoms of), there be a movement in the English Roman Catholics to break the alliance of O'Connell and of Exeter Hall,[191] strong temptations will be placed in the way of individuals, already imbued with a tone of thought congenial to Rome, to join her Communion["]....

"The *arguments* which I have published against Romanism seem to myself as cogent as ever, but men go by their sympathies, not by argument; and if I feel the force of this influence myself, who bow to the arguments, why may not others still more who never have in the same degree admitted the arguments?["] ...

Such was about my state of mind, on the publication of Tract 90 in February, 1841. The immense commotion consequent upon the publication of the Tract did not unsettle me again; for I had weathered the storm: the Tract had not been condemned: that was the great point; I made much of it....

Upon occasion of Tract 90 several Catholics wrote to me; I answered one of my correspondents thus:— ...

"The Tracts are not *suppressed*. No doctrine or principle has been conceded by us, or condemned by authority. The Bishop has but said that a certain Tract is 'objectionable,' no reason being stated. I have no intention whatever of yielding any one point which I hold on conviction; and that the authorities of the Church know full well."

---

188 Newman was vicar of St. Mary's, Oxford from 1828 to 1843.
189 Heads of Oxford colleges.
190 Latin: by that very fact.
191 Daniel O'Connell (1775–1847), Irish politician known as "the Liberator," who spurred the cause of Catholic emancipation (1829) when he was elected to parliament but could not initially take his seat because he was Catholic; Exeter Hall, London, where various religious societies regularly met.

In the summer of 1841, I found myself at Littlemore without any harass or anxiety on my mind. I had determined to put aside all controversy, and I set myself down to my translation of St. Athanasius; but, between July and November, I received three blows which broke me.

1. I had got but a little way in my work, when my trouble returned on me. The ghost had come a second time. In the Arian History[192] I found the very same phenomenon, in a far bolder shape, which I had found in the Monophysite.... Wonderful that this should come upon me! I had not sought it out; I was reading and writing in my own line of study, far from the controversies of the day, on what is called a "metaphysical" subject; but I saw clearly, that in the history of Arianism, the pure Arians were the Protestants, the semi-Arians were the Anglicans, and that Rome now was what it was. The truth lay, not with the *Via Media*, but in what was called "the extreme party." ...

2. I was in the misery of this new unsettlement, when a second blow came upon me. The Bishops one after another began to charge against me. It was a formal, determinate movement....

On October 17th, I wrote thus to a friend: "I suppose it will be necessary in some shape or other to re-assert Tract 90; else, it will seem, after these Bishops' Charges, as if it were silenced, which it has not been, nor do I intend it should be. I wish to keep quiet; but if Bishops speak, I will speak too. If the view were silenced, I could not remain in the Church, nor could many others; and therefore, since it is *not* silenced, I shall take care to show that it isn't."

A day or two after, Oct. 22, a stranger wrote to me to say, that the Tracts for the Times had made a young friend of his a Catholic, and to ask, "would I be so good as to convert him back;" I made answer:

"If conversions to Rome take place in consequence of the Tracts for the Times, I do not impute blame to them, but to those who, instead of acknowledging such Anglican principles of theology and ecclesiastical polity as they contain, set themselves to oppose them. Whatever be the influence of the Tracts, great or small, they may become just as powerful for Rome, if our Church refuses them, as they would be for our Church if she accepted them. If our rulers speak either against the Tracts, or not at all, if any number of them, not only do not favour, but even do not suffer the principles contained in them, it is plain that our members may easily be persuaded either to give up those principles, or to give up the Church. If this state of things goes on, I mournfully prophesy, not one or two, but many secessions to the Church of Rome."

Two years afterwards, looking back on what had passed, I said, "There were no converts to Rome, till after the condemnation of No. 90."

3. As if all this were not enough, there came the affair of the Jerusalem Bishopric; and, with a brief mention of it, I shall conclude.

I think I am right in saying that it had been long a desire with the Prussian Court to introduce Episcopacy[193] into the Evangelical Religion, which was intended in that country to embrace both the Lutheran and Calvinistic bodies....[194] I suppose that the idea of Episcopacy, as the Prussian king understood it, was very different from that taught in the Tractarian School; but still, I suppose also, that the chief authors of that school would have gladly seen such a measure carried out in Prussia, had it been done without compromising those principles which were necessary to the being of a Church. About the

---

192 Following Arius (c. 250–336), Arians denied the divinity of Christ.
193 Prussia, a kingdom of Germany and a major political power until Germany's defeat in World War I; episcopacy is church government.
194 Types of Protestantism, the first following the teachings of Martin Luther (1483–1546), the second those of John Calvin (1509–64).

time of the publication of Tract 90, M. Bunsen and the then Archbishop of Canterbury were taking steps for its execution,[195] by appointing and consecrating a Bishop for Jerusalem. Jerusalem, it would seem, was considered a safe place for the experiment; it was too far from Prussia to awaken the susceptibilities of any party at home; if the project failed, it failed without harm to any one; and, if it succeeded, it gave Protestantism a *status* in the East, which, in association with the Monophysite or Jacobite and the Nestorian bodies,[196] formed a political instrument for England, parallel to that which Russia had in the Greek Church, and France in the Latin....[197]

Now here, at the very time that the Anglican Bishops were directing their censure upon me for avowing an approach to the Catholic Church not closer than I believed the Anglican formularies would allow, they were on the other hand fraternizing, by their act or by their sufferance, with Protestant bodies, and allowing them to put themselves under an Anglican Bishop, without any renunciation of their errors or regard to the due reception of baptism and confirmation; while there was great reason to suppose that the said Bishop was intended to make converts from the orthodox Greeks, and the schismatical Oriental bodies, by means of the influence of England. This was the third blow, which finally shattered my faith in the Anglican Church. That Church was not only forbidding any sympathy or concurrence with the Church of Rome, but it actually was courting an intercommunion with Protestant Prussia and the heresy of the Orientals. The Anglican Church might have the Apostolical succession, as had the Monophysites; but such acts as were in progress led me to the gravest suspicion, not that it would soon cease to be a Church, but that it had never been a Church all along.

On October 12th I thus wrote to a friend:—"We have not a single Anglican in Jerusalem, so we are sending a Bishop to *make* a communion, not to govern our own people. Next, the excuse is, that there are converted Anglican Jews there who require a Bishop; I am told there are not half-a-dozen. But for *them* the Bishop is sent out, and for them he is a Bishop of the *circumcision*" (I think he was a converted Jew, who boasted of his Jewish descent), "against the Epistle to the Galatians[198] pretty nearly. Thirdly, for the sake of Prussia, he is to take under him all the foreign Protestants who will come; and the political advantages will be so great, from the influence of England, that there is no doubt they *will* come. They are to sign the Confession of Augsburg,[199] and there is nothing to show that they hold the doctrine of Baptismal Regeneration.["][200]

"As to myself, I shall do nothing whatever publicly, unless indeed it were to give my signature to a Protest; but I think it would be out of place in *me* to agitate, having been in a way silenced; but the Archbishop is really doing most grave work, of which we cannot see the end."

I did make a solemn Protest, and sent it to the Archbishop of Canterbury, and also sent it to my own Bishop....

---

195 Christian Karl Josias von Bunsen (1791–1860), Prussian diplomat; William Howley (1766–1848), archbishop of Canterbury.
196 Jacobites are members of a Monophysite sect that follows Jacobus Baradæus; Nestorians follow Nestorius (c. 400–51) and believe that Christ has two distinct natures, the divine and the human.
197 Orthodoxy and Roman Catholicism.
198 The Epistle of St. Paul the Apostle to the Galatians, a book in the New Testament.
199 The *Augsburg Confession* (1530) summarized Lutheran beliefs.
200 The belief that water baptism is necessary for spiritual salvation.

Protest.

"Whereas the Church of England has a claim on the allegiance of Catholic believers only on the ground of her own claim to be considered a branch of the Catholic Church:

And whereas the recognition of heresy, indirect as well as direct, goes far to destroy such claim in the case of any religious body advancing it:

And whereas to admit maintainers of heresy to communion, without formal renunciation of their errors, goes far towards recognizing the same:

And whereas Lutheranism and Calvinism are heresies, repugnant to Scripture, springing up three centuries since, and anathematized by East as well as West:

And whereas it is reported that the Most Reverend Primate[201] and other Right Reverend Rulers of our Church have consecrated a Bishop with a view to exercising spiritual jurisdiction over Protestant, that is, Lutheran and Calvinist congregations in the East (under the provisions of an Act made in the last session of Parliament to amend an Act made in the 26th year of the reign of his Majesty King George the Third, intituled, 'An Act to empower the Archbishop of Canterbury, or the Archbishop of York for the time being, to consecrate to the office of Bishop persons being subjects or citizens of countries out of his Majesty's dominions'), dispensing at the same time, not in particular cases and accidentally, but as if on principle and universally, with any abjuration of error on the part of such congregations, and with any reconciliation to the Church on the part of the presiding Bishop; thereby giving some sort of formal recognition to the doctrines which such congregations maintain:

And whereas the dioceses[202] in England are connected together by so close an intercommunion, that what is done by authority in one, immediately affects the rest:

On these grounds, I in my place, being a priest of the English Church and Vicar of St. Mary the Virgin's, Oxford, by way of relieving my conscience, do hereby solemnly protest against the measure aforesaid, and disown it, as removing our Church from her present ground and tending to her disorganization.

JOHN HENRY NEWMAN.
November 11, 1841."

Looking back two years afterwards on the above-mentioned and other acts, on the part of Anglican Ecclesiastical authorities, I observe: "Many a man might have held an abstract theory about the Catholic Church, to which it was difficult to adjust the Anglican,—might have admitted a suspicion, or even painful doubts about the latter,—yet never have been impelled onwards, had our Rulers preserved the quiescence of former years; but it is the corroboration of a present, living, and energetic heterodoxy, which realizes and makes them practical; it has been the recent speeches and acts of authorities, who had so long been tolerant of Protestant error, which have given to inquiry and to theory its force and its edge."

As to the project of a Jerusalem Bishopric, I never heard of any good or harm it has ever done, except what it has done for me; which many think a great misfortune, and I one of the greatest of mercies. It brought me on to the beginning of the end.

---

201 The archbishop of Canterbury.
202 A diocese is a district under the care of a particular bishop.

Leslie Stephen
from "An Agnostic's Apology" (1876)

Leslie Stephen (1832–1904), literary critic, *Cornhill Magazine* editor (1871–82), and Virginia Woolf's father, was the first editor of the *Dictionary of National Biography*. At Cambridge, Stephen excelled at rowing, distance running, and academics. Winning a university fellowship in 1854 with clerical requirements, Stephen became a deacon in 1855 and an Anglican priest in 1859. Increasingly skeptical of religion, however, he resigned his tutorship in 1862. Stephen was also an avid climber, ranking among top English mountaineers and publishing alpine essays early in his journalism career. A regular contributor to the press, Stephen edited the *Dictionary of National Biography* to much critical praise, writing 283 entries.

Essays on Freethinking and Plainspeaking (1873) contextualized Stephen's abandonment of Anglican clerical duties and established him as a prominent agnostic. Written after his first wife's death, "An Agnostic's Apology" first appeared in the *Fortnightly Review* (June 1876); revised, it became the lead essay in *An Agnostic's Apology and Other Essays* (1893).

An attempt has recently been made to obtain currency for the new nickname—Agnostic.[203] Protests against nicknames are foolish; foolish because unavailing, and foolish because nicknames are always harmless. A protest in this case would be especially foolish; for the nickname in question seems to indicate a distinct advance in the courtesies of controversy. The old theological phrase for an intellectual opponent was Atheist—a name which still retains a certain flavour as of the stake in this world and hell-fire in the next, and which, moreover, implies an inaccuracy of some importance. Dogmatic Atheism[204]—the doctrine that there is no God, whatever may be meant by God—is, to say the least, a rare phase of opinion. The word Agnosticism, on the other hand, seems to imply a fairly accurate appreciation of a form of creed already common and daily spreading. The Agnostic is one who asserts—what no one denies—that there are limits to the sphere of human intelligence. He asserts, further, what many theologians have expressly maintained, that those limits are such as to exclude at least what Mr. Lewes has so happily called "metempirical" knowledge.[205] But he goes further, and asserts, in opposition to theologians, that theology lies within this forbidden sphere. This last assertion raises the important issue; and, though I have no pretension to invent an opposition nickname, I may venture, for the purposes of this article, to describe the rival school as Gnostics.[206]

The Gnostic holds that our reason can, in some sense, transcend the narrow limits of experience. He holds that we can attain truths not capable of verification, and not needing verification, by actual experiment or observation. He holds, further, that a knowledge of those truths is essential to the highest

---

203 The belief that it is impossible to confirm any existence beyond the material.
204 Disbelief in God's existence.
205 Knowledge based on faith rather than experience; George Henry Lewes, *Problems of Life and Mind* (1873–79).
206 Gnostics are adherents of occultism or mysticism who believe that transcendental or spiritual knowledge brings redemption.

interests of mankind, and enables us in some sort to solve the dark riddle of the universe.... Overpowered, as every honest and serious thinker is at times overpowered, by the sight of pain, folly, and helplessness, by the jarring discords which run through the vast harmony of the universe, we are yet enabled to hear at times a whisper that all is well, to trust to it as coming from the most authentic source, and to know that only the temporary bars of sense prevent us from recognising with certainty that the harmony beneath the discords is a reality and not a dream. This knowledge is embodied in the central dogma of theology. God is the name of the harmony; and God is knowable. Who would not be happy in accepting this belief, if he could accept it honestly? Who would not be glad if he could say with confidence, the evil is transitory, the good eternal: our doubts are due to limitations destined to be abolished, and the world is really an embodiment of love and wisdom, however dark it may appear to our faculties? And yet, if the so-called knowledge be illusory, are we not bound by the most sacred obligations to recognise the facts? ... Dreams may be pleasanter for the moment than realities; but happiness must be won by adapting our lives to the realities. And who that has felt the burden of existence, and suffered under well-meant efforts at consolation, will deny that such consolations are the bitterest of mockeries? Pain is not an evil; death is not a separation; sickness is but a blessing in disguise. Have the gloomiest speculations of avowed pessimists ever tortured sufferers like those kindly platitudes? Is there a more cutting piece of satire in the language than the reference in our funeral service to the "sure and certain hope of a blessed resurrection"?[207] To dispel genuine hopes might be painful, however salutary. To suppress these spasmodic efforts to fly in the face of facts would be some comfort even in the distress which they are meant to alleviate.

Besides the important question whether the Gnostic can prove his dogmas, there is therefore the further question whether the dogmas, if granted, have any meaning. Do they answer our doubts or mock us with the appearance of an answer? The Gnostics pride themselves on their knowledge.... They rebuke what they call the "pride of reason"[208] in the name of a still more exalted pride. The scientific reasoner is arrogant because he sets limits to the faculty in which he trusts, and denies the existence of any other faculty. They are humble because they dare to tread in the regions which he declares to be inaccessible. But without bandying such accusations, or asking which pride is the greatest, the Gnostics are at least bound to show some ostensible justification for their complacency. Have they discovered a firm resting-place from which they are entitled to look down in compassion or contempt upon those who hold it to be a mere edifice of moonshine? If they have diminished by a scruple the weight of one passing doubt, we should be grateful: perhaps we should be converts. If not, why condemn Agnosticism?

... Trust your reason, we have been told till we are tired of the phrase, and you will become Atheists or Agnostics. We take you at your word; we become Agnostics. What right have you to turn round and rate us for being a degree more logical than yourselves? Our right, you reply, is founded upon a Divine revelation to ourselves or our church. Let us grant—it is a very liberal concession—that the right may conceivably be established; but still you are at one with us in philosophy. You say as we say that the natural man can know nothing of the Divine nature. That is Agnosticism. Our fundamental principle is not only granted, but asserted. By what logical device you succeed in overleaping the barriers which you have declared to be insuperable is another question. At least you have no *primâ facie*[209] ground for attacking

---

207 "The Order for the Burial of the Dead," *Book of Common Prayer*.
208 John Wesley, *Expository Notes* (1755, 1761); see his commentary on Acts 17:32.
209 Latin: on the face of it; in law, *prima facie* evidence appears conclusive unless proven otherwise.

our assumption that the limits of the human intellect are what you declare them to be. This is no mere verbal retort. Half, or more than half, of our adversaries agree formally with our leading principle. They cannot attack us without upsetting the very ground upon which the ablest advocates of their own case rely. The last English writer who professed to defend Christianity with weapons drawn from wide and genuine philosophical knowledge was Dean Mansel.[210] The whole substance of his argument was simply and solely the assertion of the first principles of Agnosticism. Mr. Herbert Spencer, the prophet of the Unknowable, the foremost representative of Agnosticism, professes in his programme to be carrying "a step further the doctrine put into shape by Hamilton and Mansel."[211] Nobody, I suspect, would now deny, nobody except Dean Mansel himself ever denied very seriously, that the "further step" thus taken was the logical step. Opponents both from within and without the Church, Mr. Maurice and Mr. Mill,[212] agreed that this affiliation was legitimate. The Old Testament represents Jehovah as human, as vindictive, as prescribing immoralities; therefore, Jehovah was not the true God; that was the contention of the infidel. We know nothing whatever about the true God, was the reply, for God means the Absolute and the Infinite. Any special act may come from God, for it may be a moral miracle; any attribute may represent the character of God to man, for we know nothing whatever of his real attributes, and cannot even conceive Him as endowed with attributes. The doctrine of the Atonement[213] cannot be revolting, because it cannot have any meaning. Mr. Spencer hardly goes a step beyond his original, except, indeed, in candour.

... Dr. Newman is not, like Dean Mansel, a profound metaphysician, but his admirable rhetoric expresses a far finer religious instinct. He feels more keenly, if he does not reason so systematically; and the force of one side of his case is undeniable. He holds that the unassisted reason cannot afford a sufficient support for a belief in God. He declares, as innumerable writers of less power have declared, that there is "no medium, in true philosophy, between Atheism and Catholicity, and that a perfectly consistent mind, under those circumstances in which it finds itself here below, must embrace either the one or the other." ... He looks in vain for any antagonist, except the Catholic Church, capable of baffling and withstanding "the fierce energy of passion, and the all-corroding, all-dissolving scepticism of the intellect in religious matters."[214] ... Some such doctrine is in fact but a natural corollary from the doctrine of human corruption held by all genuine theologians. The very basis of orthodox theology is the actual separation of the creation from the creator. In the "Grammar of Assent," Newman tells us that we "can only glean from the surface of the world some faint and fragmentary views" of God. "I see," he proceeds, "only a choice of alternatives in view of so critical a fact; either there is no creator or he has disowned his creatures."[215] The absence of God from his own world is the one prominent fact which startles and appals him. Dr. Newman, of course, does not see or does not admit the obvious consequence. He asserts

---

210 Henry Longueville Mansel (1820–71), dean of St. Paul's Cathedral, London. Chosen as the Bampton lecturer for 1858, Mansel spoke on "The Limits of Religious Thought Examined," lectures subsequently published in 1859. His religious thought was heavily influenced by the philosopher Sir William Hamilton (1788–1856), who was in turn indebted to Immanuel Kant (1724–1804).
211 Herbert Spencer, *First Principles* (1862).
212 Frederick Denison Maurice (1805–72), theologian, philosopher, and scholar. See Education. John Stuart Mill (1806–73), social reformer, economist, and philosopher. See Life Writing, Condition of England, Gender and Sexuality.
213 Reparation for a wrong; under the Christian doctrine of atonement, God is reconciled with sinners through the sacrifice of Christ, which atones for Original Sin.
214 John Henry Newman, *Apologia* (1864). See Faith and Doubt.
215 Author's note: [John Henry Newman,] "Grammar of Assent," [1870] p. 392.

most emphatically that he believes in the existence of God as firmly as in his own existence; and he finds the ultimate proof of this doctrine—a proof not to be put into mood and figure—in the testimony of the conscience. But he apparently admits that Atheism is as logical, that is, as free from self-contradiction, as Catholicism. He certainly declares that though the ordinary arguments are conclusive, they are not in practice convincing.... If, therefore, Dr. Newman had never heard of the Catholic Church, if, that is, he were in the position of the great majority of men now living, and of the overwhelming majority of the race which has lived since its first appearance, he would be driven to one of two alternatives. Either he would be an Atheist or he would be an Agnostic. His conscience might say, there is a God; his observation would say, there is no God.... At any rate, Dr. Newman's arguments go to prove that man, as guided by reason, ought to be an Agnostic, and that, at the present moment, Agnosticism is the only reasonable faith for at least three-quarters of the race.

All, then, who think that men should not be dogmatic about matters beyond the sphere of reason or even conceivability, who hold that reason, however weak, is our sole guide, or who find that their conscience does not testify to the divinity of the Catholic God, but declares the moral doctrines of Catholicity to be demonstrably erroneous, are entitled to claim such orthodox writers as sharing their fundamental principles, though refusing to draw the legitimate inferences.... Dr. Newman may be as much convinced of the truth of his theology as Mr. Huxley of its error. But speaking of the race and not of the individual, there is no plainer fact in history than the fact that hitherto no knowledge has been attained. There is not a single proof of natural theology of which the negative has not been maintained as vigorously as the affirmative. The fact is notorious.

You tell us to be ashamed of professing ignorance. Where is the shame of ignorance in matters still involved in endless and hopeless controversy? Is it not rather a duty? ... What theory of the universe am I to accept as demonstrably established? At the very earliest dawn of philosophy men were divided by earlier forms of the same problems which divide them now. Shall I be a Platonist or an Aristotelian?[216] A nominalist or a realist?[217] Shall I admit or deny the existence of innate ideas?[218] Shall I believe in the possibility or in the impossibility of transcending experience? ... Shall I believe in Hobbes or in Descartes?[219] Can I stop where Descartes stopped, or must I go on to Spinoza?[220] Or shall I follow Locke's guidance, and end with Hume's scepticism?[221] Or listen to Kant,[222] and, if so, shall I decide that he is right in destroying theology or in reconstructing it, or in both performances? Does Hegel[223] hold the key of the secret, or is he a mere spinner of jargon? May not Feuerbach or Schopenhauer[224] represent the true development of metaphysical inquiry? Shall I put faith in Hamilton and Mansel, and, if so, shall I read their conclusions

---

216 Plato suggested that an idea (or form) exists independently from the physical senses and can be accessed by the mind alone; Aristotle argued that no form exists independently of the thing itself, and that one must use the physical senses to access knowledge.

217 A nominalist believes that universal concepts have no relation to reality, but are names only; a Platonic realist believes that universals have an absolute existence.

218 Inborn ideas.

219 Thomas Hobbes (1588–1679), philosopher; René Descartes (1596–1650), French philosopher and mathematician.

220 Baruch de Spinoza (1632–77), Dutch philosopher.

221 John Locke (1632–1704), philosopher and political scientist; David Hume (1711–76), philosopher and economist.

222 Immanuel Kant (1724–1804), German philosopher.

223 Georg Wilhelm Friedrich Hegel (1770–1831), German philosopher.

224 Ludwig Feuerbach (1804–72) and Arthur Schopenhauer (1788–1860), German philosophers.

by the help of Mr. Spencer, or shall I believe in Mill or Mr. Lewes?[225] State any one proposition in which all philosophers agree, and I will admit it to be true; or any one which has a manifest balance of authority, and I will agree that it is probable. But so long as every philosopher flatly contradicts the first principles of his predecessors, why affect certainty? The only agreement I can discover is, that there is no philosopher of whom his opponents have not said that his opinions lead logically either to Pantheism[226] or to Atheism.

When all the witnesses thus contradict each other, the *primâ facie* result is pure scepticism.... From such scepticism there is indeed one, and, so far as I can see, but one, escape. The very hopelessness of the controversy shows that the reasoners have been transcending the limits of reason.... In short, if I would avoid utter scepticism, must I not be an Agnostic? ...

There are two questions ... about the universe which must be answered to escape from Agnosticism. The great fact which puzzles the mind is the vast amount of evil. It may be answered that evil is an illusion, because God is benevolent; or it may be answered that evil is deserved, because God is just. In one case the doubt is removed by denying the existence of the difficulty, in the other it is made tolerable by satisfying our consciences. We have seen what natural reason can do towards justifying these answers. To escape from Agnosticism we become Pantheists; then the divine reality must be the counterpart of phenomenal nature, and all the difficulties recur. We escape from Pantheism by the illogical device of freewill. Then God is indeed good and wise, but God is no longer omnipotent. By his side we erect a fetish called freewill, which is potent enough to defeat all God's good purposes, and to make his absence from his own universe the most conspicuous fact given by observation; and which, at the same time, is by its own nature intrinsically arbitrary in its action. Your Gnosticism tells us that an almighty benevolence is watching over everything, and bringing good out of all evil. Whence, then, comes the evil? By freewill; that is, by chance! It is an exception, an exception which covers, say, half the phenomena, and includes all that puzzles us. Say boldly at once no explanation can be given, and then proceed to denounce Agnosticism. If, again, we take the moral problem, the Pantheist view shows desert[227] as before God to be a contradiction in terms. We are what he has made us; nay, we are but manifestations of himself—how can he complain? Escape from the dilemma by making us independent of God, and God, so far as the observed universe can tell us, becomes systematically unjust. He rewards the good and the bad, and gives equal reward to the free agent and the slave of fate. Where are we to turn for a solution?

Let us turn to revelation; that is the most obvious reply. By all means, though this is to admit that natural reason cannot help us.... This is of course a difficulty which runs off the orthodox disputant like water from a duck's back. He appeals to his conscience, and his conscience tells him just what he wants. It reveals a Being just at that point in the scale between the two extremes which is convenient for his purposes. I open, for example, a harmless little treatise by a divine who need not be named. He knows intuitively, so he says, that there is a God, who is benevolent and wise, and endowed with personality, that is to say, conceived anthropomorphically enough to be capable of acting upon the universe, and yet so far different from man as to be able to throw a decent veil of mystery over his more questionable actions. Well, I reply, my intuition tells me of no such being. Then, says the divine, I can't prove my statements, but you would recognise their truth if your heart or your intellect were not corrupted: that is, you must

---

225 George Henry Lewes (1817–78), journalist, science writer, and philosopher.
226 The belief that God and nature are synonymous.
227 Actions deserving good or bad reward.

be a knave or a fool. This is a kind of argument to which one is perfectly accustomed in theology. I am right, and you are wrong; and I am right because I am good and wise. By all means; and now let us see what your wisdom and goodness can tell us.

The Christian revelation makes statements which, if true, are undoubtedly of the very highest importance. God is angry with man. Unless we believe and repent we shall all be damned....[228] Christianity tells us in various ways how the wrath of the Creator may be appeased and his goodwill ensured. The doctrine is manifestly important to believers; but does it give us a clearer or happier view of the universe? That is what is required for the confusion of Agnostics; and, if the mystery were in part solved, or the clouds thinned in the slightest degree, Christianity would triumph by its inherent merits. Let us, then, ask once more, Does Christianity exhibit the ruler of the universe as benevolent or as just?

If I were to assert that of every ten beings born into this world nine would be damned, that all who refused to believe what they did not hold to be proved, and all who sinned from overwhelming temptation, and all who had not had the good fortune to be the subjects of a miraculous conversion or the recipients of a grace conveyed by a magical charm, would be tortured to all eternity, what would an orthodox theologian reply? He could not say, "That is false;" I might appeal to the highest authorities for my justification; nor, in fact, could he on his own showing deny the possibility. Hell, he says, exists; he does not know who will be damned; though he does know that all men are by nature corrupt and liable to be damned if not saved by supernatural grace. He might, and probably would, now say, "That is rash. You have no authority for saying how many will be lost and how many saved: you cannot even say what is meant by hell or heaven: you cannot tell how far God may be better than his word, though you may be sure that he won't be worse than his word." And what is all this but to say, We know nothing about it? In other words, to fall back on Agnosticism? The difficulty, as theologians truly say, is not so much that evil is eternal, as that evil exists. That is in substance a frank admission that, as nobody can explain evil, nobody can explain anything. Your revelation, which was to prove the benevolence of God, has proved only that God's benevolence may be consistent with the eternal and infinite misery of most of his creatures; you escape only by saying that it is also consistent with their not being eternally and infinitely miserable. That is, the revelation reveals nothing....

The believers who desire to soften away the old dogmas ... know that God is good and just; that evil will somehow disappear and apparent injustice be somehow redressed.... We fly to religion to escape from our dark forebodings. But a religion which stifles these forebodings always fails to satisfy us. We long to hear that they are groundless. Directly we are told that they are groundless, we distrust our authority. No poetry lives which reflects only the cheerful emotions. Our sweetest songs are those which tell of saddest thought.[229] We can bring harmony out of melancholy; we cannot banish melancholy from the world. And the religious utterances, which are the highest form of poetry, are bound by the same law. There is a deep sadness in the world. Turn and twist the thought as you may, there is no escape. Optimism would be soothing if it were possible; in fact, it is impossible, and therefore a constant mockery....

Let us, however, consider for a moment what is the net result of this pleasant creed. Its philosophical basis may be sought in pure reason or in experience; but, as a rule, its adherents are ready to admit that the pure reason requires the support of the emotions before such a doctrine can be established, and are

---

228 See Ezekiel 18:30; Acts 8:22.
229 Percy Bysshe Shelley, "To a Skylark" (1820).

therefore marked by a certain tinge of mysticism. They feel rather than know.... And, meanwhile, those who have been disabused with Candide,[230] who have felt the weariness and pain of all "this unintelligible world,"[231] and have not been able to escape into any mystic rapture, have as much to say for their own version of the facts. Is happiness a dream, or misery; or is it all a dream? ... Who shall decide, and how? Of all questions that can be asked, the most important is surely this: Is the tangled web of this world composed chiefly of happiness or of misery? and of all questions that can be asked, it is surely the most unanswerable....

In any case the real appeal must be to experience.... To say that misery does not exist is to contradict the primary testimony of consciousness; to argue on *à priori* grounds[232] that misery or happiness predominates is as hopeless a task as to deduce from the principle of the excluded middle the distance from St. Paul's to Westminster Abbey.[233] Questions of fact can only be solved by examining facts. Perhaps such evidence would show, and if a guess were worth anything, I should add that I guess that it would show, that happiness predominates over misery in the composition of the known world. I am, therefore, not prejudiced against the Gnostic's conclusion; but I add that the evidence is just as open to me as to him. The whole world in which we live may be an illusion—a veil to be withdrawn in some higher state of being. But be it what it may, it supplies all the evidence upon which we can rely. If evil predominates here, we have no reason to suppose that good predominates elsewhere. All the ingenuity of theologians can never shake our conviction that facts are what we feel them to be, nor invert the plain inference from facts; and facts are just as open to one school of thought as to another....

Is it not, then, the very height of audacity, in face of a difficulty, which meets us at every turn, which has perplexed all the ablest thinkers in proportion to their ability, which vanishes in one shape only to show itself in another, to declare roundly, not only that the difficulty can be solved, but that it does not exist? Why, when no honest man will deny in private that every ultimate problem is wrapped in the profoundest mystery, do honest men proclaim in pulpits that unhesitating certainty is the duty of the most foolish and ignorant? ...

Gentlemen, we can only reply, wait till you have some show of agreement amongst yourselves. Wait till you can give some answer, not palpably a verbal answer, to some one of the doubts which oppress us as they oppress you. Wait till you can point to some single truth, however trifling, which has been discovered by your method, and will stand the test of discussion and verification. Wait till you can appeal to reason without in the same breath vilifying reason. Wait till your divine revelations have something more to reveal than the hope that the hideous doubts which they suggest may possibly be without foundation. Till then, we shall be content to admit openly what you whisper under your breath or hide in technical jargon, that the ancient secret is a secret still; that man knows nothing of the Infinite and Absolute; and that, knowing nothing, he had better not be dogmatic about his ignorance. And, meanwhile, we will endeavour to be as charitable as possible, and whilst you trumpet forth officially your contempt for our scepticism, we will at least try to believe that you are imposed upon by your own bluster.

---

230 Voltaire [François-Marie Arouet], *Candide* (1759).
231 William Wordsworth, "Tintern Abbey" (1798).
232 Latin: from what is before; to reason deductively or presumptively, independently of experience.
233 St. Paul's Cathedral and Westminster Abbey, both prominent buildings in London.

Vernon Lee
from "The Responsibilities of Unbelief: A Conversation between Three Rationalists" (1883)

Writer and critic Violet Paget (1856–1935) wrote under the pseudonym Vernon Lee. As a child, Lee moved with her family around Europe, gaining an international perspective and fluency in four languages. Her critically acclaimed *Studies of the Eighteenth Century in Italy* (1880) secured her entrance into London literary and artistic networks. During the 1880s and 1890s, Lee cultivated her literary reputation as she published fiction, personal essays, travel writing, and essays on religion, aesthetics, and literature.

Lee's essay on "The Responsibilities of Unbelief" (1883) stages a conversation between three friends who discuss the personal and moral consequences of unbelief, especially whether one should preach agnosticism to family and friends: "We unbelievers—I should rather say we believers in the believable ... should all of us be, in a fashion, priests." Published in the *Contemporary Review*, the essay prompted a critique from Frances Power Cobbe (see Faith and Doubt).

"And finally," asked Vere, "what do you think is likely to have been the result of Monsignore's[234] wonderful sermon?"

He had gone to meet his two friends in the late summer afternoon; and as they walked slowly towards the old farm on the brink of the common, they had been giving him an account of the sermon which they had just been to hear; a sermon probably intended to overcome the last scruples of one Protestant in particular, a lady on a visit to the neighbouring Catholic Earl....

... "What I want to know is, whether you suppose that Monsignore has succeeded in making another convert?"

"I think he must have succeeded," answered Baldwin; "he had evidently brought that soul to the very brink of the ditch which separates Protestantism from Catholicism; his object was to make the passage quite insensible, to fill up the ditch so that its presence could not be perceived. He tried to make it appear to Protestant listeners that Catholicism was not at all the sort of foreign, illiberal, frog-eating, Guy-Fawkesy bugbear[235] of their fancy; but, on the contrary, the simple, obvious, liberal, modern, eminently English form of belief which they think they have got (but in their hearts must have felt that they have not) in Protestantism. And I really never saw anything more ingenious than the way in which, without ever mentioning the words Catholicism or Protestantism, Monsignore contrived to leave the impression that a really sincere Protestant is already more than half a Catholic. I assure you that, if it had not been for the awful sixpenny chromo-lithographs of the Passion, the bleeding wooden Christs, the Madonnas in

---

234 A Roman Catholic title (and sometimes a position) conferred by the Pope upon a clergyman.
235 Frog-eating is a derogatory term for French; Guy Fawkes (1570–1606) was a soldier and conspirator in the 1605 Gunpowder Plot to blow up the Houses of Parliament with King James I and his ministers inside; bugbears are unnecessary fears.

muslin frocks and spangles, and all the pious tawdriness which makes Rother Chapel look like some awful Belgian or Bavarian church,[236] I might almost have believed, for the moment, that the lady in question would do very wisely to turn Catholic."

"I wonder whether she will?" mused Vere, as they walked slowly across the yielding turf of the common, which seemed in its yellow greenness to be saturated with the gleams of sunshine, breaking ever and anon through the film of white cloud against which stood out the dark and massive outline of the pine clumps, the ghost-like array of the larches, and the pale-blue undulation of the distant downs.

"She may or she may not," answered Rheinhardt, "that is no concern of mine, any more than what becomes of the actors after an amusing comedy. What is it to us unbelievers whether one more mediocrity be lost by Protestantism and gained by Catholicism? ..."

"Poor woman!" replied Vere, "it does seem a little hard that her soul should be merely an apple to be juggled with for the amusement of Professor Rheinhardt. But, after all, I agree with you that it is of no consequence to us whether she turn Catholic or remain Protestant. The matter concerns only herself, and all is right as long as she settles down in the faith best adapted to her individual spiritual wants. There ought to be as many different religions as there are different sorts of character—religions and irreligions, of course; for I think you, Rheinhardt, would have been miserable had you lived before the invention of Voltaireanism.[237] The happiness of some souls appears to consist in a sense of vigour and self-reliance, a power of censuring one's self and one's neighbours; and Protestantism, as austere and Calvinistic[238] and democratic as possible, is the right religion for them. But there are others whose highest spiritual *bien être*[239] consists in a complete stripping off of all personality, a complete letting themselves passively be swung up and down by a force greater than themselves; and such people ought, I think, to turn Catholic."

Rheinhardt looked at Vere with a droll expression of semi-paternal contempt. "My dear Vere," he asked, "is it possible that you, at your age, can still believe in such nonsense? Ladies, I admit, may require for their complete happiness to abandon their conscience occasionally into the hands of some saintly person; but do you mean to say that a man in the possession of all his faculties, with plenty to do in the world, with a library of good books, some intelligent friends, a good digestion, and a good theatre when he has a mind to go there,—do you mean to tell me that such a man can ever be troubled by the wants of his soul?"

"Such a man as that certainly would not," answered Vere, "because the name of such a man would be Hans Rheinhardt."

"It is very odd," remarked Baldwin, "that neither of you seem to consider that the lady's conversion can concern anybody except herself; Rheinhardt looks upon it as a mere piece of juggling; you, Vere, seem to regard it in a kind of æsthetic light, as if the woman ought to choose a religion upon the same principle upon which she would choose a bonnet—namely, to get something comfortable and becoming."

"Surely," interrupted Vere, "the individual soul may be permitted to seek for peace wherever there is most chance of finding it?"

---

236 A chromolithograph is a colour print produced from a stone plate; the Passion refers to Christ's suffering in the last days before his death, including the crucifixion; Rother is a small district in East Sussex.
237 Religious skepticism associated with French writer and philosopher Voltaire [François-Marie Arouet] (1694–1778).
238 Calvinism is a type of Protestantism grounded in the beliefs of French theologian John Calvin (1509–64).
239 French: well-being.

"I don't see at all why the individual soul should have a right to seek for peace regardless of the interests of society at large, any more than why the individual body should have a right to satisfy its cravings regardless of the effect on the rest of mankind," retorted Baldwin. "You cry out against this latter theory as the height of immorality, because it strikes at the root of all respect for mine and thine; but don't you see that your assumed right to gratify your soul undermines, what is quite as important, all feeling of true and false? The soul is a nobler thing than the body, you will answer. But why is it nobler? Merely because it has greater powers for good and evil, greater duties and responsibilities; and for that very reason it ought to have less right to indulge itself at the expense of what belongs not to it, but to mankind. Truth——"

"Upon my word," put in Rheinhardt, "I don't know which is the greater plague, the old-fashioned nuisance called a soul, or the newfangled bore called mankind." And he pushed open the gate of the farm-garden, where the cats rolled lazily in the neatly gravelled paths, and the hens ran cackling among the lettuces and the screens of red-flowered beans. When they entered the little farm-parlour, with its deep chimney recess, curtained with faded chintz, and its bright array of geraniums and fuchsias on the window-ledge, they found that their landlady had prepared their tea, and covered the table with all manner of home-baked cakes and fruit, jugs of freshly cut roses and sweet peas....

"... Has it never occurred to you that instead of increasing the happiness of mankind, as you intend doing by insisting that every one who can should seek for the truth in spiritual matters, you would in reality be diminishing that happiness by destroying beliefs, or half-beliefs, which afford infinite comfort and consolation and delight to a large number of men and women?"

"I have never doubted," answered Baldwin, somewhat bitterly, "that it must have been very distressing for the French nobles to have their domains confiscated in the Revolution, and for the poor, elegant, chivalric planters to have their negroes emancipated for them.[240] Still, such distressing things have to be done occasionally."

"You misunderstand me again," answered Vere, "and you might know better than to continue fancying that I am a kind of spiritual æsthete or sybarite.[241] The universe, as religion shows it, is not equally true with the universe as it really exists; but in many cases it is much more beautiful and consoling. What I mean is this: since at the bottom of the Pandora's box[242] which has been given to mankind, and out of which have issued so many cruel truths, there exists the faculty of disbelieving in some of them, of trusting in good where there is only evil, in imagining sympathy where there is indifference, and justice where there is injustice, of hoping where there is room only to despair—since this inestimable faculty of self-delusion exists, why not let mankind enjoy it, why wish to waste, to rob them of this, their most precious birthright?"

"Because," answered Baldwin, "increasing truth is the law of increasing good; because if we elect to believe that which we wish instead of believing that which is, we are deliberately degrading our nature, rendering it less excellent and useful, instead of more so, than it was; and because by being too cowardly to admit that which is, we are incapacitating ourselves, misleading and weakening others, in the great battle to make the kingdom of that which is into the kingdom of that which should be."

---

240 During the French Revolution (1789–99), revolutionaries confiscated French aristocrats' properties for the state; the American Civil War (1861–65) was partly sparked by the northern states' desire to emancipate slaves, most of whom worked on southern plantations.
241 Someone who indulges in sensual pleasures.
242 In Greek mythology, Pandora opened the box that contained all human suffering.

"I leave you to fight out your objective and subjective worlds," said Rheinhardt, taking up a book and settling himself by the lamp.

Vere was silent for a moment. "Every one," he said, "is not called upon to battle in life. Many are sent in to whom it might be merely a tolerably happy journey. What right have we to insist upon telling these things which will poison their happiness, and which will not, perhaps, make them any the more useful? You were speaking about the education of children, and this, which to you is a source of bitterness and reproach, has been to me the subject of much doubt and indecision. And I have come to the conclusion that I have no right to take it for granted that my children will necessarily be put in such positions as to require their knowing the things of which I, alas! have had the bitter certainty; that should such a position be awaiting them, disbelief in all the beautiful and consoling fictions of religion will come but too soon, and that I have no right to make such disbelief come any earlier."

"In short you deliberately teach your children things in which you disbelieve?"

Vere hesitated. "I teach them nothing; their mother is a firm believer, and I leave the children's religious instruction entirely in her hands. I have never," he added with some pride, "made the slightest attempt to undermine my wife's belief; and shall not act differently towards my children."

Baldwin fixed his eyes searchingly upon Vere. "Have you ever really cared much about your wife, Vere?" he asked.

"I married her for love; and I think that even now, I care more for her than for any one else in the world. Why do you ask?"

"Because," answered Baldwin, "it is perfectly inconceivable to me that, if you really love your wife as I should love a wife if I took one, not as my mere squaw, or odalisque,[243] or as the mother of my children, but, as you say, more than any one else in the world, you can endure that there should exist a subject, the greatest and most solemn in all the world, upon which you and your wife keep your thoughts and feelings secret from each other."

"I have friends,—men, with whom I can discuss it."

"And you can bear to be able to open your whole soul to a friend, while keeping it closed to the person whom you say you love best in the world? You can bear to feel that to your highest thoughts and hopes and fears there is a response in a man, like me, scarcely more than a stranger to you, while there is only blindness and dumbness in this woman who is constantly by your side, and to whom you are more than the whole world? Do you consider this as complete union with another, this deliberate silence and indifference, this growing and changing and maturing of your own mind, while you see her mind cramped and maimed by beliefs which you have long cast behind you?"

"I love my wife, and I respect her belief."

"You may abet her belief, Vere, but if, as you say, you consider it mere error and falsehood, you cannot respect it."

"I respect my wife's happiness, then, and my children's happiness; and for that reason I refrain from laying rough hands upon illusions which are part of that happiness. Accident has brought me into contact with what you, and I, call truth. I have been shorn of my belief; I am emancipated, free, superior—all the things which a thorough materialist is in the eyes of materialists; but," and Vere turned round upon Baldwin with a look of pity and bitterness, "I have not yet attained to the perfection of being a hypocrite,

---

[243] Squaw is a derogatory term for a North American aboriginal wife; an odalisque is a female sexual slave.

a sophist[244] to myself, of daring to pretend to my own soul that this belief of ours, this truth, is not bitter and abominable, arid and icy to our hearts."

Rheinhardt looked up from his book with a curious expression of wonder. "But, my dear friend," he said, very quietly, "why should the truth be abominable to you? A certain number of years employed as honourably and happily as possible, and after that, what preceded this life of yours; what more would you wish, and what evil is there in this that you should shrink from teaching it to your children? I am not afraid of death; why should you be?"

"You misunderstand me," answered Vere; "Heaven knows I am not afraid of death—nay, more than once it has seemed to me that to lie down and feel my soul, like my body, grow gradually numb and number, till it was chilled out of all consciousness, would be the greatest of joys. The horror of the idea of annihilation is, I think, to all, save Claudios,[245] the horror not of our own annihilation but of the annihilation of others; this Schopenhauer[246] overlooked, as you do, Rheinhardt, when he comfortably argued that after all we should not know whether we were being annihilated or not, that as long as we ourselves are awake we cannot realize sleep, and that we need only say to ourselves, 'Well, I shall sleep, be unconscious, never wake.' In this there is no horror. But Schopenhauer did not understand, having no heart, that Death is the one who robs us, who takes away the beloved, leaves us with empty arms. The worst of death is not the annihilation of ourselves;—oh, no, that is nothing; no, nor even the blank numbness of seeing the irremediable loss;—it is the sickening, gasping terror, coming by sudden unexpected starts, of foreseeing that which will inevitably be. Poets have said a great deal, especially Leopardi,[247] of Love and Death being brothers, of the desire of the one coming along with the presence of the other; it may be so. But this much is certain, that whatever may be said of the brothership of Love and Death, Love, in its larger and nobler sense, is the Wizard who has evoked for us the *fata morgana*[248] of an after life; it is Love who has taught the world, for its happiness, that there is not an endless ocean beyond this life, an ocean without shores, dark, silent, whose waters steam up in black vapours to the black heavens, a rolling chaos of disintegrated thoughts and feelings, all separate, all isolated, heaving up and down in the shapeless eternal flood. It is Love who has taught us that what has been begun here will not for ever be interrupted, nor what has been ill done for ever remain unatoned; that the affection once kindled will never cease, that the sin committed can be wiped out, and the good conceived can be achieved; that the seed sown in life will yet bloom and fructify in death, that it will not have been cast too late upon an evil soil, and the blossom of promise will not for ever have been nipped, the half-ripe fruit not for ever have fallen from the tree; that all within which is good and happy, and for ever struggling here, virtue, genius, will be free to act hereafter; that the creatures thrust asunder in the world, vainly trying to clasp one another in the crowd for ever pushing them apart, may unite for ever. All this is the wonderful phantasmagoria[249] of Love; Love has given it to mankind. What right have we to sweep it away; we—" and Vere turned reproachfully towards Baldwin—"who have perhaps never loved, and never felt the want of such a belief?"

---

244 Someone who deliberately argues falsely.
245 Claudio in Shakespeare's *Measure for Measure* spends much of the play condemned to execution and urges his sister to sacrifice her virginity to save his life.
246 Arthur Schopenhauer (1788–1860), German philosopher.
247 Giacomo Leopardi (1798–1837), Italian poet.
248 Latin: mirage.
249 A fantastic vision, usually imagined in a heightened state or dream.

Baldwin was silent for a moment, then answered, as he struck a shower of sparks out of the dull red embers,—

"I have never actually had such a belief, but I have experienced what it is to want it. I was brought up without any religious faith, with only a few general notions of right and wrong; and when I first began to read and to think for myself, my ideas naturally moved in a rationalistic, nay, a materialistic path, so that when in the course of my boyish readings I came upon disputes about an after life, it seemed to me quite impossible to conceive that there could be one. When I was very young I became engrossed in artistic and archæological subjects: it seemed to me that the only worthy interest in life was the beautiful; and, in my Olympian[250] narrowness of sympathy, people who worried themselves about other questions seemed to me poor, morbid, mediæval wretches. You see, I led a life of great solitude, and great though narrow happiness, shut up among books, and reading only such of them as favoured my perfect serenity of mind. But little by little I got to know other men, and to know somewhat more of the world; then things began gradually to change. I began to perceive the frightful dissonances in the world, the horrible false notes, the abominable harmonies of good and evil; and to meet all this I had only this kind of negative materialism, which could not suffice to give me peace of mind, but which entirely precluded my accepting any kind of theory of spiritual compensation and ultimate justice; I grew uneasy, and then unhappy. Just at that moment it so happened that I lost a friend of mine to whom I was considerably attached, whose life had been quite singularly unfortunate, indeed appeared to be growing a little happier only a few months before his death. It was the first time that death came near me, and close before my eyes. It gave me a frightful moral shock, not so much perhaps the loss of that particular individual to myself as the sense of the complete extinction of his personality, gone like the snuffed-out flame or the spent foam of the sea, gone completely, nowhere, leaving no trace, occupying no other place, become the past, the past for which we can do nothing."

Rheinhardt had put down his book for a moment, and listened, with a puzzled and wondering look. That people should be haunted by thoughts like these seemed to him almost as incomprehensible as that the dead should arise and join in a ghastly dance round the gravestones; nor would this latter phenomenon have seemed to him much the more disgusting of the two; so, after a minute, he settled down again and pulled out of his pocket a volume of Aristophanes.[251]

"You have felt all this, Baldwin," said Vere, "and you would nevertheless deliberately inflict such pain upon others? You have felt all the misery of disbelief in a future life, and you are surprised that I should be unwilling to meddle with the belief of my wife and children?"

"I am surprised at your not being almost involuntarily forced into communicating what you know to be the truth; surprised that, in your mind, there should not be an imperious sense that truth must out. Moreover, I think that the responsibility of holding back truth is always greater than any man can calculate, or any man, could he know the full consequences thereof, could support.... Do you seriously consider that a man is doing right in destroying, for the sake of the supposed happiness of his children, the spark of truth which happens to be in his power, and which belongs neither to him nor to his children, but to the whole world? Can you assert that it is honest on your part, in order to save your children the pain of knowing that they will not meet you, or their mother, or their dead friends again in heaven, to

---

250 Refers to Mount Olympus, home of the Greek gods.
251 Aristophanes (c. 450–388 BCE), Greek comic playwright.

refuse to give them that truth for which your ancestors have paid with their blood and their liberty, and which your children are bound to hand on to their children, in order that this little spark of truth may grow into a fire which shall warm and light the whole world?"

"There is something more at stake than the mere happiness or unhappiness of my children," answered Vere, "at all events than such happiness as they might get from belief in an after life. There is the happiness, the safety of their conscience."

"Do you think you can save their conscience by sacrificing your own?"

"I should not be sacrificing my conscience were I doing that which I felt bound to do, Baldwin. Would you have me teach my children that this world, which they regard as the kingdom of a just and loving God, whose supremest desire is the innocence and happiness of His creatures, is in reality the battlefield or the playground of physical forces, without thought or conscience; nay, much worse, is the creation either of a principle of good perpetually allying itself to a principle of evil, or of a dreadful unity which permits and furthers good and evil alike? What would you think of me were I to tell my children that all that they had learned of God and Christ is falsehood; and that the true gods of the world are the serenely heartless, the foully bloodthirsty gods of early Greece, of Phœnicia, and Asia Minor?[252] You would certainty think me a bad father. Yet this old mythology represents with marvellous accuracy the purely scientific view of the world, the impression given by the mere contemplation of Nature, with its conflicting and caballing[253] divinities, good and bad, black and white, resisting and assisting one another, beneficent and wicked, pure and filthy by turns. The chaos, the confusion, the utter irresponsibility, which struck the framers of old myths, is still there. All these stories seem to us very foolish and very horrible: an omniscient, omnipotent Zeus, threatened by a mysterious, impersonal Fate, looming dimly behind him; a Helios who ripens the crops and ripens the pestilence; a Cybele[254] for ever begetting and suckling and mutilating; we laugh at all this. But with what do we replace it? And if we look at our prosaic modern nature, as is shown us by science, can we accuse the chaotic and vicious fancy of those early explainers of it? Do we not see in this nature bounty and cruelty greater than that of any early gods, combats more blind than any Titan's battles,[255] marriages of good and evil more hideous than any incests of the old divinities, monster births of excellence and baseness more foul than any Centaur or Minotaur;[256] and do we not see the great gods of the universe sitting and eating the flesh of men, not unconsciously, but consciously, serenely, and without rebuke?" ...

Vere ... looked vaguely towards the window, at the ghostly billows of the downs, dark blue, bleak, unsubstantial, under the bright cold windy sky. The wind had risen, and went moaning round the farm, piping shrilly in all its chinks and crannies, and making a noise as of distant waters in the firs of the common. Suddenly in the midst of the silence within doors, there came from the adjoining room a monotonous trickle or dribble of childish voice, going on breathless, then halting suddenly exhausted, but with uniform regularity.

---

252 Phoenicia was located where present-day Lebanon now exists; Asia Minor is the Asian part of present-day Turkey.
253 Conspiring.
254 Zeus is leader of the Greek gods and the god of weather; Helios is the Greek god of the sun; Cybele is the mother goddess of Anatolia (Asia Minor).
255 The Titans were early Greek gods, later supplanted by Zeus and the Olympian gods.
256 In Greek mythology, the centaur is a creature with a horse's body and a human head and torso; the minotaur is a creature with a bull's head and a human body.

"It is Willie reading the Bible to his grandmother," remarked Rheinhardt; "the old lady is left alone at home with him on Sunday evenings, while her husband goes to the village. It is a curious accompaniment to your and Baldwin's pessimistic groanings and utilitarian jubilations."

"I think," remarked Baldwin, after a moment's fruitless listening to catch the words from next door, "I think in some matters we unbelievers might take a lesson from our neighbours. I was very much struck to-day, while listening to Monsignore's sermon, with the thought that that man feels it his duty to teach others that which he believes to be the truth, and that we do not."

"It is a priest's profession to preach, my dear Baldwin," put in Rheinhardt; "he lives by it, lives off his own preaching and off the preaching of all the other priests that live now or ever have lived."

"We unbelievers—I should rather say we believers in the believable"—answered Baldwin, "should all of us be, in a fashion, priests. You say that Monsignore lives off his own preaching and the preaching of all Catholic priests that ever have been. Well; and do we not live spiritually, do we not feed our soul upon the truth which we ourselves can find, upon the truth which generations of men have accumulated for us? If, in the course of time, there be no more priests in the world, I mean in the old sense, it will be that every man will be a priest for his own family, and every man of genius a priest for the whole of mankind. What I was thinking of just now is this: that this Monsignore, whom we consider a sort of clever deluded fool, and this old peasant woman, whose thoughts scarcely go beyond her village, are impressed with the sense of the responsibility incurred by the possession of what they consider superior truth—the responsibility of not keeping that truth to themselves, but participating it with others; and that herein they both of them assume a position far wiser, far more honest, far nobler, than do we unbelievers, who say, 'What does it matter if others know only error, as long as ourselves know truth?'"

"You forget," answered Rheinhardt, "that both Monsignore and our landlady are probably persuaded that unless they share their spiritual knowledge with their neighbours, they will be responsible for the souls of those neighbours. And if you remember what may, in the opinion of the orthodox, happen to the souls of such persons as have been slightly neglected in their religious education, I think you will admit that there is plenty to feel responsible about."

"You mean that there is nothing for us to feel responsible about. Not so. Whatever may happen to the souls of our fellows will indeed not happen in an after-world, nor will they suffer in a physical hell of Dante, or enjoy themselves in a physical Paradise of Mahomet.[257] But there is, nevertheless, for the souls which we know, for the souls which look up to us for instruction and assistance, a hell. A hell of moral doubt and despair and degradation, a hell where there is fire enough to scorch the most callous, and ice enough to numb the warmest, and mud to clog and bedraggle the most noble among us. Yes. There is a hell in the moral world, and there is heaven, and there is God; the heaven of satisfied conscience, the God of our own aspirations; and from this heaven, from the sight of this God, it is in our power to exclude those most beloved by us. Shut them out because we have not the courage to see them shiver and wince one moment in the cold and the light of truth; shut them out and leave them to wander in a world of phantoms, upon the volcano crust of that hell of moral disbelief, unaware of its existence or, aware too late, too suddenly of the crater opening beneath their feet. That old woman in the next room is teaching, feels bound to teach, her child the things which she looks upon as truth. And shall a man like you, Vere, refuse to teach your children what you know to be true? Will you leave them to believe that the world and

---

257 Dante Alighieri, *La Divina Commedia* (c. 1308–21); a "Paradise of Mahomet" refers to a Muslim idea of paradise.

man and God, the past and future and present, are wholly different from what they really are; or else to discover, unaided, with slow anguish or sudden despair, that all is different from what they thought, that there is falsehood where they relied on truth, and evil where they looked up to good; till falsehood and evil shall seem everywhere and truth and good nowhere? You spoke of the moral happiness and safety of your children; will you let them consist in falsehood, and depend upon the duration of error? Will you let your children run the risk of losing their old faith, without helping them to find a new one? Will you waste so much of their happiness for themselves, and of their usefulness for the world?"

Vere did not answer; he remained as if absorbed in thought, nervously tearing the petals off a rose which stood in the glass before him.

"Do please leave that flower alone, Vere," remonstrated Rheinhardt; "that is just the way that all you pessimists behave—pulling to pieces the few pleasant things which Nature or man has succeeded in making, because the world is not as satisfactory as it might be. Such a nice rose that was, the very apple of our landlady's eye, who picked it to afford you a pleasant surprise for supper, and you have merely made a mess of it on the tablecloth. That's what comes of thinking too much about responsibilities. One doesn't see the mischief one's fingers are up to."

And Rheinhardt, who was a tidy man, rose, and carefully swept the pink petals and the yellow seeds off the table into his hand, and thence transferred them into a little earthenware jar full of dry rose leaves, which he kept, in true eighteenth-century style, on his writing table.

"That is the difference of our philosophies," he remarked, with satisfaction; "you tear to pieces the few roses that are given us, and we pick up their leaves, and get the pleasant scent of them even when withered."

"The definition is not bad," put in Baldwin, throwing a bundle of faggots on the fire, and making it crackle and flare up lustily, flooding the room with ruddy light.

Vere turned away his face from the glow, and looked once more, vaguely and wistfully, into the bleak blueness of common and downs lying chill and dim in the moonlight.

"What you have been saying, Baldwin," he at last remarked, "may perhaps be true. It may be that it would be wiser to teach my children the things which I believe to be true. But you see I love my children a great deal; and—Well, I mean that I have not the heart to assume the responsibility of such a decision."

"You shirk your responsibilities," answered Baldwin, "and in doing so, you take upon yourself the heaviest responsibility of any."

Frances Power Cobbe
from "Agnostic Morality" (1883)

Feminist, anti-vivisectionist, and activist Frances Power Cobbe (1822–1904) contributed over her lifetime to almost every major Victorian periodical. She supported women's suffrage and campaigned against wife assault, helping to spur passage of the Matrimonial Causes Act of 1878. She enjoyed a large network of feminist friends, including Emily Davies (see Education), John Stuart Mill (see Life Writing, Condition of England, Gender and Sexuality), Helen Taylor, Lydia Becker (see Science), and Millicent Garrett Fawcett. Cobbe established the anti-vivisectionist Victoria Street Society, worked with Mary Carpenter (see Education) in the Ragged School movement, and lobbied for workhouse reform. From 1864, Cobbe lived with her life partner, Mary Lloyd, a woman she called her wife.

Raised by evangelical parents, Cobbe became agnostic in 1843 before turning to theism in 1849. She saw God as "a Father and Mother, infinite in power, wisdom, and love." In this critique, published in the *Contemporary Review*, she responds to Vernon Lee's "The Responsibilities of Unbelief" (see Faith and Doubt), arguing that "high-minded Agnostics" thought "they could rescue the compass of Duty from the wreck of Faith; but their hope was vain."

Agnosticism,[258] if we may trust some recent indications, is passing out of the jubilant stage and entering one of well-befitting seriousness. There lies the experience of a generation between the delirious exultation of Harriet Martineau over her "Spring in the Desert," and the sober sadness of the writer in the last number of this REVIEW on the "Responsibilities of Unbelief."[259] The creed that "Philosophy founded on Science is the one thing needful," which the first considered to be "the crown of experience and the joy of life,"[260] has become to the second a burden and a sorrow.... "I have been shorn of my belief," says one speaker in Vernon Lee's dialogue, "I am emancipated, free, superior; all the things which a thorough materialist is in the eyes of materialists. But I have not yet attained to the perfection of being a hypocrite, of daring to pretend to my own soul that this belief of ours, this truth, is not bitter and abominable, arid and icy to our hearts."[261]

No reader of this thoughtful and powerful paper can fail to see that the indignant antagonism which the earlier blatant Atheism[262] called forth, ought now to give place to mournful recognition of the later Agnosticism as a phase through which many of the most luminous intellects of our time are doomed to pass; the light which is in them waning till the thin crescent disappears. That it will be renewed again in the

---

258 The belief that it is impossible to confirm any existence beyond the material.
259 Harriet Martineau, *Autobiography* (1877). See Life Writing. Vernon Lee, "The Responsibilities of Unbelief" (1883). See Faith and Doubt.
260 Harriet Martineau, *Autobiography* (1877). See Life Writing.
261 Vernon Lee, "The Responsibilities of Unbelief" (1883).
262 Disbelief in God's existence.

lustre of its fulness is not to be doubted, for this Agnosticism is no unfaithfulness to the true God of love and righteousness. It is precisely because the Agnostic fails to find that God where he persists in exclusively looking for Him—namely, in the order of the physical world—that the darkness has fallen on his soul....

All methods of religious inquiry resolve themselves into two—that which seeks God in the outer world, and that which seeks Him in the world within. Out of the first came the old Nature-worship, and ... the Greek stories which Vernon Lee recalls of Zeus and Chronos and Cybele,[263] and the wilder tales of ruder races, of Moloch and Astarte, Woden and Thor.[264] In "the ages before morality," the mixed character of the gods drawn out of Nature, and who represented her mixed aspects of good and evil, was not felt to be incongruous or unworthy of worship. As morality dawned more clearly the gods were divided between good and evil, Ormuzd and Ahrimanes, Osiris and Typhon, the Devs and Asuras.[265] Some ages later, in the deeply speculative era of Alexandrian philosophy,[266] the character of the author of Nature and creator of the world[267] presented itself as so dark a problem that many schools of Gnostics—Basilidians, Marcionites, Valentinians[268]—deemed him to be an evil or fallen god, against whom the supreme and good God sent Christ to recall mankind to a higher obedience. The loftiest point ever reached, or probably attainable, by this method of religion was the Deism[269] of the seventeenth and eighteenth centuries; and to reach it two things were needful not included in the problem—namely, that those who found so good a God in Nature should have looked for Him there from the vantage ground of Christian tradition gained by the opposite method; and secondly, that they should have been yet in ignorance concerning much in Nature which is now known, and so have raised their induction from imperfect premises....

The second method of religious inquiry, which seeks for God in the inner world of spirit and conscience, leads to a very different conclusion, even though it be but "in a glass darkly"[270] that the mirror of the soul receives the Divine reflection, and many a blur of human error has been mistaken for a feature of the Divine countenance. The prophets of all time who have heard in their souls the voice of God and have cried aloud, "Thus saith the High and Holy One who inhabiteth eternity,"[271] and the faithful who have hearkened to them because their hearts echoed their prophecies, have been together keeping step, till now Christianity in all its more vitalized forms, and Theism[272] as everywhere superseding the elder Deism, alike affirm the absolute goodness of God, discarding everything in earlier dogmas repugnant

---

263 Vernon Lee, "The Responsibilities of Unbelief" (1883). See Faith and Doubt. In Greek mythology, Zeus is leader of the gods and the god of weather, Cronus is the god of time (Lee in fact refers to Helios, not Cronus), and Cybele is the mother goddess of Anatolia (Asia Minor).

264 Moloch is a false idol for whom children were burnt as offerings in the Bible and a fallen angel in John Milton's *Paradise Lost* (1667); Astarte (Queen of Heaven, Ashtoreth) is a Canaanite goddess; Odin [Woden] and Thor are Norse gods.

265 Ormuzd (Ahura Mazda) was the supreme god and Ahrimanes (Ahriman, Angra Mainyu) the supreme devil in ancient Persia; Osiris was the Egyptian god of the dead; Typhon is a mythical Greek monster with 100 dragon heads; Devs refer to Vedic gods (Devas); Asuras are Vedic demons.

266 The early centuries CE when Alexandrian philosophers viewed Hebrew texts through a neo-Platonic lens.

267 That is, the deity of the Old Testament.

268 Gnosticism was an early Christian sect whose members believed themselves to possess special spiritual knowledge and secret interpretations of sacred texts; Basilidians followed Basilides, an Alexandrian Gnostic; Marcionites followed Marcion, a Roman Gnostic; Valentinians followed Valentinus, an Egyptian Gnostic.

269 Deism developed in England and spread to France and Germany; Deists believed that God created the world and exerted no further influence.

270 1 Corinthians 13:12.

271 Isaiah 57:15.

272 Theists, unlike Deists, believed that God played an active role in the world.

thereto. The first method—the external—being the one to which Agnostics have exclusively had recourse, it follows inevitably that the result is, as we see, the denial of religion, because they do not find in Nature what Nature (consulted exclusively) cannot teach.

Of course the Agnostic may here interpose and say that the test of the truth of the second method must be to check it by the first, and see whether God, as He actually works in Nature, bears out the character which we derive from the testimony of our hearts. Such checking is every way right—nay, it is inevitable. No thoughtful man can avoid doing it, and encountering thereby all the strain of faith. But the difference lies in this, with which method do we *begin*, and to which do we assign the primary importance? If we first look for God outside of us, we shall usually stop at what we find there. If we first look for Him within, we may afterwards face with illumined eyes the mystery of Nature's shadows....

These are the obvious results of the use of the two methods of religious inquiry, as used by men in all ages. But I have attempted to define them here, because I am anxious to draw attention to the fact ... that modern Agnosticism, as distinguished from earlier forms of disbelief, has bound itself to the physical-science method, and renounced appeal to the inner witness to the character of God, by adopting the Darwinian theory of the nature of conscience....[273] According to this doctrine there is no such thing as an "eternal and immutable morality,"[274] but all orders of intelligent beings must by degrees make for themselves, what Vernon Lee aptly calls a "Rule of the Road,"[275] applicable to their particular convenience.... Thus at one and the same blow the moral *distinctions* of good and evil are exploded and reduced to the contingently expedient, or inexpedient, and the rank of the *faculty* whereby we recognize them is degraded from that of the loftiest in human nature to that of a mere inherited prejudice. How this theory overturns the foundations of morals, and by so doing deprives religion of its firmest basis, and so clears the way for Agnosticism, will become more evident the more we reflect on the matter. A better example of the working of the doctrine could not be desired than that afforded in a passage in this very article, which bears the stamp of a fragment of autobiography. "Baldwin," the character in the dialogue, who obviously represents the writer's own views, after expressing the intense desire he has felt to believe in "the beautiful dreams which console other men," goes on to say:—

"... Little by little it dawned upon me that all my misery had originated in a total misconception of the relative positions of Nature and of man; I began to perceive that the distinction between right and wrong conduct had arisen in the course of the evolution of mankind, that right and wrong meant only that which was conducive or detrimental to the increasing happiness of humanity.... Why go into details? You know that the school of philosophy to which I adhere has traced all distinctions of right and wrong to the perceptions, enforced upon man by mankind, and upon mankind by man, of the differences between such courses as are conducive to the higher development and greater happiness of men, and such other courses as are conducive only to their degradation and extinction" (p. 708).[276]

Here is the doctrine of Inherited Conscience clearly posed as lying at the very root of Vernon Lee's Agnosticism, and closing the door against the longed-for belief that his intuitions of justice and mercy had their origin in the Maker of all....

---

273 Charles Darwin, *The Descent of Man* (1871). See Science.
274 Ralph Cudworth, *A Treatise Concerning Eternal and Immutable Morality* (1731).
275 Vernon Lee, "The Responsibilities of Unbelief" (1883). See Faith and Doubt.
276 Vernon Lee, "The Responsibilities of Unbelief" (1883). See Faith and Doubt.

Hitherto religion has either been avowedly founded (as by the second method of inquiry above described) on the moral nature of man, or has appealed to it, as the ratification of the argument drawn from external Nature. The highest faculty in us—as we deemed it to be—was on all hands admitted to be the nearest to God, and the one fittest to bear witness regarding Him. "God is with mortals by conscience" has been generally assumed as an axiom in theological argument, and Christianity itself, by its dogma of the Third Person in the Trinity, only consecrated the conviction of the wisest Pagans that there is "a Holy Spirit throned within us, of our good and evil deeds the Guardian and Observer, who draws towards us as we draw towards Him."[277] ...

How changed is the view we are permitted by Darwinism to take of this crowned and sceptred impostor in our breasts, who claimed so high an origin, and has so base an one! That "still small voice"[278] to which we were wont to hearken reverently, what is it then, but the echo of the rude cheers and hisses wherewith our fathers greeted the acts which they thought useful or the reverse.... That solid ground of transcendental knowledge, which we imagined the deepest thinker of the world had sounded for us and proved firm as a rock, what is it but the shifting sand-heaps of our ancestral impressions,—nay, rather let us say, the mental *kitchen middens*[279] of generations of savages?

Is this revolution in our estimate of conscience of so little consequence, I ask, that our clergy take so little notice of it? To me it seems that it bears ruinously ... first on morals, then on religion. With the detection of conscience as a mere prejudice must end the solemn farce of moral struggle, of penitence and of remorse.... [W]ith the discrediting of conscience as a divinely constituted guide and monitor must end the possibility of approaching God through it, and of arguing from its lessons of righteousness that He who made it must be righteous likewise....

It is deeply to be deplored that this doctrine should have found acceptance on the authority of one, who, however great as a naturalist, was neither a moralist nor a metaphysician, at a juncture when the tendencies of the age all drive us only too much in the direction of physical inquiry as the road to truth.... We writhe as the long panorama of suffering and destruction is unrolled before our eyes[280] from the earliest geologic time to the present.... [I]t is a cruel enhancement of our difficulties that at such a time this hateful doctrine of Hereditary Conscience should have been broached to drive us out of the best shelter of faith—the witness of a reliable moral consciousness to the righteousness and mercy of our Maker....

Morality, on the Agnostic projection, of course limits its scope to the field of human relations. It is supposed to have risen out of them, and to have no meaning beyond them. Man has brothers, and to them he owes duty. He knows nothing of a Father, and can owe him no duty. Altruism remains the sole virtue, Piety being exploded. In the language of divines, the Second great Commandment of the Law is still in force, but we have dispensed with the First.[281]

Here at the starting-point arises a doubt whether Agnosticism does not fling away, with the obligation to love God, the best practical help towards fulfilling its own law and loving our neighbour.... Probably

---

277 Author's note: Seneca. Editor's note: Lucius Annaeus Seneca (c. 4 BCE–65 CE), Roman philosopher and tragedian.
278 1 Kings 19:12.
279 Prehistoric refuse piles.
280 A visual technology popularized during the Victorian era, the panorama gave audiences the impression of a scene passing as they viewed it from side to side.
281 Matthew 22:37–40; Mark 12:29–31; the first of the "great commandment[s] in the law" is "love the Lord thy God with all thy heart" and the second is "love thy neighbour as thyself."

every Christian and Theist who has tried conscientiously, to "love his neighbour as himself" has experienced an imperative necessity to call up ideas and feelings derived from his love of God to help him in the often difficult achievement. It has been the idea of a perfect and all-adorable Being, on which his heart has reposed when sickened with human falsehood and folly. It has been in the remembrance of God's patience and forgiveness to himself that he has learned pity and pardon for his offending brothers. One of the greatest philanthropists of the past generation, Joseph Tuckerman, told Mary Carpenter[282] that when he saw a filthy degraded creature in the streets, his feelings of repulsion were almost unconquerable, till he forcibly recalled to mind that God made that miserable man, and that he should meet him hereafter in Heaven. Then came always, he said, a revulsion of feeling, and he was enabled to go with a chastened spirit about his work of mercy. The notion (which I have heard a noted Atheist expound in a lecture) that we cannot love our brothers thoroughly till we have renounced our Father and our eternal home, seems to me simply absurd....

But it is not only on the side of God that the morality of Agnosticism stops short. All the Personal duties which, on the Kantian system, a man "owes to himself,"[283] and which were inculcated foremost of all by the older religious ethics, because they tended directly to the supreme end of creation and the approach of finite souls to Divine holiness, these lofty personal duties are retained in the new ethics only on the secondary and practically wholly insufficient grounds of their subservience to the general welfare of the community.

Thus, of the three branches of the elder morality corresponding to the threefold aspects of human life—Religious Duty, which was laid on man as a son of God, Personal Duty, laid on him as a rational free agent, and Social Duty, laid on him as a member of the community—the last alone survives in Agnostic ethics. Two-thirds of the provinces of morality have been abandoned at one sweep, as by retreating Rome in her decadence. But, I ask, is the hope of preserving the remainder from the barbarian hosts of selfishness and passion any the better? ... Surely it is nothing of the kind. Even for our neighbour's own sake there is nothing we can ever do for him half so useful as to *be* ourselves the very noblest, purest, holiest men and women we know how. The recognition of the supremacy of Personal Duties appears to be the first step towards the right performance of the highest Social Duties.

Deprived of two-thirds of its original empire and dethroned from its high seat of judgment, does there yet perchance remain for Duty, as understood by the Agnostic, some special sanctions, some more close and tender, if not equally lofty and solemn claim, than those which belonged to it under the older Theistic schemes? Such would seem to be the persuasion of many amongst those who have felt the "Responsibilities of Unbelief,"[284] perhaps of all the best minds amongst them—Mr. Morley, Mr. Harrison, George Eliot,[285] and now, obviously, of Vernon Lee. This thoughtful writer is actually of opinion that the belief in an immortal life is an "enervating"[286] one, and that there is a "moral tonic" in believing that "there is no place beyond the grave where folly and selfishness may be expiated and retrieved, and that,

---

282 Joseph Tuckerman (1778–1840), American philanthropist; Mary Carpenter (1807–77) (see Education), philanthropist and social reformer; Mary Carpenter, *Memoir of Joseph Tuckerman* (1848).
283 Immanuel Kant (1724–1804), German philosopher; Kant, *The Metaphysic of Ethics*, trans. J.W. Semple (1836).
284 Vernon Lee, "The Responsibilities of Unbelief" (1883).
285 John Morley (1838–1923), writer and politician; Frederic Harrison (1831–1923), writer, professor, and positivist; George Eliot (1819–80), writer. See Aesthetics and Culture.
286 Morally weakening.

whatever good may be done, must be done in this world."[287] ... But these mournful feelings are assuredly the "enervating" ones, for nothing can be so enervating as despair. What "moral tonic" can there be in the conviction that, whether we labour or sit still, sacrifice our life-blood for our brother, or sacrifice him to our selfishness, it will soon be all one to him and to us? ...

But if Agnostic ethics be thus miserably defective—if they be narrow in their scope and poor in their aim of conferring transitory happiness on a perishing race—if they have no basis in a pure reason or a divinely taught conscience, but appeal only to a shifting and semi-barbarous prejudice—if, even from the point of view of sentiment, they lack the motives which are best calculated to inspire zeal and self-sacrifice; then it is surely time for high-minded Agnostics to recognize that their laudable efforts to construct a morality on the ruins of religion [have] failed, and must ever fail. The dilemma is more terrible than they have yet contemplated. They have imagined that they had merely to choose between morality with religion, or morality without religion. But the only choice for them is between morality and religion together, or the relinquishment both of morality and religion. They were sanguine enough to think they could rescue the compass of Duty from the wreck of Faith; but their hope was vain, and the well-meaning divers among them who have gone in search of it have come up with a handful of sea-tangle.

Much false lustre has, I think, been cast over a creed which is in truth the "City of Dreadful Night,"[288] by the high Altruistic sentiments and hopes of certain illustrious Agnostics. George Eliot's aspiration to join the "choir invisible," whose voices are "the music of the world;"[289] Mr. Frederic Harrison's generous desire for "posthumous beneficent activity,"[290] have thrown, for a time, over it a light as from a sun which has set. For myself, I confess there seems to me something infinitely pathetic in these longings of men and women, who once hoped for a "house, not made with hands, eternal in the heavens," amid "the spirits of the just made perfect," but who are fain now to be content with such ghosts of Hope as these.[291] The millennium of Darwinism for the "surviving fittest"[292] of the human race—those toothless, hairless, slow-moving creatures, with all peaceful sentiments bred in, and all combative ones bred out—is, after all, no such vision of paradise as that even the purest Altruist can find in it compensation for the belief that all the men and women whom he has ever known or loved, are doomed to annihilation long before that new race—such as it will be—can arise....

---

287 Vernon Lee, "The Responsibilities of Unbelief" (1883).
288 James Thomson, "The City of Dreadful Night" (1874).
289 George Eliot, "O, May I Join the Choir Invisible" (1867).
290 Frederic Harrison, "The Soul and Future Life," *A Modern Symposium* (1878).
291 2 Corinthians 5:1; Hebrews 12:23.
292 The phrase "survival of the fittest" was first used by Herbert Spencer in *Principles of Biology* (1864) and then by Charles Darwin in later editions of *On the Origin of Species* (first published in 1859).

SCIENCE

Introduction
Bernard Lightman

At the time Victoria ascended the throne in 1837, Oxford- and Cambridge-educated Anglicans dominated British science. Referred to as the "gentlemen of science," they included geologists William Buckland, Charles Lyell, and Adam Sedgwick, mathematicians Charles Babbage and Augustus De Morgan, biologist Richard Owen, chemist Humphry Davy, astronomer John Herschel, and polymath William Whewell. The "young Turks" of their era, they attempted to reform British science, then led by members of the Royal Society, many of them aristocrats and wealthy members with no scientific background. When these attempts failed, they established the British Association for the Advancement of Science in 1831.

To the gentlemen of science, everything in nature reflected God's purpose. Showing their allegiance to the Anglican establishment, they grounded their science on the theological and political principles formulated by Anglican divine William Paley, author of *Natural Theology* (1802). According to Paley's theology, living things revealed the hand of a benevolent God. These marks of God's design had been put there from the beginning of creation. Nature was static, species immutable. Design in the natural world was paralleled by design in the social world. Writing in the shadow of the French Revolution, Paley urged British workers to be content with their lot: it was impious to complain about the social order since God had sanctioned it. The gentlemen of science argued that natural theology shored up the political and social status quo.

Various groups contested this vision of science. Middle-class philosophical radicals challenged it with their Utilitarian ideology—based on Jeremy Bentham's principle of the greatest happiness for the greatest number—and with their theory of knowledge grounded in bodily sensation. More radical Nonconformists attacked the Anglican church by drawing on egalitarian political ideas imported from continental anatomy and from Lamarckian evolution, which emphasized progressive development due to the inheritance of acquired characteristics. The gentlemen of science were hard-pressed to defend the legitimacy of their vision and the conservative notion of society it buttressed. Whereas they were convinced that knowledge would lead to the recognition of a divine, static, and hierarchical natural order, the science of their enemies was naturalistic, emphasizing an egalitarian natural and social world characterized by progress.

The gentlemen of science therefore encouraged the production of popular books promoting natural theology. Buckland, Whewell, and others contributed to the eight volumes of the Bridgewater Treatises (1833–36), which all demonstrated God's goodness as manifested in creation. Herschel and Whewell supported the work of Mary Somerville, the most famous female popularizer of the first half of the century. Already, by the mid-1830s, she was an icon to the Whigs, members of the upper class who supported gradual social and political reform in order to avoid revolution. To them, she symbolized self-education, liberalism, and women's rights. In *Mechanism of the Heavens* (1831), she translated and interpreted the mathematics of the French astronomer Pierre-Simon Laplace, sanitizing the impious implications of the French Enlightenment in the process. Somerville aimed to demonstrate that leading French science could enhance understanding of God's divine goodness. In her *Connexion of the Physical Sciences* (1834), she presented an overview of rapidly advancing scientific fields to show how they illuminated God's divine nature.

"A Passion for Astronomy." *Punch* (1 Dec. 1866): 222.

Before the mid-nineteenth century, there were few science writers because there was little demand for popular scientific books and journals. It was only in the Victorian period that "popular science" emerged for the first time. Popular science publications began in the early nineteenth century and many were commercial failures. A British market did not exist for such works until later in the century, when rising literacy rates created a new readership composed of middle-class and wealthier working-class members. The development of cheap, mass-produced books, combined with the expanded British reading audience, led to the demand for professional writers who could churn out scientific books and articles for a popular readership.

The success of the anonymously published *Vestiges of the Natural History of Creation* in 1844 signalled that a new readership existed, making the production of cheap science books financially viable. The author was Robert Chambers, one of the brothers behind the Scottish firm W. and R. Chambers, a publishing house that had moved into large-scale cheap book publishing in the 1830s. When Chambers wrote *Vestiges*, he drew on his experience as publisher and journalist. It allowed him to present evolutionary theory, hitherto linked to working-class radicalism, as suitable drawing-room reading. The result was a sensational bestseller. Guessing the author's identity became a fashionable game, with Prince Albert and

Charles Darwin among the suspects. Within a decade, the book sold 21,250 copies in Britain, continuing to sell well throughout the nineteenth century despite efforts by men of science to demolish its scientific credibility. By 1890 it had sold 38,750 copies.

The hoopla surrounding *Vestiges* was the first indication that scientific subjects had captured the British imagination by mid-century. Huge crowds flocked to visit the Great Exhibition, held in London in 1851. The Exhibition was housed in an immense glass and iron building, earning the nickname the "Crystal Palace." The natural history crazes of the 1850s also indicated growing curiosity about nature. The marine aquarium became a national craze while enthusiasts combed beaches for specimens. Fern collecting became a fad, followed by intense curiosity about dinosaurs. When the Crystal Palace Company relocated the Great Exhibition to Sydenham, just south of London, an exhibition of extinct reptiles and mammals became one of the most popular attractions. The public was treated to life-sized restorations of the plesiosaurus, the pterodactyl, the megalosaurus, and the iguanodon. After the exhibition's opening in June 1854, over a million people a year for the next 50 years saw these models and the dinosaur entered the popular imagination.

A new group of scientists from outside Oxford and Cambridge arrived on the scene during the 1850s, taking advantage of the growing interest in science. Referred to by scholars as "scientific naturalists," these men vied with the gentlemen of science for leadership of British science. At the same time, led by

"The Naturalist. From the picture by Stacey Marks, R.A." (detail). *Graphic* (31 Oct. 1891): 517.

biologist T.H. Huxley, physicist John Tyndall, and botanist Joseph Dalton Hooker, the scientific naturalists engaged in a debate with Anglican clergy over who would provide the best leadership for modern British society. The scientific naturalists advanced new interpretations of nature, society, and humanity derived from empirical science and cast doubt on a science based on natural theology. They were naturalistic in ruling out causes not present in empirically observed nature. They were scientific in interpreting nature in accordance with three major mid-century scientific theories: the atomic theory of matter, the conservation of energy, and evolution.

This group of elite scientists gained coherence when some of its most active members formed the X Club. Starting in 1864, George Busk, Edward Frankland, Thomas Hirst, John Lubbock, Herbert Spencer, William Spottiswoode, Hooker, Huxley, and Tyndall met for dinner every month to strategize how to accomplish their objectives. They sought to redefine British science, turning it into a professional, merit-based, publicly respected, and state-endowed activity. In order to succeed, they had to be aggressive, opportunistic, and politically savvy. They served on various government commissions related to science; angled for, and won, high posts in scientific societies; participated in reforms of scientific education; and remade the scientific institutions in which they worked. They engaged supporters of the Anglican Church in the periodical press or in public debate. The controversy surrounding Charles Darwin's *On the Origin of Species* (1859) was a godsend to them. It allowed them to defend scientists' right to posit naturalistic theories without fear of reprisal from scientifically unqualified Anglican intellectuals and to be judged by their scientific peers on an evidentiary basis.

"The Museum of Practical Geology.—The Great Hall."
Illustrated London News (24 May 1851): 446.

Though eventually allied with the scientific naturalists, Darwin was at first a typical gentleman of science. He attended Cambridge intending to become a clergyman. There, John Stevens Henslow, a botanist, and Adam Sedgwick, a geologist, taught him about science informally. It was Henslow who arranged for him to be a part of the *Beagle* Voyage (1831–36) as the captain's companion. Darwin used the opportunity to collect fossils and exotic specimens. He also undertook an extensive study of the geology of South America guided by Charles Lyell's *Principles of Geology* (1830–33). From Darwin's point of view, his observations on the *Beagle* Voyage confirmed Lyell's emphasis on the gradual change of the earth's crust through the uniform agency of secondary causes. Later, Darwin applied the same principles to understanding how living beings evolved. When he returned to England, he began to analyze the specimens he had sent home. Questions about the immutability of species that had plagued him during the voyage continued to percolate. In 1837, he opened his first notebook on transmutation. In September 1838, after reading Thomas Malthus's *Essay on the Principle of Population* (1798), Darwin formulated his theory of natural selection, a naturalistic explanation of how species evolve. Since evolution was associated with unrespectable lower-class unbelief, Darwin kept his theory to himself for 20 years. A letter in 1858 by Alfred Russel Wallace to Darwin, outlining a theory of evolution similar to the one that Darwin had been working on, forced Darwin to write what became *On the Origin of Species* (1859).

In the ensuing controversy, the scientific naturalists defended Darwin. They also explored the implications of Darwin's biological theories for ethics, religion, race, gender, and politics. Darwin's cousin, Francis

"Darwinian." *Punch* (25 Nov. 1876): 228.

Galton, argued that natural selection determined the development of human intelligence. Using what he claimed were scientific methods, he ranked the intellectual standard of each race and offered suggestions on how to raise average intelligence through eugenics (the science of breeding). Huxley linked evolution to religious unbelief. He was responsible for coining the term "agnostic." Huxley also wrote several essays on the meaning of evolution for social ethics. He rejected the notion that the evolutionary process tended towards a final good and that humans should allow natural selection to run its course without hindrance. Huxley was responding to one of his fellow scientific naturalists, Herbert Spencer, who saw social and biological evolution as part of the same process. Spencer had been pushing evolutionary theory even before Darwin's *On the Origin of Species* had appeared. He linked evolution to liberalism. Affected by his Nonconformist roots, Spencer never entirely rejected the notion of a divine being, though he often referred to it as the "Unknowable."

Some important literary figures embraced elements of scientific naturalism. Both the scientific naturalists and the realist novelists shared a common scientific perspective. Realist novelists, including George Eliot and Thomas Hardy, attempted to bring out the hitherto unseen complexity of ordinary life. They presented human existence in ways that paralleled the scientists' approach to understanding the natural world. This shared perspective is most evident in the way that Victorian literary figures attempted to know the world. The scientific naturalists and their literary twins both held an epistemological ideal of self-sacrifice, or self-annihilation, in order to reach a position of objectivity from which to locate truth or describe reality. This epistemology required that the individual begin by putting aside religion as an authority in the quest for knowledge and demanded a willingness to suffer the consequences of finding out the unpleasant truth that the world was not made for humanity. In many Victorian novels, knowledge-seeking and truth-telling lie at the heart of the story. The plot often turns on the protagonist's ability to develop the proper temper and objective state of mind to permit a realistic confrontation with the world.

Although scientific naturalists and their literary allies constituted a formidable cadre in the second half of the century, their views on the cultural implications of evolution were contested by many groups, as were their claims to cultural authority. First, there were opponents within the scientific community, including the physicists based in Scotland, among them William Thomson and James Clerk Maxwell, who wanted to retain a religious framework for science, as well as the gentlemen of science who were still active in this period, including the anatomist Richard Owen. Many of the self-educated popularizers of science, including Philip Henry Gosse, Richard Proctor, and Mary Ward, were also keen to perpetuate the tradition of natural theology. British intellectual and religious leaders were also opposed to scientific naturalism, including representatives of the old aristocratic-Anglican establishment, such as Bishop Samuel Wilberforce and distinguished Tory politician A.J. Balfour. They were joined by leading Catholics, including John Henry Newman, and prominent Nonconformists such as Congregationalist minister Robert William Dale and Robert Flint, a philosopher and theologian in the Church of Scotland. Idealists such as Thomas Henry Green, spiritualists, including Oliver Lodge, and literary figures such as John Ruskin were among those who challenged the worldview championed by the scientific naturalists. Frances Power Cobbe, like other feminists and anti-vivisectionists, clashed with scientific naturalists over their views on women's social roles and animal experimentation. Lydia Becker, who began as a popularizer of science before becoming a leading figure in the suffragette movement, was one of Darwin's correspondents. But even before *The Descent of Man* (1871) appeared, she wrote a series of essays rejecting the idea that women were by their very nature prohibited from studying science. Socialist intellectuals, including Henry

Mayers Hyndman, dismissed Darwin and Huxley as pro-capitalist due to their emphasis on competition in the evolutionary process.

The cultural authority of scientific naturalists reached its highest point during the 1860s and 1870s, when figures such as Huxley and Tyndall were in their prime. Despite their many critics, by the 1870s they were prominent members of the scientific establishment holding key positions in the important scientific societies. The 1880s brought a series of social and cultural changes that led to the decline of scientific naturalism. They were perceived as defenders of the status quo when working-class support for socialism and trade unionism increased in the final decades of the century. The worship of science, inaugurated by the Crystal Palace in 1851, drew to a close by the end of the 1880s. During the 1890s, eminent thinkers from around the Western world, including William James of the United States, Henri Bergson of France, Edmund Husserl of Germany, and James Ward of England, critiqued the naturalistic analysis of nature. By then, the scientists who had first championed scientific naturalism were dying off, but in their heyday, they constructed a powerful notion of culture that was based more on scientific than on religious principles.

Works Cited and Further Reading

Browne, Janet. *Charles Darwin: Voyaging*. New York: Knopf, 1995. Print.

——. *Charles Darwin: The Power of Place*. New York: Knopf, 2002. Print.

Dawson, Gowan. *Darwin, Literature, and Victorian Respectability*. Cambridge: Cambridge UP, 2007. Print.

Desmond, Adrian. *The Politics of Evolution: Medicine, Morphology, and Reform in Radical London*. Chicago: U of Chicago P, 1989. Print.

Desmond, Adrian, and James R. Moore. *Darwin*. New York: Norton, 1991. Print.

——. *Huxley: From Devil's Disciple to Evolution's High Priest*. Reading, MA: Addison-Wesley, 1997. Print.

Gates, Barbara T. *Kindred Nature: Victorian and Edwardian Women Embrace the Living World*. Chicago: U of Chicago P, 1998. Print.

Le-May Sheffield, Suzanne. *Revealing New Worlds: Three Victorian Women Naturalists*. London: Routledge, 2001. Print.

Levine, George. *Darwin and the Novelists: Patterns of Science in Victorian Fiction*. Cambridge, MA: Harvard UP, 1988. Print.

——. *Dying to Know: Scientific Epistemology and Narrative in Victorian England*. Chicago: U of Chicago P, 2002. Print.

Lightman, Bernard, ed. *Victorian Science in Context*. Chicago: U of Chicago P, 1997. Print.

——. *Victorian Popularizers of Science: Designing Nature for New Audiences*. Chicago: U of Chicago P, 2007. Print.

Morrell, Jack, and Arnold Thackray. *Gentlemen of Science: Early Years of the British Association for the Advancement of Science*. Oxford: Clarendon, 1981. Print.

Secord, James. *Victorian Sensation: The Extraordinary Publication, Reception, and Secret Authorship of Vestiges of the Natural History of Creation*. Chicago: U of Chicago P, 2000. Print.

Smith, Crosbie. *The Science of Energy: A Cultural History of Energy Physics in Victorian Britain*. Chicago: U of Chicago P, 1998. Print.

Smith, Jonathan. *Charles Darwin and Victorian Visual Culture*. Cambridge: Cambridge UP, 2006. Print.

Turner, Frank. *Between Science and Religion: The Reaction to Scientific Naturalism in Late Victorian England*. New Haven: Yale UP, 1974. Print.

——. *Contesting Cultural Authority: Essays in Victorian Intellectual Life*. Cambridge: Cambridge UP, 1993. Print.

Charles Lyell

from *Principles of Geology, being an Attempt to Explain the Former Changes of the Earth's Surface, by Reference to Causes Now in Operation* (1830)

Geologist Sir Charles Lyell (1797–1875) studied geology at Oxford before briefly pursuing law, which he abandoned to undertake geological studies of the earth's formation. He admired Jean Baptiste de Lamarck's evolutionary theories and became a supporter of Charles Darwin (see Science, Travel and Exploration). Lyell served as secretary (later president) of the Geological Society of London and as professor of geology at King's College; knighted in 1848, he received the Geological Society's Wollaston Medal (its highest award) in 1866. He was buried in Westminster Abbey.

Opposing current theory that geological changes occur through sudden catastrophic events, Lyell argued in *Principles of Geology* (3 vols., 1830–33) that such changes could be accounted for by "modern causes" still "in operation." He fought against those who endorsed biblical accounts of the earth's formation, seeking "to free the science from Moses." *Principles* went through numerous editions and translations in Britain, France, and America, enjoying wide general and scientific readership.

Volume 1, Chapter 5: Review of the Causes Which Have Retarded the Progress of Geology ...

We have seen that, during the progress of geology, there have been great fluctuations of opinion respecting the nature of the causes to which all former changes of the earth's surface are referrible. The first observers conceived that the monuments which the geologist endeavours to decipher, relate to a period when the physical constitution of the earth differed entirely from the present, and that, even after the creation of living beings, there have been causes in action distinct in kind or degree from those now forming part of the economy of nature. These views have been gradually modified, and some of them entirely abandoned in proportion as observations have been multiplied, and the signs of former mutations more skilfully interpreted. Many appearances, which for a long time were regarded as indicating mysterious and extraordinary agency, are finally recognized as the necessary result of the laws now governing the material world; and the discovery of this unlooked for conformity has induced some geologists to infer that there has never been any interruption to the same uniform order of physical events. The same assemblage of general causes, they conceive, may have been sufficient to produce, by their various combinations, the endless diversity of effects, of which the shell of the earth has preserved the memorials, and, consistently with these principles, the recurrence of analogous changes is expected by them in time to come.

Whether we coincide or not in this doctrine, we must admit that the gradual progress of opinion concerning the succession of phenomena in remote eras, resembles in a singular manner that which accompanies the growing intelligence of every people, in regard to the economy of nature in modern times. In an early stage of advancement, when a great number of natural appearances are unintelligible, an eclipse, an earthquake, a flood, or the approach of a comet, with many other occurrences afterwards found to belong to the regular course of events, are regarded as prodigies. The same delusion prevails as to moral phenomena, and many of these are ascribed to the intervention of demons, ghosts, witches, and other immaterial and supernatural agents. By degrees, many of the enigmas of the moral and physical world are explained, and, instead of being due to extrinsic and irregular causes, they are found to depend on fixed and invariable laws. The philosopher at last becomes convinced of the undeviating uniformity of secondary causes, and, guided by his faith in this principle, he determines the probability of accounts transmitted to him of former occurrences, and often rejects the fabulous tales of former ages, on the ground of their being irreconcilable with the experience of more enlightened ages.

As a belief in want of conformity in the physical constitution of the earth, in ancient and modern times, was for a long time universally prevalent, and that too amongst men who were convinced that the order of nature is *now* uniform, and has continued so for several thousand years; every circumstance which could have influenced their minds and given an undue bias to their opinions deserves particular attention. Now the reader may easily satisfy himself, that, however undeviating the course of nature may have been from the earliest epochs, it was impossible for the first cultivators of geology to come to such a conclusion, so long as they were under a delusion as to the age of the world, and the date of the first creation of animate beings. However fantastical some theories of the sixteenth century may now appear to us,—however unworthy of men of great talent and sound judgment, we may rest assured that, if the same misconceptions now prevailed in regard to the memorials of human transactions, it would give rise to a similar train of absurdities. Let us imagine, for example, that Champollion, and the French and Tuscan literati now engaged in exploring the antiquities of Egypt,[1] had visited that country with a firm belief that the banks of the Nile were never peopled by the human race before the beginning of the nineteenth century, and that their faith in this dogma was as difficult to shake as the opinion of our ancestors, that the earth was never the abode of living beings until the creation of the present continents, and of the species now existing,—it is easy to perceive what extravagant systems they would frame, while under the influence of this delusion, to account for the monuments discovered in Egypt. The sight of the pyramids, obelisks, colossal statues, and ruined temples, would fill them with such astonishment, that for a time they would be as men spell-bound—wholly incapacitated to reason with sobriety. They might incline at first to refer the construction of such stupendous works to some superhuman powers of a primeval world....

---

1   Jean-François Champollion (1790–1832), French linguist and historian who decoded the Rosetta Stone, allowing the translation of hieroglyphics; there was an archaeological renaissance in the early to mid-nineteenth century.

... Incredible as such scepticism may appear, it would be rivalled by many systems of the sixteenth and seventeenth centuries, and among others by that of the learned Falloppio,[2] who regarded the tusks of fossil elephants as earthy concretions, and the vases of Monte Testaceo, near Rome, as works of nature, and not of art. But when one generation had passed away, and another not compromised to the support of antiquated dogmas had succeeded, they would review the evidence afforded by mummies more impartially, and would no longer controvert the preliminary question, that human beings had lived in Egypt before the nineteenth century: so that when a hundred years perhaps had been lost, the industry and talents of the philosopher would be at last directed to the elucidation of points of real historical importance.

But we have adverted to one only of many prejudices with which the earlier geologists had to contend. Even when they conceded that the earth had been peopled with animate beings at an earlier period than was at first supposed, they had no conception that the quantity of time bore so great a proportion to the historical era as is now generally conceded. How fatal every error as to the quantity of time must prove to the introduction of rational views concerning the state of things in former ages, may be conceived by supposing that the annals of the civil and military transactions of a great nation were perused under the impression that they occurred in a period of one hundred instead of two thousand years. Such a portion of history would immediately assume the air of a romance; the events would seem devoid of credibility, and inconsistent with the present course of human affairs. A crowd of incidents would follow each other in thick succession. Armies and fleets would appear to be assembled only to be destroyed, and cities built merely to fall in ruins. There would be the most violent transitions from foreign or intestine[3] war to periods of profound peace, and the works effected during the years of disorder or tranquillity would be alike superhuman in magnitude.

He who should study the monuments of the natural world under the influence of a similar infatuation, must draw a no less exaggerated picture of the energy and violence of causes, and must experience the same insurmountable difficulty in reconciling the former and present state of nature. If we could behold in one view all the volcanic cones thrown up in Iceland, Italy, Sicily, and other parts of Europe, during the last five thousand years, and could see the lavas which have flowed during the same period; the dislocations, subsidences and elevations caused by earthquakes; the lands added to various deltas, or devoured by the sea, together with the effects of devastation by floods, and imagine that all these events had happened in one year, we must form most exalted ideas of the activity of the agents, and the suddenness of the revolutions. Were an equal amount of change to pass before our eyes in the next year, could we avoid the conclusion that some great crisis of nature was at hand? If geologists, therefore, have misinterpreted the signs of a succession of events, so as to conclude that centuries were implied where the characters imported thousands of years, and thousands of years where the language of nature signified millions, they could not, if they reasoned logically from such false premises, come to any other conclusion, than that the system of the natural world had undergone a complete revolution....

... We inhabit about a fourth part of the surface [of the globe]; and that portion is almost exclusively the theatre of decay and not of reproduction. We know, indeed, that new deposits are annually formed in seas and lakes, and that every year some new igneous rocks are produced in the bowels of the earth, but we cannot watch the progress of their formation; and, as they are only present to our minds by the aid of reflection, it requires an effort both of the reason and the imagination to appreciate duly their importance.

---

2   Gabriele Falloppio (c. 1523–62), Italian anatomist, botanist, and professor of medicine.
3   Civil wars.

It is, therefore, not surprising that we imperfectly estimate the result of operations invisible to us; and that, when analogous results of some former epoch are presented to our inspection, we cannot recognise the analogy. He who has observed the quarrying of stone from a rock, and has seen it shipped for some distant port, and then endeavours to conceive what kind of edifice will be raised by the materials, is in the same predicament as a geologist, who, while he is confined to the land, sees the decomposition of rocks, and the transportation of matter by rivers to the sea, and then endeavours to picture to himself the new strata[4] which Nature is building beneath the waters. Nor is his position less unfavourable when, beholding a volcanic eruption, he tries to conceive what changes the column of lava has produced, in its passage upwards, on the intersected strata; or what form the melted matter may assume at great depths on cooling down; or what may be the extent of the subterranean rivers and reservoirs of liquid matter far beneath the surface. It should, therefore, be remembered, that the task imposed on those who study the earth's history requires no ordinary share of discretion, for we are precluded from collating the corresponding parts of a system existing at two different periods. If we were inhabitants of another element—if the great ocean were our domain, instead of the narrow limits of the land, our difficulties would be considerably lessened; while, on the other hand, there can be little doubt, although the reader may, perhaps, smile at the bare suggestion of such an idea, that an amphibious being, who should possess our faculties, would still more easily arrive at sound theoretical opinions in geology, since he might behold, on the one hand, the decomposition of rocks in the atmosphere, and the transportation of matter by running water; and, on the other, examine the deposition of sediment in the sea, and the imbedding of animal remains in new strata. He might ascertain, by direct observation, the action of a mountain torrent, as well as of a marine current; might compare the products of volcanos on the land with those poured out beneath the waters; and might mark, on the one hand, the growth of the forest, and on the other that of the coral reef. Yet, even with these advantages, he would be liable to fall into the greatest errors when endeavouring to reason on rocks of subterranean origin. He would seek in vain, within the sphere of his observation, for any direct analogy to the process of their formation, and would therefore be in danger of attributing them, wherever they are upraised to view, to some "primeval state of nature." ...

For more than two centuries the shelly strata of the Subapennine hills[5] afforded matter of speculation to the early geologists of Italy, and few of them had any suspicion that similar deposits were then forming in the neighbouring sea. They were as unconscious of the continued action of causes still producing similar effects, as the astronomers, in the case supposed by us, of the existence of certain heavenly bodies still giving and reflecting light, and performing their movements as in the olden time. Some imagined that the strata, so rich in organic remains, instead of being due to secondary agents, had been so created in the beginning of things by the fiat of the Almighty; and others ascribed the imbedded fossil bodies to some plastic power which resided in the earth in the early ages of the world. At length Donati explored the bed of the Adriatic, and found the closest resemblance between the new deposits there forming, and those which constituted hills above a thousand feet high in various parts of the peninsula.[6] He ascertained that certain genera of living testacea were grouped together at the bottom of the sea in precisely the same manner as were their fossil analogues in the strata of the hills, and that some species were common to the

---

4   Rock layers.
5   A series of hills that surround the Apennine Mountains in Italy.
6   Vitaliano Donati (1717–63), Italian botanist; the Adriatic Sea is the section of the Mediterranean that separates the Italian and Balkan peninsulas.

recent and fossil world.[7] Beds of shells, moreover, in the Adriatic, were becoming incrusted with calcareous rock;[8] and others were recently enclosed in deposits of sand and clay, precisely as fossil shells were found in the hills. This splendid discovery of the identity of modern and ancient submarine operations was not made without the aid of artificial instruments, which, like the telescope, brought phenomena into view not otherwise within the sphere of human observation.

In like manner, in the Vicentin,[9] a great series of volcanic and marine sedimentary rocks were examined in the early part of the last century; but no geologist suspected, before the time of Arduino,[10] that these were partly composed of ancient submarine lavas. If, when these enquiries were first made, geologists had been told that the mode of formation of such rocks might be fully elucidated by the study of processes then going on in certain parts of the Mediterranean, they would have been as incredulous as geometers would have been before the time of Newton,[11] if any one had informed them that, by making experiments on the motion of bodies on the earth, they might discover the laws which regulated the movements of distant planets.

The establishment, from time to time, of numerous points of identification, drew at length from geologists a reluctant admission, that there was more correspondence between the physical constitution of the globe, and more uniformity in the laws regulating the changes of its surface, from the most remote eras to the present, than they at first imagined....

Charles Bell
from *The Hand: Its Mechanism and Vital Endowments as Evincing Design* (1833)

Anatomist and surgeon Sir Charles Bell (1774–1842) claimed he saw God's work in the human body's perfection. Trained in medicine at the University of Edinburgh, he taught anatomy and surgery in Edinburgh before taking up positions as surgeon to the Middlesex Hospital; member (later, senior professor) of the Royal College of Surgeons; and professor of anatomy, surgery, and physiology at the newly established London University. Valuing the importance of anatomical drawings, he illustrated many of his own books: *System of Dissections* (1798), *Anatomy of the Brain* (1802), *Anatomy of the Human Body* (with brother John Bell, 1804), *Anatomy of Expression* (1806), and *A Dissertation on Gun-Shot Wounds* (1814), published during the Napoleonic wars.

Bell's treatise *The Hand* (1833) was published thanks to a bequest from the Earl of Bridgewater, who left £8,000 to support scientific works illustrating divine wisdom "as manifested in the creation." *The Hand* enjoyed wide readership and was published in many editions.

---

7   Testacea are shelled molluscs; Vitaliano Donati, *Della storia naturale marina dell'Adriatico* (1750).
8   Rocks containing mainly calcium.
9   A coastal area in northeast Italy.
10 Giovanni Arduino (1714–95), Italian geologist and engineer.
11 Isaac Newton (1642–1727), theoretical physicist and mathematician.

Chapter 10: The Hand Not the Source of Ingenuity or Contrivance, nor Consequently of Man's Superiority

Seeing the perfection of the hand, we can hardly be surprised that some philosophers should have entertained the opinion with Anaxagoras,[12] that the superiority of man is owing to his hand. We have seen that the system of bones, muscles, and nerves of this extremity is suited to every form and condition of vertebrated animals; and we must confess that it is in the human hand that we have the consummation of all perfection as an instrument. This, we perceive, consists in its power, which is a combination of strength with variety and extent of motion; we see it in the forms, relations, and sensibility of the fingers and thumb; in the provisions for holding, pulling, spinning, weaving, and constructing; properties which may be found in other animals, but which are combined to form this more perfect instrument.

In these provisions the instrument corresponds with the superior mental capacities, the hand being capable of executing whatever man's ingenuity suggests. Nevertheless, the possession of the ready instrument is not the cause of the superiority of man, nor is its aptness the measure of his attainments. So that we rather say with Galen—that man had hands given to him because he was the wisest creature, than ascribe his superiority and knowledge to the use of his hands....[13]

This question has arisen from observing the perfect correspondence between the propensities of animals and their forms and outward organization. When we see a heron standing by the water side, still as a grey stone, and hardly distinguishable from it, we may ascribe this habit to the acquired use of its feet, constructed for wading, and to its long bill and flexible neck; for the neck and bill are as much suited to its wants as the lister[14] is to the fisherman. But there is nothing in the configuration of the black-bear particularly adapted to catch fish; yet he will sit on his hinder extremities by the side of a stream, in the morning or evening, like a practised fisher; there he will watch, so motionless as to deceive the eye of the Indian, who mistakes him for the burnt trunk of a tree; and with his fore paw he will seize a fish with incredible celerity. The exterior organ is not, in this instance, the cause of the habit or of the propensity; and if we see the animal in possession of the instinct without the appropriate organ, we can the more readily believe that, in other examples, the habit exists with the instrument, although not through it.

The canine teeth are not given without the carnivorous appetite, nor is the necessity of living by carnage joined to a timid disposition; but boldness and fierceness, as well as cunning, belong to the animal with retractile claws and sharp teeth, and which prey on living animals.... On the other hand, the timid vegetable feeder has not his propensities produced by the erect ears and prominent eyes: though his disposition corresponds with them in his suspiciousness and timidity. The boldness of the bison or buffalo may be as great as that of the lion; but the impulse is different—there is a direction given to him by instinct to strike with his horns: and he will so push whether he has horns or not.... It would, indeed, be strange, where all else is perfect, if the instinctive character or disposition of the animal were at variance with its arms or instruments.

But the idea may still be entertained that the accidental use of the organ may conduce to its more frequent exercise and to the production of a corresponding disposition. Such an hypothesis would not explain the facts. The late Sir Joseph Banks,[15] in his evening conversations, told us that he had seen, what

---

12   Anaxagoras (c. 500–428 BCE), Greek philosopher.
13   Galen, *De Usu Partium* (second century).
14   A spear used for fishing.
15   Joseph Banks (1743–1820), naturalist and botanist.

many perhaps have seen, a chicken catch at a fly whilst the shell stuck to its tail. Sir Humphry Davy[16] relates that a friend of his having discovered under the burning sand of Ceylon, the eggs of the alligator, he had the curiosity to break one of them; when a young alligator came forth, perfect in its motions and in its passions; for although hatched under the influence of the sunbeams in the burning sand, it made towards the water, its proper element: when hindered, it assumed a threatening aspect and bit the stick presented to it....

In every change which the globe has undergone, we see an established relation between the animal created, and the elements around it[.] It is idle to suppose this a matter of chance. Either the structure and functions of the animal must have been formed to correspond with the condition of the elements, or the elements must have been controlled to minister to the necessities of the animal; and if the most careful investigation lead us to this conclusion, in contemplating all the inferior gradations of animal existence, what is it that makes us so unwilling to admit such an influence in the last grand work of creation?

We cannot resist those proofs of a beginning, or of design prevailing everywhere, or of a First Cause.[17] When we are bold enough to extend our enquiries into the great revolutions which have taken place, whether in the condition of the earth or in the structure of the animals which have inhabited it, our notions of the uniformity of the course of nature must suffer some modification. Changes must, at certain epochs, have been wrought, and new beings brought into existence, different from the order of things previously existing, or now existing: and such interference is not contrary to the great scheme of creation. It is not contrary to that scheme, but only to our present state. For the most wise and benevolent purposes, a conviction is implanted in our nature that we should rely on the course of events, as permanent and necessary. We belong to a certain epoch; and it is when our ambitious thoughts carry us beyond our natural condition, that we feel how much our faculties are constrained, and our conceptions, as well as our language, imperfect. We must either abandon these speculations altogether, or cease to argue purely from our present situation.

It has been made manifest that man and the animals inhabiting the earth have been created with reference to the magnitude of the globe itself;—that their living endowments bear a relation to their state of existence and to the elements around them. We have learnt that the system of animal bodies is simple and universal, notwithstanding the amazing diversity of forms that meet the eye—and that this system not only embraces all living creatures, but that it has been in operation at periods of great antiquity, before the last revolution of the earth's surface had been accomplished.

The most obvious appearances and the labours of the geologist give us reason to believe that the earth has not always been in the state in which it is now presented to us. Every substance which we see is compound; we nowhere obtain the elements of things: the most solid materials of the globe are formed of decompounded and reunited parts. Changes have been wrought on the general surface, and the proofs of these changes are as distinct as the furrows on a field are indicative that the plough has passed over it. The deeper parts of the crust of the earth and the animal remains imbedded, also give proofs of revolutions: and that in the course of these revolutions there have been long periods or epochs. In short, progressive

---

16 Humphry Davy (1778–1829), chemist.
17 The belief in God as creator.

changes, from the lowest to the highest state of existence, of organization and of enjoyment, point to the great truth that there was a beginning.

When the geologist sees a succession of stratified rocks—the lowest simple, or perhaps chemical; the strata[18] above these, compound; and successively others more conglomerated, or more distinctly composed of the fragments of the former—it is not easy to contradict the hypothesis of an eternal succession of causes. But there is nothing like this in the animal body, the material is the same in all, the general design too is the same: but each family, as it is created, is submitted to such new and fundamental arrangements in its construction as implies the presence of the hand of the Creator.

There is nothing in the inspection of the species of animals, which countenances the notion of a return of the world to any former condition. When we acknowledge that animals have been created in succession and with an increasing complexity of parts, we are not to be understood as admitting that there is here proof of a growing maturity of power, or an increasing effort in the Creator; and for this very plain reason, which we have stated, that the bestowing of life or the union of the vital principle with the material body, is the manifestation of a power superior to that displayed in the formation of an organ or the combination of many organs, or construction of the most complex mechanism. It is not, therefore, a greater power that we see in operation, but a power manifesting itself in the perfect and successive adaptation of one thing to another—of vitality and organization to inorganic matter....

We mark changes in the earth's surface, and observe, at the same time, corresponding changes in the animal creation. We remark varieties in the outward form, size, and general condition of animals, and corresponding varieties in the internal organization,—until we find men created of undoubted preeminence over all, and placed suitably in a bounteous condition of the earth....

There is extreme grandeur in the thought of an anticipating or prospective intelligence: in reflecting that what was finally accomplished in man, was begun in times incalculably remote, and antecedent to the great revolutions which the earth's surface has undergone. Nor are these conclusions too vast to be drawn from the examination of a part so small as the bones of the hand....

Mary Somerville

from *On the Connexion of the Physical Sciences* (1834)

Scientist, mathematician, and author Mary Somerville (1780–1872) fought to attain education in "unfeminine" subjects such as Latin, Greek, and algebra. She published on astronomy, geography, and physical, molecular, and microscopic science. Her friend John Herschel, and other men presented her research to scientific associations. In 1826, Somerville's paper on light and magnetism appeared in *Philosophical Transactions*, the second paper written by a woman ever to be published by the Royal Society. Constrained by familial responsibilities, she undertook work on *Mechanism of the Heavens* (1831)—later adopted at Cambridge—between social duties. She was honoured in 1879 when Somerville College, Oxford was named after her.

---

18   Rock layers.

Somerville dedicated *On the Connexion of the Physical Sciences* (1834) to Queen Adelaide, hoping that it would make "the laws by which the material world is governed more familiar to [her] countrywomen." Devoutly Christian, Somerville saw the universe as reflecting the "eternal Mind, which contains all truth and wisdom."

~

To the Queen.

Madam,
If I have succeeded in my endeavour to make the laws by which the material world is governed more familiar to my countrywomen, I shall have the gratification of thinking, that the gracious permission to dedicate my book to your Majesty has not been misplaced.
I am,
With the greatest respect,
Your Majesty's
Obedient and humble servant,
Mary Somerville.

Royal Hospital, Chelsea,
1 *Jan.* 1834.

Section 1

... Science, regarded as the pursuit of truth, which can only be attained by patient and unprejudiced investigation, wherein nothing is too great to be attempted, nothing so minute as to be justly disregarded, must ever afford occupation of consummate interest and subject of elevated meditation. The contemplation of the works of creation elevates the mind to the admiration of whatever is great and noble; accomplishing the object of all study,—which, in the eloquent language of Sir James Mackintosh, "is to inspire the love of truth, of wisdom, of beauty, especially of goodness, the highest beauty, and of that supreme and eternal Mind, which contains all truth and wisdom, all beauty and goodness. By the love or delightful contemplation and pursuit of these transcendent aims, for their own sake only, the mind of man is raised from low and perishable objects, and prepared for those high destinies which are appointed for all those who are capable of them."[19]

The heavens afford the most sublime subject of study which can be derived from science. The magnitude and splendour of the objects, the inconceivable rapidity with which they move, and the enormous distances between them, impress the mind with some notion of the energy that maintains them in their motions with a durability to which we can see no limit. Equally conspicuous is the goodness of the great First Cause,[20] in having endowed man with faculties by which he can not only appreciate

---

19 James Mackintosh, *Progress of Ethical Philosophy* (1830).
20 The belief in God as creator.

the magnificence of His works, but trace, with precision, the operation of his laws; use the globe he inhabits as a base wherewith to measure the magnitude and distance of the sun and planets, and make the diameter of the earth's orbit the first step of a scale by which he may ascend to the starry firmament. Such pursuits, while they ennoble the mind, at the same time inculcate humility, by showing that there is a barrier which no energy, mental or physical, can ever enable us to pass: that however profoundly we may penetrate the depths of space, there still remain innumerable systems, compared with which those apparently so vast must dwindle into insignificance, or even become invisible; and that not only man, but the globe he inhabits,—nay, the whole system of which it forms so small a part,—might be annihilated, and its extinction be unperceived in the immensity of creation.

Although it must be acknowledged that a complete acquaintance with physical astronomy can be attained by those only who are well versed in the higher branches of mathematical and mechanical science, and that they alone can appreciate the extreme beauty of the results, and of the means by which these results are obtained, it is nevertheless true that a sufficient skill in analysis to follow the general outline,—to see the mutual dependence of the different parts of the system, and to comprehend by what means some of the most extraordinary conclusions have been arrived at,—is within the reach of many who shrink from the task, appalled by difficulties, which, perhaps, are not more formidable than those incident to the study of the elements of every branch of knowledge; and who possibly overrate them from disregarding the distinction between the degree of mathematical acquirement necessary for making discoveries, and that which is requisite for understanding what others have done....

Section 19

The action of the atmosphere on light is not less interesting than the theory of sound, for in consequence of the refractive power of the air, no distant object is seen in its true position.

All the celestial bodies appear to be more elevated than they really are, because the rays of light, instead of moving through the atmosphere in straight lines, are continually inflected towards the earth. Light passing obliquely out of a rare into a denser medium, as from vacuum into air, or from air into water, is bent or refracted from its course towards a perpendicular to that point of the denser surface where the light enters it. In the same medium, the sine of the angle contained between the incident ray and the perpendicular is in a constant ratio to the sine of the angle contained by the refracted ray and the same perpendicular; but this ratio varies with the refracting medium. The denser the medium the more the ray is bent. The barometer shows that the density of the atmosphere decreases as the height above the earth increases; and direct experiments prove, that the refractive power of the air increases with its density; it follows, therefore, that if the temperature be uniform, the refractive power of the air is greatest at the earth's surface and diminishes upwards.

A ray of light from a celestial object falling obliquely on this variable atmosphere, instead of being refracted at once from its course, is gradually more and more bent during its passage through it, so as to move in a vertical curved line.... The object is seen in the direction of a tangent to that part of the curve which meets the eye, consequently the apparent altitude of the heavenly bodies is always greater than their true altitude. Owing to this circumstance, the stars are seen above the horizon after they are set, and the day is lengthened from a part of the sun being visible, though he really is behind the rotundity of the earth. It would be easy to determine the direction of a ray of light through the atmosphere, if the law of the density were known; but as this law is perpetually varying with the temperature, the cause is very complicated. When rays pass perpendicularly from one medium into another, they are not bent; and experience shows, that in the same surface, though the sines of the angles of incidence and refraction retain the same ratio, the refraction increases with the obliquity of incidence. Hence it appears, from what precedes, that the refraction is greatest at the horizon, and at the zenith there is none....

Bodies, whether luminous or not, are only visible by the rays which proceed from them; and as the rays must pass through strata of different densities in coming to us, it follows that, with the exception of stars in the zenith, no object either in or beyond our atmosphere is seen in its true place; but the deviation is so small in ordinary cases, that it causes no inconvenience....

Some very singular appearances occur from the occidental expansion or condensation of the strata[21] of the atmosphere contiguous to the surface of the earth, by which distant objects, instead of being elevated, are depressed; and sometimes, being at once both elevated and depressed, they appear double, one of the images being direct, and the other inverted. In consequence of the upper edges of the sun and moon being less refracted than the lower, they often appear to be oval when near the horizon. The looming also, or elevation of coasts, mountains and ships, when viewed across the sea, arises from unusual refraction. A friend of the author's, on the plains of Hindostan, saw the whole upper chain of the Himalaya mountains start into view, from a sudden change in the density of the air, occasioned by a heavy shower after a very long course of dry and hot weather. Single and double images of objects at sea, arising from sudden changes of temperature, which are not so soon communicated to the water on account of its density as to the air, occur more rarely, and are of shorter duration than similar appearances on land. In 1818, Captain Scoresby, whose observations on the phenomena of the polar seas are so valuable, recognised his father's ship by its inverted image in the air, although the vessel itself was below the horizon. He afterwards found that she was seventeen miles beyond the horizon and thirty miles distant.[22] Two images are sometimes seen suspended in the air over a ship, one direct and the other inverted, with their topmasts or their hulls meeting, according as the inverted image is above or below the direct image. Dr. Wollaston has proved that these appearances are owing to the refraction of the rays through media of different densities, by the very simple experiment of looking along a red hot poker at a distant object. Two images are seen, one direct and another inverted, in consequence of the change induced by the heat in the density of the adjacent air....[23]

Many of the phenomena that have been ascribed to extraordinary refraction seem to be occasioned by a partial or total reflection of the rays of light at the surfaces of strata of different densities. It is well known that when light falls obliquely upon the external surface of a transparent medium, as on a plate of glass, or stratum of air, one portion is reflected and the other transmitted, but when light falls very obliquely upon the internal surface, the whole is reflected and not a ray is transmitted; in all cases the angles made by the incident and reflected rays with a perpendicular to the surface being equal. As the brightness of the reflected image depends on the quantity of light, those arising from total reflection must be by far the most vivid. The delusive appearance of water, so well known to African travellers, and to the Arab of the desert, as the Lake of the Gazelles,[24] is ascribed to the reflection which takes place between strata of air of

---

21 Rock layers.
22 William Scoresby Junior, *Journal of a Voyage to the Northern Whale-Fishery* (1823).
23 William Hyde Wollaston, "On Double Images Caused by Atmospherical Refraction" (1800).
24 A name for a mirage.

different densities, owing to radiation of heat from the arid sandy plains. The mirage described by Captain Mundy, in his Journal of a Tour in India, probably arises from this cause. "A deep precipitous valley below us, at the bottom of which I had seen one or two miserable villages in the morning, bore in the evening a complete resemblance to a beautiful lake; the vapour, which played the part of water, ascending nearly half way up the sides of the vale, and on its bright surface trees and rocks being distinctly reflected. I had not been long contemplating the phenomenon, before a sudden storm came on and dropped a curtain of clouds over the scene."[25]

An occurrence which happened on the 18th of November, 1804, was probably produced by reflection. Dr. Buchan, while watching the rising sun from the cliff about a mile to the east of Brighton, at the instant the solar disc emerged from the surface of the ocean, saw the cliff on which he was standing, a wind-mill, his own figure and that of a friend, depicted immediately opposite to him on the sea. This appearance lasted about ten minutes, till the sun had risen nearly his own diameter above the surface of the waves.[26] The whole then seemed to be elevated into the air and successively vanished. The rays of the sun fell upon the cliff at an incidence of 73° from the perpendicular, and the sea was covered with a dense fog many yards in height, which gradually receded before the rising sun. When extraordinary refraction takes place laterally, the strata of variable density are perpendicular to the horizon, and when it is combined with vertical refraction, the objects are magnified as if seen through a telescope. From this cause, on the 26th of July, 1798, the cliffs of France, fifty miles off, were seen as distinctly from Hastings as if they had been close at hand, and even Dieppe was said to have been visible in the afternoon.

The stratum of air in the horizon is so much thicker and more dense than the stratum in the vertical, that the sun's light is diminished 1300 times in passing through it, which enables us to look at him when setting without being dazzled. The loss of light, and consequently of heat, by the absorbing power of the atmosphere, increases with the obliquity of incidence. Of ten thousand rays falling on its surface, 8123 arrive at a given point of the earth if they fall perpendicularly; 7024 arrive if the angle of direction be fifty degrees; 2831 if it be seven degrees; and only five rays will arrive through a horizontal stratum. Since so great a quantity of light is lost in passing through the atmosphere, many celestial objects may be altogether invisible from the plain, which may be seen from elevated situations. Diminished splendour and the false estimate we make of distance from the number of intervening objects, lead us to suppose the sun and moon to be much larger when in the horizon than at any other altitude, though their apparent diameters are then somewhat less. Instead of the sudden transitions of light and darkness, the reflective power of the air adorns nature with the rosy and golden hues of the Aurora,[27] and twilight. Even when the sun is eighteen degrees below the horizon, a sufficient portion of light remains to show that, at the height of thirty miles, it is still dense enough to reflect light. The atmosphere scatters the sun's rays, and gives all the beautiful tints and cheerfulness of day. It transmits the blue light in greatest abundance; the higher we ascend, the sky assumes a deeper hue, but in the expanse of space, the sun and stars must appear like brilliant specks in profound blackness.

---

25 Captain Mundy, *Pen and Pencil Sketches: Being the Journal of a Tour of India* (1832).
26 Alexander Buchan, "Account of an Appearance off Brighton Cliff, Seen in the Air by Reflection" (1806).
27 Dawn.

Robert Chambers
from *Vestiges of the Natural History of Creation* (1844)

Writer, editor, and publisher Robert Chambers (1802–71) anonymously authored the controversial *Vestiges of the Natural History of Creation* (1844), a popular scientific work asserting that Earth developed through evolution rather than by divine creation. Son of a bankrupt Scottish cotton manufacturer, Chambers started a bookstall; he joined forces with his brother William in 1832 to launch the successful *Chambers's Edinburgh Journal*, an affordable weekly paper, and subsequently to form the publishing firm W. and R. Chambers. Robert worked as publisher by day and wrote in the mornings and evenings; he authored over 20 books, including the *Cyclopaedia of English Literature* (1840–43) and biographies of Walter Scott and Robert Burns.

    Vestiges was the work not of a scientist but of a writer who popularized science; it appeared in four editions over seven months. Chambers did not disclose his authorship for fear of damaging the publishing firm's reputation. Speculations about the work's author pointed to Harriet Martineau (see Life Writing, Condition of England, Education) and Prince Albert.

Chapter 12: General Considerations Respecting the Origin of the Animated Tribes

Thus concludes the wondrous chapter of the earth's history which is told by geology. It takes up our globe at the period when its original incandescent state had nearly ceased; conducts it through what we have every reason to believe were vast, or at least very considerable, spaces of time, in the course of which many superficial changes took place, and vegetable and animal life was gradually developed; and drops it just at the point when man was apparently about to enter on the scene. The compilation of such a history, from materials of so extraordinary a character, and the powerful nature of the evidence which these materials afford, are calculated to excite our admiration, and the result must be allowed to exalt the dignity of science, as a product of man's industry and his reason. If there is any thing more than another impressed on our minds by the course of the geological history, it is, that the same laws and conditions of nature now apparent to us have existed throughout the whole time, though the operation of some of these laws may now be less conspicuous than in the early ages.... That seas have flowed and ebbed, and winds disturbed their surfaces, in the time of the secondary rocks, we have proof on the yet preserved surfaces of the sands which constituted margins of the seas in those days.... To turn to organic nature, vegetation seems to have proceeded then exactly as now. The very alternations of the seasons has been read in unmistakable characters in sections of the trees of those days, precisely as it might be read in a section of a tree cut down yesterday. The system of prey amongst animals flourished throughout the whole of the pre-human period; and the adaptation of all plants and animals to their respective spheres of existence was as perfect in those early ages as it is still.

But, as has been observed, the operation of the laws may be modified by conditions. At one early age, if there was any dry land at all, it was perhaps enveloped in an atmosphere unfit for the existence of terrestrial animals, and which had to go through some changes before that condition was altered.... Volcanic forces, and perhaps also the disintegrating power, seem to have been on the decrease since the first, or we have at least long enjoyed an exemption from such paroxysms of the former, as appear to have prevailed at the close of the coal formation in England and throughout the tertiary era.[28] The surface has also undergone a gradual progress by which it has become always more and more variegated, and thereby fitted for the residence of a higher class of animals.

In pursuing the progress of the development of both plants and animals upon the globe, we have seen an advance in both cases, along the line leading to the higher forms of organization. Amongst plants, we have first sea-weeds, afterwards land plants; and amongst these the simpler ... before the more complex. In the department of zoology, we see zoophytes, radiata, mollusca, articulata,[29] existing for ages before there were any higher forms. The first step forward gives fishes.... Afterwards come land animals, of which the first are reptiles, universally allowed to be the type next in advance from fishes, and to be connected with these by the links of an insensible gradation. From reptiles we advance to birds, and thence to mammalia, which are commenced by marsupialia,[30] acknowledgedly low forms in their class. That there is thus a progress of some kind, the most superficial glance at the geological history is sufficient to convince us. Indeed the doctrine of the gradation of animal forms has received a remarkable support from the discoveries of this science, as several types formerly wanting to a completion of the series have been found in a fossil state.[31]

It is scarcely less evident, from the geological record, that the progress of organic life has observed some correspondence with the progress of physical conditions on the surface. We do not know for certain that the sea, at the time when it supported radiated, molluscous, and articulated families,[32] was incapable of supporting fishes; but causes for such a limitation are far from inconceivable. The huge saurians[33] appear to have been precisely adapted to the low muddy coasts and sea margins of the time when they flourished. Marsupials appear at the time when the surface was generally in that flat, imperfectly variegated state in which we find Australia, the region where they now live in the greatest abundance, and one which has no higher native mammalian type. Finally, it was not till the land and sea had come into their present relations, and the former, in its principal continents, had acquired the irregularity of surface necessary for man, that man appeared. We have likewise seen reason for supposing that land animals could not

---

28 Coal formed geologically before and during the tertiary period, now known as the "Cenozoic" period.
29 Zoophytes are animals that imitate plants, such as corals or sponges; radiata are radially symmetric invertebrates, such as jellyfish or worms; mollusca are molluscs, invertebrates with a muscular foot and a mantle, such as clams or octopi; articulata (now an antiquated term) are invertebrates with an external skeleton and segmented bodies and limbs, such as trilobites or shrimp.
30 Mammals (e.g., cats) and marsupials (e.g., kangaroos); marsupials have an exterior pouch in which they carry their young.
31 Author's note: Intervals in the series were numerous in the department of the pachydermata; many of these gaps are now filled up from the extinct genera found in the tertiary formation. Editors' note: pachydermata are pachyderms, animals such as elephants.
32 Radiated animals are those displaying radial symmetry; molluscous animals are invertebrates, like molluscs; articulated animals consist of attached segments.
33 Reptiles such as crocodiles and the now extinct ichthyosauri.

have lived before the carbonigenous era,[34] owing to the great charge of carbonic acid gas presumed to have been contained in the atmosphere down to that time....

In examining the fossils of the lower marine creation, with a reference to the kind of rock in connexion, with which they are found, it is observed that some strata[35] are attended by a much greater abundance of both species and individuals than others. They abound most in calcareous rocks,[36] which is precisely what might be expected, since lime is necessary for the formation of the shells of the mollusks and articulata, and the hard substance of the crinoidea[37] and corals; next in the carboniferous series; next in the tertiary; next in the new red sandstone; next in slates; and lastly, least of all, in the primary rocks.... Nor is it less remarkable how various species are withdrawn from the earth, when the proper conditions for their particular existence are changed.... Not one species of any creature which flourished before the tertiary (Ehrenberg's infusoria[38] excepted) now exists; and of the mammalia which arose during that series, many forms are altogether gone, while of others we have now only kindred species. Thus to find not only frequent additions to the previously existing forms, but frequent withdrawals of forms which had apparently become inappropriate ... is a fact calculated very forcibly to arrest attention.

A candid consideration of all these circumstances can scarcely fail to introduce into our minds a somewhat different idea of organic creation from what has hitherto been generally entertained. That God created animated beings, as well as the terraqueous theatre[39] of their being, is a fact so powerfully evidenced, and so universally received, that I at once take it for granted. But in the particulars of this so highly supported idea, we surely here see cause for some re-consideration. It may now be inquired,—In what way was the creation of animated beings effected? The ordinary notion may, I think, be not unjustly described as this,—that the Almighty author produced the progenitors of all existing species by some sort of personal or immediate exertion. But how does this notion comport with what we have seen of the gradual advance of species, from the humblest to the highest? How can we suppose an immediate exertion of this creative power at one time to produce zoophytes, another time to add a few marine mollusks, another to bring in one or two conchifers,[40] again to produce crustaceous fishes, again perfect fishes, and so on to the end? This would surely be to take a very mean view of the Creative Power—to, in short, anthropomorphize it, or reduce it to some such character as that borne by the ordinary proceedings of mankind. And yet this would be unavoidable; for that the organic creation was thus progressive through a long space of time, rests on evidence which nothing can overturn or gainsay. Some other idea must then be come to with regard to *the mode* in which the Divine Author proceeded in the organic creation. Let us seek in the history of the earth's formation for a new suggestion on this point. We have seen powerful evidence, that the construction of this globe and its associates, and inferentially that of all the other globes of space, was the result, not of any immediate or personal exertion on the part of the Deity, but of natural laws which are expressions of his will. What is to hinder our supposing that the organic creation is also a result of natural laws, which are in like manner an expression of his will? ...

---

34 A geological period within the Palaeozoic era.
35 Rock layers.
36 Rocks containing calcium.
37 A type of invertebrate with arms, such as feather stars, that was common in the Palaeozoic era.
38 Protozoa; Christian Gottfried Ehrenberg, *Die Infusionsthierchen als vollkommene Organismen* (1838).
39 Earth, including its oceans.
40 Conchifera are a type of mollusc.

It will be objected that the ordinary conceptions of Christian nations on this subject are directly derived from Scripture, or, at least, are in conformity with it. If they were clearly and unequivocally supported by Scripture, it may readily be allowed that there would be a strong objection to the reception of any opposite hypothesis. But the fact is, however startling the present announcement of it may be, that the first chapter of the Mosaic record[41] is not only not in harmony with the ordinary ideas of mankind respecting cosmical and organic creation, but is opposed to them, and only in accordance with the views here taken. When we carefully peruse it with awakened minds, we find that all the procedure is represented primarily and pre-eminently as flowing *from commands and expressions of will, not from direct acts.* Let there be light—let there be a firmament—let the dry land appear—let the earth bring forth grass, the herb, the tree—let the waters bring forth the moving creature that hath life—let the earth bring forth the living creature after his kind—these are the terms in which the principal acts are described. The additional expressions,—God made the firmament—God made the beast of the earth, &c.,[42] occur subordinately, and only in a few instances; they do not necessarily convey a different idea of the mode of creation, and indeed only appear as alternative phrases, in the usual duplicative manner of Eastern narrative. Keeping this in view, the words used in a subsequent place, "*God formed* man in his own image,"[43] cannot well be understood as implying any more than what was implied before,—namely, that man was produced in consequence of an expression of the Divine will to that effect. Thus, the scriptural objection quickly vanishes, and the prevalent ideas about the organic creation appear only as a mistaken inference from the text, formed at a time when man's ignorance prevented him from drawing therefrom a just conclusion. At the same time, I freely own that I do not think it right to adduce the Mosaic record, either in objection to, or support of any natural hypothesis, and this for many reasons, but particularly for this, that there is not the least appearance of an intention in that book to give philosophically exact views of nature.

To a reasonable mind the Divine attributes must appear, not diminished or reduced in any way, by supposing a creation by law, but infinitely exalted. It is the narrowest of all views of the Deity, and characteristic of a humble class of intellects, to suppose him acting constantly in particular ways for particular occasions.... When all is seen to be the result of law, the idea of an Almighty Author becomes irresistible, for the creation of a law for an endless series of phenomena—an act of intelligence above all else that we can conceive—could have no other imaginable source, and tells, moreover, as powerfully for a sustaining as for an originating power. On this point a remark of Dr. Buckland seems applicable: "If the properties adopted by the elements at the moment of their creation adapted them beforehand to the infinity of complicated useful purposes which they have already answered, and may have still farther to answer, under many dispensations of the material world, such an aboriginal constitution, so far from superseding an intelligent agent, would only exalt our conceptions of the consummate skill and power that could comprehend such an infinity of future uses under future systems, in the original groundwork of his creation."[44] ...

It may here be remarked that there is in our doctrine that harmony in all the associated phenomena which generally marks great truths. First, it agrees, as we have seen, with the idea of planet-creation by natu-

---

41 The writings attributed to Moses: the Pentateuch, or first five books of the Old Testament.
42 See Genesis 1, the "first chapter" of the Mosaic record.
43 Genesis 1:27; 2:7.
44 William Buckland, *Geology and Mineralogy Considered with Reference to Natural Theology* (1836), Treatise 6 of *The Bridgewater Treatises on the Power, Wisdom and Goodness of God as Manifested in the Creation*.

ral law. Secondly, upon this supposition, all that geology tells us of the succession of species appears natural and intelligible. Organic life *presses in*, as has been remarked, wherever there was room and encouragement for it, the forms being always such as suited the circumstances, and in a certain relation to them, as, for example, where the limestone-forming seas produced an abundance of corals, crinoidea, and shell-fish....

It is also to be observed, that the thing to be accounted for is not merely the origination of organic being upon this little planet, third of a series which is but one of hundreds of thousands of series, the whole of which again form but one portion of an apparently infinite globe-peopled space, where all seems analogous. We have to suppose, that every one of these numberless globes is either a theatre of organic being, or in the way of becoming so. This is a conclusion which every addition to our knowledge makes only the more irresistible. Is it conceivable, as a fitting mode of exercise for creative intelligence, that it should be constantly moving from one sphere to another, to form and plant the various species which may be required in each situation at particular times? Is such an idea accordant with our general conception of the dignity, not to speak of the power, of the Great Author? Yet such is the notion which we must form, if we adhere to the doctrine of special exercise. Let us see, on the other hand, how the doctrine of a creation by law agrees with this expanded view of the organic world.

Unprepared as most men may be for such an announcement, there can be no doubt that we are able, in this limited sphere, to form some satisfactory conclusions as to the plants and animals of those other spheres which move at such immense distances from us. Suppose that the first persons of an early nation who made a ship and ventured to sea in it, observed, as they sailed along, a set of objects which they had never before seen—namely, a fleet of other ships—would they not have been justified in supposing that those ships were occupied, like their own, by human beings possessing hands to row and steer, eyes to watch the signs of the weather, intelligence to guide them from one place to another—in short, beings in all respects like themselves, or only shewing such differences as they knew to be producible by difference of climate and habits of life. Precisely in this manner we can speculate on the inhabitants of remote spheres. We see that matter has originally been diffused in one mass, of which the spheres are portions. Consequently, inorganic matter must be presumed to be everywhere the same, although probably with differences in the proportions of ingredients in different globes, and also some difference of conditions. Out of a certain number of the elements of inorganic matter are composed organic bodies, both vegetable and animal; such must be the rule in Jupiter and in Sirius,[45] as it is here. We, therefore, are all but certain that herbaceous and ligneous fibre,[46] that flesh and blood, are the constituents of the organic beings of all those spheres which are as yet seats of life. Gravitation we see to be an all-pervading principle: therefore there must be a relation between the spheres and their respective organic occupants, by virtue of which they are fixed, as far as necessary, on the surface.... Electricity we also see to be universal; if, therefore, it be a principle concerned in life and in mental action, as science strongly suggests, life and mental action must everywhere be of one general character. We come to comparatively a matter of detail, when we advert to heat and light; yet it is important to consider that these are universal agents, and that, as they bear marked relations to organic life and structure on earth, they may be presumed to do so in other spheres also. The considerations as to light are particularly interesting, for, on our globe, the structure of one important organ, almost universally distributed in the animal kingdom, is in direct and precise relation to it. Where there is light there will be

---

45 Sirius is the brightest star.
46 Wood fibre.

eyes.... It is but a small stretch of the argument to suppose that, one conspicuous organ of a large portion of our animal kingdom being thus universal, a parity in all the other organs—species for species, class for class, kingdom for kingdom—is highly likely, and that thus the inhabitants of all the other globes of space bear not only a general, but a particular resemblance to those of our own.

Assuming that organic beings are thus spread over all space, the idea of their having all come into existence by the operation of laws everywhere applicable, is only conformable to that principle, acknowledged to be so generally visible in the affairs of Providence, to have all done by the employment of the smallest possible amount of means. Thus, as one set of laws produced all orbs and their motions and geognostic[47] arrangements, so one set of laws overspread them all with life. The whole productive or creative arrangements are therefore in perfect unity.

Herbert Spencer
from *Social Statics: or, The Conditions Essential to Human Happiness Specified, and the First of Them Developed* (1850)

Agnostic philosopher and sociologist Herbert Spencer (1820–1903) participated in the 1850s' intellectual ferment that anticipated Darwinism; he coined the term "survival of the fittest." Educated at home, then tutored by his uncle (an evangelical rector and reformer), Spencer trained in Euclid, Latin, French, Greek, algebra, political economy, physics, and chemistry. After teaching and apprenticing as a railway engineer, he became sub-editor at *The Economist* (1848–53) until his uncle's legacy freed him to write independently. Mixing in intellectual circles, Spencer enjoyed friendships with George Henry Lewes, George Eliot (see Aesthetics and Culture), John Tyndall, and T.H. Huxley (see Science), who introduced him to elite scientists. His *The Principles of Psychology* (1855) stirred controversy with its materialism and ostensible atheism.

Social Statics (1850) launched his theory of human societies as regulated by natural laws. Here Spencer views moral qualities through an evolutionary lens; "evil" thus arises from an incongruity between a species and its conditions.

Chapter 2: The Evanescence of Evil

1

All evil results from the non-adaptation of constitution to conditions. This is true of everything that lives. Does a shrub dwindle in poor soil, or become sickly when deprived of light, or die outright if removed to a cold climate? it is because the harmony between its organization and its circumstances has been

---

47 Of rocks.

destroyed. Those experiences of the farmyard and the menagerie which show that pain, disease, and death, are entailed upon animals by certain kinds of treatment, may all be generalised under the same law. Every suffering incident to the human body, from a headache up to a fatal illness—from a burn or a sprain, to accidental loss of life, is similarly traceable to the having placed that body in a situation for which its powers did not fit it. Nor is the expression confined in its application to physical evil; it comprehends moral evil also. Is the kindhearted man distressed by the sight of misery? is the bachelor unhappy because his means will not permit him to marry? does the mother mourn over her lost child? does the emigrant lament leaving his fatherland? are some made uncomfortable by having to pass their lives in distasteful occupations, and others from having no occupation at all? the explanation is still the same. No matter what the special nature of the evil, it is invariably referable to the one generic cause—want of congruity between the faculties and their spheres of action.

2

Equally true is it that evil perpetually tends to disappear. In virtue of an essential principle of life, this non-adaptation of an organism to its conditions is ever being rectified; and modification of one or both, continues until the adaptation is complete. Whatever possesses vitality, from the elementary cell up to man himself, inclusive, obeys this law. We see it illustrated in the acclimatization of plants, in the altered habits of domesticated animals, in the varying characteristics of our own race. Accustomed to the brief arctic summer, the Siberian herbs and shrubs spring up, flower, and ripen their seeds, in the space of a few weeks. If exposed to the rigour of northern winters, animals of the temperate zone get thicker coats, and become white.... Ambling is a pace not natural to the horse; yet there are American breeds that now take to it without training.

Man exhibits just the same adaptability. He alters in colour according to temperature—lives here upon rice, and there upon whale oil—gets larger digestive organs if he habitually eats innutritious food—acquires the power of long fasting if his mode of life is irregular, and loses it when the supply of food is certain—becomes fleet and agile in the wilderness and inert in the city—attains acute vision, hearing, and scent, when his habits of life call for them, and gets these senses blunted when they are less needful. That such changes are towards fitness for surrounding circumstances no one can question. When he sees that the dweller in marshes lives in an atmosphere which is certain death to a stranger—when he sees that the Hindoo can lie down and sleep under a tropical sun, whilst his white master with closed blinds, and water sprinklings, and punkah,[48] can hardly get a doze—when he sees that the Greenlander and the Neapolitan[49] subsist comfortably on their respective foods—blubber and macaroni, but would be made miserable by an interchange of them—when he sees that in other cases there is still this fitness to diet, to climate, and to modes of life, even the most sceptical must admit that some law of adaptation is at work....

This universal law of physical modification, is the law of mental modification also. The multitudinous differences of capacity and disposition that have in course of time grown up between the Indian, African, Mongolian and Caucasian races, and between the various subdivisions of them, must all be ascribed to the acquirement in each case of fitness for surrounding circumstances. Those strong contrasts between the characters of nations and of times awhile since exemplified ... admit of no other conceivable explanation.

48　Ceiling fan.
49　Someone who lives in Naples, Italy.

Why all this divergence from the one common original type? If adaptation of constitution to conditions is not the cause, what is the cause? ...

In fact, if we consider the question closely, no other arrangement of things can be imagined. For we must adopt one of three propositions. We must either affirm that the human being is wholly unaltered by the influences that are brought to bear upon him—his circumstances as we call them; or that he perpetually tends to become more and more *un*fitted to those circumstances; or that he tends to become fitted to them. If the first is true, then all schemes of education, of government, of social reform—all instrumentalities by which it is proposed to act upon man, are utterly useless, seeing that he cannot be acted upon at all. If the second is true, then the way to make a man virtuous is to accustom him to vicious practices, and *vice versâ*. Both of which propositions being absurd, we are compelled to admit the remaining one.

3

Keeping in mind then the two facts, that all evil results from the non-adaptation of constitution to conditions; and that where this non-adaptation exists it is continually being diminished by the changing of constitution to suit conditions, we shall be prepared for comprehending the present position of the human race.

By the increase of population the state of existence we call social has been necessitated. Men living in this state suffer under numerous evils. By the hypothesis it follows that their characters are not completely adapted to such a state.

In what respect are they not so adapted? what is the special qualification which the social state requires?

It requires that each individual shall have such desires only, as may be fully satisfied without trenching upon the ability of other individuals to obtain like satisfaction. If the desires of each are not thus limited, then either all must have certain of their desires ungratified; or some must get gratification for them at the corresponding expense of others. Both of which alternatives necessitating pain, imply non-adaptation.

But why is not man adapted to the social state?

Simply because he yet partially retains the characteristics that adapted him for an antecedent state. The respects in which he is not fitted to society are the respects in which he is fitted for his original predatory life. His primitive circumstances required that he should sacrifice the welfare of other beings to his own; his present circumstances require that he should not do so; and in as far as his old attribute still clings to him, in so far is he unfit for the social state. All sins of men against each other, from the cannibalism of the Carrib[50] to the crimes and venalities that we see around us; the felonies that fill our prisons, the trickeries of trade, the quarrelings of nation with nation, and of class with class, the corruptness of institutions, the jealousies of caste, and the scandal of drawing-rooms, have their causes comprehended under this generalization.

Concerning the present position of the human race, we must therefore say, that man needed one moral constitution to fit him for his original state; that he needs another to fit him for his present state; and that he has been, is, and will long continue to be, in process of adaptation. By the term *civilization* we signify

---

50 Caribs are natives of the West Indies' southern islands; in the nineteenth century, they were often associated with cannibalism.

the adaptation that has already taken place. The changes that constitute *progress* are the successive steps of the transition. And the belief in human perfectibility, merely amounts to the belief, that in virtue of this process, man will eventually become completely suited to his mode of life.

4

If there be any conclusiveness in the foregoing arguments, such a faith is well founded. As commonly supported by evidence drawn from history, it cannot be considered indisputable. The inference that as advancement has been hitherto the rule, it will be the rule henceforth, may be called a plausible speculation. But when it is shown that this advancement is due to the working of a universal law; and that in virtue of that law it must continue until the state we call perfection is reached, then the advent of such a state is removed out of the region of probability into that of certainty. If any one demurs to this, let him point out the error. Here are the several steps of the argument.

All imperfection is unfitness to the conditions of existence.

This unfitness must consist either in having a faculty or faculties in excess; or in having a faculty or faculties deficient; or in both.

A faculty in excess, is one which the conditions of existence do not afford full exercise to; and a faculty that is deficient, is one from which the conditions of existence demand more than it can perform.

But it is an essential principle of life that a faculty to which circumstances do not allow full exercise diminishes; and that a faculty on which circumstances make excessive demands increases.

And so long as this excess and this deficiency continue, there must continue decrease on the one hand, and growth on the other.

Finally all excess and all deficiency must disappear; that is, all unfitness must disappear; that is, all imperfection must disappear.

Thus the ultimate development of the ideal man is logically certain—as certain as any conclusion in which we place the most implicit faith; for instance, that all men will die. For why do we infer that all men will die? Simply because, in an immense number of past experiences, death has uniformly occurred. Similarly then as the experiences of all people in all times—experiences that are embodied in maxims, proverbs, and moral precepts, and that are illustrated in biographies and histories, go to prove that organs, faculties, powers, capacities, or whatever else we call them, grow by use and diminish from disuse, it is inferred that they will continue to do so. And if this inference is unquestionable, then is the one above deduced from it—that humanity must in the end become completely adapted to its conditions—unquestionable also.

Progress, therefore, is not an accident, but a necessity. Instead of civilization being artificial, it is a part of nature; all of a piece with the development of the embryo or the unfolding of a flower. The modifications mankind have undergone, and are still undergoing, result from a law underlying the whole organic creation; and provided the human race continues, and the constitution of things remains the same, those modifications must end in completeness. As surely as the tree becomes bulky when it stands alone, and slender if one of a group; as surely as the same creature assumes the different forms of cart-horse and race-horse, according as its habits demand strength or speed; as surely as a blacksmith's arm grows large, and the skin of a labourer's hand thick; as surely as the eye tends to become long-sighted in the sailor, and short-sighted in the student; as surely as the blind attain a more delicate sense of touch; as surely as a clerk acquires rapidity in writing and calculation; as surely as the musician learns to detect an error of a semitone amidst what seems to others a very babel[51] of sounds; as surely as a passion grows by indulgence and diminishes when restrained; as surely as a disregarded conscience becomes inert, and one that is obeyed active; as surely as there is any efficacy in educational culture, or any meaning in such terms as habit, custom, practice;—so surely must the human faculties be moulded into complete fitness for the social state; so surely must the things we call evil and immorality disappear; so surely must man become perfect.

Philip Henry Gosse
from *Evenings at the Microscope* (1859)

Naturalist and writer Philip Henry Gosse (1810–88) travelled widely, being indentured as a clerk in Newfoundland, farming in Quebec (then called Lower Canada), teaching in Alabama, and collecting specimens in Jamaica. He wrote on Newfoundland entomology, Lower Canada's natural history, and Jamaican birds. In 1848, he married Emily Bowes, an evangelical writer; their only son was Edmund Gosse (see Life Writing). Philip Henry Gosse's highly successful books *A Naturalist's Rambles on the Devonshire Coast* (1853) and *The Aquarium* (1854) inspired Victorian fads for seashore exploration and aquariums. The preeminent Victorian natural history popularizer, Gosse was elected to the Royal Society in 1856. He compromised his scientific reputation with *Omphalos: An Attempt to Untie the Geological Knot* (1857), which argued against evolutionary theory, positing that God had placed fossils in the earth upon creation.

In this selection from *Evenings at the Microscope* (1859), Gosse encourages the worship of God through meticulous observation of nature; such observations influenced Victorian realist novelists' detailed analyses of human actions and interactions.

Chapter 12: Barnacles

You cannot have wandered among the rocks on our southern or western coasts, when the tide is out, without having observed that their whole surface, up to a certain level ..., is roughened with an innumerable multitude of little brownish cones. If you have ever thought it worth while to examine them with more care, you have seen that, crowded as they are, so thickly that frequently they crush each other out of their proper form and proportions, they are all constructed on the same model. Each cone is seen to be a little castle, built up of stony plates that lean toward each other, but which leave an orifice at the top....

Perhaps you have never pushed your investigations further than this, having a courteous respect for the feelings of the inmate, which has prevented your intruding on a privacy so recluse. But I have been less considerate; many a time have I applied the steel chisel and hammer to the solid rock, and having cut

---

51 Babel, city and tower where God confused the universal language, making people unintelligible to one another (Genesis 11:1–9).

off some projecting piece or angle, have transferred it, all covered with its stony cones, to the interior of a glass tank of sea-water, for more intimate acquaintance with the little builders at leisure.

These are Barnacles.... Such a colony I have now in my possession, which I will submit to you, for they present a beautiful and highly interesting spectacle, when engaged in their ordinary employment of fishing for a subsistence....

Without disturbing the busy fishers, then, just take your seat in front of this tank, and with a lens before your eye watch the colony.... From one and another, every instant, a delicate hand is thrust forth, and presently withdrawn. Fix your attention on some one conveniently placed for observation. It is now closed; but in a moment a slit opens in the valves within the general orifice, displaying a black lining with pale blue edges; it widens to an oval; the pointed valves are projected, and an apparatus of delicate curled filaments is thrust quickly out, expanding and uncurling as it comes, to the form of a fan; then in an instant more the tips of all the threads again curl up, the threads collapse, and the whole apparatus is quickly withdrawn, and disappears beneath the closing valves. The next moment, however, they reopen, and the little hand of delicate fingers makes another grasp, and so the process is continually repeated while this season of activity endures.

Now, by putting this specimen into a glass trough, and placing it under a low power of the microscope, we shall see what an exquisite piece of mechanism it is. The little hand consists of twenty-four long fingers, ... each composed of a great number of joints, and much resembling in this respect the antennæ of a Beetle. These fingers surround the mouth, which is placed at the bottom of the sort of imperfect funnel formed by their divergence. They resolve themselves into six pairs of arms.... Those nearest the mouth are the shortest, and each pair increases regularly in length to the most distant, which are the central pair when the hand is extended. Each division of each of this longest and most extensile pair comprises, in the specimen before us, thirty-two joints, while the shortest consists of about ten, the intermediate ones being in proportion; so that the whole apparatus includes nearly five hundred distinct articulations, a wonderful provision for flexibility, seeing that every joint is worked by its own proper system of muscles.

Moreover, every separate joint is furnished with its own system of spinous hairs, which are doubtless delicate organs of touch.... These hairs project at a more or less wide angle from the axis of the finger-like filament, and are graduated in length; and what is very striking, as illustrating the exquisite workmanship of the Divine hand, the hairs themselves are compound structures; for under a high power they seem to be composed of numerous joints—an illusory appearance probably, what look like joints being rather successive shoulders, or projections and constrictions of the outline—while each shoulder carries a whorl of finer spines, lying nearly close to the main hair, and scarcely deviating from its general direction....

And now do you ask—What is the object of this elaborate contrivance, or rather series of contrivances? I answer—It is the net with which the fisher takes his food—it is his means of living. You have seen that the animal has no power of pursuing prey: he is immovably fixed to the walls of his castle, which is immovably fixed to the solid rock. He is compelled therefore to subsist on what passes his castle, and on what he can catch as he sits in his doorway and casts his net at random....

Fixed and immovable as the Barnacles are in their adult and final stage, they have passed by metamorphosis through conditions of life in which they were active roving little creatures, endowed with the power of swimming freely in the wide sea. In this condition they present the closest resemblance to familiar forms of *Crustacea*,[52] as you will perceive when you examine some specimens of the larvæ that I am able to show you.

I have in one of my tanks an individual of the fine and large Barnacle, *Balanus porcatus*,[53] which for several days past has been at intervals throwing out from the orifice of its shell dense clouds of atoms, which form compact columns reaching from the animal to the surface of the water. One of these cloudy columns, when examined with a lens, is seen to be composed of thousands of dancing creatures.... They maintain a vivacious motion, and yet at the same time keep their association and the general form of the column.

Taking out a few of the dancing atoms, and isolating them in this glass stage-cell, we see that they have exactly the figure, appearance, and character of the young of the common *Cyclops*....[54] Their movements are almost incessant, a series of jerking progressions performed by quick but apparently laborious flappings of the limbs, right and left together. They occasionally rest from their exertions for a few moments, but seem to have no power of alighting on any object.

But in order to obtain a more precise idea of the structure of this tiny creature, we must manage to restrain its liberty a little, by applying gentle pressure with the compressorium,[55] just sufficient to confine it without hurting it. The body is enclosed in a broad carapace,[56] shaped much like a heraldic shield, but very convex on the back, and terminating behind in a slender point or spine, which is cut into minute teeth along the edges. Below this shield is seen the body, with three pairs of legs, a great proboscis[57] in the middle pointing downward and backward, and the anal fork, which consists of a bulbous base and two diverging points, which project behind under the spine of the shield.

The legs are exclusively swimming organs; they have no provision for grasping, no claws or hooks, nor do they appear to be capable of being used for crawling on the ground or for climbing among the sea-weeds.... In the fore part of the body a large eye is placed, deep-seated, which is of a roundish form, and is intensely black, both by reflected and transmitted light. On the summit of the forehead are placed a pair of thick flexible horn-like organs, which are abruptly bent in the middle, and which I believe represent the first pair of antennæ. This then is the first stage of the Barnacle—the form under which it appears when it is hatched from the egg.

Among the multitudes which have been evolved during these last few days, and which are now swimming at large in the tank, we may be able to detect some that have passed through their first stage, and having moulted their skin have attained a more advanced form. Here is one, which by its superior size seems to have made some progress toward maturity.

Yes, here are more. These are evidently in their second stage. There is an increase in length; for whereas the former was only 1/100th of an inch in length, these have attained to a length of 1/70th of an inch....

A specimen nearly twice as large as this last affords us an opportunity of tracing the Barnacle to another point of its transformations. The modifications are chiefly in the proboscis and the anal fork. The former now points directly downward, is furnished with a pair of minute spines on its anterior side, and with a

---

52 Crustaceans, such as crab, shrimp, and crayfish.
53 Acorn barnacle.
54 A type of copepod, which is a crustacean.
55 A microscope part used by Victorians to control the thickness of a liquid film on a slide or to exert pressure on an observed specimen.
56 A crustacean's shell.
57 A tube-like mouth.

terminal hook; while its posterior side is set with strong vibrating cilia.[58] The anal fork is greatly increased in dimensions, has its edges armed with spines articulated to its surface, and is marked with longitudinal lines which resemble corrugations. The under surface of the body is also much corrugated transversely.

In the first moult the spine of the shield was greatly increased, the size of the body itself remaining stationary; in the second moult the ratio is reversed, the body has largely increased, but the spine is nearly *in statu quo*.[59]

We cannot follow the metamorphosis any further by personal observation, but from the researches of others, and especially of Mr. Darwin,[60] we know that other stages have to be passed before the final fixed condition is attained. As yet no appreciable advance has been made, by either of the two moultings which we have traced, from the free, jerking, dancing Water-flea that was first hatched, toward the sessile Barnacle[61] enclosed in its shelly cone of several valves, and firmly fixed to the solid rock; and we are yet at a loss to imagine how such a change can be effected.

Nor is the matter apparently helped by the next moult; for though there now ensues a great change of form, it does not seem to resemble the adult Barnacle much (if at all) more than before. If described without reference to its parentage, it would still be considered an Entomostracous Crustacean,[62] or Water-flea, but removed to another tribe....

It is in this second form, which may be considered the pupa of the Barnacle, that the animal quits its free roving life, and becomes a fixture for the remainder of its days. And this is a most wonderful process; so wonderful, that it would be utterly incredible, but that the researches of Mr. Darwin have proved it incontestably to be the means by which the wisdom of God has ordained that the little Water-flea should be transformed into a stony Acorn Barnacle.

Having selected a suitable place for fixing its residence—such as those massive rocks which sustain the impetuous billows on our sea-worn coasts—the great projecting antennæ manifest a new and unprecedented function. Glands situated at their base secrete a tenacious glue, which, being poured out in great profusion, cements the whole front of the head to the rock, including and concealing the antennæ themselves. The cement rapidly *sets* under water, and the animal is henceforth immovable.

It now moults its skin once more. Another great change takes place; the bivalve shell[63] is thrown off, as are also the eyes with their bent supports, and it is seen to be a true Barnacle, though as yet of minute dimensions, and with its valves in a very rudimentary condition. It is now the representative of a third type among the Crustacean forms, for it is in effect a Stomapod;[64] such as the Opossum Shrimp (*Mysis*),[65] for example, with the shield composed of several pieces, stony in texture, on account of the great development of their calcareous[66] element, and so modified in form as to make a low cone, the legs (become the *cirri*, or what I have above called the "fingers") made to perform their movements backward instead of forward, and the whole abdomen reduced to an almost invisible point.

---

58 Small filaments.
59 Latin: the same as before.
60 Charles Darwin (1809–82), scientist. See Science, Travel and Exploration.
61 Stationary, adult barnacle.
62 One of the two major classes of crustacean in the Victorian period.
63 A shell with two parts connected by a hinge.
64 Colloquially "mantis shrimp," a shrimp-like order of crustacean.
65 Mysidacea, colloquially "opossum shrimp," a shrimp-like subclass of crustacean.
66 Containing calcium carbonate.

Marvellous indeed are these facts. If such changes as these, or anything approaching to them, took place in the history of some familiar domestic animal—if the horse, for instance, was invariably born under the form of a fish, passed through several modifications of this form, imitating the shape of the perch, then the pike, then the eel, by successive castings of its skin; then by another shift appeared as a bird, and then, gluing itself by its forehead to some stone, with its feet in the air, threw off its covering once more; and became a foal, which then gradually grew into a horse—or if some veracious traveller, some Livingstone or Barth,[67] were to tell us that such processes were the invariable conditions under which some beast of burden largely used in the centre of Africa passed—should we not think them very wonderful? Yet they would not be a whit more wonderful in this supposed case than in the case of the Barnacle, in whose history they are constantly exhibited in millions of individuals, and have been for ages—even in creatures so common that we cannot take a walk beneath our sea-cliffs, without treading on them by hundreds!

Mary Ward

from *Telescope Teachings: A Familiar Sketch of Astronomical Discovery; Combining a Special Notice of Objects Coming within the Range of a Small Telescope, Illustrated by the Author's Original Drawings; with a Detail of the Most Interesting Discoveries Which Have Been Made with the Assistance of Powerful Telescopes, Concerning the Phenomena of the Heavenly Bodies, Including the Recent Comet* (1859)

Science writer Mary Ward (1827–69) popularized astronomy and microscopy in her successful self-illustrated books *Telescope Teachings* (1859) and *Microscope Teachings* (1864). Her parents educated her, encouraging her interest in natural history, astronomy, and drawing, and buying her a high-quality microscope, which she demonstrated to family, friends, and estate workers. Ward's marriage (to Henry Ward in 1854) produced eight children; unable to live on her dowry income, the couple struggled financially. While Ward had the knowledge to write on scientific subjects, publishing on such subjects was often barred to women. She hand-printed *A Windfall for the Microscope* (1856), intending it for private distribution; she then published 250 copies of *Sketches with the Microscope* (1857). A relative showed it to a London publisher who reprinted it as *A World of Wonders Revealed by the Microscope* (1858). Ward died tragically when she was thrown from a steam-powered automobile invented by her cousin.

---

67   David Livingstone (1813–73), explorer, scientist, and missionary. See Travel and Exploration. Heinrich Barth (1821–65), German explorer, linguist, and scholar.

In this selection from *Telescope Teachings*, Ward describes the sun's features, offering pragmatic instructions on how not to damage vision when examining the sun.

∼

Preface

Can Astronomy be presented to the young as an entertaining study? Has any one attempted to cull from treatises addressed to the not wholly unlearned in science, facts and anecdotes, the "light literature" of this sublime study, and to tell these things in simple words to the young?

And to give the interest of *reality* to these facts, has it been suggested to those who can admire and wonder at the splendour of the firmament, to try how much they can improve their view of star or planet, by examining them with the help of a small telescope, such as one may see, perchance, at every sixth window, on a fine summer's day, at a watering-place, its object-glass, capable of better things, idly directed to fishing-boat or distant steamer, or still more idly, to unconscious group on the pier?

As we believe that these attempts, namely, to relate a few of the discoveries of the learned, in words which the unlearned can understand, and to tell how much may be seen of the heavenly bodies with a small telescope, have not been hitherto combined, we now venture on the task....

Chapter 2
The Sun

Let us place at the beginning of our observations this magnificent orb. It is, of all the heavenly bodies, the one most frequently in our thoughts. It is the brightest thing which the Lord of Glory has been pleased to shew us in this life. It is the source of light and heat to our earth, and to eighty-four planets besides!... The reader will possibly feel surprised at this latter statement, which would doubtless have appeared to the ancients to be fairly incredible. Some philosophers of the seventeenth century, for instance, held that the number of planets could not and ought not to exceed seven, ... namely, our Earth and Moon, Mercury, Venus, Mars, Jupiter, and Saturn, which were the only planetary bodies known to mankind before the invention of the telescope.

In the present state of knowledge, astronomers give us the following list:—

Sixty-four "primary planets" revolving round the Sun as our Earth does.

Twenty satellites, including our Moon.

Of the sixty-four primary planets fifty-six are asteroids, comparatively small bodies, all of which were discovered in this century, and fifty-two since the year 1844. The others are—Mercury, Venus, the Earth, Mars, Jupiter, Saturn, known to the ancients, Uranus, discovered by Sir William Herschel, 1781, and Neptune, discovered by Le Verrier and Adams,[68] 1846....

---

68 William Herschel (1738–1822), astronomer, discovered the planet Uranus in 1781; Urbain-Jean-Joseph Le Verrier (1811–77), French astronomer; John C. Adams (1819–92), mathematician and astronomer, independently predicted the position and existence of the planet Neptune using only mathematics.

The satellites are as follows:—One belonging to the Earth, four to Jupiter, eight to Saturn, six to Uranus, and one to Neptune....

The Sun also dispenses light and heat to a very great number of comets.

We now proceed to narrate some of the discoveries, which, by means of the telescope, have hitherto been made concerning this stupendous globe; and first let us describe its appearance as seen through our little instrument.

We must place a piece of dark-coloured glass before the eye-piece of the telescope, as the Sun is far too bright to be looked at without this protection. There are two other little precautions which we would recommend to the observer; firstly, to point the telescope by observing its shadow on a piece of paper, held to receive it; when this shadow is perfectly round, it will be found that the instrument is exactly pointing to the Sun: secondly, prepare a flat piece of pasteboard, with a hole cut through it of the diameter of the telescope, and when the instrument is properly adjusted, slip on the pasteboard to screen the unemployed eye and the head and face from the heat of the Sun. The first precaution is recommended to save the observer from being dazzled in vain endeavours to "hit the Sun" in the ordinary way, and both are more easily and quickly done in practice than in description.

Looking now through the telescope, should the dark glass used be of a reddish shade, we shall see a round orange-coloured disc in a black sky. On this disc there are generally a few black spots, somewhat resembling small blots or splashes of ink. When examined with care the larger spots prove to be not uniformly black, and not circular in shape, but of two dark shades, and of irregular outline.... It is sometimes practicable to look at the Sun through a fog or thin cloud without using the coloured glass. Its disc then appears white, and the spots are of two shades of brown.

The opinion generally held by astronomers concerning these spots is, that they are the *comparatively dark solid body of the Sun*, laid bare to our view by immense fluctuations in its luminous atmosphere; ... that the Sun has at least two atmospheres, upper and lower, and that the *darker* part of the spots is where the Sun is seen through a rent in *both* layers of atmosphere; the *lighter*, where one layer still covers it.... Recent observations have indicated that there are *three* gradations of shade, in some spots at least, the centre being the darkest....

The solar spots are not permanent. When watched from day to day, they are observed to enlarge or contract, to change their forms, and at length to disappear altogether; and new ones appear where previously there were none. These changes can be detected with a very small telescope. Another phenomenon on the Sun's disc is the occasional appearance of certain branching streaks of light on its luminous surface, curved in shape, and distinguished by their superior brightness. These are called *faculæ*, and are often observed in the neighbourhood of great spots, or on parts of the solar disc, where spots shortly afterwards break out. These have been supposed to be the ridges of immense waves in the luminous regions of the Sun's atmosphere, indicative of violent agitation in their vicinity....

With powerful instruments the whole surface of the Sun may be seen to be finely mottled with minute dark dots or pores, which fluctuate in their appearance like the rest of the markings....

The changes in these spots are truly surprising when we consider the size of the Sun; and its size is known with considerable exactness, having been calculated by comparing its apparent diameter by its known distance....

And how is the Sun's distance known? It is no doubt difficult to conceive the way in which the distance of *any* inaccessible point can be ascertained. Surveyors use an instrument by which they can tell *the direction* of any far-off tree or building, *as seen from each end of a line, which they have actually measured on the ground*, and knowing the two directions, and the length of the "base line," they can by arithmetical calculations tell the *distance* of a tree or building; ... and it is by a nearly similar process, on a far larger scale, and performed with excellent instruments, that the distances of the Sun and planets have been computed. The *base line*, answering to the surveyors' line measured on the ground, has been as long as from Britain to the Cape of Good Hope....[69]

And the Sun is so far off that its light takes more than eight minutes to reach the Earth, ... and yet light requires *but one second* to travel one hundred and ninety-two thousand miles....

It must then be of stupendous size to appear so large as it does at such a distance. Some spots have frequently appeared on it large enough to be visible to the naked eye.... One of these was forty-five thousand miles in diameter, three times as long as the voyage from England to Australia! "That such a spot should close up in six weeks time (for they hardly ever last longer) its borders must approach at the rate of more than a thousand miles a day."[70] ...

We have now described at some length the Sun's thinly-scattered *spots*, but what shall we say of its *brightness*, its radiant beams, which return to our eyes in such splendour even when reflected from the far-distant orb of Saturn? What of its genial life-dispensing heat?

"The question, 'Whence are thy beams, O Sun?' remains as unanswered now as in the days of Ossian,[71] and the manner in which this perpetual light and heat are kept undimmed, is as great a mystery as life itself."[72] ... A mystery to us, but no mystery to "the Father of Lights," who "maketh his Sun to rise on the evil and on the good." The venerable Humboldt thus eulogises the solar rays in a charming passage in Cosmos....[73] He says they "act not alone on the material world, decomposing and re-uniting its substances in fresh combination, they do not merely call forth from the bosom of the earth the tender germs of plants, elaborate in leaves the substance (chlorophyll) to which they owe their verdure, and in flowers their tints and fragrance, and repeat a thousand, and again a thousand times the Sun's bright image in the sparkling play of the waves of the sea, and in the dew-drops on the blades of grass, as the breeze sweeps over the meadow; the light of heaven in the various degrees of its intensity and duration, also connects itself by mysterious links with man's inner being—with his intellectual susceptibilities, and with the cheerful and serene, or the melancholy tone of his disposition."

The subject has been not less eloquently treated in English poetry. The following beautiful lines may appropriately close our chapter on the Sun:—

THE SUNBEAM....[74]

> Thou art no lingerer in monarch's hall;
> A joy thou art, and a wealth to all;

---

69 The southern tip of the African continent.
70 William Herschel, *A Treatise on Astronomy* (1833).
71 James MacPherson, *The Poems of Ossian* (1760–63). These poems, purportedly translations of the works of the ancient bard Ossian, were later shown to have been written largely by MacPherson himself.
72 James Breen, *Planetary Worlds: The Topography and Telescopic Appearances of the Sun, Planets, Moon, and Comets* (1854).
73 Alexander von Humboldt, *Cosmos: A Sketch of the Physical Description of the Universe* (1845–62).
74 Felicia Hemans, "The Sunbeam" (1808).

A bearer of hope unto land and sea—
Sunbeam! what gift has the world like thee?

Thou art walking the billows, and ocean smiles,
Thou hast touched with glory his thousand isles;
Thou hast lit up the ships, and the feathery foam,
And gladdened the sailor like words from home.

To the solemn depths of the forest shades,
Thou art streaming on through their green arcades,
And the quivering leaves that have caught thy glow,
Like fire-flies glance to the pools below.

I looked on the mountains—a vapour lay,
Folding their heights in its dark array;
Thou brokest forth—and the mist became
A crown and a mantle of living flame.

I looked on the peasant's lowly cot,
Something of sadness had wrapped the spot;
But a gleam of *thee* on its casement fell,
And it laugh'd into beauty at that bright spell.

To the earth's wild places a guest thou art,
Flushing the waste like the rose's heart;
And thou scornest not, from thy pomp, to shed
A tender light on the ruin's head.

Thou tak'st through the dim church-aisle thy way,
And its pillars from twilight flash forth to day;
And its high pale tombs, with their trophies old,
Are bathed in a flood as of burning gold.

And thou turnest not from the humblest grave,
Where a flower to the sighing winds may wave;
Thou scatter'st its gloom like the dreams of rest,
Thou sleepest in love on its grassy breast.

Sunbeam of summer! Oh, what is like thee?
Hope of the wilderness, joy of the sea!
One thing is like thee, to mortals given,
The faith touching all things with hues of heaven.

Charles Darwin

from *On the Origin of Species by Means of Natural Selection, or the Preservation of Favoured Races in the Struggle for Life* (1859)

Naturalist and geologist Charles Darwin (1809–82) authored the groundbreaking theory of natural selection. Darwin started medical training in Edinburgh but moved to Cambridge University, where botany and natural history fascinated him. A five-year circumnavigation on board the *Beagle* (1831–36) confirmed Darwin's commitment to natural history and geology, providing evidence for later publications. Marrying his cousin Emma and living on family wealth, he embraced a rural scientific life that permitted studies of barnacles, bees, earthworms, birds, and seeds. His theory of natural selection (conceived 1830s, in essay form 1840s, and published 1850s) was influenced by Lyell's geology (see Science) and Malthusian population theory. Friends who had read Alfred Russel Wallace's (see Travel and Exploration) evolutionary theory encouraged him to publish.

On the Origin of Species (1859) addressed a general rather than scientific audience. Its tenets (the mutability of species, struggle for existence, emphasis on chance, and implicit conclusion of human descent from animals) aroused controversy and proved vastly influential.

∼

Chapter 4: Natural Selection

How will the struggle for existence, discussed too briefly in the last chapter, act in regard to variation? Can the principle of selection, which we have seen is so potent in the hands of man, apply in nature? I think we shall see that it can act most effectually. Let it be borne in mind in what an endless number of strange peculiarities our domestic productions, and, in a lesser degree, those under nature, vary; and how strong the hereditary tendency is. Under domestication, it may be truly said that the whole organisation becomes in some degree plastic.[75] Let it be borne in mind how infinitely complex and close-fitting are the mutual relations of all organic beings to each other and to their physical conditions of life. Can it, then, be thought improbable, seeing that variations useful to man have undoubtedly occurred, that other variations useful in some way to each being in the great and complex battle of life, should sometimes occur in the course of thousands of generations? If such do occur, can we doubt ... that individuals having any advantage, however slight, over others, would have the best chance of surviving and of procreating their kind? On the other hand, we may feel sure that any variation in the least degree injurious would be rigidly destroyed. This preservation of favourable variations and the rejection of injurious variations, I call Natural Selection....

We shall best understand the probable course of natural selection by taking the case of a country undergoing some physical change, for instance, of climate. The proportional numbers of its inhabitants

---

75 Capable of being moulded or changed.

would almost immediately undergo a change, and some species might become extinct.... If the country were open on its borders, new forms would certainly immigrate, and this also would seriously disturb the relations of some of the former inhabitants. Let it be remembered how powerful the influence of a single introduced tree or mammal has been shown to be. But in the case of an island, or of a country partly surrounded by barriers, into which new and better adapted forms could not freely enter, we should then have places in the economy of nature which would assuredly be better filled up, if some of the original inhabitants were in some manner modified.... In such case, every slight modification, which in the course of ages chanced to arise, and which in any way favoured the individuals of any of the species, by better adapting them to their altered conditions, would tend to be preserved; and natural selection would thus have free scope for the work of improvement.

We have reason to believe ... that a change in the conditions of life, by specially acting on the reproductive system, causes or increases variability; and in the foregoing case the conditions of life are supposed to have undergone a change, and this would manifestly be favourable to natural selection, by giving a better chance of profitable variations occurring; and unless profitable variations do occur, natural selection can do nothing. Not that, as I believe, any extreme amount of variability is necessary; as man can certainly produce great results by adding up in any given direction mere individual differences, so could Nature, but far more easily, from having incomparably longer time at her disposal. Nor do I believe that any great physical change, as of climate, or any unusual degree of isolation to check immigration, is actually necessary to produce new and unoccupied places for natural selection to fill up by modifying and improving some of the varying inhabitants. For as all the inhabitants of each country are struggling together with nicely balanced forces, extremely slight modifications in the structure or habits of one inhabitant would often give it an advantage over others; and still further modifications of the same kind would often still further increase the advantage. No country can be named in which all the native inhabitants are now so perfectly adapted to each other and to the physical conditions under which they live, that none of them could anyhow be improved; for in all countries, the natives have been so far conquered by naturalised productions, that they have allowed foreigners to take firm possession of the land. And as foreigners have thus everywhere beaten some of the natives, we may safely conclude that the natives might have been modified with advantage, so as to have better resisted such intruders.

As man can produce and certainly has produced a great result by his methodical and unconscious means of selection, what may not nature effect? Man can act only on external and visible characters: nature cares nothing for appearances, except in so far as they may be useful to any being. She can act on every internal organ, on every shade of constitutional difference, on the whole machinery of life. Man selects only for his own good; Nature only for that of the being which she tends. Every selected character is fully exercised by her; and the being is placed under well-suited conditions of life. Man keeps the natives of many climates in the same country; he seldom exercises each selected character in some peculiar and fitting manner; he feeds a long and a short beaked pigeon on the same food; ... he exposes sheep with long and short wool to the same climate. He does not allow the most vigorous males to struggle for the females. He does not rigidly destroy all inferior animals, but protects during each varying season, as far as lies in his power, all his productions. He often begins his selection by some half-monstrous form; or at least by some modification prominent enough to catch his eye, or to be plainly useful to him. Under nature, the slightest difference of structure or constitution may well turn the nicely-balanced scale in the struggle for life, and so be preserved. How fleeting are the wishes and efforts of man! how short his time!

and consequently how poor will his products be, compared with those accumulated by nature during whole geological periods. Can we wonder, then, that nature's productions should be far "truer" in character than man's productions; that they should be infinitely better adapted to the most complex conditions of life, and should plainly bear the stamp of far higher workmanship?

It may be said that natural selection is daily and hourly scrutinising, throughout the world, every variation, even the slightest; rejecting that which is bad, preserving and adding up all that is good; silently and insensibly working, whenever and wherever opportunity offers, at the improvement of each organic being in relation to its organic and inorganic conditions of life. We see nothing of these slow changes in progress, until the hand of time has marked the long lapse of ages, and then so imperfect is our view into long past geological ages, that we only see that the forms of life are now different from what they formerly were.

Although natural selection can act only through and for the good of each being, yet characters and structures, which we are apt to consider as of very trifling importance, may thus be acted on. When we see leaf-eating insects green, and bark-feeders mottled-grey; the alpine ptarmigan white in winter, the red-grouse the colour of heather, and the black-grouse that of peaty earth,[76] we must believe that these tints are of service to these birds and insects in preserving them from danger....

As we see that those variations which under domestication appear at any particular period of life, tend to reappear in the offspring at the same period;—for instance, in the seeds of the many varieties of our culinary and agricultural plants; in the caterpillar and cocoon stages of the varieties of the silkworm; in the eggs of poultry, and in the colour of the down of their chickens; in the horns of our sheep and cattle when nearly adult;—so in a state of nature, natural selection will be enabled to act on and modify organic beings at any age, by the accumulation of profitable variations at that age, and by their inheritance at a corresponding age.... Natural selection may modify and adapt the larva of an insect to a score of contingencies, wholly different from those which concern the mature insect. These modifications will no doubt affect, through the laws of correlation, the structure of the adult; and probably in the case of those insects which live only for a few hours, and which never feed, a large part of their structure is merely the correlated result of successive changes in the structure of their larvæ. So, conversely, modifications in the adult will probably often affect the structure of the larva; but in all cases natural selection will ensure that modifications consequent on other modifications at a different period of life, shall not be in the least degree injurious: for if they became so, they would cause the extinction of the species.

Natural selection will modify the structure of the young in relation to the parent, and of the parent in relation to the young.... What natural selection cannot do, is to modify the structure of one species, without giving it any advantage, for the good of another species; and though statements to this effect may be found in works of natural history, I cannot find one case which will bear investigation. A structure used only once in an animal's whole life, if of high importance to it, might be modified to any extent by natural selection; for instance, the great jaws possessed by certain insects, and used exclusively for opening the cocoon—or the hard tip to the beak of nestling birds, used for breaking the egg. It has been asserted, that of the best short-beaked tumbler-pigeons more perish in the egg than are able to get out of it; so that fanciers[77] assist in the act of hatching. Now, if nature had to make the beak of a

---

76 These game birds' feathers change colour according to their surroundings.
77 Someone who enjoys and is knowledgeable about a subject.

full-grown pigeon very short for the bird's own advantage, the process of modification would be very slow, and there would be simultaneously the most rigorous selection of the young birds within the egg, which had the most powerful and hardest beaks, for all with weak beaks would inevitably perish: or, more delicate and more easily broken shells might be selected, the thickness of the shell being known to vary like every other structure.

Sexual Selection.—Inasmuch as peculiarities often appear under domestication in one sex and become hereditarily attached to that sex, the same fact probably occurs under nature, and if so, natural selection will be able to modify one sex in its functional relations to the other sex, or in relation to wholly different habits of life in the two sexes, as is sometimes the case with insects. And this leads me to say a few words on what I call Sexual Selection. This depends, not on a struggle for existence, but on a struggle between the males for possession of the females; the result is not death to the unsuccessful competitor, but few or no offspring. Sexual selection is, therefore, less rigorous than natural selection. Generally, the most vigorous males, those which are best fitted for their places in nature, will leave most progeny. But in many cases, victory will depend not on general vigour, but on having special weapons, confined to the male sex. A hornless stag or spurless cock[78] would have a poor chance of leaving offspring....

Thus it is, as I believe, that when the males and females of any animal have the same general habits of life, but differ in structure, colour, or ornament, such differences have been mainly caused by sexual selection; that is, individual males have had, in successive generations, some slight advantage over other males, in their weapons, means of defence, or charms; and have transmitted these advantages to their male offspring....

Illustrations of the action of Natural Selection.—In order to make it clear how, as I believe, natural selection acts, I must beg permission to give one or two imaginary illustrations. Let us take the case of a wolf, which preys on various animals, securing some by craft, some by strength, and some by fleetness; and let us suppose that the fleetest prey, a deer for instance, had from any change in the country increased in numbers, or that other prey had decreased in numbers, during that season of the year when the wolf is hardest pressed for food. I can under such circumstances see no reason to doubt that the swiftest and slimmest wolves would have the best chance of surviving.... I can see no more reason to doubt this, than that man can improve the fleetness of his greyhounds by careful and methodical selection, or by that unconscious selection which results from each man trying to keep the best dogs without any thought of modifying the breed.

Even without any change in the proportional numbers of the animals on which our wolf preyed, a cub might be born with an innate tendency to pursue certain kinds of prey.... Now, if any slight innate change of habit or of structure benefited an individual wolf, it would have the best chance of surviving and of leaving offspring. Some of its young would probably inherit the same habits or structure, and by the repetition of this process, a new variety might be formed which would either supplant or coexist with the parent-form of wolf....

I am well aware that this doctrine of natural selection, exemplified in the above imaginary instances, is open to the same objections which were at first urged against Sir Charles Lyell's noble views on "the

---

78   Rooster with no spur (claw that grows on the back of the foot).

modern changes of the earth, as illustrative of geology;"[79] but we now very seldom hear the action, for instance, of the coast-waves, called a trifling and insignificant cause, when applied to the excavation of gigantic valleys or to the formation of the longest lines of inland cliffs. Natural selection can act only by the preservation and accumulation of infinitesimally small inherited modifications, each profitable to the preserved being; and as modern geology has almost banished such views as the excavation of a great valley by a single diluvial wave,[80] so will natural selection, if it be a true principle, banish the belief of the continued creation of new organic beings, or of any great and sudden modification in their structure....

Circumstances favourable to Natural Selection.—This is an extremely intricate subject. A large amount of inheritable and diversified variability is favourable, but I believe mere individual differences suffice for the work. A large number of individuals, by giving a better chance for the appearance within any given period of profitable variations, will compensate for a lesser amount of variability in each individual, and is, I believe, an extremely important element of success. Though nature grants vast periods of time for the work of natural selection, she does not grant an indefinite period; for as all organic beings are striving, it may be said, to seize on each place in the economy of nature, if any one species does not become modified and improved in a corresponding degree with its competitors, it will soon be exterminated.

In man's methodical selection, a breeder selects for some definite object, and free intercrossing[81] will wholly stop his work. But when many men, without intending to alter the breed, have a nearly common standard of perfection, and all try to get and breed from the best animals, much improvement and modification surely but slowly follow from this unconscious process of selection, notwithstanding a large amount of crossing with inferior animals. Thus it will be in nature; for within a confined area ... natural selection will always tend to preserve all the individuals varying in the right direction, though in different degrees, so as better to fill up the unoccupied place. But if the area be large, its several districts will almost certainly present different conditions of life; and then if natural selection be modifying and improving a species in the several districts, there will be intercrossing with the other individuals of the same species on the confines of each....

Intercrossing plays a very important part in nature in keeping the individuals of the same species, or of the same variety, true and uniform in character. It will obviously thus act far more efficiently with those animals which unite for each birth; but I have already attempted to show that we have reason to believe that occasional intercrosses take place with all animals and with all plants. Even if these take place only at long intervals, I am convinced that the young thus produced will gain so much in vigour and fertility over the offspring from long-continued self-fertilisation, that they will have a better chance of surviving and propagating their kind; and thus, in the long run, the influence of intercrosses, even at rare intervals, will be great. If there exist organic beings which never intercross, uniformity of character can be retained amongst them, as long as their conditions of life remain the same, only through the principle of inheritance, and through natural selection destroying any which depart from the proper type; but if their conditions of life change and they undergo modification, uniformity of character can be given to their modified offspring, solely by natural selection preserving the same favourable variations.

---

79 Charles Lyell, *Principles of Geology* (1830–33). See Science.
80 The wave of a catastrophic flood.
81 Cross-breeding.

Isolation, also, is an important element in the process of natural selection. In a confined or isolated area, if not very large, the organic and inorganic conditions of life will generally be in a great degree uniform; so that natural selection will tend to modify all the individuals of a varying species throughout the area in the same manner in relation to the same conditions. Intercrosses, also, with the individuals of the same species, which otherwise would have inhabited the surrounding and differently circumstanced districts, will be prevented. But isolation probably acts more efficiently in checking the immigration of better adapted organisms, after any physical change, such as of climate or elevation of the land, &c.; and thus new places in the natural economy of the country are left open for the old inhabitants to struggle for, and become adapted to, through modifications in their structure and constitution. Lastly, isolation, by checking immigration and consequently competition, will give time for any new variety to be slowly improved; and this may sometimes be of importance in the production of new species. If, however, an isolated area be very small, either from being surrounded by barriers, or from having very peculiar physical conditions, the total number of the individuals supported on it will necessarily be very small; and fewness of individuals will greatly retard the production of new species through natural selection, by decreasing the chance of the appearance of favourable variations....

Although I do not doubt that isolation is of considerable importance in the production of new species, on the whole I am inclined to believe that largeness of area is of more importance, more especially in the production of species, which will prove capable of enduring for a long period, and of spreading widely. Throughout a great and open area, not only will there be a better chance of favourable variations arising from the large number of individuals of the same species there supported, but the conditions of life are infinitely complex from the large number of already existing species; and if some of these many species become modified and improved, others will have to be improved in a corresponding degree or they will be exterminated. Each new form, also, as soon as it has been much improved, will be able to spread over the open and continuous area, and will thus come into competition with many others.... I conclude that, although small isolated areas probably have been in some respects highly favourable for the production of new species, yet that the course of modification will generally have been more rapid on large areas; and what is more important, that the new forms produced on large areas, which already have been victorious over many competitors, will be those that will spread most widely, will give rise to most new varieties and species, and will thus play an important part in the changing history of the organic world....

To sum up the circumstances favourable and unfavourable to natural selection, as far as the extreme intricacy of the subject permits. I conclude, looking to the future, that for terrestrial productions a large continental area, which will probably undergo many oscillations of level, and which consequently will exist for long periods in a broken condition, will be the most favourable for the production of many new forms of life, likely to endure long and to spread widely. For the area will first have existed as a continent, and the inhabitants, at this period numerous in individuals and kinds, will have been subjected to very severe competition. When converted by subsidence[82] into large separate islands, there will still exist many individuals of the same species on each island: intercrossing on the confines of the range of each species will thus be checked: after physical changes of any kind, immigration will be prevented, so that new places in the polity[83] of each island will have to be filled up by modifications of the old inhabitants; and

---

82   Gradual sinking.
83   Organization.

time will be allowed for the varieties in each to become well modified and perfected. When, by renewed elevation, the islands shall be re-converted into a continental area, there will again be severe competition: the most favoured or improved varieties will be enabled to spread: there will be much extinction of the less improved forms, and the relative proportional numbers of the various inhabitants of the renewed continent will again be changed; and again there will be a fair field for natural selection to improve still further the inhabitants, and thus produce new species.

That natural selection will always act with extreme slowness, I fully admit. Its action depends on there being places in the polity of nature, which can be better occupied by some of the inhabitants of the country undergoing modification of some kind. The existence of such places will often depend on physical changes, which are generally very slow, and on the immigration of better adapted forms having been checked. But the action of natural selection will probably still oftener depend on some of the inhabitants becoming slowly modified; the mutual relations of many of the other inhabitants being thus disturbed. Nothing can be effected, unless favourable variations occur, and variation itself is apparently always a very slow process.... I further believe, that this very slow, intermittent action of natural selection accords perfectly well with what geology tells us of the rate and manner at which the inhabitants of this world have changed.

Slow though the process of selection may be, if feeble man can do much by his powers of artificial selection, I can see no limit to the amount of change, to the beauty and infinite complexity of the coadaptations between all organic beings, one with another and with their physical conditions of life, which may be effected in the long course of time by nature's power of selection....

Divergence of Character.—The principle, which I have designated by this term, is of high importance on my theory, and explains, as I believe, several important facts. In the first place, varieties, even strongly-marked ones, though having somewhat of the character of species—as is shown by the hopeless doubts in many cases how to rank them—yet certainly differ from each other far less than do good and distinct species. Nevertheless, according to my view, varieties are species in the process of formation, or are, as I have called them, incipient species. How, then, does the lesser difference between varieties become augmented into the greater difference between species? ... Mere chance, as we may call it, might cause one variety to differ in some character from its parents, and the offspring of this variety again to differ from its parent in the very same character and in a greater degree; but this alone would never account for so habitual and large an amount of difference as that between varieties of the same species and species of the same genus.

As has always been my practice, let us seek light on this head from our domestic productions.... [W]e may suppose that at an early period one man preferred swifter horses; another stronger and more bulky horses. The early differences would be very slight; in the course of time, from the continued selection of swifter horses by some breeders, and of stronger ones by others, the differences would become greater, and would be noted as forming two sub-breeds; finally, after the lapse of centuries, the sub-breeds would become converted into two well-established and distinct breeds. As the differences slowly become greater, the inferior animals with intermediate characters, being neither very swift nor very strong, will have been neglected, and will have tended to disappear. Here, then, we see in man's productions the action of what may be called the principle of divergence, causing differences, at first barely appreciable, steadily to increase, and the breeds to diverge in character both from each other and from their common parent.

But how, it may be asked, can any analogous principle apply in nature? I believe it can and does apply most efficiently, from the simple circumstance that the more diversified the descendants from any one species become in structure, constitution, and habits, by so much will they be better enabled to seize on many and widely diversified places in the polity of nature, and so be enabled to increase in numbers....

The truth of the principle, that the greatest amount of life can be supported by great diversification of structure, is seen under many natural circumstances. In an extremely small area, especially if freely open to immigration, and where the contest between individual and individual must be severe, we always find great diversity in its inhabitants. For instance, I found that a piece of turf, three feet by four in size, which had been exposed for many years to exactly the same conditions, supported twenty species of plants, and these belonged to eighteen genera[84] and to eight orders, which shows how much these plants differed from each other.... Most of the animals and plants which live close round any small piece of ground, could live on it (supposing it not to be in any way peculiar in its nature), and may be said to be striving to the utmost to live there; but, it is seen, that where they come into the closest competition with each other, the advantages of diversification of structure, with the accompanying differences of habit and constitution, determine that the inhabitants, which thus jostle each other most closely, shall, as a general rule, belong to what we call different genera and orders....

... [I]n the general economy of any land, the more widely and perfectly the animals and plants are diversified for different habits of life, so will a greater number of individuals be capable of there supporting themselves. A set of animals, with their organisation but little diversified, could hardly compete with a set more perfectly diversified in structure....

We have seen that in each country it is the species of the larger genera which oftenest present varieties or incipient species. This, indeed, might have been expected; for as natural selection acts through one form having some advantage over other forms in the struggle for existence, it will chiefly act on those which already have some advantage; and the largeness of any group shows that its species have inherited from a common ancestor some advantage in common. Hence, the struggle for the production of new and modified descendants, will mainly lie between the larger groups, which are all trying to increase in number. One large group will slowly conquer another large group, reduce its numbers, and thus lessen its chance of further variation and improvement. Within the same large group, the later and more highly perfected sub-groups, from branching out and seizing on many new places in the polity of Nature, will constantly tend to supplant and destroy the earlier and less improved sub-groups. Small and broken groups and sub-groups will finally tend to disappear. Looking to the future, we can predict that the groups of organic beings which are now large and triumphant, and which are least broken up, that is, which as yet have suffered least extinction, will for a long period continue to increase. But which groups will ultimately prevail, no man can predict.... Although extremely few of the most ancient species may now have living and modified descendants, yet at the most remote geological period, the earth may have been as well peopled with many species of many genera, families, orders, and classes, as at the present day.

Summary of Chapter.—If during the long course of ages and under varying conditions of life, organic beings vary at all in the several parts of their organisation, and I think this cannot be disputed; if there be, owing to the high geometrical powers of increase of each species, at some age, season, or year, a severe struggle for life, and this certainly cannot be disputed; then, considering the infinite complexity of the relations of all organic beings to each other and to their conditions of existence, causing an

---

84 Plural of genus.

infinite diversity in structure, constitution, and habits, to be advantageous to them, I think it would be a most extraordinary fact if no variation ever had occurred useful to each being's own welfare, in the same way as so many variations have occurred useful to man. But if variations useful to any organic being do occur, assuredly individuals thus characterised will have the best chance of being preserved in the struggle for life; and from the strong principle of inheritance they will tend to produce offspring similarly characterised. This principle of preservation, I have called, for the sake of brevity, Natural Selection. Natural selection, on the principle of qualities being inherited at corresponding ages, can modify the egg, seed, or young, as easily as the adult. Amongst many animals, sexual selection will give its aid to ordinary selection, by assuring to the most vigorous and best adapted males the greatest number of offspring. Sexual selection will also give characters useful to the males alone, in their struggles with other males.

Whether natural selection has really thus acted in nature, in modifying and adapting the various forms of life to their several conditions and stations, must be judged of by the general tenour and balance of evidence given in the following chapters. But we already see how it entails extinction; and how largely extinction has acted in the world's history, geology plainly declares. Natural selection, also, leads to divergence of character; for more living beings can be supported on the same area the more they diverge in structure, habits, and constitution, of which we see proof by looking at the inhabitants of any small spot or at naturalised productions. Therefore during the modification of the descendants of any one species, and during the incessant struggle of all species to increase in numbers, the more diversified these descendants become, the better will be their chance of succeeding in the battle of life. Thus the small differences distinguishing varieties of the same species, will steadily tend to increase till they come to equal the greater differences between species of the same genus, or even of distinct genera.

We have seen that it is the common, the widely-diffused, and widely-ranging species, belonging to the larger genera, which vary most; and these will tend to transmit to their modified offspring that superiority which now makes them dominant in their own countries. Natural selection, as has just been remarked, leads to divergence of character and to much extinction of the less improved and intermediate forms of life....

The affinities of all the beings of the same class have sometimes been represented by a great tree.... The green and budding twigs may represent existing species; and those produced during each former year may represent the long succession of extinct species. At each period of growth all the growing twigs have tried to branch out on all sides, and to overtop and kill the surrounding twigs and branches, in the same manner as species and groups of species have tried to overmaster other species in the great battle for life. The limbs divided into great branches, and these into lesser and lesser branches, were themselves once, when the tree was small, budding twigs; and this connexion of the former and present buds by ramifying branches may well represent the classification of all extinct and living species in groups subordinate to groups. Of the many twigs which flourished when the tree was a mere bush, only two or three, now grown into great branches, yet survive and bear all the other branches; so with the species which lived during long-past geological periods, very few now have living and modified descendants. From the first growth of the tree, many a limb and branch has decayed and dropped off; and these lost branches of various sizes may represent those whole orders, families, and genera which have now no living representatives, and which are known to us only from having been found in a fossil state. As we here and there see a thin straggling branch springing from a fork low down in a tree, and which by some chance has been favoured and is still alive on its summit, so we occasionally see an animal like the Ornithorhynchus or Lepidosiren,[85] which in some small degree connects by its affinities two large branches of life, and which has apparently been saved from fatal competition by having inhabited a protected station. As buds give rise by growth to fresh buds, and these, if vigorous, branch out and overtop on all sides many a feebler branch, so by generation I believe it has been with the great Tree of Life,[86] which fills with its dead and broken branches the crust of the earth, and covers the surface with its ever branching and beautiful ramifications.

Lydia Becker
from "On the Study of Science by Women" (1869)

Feminist activist and science writer Lydia Becker (1827–90) was the "visible head" of the women's suffrage movement. Inspired by Barbara Leigh Smith Bodichon (see Gender and Sexuality), she edited the *Women's Suffrage Journal* (1870–90), contributed widely to the periodical press, and advocated for suffrage in numerous public lectures. Renowned as a speaker, Becker was elected to the Manchester school board following the Education Act of 1870. Also known for her plant collecting and writings on botany for general audiences, she corresponded in the 1860s and 1870s with Charles Darwin (see Science, Travel and Exploration).

Becker's 1869 article, published in the *Contemporary Review*, promotes scientific education for both men and women. She argues that women's minds are "starved" for want of "mental food" and that their scientific contributions would help humanity. She characterizes the women's movement as international and egalitarian—it "arises from no spirit of opposition or rivalry with men, but from deep and intense sympathy in their noblest aims and aspirations."

In speaking of the study of science by women, I desire, at the outset, to guard against the supposition that I consider such study to present any exceptional peculiarity to distinguish it from the study of science by men. Male and female students, in any branch of science, must go through the same training, and have their qualifications and capacities tested by precisely the same rules; neither is there anything in these studies which is naturally more attractive or advantageous to persons of one sex than of the other.

Nevertheless, the fact is indisputable that at the present time the students of science among men greatly outnumber those among women. Some persons attribute this circumstance to an inherent specific distinction in the minds of the two sexes of man. They assume the existence of a natural distaste or incapacity for scientific pursuits among women, and they consider it neither possible nor desirable to encourage them in the successful prosecution of such studies.

---

85 An ornithorhynchus is a platypus; a lepidosiren is a lung-fish.
86 In the Bible, God creates the tree of life in the garden of Eden.

Others perceive in existing social and conventional arrangements, which exclude women from those opportunities of cultivating their intellectual faculties which are freely enjoyed by men, a perfectly sufficient explanation of the difference in the numbers and the proficiency of persons of each sex engaged in scientific pursuits.

The last is, I think, the true solution of the question, "Why are there fewer scientific women than scientific men?" The assumed difference in the minds of the two sexes is purely hypothetical; the practical difference in the training and advantages given to each is a fact as indisputable as the one which it explains.

I do not deny the existence of distinct types or orders of mind among mankind—all I deny is the coincidence of any one of these types with the physical distinction of sex.

If we take an assemblage of persons of both sexes, and test the differences of thought, opinion or capacity existing among them, by putting before them any proposition on which opposite views can be held, I believe it would be impossible to find one which would range all the men on one side, and all the women on the other. If it were true that there is a specific difference, however slight, between the minds of men and women, it would be possible to find such a proposition, if we took one which corresponded to this distinction. When a naturalist seeks to group a number of individuals into a distinct class, he fixes on some character or set of characters common to them all, and distinguishing them from other individuals. When he finds such a group distinctly defined, he calls it a species. But when he finds two individuals differing very widely from each other, yet so connected by intermediate forms that he can pass from one extreme to the other without a violent break any where in the series, he considers them to be of one and the same kind. If we apply this principle as an illustration of the variety in human intellects, taking the conventional masculine type of mind as one end of the scale, and the conventional feminine type as the other, we shall find them connected by numerous intermediate varieties, distributed indiscriminately among male and female persons; that what is called a masculine mind is frequently found united to a feminine body, and sometimes the reverse, and that there is no necessary nor even presumptive connection between the sex of a human being and the type of intellect and character he possesses.

The equality of men and women, as regards intellect, resembles the equality of men among themselves, or women among themselves. No two are alike, no two are equal, but all start fair, and all have an equal right to advance as far as they can. Like a crowd of men and women on a level floor, all stand on the same plane, but some overtop the others. If we measure them by physical stature, there will be a considerable disparity between the sexes, and it will take an unusually tall woman to reach the height of the men. If we measure them by mental stature we shall find a different result. A woman who is somewhat taller than the masses of her sisters will be found to overtop the majority of the men.

The existence of a difference in the intellectual powers of the sexes is a question fertile in endless disputations, which can only be satisfactorily set at rest by the test of observation and experiment. Wherever this test has been impartially applied, by studies and examinations conducted without reference to the sex of the student, the honours have been fairly divided between men and women, and no line of demarcation has made itself apparent between the character of the subjects chosen or the degree of proficiency attained....

Most of the inducements for pursuing scientific studies are common to men and women. But there are some considerations which render such pursuits of greater value to women than to men. Prevalent opinions and customs impose on women so much more monotonous and colourless lives.... In default of mental food and exercise, the minds of women get starved out.... Many women might be saved from the evil of the life of intellectual vacuity, to which their present position renders them so peculiarly liable, if they had a thorough training in some branch of science, and the opportunity of carrying it on as a serious pursuit, in concert with others having similar tastes. Many a passing moment would then be made bright with a flash of thought which would otherwise have stolen away unmarked into the irrevocable past.

Men, who have been in the habit of enjoying the advantages attending systematic study and of the liberty of thought and speech not yet attained by women, do not need to be reminded of the benefits they derive from them. But women, who have never had the opportunity of finding out by experience the value of these conditions of mental life, do not always appreciate the magnitude of the loss they endure. If they did, I think they would not be content with their enforced exclusion from the pale of scientific society.

One of the greatest benefits which intellectual pursuits bring in their train is that of affording a peaceful neutral ground in which the mind can take refuge from the petty cares and annoyances of life, or even find diversion from more serious troubles. Like prudent investors, who keep a part of their capital in the funds,[87] those who place the sources of a portion of their income of enjoyment in some pursuit wholly unconnected with their personal affairs, will find they have an interest which is perfectly safe amid the chances and changes of life. I do not for a moment maintain that intellectual pursuits can afford consolation in sorrow ... ; but they are undoubtedly capable of giving solace and diversion to the mind which might otherwise dwell too long on the gloomy side of things, and of beguiling the tedium of enforced solitude, or of confinement to a sick room....

If we turn from the consideration of the advantages women would gain from taking an active part in scientific pursuits, to the means accessible to them for prosecuting these studies we perceive a very deplorable state of affairs.

The necessity for some common ground on which all interested in intellectual pursuits may meet, has been so strongly felt, that there exist all over the country institutions and societies, devoted either to literature and philosophy in general, or to the cultivation of special departments of knowledge. But most of these institutions, especially such as are devoted to the higher branches of scientific investigation, have one strange and injurious deficiency. They do not throw open such opportunities as they afford for acquiring knowledge freely to all who desire it; they ... say to one half of the human race, "You shall not enter into the advantages we have to offer; ... should any of you, in spite of this drawback, reach such a measure of attainments as would entitle one of us to the honour of membership or fellowship in any learned society, we will not, by conferring such distinctions on any of you, recognise your right to occupy your minds with such studies at all." ...

In order to have definite information on this head, I applied to the secretaries of one or two of the scientific societies of the metropolis, with the following result. Mr. White, Assistant-Secretary of the Royal Society,[88] writes:—

> In answer to your inquiry as to what is the position of women with regard to the Royal Society, I beg leave to say that the Society is not open to women: that ladies are not admitted to the meetings, and have never been elected Fellows.

---

87 Stock in the national debt similar to government bonds.
88 A British scientific society (founded 1662) with the aim of promoting and furthering scientific inquiry.

Mrs. Somerville[89] many years ago was elected honorary member of the Astronomical Society, but I am not aware that she has ever written F.R.A.S.[90] after her name....

Besides the special benefits to women themselves, results of a yet more important nature with respect to the happiness and welfare of mankind, would follow from making them acquainted with the results of scientific inquiry, and imbuing their minds with the principles on which such researches are based. The importance of scientific knowledge is not yet appreciated by the general public. A knowledge of science is frequently treated as if it were merely a branch of learning, like Latin or Greek, and the question of making it a part of general education is regarded as if it were simply a question of what course of study was best fitted to train the faculties or suit the taste of the student.

But surely there is a more important aspect of the study of science than that which regards it as merely a mass of curious and interesting information. Men and women constitute an integral portion of a universe governed by uniform and undeviating laws. It is the object of scientific explorers to discover these laws, a pursuit in which they may be said as yet to have hardly made a beginning. Every step gained in advance reveals something which can be turned to account in ameliorating the hardships and discomforts of life, and promoting the happiness of mankind. With complete knowledge of the conditions under which we live, and complete conformity to these conditions, we might hope to see most of the evils that afflict our race entirely disappear.... The greater the number of minds that are impressed with this belief, the greater the encouragement that will be given to the inquiry, and the greater the probability and the proximity of success. When the conviction of the preventability of misery shall have become the prevailing one, men and women will cease to meet its existence chiefly with endeavours to palliate its effects, but will set resolutely to work to remove its causes. They will then no longer accuse either chance or Providence of sending the ills that afflict mankind, but perceive that they are traceable to the action of inexorable and undeviating law, and that most, if not all of them, may be averted or avoided by human foresight acting on human knowledge....

There is a strong tendency greatly to undervalue the extent and the intensity of the feeling that exists among women of dissatisfaction with their present condition, and with their exclusion from participation in the pursuits that interest and occupy men. It is assumed that the majority are contented, and that the desire for an amelioration of their lot is felt only by a few exceptional natures. But let not those in whose hands the power lies, pass over the cry so lightly. Many are the signs of the times[91] which tell a different story. Among many voices, one has been raised that had no strength in itself, but in the truth of the note that it rang. That note has found an answering chord in thousands of women's hearts, and has come back from near and far, over the length and breadth of the land. Not in loud and turbulent cries, but in tones unmistakably clear to an ear attuned to catch the delicate harmonics that breathe from sorrowful and suffering souls. And not from our land alone, for women's hearts are everywhere the same. Voices have resounded from the Alps: signs have reached over the Pyrenees; echoes have bridged the Atlantic. No false note could awaken so deep and so wide a response; no harsh tone could evoke such loving sympathy.

The cry for equal rights for all human beings proceeds from the irrepressible consciousness of equal needs, and the possession of common feelings. The movement now hourly gaining strength for the social, educational, and political enfranchisement of women, arises from no spirit of opposition or rivalry with men, but from deep and intense sympathy in their noblest aims and aspirations.

---

89 Mary Somerville (1780–1872), physicist, astronomer, and mathematician. See Science.
90 Fellow of the Royal Astronomical Society.
91 Matthew 16:3.

Francis Galton
from *Hereditary Genius: An Inquiry into Its Laws and Consequences* (1869)

Francis Galton (1822–1911), cousin of Charles Darwin (see Science, Travel and Exploration), spent a lifetime investigating genetics and heredity. Abandoning medicine to study mathematics at Cambridge, he inherited wealth, thereafter travelling in the Middle East and Africa and pursuing quantitative scientific studies. He counted the number of attractive women on a street and how often colleagues fidgeted at meetings; he collected and correlated data on the characteristics of parents and offspring at his "anthropometric laboratory"; he analyzed biographical dictionary entries to uncover how often "eminent" people came from eminent as opposed to undistinguished origins. In 1883, he coined the word "eugenics" from the Greek for "beautiful" and "heredity"; he believed in the importance of improving the race through breeding from its best. His work inspired scientists to study human heredity and use statistics.

Here, Galton attempts to quantify differences among races, arguing for ancient Greek superiority and the need to improve British stock.

Chapter 20: The Comparative Worth of Different Races

I have now completed what I have to say concerning the kinships of individuals, and proceed, in this chapter, to attempt a wider treatment of my subject, through a consideration of nations and races.

Every long-established race has necessarily its peculiar fitness for the conditions under which it has lived, owing to the sure operation of Darwin's law of natural selection.[92] However, I am not much concerned, for the present, with the greater part of those aptitudes, but only with such as are available in some form or other of high civilization. We may reckon upon the advent of a time, when civilization, which is now sparse and feeble ... , shall overspread the globe. Ultimately it is sure to do so, because civilization is the necessary fruit of high intelligence when found in a social animal, and there is no plainer lesson to be read off the face of Nature than that the result of the operation of her laws is to evoke intelligence in connexion with sociability. Intelligence is as much an advantage to an animal as physical strength or any other natural gift, and therefore, out of two varieties of any race of animal who are equally endowed in other respects, the most intelligent variety is sure to prevail in the battle of life. Similarly, among animals as intelligent as man, the most social race is sure to prevail, other qualities being equal.

Under even a very moderate form of material civilization, a vast number of aptitudes acquired through the "survivorship of the fittest"[93] and the unsparing destruction of the unfit ... have become ... hindrances,

---

92 Charles Darwin, *On the Origin of Species by Means of Natural Selection* (1859). See Science.
93 Herbert Spencer, *Principles of Biology* (1864). Spencer's expression "survival of the fittest" is often attributed to Darwin, who used it in the 6th edition of *On the Origin of Species*; the phrase is synonymous with "natural selection."

and not gains, to civilization. I shall refer to some of these a little further on, but I will first speak of the qualities needed in civilized society. They are, speaking generally, such as will enable a race to supply a large contingent to the various groups of eminent men, of whom I have treated in my several chapters....

In comparing the worth of different races, I shall make frequent use of the law of deviation from an average, to which I have already been much beholden.... I shall assume that the *intervals* between the grades of ability are the *same* in all the races—that is, if the ability of class A of one race be equal to the ability of class C in another, then the ability of class B of the former shall be supposed equal to that of class D of the latter, and so on. I know this cannot be strictly true, for it would be in defiance of analogy if the variability of all races were precisely the same; but, on the other hand, there is good reason to expect that the error introduced by the assumption cannot sensibly affect the off-hand results for which alone I propose to employ it....

Let us, then, compare the negro race with the Anglo-Saxon, with respect to those qualities alone which are capable of producing judges, statesmen, commanders, men of literature and science, poets, artists, and divines. If the negro race in America had been affected by no social disabilities, a comparison of their achievements with those of the whites in their several branches of intellectual effort, having regard to the total number of their respective populations, would give the necessary information. As matters stand, we must be content with much rougher data.

First, the negro race has occasionally, but very rarely, produced such men as Toussaint l'Ouverture,[94] who are of our class F; that is to say, its X, or its total classes above G, appear to correspond with our F, showing a difference of not less than two grades between the black and white races, and it may be more.

Secondly, the negro race is by no means wholly deficient in men capable of becoming good factors, thriving merchants, and otherwise considerably raised above the average of whites—that is to say, it can not unfrequently supply men corresponding to our class C, or even D.... In short, classes E and F of the negro may roughly be considered as the equivalent of our C and D—a result which again points to the conclusion, that the average intellectual standard of the negro race is some two grades below our own.

Thirdly, we may compare, but with much caution, the relative position of negroes in their native country with that of the travellers who visit them.... A native chief has as good an education in the art of ruling men, as can be desired; he is continually exercised in personal government, and usually maintains his place by the ascendency of his character, shown every day over his subjects and rivals. A traveller in wild countries also fills, to a certain degree, the position of a commander, and has to confront native chiefs at every inhabited place. The result is familiar enough—the white traveller almost invariably holds his own in their presence....

Fourthly, the number among the negroes of those whom we should call half-witted men, is very large.... I was myself much impressed by this fact during my travels in Africa. The mistakes the negroes made in their own matters, were so childish, stupid, and simpleton-like, as frequently to make me ashamed of my own species. I do not think it any exaggeration to say, that their C is as low as our E, which would be a difference of two grades, as before....

The Australian type is at least one grade below the African negro. I possess a few serviceable data about the natural capacity of the Australian, but not sufficient to induce me to invite the reader to consider them.

---

94 François Dominique Toussaint L'Ouverture (c. 1743–1803), Haitian, former slave and revolutionary leader for Haitian independence.

The average standard of the Lowland Scotch and the English North-country men is decidedly a fraction of a grade superior to that of the ordinary English, because the number of the former who attain to eminence is far greater than the proportionate number of their race would have led us to expect. The same superiority is distinctly shown by a comparison of the well-being of the masses of the population; for the Scotch labourer is much less of a drudge than the Englishman of the Midland counties.... The peasant women of Northumberland work all day in the fields, and are not broken down by the work; ... and, when married, they attend well to the comfort of their homes. It is perfectly distressing to me to witness the draggled, drudged, mean look of the mass of individuals, especially of the women, that one meets in the streets of London and other purely English towns. The conditions of their life seem too hard for their constitutions, and to be crushing them into degeneracy.

The ablest race of whom history bears record is unquestionably the ancient Greek, partly because their master-pieces in the principal departments of intellectual activity are still unsurpassed ... and partly because the population that gave birth to the creators of those master-pieces was very small. Of the various Greek sub-races, that of Attica[95] was the ablest, and she was no doubt largely indebted to the following cause, for her superiority. Athens opened her arms to immigrants, but not indiscriminately, for her social life was such that none but very able men could take any pleasure in it; on the other hand, she offered attractions such as men of the highest ability and culture could find in no other city. Thus, by a system of partly unconscious selection, she built up a magnificent breed of human animals, which, in the space of one century—viz. between 530 and 430 B.C.—produced the following illustrious persons, fourteen in number:—

Statesmen and Commanders.—Themistocles (mother an alien), Miltiades, Aristeides, Cimon (son of Miltiades), Pericles (son of Xanthippus, the victor at Mycale).[96]

Literary and Scientific Men.—Thucydides, Socrates, Xenophon, Plato.[97]

Poets.—Æschylus, Sophocles, Euripides, Aristophanes.[98]

Sculptor.—Phidias.[99]

We are able to make a closely-approximate estimate of the population that produced these men, because the number of the inhabitants of Attica has been a matter of frequent inquiry, and critics appear at length to be quite agreed in the general results. It seems that the little district of Attica contained, during its most flourishing period ... , less than 90,000 native free-born persons, 40,000 resident aliens, and a ... population of 400,000 slaves. The first item is the only one that concerns us here, namely, the 90,000 free-born persons. Again, the common estimate that population renews itself three times in a century is very close to the truth, and may be accepted in the present case. Consequently, we have to deal with a total population of 270,000 free-born persons, or 135,000 males, born in the century I have named. Of these, about one-half, or 67,500, would survive the age of 26, and one-third, or 45,000, would survive

---

95 The area surrounding and including Athens.
96 Themistocles (c. 528–462 BCE), politician and naval leader; Miltiades (c. 540–489 BCE), military leader; Aristeides (d. c. 468 BCE), politician and military strategist; Cimon (d. c. 450 BCE), politician and military leader; Pericles (c. 495–429 BCE), politician and military leader; Xanthippus (d. c. 472 BCE), naval leader during the Persian Wars; Mycale, a battle in the Persian Wars won by the Athenian fleet under Xanthippus.
97 Thucydides (c. 455–c. 400 BCE), historian and military leader; Socrates (469–399 BCE), philosopher; Xenophon (c. 435–c. 354 BCE), military leader, historian, and writer; Plato (c. 429–c. 347 BCE), philosopher.
98 Dramatists Æschylus (c. 525–c. 456 BCE), Sophocles (c. 496–406 BCE), Euripides (480–c. 406 BCE), and Aristophanes (c. 450–c. 385 BCE).
99 Phidias (c. 490–c. 430 BCE), sculptor famous for his statue of Zeus at Olympia, a wonder of the ancient world.

that of 50. As 14 Athenians became illustrious, the selection is only as 1 to 4,822 in respect to the former limitation, and as 1 to 3,214 in respect to the latter. Referring to the table [on page 467], it will be seen that this degree of selection corresponds very fairly to the classes F (1 in 4,300) and above, of the Athenian race. Again, as G is one-sixteenth or one-seventeenth as numerous as F, it would be reasonable to expect to find one of class G among the fourteen; we might, however, by accident, meet with two, three, or even four of that class—say Pericles, Socrates, Plato, and Phidias.

Now let us attempt to compare the Athenian standard of ability with that of our own race and time. We have no men to put by the side of Socrates and Phidias, because the millions of all Europe, breeding as they have done for the subsequent 2,000 years, have never produced their equals. They are, therefore, two or three grades above our G—they might rank as I or J. But, supposing we do not count them at all, saying that some freak of nature acting at that time, may have produced them, what must we say about the rest? Pericles and Plato would rank, I suppose, the one among the greatest of philosophical statesmen, and the other as at least the equal of Lord Bacon.[100] They would, therefore, stand somewhere among our unclassed X, one or two grades above G—let us call them between H and I. All the remainder—the F of the Athenian race—would rank above our G, and equal to or close upon our H. It follows from all this, that the average ability of the Athenian race is, on the lowest possible estimate, very nearly two grades higher than our own—that is, about as much as our race is above that of the African negro....

We know, and may guess something more, of the reason why this marvellously-gifted race declined. Social morality grew exceedingly lax; marriage became unfashionable, and was avoided; many of the more ambitious and accomplished women were avowed courtesans, and consequently infertile, and the mothers of the incoming population were of a heterogeneous class.... It can be, therefore, no surprise to us, though it has been a severe misfortune to humanity, that the high Athenian breed decayed and disappeared; for if it had maintained its excellence, and had multiplied and spread over large countries ... , it would assuredly have accomplished results advantageous to human civilization, to a degree that transcends our powers of imagination.

If we could raise the average standard of our race only one grade, what vast changes would be produced!...

It seems to me most essential to the well-being of future generations, that the average standard of ability of the present time should be raised. Civilization is a new condition imposed upon man by the course of events, just as in the history of geological changes new conditions have continually been imposed on different races of animals. They have had the effect either of modifying the nature of the races through the process of natural selection ... or of destroying them altogether, when the changes were too abrupt or the race unyielding. The number of the races of mankind that have been entirely destroyed under the pressure of the requirements of an incoming civilization, reads us a terrible lesson. Probably in no former period of the world has the destruction of the races of any animal whatever, been effected over such wide areas and with such startling rapidity as in the case of savage man. In the North American Continent, in the West Indian Islands, in the Cape of Good Hope, in Australia, New Zealand, and Van Diemen's Land,[101] the human denizens of vast regions have been entirely swept away in the short space of three centuries,

---

100 Francis Bacon (1561–1626), politician, scientist, lawyer, writer, and philosopher.
101 The West Indies are now known as the Caribbean Islands; the Cape of Good Hope is in South Africa; Van Diemen's Land is now known as Tasmania.

CLASSIFICATION OF MEN ACCORDING TO THEIR NATURAL GIFTS.

Grades of natural ability, separated by equal intervals.		Proportionate, viz. one in	Numbers of men comprised in the several grades of natural ability, whether in respect to their general powers, or to special aptitudes.							
			In each million of the same age.	In total male population of the United Kingdom, viz. 15 millions, of the undermentioned ages:—						
Below average.	Above average.			20—30	30—40	40—50	50—60	60—70	70—80	
a	A	4	256,791	651,000	495,000	391,000	268,000	171,000	77,000	
b	B	6	162,279	409,000	312,000	246,000	168,000	107,000	48,000	
c	C	16	62,563	161,000	123,000	97,000	66,000	42,000	19,000	
d	D	64	15,696	39,800	30,300	23,900	16,400	10,400	4,700	
e	E	413	2,423	6,100	4,700	3,700	2,520	1,600	729	
f	F	4,300	233	590	450	355	243	155	70	
g	G	79,000	14	35	27	21	15	9		
x	X									
all grades below g	all grades above G	1,000,000	1	3	2	2	2	—	—	
On either side of average			500,000	1,268,000	964,000	761,000	521,000	332,000	149,000	
Total, both sides			1,000,000	2,536,000	1,928,000	1,522,000	1,042,000	664,000	298,000	

FRANCIS GALTON

less by the pressure of a stronger race than through the influence of a civilization they were incapable of supporting. And we too, the foremost labourers in creating this civilization, are beginning to show ourselves incapable of keeping pace with our own work. The needs of centralization, communication, and culture, call for more brains and mental stamina than the average of our race possess. We are in crying want for a greater fund of ability in all stations of life; for neither the classes of statesmen, philosophers, artisans, nor labourers are up to the modern complexity of their several professions.... Our race is overweighted, and appears likely to be drudged into degeneracy by demands that exceed its powers. If its average ability were raised a grade or two, our new classes F and G would conduct the complex affairs of the state at home and abroad as easily as our present F and G, when in the position of country squires, are able to manage the affairs of their establishments and tenantry. All other classes of the community would be similarly promoted to the level of the work required by the nineteenth century, if the average standard of the race were raised.

When the severity of the struggle for existence is not too great for the powers of the race, its action is healthy and conservative, otherwise it is deadly, just as we may see exemplified in the scanty, wretched vegetation that leads a precarious existence near the summer snow line of the Alps, and disappears altogether a little higher up. We want as much backbone as we can get, to bear the racket to which we are henceforth to be exposed, and as good brains as possible to contrive machinery, for modern life to work more smoothly than at present. We can, in some degree, raise the nature of man to a level with the new conditions imposed upon his existence, and we can also, in some degree, modify the conditions to suit his nature. It is clearly right that both these powers should be exerted, with the view of bringing his nature and the conditions of his existence into as close harmony as possible....

Charles Darwin

from *The Descent of Man, and Selection in Relation to Sex* (1871)

Naturalist and geologist Charles Darwin (1809–82) authored the groundbreaking theory of natural selection. Darwin started medical training in Edinburgh but moved to Cambridge University, where botany and natural history fascinated him. A five-year circumnavigation on board the *Beagle* (1831–36) confirmed Darwin's commitment to natural history and geology, providing evidence for later publications. Marrying his cousin Emma and living on family wealth, he embraced a rural scientific life that permitted studies of barnacles, bees, earthworms, birds, and seeds. His theory of natural selection was influenced by Lyell's geology (see Science) and Malthusian population theory. *On the Origin of Species* (1859) addressed a general rather than scientific audience. Its tenets (the mutability of species, struggle for existence, emphasis on chance, and implicit conclusion of human descent from animals) aroused controversy and proved vastly influential.

Intended as a sequel to *Origin*, *The Descent of Man* (1871) examined sexual selection and the expression of emotion in animals and humans.

Chapter 19: Secondary Sexual Characters of Man[102]

With mankind the differences between the sexes are greater than in most species of Quadrumana, but not so great as in some, for instance, the mandrill.[103] Man on an average is considerably taller, heavier, and stronger than woman, with squarer shoulders and more plainly-pronounced muscles. Owing to the relation which exists between muscular development and the projection of the brows, ... the superciliary ridge[104] is generally more strongly marked in man than in woman. His body, and especially his face, is more hairy, and his voice has a different and more powerful tone. In certain tribes the women are said, whether truly I know not, to differ slightly in tint from the men; and with Europeans, the women are perhaps the more brightly coloured of the two, as may be seen when both sexes have been equally exposed to the weather.

Man is more courageous, pugnacious, and energetic than woman, and has a more inventive genius. His brain is absolutely larger, but whether relatively to the larger size of his body, in comparison with that of woman, has not, I believe been fully ascertained. In woman the face is rounder; the jaws and the base of the skull smaller; the outlines of her body rounder, in parts more prominent; and her pelvis is broader than in man; ... but this latter character may perhaps be considered rather as a primary than a secondary sexual character. She comes to maturity at an earlier age than man.

As with animals of all classes, so with man, the distinctive characters of the male sex are not fully developed until he is nearly mature; and if emasculated they never appear. The beard, for instance, is a secondary sexual character, and male children are beardless, though at an early age they have abundant hair on their heads. It is probably due to the rather late appearance in life of the successive variations, by which man acquired his masculine characters, that they are transmitted to the male sex alone. Male and female children resemble each other closely, like the young of so many other animals in which the adult sexes differ; they likewise resemble the mature female much more closely, than the mature male. The female, however, ultimately assumes certain distinctive characters, and in the formation of her skull, is said to be intermediate between the child and the man.... Again, as the young of closely allied though distinct species do not differ nearly so much from each other as do the adults, so it is with the children of the different races of man. Some have even maintained that race-differences cannot be detected in the infantile skull.... In regard to colour, the new-born negro child is reddish nut-brown, which soon becomes slaty-grey; the black colour being fully developed within a year in the Sudan, but not until three years in Egypt. The eyes of the negro are at first blue, and the hair chestnut-brown rather than black, being curled only at the ends. The children of the Australians immediately after birth are yellowish-brown, and become dark at a later age. Those of the Guaranys of Paraguay are whitish-yellow, but they acquire in the course of a few weeks the yellowish-brown tint of their parents. Similar observations have been made in other parts of America....

I have specified the foregoing familiar differences between the male and female sex in mankind, because they are curiously the same as in the Quadrumana. With these animals the female is mature at an earlier age than the male.... With most of the species the males are larger and much stronger than

---

102 The author's footnotes have been deleted except as indicated.
103 Quadrumana are primates with opposable digits on both hands and feet; the mandrill is an African baboon.
104 Eyebrow ridge.

the females, of which fact the gorilla offers a well-known instance. Even in so trifling a character as the greater prominence of the superciliary ridge, the males of certain monkeys differ from the females, ... and agree in this respect with mankind. In the gorilla and certain other monkeys, the cranium of the adult male presents a strongly-marked sagittal crest,[105] which is absent in the female; and Ecker[106] found a trace of a similar difference between the two sexes in the Australians.... With monkeys when there is any difference in the voice, that of the male is the more powerful. We have seen that certain male monkeys, have a well-developed beard, which is quite deficient, or much less developed in the female. No instance is known of the beard, whiskers, or moustache being larger in a female than in the male monkey....

In regard to the general hairyness of the body, the women in all races are less hairy than the men, and in some few Quadrumana the under side of the body of the female is less hairy than that of the male.... Lastly, male monkeys, like men, are bolder and fiercer than the females. They lead the troop, and when there is danger, come to the front. We thus see how close is the parallelism between the sexual differences of man and the Quadrumana. With some few species, however, as with certain baboons, the gorilla and orang, there is a considerably greater difference between the sexes, in the size of the canine teeth, in the development and colour of the hair, and especially in the colour of the naked parts of the skin, than in the case of mankind.

The secondary sexual characters of man are all highly variable, even within the limits of the same race or sub-species; and they differ much in the several races. These two rules generally hold good throughout the animal kingdom. In the excellent observations made on board the *Novara*,[107] ... the male Australians were found to exceed the females by only 65 millim. in height, whilst with the Javanese the average excess was 218 millim., so that in this latter race the difference in height between the sexes is more than thrice as great as with the Australians. The numerous measurements of various other races, with respect to stature, the circumference of the neck and chest, and the length of the back-bone and arms, which were carefully made, nearly all shewed that the males differed much more from each other than did the females. This fact indicates that, as far as these characters are concerned, it is the male which has been chiefly modified, since the races diverged from their common and primeval source....

In the previous chapters we have seen that with mammals, birds, fishes, insects, &c., many characters, which there is every reason to believe were primarily gained through sexual selection by one sex alone, have been transferred to both sexes. As this same form of transmission has apparently prevailed to a large extent with mankind, it will save much useless repetition if we consider the characters peculiar to the male sex together with certain other characters common to both sexes.

Law of Battle.—With barbarous nations, for instance with the Australians, the women are the constant cause of war both between the individuals of the same tribe and between distinct tribes. So no doubt it was in ancient times.... With the North American Indians, the contest is reduced to a system. That excellent observer, Hearne, ... says:—"It has ever been the custom among these people for the men to wrestle for any woman to whom they are attached; and, of course, the strongest party always carries off the prize. A weak man, unless he be a good hunter, and well-beloved, is seldom permitted to keep a wife that a stronger

---

105 Skulltop protrusion where jaw muscles attach.
106 Johann Alexander Ecker (1816–87), German anthropologist.
107 This Austrian ship circumnavigated the globe on a scientific expedition from 1857 to 1859.

man thinks worth his notice. This custom prevails throughout all the tribes, and causes a great spirit of emulation among their youth, who are upon all occasions, from their childhood, trying their strength and skill in wrestling."[108] With the Guanas of South America, Azara states that the men rarely marry till twenty or more years old, as before that age they cannot conquer their rivals.[109]

Other similar facts could be given; but even if we had no evidence on this head, we might feel almost sure, from the analogy of the higher Quadrumana, ... that the law of battle had prevailed with man during the early stages of his development.... It was remarked in a former chapter that as man gradually became erect, and continually used his hands and arms for fighting with sticks and stones, as well as for the other purposes of life, he would have used his jaws and teeth less and less. The jaws, together with their muscles, would then have become reduced through disuse.... By such steps the original inequality between the jaws and teeth in the two sexes of mankind would ultimately have been quite obliterated.... As the prodigious difference between the skulls of the two sexes in the gorilla and orang, stands in close relation with the development of the immense canine teeth in the males, we may infer that the reduction of the jaws and teeth in the early male progenitors of man led to a most striking and favourable change in his appearance.

There can be little doubt that the greater size and strength of man, in comparison with woman, together with his broader shoulders, more developed muscles, rugged outline of body, his greater courage and pugnacity, are all due in chief part to inheritance from some early male progenitor, who, like the existing anthropoid apes, was thus characterised. These characters will, however, have been preserved or even augmented during the long ages whilst man was still in a barbarous condition, by the strongest and boldest men having succeeded best in the general struggle for life, as well as in securing wives, and thus having left a large number of offspring. It is not probable that the greater strength of man was primarily acquired through the inherited effects of his having worked harder than woman for his own subsistence and that of his family; for the women in all barbarous nations are compelled to work at least as hard as the men. With civilised people the arbitrament of battle[110] for the possession of the women has long ceased; on the other hand, the men, as a general rule, have to work harder than the women for their mutual subsistence; and thus their greater strength will have been kept up.

Difference in the Mental Powers of the two Sexes.—With respect to differences of this nature between man and woman, it is probable that sexual selection has played a very important part. I am aware that some writers doubt whether there is any inherent difference; but this is at least probable from the analogy of the lower animals which present other secondary sexual characters. No one will dispute that the bull differs in disposition from the cow, the wild-boar from the sow, the stallion from the mare, and, as is well known to the keepers of menageries, the males of the larger apes from the females. Woman seems to differ from man in mental disposition, chiefly in her greater tenderness and less selfishness; and this holds good even with savages, as shewn by a well-known passage in Mungo Park's Travels,[111] and by statements made by many other travellers. Woman, owing to her maternal instincts, displays these qualities towards her infants in an eminent degree; therefore it is likely that she should often extend them towards her fellow-creatures. Man is the rival of other men; he delights in competition, and this leads to ambition which passes too easily

---

108 Samuel Hearne, *A Journey from Prince of Wales's Fort in Hudson's Bay to the Northern Ocean* (1795).
109 Félix de Azara, *Voyage dans l'Amérique méridionale depuis 1781 jusqu'en 1801* (1809).
110 Resolving a dispute by physical confrontation.
111 Mungo Park, *Travels in the Interior Districts of Africa* (1799).

into selfishness. These latter qualities seem to be his natural and unfortunate birthright. It is generally admitted that with woman the powers of intuition, of rapid perception, and perhaps of imitation, are more strongly marked than in man; but some, at least, of these faculties are characteristic of the lower races, and therefore of a past and lower state of civilisation.

The chief distinction in the intellectual powers of the two sexes is shewn by man attaining to a higher eminence, in whatever he takes up, than woman can attain—whether requiring deep thought, reason, or imagination, or merely the use of the senses and hands. If two lists were made of the most eminent men and women in poetry, painting, sculpture, music,—comprising composition and performance, history, science, and philosophy, with half-a-dozen names under each subject, the two lists would not bear comparison. We may also infer, from the law of the deviation of averages, so well illustrated by Mr. Galton, in his work on "Hereditary Genius,"[112] that if men are capable of decided eminence over women in many subjects, the average standard of mental power in man must be above that of woman.

The half-human male progenitors of man, and men in a savage state, have struggled together during many generations for the possession of the females. But mere bodily strength and size would do little for victory, unless associated with courage, perseverance, and determined energy. With social animals, the young males have to pass through many a contest before they win a female, and the older males have to retain their females by renewed battles. They have, also, in the case of man, to defend their females, as well as their young, from enemies of all kinds, and to hunt for their joint subsistence. But to avoid enemies, or to attack them with success, to capture wild animals, and to invent and fashion weapons, requires the aid of the higher mental faculties, namely, observation, reason, invention, or imagination. These various faculties will thus have been continually put to the test, and selected during manhood; they will, moreover, have been strengthened by use during this same period of life. Consequently, in accordance with the principle often alluded to, we might expect that they would at least tend to be transmitted chiefly to the male offspring at the corresponding period of manhood.

Now, when two men are put into competition, or a man with a woman, who possess every mental quality in the same perfection, with the exception that the one has higher energy, perseverance, and courage, this one will generally become more eminent, whatever the object may be, and will gain the victory....[113] These latter as well as the former faculties will have been developed in man, partly through sexual selection,—that is, through the contest of rival males, and partly through natural selection,—that is, from success in the general struggle for life; and as in both cases the struggle will have been during maturity, the characters thus gained will have been transmitted more fully to the male than to the female offspring. It accords with the view that some of our mental faculties have been modified or strengthened through sexual selection, that, firstly, they undergo, as is generally admitted, a considerable change at puberty, and, secondly, that eunuchs remain throughout life inferior in these same qualities. Thus man has ultimately become superior to woman. It is, indeed, fortunate that the law of the equal transmission of characters to both sexes has commonly prevailed throughout the whole class of mammals; otherwise it is probable that man would have become as superior in mental endowment to woman, as the peacock is in ornamental plumage to the peahen.

---

112 Francis Galton, *Hereditary Genius* (1869). See Science.
113 Author's note: J. Stuart Mill remarks ("The Subjection of Women," 1869, p. 122), "the things in which man most excels women are those which require most plodding, and long hammering at single thoughts." What is this but energy and perseverance?

It must be borne in mind that the tendency in characters acquired at a late period of life by either sex, to be transmitted to the same sex at the same age, and of characters acquired at an early age to be transmitted to both sexes, are rules which, though general, do not always hold good. If they always held good, we might conclude (but I am here wandering beyond my proper bounds) that the inherited effects of the early education of boys and girls would be transmitted equally to both sexes; so that the present inequality between the sexes in mental power could not be effaced by a similar course of early training; nor can it have been caused by their dissimilar early training. In order that woman should reach the same standard as man, she ought, when nearly adult, to be trained to energy and perseverance, and to have her reason and imagination exercised to the highest point; and then she would probably transmit these qualities chiefly to her adult daughters. The whole body of women, however, could not be thus raised, unless during many generations the women who excelled in the above robust virtues were married, and produced offspring in larger numbers than other women. As before remarked with respect to bodily strength, although men do not now fight for the sake of obtaining wives, and this form of selection has passed away, yet they generally have to undergo, during manhood, a severe struggle in order to maintain themselves and their families; and this will tend to keep up or even increase their mental powers, and, as a consequence, the present inequality between the sexes....

Richard Proctor
from "A Voyage to the Ringed Planet" (1872)

Astronomy writer Richard Proctor (1837–88) studied mathematics and theology at Cambridge, eventually finding science and religion incompatible and taking up law. He taught his eldest son mathematics and astronomy, abandoning law for astronomy upon the boy's death. After losing his savings in a bank failure, he taught mathematics to support his family. Proctor's first lucrative publication was *Other Worlds than Ours* (1870). Writing success allowed him to publish and lecture full-time. He also emphasized accuracy in celestial charting, exposing other astronomers' errors. Proctor's output was enormous: he published more than 500 essays and almost 60 books. Elected a Royal Astronomical Society fellow in 1866, Proctor was admired by scientific and general readers alike, becoming an influential popularizer of astronomy.

Proctor's article "A Voyage to the Ringed Planet," published in the *Cornhill Magazine* in 1872, covers his favourite topic, the possibility of extraterrestrial life.

At midnight on the 9th of July, 1872, Saturn being at the time due south and not far above the horizon, we set forth on our voyage across the depths of space which separate this earth from the Ringed Planet. The voyage we were now undertaking was of far greater extent than that to the sun which I have already described....[114] Yet I must confess that, deeply as I had been interested when we set forth on our journey

---

114 Richard Proctor, "A Voyage to the Sun," *Cornhill Magazine* 25 (1872): 322–35.

to the sun, I was yet more interested on this occasion.... The grandeur of the universe is incomprehensible, "the glory of God is insufferable;" but in other worlds we may find creatures as imperfect as ourselves; there we may witness phenomena that we can understand because they are comparable with those already known to us—in such worlds, in fine, we may find safety from "the persecution of the infinite."[115]

It was with a strange feeling that we watched the earth gradually passing from our view.... Our course was directed towards the darkest region of the heavens, and as the faint lights which shone from towns and villages beneath us grew undiscernible with distance, we were immersed in a profound darkness....

... The earth's globe at this time presented a marvellous appearance. Its apparent diameter was about four times as great as the moon's (not as then appearing to us, but as she appears when seen from the earth); but all round this large dark disc we could see a ruddy light of extreme brightness, and growing gradually brighter as we receded....

... Later we reached a stage on our journey when the earth began to be presented as a vast black disc upon the solar face, now no longer magnified by the effect of the earth's atmosphere. This black disc grew smaller and smaller, until presently another smaller disc—the moon's—appeared along with it on the sun's face. At this time we had passed somewhat beyond the path of Mars, and we turned from the further contemplation of the earth and moon, in order to give all our attention to the circumstances of our journey towards the ringed planet.

... We could not at present see the ring, nor, indeed, any sign that the planet is not like other planets. Saturn shone there before us, distinguished only from the stars by his superior brightness, and a certain indescribable contrast between his light and theirs. For though the stars were not twinkling, but shining with "purest ray serene,"[116] yet was there something in the stellar light which caused it to differ unmistakably from that of Saturn. It may have been partly, perhaps, that, owing to the exceeding swiftness of our onward flight, we unconsciously recognized the comparative nearness of Saturn; and were thus impressed by the distinction between the light from suns millions of times farther from us, and that from an orb which, vast though it is, is yet insignificant, compared with the least of the suns which people space....

As we neared the planet, though as yet we were far beyond the path of the outermost satellite, we could perceive that the golden colour which had formed so beautiful a feature of Saturn, came from certain parts only of his globe; or rather, a much deeper tint, a burning cinnamon ... came from certain zones of the planet.... The actual aspect of the planet may be thus described: the great central zone, occupying the position of the planet's equator, was of a bright yellow, so flecked with spots of pure white that when we had been somewhat farther away it had appeared almost perfectly white. Then came on either side zones of a rich purple flecked with yellow spots, between which were the "burning cinnamon" bands already mentioned. But the purple of the zones became more and more bluish the farther the zones were from the equatorial belt. Close by the north pole were several narrow zones of a delicate blue; and the pole itself was occupied by a wide region of rich cobalt blue, flecked with purple and olive-green spots. The southern polar regions were as yet concealed from our view by the rings....

To our amazement we found, as we drew nearer to Saturn, that his whole surface presented a scene of indescribable agitation. The white clouds on the equatorial belt appeared and changed in shape and

---

115 Jean Paul [Johann Paul Friedrich] Richter, *The Comet* (1820–22).
116 Thomas Gray, *Elegy Written in a Country Church-Yard* (1751).

vanished with startling rapidity. And the whole of this belt seemed opalescent, the colour and brightness of the different parts varying continuously....

These appearances were so remarkable, and seemed so obviously to belong to the planet itself, and not to be caused by the varying effects of the sun's light, that we determined as we drew near the planet (and when we were already past the inner edge of the dark ring) to circle round Saturn's globe so as to reach its unillumined side, before passing beneath the planet's atmosphere.

We did so, penetrating into the vast shadow projected by the planet into space. Instead, however, of the black darkness which might have been expected, we found that all the parts of the planet which at the moment was turned from the sun, was aglow with a somewhat dull luminosity, like that of fire shining through smoke or vapour....

We began to perceive that whatever else of interest we might find in the globe of Saturn, we need certainly not look for living creatures there. It was plain that we were about to visit a region where nature's forces were working too intensely to admit of other and less active forms of force. We became cognizant indeed of another circumstance, which confirmed this impression. As we approached the globe of Saturn, we could perceive that myriads of meteors and small comets were circling close around him, or streaming in upon his surface.... [T]heir velocity was enormous, insomuch that their fall upon the planet or their swift rush through his atmosphere would have sufficed to destroy all living creatures on his globe. But the fiery glow of so large a proportion of Saturn's visible surface, seemed of itself sufficient to show that it could not be inhabited.

When at length we passed within the Saturnian atmosphere,—which extends but a small distance relatively above his visible surface,—we obtained at once the most convincing evidence that he cannot possibly be the abode of life. Immediately a strange uproar surrounded us.... Repeated reverberations seemed to announce either the collision of enormous masses or the occurrence of tremendous volcanic outbursts. But the most characteristic of the noises which greeted us was an intense and persistent hissing, as though steam were rushing from a million outlets at once.

Passing to the illuminated portion of the planet and remaining on the equatorial zone we found ourselves still unable to tell whence this hideous noise proceeded. On all sides of us were immense masses and columns of whitish vapour.... Directing our perceptions towards the depths beneath us, we could recognize no sign of any surface. We passed downwards for hundreds and hundreds of miles, until we had lost the light of the sun, which was replaced by the continually increasing glow of the fires we were approaching. At length, as we passed through a layer of clouds, which could scarcely have been less than twenty thousand miles below what we had regarded as the surface of the planet, we suddenly beheld a scene so startling that we stayed our course as by common consent to gaze upon it. We at length saw the true surface of Saturn. And what a surface! ... Vast seas of fire, tossed by furious gales whose breath was flame, coruscated with a thousand colours as their condition underwent continual change. Then over a wide extent of those oceans the intense lustre would die out, to be replaced by a dull almost imperceptible glow, where the surface of the fiery ocean was changing into a crust of red-hot rock. But then came fresh disturbance; the crust broke in a thousand places, showing the intensely hot sea beneath....

We should have wished, perhaps, under other circumstances to extend our survey over the rest of Saturn's surface; though from what we had already witnessed, we felt well assured that the whole planet is the scene of a turmoil and confusion resembling that now before us. At the poles indeed there is an approach to quiescence,[117] and it would even appear that before many ages are past, the polar Saturnian regions may be fit to be the abode of living creatures.... But though local peculiarities of this sort exist, yet, in a general sense, it may be said that the whole bulk of Saturn is instinct with fiery energy, rendering it altogether unsuited to be the abode of living creatures, or at least of creatures resembling any existing on the earth....

We now passed to the so-called dark ring. This ring is, however, no darker, in one sense, than the others.... The fact really is, that the dark ring consists of a number of very small bodies, all travelling nearly in the same level, and so widely scattered that one can see through the ring the deep blue background of the sky. This deep blue background, combined with the yellowish red light which these bodies reflect, produces the purplish brown colour which terrestrial telescopists recognize in this ring....

We passed through the outer bright ring, noticing nothing that in any remarkable degree distinguished it from the inner bright ring. In both these rings the satellites showed a tendency to travel in long flights, so as to form as it were subordinate rings, or rather parts of rings, for these flights nowhere extended more than a few thousand miles in length.

All the most interesting part of our voyage was now as we supposed past. We had only to pay a hasty visit to each of Saturn's eight satellites,[118] and then to return, heartily disappointed, so far as our main object was concerned, to the world we had left in such high hope.

As Mimas,[119] the innermost satellite, was close by the part of the ring-system we had now reached, we passed over at once to this small orb.

Prepared to find in Mimas a miniature moon, even less interesting than it might otherwise have been, because we knew now that it could serve no useful part to living creatures in Saturn, our amazement will be conceived when we discovered as we approached that Mimas is a miniature world. We saw before us land and water; we could perceive clouds floating in the Mimasian air; and presently as we passed the confines of this air, we began to hear the sounds of busy life. Descending through a cloud veil which hid from our view the land and water immediately beneath us, we saw at length the beings of another world!

At first all was perplexing to us. We perceived living creatures utterly unlike any with which we had hitherto been familiar. They were busy in their several ways, but the nature of their ways and the object of their actions we could not comprehend. It would only confuse those whom this narrative will reach to describe all that we saw, or to attempt to explain how what we saw became gradually intelligible to us. The forms of life are probably almost as numerous in Mimas as on the earth; and the relations between the several orders of living creatures are as interesting and as complicated. It would require a whole treatise to present aright all that a Huxley or an Owen[120] in Mimas could teach about the living creatures which exist there. It is clear that to convey accurate ideas respecting the whole economy of another world would be quite impossible, unless those to whom we commit this narrative were prepared to devote a whole volume to such matters.

But certain circumstances may be related, as likely to prove interesting to the inhabitants of another world.

---

117 Stillness.
118 That is, Saturn's moons.
119 A moon of Saturn, discovered in 1789.
120 T.H. Huxley (1825–95), biologist and surgeon. See Science. Richard Owen (1804–92), palaeontologist and comparative anatomist.

The Mimasians are somewhat smaller than men, but like men, they carry the head erect, and have four chief limbs, two upper and two lower, the latter chiefly used in progression. The trunk is shorter in proportion to the total height, and the frame appears to be more muscular and powerful. It is difficult, however, to form a judgment on this point, because the circumstances under which these beings live are altogether unlike those which prevail on the earth. Indeed, so soon as we had learned that Mimas is inhabited, we expected to find the creatures living here either gigantic in stature or else of surpassing agility, simply because we knew that Mimasian gravitation must be very much less energetic than the attraction of gravity on the earth. But we found none of them to exceed in dimensions the creatures most nearly corresponding to them on the earth; while there is nothing very remarkable about the activity of any Mimasian animals. It would seem likely that the question of actual strength and activity depends quite as much on other circumstances as on those which have usually been considered by writers on the subject of other worlds....

But it was in the configuration of the head that these beings were most markedly distinguished from the human race. The ears are large and quite round, somewhat resembling conch-shells, and capable of changing in shape so as to gather in a greater or smaller quantity of sound as the Mimasian may desire. But the most remarkable feature of the Mimasian face consists of two orbits immediately above the large eye-orbits, and occupied by a series of delicate thread-like appendages radially arranged. For a long time we were quite unable to understand what this feature might signify, especially as the Mimasian animals exhibit a like peculiarity, though with characteristic differences of structure. We found at length, however, that the feature represents a sixth sense possessed by the Mimasians, and bearing the same relation to heat which eyesight bears to light. By means of this peculiar sense the Mimasian can as readily distinguish the shape of objects which approach him, as a man can tell the shape of an object lying within the range of his vision. But the sense enables the Mimasian to ascertain more than the mere shape of objects, for while his eyesight enables him to distinguish the appearance of objects, this sixth sense tells him of their constitution and physical condition. It is also as available in the darkest Mimasian night as in full day.

The axis of Mimas being inclined as well to the level in which Saturn travels as to the plane of the ring-system (in which plane, as you are aware, Mimas circles), they have two chief seasonal influences. During the long Mimasian year (the same, of course, as the Saturnian) the sun's midday altitude changes much as on the earth; only the four quarters of the year are each rather more than seven of our years in length. But these changes do not greatly affect the Mimasians, though they commonly live some ten or twelve years, that is from about 300 to about 350 of our years.... Their chief season-ruler is Saturn himself, who supplies them with an enormous amount of heat. Indeed, the heat supplied by Saturn is so great that (as we afterwards learned) the inhabitants of Tethys, Dione, and Rhea hold life to be impossible not only in Mimas but in Enceladus,[121] the next in order of distance from Saturn. It will be understood how important a part the heat of Saturn plays in the economy of Mimas, when I mention that he looks about nine hundred times as large as the sun appears to us. He does not indeed shine very conspicuously; the light he gives being such as I have already described in speaking of our approach to his globe. But the Mimasians have to shade their heat-eyes (so to name the feature already mentioned) when the vast orb of Saturn is in the fulness of his meridian heat-glow. Particularly is this the case when he is high above the horizon, at this heat-noon. For, owing to the inclination of the axis of Mimas to the plane in which

---

121 The moons of Saturn known at the time were Mimas, Enceladus, Tethys, Dione, Rhea, Titan, Hyperion, and Japetus.

this world travels round Saturn, the orb of the latter has a variable course on the Mimasian sky. Most perplexing are the relations thus presented. For Mimas turns once on its axis in about six hours, and travels once round Saturn in something short of twenty-three hours; so that even while Saturn is passing across the Mimasian sky, he can be seen to traverse a large space among the stars. X., who, as you know, is well versed in terrestrial astronomy, expressed the opinion that Mimasian astronomy must be difficult to master.

However, the Mimasians, though good observers (their instruments I shall describe on another occasion), have as yet very imperfect ideas respecting astronomical subjects. They suppose Mimas to be the centre of the universe; and though some of the more travelled Mimasians maintain that Mimas is either a globe or a cylinder in shape, yet the majority conceive that its surface is quite flat....

I must leave to another occasion a fuller description of what we saw and learned in Mimas. It will be as well also that for the present I should say nothing respecting the creatures which inhabit Enceladus, Tethys, Dione, Rhea, Titan, and Japetus, for already this account has extended to a sufficient length. Let it be sufficient for the present to remark that all these satellites are inhabited, and that the peculiarities which distinguish their inhabitants from each other and from those of Mimas, are as remarkable as those which distinguish Mimasian creatures from the inhabitants of the earth.

Thomas Henry Huxley
from "The Struggle for Human Existence: A Programme" (1888)

"Darwin's Bulldog," Thomas Henry Huxley (1825–95) was an important scientific educator and defender of evolutionary theory. He established his reputation through a four-year voyage as a naturalist aboard HMS *Rattlesnake*, returning home in 1850 to adulation by London scientists. Educated as an evangelical, he experienced religious skepticism and later became agnostic. He contributed to science education through his lectures to Working Men's Colleges, and, importantly, by his training of future science teachers. When Darwin's *On the Origin of Species* (see Science) appeared in 1859, Huxley lauded it in the *Times*, *Westminster Review*, and *Macmillan's*. While Darwin avoided discussing humanity's animal origins, Huxley viewed them as crucial, declaring to Bishop Wilberforce that he would rather have an ape for a grandfather than a man who used his influence to oppose scientific discussion. In 1870, he asserted that science is "neither Christian, nor Unchristian, but ... Extra-christian."

In the following selection, published in 1888 in *The Nineteenth Century*, he argues that nature's governing principle is a "materialized logical process."

The vast and varied procession of events which we call Nature affords a sublime spectacle and an inexhaustible wealth of attractive problems to the speculative observer. If we confine our attention to that aspect which engages the attention of the intellect, nature appears a beautiful and harmonious whole....

But if she be regarded from a less elevated, but more human, point of view; if our moral sympathies are allowed to influence our judgment, and we permit ourselves to criticise our great mother as we criticise one another;—then our verdict, at least so far as sentient nature is concerned, can hardly be so favourable.

In sober truth, to those who have made a study of the phenomena of life as they are exhibited by the higher forms of the animal world, the optimistic dogma that this is the best of all possible worlds will seem little better than a libel upon possibility. It is really only another instance to be added to the many extant, of the audacity of *à priori* speculators[122] who, having created God in their own image, find no difficulty in assuming that the Almighty must have been actuated by the same motives as themselves. They are quite sure that, had any other course been practicable, He would no more have made infinite suffering a necessary ingredient of His handiwork than a respectable philosopher would have done the like.

But even the modified optimism of the time-honoured thesis of physico-theology,[123] that the sentient world is, on the whole, regulated by principles of benevolence, does but ill stand the test of impartial confrontation with the facts of the case. No doubt it is quite true that sentient nature affords hosts of examples of subtle contrivances directed towards the production of pleasure or the avoidance of pain; and it may be proper to say that these are evidences of benevolence. But if so, why is it not equally proper to say of the equally numerous arrangements, the no less necessary result of which is the production of pain, that they are evidences of malevolence?

If a vast amount of that which, in a piece of human workmanship, we should call skill, is visible in those parts of the organisation of a deer to which it owes its ability to escape from beasts of prey, there is at least equal skill displayed in that bodily mechanism of the wolf which enables him to track, and sooner or later to bring down, the deer. Viewed under the dry light of science, deer and wolf are alike admirable; and if both were non-sentient automata, there would be nothing to qualify our admiration of the action of the one on the other. But the fact that the deer suffers while the wolf inflicts suffering engages our moral sympathies. We should call men like the deer innocent and good, men such as the wolf malignant and bad; we should call those who defended the deer and aided him to escape brave and compassionate, and those who helped the wolf in his bloody work base and cruel. Surely, if we transfer these judgments to nature outside the world of man at all, we must do so impartially. In that case, the goodness of the right hand which helps the deer, and the wickedness of the left hand which eggs on the wolf, will neutralize one another: and the course of nature will appear to be neither moral nor immoral, but non-moral.

This conclusion is thrust upon us by analogous facts in every part of the sentient world; yet, inasmuch as it not only jars upon prevalent prejudices, but arouses the natural dislike to that which is painful, much ingenuity has been exercised in devising an escape from it.

From the theological side, we are told that this is a state of probation, and that the seeming injustices and immoralities of nature will be compensated by-and-by. But how this compensation is to be effected, in the case of the great majority of sentient things, is not clear. I apprehend that no one is seriously prepared to maintain that the ghosts of all the myriads of generations of herbivorous animals which lived during the millions of years of the earth's duration before the appearance of man, and which have all that time been tormented and devoured by carnivores, are to be compensated by a perennial existence in clover; while the ghosts of carnivores are to go to some kennel where there is neither a pan of water nor a bone

---

122 Those whose speculations are based on theoretical rather than empirical evidence.
123 Theology based on evidence of divine design in nature.

with any meat on it. Besides, from the point of view of morality, the last state of things would be worse than the first. For the carnivores, however brutal and sanguinary, have only done that which, if there is any evidence of contrivance in the world, they were expressly constructed to do....

From the point of view of the moralist the animal world is on about the same level as a gladiator's show. The creatures are fairly well treated, and set to fight—whereby the strongest, the swiftest, and the cunningest live to fight another day. The spectator has no need to turn his thumbs down, as no quarter is given. He must admit that the skill and training displayed are wonderful. But he must shut his eyes if he would not see that more or less enduring suffering is the meed[124] of both vanquished and victor....

This may not be the best of all possible worlds, but to say that it is the worst is mere petulant nonsense. A worn-out voluptuary[125] may find nothing good under the sun, or a vain and inexperienced youth, who cannot get the moon he cries for, may vent his irritation in pessimistic moanings; but there can be no doubt in the mind of any reasonable person that mankind could, would, and in fact do, get on fairly well with vastly less happiness and far more misery than find their way into the lives of nine people out of ten.... Men with any manhood in them find life quite worth living under worse conditions than these.

There is another sufficiently obvious fact which renders the hypothesis that the course of sentient nature is dictated by malevolence quite untenable. A vast multitude of pleasures, and these among the purest and the best, are superfluities, bits of good which are to all appearance unnecessary as inducements to live, and are, so to speak, thrown into the bargain of life. To those who experience them, few delights can be more entrancing than such as are afforded by natural beauty or by the arts and especially by music; but they are products of, rather than factors in, evolution, and it is probable that they are known, in any considerable degree, to but a very small proportion of mankind.

The conclusion of the whole matter seems to be that ... [p]essimism is as little consonant with the facts of sentient existence as optimism. If we desire to represent the course of nature in terms of human thought, and assume that it was intended to be that which it is, we must say that its governing principle is intellectual and not moral; that it is a materialized logical process accompanied by pleasures and pains, the incidence of which, in the majority of cases, has not the slightest reference to moral desert....

In the strict sense of the word "nature," it denotes the sum of the phenomenal world, of that which has been, and is, and will be; and society, like art, is therefore a part of nature. But it is convenient to distinguish those parts of nature in which man plays the part of immediate cause, as something apart; and, therefore, society, like art, is usefully to be considered as distinct from nature. It is the more desirable, and even necessary, to make this distinction, since society differs from nature in having a definite moral object; whence it comes about that the course shaped by the ethical man—the member of society or citizen—necessarily runs counter to that which the non-ethical man—the primitive savage, or man as a mere member of the animal kingdom—tends to adopt. The latter fights out the struggle for existence to the bitter end, like any other animal; the former devotes his best energies to the object of setting limits to the struggle.

In the cycle of phenomena presented by the life of man, the animal, no more moral end is discernible than in that presented by the lives of the wolf and of the deer. However imperfect the relics of prehistoric men may be, the evidence which they afford clearly tends to the conclusion that, for thousands and thousands of years, before the origin of the oldest known civilisations, men were savages of a very low

---

124 Reward.
125 Someone who indulges in sensuous pleasures.

type. They strove with their enemies and their competitors; they preyed upon things weaker or less cunning than themselves; they were born, multiplied without stint, and died, for thousands of generations, alongside the mammoth, the urus,[126] the lion, and the hyæna ... ; and they were no more to be praised or blamed, on moral grounds, than their less erect and more hairy compatriots....

The history of civilisation—that is of society—on the other hand, is the record of the attempts which the human race has made to escape from this position. The first men who substituted the state of mutual peace for that of mutual war, whatever the motive which impelled them to take that step, created society. But, in establishing peace, they obviously put a limit upon the struggle for existence.... The primitive savage ... appropriated whatever took his fancy, and killed whomsoever opposed him, if he could. On the contrary, the ideal of the ethical man is to limit his freedom of action to a sphere in which he does not interfere with the freedom of others; he seeks the common weal as much as his own; and, indeed, as an essential part of his own welfare.... He tries to escape from his place in the animal kingdom, founded on the free development of the principle of non-moral evolution, and to found a kingdom of man, governed upon the principle of moral evolution....

But the effort of ethical man to work towards a moral end by no means abolished, perhaps has hardly modified, the deep-seated organic impulses which impel the natural man to follow his non-moral course. One of the most essential conditions, if not the chief cause, of the struggle for existence, is the tendency to multiply without limit, which man shares with all living things.... But, in civilised society, the inevitable result ... is the re-establishment, in all its intensity, of that struggle for existence—the war of each against all—the mitigation or abolition of which was the chief end of social organisation.

It is conceivable that, at some period in the history of the fabled Atlantis,[127] the production of food should have been exactly sufficient to meet the wants of the population.... And ... let it be imagined that every man, woman, and child was perfectly virtuous, and aimed at the good of all as the highest personal good. In that happy land, the natural man would have been finally put down by the ethical man.... But it is obvious that this state of things could have been permanent only with a stationary population. Add ten fresh mouths; and as, by the supposition, there was only exactly enough before, somebody must go on short rations. The Atlantis society might have been a heaven upon earth, the whole nation might have consisted of just men, needing no repentance, and yet somebody must starve.... [N]on-moral Nature ... would have riven the social fabric....

Our Atlantis may be an impossible figment, but the antagonistic tendencies which the fable adumbrates[128] have existed in every society which was ever established, and, to all appearance, must strive for the victory in all that will be.... No doubt immoral motives of all sorts have figured largely among the minor causes of these events. But, beneath all this superficial turmoil, lay the deep-seated impulse given by unlimited multiplication....

In the ancient world and in a large part of that in which now live, the practice of infanticide was or is a regular and legal custom; the steady recurrence of famine, pestilence, and war were and are normal factors in the struggle for existence, and have served, in a gross and brutal fashion, to mitigate the intensity of its chief cause.

---

126 Prehistoric ox.
127 A prosperous mythical island overwhelmed by natural disaster.
128 Prefigures.

But, in the more advanced civilisations, the progress of private and public morality has steadily tended to remove all these checks. We declare infanticide murder, and punish it as such; we decree, not quite successfully, that no one shall die of hunger; we regard death from preventible causes of other kinds as a sort of constructive murder, and eliminate pestilence to the best of our ability; we declaim against the curse of war, ... and we are never weary of dilating on the blessedness of peace and the innocent beneficence of Industry.... The finer spirits look to an ideal "civitas Dei;"[129] a state when, every man having reached the point of absolute self-negation, and having nothing but moral perfection to strive after, peace will truly reign, not merely among nations, but among men, and the struggle for existence will be at an end.

... And that which I wish to point out is that, so long as the natural man increases and multiplies without restraint, so long will peace and industry not only permit, but they will necessitate, a struggle for existence as sharp as any that ever went on under the *régime* of war....

Let us look at home. For seventy years, peace and industry have had their way among us with less interruption and under more favourable conditions than in any other country on the face of the earth. The wealth of Crœsus[130] was nothing to that which we have accumulated, and our prosperity has filled the world with envy. But Nemesis[131] did not forget Crœsus: has she forgotten us?

I think not. There are now 36,000,000 of people in our island, and every year considerably more than 300,000 are added to our numbers.[132] That is to say, about every hundred seconds, or so, a new claimant to a share in the common stock or maintenance presents him or herself among us. At the present time, the produce of the soil does not suffice to feed half its population....

Judged by an ethical standard, nothing can be less satisfactory than the position in which we find ourselves. In a real, although incomplete, degree we have attained the condition of peace which is the main object of social organisation.... And lo! in spite of ourselves, we are in reality engaged in an internecine struggle for existence with our presumably no less peaceful and well-meaning neighbours.... Let us be under no illusions then. So long as unlimited multiplication goes on, no social organisation which has ever been devised, or is likely to be devised; no fiddle-faddling with the distribution of wealth, will deliver society from the tendency to be destroyed by the reproduction within itself, in its intensest form, of that struggle for existence, the limitation of which is the object of society. And however shocking to the moral sense this eternal competition of man against man and of nation against nation may be; however revolting may be the accumulation of misery at the negative pole of society, in contrast with that of monstrous wealth at the positive pole; this state of things must abide, and grow continually worse.... It is the true riddle of the Sphinx;[133] and every nation which does not solve it will sooner or later be devoured by the monster itself has generated.

---

129 Latin: city of God.
130 Croesus (reigned c. 560–546 BCE), wealthy Lydian king.
131 Ancient Greek goddess of retribution.
132 Author's note: These numbers are only approximately accurate. In 1881, our population amounted to 35,241,482, exceeding the number in 1871 by 3,396,103. The average annual increase in the decennial period 1871–1881 is therefore 339,610. The number of minutes in a calendar year is 525,600.
133 In Greek mythology, the Sphinx is a creature with wings, a woman's head, and a lion's body. It guards the entrance to Thebes with a riddle and eats all who cannot answer.

TRAVEL AND EXPLORATION

Introduction
Laura Franey

Various motives impelled British Victorians to travel outside their home islands. For some, poor health demanded visits to warmer, drier climates. Others sought fame and glory by exploring foreign lands, establishing new trade routes or new markets for British goods, or winning converts to Christianity. Some wanted to find and describe flora, fauna, or Indigenous peoples previously unknown or little-known to Europeans. In some cases, escape was the prime motivation for travel—escape from unpromising economic circumstances, difficult relationships, or restrictions associated with class status or gender identity. Toward the end of the century, more leisure travel occurred beyond conventional European tourist spots as railroads and steamships became more widespread and Britain extended its influence in the world.

The rich history of travel writing stretches back to the ancient world and each era boasts its own subtypes within the larger genre. British travel writing written during Queen Victoria's reign can be divided into two main categories: (1) the formal chronological account of a journey made for scientific, political, or missionary purposes, with descriptions of places or peoples encountered by the traveller; and (2) the letters or journals of a journey taken mostly for pleasure, written by one who seeks to entertain and educate the reader. Of course, there are texts—some of which are represented in this anthology—that defy this binary categorization, but these subtypes provide a helpful way to think about travel writers' intentions and readers' expectations in the nineteenth century.

We also see two very different tones in Victorian travel writing. Most of the travel narratives from the period display a consistent seriousness meant to reflect the significance of the traveller and the journey. By contrast, some narratives feature comic episodes and maintain an ironic stance. Such variation is to be expected in such a wide-ranging genre. After all, Victorian writing about travel and exploration entailed everything from cutting observations about socialites gathered at German watering holes to geographic findings collected as part of the "Great Game" in which Russia and Britain competed for authority in Central Asia.

Many of the excerpts in this anthology feature "heroic" exploration rather than leisure travel. This choice reflects the great appeal that travel writing about the "unknown" possessed for Victorian readers. According to James Buzard, Victorians privileged the explorer over the tourist: "The traveller exhibits boldness and gritty endurance under all conditions (being true to the etymology of 'travel' in the word 'travail'); the tourist is the cautious, pampered unit of a leisure industry" (2). Indeed, most of the excerpts emphasize travellers' endurance in dealing with the setbacks accompanying their attempts to forge into little-explored areas. Some of the explorers understood themselves as harbingers of progress, leading the introduction of "civilization" to supposedly backwards areas of the globe. As Samuel Baker states

"The West Coast of Africa—Landing in a Surf Boat at Accra."
The Graphic (15 Aug. 1891): 198.

forthrightly in *The Albert N'yanza, Great Basin of the Nile*, a chronicle of the travails he and his wife faced as they searched for additional sources of the Nile River, "The explorer is the precursor of the colonist; and the colonist is the human instrument by which the great work must be constructed—that greatest and most difficult of all undertakings—the civilization of the world" (xli).

Victorian travel narratives often contain long passages of ethnography and descriptions of animals and plants that may seem out of place to readers today. Travel writers knew that people in Britain eagerly devoured information about the rest of the world. They therefore provided the desired information in weighty tomes that usually included not only extensive written accounts but also maps, charts, tables, and other illustrations (as either drawings in the early part of Victoria's reign or photographs as photographic reproduction became more accessible later in the period). Visual elements served to authenticate travellers' sojourns, pull readers into the narrative, and provide evidence for scientific claims.

In terms of travellers' tendencies to make scientific claims, we should keep in mind that a stark division between amateurs and professionals did not really exist in the nineteenth century. No matter what their objectives, intentions, or educational training, almost all travellers were seen as reliable sources of the photographs, specimens, artifacts, and maps used by Victorians as they sought to catalogue human, animal, and plant species. Sometimes, big scientific puzzles were solved largely by travellers. For example, two of the most significant nineteenth-century evolutionary theorists, Charles Darwin and Alfred Russel Wallace, were themselves travellers and travel writers. Darwin (in *Voyage of the Beagle*) and Wallace (in *The Malay Archipelago*) asked significant questions about the flora and fauna they witnessed during their travels in Southeast Asia as well as in Central and South America. International travel gave scientific thinkers like Darwin and Wallace an opportunity to observe animals and plants not found in the British Isles or on the European mainland and provided the impetus for new discoveries and theories in various scientific fields.

Of course, not all of the new ideas and theories that arose out of the experiences and writings of travellers are still as scientifically valuable today as is the theory of evolution. This is especially true of theories of race formation and differentiation. In their quest to understand racial difference, Victorian travellers frequently collected human skulls, skeletons, and cultural artifacts; these material items were studied and used to support conclusions about racial hierarchies. Usually these hierarchies privileged Europeans and ancient Greeks and saw Australian Aborigines, Africans, Asians, and American Indigenous peoples as low on the evolutionary scale. Readers of this anthology will probably note the sense of racial and cultural superiority expressed by many Victorian British travellers, a sense of superiority that went hand-in-hand with these contemporary racial theories. These writers' usual characterization of non-Europeans as deficient in their moral, industrial, artistic, or intellectual qualities is likely to disturb us today, but it is helpful to remember that the very travels described may have planted seeds for later non-hierarchical approaches to race and ethnicity. In describing the vibrant cultural, religious, and political life of other nations, Victorian travellers showed readers that other ways of living were possible. As Mary Louise Pratt reminds us, the "contact zones" (4) explored by travellers functioned not only as arenas for the exercise of power and control but also as areas of exchange and learning.

Establishing and maintaining relationships with local peoples (including guides) was crucial for British travellers' successes in the nineteenth century, yet these relationships are often downplayed or occluded from travel narratives. Despite our popular imagining of a solitary traveller in a forbidding jungle or desert, most sojourners were part of large entourages that included both fellow Europeans and Indigenous people. Some travellers, such as Mary Kingsley, Isabella Bird, and David Livingstone, employed only a handful of local people to carry goods or to act as guides and interpreters. In contrast, the expeditionary parties of travellers such as Richard Burton and Henry Morton Stanley in Africa and the official travelling parties of government figures such as George Eden, governor general of India (whose travels in the 1830s are chronicled by his sister, Emily Eden, in *Up the Country*), could boast hundreds or even thousands of participants, both European and Indigenous. Yet most of the companion travellers and camp followers do not have nearly as much name recognition as the travellers who organized and wrote about the trips. Two examples from this anthology illustrate this downplaying of such relationships. The first comes from the travels of David Livingstone (*Missionary Travels and Researches in South Africa, 1875–1885*). An African man known as Susi accompanied Livingstone on his missionary and geographic journeys, even bringing Livingstone's body to the East African coast after his death. Those who study African travel might be familiar with Susi and his exploits, but Livingstone enjoys much greater name recognition in the United States and Britain than does Susi. Another example is Ada Field, an Englishwoman who travelled with Kate Marsden in Russia, but who fell ill and was left behind about 600 miles into the approximately 14,000-mile journey described in Marsden's *On Sledge and Horseback to Outcast Siberian Lepers* (1893). Like the numerous Indigenous people who travelled with Marsden, carrying equipment, clothing, medicine, and food, Field is not remembered as a daring adventurer.

Non-fiction travel narratives of the type included in this anthology heavily informed the creation of fictional travel literature, especially the adventure story. Writers of this still-popular genre include Joseph Conrad, Robert Louis Stevenson, G.A. Henty, and H. Rider Haggard. The thrilling story of an explorer (almost always male and of European descent) fighting his way through obstacles to gain some objective—whether the compassionate rescue of a captive, the spreading of Christianity, or the

"At the Mouth of the Rusizi, Lake Tanganyika" in H.M. Stanley, "How I Found Livingstone," *Illustrated London News* (9 Nov. 1872): 445.

discovery of natural resources such as gold—is so familiar as to be a cliché. But adventure yarns did attract a considerable audience, whether they appeared in family magazines or in volumes destined for bookshops or circulating libraries. Victorian readers of all ages, not just young boys, enjoyed tales that featured geographical exploits, narrow escapes, and love affairs that often ended with an Indigenous woman sacrificing herself to save the hero's life.

The literature of travel was a wonderfully diverse field in the nineteenth century. The following selections, each compelling in its own right, provide a glimpse into the range of peoples, landscapes, and animals encountered by British Victorian travellers. They also demonstrate the various styles employed by these travellers in transforming raw experiences into word-pictures that they hoped would entertain, inform, and surprise their Victorian readers.

"Houseboat Life in Kashmir." *The Graphic* (8 Aug. 1891): 163.

Works Cited and Further Reading

Baker, Samuel White. *The Albert N'yanza, Great Basin of the Nile and Explorations of the Nile Sources*. 2 vols. 1866. London: Sidgwick and Jackson, 1962. Print.

Birkett, Dea. *Victorian Women Explorers*. London: Basil Blackwell, 1990. Print.

Bivona, Daniel. *British Imperial Literature 1870–1940: Writing and the Administration of Empire*. Cambridge: Cambridge UP, 1998. Print.

Brantlinger, Patrick. *Rule of Darkness: British Literature and Imperialism, 1830–1914*. Ithaca: Cornell UP, 1988. Print.

Buzard, James. *The Beaten Track: European Tourism, Literature, and the Ways to "Culture," 1800–1918*. Oxford: Oxford UP, 1993. Print.

Foster, Shirley, and Sara Mills, eds. *An Anthology of Women's Travel Writing*. Manchester: Manchester UP, 2002. Print.

Pratt, Mary Louise. *Imperial Eyes: Travel Writing and Transculturation*. London: Routledge, 1992. Print.

Speake, Jennifer, ed. *Literature of Travel and Exploration: An Encyclopedia*. New York: Fitzroy Dearborn, 2003. Print.

James Holman

from *A Voyage Round the World Including Travels in Africa, Asia, Australasia, America, etc. etc. from 1827 to 1832* (1834)

Naval Lieutenant James Holman (1786–1857) left active service in 1810 because of rheumatism; he later became blind. Appointed a naval knight of Windsor (1812), Holman received a stipend and lived with other lieutenants with disabilities. He obtained leaves of absence for university study (1813–18) and travel to Europe, Siberia, Africa, Asia, Australasia, America, Iberia, Turkey, and Scandinavia. He used a "noctograph" (a metal grid placed over chemically treated paper) to take notes. His blindness fascinated readers of his publications, *A Narrative of a Journey Undertaken in the Years 1819, 1820, and 1821* (1822), *Travels through Russia* (1825), and *A Voyage Round the World* (4 vols., 1834–35). A fellow of the Linnean Society, the Royal Society, and the Raleigh Club (the Royal Geographical Society's forerunner), Holman died while compiling his autobiography.

In *Voyage*, Holman describes the onset of blindness and the "intellectual gratification" of travel; his account of a meeting with native leaders in Fernando Pó is surprisingly visual.

Chapter 1

The passion for travelling is, I believe, instinctive in some natures.... For my own part, I have been conscious from my earliest youth of the existence of this desire to explore distant regions, to trace the varieties exhibited by mankind under the different influences of different climates, customs, and laws, and to investigate with unwearied solicitude the moral and physical distinctions that separate and diversify the various nations of the earth.

I am bound to believe that this direction of my faculties and energies has been ordained by a wise and benevolent Providence, as a source of consolation under an affliction which closes upon me all the delights and charms of the visible world. The constant occupation of the mind, and the continual excitement of mental and bodily action, contribute to diminish, if not to overcome, the sense of deprivation which must otherwise have pressed upon me.... When I entered the naval service I felt an irresistible impulse to become acquainted with as many parts of the world as my professional avocations would permit, and I was determined not to rest satisfied until I had completed the circumnavigation of the globe. But at the early age of twenty-five, while these resolves were strong, and the enthusiasm of youth was fresh and sanguine, my present affliction came upon me. It is impossible to describe the state of my mind at the prospect of losing my sight, and of being, as I then supposed, deprived by that misfortune of the power of indulging in my cherished project. Even the suspense which I suffered, during the period when my medical friends were uncertain of the issue, appeared to me a greater misery than the final knowledge of the calamity itself. At last I entreated them to be explicit, and to let me know the worst, as that could be more easily endured than the agonies of doubt. Their answer, instead of increasing my uneasiness, dispelled it. I felt a comparative relief in being no longer deceived by false hopes; and the certainty that my case was beyond remedy determined me to seek, in some pursuit adapted to my new state of existence, a congenial field of employment and consolation.... [T]he return of strength and vigour, and the concentration of my views upon one object, gradually brought back my old passion, which at length became as firmly established as it was before.... I ventured, alone and sightless, upon my dangerous and novel course; and I cannot look back upon the scenes through which I have passed, the great variety of circumstances by which I have been surrounded, and the strange experiences with which I have become familiar, without an intense aspiration of gratitude for the bounteous dispensation of the Almighty, which enabled me to conquer the greatest of human evils by the cultivation of what has been to me the greatest of human enjoyments, and to supply the void of sight with countless objects of intellectual gratification....

I am constantly asked, and I may as well answer the question here once for all, what is the use of travelling to one who cannot see? I answer, Does every traveller see all that he describes?—and is not every traveller obliged to depend upon others for a great proportion of the information he collects? Even Humboldt[1] himself was not exempt from this necessity.

The picturesque in nature, it is true, is shut out from me, and works of art are to me mere outlines of beauty, accessible only to one sense; but perhaps this very circumstance affords a stronger zest to curiosity, which is thus impelled to a more close and searching examination of details than would be considered necessary to a traveller who might satisfy himself by the superficial view, and rest content with the first impressions conveyed through the eye. Deprived of that organ of information, I am compelled to adopt a more rigid and less suspicious course of inquiry, and to investigate analytically, by a train of patient examination, suggestions, and deductions, which other travellers dismiss at first sight; so that, freed from the hazard of being misled by appearances, I am the less likely to adopt hasty and erroneous conclusions....

I am frequently asked how I take my notes. It is simply thus: I keep a sort of rough diary, which I fill up from time to time as opportunities offer ... but I always vividly remember the daily occurrences which I wish to retain, so that it is not possible that any circumstances can escape my attention. I also collect distinct notes on various subjects, as well as particular descriptions of interesting objects, and when I cannot meet with a friend to act as my amanuensis,[2] I have still a resource in my own writing apparatus....

---

1   Alexander von Humboldt (1769–1859), German traveller and naturalist.
2   Someone who transcribes from dictation.

... This apparatus, which is called the "Nocto via Polygraph," by Mr. Wedgwood, the inventor,[3] is not only useful to the blind, but is equally capable of being rendered available to all persons suffering under diseases of the eyes; for, although it does not assist you to commit your thoughts to paper with the same facility that is attained by the use of pen and ink, it enables you to write very clearly and legibly....

Having given these personal explanations—rendered necessary by the peculiarity of my situation, and the very general curiosity which appears to exist on the subject, if I may judge by the frequency of the interrogatories that are put to me—I will now conclude my preliminary observations ... but place myself at once on board H.M.S. Eden, at Woolwich,[4] on the 1st of July, 1827, having been previously invited to take a passage to the coast of Africa, by her captain, W.F.W. Owen, Esq., who was appointed superintendent of a new settlement about to be established on the island of Fernando Po....[5]

Chapter 8

... The island of Fernando Po, situated off the western coast of Africa, ... is about one hundred and twenty miles in circumference. It is generally believed to have been discovered in the year 1471, by a Portuguese navigator,[6] who gave it the name of Ilha Formosa, or the Beautiful Isle, afterwards changed for that of its discoverer, which it now retains. The Portuguese first established a settlement upon it which they, however, abandoned, and subsequently transferred the right of possession to Spain, receiving in exchange the Island of Trinidad, off the coast of Brazil.

In the year 1764, a new settlement was founded by Spain, which, after a lapse of eighteen years, was also abandoned, for causes which have not been satisfactorily explained, although it is generally believed that a series of misunderstandings with the natives took place, which principally produced that result....

Since this period the island has been left to its native inhabitants, excepting that various European, and particularly English vessels, have occasionally touched at it for the purpose of procuring water and yams....

At length, a variety of considerations determined the British Government to attempt a new settlement on this island....

In the first place, the convenient situation of the island, at the distance of only twenty miles from the main-land of Africa, and in the immediate neighbourhood of the mouths of the many large rivers which pour their waters into the Gulf of Biafra,[7] appeared to afford a most eligible point for checking the slave-trade, of which this position may be considered the very centre.[8]

Secondly, it was imagined ... that the adoption of the measure would tend materially to diminish the sufferings of the miserable objects of human traffic—the unfortunate slaves—who too frequently

---

3   Ralph Wedgwood's "manifold writer" (invented in 1806) allowed the blind to write without ink, using carbon paper and a metal quill.
4   A town in Greater London on the south bank of the Thames River; it housed the Royal Dockyards, which closed in 1869.
5   Bioko (formerly Fernando Pó), an island off the west coast of Africa that is currently part of Equatorial Guinea.
6   Fernão do Pó (Fernando Pó) discovered Bioko c. 1472.
7   The Bight of Biafra (also Bight of Bonny), one of two large bays in the Gulf of Guinea.
8   In 1807, Britain's Abolition of the Slave Trade Act established stiff fines for slave trading; other European nations and the United States swiftly joined the abolitionist movement. Britain's powerful navy played a major role in policing smugglers of slaves.

sank under the confinement and disease incidental to a protracted voyage to Sierra Leone,[9] before their liberation could be legally accomplished.

In the third place, it was hoped that the greater salubrity[10] of the new colony would lead to the eventual abandonment of the settlements of Sierra Leone and Cape Coast Castle,[11] the direful effects of whose climates upon European life have long been proverbial....

To carry the proposed object into effect, an expedition was fitted out in the early part of the summer of 1827, under the command of Captain William Fitzwilliam Owen, of His Majesty's ship *Eden*, who received the appointment of superintendent of the colony....

On first approaching the island, its mountains were shrouded from view by heavy clouds and a hazy atmosphere; which, however, gradually dispersed as we neared the shore, and revealed to the eyes of my companions a magnificent display of mountain scenery, closely studded with large trees, and thick with underwood, whose luxuriant foliage of various tints and hues, blending with the scarcely ruffled bosom of the ocean, and the retiring clouds, making the sky each moment become more lucid and transparent, formed such a variegated picture of natural beauty, that we unanimously hailed it as the land of promise.

It was not long before the scene began to assume an aspect of animation, the immediate consequence of our arrival; for, in less than half an hour after we anchored, a number of canoes, with several natives in each ... approached us for the purpose of bartering the productions of their island, namely, yams, fowls, palm-wine in calabashes,[12] fish, some boxes made of split cane, monkey and snake skins, with other trifling articles; for pieces of iron hoop, a few inches long, which we afterwards found they made into two-edged knives.... It was easy to perceive that the natives were fine-looking, active, middle-sized men, with an agreeable and animated expression of countenance. The natural colour of their skin was not ascertainable, the whole body being painted, or rather daubed over with a composition of clay, or ochre,[13] mixed up with palm-oil. The prevailing colour was red, which seems to belong more exclusively to the lower classes: some few, however, had used a yellow, and others a grey pigment, probably as a mark of distinction, and which we afterwards found appropriated to the kings, or chief men. The faces were much seamed or scarified, while other parts of the body, and particularly the abdomen, were more or less tattoed....

Their weapons were wooden well-barbed spears, with their points hardened by fire, each individual being provided with three or four. We afterwards, however, found that these were not the only means of defence, as they are possessed of slings, in the use of which they acquire no inconsiderable expertness. The canoes appeared to be from 15 to 30 feet in length, and each capable of carrying from three to twelve persons; these were provided with sails made of a kind of split rattan matting, of an oblong square form, the longer side placed perpendicularly, and some of them had a staff erected in the bow, with a bunch of feathers at the top of it....

---

9   A British colony of freed slaves on the west African coast.
10 Health-giving environment.
11 A Swedish castle in present-day Ghana, built in 1655 and seized by the British in 1663; it was the seat of British colonial government in the Gold Coast until 1877.
12 Gourd shells used to carry liquids.
13 Clay or earth containing much iron oxide and ranging in colour from yellow to red and brown.

Sunday, October 28.— ...
In the course of the day, Captain Owen landed at various points for the purpose of investigating the localities of the neighbourhood, and with a view of selecting the most eligible situation for our intended establishment. Lieutenant Robinson also went on shore to take sights for comparing the chronometers....[14]

Tuesday, Oct. 30.—Captain Owen, having now thoroughly investigated the vicinity of this place, determined upon the site of our future settlement. For this purpose, Maidstone Bay, in consequence of its capacity, (being about four miles and a half from Cape Bullen, its north-western limit, to Point William); the excellency of its anchorage, and the smoothness of its water, offered peculiar advantages; to which may be added, its reception of the waters of the Baracouta[15] river, with other smaller streams, and the abundance of its fine fish of various kinds, including two or three species of turtle. On the south-eastern side, adjoining to coves which have received the respective names of Clarence and Cockburn Coves, two necks of land project into the bay, the one named Point Adelaide, with two small islands off it, bearing the same name; the other Point William. It was on the latter, constituting a kind of peninsula, projecting nearly six hundred yards into the sea, that Captain Owen decided upon fixing the infant settlement, which is probably destined to become the future emporium of the commerce, as well as the centre of civilization of this part of the globe,—giving it, out of compliment to His Royal Highness the Lord High Admiral, the name of Clarence....[16]

The above situation having been finally decided upon, Captain Owen determined to lose no time in commencing operations, and, in the course of the day, notwithstanding it proved rainy, a party of a hundred Kroomen[17] and other black labourers, were landed, under the command of Mr. Vidal, the senior lieutenant, and immediately began to clear a road through the jungle, to the spot selected for the new town....

Wednesday, Oct. 31.—The steam-vessel (*African*) arrived to-day, and brought in two vessels under Brazilian colours, which Lieutenant Badgeley had boarded and detained, under strong suspicion of their being engaged in the slave-trade.

At nine o'clock, the King of Baracouta, accompanied by his brother and five or six other chiefs, came on board according to promise, and without betraying any symptoms of timidity. The party were immediately conducted to the captain's cabin, and entertained with wine and biscuit, which they appeared to partake of with considerable relish....

A description of their dress, which was in the most fanciful savage taste, cannot fail to be interesting. In the first place, the body was completely smeared over with the kind of paint I have before described: His Majesty's colour, like that which distinguishes the imperial family of China, being yellow, while the livery of his attendants was dark red. The hair of the head was dressed in long small curls hanging down behind, and which, instead of hair powder and pomatum,[18] were well stiffened with ochre and oil: in front, similar curls dividing from the forehead, hung down on each side below the ears, somewhat in the style of

---

14 A timekeeper that functions in extreme temperatures and can be used to determine a ship's longitude.
15 Barracuda.
16 William IV (1765–1837) was Duke of Clarence before he acceded to the throne in 1830.
17 An African people living on the Liberian coast.
18 Hair ointment.

Vandyke's[19] female portraits of the age of Charles I. The forehead was generally round, sufficiently elevated to give phrenological[20] indications of a fair portion of intellect.... The neck, arms, body above the hips, and the legs below the knee, were encircled by ornamental bands, in the form of bracelets, which were, for the most part, composed of strings of beads, or the vertebræ of small snakes; to the girdle, which thus surrounded the body, was appended, hanging down in front, the only article of covering which they can be said to wear, consisting of the skin of some animal, and which, in many instances, was decorated with a bunch of herbage. His Majesty, however, as a mark of distinction, wore also a similar covering behind....

Our more difficult task was yet to be encountered—the distribution of presents. His yellow Majesty was in the first place complimented with the whole of an iron hoop straightened out for the occasion, and also with half a dozen fishing-hooks; to his brother we gave half the quantity: while the minor chiefs received about a foot in length each. Some squabbling occurred during this arrangement, which was, at length, happily concluded, pretty much to the satisfaction of the whole party, and they left the ship in apparent good humour, evidently highly gratified with their visit.

Charles Darwin

from *Journal of Researches into the Geology and Natural History of the Various Countries Visited by H.M.S. Beagle, under the Command of Captain FitzRoy, R.N. from 1832 to 1836* (1839)

Naturalist and geologist Charles Darwin (1809–82) authored the groundbreaking theory of natural selection. Darwin studied at Cambridge, where botany and natural history fascinated him. In 1831, botany professor John Henslow proposed him for a circumnavigation of the globe on board the *Beagle*, whose captain, Robert FitzRoy, sought a gentleman to undertake scientific research en route. The voyage (1831–36) crossed the Atlantic to South America, rounding the Horn and visiting the Pacific Islands, Australia, New Zealand, and Cape Town. Darwin published a zoological account (1838–43), then a travel narrative, *Journal of Researches into the Geology and Natural History of the Various Countries Visited by H.M.S. Beagle* (1839). The journey confirmed Darwin's commitment to natural history and geology, providing evidence for later publications, including *On the Origin of Species* (1859).

This excerpt narrates the *Beagle*'s encounter with Tierra del Fuegian natives and the return of three anglicized Fuegians whom the captain had taken aboard on an earlier voyage.

---

19 Anthony van Dyck (1599–1641), Flemish artist.
20 An early nineteenth-century theory that posited that mental attributes were linked to the shapes of people's heads.

Chapter 11

... December 17th, 1832.—Having now finished with Patagonia, I will describe our first arrival in Tierra del Fuego.[21] A little after noon we doubled Cape St. Diego, and entered the famous strait of Le Maire.[22] We kept close to the Fuegian shore, but the outline of the rugged, inhospitable Statenland was visible amidst the clouds. In the afternoon we anchored in the bay of Good Success.[23] While entering we were saluted in a manner becoming the inhabitants of this savage land. A group of Fuegians partly concealed by the entangled forest, were perched on a wild point overhanging the sea; and as we passed by, they sprang up, and waving their tattered cloaks sent forth a loud and sonorous shout. The savages followed the ship, and just before dark we saw their fire, and again heard their wild cry....

In the morning, the Captain sent a party to communicate with the Fuegians. When we came within hail, one of the four natives who were present advanced to receive us, and began to shout most vehemently, wishing to direct us where to land. When we were on shore the party looked rather alarmed, but continued talking and making gestures with great rapidity. It was without exception the most curious and interesting spectacle I had ever beheld. I could not have believed how wide was the difference, between savage and civilised man. It is greater than between a wild and domesticated animal, inasmuch as in man there is a greater power of improvement. The chief spokesman was old, and appeared to be the head of the family; the three others were powerful young men, about six feet high. The women and children had been sent away. These Fuegians are a very different race from the stunted miserable wretches further to the westward. They are much superior in person, and seem closely allied to the famous Patagonians of the Strait of Magellan.[24] Their only garment consists of a mantle made of guanaco[25] skin, with the wool outside; this they wear just thrown over their shoulders, as often leaving their persons exposed as covered. Their skin is of a dirty coppery red colour.

The old man had a fillet[26] of white feathers tied round his head, which partly confined his black, coarse, and entangled hair. His face was crossed by two broad transverse bars; one painted bright red reached from ear to ear, and included the upper lip; the other, white like chalk, extended parallel and above the first, so that even his eyelids were thus coloured. Some of the other men were ornamented by streaks of black powder, made of charcoal. The party altogether closely resembled the devils which come on the stage in such plays as Der Freischuts.[27]

Their very attitudes were abject, and the expression of their countenances distrustful, surprised, and startled. After we had presented them with some scarlet cloth, which they immediately tied round their necks, they became good friends. This was shown by the old man patting our breasts, and making a chuckling kind of noise, as people do when feeding chickens. I walked with the old man, and this demonstration of friendship was repeated several times; it was concluded by three hard slaps, which

---

21 Tierra del Fuego is an archipelago at the southern tip of South America.
22 The Cabo (Cape) San Diego is the southeastern tip of Isla Grande de Tierra del Fuego; the Strait of Le Maire is between Cabo San Diego and Staten Island, also in the archipelago.
23 A bay on Isla Grande de Tierra del Fuego, in the Strait of Le Maire.
24 Patagonians are the natives of the southern tip of the South American mainland, who were said to be giants (see Dixie, Travel and Exploration); the Strait of Magellan is between the Tierra del Fuego archipelago and the mainland.
25 A wild quadruped, similar to a llama or alpaca.
26 Head band.
27 Carl Maria von Weber, *Der Freischütz* (1821), a popular German opera in which souls are bartered to the Devil.

were given me on the breast and back at the same time. He then bared his bosom for me to return the compliment, which being done, he seemed highly pleased. The language of these people, according to our notions, scarcely deserves to be called articulate. Captain Cook[28] has compared it to a man clearing his throat, but certainly no European ever cleared his throat with so many hoarse, guttural, and clicking sounds....

It was interesting to watch the conduct of these people towards Jemmy Button (one of the Fuegians[29] who had been taken, during the former voyage, to England): they immediately perceived the difference between him and the rest, and held much conversation between themselves on the subject. The old man addressed a long harangue to Jemmy, which it seems was to invite him to stay with them. But Jemmy understood very little of their language, and was, moreover, thoroughly ashamed of his countrymen. When York Minster (another of these men) came on shore, they noticed him in the same way, and told him he ought to shave; yet he had not twenty dwarf hairs on his face, whilst we all wore our untrimmed beards. They examined the colour of his skin, and compared it with ours. One of our arms being bared, they expressed the liveliest surprise and admiration at its whiteness....

December 25th.... At a subsequent period the Beagle anchored for a couple of days near Wollaston Island....[30] [G]oing on shore we pulled alongside a canoe with six Fuegians. These were the most abject and miserable creatures I any where beheld.[31] On the east coast the natives, as we have seen, have guanaco cloaks, and on the west, they possess seal-skins. Amongst these central tribes the men generally possess an otter-skin, of some small scrap about as large as a pocket-handkerchief, which is barely sufficient to cover their backs as low down as their loins. It is laced across the breast by strings, and according as the wind blows, it is shifted from side to side. But these Fuegians in the canoe were quite naked, and even one full-grown woman was absolutely so. It was raining heavily, and the fresh water, together with the spray, trickled down her body. In another harbour not far distant, a woman, who was suckling a recently-born child, came one day alongside the vessel, and remained there whilst the sleet fell and thawed on her naked bosom, and on the skin of her naked child. These poor wretches were stunted in their growth, their hideous faces bedaubed with white paint, their skins filthy and greasy, their hair entangled, their voices discordant, their gestures violent and without dignity. Viewing such men, one can hardly make oneself believe they are fellow-creatures, and inhabitants of the same world.... At night, five or six human beings, naked and scarcely protected from the wind and rain of this tempestuous climate, sleep on the wet ground coiled up like animals. Whenever it is low water, they must rise to pick shell-fish from the rocks; and the women, winter and summer, either dive to collect sea eggs, or sit patiently in their canoes,

---

28 James Cook (1728–79), explorer.
29 Author's note: Captain FitzRoy has given a history of these people. Four were taken to England; one died there, and the three others (two men and one woman) were now brought back and settled in their own country.
30 One of the Wollaston Islands, the southernmost in the archipelago.
31 Author's note: I believe, in this extreme part of South America, man exists in a lower state of improvement than in any other part of the world. The South Sea islander, of either race is comparatively civilized. The Esquimaux [Eskimo], in his subterranean hut, enjoys some of the comforts of life, and in his canoe, when fully equipped, manifests much skill. Some of the tribes of Southern Africa, prowling about in search of roots, and living concealed on the wild and arid plains, are sufficiently wretched. But the Australian, in the simplicity of the arts of life, comes nearest the Fuegian. He can, however, boast of his boomerang, his spear and throwing-stick, his method of climbing trees, tracking animals, and scheme of hunting. Although thus superior in acquirements, it by no means follows that he should likewise be so in capabilities. Indeed, from what we saw of the Fuegians, who were taken to England, I should think the case was the reverse.

and, with a baited hair-line, jerk out small fish. If a seal is killed, or the floating carcass of a putrid whale discovered, it is a feast: such miserable food is assisted by a few tasteless berries and fungi. Nor are they exempt from famine, and, as a consequence, cannibalism accompanied by parricide.[32]

The tribes have no government or head, yet each is surrounded by other hostile ones, speaking different dialects; and the cause of their warfare would appear to be the means of subsistence. Their country is a broken mass of wild rock, lofty hills, and useless forests: and these are viewed through mists and endless storms. The habitable land is reduced to the stones which form the beach; in search of food they are compelled to wander from spot to spot, and so steep is the coast, that they can only move about in their wretched canoes. They cannot know the feeling of having a home, and still less that of domestic affection; unless indeed the treatment of a master to a laborious slave can be considered as such. How little can the higher powers of the mind be brought into play! What is there for imagination to picture, for reason to compare, for judgment to decide upon? to knock a limpet[33] from the rock does not even require cunning, that lowest power of the mind. Their skill in some respects may be compared to the instinct of animals; for it is not improved by experience: the canoe, their most ingenious work, poor as it is, has remained the same, for the last two hundred and fifty years.

Whilst beholding these savages, one asks, whence have they come? What could have tempted, or what change compelled a tribe of men to leave the fine regions of the north, to travel down the Cordillera or backbone of America,[34] to invent and build canoes, and then to enter on one of the most inhospitable countries within the limits of the globe? Although such reflections must at first occupy one's mind, yet we may feel sure that many of them are quite erroneous. There is no reason to believe that the Fuegians decrease in number; therefore we must suppose that they enjoy a sufficient share of happiness (of whatever kind it may be) to render life worth having. Nature by making habit omnipotent, and its effects hereditary, has fitted the Fuegian to the climate and the productions of his country....

[January] 22D.—.... At night we slept close to the junction of Ponsonby Sound with the Beagle channel.[35] A small family of Fuegians, who were living in the cove, were very quiet and inoffensive, and soon joined our party round the blazing fire....

... [E]arly in the morning (23d) a fresh party arrived. Several of them had run so fast that their noses were bleeding, and their mouths frothed from the rapidity with which they talked, and with their naked bodies all bedaubed with black, white, and red, they looked like so many demoniacs who had been fighting. We then proceeded down Ponsonby Sound to the spot where poor Jemmy expected to find his mother and relations....

During the succeeding year we paid another visit to the Fuegians, and the Beagle herself followed the same course which I have just described as having been taken in the boats.[36] I was amused by finding what a difference the circumstance of being quite superior in force made, in the interest of beholding these savages. While in the boats I got to hate the very sound of their voices, so much trouble

---

32 The act of murdering a parent or other near relative.
33 Small mollusc that clings to rocks.
34 A mountain chain; here referring to the Andes.
35 Ponsonby Sound is between Navarino Island and Hoste Island; the Beagle Channel is between these two islands and Isla Grande del Tierra del Fuego.
36 The *Beagle* carried small vessels for inshore expeditions.

did they give us. The first and last word was "yammerschooner."[37] When, entering some quiet little cove, we have looked round and thought to pass a quiet night, the odious word "yammerschooner" has shrilly sounded from some gloomy nook, and then the little signal smoke has curled upwards to spread the news. On leaving some place we have said to each other, "Thank Heaven, we have at last fairly left these wretches!" when one more faint halloo from an all-powerful voice, heard at a prodigious distance, would reach our ears, and clearly could we distinguish—"yammerschooner." But on the latter occasion, the more Fuegians the merrier; and very merry work it was. Both parties laughing, wondering, gaping at each other; we pitying them, for giving us good fish and crabs for rags, &c.; they grasping at the chance of finding people so foolish as to exchange such splendid ornaments for a good supper. It was most amusing to see the undisguised smile of satisfaction with which one young woman, with her face painted black, tied with rushes several bits of scarlet cloth round her head. Her husband, who enjoyed the very universal privilege in this country of possessing two wives, evidently became jealous of all the attention paid to his young wife; and, after a consultation with his naked beauties, was paddled away by them.

Some of the Fuegians plainly showed that they had a fair idea of barter. I gave one man a large nail (a most valuable present) without making any signs for a return; but he immediately picked out two fish, and handed them up on the point of his spear. If any present was designed for one canoe, and it fell near another, it was invariably given to the right owner. We were always much surprised at the little notice, or rather none whatever, which was evinced respecting many things, even such as boats, the use of which must have been evident. Simple circumstances,—such as the whiteness of our skins, the beauty of scarlet cloth or blue beads, the absence of women, our care in washing ourselves,—excited their admiration far more than any grand or complicated object, such as the ship....

The perfect equality among the individuals composing these tribes, must for a long time retard their civilization. As we see those animals, whose instinct compels them to live in society and obey a chief, are most capable of improvement, so is it with the races of mankind. Whether we look at it as a cause or a consequence, the more civilized always have the most artificial governments. For instance, the inhabitants of Otaheite,[38] who, when first discovered, were governed by hereditary kings, had arrived at a far higher grade than another branch of the same people, the New Zealanders,[39]—who although benefited by being compelled to turn their attention to agriculture, were republicans in the most absolute sense. In Tierra del Fuego, until some chief shall arise with power sufficient to secure any acquired advantages, such as the domesticated animals or other valuable presents, it seems scarcely possible that the political state of the country can be improved. At present, even a piece of cloth is torn into shreds and distributed; and no one individual becomes richer than another. On the other hand, it is difficult to understand how a chief can arise till there is property of some sort by which he might manifest and still increase his authority.

---

37   Previously defined by Darwin as "Give me"; an indication of a desire to trade or be given gifts.
38   Tahitians.
39   Maori; the Tahitians and Maori are both of Polynesian descent.

Richard F. Burton
from *Personal Narrative of a Pilgrimage to El-Medinah and Meccah* (1855)

Explorer and writer Richard Burton (1821–90), though expelled from Oxford in 1842, proved linguistically gifted, learning over 40 languages and dialects. While serving in the army in India, he passed as native to gain intelligence for the British. Returning to England in 1849, he started a prolific writing career, producing articles, sketches, diaries, and travel books (on Africa, North and South America, and elsewhere). In 1853, Burton sailed for the Middle East, passing as Muslim to enter Mecca and Medina; in 1854, masquerading as a Turkish merchant, he entered Harar, centre of the Somalian slave trade. Supported by the Royal Geographical Society, Burton and John Speke searched for the White Nile's source (1857–59). After Burton fell ill, Speke discovered Lake Victoria and was hailed as a hero in Britain.

In this selection from his *Personal Narrative of a Pilgrimage to El-Medinah and Meccah*, Burton describes how he passed as Muslim in order to gain access to mosques and holy sites.

~

Chapter 1: To Alexandria

A Few Words Concerning What Induced Me to a Pilgrimage
In the autumn of 1852, through the medium of General Monteith,[40] I offered my services to the Royal Geographical Society of London, for the purpose of removing that opprobrium[41] to modern adventure, the huge white blot which in our maps still notes the eastern and the central regions of Arabia....

... The "experimentum crucis"[42] was a visit to El Hejaz, at once the most difficult and the most dangerous point by which a European can enter Arabia.... [B]eing liberally supplied with the means of travel by the Royal Geographical Society; thoroughly tired of "progress" and of "civilisation;" curious to see with my eyes what others are content to "hear with ears," namely, Moslem's inner life in a really Mohammedan country; and longing, if truth be told, to set foot on that mysterious spot which no tourist had yet described, measured, sketched and daguerreotyped,[43] I resolved to resume my old character of a Persian wanderer,[44] and to make the attempt....

On the evening of April 3, 1853, I left London for Southampton. By the advice of a brother officer—little thought at that time the adviser or the advised how valuable was the suggestion—my Eastern

---

40 William Monteith (1790–1864), army officer, diplomat, and historian.
41 Disapproval.
42 Latin: A decisive experiment, one capable of proving which hypothesis is correct.
43 To daguerreotype means to reproduce an image by the earliest photographic process.
44 Author's note: The vagrant, the merchant, and the philosopher, amongst Orientals, are frequently united in the same person.

dress was called into requisition[45] before leaving town, and all my "impedimenta"[46] were taught to look exceedingly Oriental. Early the next day a "Persian Prince" embarked on board the Peninsular and Oriental Company's magnificent screw steamer[47] "Bengal."

A fortnight was profitably spent in getting into the train of Oriental manners. For what polite Chesterfield[48] says of the difference between a gentleman and his reverse,—namely, that both perform the same offices of life, but each in a several and widely different way—is notably as applicable to the manners of the Eastern as of the Western man. Look, for instance, at that Indian Moslem drinking a glass of water. With us the operation is simple enough, but his performance includes no fewer than five novelties. In the first place he clutches his tumbler as though it were the throat of a foe; secondly, he ejaculates, "In the name of Allah the Compassionate, the Merciful!" before wetting his lips; thirdly, he imbibes the contents, swallowing them, not drinking, and ending with a satisfied grunt; fourthly, before setting down the cup, he sighs forth, "Praise be to Allah"—of which you will understand the full meaning in the Desert; and, fifthly, he replies, "May Allah make it pleasant to thee!" in answer to his friend's polite "Pleasurably and health!" Also he is careful to avoid the irreligious action of drinking the pure element in a standing position ...

Our voyage over the "summer sea"[49] was an eventless one.... On the evening of the thirteenth day after our start, the big-trowsered pilot, so lovely in his deformities to western eyes, made his appearance, and the good screw "Bengal," found herself at anchor off the Headland of Figs.[50]

Having been invited to start from the house of a kind friend, John Larking,[51] I disembarked with him, and rejoiced to see that by dint of a beard and a shaven head I had succeeded, like the Lord of Geesh,[52] in "misleading the inquisitive spirit of the populace." The mingled herd of spectators before whom we passed in review on the landing-place, hearing an audible "Alhamdulillah"[53] whispered "Moslem!" The infant population spared me the compliments usually addressed to hatted heads; and when a little boy, presuming that the occasion might possibly open the hand of generosity, looked in my face and exclaimed "Bakhshish,"[54] he obtained in reply a "Mafish;"[55] which convinced the bystanders that the sheep-skin contained a real sheep. We then mounted a carriage, fought our way through the donkeys, and in half an hour found ourselves, chibouque[56] in mouth and coffee-cup in hand, seated on the divans[57] in my friend's hospitable house....

---

45 Called into service.
46 Travelling equipment.
47 A modern steamer with a screw propeller.
48 Philip Dormer Stanhope, Lord Chesterfield (1694–1773), politician, writer, and diplomat.
49 Bion of Smyrna (fl. 100 BCE).
50 Author's note: In Arabic "Ras el Tin," the promontory upon which immortal Pharohs once stood.
51 John Wingfield Larking (1801–91), the British consul at Alexandria.
52 James Bruce of Kinnaird, Lord of Geesh (1730–94), African traveller.
53 Author's note: "Praise be to Allah, Lord of the (three) worlds!" a pious ejaculation which leaves the lips of the True Believer on all occasions of concluding actions.
54 Author's note: ... a fee or present....
55 Author's note: ... "there is none," equivalent to, "I have left my purse at home".... Egyptian: I don't have anything to give.
56 Tobacco pipe.
57 A kind of couch.

Chapter 5: The Ramazan[58]

This year the Ramazan befel in June, and a fearful infliction was that "blessed month." For the space of sixteen consecutive hours and a quarter, we were forbidden to eat, drink, smoke, snuff, and even to swallow our saliva designedly. I say forbidden, for although the highest orders of Turks ... may break the ordinance in strict privacy, popular opinion would condemn any open infraction of it with uncommon severity....

Like the Italian and Greek fasts, the chief effect of the "blessed month" upon true believers is to darken their tempers into positive gloom. Their voices, never of the softest, acquire, especially after noon, a terribly harsh and creaking tone. The men curse one another ... and beat the women. The women slap and abuse the children, and these in their turn cruelly entreat, and use harsh language to the dogs and cats. You can scarcely spend ten minutes in any populous part of the city without hearing some violent dispute. The "Karakun," or station-houses, are filled with lords who have administered an undue dose of chastisement to their ladies, and with ladies who have scratched, bitten, and otherwise injured the bodies of their lords. The Mosques are crowded with a sulky, grumbling population, making themselves offensive to one another on earth, whilst working their way to heaven; and in the shade, under the outer walls, the little boys who have been expelled the church attempt to forget their miseries in spiritless play.... [A]s a rule the shops are either shut or destitute of shopmen, merchants will not purchase, and students will not study. In fine, the Ramazan, for many classes, is one-twelfth of the year wantonly thrown away.

The following is the routine of a fast day. About half an hour after midnight, the gun sounds its warning to faithful men that it is time to prepare for the "Sahur," or morning meal.... It is some time before the stomach becomes accustomed to such hours, but in matters of appetite, habit is everything, and for health's sake one should strive to eat as plentifully as possible. Then sounds the Salam, or Blessings on the Prophet ... an introduction to the call of morning prayer. Smoking sundry pipes with tenderness, as if taking leave of a friend, and until the second gun, fired at about half past two A.M., gives the Insak ... —the order to abstain from food,—I wait the Azan,[59] which in this month is called somewhat earlier than usual. Then, after a ceremony termed the Niyat[60] of fasting, I say my prayers, and prepare for repose.... At 7 A.M. the labours of the day begin for the working classes of society; the rich spend the night in revelling, and rest from dawn to noon.

The first thing on rising is to perform the Wuzu, or lesser ablution, which invariably follows sleep in a reclining position; without this it would be improper to pray, to enter the mosques, to approach a religious man, or to touch the Koran.... At 9 A.M. Shaykh Mohammed enters, with "lecture" written upon his wrinkled brow, or I pick him up on the way, and proceed straight to the Mosque El Azhar. After three hours' hard reading with little interruption from by-standers ... comes the call to mid-day prayer. The founder of Islam ordained but few devotions for the morning, which is the business part of the Eastern day, but during the afternoon and evening they succeed one another rapidly, and their length increases. It is then time to visit my rich patients, and afterwards, in order to accustom myself to the sun, to wander

---

58 This section takes place in Cairo, Egypt; Ramadan is the ninth month of the Islamic calendar and a period in which Muslims fast from dawn to sunset.
59 Author's note: The summons to prayer.
60 Author's note: in the Mohammedan church, every act of devotion must be preceded by what is called its Niyat, or purpose....

through the bookshops for an hour or two, or simply to idle in the street. At 3 P.M. I return home, recite the afternoon prayers, and re-apply myself to study.

This is the worst part of the day. In Egypt the summer nights and mornings are, generally speaking, pleasant, but the forenoons are sultry, and the afternoons serious. A wind wafting the fine dust and furnace heat of the desert blows over the city ... and not a cloud or a vapour breaks the dreary expanse of splendour on high.... Weakened with fasting, the body feels the heat trebly, and the disordered stomach almost affects the brain. Every minute is counted with morbid fixity of idea as it passes on towards the blessed sunset, especially by those whose terrible lot is manual labour at such a season....

As the Maghrib, the sunset hour, approaches—and how slowly it comes!—the town seems to recover from a trance. People flock to the windows and balconies, in order to watch the moment of their release. Some pray, others tell their beads, while others, gathering together in groups or paying visits, exert themselves to while away the lagging time.

O gladness! at length it sounds, that gun from the citadel. Simultaneously rises the sweet cry of the Muezzin,[61] calling men to prayer, and the second cannon booms from the Abbasiyah Palace ... , —"Al fitar! al fitar!" fast-breaking! fast-breaking! shout the people, and a hum of joy rises from the silent city. Your acute ears waste not a moment in conveying the delightful intelligence to your parched tongue, empty stomach, and languid limbs. You exhaust a pot full of water, no matter its size. You clap hurried hands ... for a pipe, you order coffee, and, provided with these comforts, you sit down, and calmly contemplate the coming pleasures of the evening.

Poor men eat heartily at once. The rich break their fast with a light meal,—a little bread and fruit, fresh or dry, especially water-melon, sweetmeats, or such digestible dishes as "Muhallabah"—a thin jelly of milk, starch, and rice-flour. They then smoke a pipe, drink a cup of coffee or a glass of sherbet, and recite the evening prayers; for the devotions of this hour are delicate things, and while smoking a first pipe after sixteen hours' abstinence, time easily slips away. Then they sit down to the Fatúr (breakfast), *the* meal of the twenty-four hours, and eat plentifully, if they would avoid an illness....

The streets are now crowded with a good-humoured throng of strollers; the many bent on pleasure, the few wending their way to mosque, where the Imam[62] recites "Tarawih" prayers.[63] They saunter about, the accustomed pipe in hand, shopping, for the stalls are open till a late hour, or they sit in crowds at the coffee-house entrance, smoking Shishas,[64] chatting, and listening to storytellers, singers and itinerant preachers. Here a bare-footed girl trills and quavers, accompanied by a noisy tambourine and a "scrannel pipe"[65] of abominable discordance, in honour of a perverse saint whose corpse insisted upon being buried inside some respectable man's dwelling-house.... A steady stream of loungers sets through the principal thoroughfares towards the Ezbekiyah,[66] which skirts the Frank quarter, where they sit in the moonlight, listening to Greek and Turkish bands, or making merry with cakes, toasted grains, coffee, sugared-drinks, and the broad pleasantries of Kara Gyuz....[67]

---

61   Person chosen by the mosque to lead the call for prayer.
62   Leader of the mosque.
63   Author's note: Extra prayers repeated in the Ramazan....
64   Author's note: The Shisha, or Egyptian water-pipe....
65   Unmelodious pipe.
66   Gardens.
67   Author's note: ... [T]he Turkish Punch ... [of Punch and Judy].

Returning to the Moslem quarter, you are bewildered by its variety of sounds. Everyone talks, and talking here is always in extremes, either in a whisper, or in a scream; gesticulation excites the lungs, and strangers cannot persuade themselves that men so converse without being or becoming furious. All the street cries, too, are in the soprano key. "In thy protection! in thy protection!" shouts a Fellah[68] to a sentinel, who is flogging him towards the station-house, followed by a tail of women, screaming, "O my calamity! O my shame!" The boys have elected a Pacha,[69] whom they are conducting in procession, with wisps of straw for Mashals, or Cressets,[70] and outrunners, all huzzaing with ten-schoolboy power. "O thy right! O thy left! O thy face! O thy heel! O thy back, thy back!" cries the panting footman, who, huge torch on shoulder, runs before the grandee's carriage; "bless the Prophet, and get out of the way!" "O Allah bless him!" respond the good Moslems, some shrinking up to the walls to avoid the stick, others rushing across the road, so as to give themselves every chance of being knocked down.... "Sweetwater, and gladden thy soul, O lemonade!" pipes the seller of that luxury, clanging his brass cups together. Then come the beggars, intensely Oriental. "My supper is in Allah's hands, my supper is in Allah's hands! whatever thou givest, that will go with thee!" chaunts the old vagrant, whose wallet perhaps contains more provision than the basket of many a respectable shopkeeper....

And sometimes, high above the hubbub, rises the melodious voice of the blind muezzin,[71] who from his balcony in the beetling tower rings forth, "Hie ye to devotion! Hie ye to salvation. Devotion is better than sleep! Devotion is better than sleep!" Then good Moslems piously stand up, and mutter, previous to prayer, "Here am I at thy call, O Allah! here am I at thy call!"

Sometimes I walked with my friend to the citadel,[72] and sat upon a high wall, one of the outworks of Mahommed Ali's mosque,[73] enjoying a view which, seen by night, when the summer moon is near the full, has a charm no power of language can embody. Or escaping from "stifled Cairo's filth ... ,"[74] we passed, through the Gate of Victory, into the wilderness beyond the city of the dead....[75] Seated upon some mound of ruins, we inhaled the fine air of the desert, inspiriting as a cordial,[76] when star-light and dew mists diversified a scene, which, by day, is one broad sea of yellow loam[77] with billows of chalk rock, thinly covered by a film-like spray of sand floating in the fiery wind. There, within a mile of crowded life, all is desolate, the town walls seem crumbling to decay, the hovels are tenantless, and the paths untrodden; behind you lies the wild, before, the thousand tomb-stones, ghastly in their whiteness, and beyond them the tall dark forms of the Mameluke Sultan's towers[78] rise from the low and hollow ground like the spirits of kings guarding ghostly subjects in the shadowy realm. Nor less weird than the scene are the sounds!—the hyæna's laugh, the howl of the wild dog, and the screech of the low-flying owl....

---

68 Peasant.
69 Highest title in the Ottoman empire.
70 Iron baskets or vessels, usually mounted on poles and containing fuel to be burned for light; here the straw represents such torches.
71 By tradition, blind people were chosen as muezzin because they were unable to look into people's private courtyards from the minaret.
72 The Cairo Citadel.
73 The mosque sits at the pinnacle of the Cairo Citadel.
74 James Thomson, *The Seasons* (1726–30).
75 Gate of Victory: the gate of Cairo; the city of the dead is a huge cemetery in southeastern Cairo.
76 Stimulating medicine or drink.
77 Soil.
78 Towers of the Cairo Citadel.

About half an hour before midnight sounds the Abrar ... or call to prayer, at which time the latest wanderers return home to prepare for the Sahur, their morning meal. You are careful on the way to address each sentinel with a "peace be upon thee!" especially if you have no lantern, otherwise you may chance to sleep in the guard-house. And, *chemin faisant*,[79] you cannot but stop to gaze at streets as little like what civilised Europe understands by that name as is an Egyptian temple to the new Houses of Parliament.[80]

There are certain scenes, cannily termed "Kenspeckle,"[81] that print themselves upon memory, and which endure as long as memory endures,—a thundercloud bursting upon the Alps, a night of stormy darkness off the Cape, and, perhaps, most awful of all, a solitary journey over the sandy desert.

Of this class is a stroll through the streets of old Cairo by night. All is squalor in the brilliancy of noon-day. In darkness you see nothing but a mere silhouette. But when the moon is high in the heavens, with the summer stars raining light upon God's world, there is something not of earth in the view. A glimpse at the strip of pale blue sky above scarcely reveals "three ells[82] of breadth:" in many places the interval is less; here the copings[83] meet, and there the outriggings[84] of the houses seem to be interlaced. Now they are parted by a pencil, then by a flood of silvery splendour, while under the projecting cornices and the huge hanging windows of fantastic wood-work, supported by gigantic corbels, and deep verandas, and gateways huge enough for Behemoth to pass through, and blind wynds[85] and long cul-de-sacs, lie patches of thick darkness, made visible by the dimmest of oil lights. The arch is a favourite feature: in one place you see it a mere skeleton of stone opening into some huge deserted hall; in another it is full of fretted stone and carved wood. Not a line is straight, the huge dead walls of the mosques slope over their massy buttresses, and the thin minarets seem about to fall across your path. The cornices project crookedly from the houses, and the great gables stand merely by force of cohesion. And that the line of beauty may not be wanting, the graceful bending form of the palm, on whose topmost feathers, quivering in the breeze, the moonbeam glistens, springs from a gloomy mound, or from the darkness of a mass of houses almost level with the ground. Briefly the whole view is so drear, so fantastic, so ghostly, that it seems rather preposterous to imagine that in such places human beings like ourselves can be born, and live through life, to carry out the command "increase and multiply,"[86] and die.

---

79   French: as you go along.
80   The British Houses of Parliament were rebuilt following a fire in 1834.
81   Conspicuous.
82   An ell is a unit of measurement varying in length between different countries; in England, about 114 cm.
83   The highest layer of masonry in a wall.
84   A structure projecting from the outside of a building.
85   Narrow street or alley.
86   Genesis 1:22.

David Livingstone
from *Missionary Travels and Researches in South Africa* (1857)

Missionary and African explorer David Livingstone (1813–73) came from a poor Scottish family. Working in cotton mills from age ten, he read at his spinning jenny, attended school after work, and financed his medical education. He joined the London Missionary Society, whose work took him to South Africa in 1840 and initiated a life of exploration, anti-slavery activism, and Christian service. In three journeys, he explored the Zambesi River, gave Victoria Falls its name, and sought the Nile's source as well as a route to the coast from the Zambesi. Hailed as a British hero, he won the Royal Geographical Society's gold medal and met Queen Victoria.

His *Missionary Travels and Researches in South Africa* (1857) sold out before publication. This excerpt details his call to Christian service, his arrival in South Africa, and his conversations with Sechele, a Christian convert. These accounts provide a glimpse of how he nurtured relationships with Africans, learning Setswana and discussing the cultural dimensions of Christian conversion.

~

Introduction

… The earliest recollection of my mother recalls a picture so often seen among the Scottish poor—that of the anxious housewife striving to make both ends meet. At the age of ten I was put into the factory as a "piecer,"[87] to aid by my earnings in lessening her anxiety. With a part of my first week's wages I purchased Ruddiman's "Rudiments of Latin,"[88] and pursued the study of that language for many years afterwards, with unabated ardour, at an evening school, which met between the hours of eight and ten. The dictionary part of my labours was followed up till twelve o'clock, or later, if my mother did not interfere by jumping up and snatching the books out of my hands. I had to be back in the factory by six in the morning, and continue my work, with intervals for breakfast and dinner, till eight o'clock at night. I read in this way many of the classical authors, and knew Virgil and Horace[89] better at sixteen than I do now. Our schoolmaster—happily still alive—was supported in part by the company;[90] he was attentive and kind, and so moderate in his charges that all who wished for education might have obtained it….

In the glow of love which Christianity inspires, I soon resolved to devote my life to the alleviation of human misery. Turning this idea over in my mind, I felt that to be a pioneer of Christianity … might lead to the material benefit of some portions of that immense empire; and therefore set myself to obtain a medical education, in order to be qualified for that enterprise….

---

87   A small person or child employed in a textile factory to join any yarn or threads that broke during production.
88   Thomas Ruddiman, *Rudiments of the Latin Tongue* (1714).
89   Virgil (70–19 BCE) and Horace (65–8 BCE), Roman poets.
90   Henry Monteith & Co., a cotton company, supported the schooling of the children working there by building a school for child-workers and workers' children, which was used on the weekends as a chapel.

My reading while at work was carried on by placing the book on a portion of the spinning jenny,[91] so that I could catch sentence after sentence as I passed at my work; I thus kept up a pretty constant study undisturbed by the roar of the machinery.... The toil of cotton-spinning, to which I was promoted in my nineteenth year, was excessively severe on a slim loose-jointed lad, but it was well paid for; and it enabled me to support myself while attending medical and Greek classes in Glasgow in winter, as also the divinity lectures of Dr. Wardlaw,[92] by working with my hands in summer. I never received a farthing of aid from any one, and should have accomplished my project of going to China as a medical missionary in the course of time by my own efforts, had not some friends advised my joining the London Missionary Society on account of its perfectly unsectarian character.[93] It "sends neither episcopacy, nor presbyterianism, nor independency, but the gospel of Christ to the heathen."[94] This exactly agreed with my ideas of what a Missionary Society ought to do....

Chapter 1

The general instructions I received from the Directors of the London Missionary Society led me, as soon as I reached Kuruman or Lattakoo, then, as it is now, their farthest inland station from the Cape,[95] to turn my attention to the north. Without waiting longer at Kuruman than was necessary to recruit the oxen,[96] which were pretty well tired by the long journey from Algoa Bay, I proceeded, in company with another missionary, to the Bakuéna or Bakwain country, and found Sechele, with his tribe, located at Shokuáne.[97] We shortly after retraced our steps to Kuruman; but as the objects in view were by no means to be attained by a temporary excursion of this sort, I determined to make a fresh start into the interior as soon as possible. Accordingly, after resting three months at Kuruman, which is a kind of head station in the country, I returned to a spot about fifteen miles south of Shokuane, called Lepelóle (now Litubarúba). Here, in order to obtain an accurate knowledge of the language, I cut myself off from all European society for about six months, and gained by this ordeal an insight into the habits, ways of thinking, laws, and language of that section of the Bechuanas, called Bakwains,[98] which has proved of incalculable advantage in my intercourse with them ever since....

---

91 An industrial spinning wheel.
92 Livingstone studied both medicine, at Anderson's College, and Greek, at Glasgow University; Ralph Wardlaw (1779–1853), theologian.
93 Livingstone joined the London Missionary Society in 1838, after the termination of his summer work at the mill; they discontinued sending missionaries to China due to the Opium Wars (1839–42); unsectarian (non-sectarian) means unaffiliated with a specific religious group.
94 The latter part of this quotation ("the gospel of Christ to the heathen") is drawn from Adam Clarke, *Commentary on the Whole of Scripture* (8 vols., 1810–24).
95 The Cape of Good Hope, the southernmost point in Africa and a major port of South Africa (then Cape Colony); Kuruman is inland, north of the Orange River and northeast of the Cape.
96 To allow the oxen to recuperate.
97 Algoa Bay is east of the Cape's tip, near Port Elizabeth; the Bechuanaland Protectorate (also Bakuéna and Bakwain Land) was a British colony established in 1885; Shokuane (present-day Molepolole) is to the northwest of Gabrone in Botswana.
98 Now known as the Batswana or Tswana peoples; natives of present-day Botswana.

I attached myself to the tribe called Bakuena, or Bakwains, the chief of which, named Sechele, was then living with his people at a place called Shokuane. I was from the first struck by his intelligence, and by the marked manner in which we both felt drawn to each other....

Sechele was ... seated in his chieftainship when I made his acquaintance. On the first occasion in which I ever attempted to hold a public religious service, he remarked that it was the custom of his nation, when any new subject was brought before them, to put questions on it; and he begged me to allow him to do the same in this case. On expressing my entire willingness to answer his questions, he inquired if my forefathers knew of a future judgment. I replied in the affirmative, and began to describe the scene of the "great white throne, and Him who shall sit on it, from whose face the heaven and earth shall flee away,"[99] &c. He said, "You startle me—these words make all my bones to shake—I have no more strength in me: but my forefathers were living at the same time yours were, and how is it that they did not send them word about these terrible things sooner? ..." I got out of the difficulty by explaining the geographical barriers in the North, and the gradual spread of knowledge from the South, to which we first had access by means of ships; and I expressed my belief that, as Christ had said, the whole world would yet be enlightened by the Gospel.[100] Pointing to the great Kalahári desert,[101] he said, "You never can cross that country to the tribes beyond; it is utterly impossible even for us black men, except in certain seasons, when more than the usual supply of rain falls, and an extraordinary growth of water-melons follows. Even we who know the country would certainly perish without them." Re-asserting my belief in the words of Christ, we parted; and it will be seen further on that Sechele himself assisted me in crossing that desert which had previously proved an insurmountable barrier to so many adventurers.

As soon as he had an opportunity of learning, he set himself to read with such close application that, from being comparatively thin, the effect of having been fond of the chase, he became quite corpulent from want of exercise. Mr. Oswell[102] gave him his first lesson in figures, and he acquired the alphabet on the first day of my residence at Chonuane.[103] He was by no means an ordinary specimen of the people, for I never went into the town but I was pressed to hear him read some chapters of the Bible....

Seeing me anxious that his people should believe the words of Christ, he once said, "Do you imagine these people will ever believe by your merely talking to them? I can make them do nothing except by thrashing them; and if you like, I shall call my head men, and with our litupa (whips of rhinoceros-hide) we will soon make them all believe together." The idea of using entreaty and persuasion to subjects to become Christians—whose opinion on no other matter would he condescend to ask—was especially surprising to him. He considered that they ought only to be too happy to embrace Christianity at his command. During the space of two years and a half he continued to profess to his people his full conviction of the truth of Christianity; and in all discussions on the subject he took that side, acting at the same time in an upright manner in all the relations of life. He felt the difficulties of his situation long before I did, and often said, "O, I wish you had come to this country before I became entangled in the meshes of our customs!" In fact, he could not get rid of his superfluous wives, without appearing to be ungrateful to their parents, who had done so much for him in his adversity.

---

99 Revelation 20:11.
100 Romans 10:17–18.
101 The desert begins north of the Orange River, extending through South Africa, Namibia, and Botswana.
102 William Cotton Oswell (1818–93), explorer.
103 In South Africa, near the border with Botswana.

In the hope that others would be induced to join him in his attachment to Christianity, he asked me to begin family worship with him in his house. I did so; and by-and-by was surprised to hear how well he conducted the prayer in his own simple and beautiful style, for he was quite a master of his own language....

When he at last applied for baptism,[104] I simply asked him how he, having the Bible in his hand, and able to read it, thought he ought to act. He went home, gave each of his superfluous wives new clothing, and all his own goods, which they had been accustomed to keep in their huts for him, and sent them to their parents with an intimation that he had no fault to find with them, but that in parting with them he wished to follow the will of God.... Here commenced an opposition which we had not previously experienced. All the friends of the divorced wives became the opponents of our religion. The attendance at school and church diminished to very few besides the chief's own family. They all treated us still with respectful kindness, but to Sechele himself they said things which, as he often remarked, had they ventured on in former times, would have cost them their lives. It was trying, after all we had done, to see our labours so little appreciated; but we had sown the good seed,[105] and have no doubt but it will yet spring up, though we may not live to see the fruits....

In our relations with this people we were simply strangers exercising no authority or control whatever. Our influence depended entirely on persuasion; and, having taught them by kind conversation as well as by public instruction, I expected them to do what their own sense of right and wrong dictated. We never wished them to do right merely because it would be pleasing to us, nor thought ourselves to blame when they did wrong, although we were quite aware of the absurd idea to that effect. We saw that our teaching did good to the general mind of the people by bringing new and better motives into play. Five instances are positively known to me in which by our influence on public opinion war was prevented; and where, in individual cases, we failed, the people did no worse than they did before we came into the country. In general they were slow, like all the African people hereafter to be described, in coming to a decision on religious subjects; but in questions affecting their worldly affairs they were keenly alive to their own interests. They might be called stupid in matters which had not come within the sphere of their observation, but in other things they showed more intelligence than is to be met with in our own uneducated peasantry. They are remarkably accurate in their knowledge of cattle, sheep, and goats, knowing exactly the kind of pasturage suited to each; and they select with great judgment the varieties of soil best suited to different kinds of grain. They are also familiar with the habits of wild animals, and in general are well up in the maxims which embody their ideas of political wisdom....

The belief in the gift or power of *rain-making* is one of the most deeply-rooted articles of faith in this country. The chief Sechele was himself a noted rain-doctor, and believed in it implicitly. He has often assured me that he found it more difficult to give up his faith in that than in anything else which Christianity required him to abjure. I pointed out to him that the only feasible way of watering the gardens was to select some good never-failing river, make a canal, and irrigate the adjacent lands. This suggestion was immediately adopted, and soon the whole tribe was on the move to the Kolobeng, a stream about forty miles distant. The experiment succeeded admirably during the first year. The Bakwains made the canal and dam in exchange for my labour in assisting to build a square house for their chief. They also built their own school under my superintendence.... But in our second year again no rain fell. In the third the

---

104 The Christian rite of baptism signals the cleansing of sin.
105 Matthew 13:37.

same extraordinary drought followed. Indeed, not ten inches of water fell during these two years, and the Kolobeng ran dry; so many fish were killed that the hyænas from the whole country round collected to the feast, and were unable to finish the putrid masses. A large old alligator, which had never been known to commit any depredations, was found left high and dry in the mud among the victims. The fourth year was equally unpropitious, the fall of rain being insufficient to bring the grain to maturity.... The leaves of indigenous trees were all drooping, soft, and shrivelled, though not dead; and those of the mimosæ were closed at midday, the same as they are at night....

As the Bakwains believed that there must be some connection between the presence of "God's Word" in their town and these successive and distressing droughts, they looked with no good will at the church-bell, but still they invariably treated us with kindness and respect. I am not aware of ever having had an enemy in the tribe. The only avowed cause of dislike was expressed by a very influential and sensible man, the uncle of Sechele. "We like you as well as if you had been born among us; you are the only white man we can become familiar with (thoaëla); but we wish you to give up that everlasting preaching and praying; we cannot become familiar with that at all. You see we never get rain, while those tribes who never pray as we do obtain abundance." ...

The conduct of the people during this long-continued drought was remarkably good. The women parted with most of their ornaments to purchase corn from more fortunate tribes. The children scoured the country in search of the numerous bulbs and roots which can sustain life, and the men engaged in hunting....

In addition to other adverse influences, the general uncertainty, though not absolute want, of food, and the necessity of frequent absence for the purpose of either hunting game or collecting roots and fruits, proved a serious barrier to the progress of the people in knowledge. Our own education in England is carried on at the comfortable breakfast and dinner table and by the cosy fire, as well as in the church and school. Few English people with stomachs painfully empty would be decorous at church any more than they are when these organs are overcharged. Ragged schools[106] would have been a failure had not the teachers wisely provided food for the body as well as food for the mind; and not only must we show a friendly interest in the bodily comfort of the objects of our sympathy as a Christian duty, but we can no more hope for healthy feelings among the poor, either at home or abroad, without feeding them into them, than we can hope to see an ordinary working-bee reared into a queen-mother by the ordinary food of the hive.

Sending the Gospel to the heathen must, if this view be correct, include much more than is implied in the usual picture of a missionary, namely, a man going about with a Bible under his arm. The promotion of commerce ought to be specially attended to, as this, more speedily than anything else, demolishes that sense of isolation which heathenism engenders, and makes the tribes feel themselves mutually dependent on, and mutually beneficial to, each other. With a view to this the missionaries at Kuruman got permission from the Government for a trader to reside at the station, and a considerable trade has been the result; the trader himself has become rich enough to retire with a competence.[107] Those laws which still prevent free commercial intercourse among the civilized nations seem to be nothing else but the remains of our own heathenism. My observations on this subject make me extremely desirous to promote the preparation of the raw materials of European manufactures in Africa, for by that means we may not only put a stop

---

106 Free schools for poor children.
107 Adequate means for living in comfort.

to the slave-trade, but introduce the negro family into the body corporate of nations, no one member of which can suffer without the others suffering with it. Success in this, in both Eastern and Western Africa, would lead, in the course of time, to a much larger diffusion of the blessings of civilization than efforts exclusively spiritual and educational confined to any one small tribe.[108] These, however, it would of course be extremely desirable to carry on at the same time at large central and healthy stations, for neither civilization nor Christianity can be promoted alone. In fact, they are inseparable.

Henry Walter Bates

from *The Naturalist on the River Amazons, a Record of Adventures, Habits of Animals, Sketches of Brazilian and Indian Life, and Aspects of Nature under the Equator, during Eleven Years of Travel* (1863)

Naturalist Henry Walter Bates (1825–92) attended a village academy; in 1838, he continued school at a mechanics' institute while working as a hosier. As a self-taught naturalist, he collected insects after work. In 1844, Bates met Alfred Russel Wallace (see Travel and Exploration), schoolteacher and naturalist; they planned an Amazon expedition, sailing in 1848. Wallace returned in 1852, but Bates remained for 11 years, shipping specimens for sale to museums and collectors. He collected almost 15,000 species, 8,000 previously undiscovered. After his return in 1859, he published on these collections (1859–62). An article caught the attention of Charles Darwin (see Science, Travel and Exploration), who became a correspondent and suggested that Bates publish his travels, recommending publisher John Murray. In 1864, Bates became the Royal Geographical Society's assistant secretary.

The Naturalist on the River Amazons (2 vols., 1863) enjoyed success, remaining in print for decades. Here, Bates vividly describes his interactions with a native family and laments the tribe's devastation by European diseases.

Volume 2, Chapter 4: Excursions in the Neighbourhood of Ega[109]

I will now proceed to give some account of the more interesting of my shorter excursions in the neighbourhood of Ega. The incidents of the longer voyages, which occupied each several months, will be narrated in a separate chapter....

---

108 Livingstone's accounts of the brutalities of the Arab slave trade in Africa reawakened British abolitionist fervour; he promoted legitimate trade instead as a means of spreading civilization.
109 Now known as Tefé, Brazil, on the banks of the Tefé and Amazon Rivers.

On the 23rd of May, 1850, I visited ... the Delegado, a family of the Passé tribe,[110] who live near the head waters of the [I]garapé, which flows from the south into the Teffé, entering it at Ega. The creek is more than a quarter of a mile broad near the town, but a few miles inland it gradually contracts, until it becomes a mere rivulet flowing through a broad dell in the forest. When the river rises it fills this dell; the trunks of the lofty trees then stand many feet deep in the water, and small canoes are able to travel the distance of a day's journey under the shade, regular paths or alleys being cut through the branches and lower trees. This is the general character of the country of the Upper Amazons;[111] a land of small elevation and abruptly undulated, the hollows forming narrow valleys in the dry months, and deep navigable creeks in the wet months. In retired nooks on the margins of these shady rivulets, a few families or small hordes of aborigines still linger in nearly their primitive state, the relicts of their once numerous tribes. The family we intended to visit on this trip was that of Pedro-uassú (Peter the Great, or Tall Peter), an old chieftain or Tushaúa of the Passés.

We set out at sunrise, in a small igarité,[112] manned by six young Indian paddlers. After travelling about three miles along the broad portion of the creek—which, being surrounded by woods, had the appearance of a large pool—we came to a part where our course seemed to be stopped by an impenetrable hedge of trees and bushes. We were some time before finding the entrance, but when fairly within the shades, a remarkable scene presented itself.... A narrow and tolerably straight alley stretched away for a long distance before us; on each side were the tops of bushes and young trees, forming a kind of border to the path, and the trunks of the tall forest trees rose at irregular intervals from the water, their crowns interlocking far over our heads, and forming a thick shade.... We travelled at good speed for three hours along this shady road; the distance of Pedro's house from Ega being about twenty miles. When the paddlers rested for a time, the stillness and gloom of the place became almost painful: our voices waked dull echoes as we conversed, and the noise made by fishes occasionally whipping the surface of the water was quite startling....

At length we arrived at our journey's end. We were then in a very dense and gloomy part of the forest: we could see, however, the dry land on both sides of the creek, and to our right a small sunny opening appeared, the landing-place to the native dwellings....

As we landed, Pedro-uassú himself came down to the port to receive us; our arrival having been announced by the barking of dogs. He was a tall and thin old man, with a serious, but benignant expression of countenance, and a manner much freer from shyness and distrust than is usual with Indians. He was clad in a shirt of coarse cotton cloth, dyed with murishí,[113] and trowsers of the same material turned up to the knee. His features were sharply delineated—more so than in any Indian face I had yet seen; the lips thin and the nose rather high and compressed. A large, square, blue-black tattooed patch occupied the middle of his face, which, as well as the other exposed parts of his body, was of a light reddish-tan colour, instead of the usual coppery-brown hue.... The language used was Tupí:[114] I heard no other spoken all the day. It must be borne in mind that Pedro-uassú had never had much intercourse with whites: he was, although

---

110 Arawakan natives of Brazil.
111 The upper area of the Amazonas State, which occupies the northwestern region of Brazil.
112 Single-masted river boat.
113 A reddish brown dye, extracted from the bark of a Byrsonima plant.
114 An extinct Tupí-Guarani language.

baptised,[115] a primitive Indian, who had always lived in retirement; the ceremony of baptism having been gone through, as it generally is by the aborigines, simply from a wish to stand well with the whites.

Arrived at the house, we were welcomed by Pedro's wife: a thin, wrinkled, active old squaw,[116] tattooed in precisely the same way as her husband. She had also sharp features, but her manner was more cordial and quicker than that of her husband: she talked much, and with great inflection of voice; whilst the tones of the old man were rather drawling and querulous. Her clothing was a long petticoat of thick cotton cloth, and a very short chemise, not reaching to her waist. I was rather surprised to find the grounds around the establishment in neater order than in any sitio,[117] even of civilised people, I had yet seen on the Upper Amazons: the stock of utensils and household goods of all sorts was larger, and the evidences of regular industry and plenty more numerous than one usually perceives in the farms of civilised Indians and whites. The buildings were of the same construction as those of the humbler settlers in all other parts of the country. The family lived in a large, oblong, open shed built under the shade of trees. Two smaller buildings, detached from the shed and having mud-walls with low doorways, contained apparently the sleeping apartment of different members of the large household. A small mill for grinding sugar-cane, having two cylinders of hard notched wood; wooden troughs, and kettles for boiling the *guarápa* (cane juice), to make treacle, stood under a separate shed, and near it was a large enclosed mud-house for poultry. There was another hut and shed a short distance off, inhabited by a family dependent on Pedro, and a narrow pathway through the luxuriant woods led to more dwellings of the same kind. There was an abundance of fruit trees around the place, including the never-failing banana, with its long, broad, soft green leaf-blades, and groups of full-grown Pupúnhas, or peach palms. There was also a large number of cotton and coffee trees. Amongst the utensils I noticed baskets of different shapes, made of flattened maranta[118] stalks, and dyed various colours. The making of these is an original art of the Passés, but I believe it is also practised by other tribes, for I saw several in the houses of semi-civilised Indians on the Tapajos.[119]

There were only three persons in the house besides the old couple, the rest of the people being absent; several came in, however, in the course of the day. One was a daughter of Pedro's, who had an oval tattooed spot over her mouth; the second was a young grandson; and the third the son-in-law from Ega, Cardozo's *compadre*.[120] The old woman was occupied, when we entered, in distilling spirits from cará, an edible root similar to the potato, by means of a clay still, which had been manufactured by herself. The liquor had a reddish tint, but not a very agreeable flavour. A cup of it warm from the still, however, was welcome after our long journey.... The old lady was very talkative, and almost fussy in her desire to please her visitors. We sat in tucúm[121] hammocks, suspended between the upright posts of the shed. The young woman with the blue mouth—who, although married, was as shy as any young maiden of her race—soon became employed in scalding and plucking fowls for the dinner, near the fire on the ground at the other end of the dwelling....

---

115 The Christian rite of baptism signals the cleansing of sin.
116 Derogatory term for an aboriginal wife.
117 Spanish: space; site.
118 An evergreen plant with broad, flat leaves, species of which are native to almost all tropical areas in the world.
119 A river in central Brazil that flows north into the Amazon River.
120 Spanish: godfather.
121 Fibres taken from the leaves of a Brazilian palm tree.

I left them ... and went a long ramble into the forest, Pedro sending his grandson, a smiling well-behaved lad of about fourteen years of age, to show me the paths, my companion taking with him his *Zarabatana*, or blowpipe. This instrument is used by all the Indian tribes on the Upper Amazons. It is generally nine or ten feet long, and is made of two separate lengths of wood, each scooped out so as to form one half of the tube. To do this with the necessary accuracy requires an enormous amount of patient labour, and considerable mechanical ability, the tools used being simply the incisor teeth of the Páca and Cutía.[122] The two half tubes, when finished, are secured together by a very close and tight spirally-wound strapping, consisting of long flat strips of Jacitára, or the wood of the climbing palm-tree; and the whole is smeared afterwards with black wax, the production of a Melipona bee.[123] The pipe tapers towards the muzzle, and a cup-shaped mouthpiece, made of wood, is fitted in the broad end. A full-sized *Zarabatana* is heavy, and can only be used by an adult Indian who has had great practice. The young lads learn to shoot with smaller and lighter tubes....

We walked about two miles along a well-trodden pathway, through high caäpoeira (second-growth forest). A large proportion of the trees were Melastomas,[124] which bore a hairy yellow fruit, nearly as large and as well flavoured as our gooseberry. The season, however, was nearly over for them. The road was bordered every inch of the way by a thick bed of elegant Lycopodiums.[125] An artificial arrangement of trees and bushes could scarcely have been made to wear so finished an appearance as this naturally decorated avenue. The path at length terminated at a plantation of mandioca,[126] the largest I had yet seen since I left the neighbourhood of Pará. There were probably ten acres of cleared land, and part of the ground was planted with Indian corn, water-melons, and sugar-cane. Beyond this field there was only a faint hunter's track, leading towards the untrodden interior. My companion told me he had never heard of there being any inhabitants in that direction (the south). We crossed the forest from this place to another smaller clearing, and then walked, on our road home, through about two miles of caäpoeira of various ages, the sites of old plantations. The only fruits of our ramble were a few rare insects and a Japú (Cassicus cristatus), a handsome bird with chestnut and saffron-coloured plumage, which wanders through the tree-tops in large flocks. My little companion brought this down from a height which I calculated at thirty yards. The blowpipe, however, in the hands of an expert adult Indian, can be made to propel arrows so as to kill at a distance of fifty and sixty yards. The aim is most certain when the tube is held vertically, or nearly so. It is a far more useful weapon in the forest than a gun, for the report of a firearm alarms the whole flock of birds or monkeys feeding on a tree, whilst the silent poisoned dart brings the animals down one by one until the sportsman has a heap of slain by his side. None but the stealthy Indian can use it effectively. The poison, which must be fresh to kill speedily, is obtained only of the Indians who live beyond the cataracts of the rivers flowing from the north, especially the Rio Negro and the Japurá. Its principal ingredient is the wood of the Strychnos toxifera,[127] a tree which does not grow in the humid forests of the river plains....

When we returned to the house after mid-day ... [t]he widower was asleep; the stirring, managing old lady with her daughter were preparing dinner. This, which was ready soon after I entered, consisted

---

122 Both are South American rodents.
123 A stingless South and Central American honey bee.
124 A shrub with bright purple flowers.
125 Clubmoss, a fern-like creeping plant.
126 Cassava, a plant cultivated for its tubers, which are the staple of many native South American diets.
127 The plant is a source of curare, a paralyzing poison.

of boiled fowls and rice, seasoned with large green peppers and lemon juice, and piles of new, fragrant farinha[128] and raw bananas. It was served on plates of English manufacture on a tupé, or large plaited rush mat, such as is made by the natives pretty generally on the Amazons. Three or four other Indians, men and women of middle age, now made their appearance, and joined in the meal....

The horde of Passés of which Pedro-uassú was Tushaúa or chieftain, was at this time reduced to a very small number of individuals. The disease mentioned in the last chapter[129] had for several generations made great havoc amongst them; many, also, had entered the service of whites at Ega, and, of late years, intermarriages with whites, half-castes, and civilised Indians had been frequent. The old man bewailed the fate of his race ... with tears in his eyes. "The people of my nation," he said, "have always been good friends to the Caríwas (whites), but before my grandchildren are old like me the name of Passé will be forgotten." In so far as the Passés have amalgamated with European immigrants or their descendants, and become civilised Brazilian citizens, there can scarcely be ground for lamenting their extinction as a nation; but it fills one with regret to learn how many die prematurely of a disease which seems to arise on their simply breathing the same air as the whites....

The Passés are always spoken of in this country as the most advanced of all the Indian nations in the Amazons region. I saw altogether about thirty individuals of the tribe, and found them generally distinguishable from other Indians by their lighter colour, sharper features, and more open address. But these points of distinction were not invariable, for I saw individuals of the Jurí and Miránha tribes from the Upper Japurá; of the Catoquínos, who inhabit the banks of the Jurúa, 300 miles from its mouth; and of the Tucúnas of St. Paulo, who were scarcely distinguishable from Passés in all the features mentioned. It is remarkable that a small tribe, the Caishánas, who live in the very midst of all these superior tribes, are almost as debased physically and mentally as the Múras, the lowest of all the Indian tribes on the Amazons. Yet were they seen separately, many Caishánas could not be distinguished from Miránhas or Jurís, although none have such slender figures or are so frank in their ways as to be mistaken for Passés. I make these remarks to show that the differences between the nations or tribes of Indians are not absolute, and therefore that there is no ground for supposing any of them to have had an origin entirely different from the rest. Under what influences certain tribes, such as the Passés, have become so strongly modified in mental, social, and bodily features, it is hard to divine. The industrious habits, fidelity, and mildness of disposition of the Passés, their docility and, it may be added, their personal beauty, especially of the children and women, made them from the very first attractive to the Portuguese colonists. They were, consequently, enticed in great number from their villages and brought to Barra[130] and other settlements of the whites. The wives of governors and military officers from Europe were always eager to obtain children for domestic servants: the girls being taught to sew, cook, weave hammocks, manufacture pillow-lace, and so forth. They have been generally treated with kindness, especially by the educated families in the settlements. It is pleasant to have to record that I never heard of a deed of violence perpetrated, on the one side or the other, in the dealings between European settlers and this noble tribe of savages....

We started on our return to Ega at half-past four o'clock in the afternoon. Our generous entertainers loaded us with presents. There was scarcely room for us to sit in the canoe, as they had sent down ten

---

128 Starch or flour obtained from cassava roots.
129 From the previous chapter: "Nearly all the people were disfigured by dark blotches on the skin, the effect of a cutaneous disease very prevelant in this part of the country.... The disease would seem to be contagious."
130 Located where the Rio Grande joins the Rio São Francisco.

large bundles of sugar-cane, four baskets of farinha, three cedar planks, a small hamper of coffee, and two heavy bunches of bananas. After we were embarked the old lady came with a parting gift for me—a huge bowl of smoking-hot banana porridge. I was to eat it on the road "to keep my stomach warm." Both stood on the bank as we pushed off, and gave us their adios,[131] "Ikuána Tupána eirúm" (Go with God): a form of salutation taught by the old Jesuit missionaries.[132]

Emily Eden

from *"Up the Country": Letters Written to Her Sister from the Upper Provinces of India* (1866)

Writer and watercolour artist Emily Eden (1797–1869) came from an aristocratic family whose circle included politicians and diplomats; her father's career included ambassadorships to Spain and Holland. Educated at home, Eden read widely and honed her talents in watercolour sketching. After her parents died, she and sister Frances sailed to Calcutta with their brother George, who had been appointed governor general of India (1836–42). Eden's first book, *Portraits of the Princes and People of India* (1844), presented her lithographs; she also authored two novels and published letters (some of which appeared posthumously).

The Edens' extensive tour of northwest India became the foundation of *"Up the Country": Letters Written to Her Sister from the Upper Provinces of India* (1866). This excerpt from the book's opening contrasts colonial and British life, notes the delays in the reception of British news in India, and suggests the penetration of British fiction and popular science into imperial contexts.

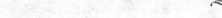

Chapter 1

On board the "Megna" flat,[133] *Saturday, Oct. 21, 1837.*
"Once more upon the waters, yet once more,"[134] and so on. We are now fairly off for eighteen months' of travelling by steamers, tents, and mountains—and every day of a cabin seems to me like so much waste.... Well, I am sure it is all for the best—I make no objection—I like to see things take their course; but still I do say, that for a person who required nothing but to be allowed the undisturbed enjoyment of that small Greenwich house and garden, with all its little Cockney[135] pleasures and pursuits, I have been very

---

131 Spanish: *adios*, literally meaning "to God," came to mean "goodbye."
132 Jesuits were active in Brazil in the sixteenth, seventeenth, and eighteenth centuries.
133 The Meghna (then Megna) Estuary and the Ganges Delta are comprised of sedimentary islands at the mouths of the Brahmaputra and Ganges rivers, on the Bay of Bengal; the Meghna River is a major tributary of the Brahmaputra.
134 George Gordon Byron, *Childe Harold's Pilgrimage* (1812–18).
135 Greenwich is a borough in London; cockneys are born Londoners.

hardly treated and rather over-worked. We got up at five this morning; the servants were all in a fuss, and Wright[136] was in all the delusions of carpet-bags and nice bandboxes,[137] in which she may be indulged till we leave the steamer, and then she will be obliged to wake from them, as the coolie[138] is yet to be discovered who would carry a carpet-bag, and a bandbox does not precisely meet the views of a camel.

When we came down for some coffee, the great hall was full of gentlemen who had come to accompany his lordship to the ghaut[139]—even Mr. Macaulay[140] had turned out for it. F.[141] and I, with Captain P., soon took ourselves off, and drove down to the landing-place. There were two lines of troops from the door of Government House[142] to the river, and the band was playing that march in the "Puritani"[143] which, when we were at the Admiralty,[144] used to be played every morning by the Guards' band, and which, consequently, always carries me back to the horrid time of our preparations for leaving England, so I can always cry it all over again to that tune. The road was covered with carriages and riders; and, at the ghaut, a large set of our particular acquaintances were waiting for us, so we got out and stood with them while G.[145] made his progress on foot. It was really a very pretty procession: such crowds of people and such diversities of dress. He is not so shy as he used to be at these ceremonies, though I think a long walk through troops presenting arms is trying to everybody. The instant he arrived at the ghaut, he gave a general good-bye, offered me his arm, and we walked off to the boats as fast as we could. The guns fired, the gentlemen waved their hats, and so we left Calcutta. It has really done handsomely by us, and we ought to be obliged to them for *saying*—if it is no more—that they are sorry we are going. But I dare-say we are an amusement to them. They liked our balls and parties, and whatever we did or said was the subject of an anecdote; and if we said or did nothing they invented something for us—and it all served to wonder at—which, in a country where there is little society and few topics, was an advantage.

The Sunderbunds,[146] *Monday, Oct. 23.*

We came into these lovely riant[147] scenes on Sunday morning. They are a composition of low stunted trees, marsh, tigers and snakes, with a stream that sometimes looks like a very wide lake and then becomes so narrow that the jungle wood scrapes against the sides of the flat—and this morning scraped away all G.'s jalousies,[148] which are a great loss. I never saw such a desolate scene: no birds flying about—there is no grain for them to eat. We have met only one native boat, which must have been there since the Deluge.[149] Occasionally there is a bamboo stuck up with a bush tied to it, which is to recall the cheerful fact that

---

136 Eden's lady's maid.
137 Hat boxes.
138 Hired native; a porter.
139 Landing for a boat; steps to a river.
140 Thomas Babington Macaulay (1800–59), writer who served in the supreme council of India, 1834–38.
141 Frances Eden (1801–49), Eden's sister.
142 The residence of the governor general.
143 Vincenzo Bellini's opera *I Puritani* (1835).
144 British navy headquarters.
145 George Eden (1784–1849), governor general of India and Eden's brother.
146 The Sunderbunds (also Sunderbans) is an area both of jungle and swamp and of agriculture between the Hooghly and Meghna rivers, at the mouth of the Ganges Delta.
147 Pleasant.
148 Shutters or blinds.
149 The biblical flood: Genesis 6–8.

there a tiger has carried off a man. None of our Hindus, though they are starving, will go on shore to cook—and, indeed, it would be very unsafe. It looks as if this bit of world had been left unfinished when land and sea were originally parted. The flat is dreadfully hot at night; but not more uncomfortable than a boat must necessarily be in this climate....

Wednesday, Oct. 25.
We stopped at Koolna yesterday for coals,[150] and stayed an hour to let the Hindus cook their dinner. We are out of the Sunderbunds now, and steaming between two banks not quite so elevated, nor nearly so picturesque as those flat marshes between Eastcombe and the river;[151] and, they say, we shall see nothing prettier, or rather less hideous, between this and Simla, except at Raj Mahl.[152] G. is already bored to death with having nothing to do. He has read two novels and cannot swallow any more, and is longing for his quiet cool room at Government House. The nights are dreadful—all for want of a punkah[153]—and hardly any of us get a wink of sleep. However, we shall soon overtake cooler weather. The six gentlemen passed the three first nights on deck, owing to the heat below, and I sat up in bed fanning myself. The native servants sleep any and everywhere, over our heads, under our feet, or at our doors, and as there are no partitions but green blinds at the sides and gratings above, of course we hear them coughing all night.

Thursday, Oct. 26.
They are steering us very badly; we go rolling about from one side of the river to the other, and every now and then thump against the bank, and then the chairs and table all shake and the inkstand tips over. I think I feel a little seasick. Our native servants look so unhappy. They hate leaving their families, and possibly leaving two or three wives is two or three times as painful as leaving one, and they cannot endure being parted from their children. Then they are too crowded here to sleep comfortably. Major J. observed in a gentle, ill-used voice: "I think Captain K. behaved very ill to us; he said that between both steamers and the flat he could lodge all the servants that were indispensably and absolutely necessary to us, so I only brought one hundred and forty, and now he says there is not room even for them." Certainly this boat must be drunk, she reels about in such a disorderly fashion. I wish I had my cork jacket[154] on.

I am glad that in your last letter you deigned for once to comment on the "Pickwick Papers."[155] I collected all the stray numbers, and began reading them straight through to-day,[156] because hitherto I have never had time to make out exactly what they were about, delightful as they were. I wish you would read over again that account of Winkle and the horse which will not go on—"Poor fellow! good old horse!"—and Pickwick saying, "It is like a dream, a horrid dream, to go about all day with a horrid horse that we cannot get rid of."[157] That book makes me laugh till I cry, when I am sitting quite by myself.—— There! I thought so. We are aground, and the other steamer is going flourishing by, in grinning delight.

---

150 Koolna was a coal depot on the Hooghly; coal was used to power steamships.
151 Southern Gloucestershire, between Wiltshire and the Severn River and Estuary.
152 Shimla (Simla), located in northernmost India, was the summer capital of India when it was a British colony; the Rajmahal, in northeastern India, is upriver from Calcutta, on the Ganges.
153 Large fan.
154 Life vest.
155 Charles Dickens, *The Pickwick Papers* (1836–37).
156 The *Pickwick Papers* were published serially; she is reading them in numerical order.
157 Eden paraphrases the scene from Part 2, Chapter 5 of the *Pickwick Papers* (April 1836).

Friday, Oct. 27.

We remained aground for two hours, and *touched* several times after we were afloat. Some of the other party visited us in the evening, and I lent General E. a novel to help him on. I have been reading "Astoria," out of that last box you sent us, and that great fat "Johnsoniana."[158] The anecdotes are not very new, but anything about Johnson is readable. G. has got some Bridgewater Treatises,[159] which he likes.

Beanleah,[160] *Saturday, Oct. 28.*

We stopped at Surder[161] yesterday, to take in some sheep. We ought to have been there two days ago, if we had had better pilots and fewer groundings. G. said, last night, when we again failed in landing there, that it seemed to him Absurder rather than Surder. He made another good pun to-day. How our intellects are weakened by the climate!—we make and relish puns! The A.D.C.'s[162] are very apt to assemble over our cabins at night, to smoke and to talk, and we hear every word they say. When it is really time to go to sleep, I generally send old Rosina up to disperse them, in her civilest manner. I was telling W.O.[163] that they were like so many old Chelsea pensioners;[164] they go on prosing night after night exclusively about the army, the king's army, and the company's army; and that if there were only a little levity in their talk, I should not so much mind being kept awake by it. He said, "Ah, yes, we were very animated last night about the company's army, and your old Rosina came creeping up with 'O sahib, *astai* bolo' (*gently* speak), upon which G. observed, 'Ah, if she had said, O sahib, *nasty* bolo!' that would have satisfied Emily much better." This joke being founded on Hindustani, and coming from the Governor-General, kept the whole suite in a roar of laughter for half an hour. They really relished it.

Two young writers whom we had known at Calcutta came to Surder to meet us, and we took them on board and took them back to Baulyah. How some of these young men must detest their lives! Mr.—— was brought up entirely at Naples and Paris, came out in the world when he was quite a boy, and cares for nothing but society and Victor Hugo's novels,[165] and that sort of thing. He is now stationed at B., and supposed to be very lucky in being appointed to such a cheerful station. The whole concern consists of five bungalows, very much like the thatched lodge at Langley. There are three married residents: one lady has bad spirits (small blame to her), and she has never been seen; another has weak eyes, and wears a large shade about the size of a common verandah; and the other has bad health, and has had her head shaved. A tour[166] is not to be had here for love or money, so she wears a brown silk cushion with a cap pinned to the top of it. The Doctor and our friend make up the rest of the society. He goes every morning to hear causes[167] between natives about strips of land or a few rupees—that lasts till five; then he rides about an

---

158 Washington Irving, *Astoria* (1836); James Boswell, *Johnsoniana; from Boswell's Life of the Great Lexicographer and Moralist* (1820).
159 A series of treatises "On the Power, Wisdom, and Goodness of God, as manifested in the Creation," funded through trust by the late Francis Henry, Earl of Bridgewater, and published by the Royal Society; see Bell (Science).
160 In northwestern Bangladesh, on the Indian border, on the Ganges.
161 Sardah, in northwestern Bangladesh, on the Indian border, on the Ganges.
162 *Aides-de-camp*, assistant officers to senior military officers.
163 Lord William Osborne, Eden's nephew.
164 Retired British Army members; a reference to the Royal Hospital Chelsea, a retirement home for army pensioners.
165 Victor Hugo (1802–85), French writer.
166 A front of false hair to be worn under a bonnet.
167 The case of one party in a lawsuit.

uninhabited jungle till seven; dines; reads a magazine, or a new book when he can afford one, and then goes to bed. A lively life, with the thermometer at several hundred!

Raj Mahl, Monday, Oct. 30.
We are now, after ten days' hard steaming, only 200 miles from Calcutta. G. sighs for the Salisbury "Highflyer"[168] and a good roadside inn; but to-day we have come to some hills and a pretty bit of country. We landed at four, saw the ruins, which are very picturesque, gave Chance[169] a run on shore, and we had time for one sketch. But the real genuine charm and beauty of Raj Mahl were a great fat Baboo[170] standing at the ghaut, with two bearers behind him carrying the post-office packet. There were letters by the "Madagascar," which left London the 20th July, and was only three months on her passage. I had your large packet, and ten letters. Altogether it was a great prize, was not it? and just at such an interesting period. I think the young Queen a charming invention,[171] and I can fancy the degree of enthusiasm she must excite. Even here we feel it. The account of her proroguing Parliament[172] gave me a lump in my throat; and then why is the Duchess of Kent[173] not with her in all these pageants? There is something mysterious about that. Probably nothing is more simple, or obvious, but still I should like to know what the mother and daughter say to each other when they meet in private. To return to your letters. There must have been one missing, because Newsalls suddenly burst upon me as your actual residence, whereas I did not know that there was such a place, that it had ever been built, or that you ever thought of taking it....

Alfred Russel Wallace
from *The Malay Archipelago: The Land of the Orang-utan, and the Bird of Paradise. A Narrative of Travel, with Studies of Man and Nature* (1869)

Self-taught naturalist Alfred Russel Wallace (1823–1913) trained in practical trades (surveying, watchmaking, and building), attended Mechanics' Institutes, studied in libraries, and lectured on science. Having become a schoolmaster in 1843, he met Henry Walter Bates (see Travel and Exploration). They planned an 1848 Amazon expedition, hoping to earn money by collecting specimens. They also wished to investigate evolution, an idea they had encountered in *Vestiges of the Natural History of Creation* (1844) by Robert Chambers (see Science). In 1852, Wallace returned to England and published a travel account and a study of palm trees (both 1853). In 1858, Wallace sent Charles

---

168 Salisbury is in Wiltshire; the Highflyer is a fast stagecoach.
169 Eden's dog.
170 Also Babu; an elderly Indian gentleman.
171 Victoria acceded to the throne on 20 June 1837, at age 18.
172 Proroguing is the ending of a parliamentary session, usually done by a speech from the throne; Queen Victoria delivered her prorogation speeches in person rather than through a representative.
173 Victoria's mother, whom Victoria greatly disliked; although convention required her to continue to live with her mother until marriage, Victoria had banned her mother from her presence upon assuming the role of queen.

Darwin (see Science, Travel and Exploration) an essay that outlined his basic theory of evolution; Charles Lyell (see Science) and Joseph Hooker presented it with two of Darwin's unpublished papers to the Linnean Society.

Wallace's journey to the Malay archipelago (1854–62) netted 126,500 specimens, including over 1,200 new species of birds and insects. This selection from *The Malay Archipelago* (1869) describes Wallace's efforts to collect orangutan specimens.

∼

Volume 1, Chapter 4: Borneo—The Orang-utan

I arrived at Sarawak[174] on November 1st, 1854, and left it on January 25th, 1856. In the interval I resided at many different localities, and saw a good deal of the Dyak tribes as well as of the Bornean Malays....[175] [S]o many books have been written about this part of Borneo[176] since I was there, that I shall avoid going into details of what I saw and heard and thought of Sarawak and its ruler, confining myself chiefly to my experiences as a naturalist in search of shells insects birds and the Orang-utan, and to an account of a journey through a part of the interior seldom visited by Europeans....

One of my chief objects in coming to stay at Simunjon[177] was to see the Orang-utan (or great man-like ape of Borneo) in his native haunts, to study his habits, and obtain good specimens of the different varieties and species of both sexes, and of the adult and young animals. In all these objects I succeeded beyond my expectations, and will now give some account of my experience in hunting the Orang-utan, or "Mias," as it is called by the natives; and as this name is short, and easily pronounced, I shall generally use it in preference to Simia satyrus,[178] or Orang-utan.

Just a week after my arrival at the mines, I first saw a Mias. I was out collecting insects, not more than a quarter of a mile from the house, when I heard a rustling in a tree near, and, looking up, saw a large red-haired animal moving slowly along, hanging from the branches by its arms. It passed on from tree to tree till it was lost in the jungle, which was so swampy that I could not follow it....

On the 12th of May I found another, ... howling and hooting with rage, and throwing down branches. I shot at it five times, and it remained dead on the top of the tree, supported in a fork in such a manner that it would evidently not fall. I therefore returned home, and luckily found some Dyaks, who came back with me, and climbed up the tree for the animal. This was the first full-grown specimen I had obtained; but it was a female, and not nearly so large or remarkable as the full-grown males. It was, however, 3 ft. 6 in. high, and its arms stretched out to a width of 6 ft. 6 in. I preserved the skin of this specimen in a cask of arrack,[179] and prepared a perfect skeleton, which was afterwards purchased for the Derby Museum.

---

174 Malaysian state in northwestern Borneo.
175 The Dyaks (also Dayaks) are natives of Borneo; the Malays are an ethnic group of Oceanic and Southeast Asian peoples living in various areas of the Malay Peninsula, including Borneo.
176 An island in the Malay Peninsula, in Southeast Asia.
177 An inland city in southwestern Sarawak.
178 The scientific classification for the Bornean Orangutan.
179 A Southeast Asian alcohol.

Only four days afterwards some Dyaks saw another Mias near the same place, and came to tell me. We found it to be a rather large one, very high up on a tall tree. At the second shot it fell rolling over, but almost immediately got up again and began to climb. At a third shot it fell dead. This was also a full-grown female, and while preparing to carry it home, we found a young one face downwards in the bog.... Luckily it did not appear to have been wounded, and after we had cleaned the mud out of its mouth it began to cry out, and seemed quite strong and active. While carrying it home it got its hands in my beard, and grasped so tightly that I had great difficulty in getting free, for the fingers are habitually bent inwards at the last joint so as to form complete hooks. At this time it had not a single tooth, but a few days afterwards it cut its two lower front teeth. Unfortunately, I had no milk to give it.... I was therefore obliged to give it rice-water from a bottle with a quill in the cork, which after a few trials it learned to suck very well. This was very meagre diet, and the little creature did not thrive well on it....

After five weeks it cut its two upper front teeth, but in all this time it had not grown the least bit, remaining both in size and weight the same as when I first procured it. This was no doubt owing to the want of milk or other equally nourishing food. Rice-water, rice, and biscuits were but a poor substitute, and the expressed milk of the cocoa-nut which I sometimes gave it did not quite agree with its stomach. To this I imputed an attack of diarrhœa from which the poor little creature suffered greatly, but a small dose of castor-oil[180] operated well, and cured it. A week or two afterwards it was again taken ill, and this time more seriously.... It lost all appetite for its food, and, after lingering for a week a most pitiable object, died, after being in my possession nearly three months.... I preserved its skin and skeleton, and in doing so found that when it fell from the tree it must have broken an arm and a leg, which had, however, united so rapidly that I had only noticed the hard swellings on the limbs where the irregular junction of the bones had taken place.

Exactly a week after I had caught this interesting little animal I succeeded in shooting a full-grown male Orang-utan. I had just come home from an entomologising[181] excursion when Charles[182] rushed in out of breath with running and excitement, and exclaimed, interrupted by gasps, "Get the gun, sir,—be quick,—such a large Mias!" "Where is it?" I asked, taking hold of my gun as I spoke, which happened luckily to have one barrel loaded with ball. "Close by, sir—on the path to the mines—he can't get away." ...

... After a short time I heard a very slight rustling sound overhead, but on gazing up could see nothing. I moved about in every direction to get a full view into every part of the tree under which I had been standing, when I again heard the same noise but louder, and saw the leaves shaking as if caused by the motion of some heavy animal which moved off to an adjoining tree. I immediately shouted for all [the others] to come up and try and get a view, so as to allow me to have a shot. This was not an easy matter, as the Mias had a knack of selecting places with dense foliage beneath. Very soon, however, one of the Dyaks called me and pointed upwards, and on looking I saw a great red hairy body and a huge black face gazing down from a great height, as if wanting to know what was making such a disturbance below. I instantly fired, and he made off at once, so that I could not then tell whether I had hit him.

... Once while loading I had a splendid view of him, moving along a large limb of a tree in a semi-erect posture, and showing him to be an animal of the largest size. At the path he got on to one of the loftiest

---

180 This oil was used medicinally, although it is a laxative and would not, therefore, cure diarrhea.
181 Insect studying.
182 Author's note: Charles Allen, an English lad of sixteen, accompanied me as an assistant.

trees in the forest, and we could see one leg hanging down useless, having been broken by a ball. He now fixed himself in a fork, where he was hidden by thick foliage, and seemed disinclined to move. I was afraid he would remain and die in this position, and as it was nearly evening I could not have got the tree cut down that day. I therefore fired again, and he then moved off, and going up the hill was obliged to get on to some lower trees, on the branches of one of which he fixed himself in such a position that he could not fall, and lay all in a heap as if dead, or dying.

I now wanted the Dyaks to go up and cut off the branch he was resting on, but they were afraid, saying he was not dead, and would come and attack them. We then shook the adjoining tree, pulled the hanging creepers, and did all we could to disturb him, but without effect, so I thought it best to send for two Chinamen with axes to cut down the tree.... The tree was luckily a small one, so when the axes came we soon had it cut through; but it was so held up by jungle ropes and climbers to adjoining trees that it only fell into a sloping position. The Mias did not move, and I began to fear that after all we should not get him, as it was near evening, and half a dozen more trees would have to be cut down before the one he was on would fall. As a last resource we all began pulling at the creepers, which shook the tree very much, and, after a few minutes, when we had almost given up all hopes, down he came with a crash and a thud like the fall of a giant. And he was a giant, his head and body being full as large as a man's. He was of the kind called by the Dyaks "Mias Chappan," or "Mias Pappan," which has the skin of the face broadened out to a ridge or fold at each side. His outstretched arms measured seven feet three inches across, and his height, measuring fairly from the top of the head to the heel, was four feet two inches. The body just below the arms was three feet two inches round, and was quite as long as a man's, the legs being exceedingly short in proportion. On examination we found he had been dreadfully wounded. Both legs were broken, one hip-joint and the root of the spine completely shattered, and two bullets were found flattened in his neck and jaws. Yet he was still alive when he fell. The two Chinamen carried him home tied to a pole, and I was occupied with Charley the whole of the next day, preparing the skin and boiling the bones to make a perfect skeleton, which are now preserved in the Museum at Derby....

The Dyaks all declare that the Mias is never attacked by any animal in the forest, with two rare exceptions; and the accounts I received of these are so curious that I give them nearly in the words of my informants, old Dyak chiefs, who had lived all their lives in the places where the animal is most abundant. The first of whom I inquired said: "No animal is strong enough to hurt the Mias, and the only creature he ever fights with is the crocodile. When there is no fruit in the jungle, he goes to seek food on the banks of the river, where there are plenty of young shoots that he likes, and fruits that grow close to the water. Then the crocodile sometimes tries to seize him, but the Mias gets upon him, and beats him with his hands and feet, and tears him and kills him." He added that he had once seen such a fight, and that he believes that the Mias is always the victor.

My next informant was the Orang Kaya, or chief of the Balow Dyaks, on the Simūnjon River.[183] He said: "The Mias has no enemies; no animals dare attack it but the crocodile and the python. He always kills the crocodile by main strength, standing upon it, pulling open its jaws, and ripping up its throat. If a python attacks a Mias, he seizes it with his hands, and then bites it, and soon kills it. The Mias is very strong; there is no animal in the jungle so strong as he."

---

183 A tributary of the Sadong River, in southwestern Sarawak.

It is very remarkable that an animal so large, so peculiar, and of such a high type of form as the Orang-utan, should be confined to so limited a district—to two islands, and those almost the last inhabited by the higher Mammalia;[184] for, eastward of Borneo and Java,[185] the Quadrumania, Ruminants, Carnivora,[186] and many other groups of Mammalia, diminish rapidly, and soon entirely disappear. When we consider, further, that almost all other animals have in earlier ages been represented by allied yet distinct forms—that, in the latter part of the tertiary period,[187] Europe was inhabited by bears, deer, wolves, and cats; Australia by kangaroos and other marsupials; South America by gigantic sloths and ant-eaters; all different from any now existing, though intimately allied to them—we have every reason to believe that the Orang-utan, the Chimpanzee, and the Gorilla have also had their forerunners. With what interest must every naturalist look forward to the time when the caves and tertiary deposits of the tropics may be thoroughly examined, and the past history and earliest appearance of the great man-like apes be at length made known.

Henry M. Stanley

from *How I Found Livingstone; Travels, Adventures, and Discoveries in Central Africa; Including Four Months' Residence with Dr. Livingstone*[188] (1872)

Journalist and explorer Henry Morton Stanley (1841–1904) was baptized John Rowlands. An illegitimate child, he was placed in a workhouse (1847–56), where he acquired a basic education. He subsequently worked as a pupil teacher, farm-hand, butcher's assistant, and cabin boy. Having jumped ship in New Orleans, he took the name of the cotton trader Henry Hope Stanley, whom he considered a father figure. Stanley fought in the Civil War (for South *and* North) before his career in journalism. In 1867, he convinced the *New York Herald*'s James Gordon Bennett to appoint him special correspondent; he reported from Abyssinia, Suez, Spain, and Turkey. In 1868, Bennett dispatched Stanley to Africa to interview David Livingstone (see Travel and Exploration), then unheard of for two years. Stanley located Livingstone at Ujiji, on Lake Tanganyika.

This excerpt from *How I Found Livingstone* (1872) records their meeting. Stanley's well-known greeting, "Dr. Livingstone, I presume?" was probably scripted after the fact.

---

184 Mammals, including marsupials.
185 Indonesian islands.
186 Quadrumana is an outdated term for non-human primates; ruminants are hoofed mammals, such as cows, goats, and antelopes; Carnivora are carnivores, such as tigers, foxes, and badgers.
187 The first period of the Cenozoic era and the formative period for modern plants and animals.
188 David Livingstone (1813–73), doctor, missionary, and African explorer; he had set off from England in 1866 to Zanzibar, to seek the source of the Nile River; see Travel and Exploration.

Introductory

On the sixteenth day of October, in the year of our Lord one thousand eight hundred and sixty-nine, I am in Madrid, fresh from the carnage at Valencia.[189] At 10 A.M. Jacopo, at No.—Calle de la Cruz, hands me a telegram: on opening it I find it reads, "Come to Paris on important business." The telegram is from Jas. Gordon Bennett, jun.,[190] the young manager of the "New York Herald." ...

At 3 P.M. I was on my way, and being obliged to stop at Bayonne[191] a few hours, did not arrive at Paris until the following night. I went straight to the "Grand Hotel," and knocked at the door of Mr. Bennett's room.

"Come in," I heard a voice say.

Entering, I found Mr. Bennett in bed.

"Who are you?" he asked.

"My name is Stanley!" I answered.

"Ah, yes! sit down; I have important business on hand for you."

After throwing over his shoulders his robe-de-chambre,[192] Mr. Bennett asked, "Where do you think Livingstone is?"

"I really do not know, sir!"

"Do you think he is alive?"

"He may be, and he may not be!" I answered.

"Well, I think he is alive, and that he can be found, and I am going to send you to find him."

"What!" said I, "do you really think I can find Dr. Livingstone? Do you mean me to go to Central Africa?"

"Yes; I mean that you shall go, and find him wherever you may hear that he is, and to get what news you can of him, and perhaps ... the old man may be in want:—take enough with you to help him should he require it. Of course you will act according to your own plans, and do what you think best—BUT FIND LIVINGSTONE![*] ...

"Good-night, sir," I said; "what it is in the power of human nature to do I will do; and on such an errand as I go upon, God will be with me." ...

Chapter 11: Through Ukawendi, Uvinza, and Uhha, to Ujiji[193]

... *November 3rd.*—What contention have we not been a witness to these last three days! What anxiety have we not suffered ever since our arrival in Uvinza!... We got the donkey across[194] with the aid of a mganga, or medicine man, who spat some chewed leaves of a tree which grows close to the stream over

---

189 Madrid, in central Spain; Valencia, on the eastern coast of Spain; Stanley was in Spain following the deposition of Queen Isabella of Spain (1868) and reported on the Republican uprisings of 1869, the seat of which was in Valencia.
190 James Gordon Bennett, Jr. (1841–1918), manager of the *New York Herald*.
191 On the southwestern coast of France, just north of the Spanish border.
192 French: bathrobe, dressing gown.
193 Uvinza is east of Lake Tanganyika, in present-day Tanzania; Ujiji is a village on the northeastern shore of Lake Tanganyika.
194 Across the Malagarasi River; the group had lost another donkey to crocodiles while crossing the river on the previous day.

him. He informed me he could cross the river at any time, day or night, after rubbing his body with these chewed leaves, which he believed to be a most potent medicine.

About 10 A.M. appeared from the direction of Ujiji a caravan of eighty Waguhha, a tribe which occupies a tract of country on the south-western side of the Lake Tanganika.[195] We asked the news, and were told a white man had just arrived at Ujiji from Manyuema.[196] This news startled us all.

"A white man?" we asked.

"Yes, a white man," they replied.

"How is he dressed?"

"Like the master," they answered, referring to me.

"Is he young, or old?"

"He is old. He has white hair on his face, and is sick."

"Where has he come from?"

"From a very far country away beyond Uguhha,[197] called Manyuema."

"Indeed! and is he stopping at Ujiji now?"

"Yes, we saw him about eight days ago."

"Do you think he will stop there until we see him?"

"*Sigue*" (don't know).

"Was he ever at Ujiji before?"

"Yes, he went away a long time ago."

Hurrah! This is Livingstone! He must be Livingstone! He *can* be no other; but still;—he may be some one else—some one from the West Coast—or perhaps he is Baker![198] No; Baker has no white hair on his face. But we must now march quick, lest he hears we are coming, and runs away.

I addressed my men, and asked them if they were willing to march to Ujiji without a single halt, and then promised them, if they acceded to my wishes, two doti[199] each man. All answered in the affirmative, almost as much rejoiced as I was myself. But I was madly rejoiced; intensely eager to resolve the burning question, "Is it Dr. David Livingstone?" God grant me patience, but I do wish there was a railroad, or, at least, horses in this country....

November 7th.— ... Bravely toiled the men, without murmur, though their legs were bleeding from the cruel grass. "Ambrosial morn"[200] at last appeared, with all its beautiful and lovely features.... The men, though fatigued at the unusual travel, sped forward with quicker pace as daylight broke, until, at 8 A.M., we sighted the swift Rusugi River,[201] when a halt was ordered in a clump of jungle near it, for breakfast and rest....

---

195 Lake Tanganyika, one of the largest and deepest lakes in the world, is on the border between the present-day countries of the Democratic Republic of the Congo, Zambia, Tanzania, and Burundi.
196 Now called Maniema; an area about 300 kilometres west of the northern tip of Lake Tanganyika in the present-day Congo.
197 A village on the northwestern side of Lake Tanganyika.
198 Samuel White Baker (1821–93), explorer.
199 A measure of cloth; two doti would be about seven metres of cloth.
200 William Mason, *Elfrida* (1752).
201 A northern tributary of the Malagarasi River, in present-day Tanzania, just south of Ujiji.

November 10th. Friday.— ... In two hours I am warned to prepare for a view of the Tanganika, for, from the top of a steep mountain the kirangozi[202] says I can see it.... And we press forward and up the hill breathlessly, lest the grand scene hasten away.... A little further on—just yonder, oh! there it is—a silvery gleam. I merely catch sight of it between the trees, and—but here it is at last! True—THE TANGANIKA! and there are the blue-black mountains of Ugoma and Ukaramba.[203] An immense broad sheet, a burnished bed of silver—lucid canopy of blue above—lofty mountains are its valances, palm forests form its fringes!...

"Was this the place where Burton and Speke[204] stood, Bombay, when they saw the lake first?"

"I don't remember, master; it was somewhere about here, I think."

"Poor fellows! The one was half-paralyzed, the other half-blind,"[205] said Sir Roderick Murchison,[206] when he described Burton and Speke's arrival in view of the Tanganika.

And I? Well, I am so happy that, were I quite paralyzed and blinded, I think that at this supreme moment I could take up my bed and walk,[207] and all blindness would cease at once. Fortunately, however, I am quite well; I have not suffered a day's sickness since the day I left Unyanyembe....[208]

We push on rapidly.... We arrive at the summit, travel across and arrive at its western rim, and—pause, reader—the port of Ujiji is below us, embowered in the palms, only five hundred yards from us!... At last the sublime hour has arrived!—our dreams, our hopes, and anticipations are now about to be realized! Our hearts and our feelings are with our eyes, as we peer into the palms and try to make out in which hut or house lives the white man with the grey beard we heard about on the Malagarazi.[209]

"Unfurl the flags, and load your guns!"

"Ay Wallah, ay Wallah, bana!"[210] respond the men, eagerly....

A volley from nearly fifty guns roars like a salute from a battery of artillery: we shall note its effect presently on the peaceful-looking village below.

"Now, kirangozi, hold the white man's flag up high, and let the Zanzibar flag bring up the rear. And you men keep close together, and keep firing until we halt in the market-place, or before the white man's house...."

Before we had gone a hundred yards our repeated volleys had the effect desired. We had awakened Ujiji to the knowledge that a caravan was coming, and the people were witnessed rushing up in hundreds to meet us. The mere sight of the flags informed every one immediately that we were a caravan, but the American flag borne aloft by gigantic Asmani, whose face was one vast smile on this day, rather staggered them at first. However, many of the people who now approached us remembered the flag. They had seen it float above the American Consulate, and from the masthead of many a ship in the harbor of Zanzibar,

---

202 Swahili: head guide.
203 The Ugoma are a chain of mountains on the western side of Lake Tanganyika; Ukaramba may refer to Karamba, a mountain at the northern tip of Lake Tanganyika.
204 Richard Burton (1821–90) (see Travel and Exploration) and John Speke (1827–64) were the first Europeans to find Lake Tanganyika (1858).
205 Upon reaching the lake, Speke and Burton both had malaria: Burton couldn't stand; Speke was almost blind, a recurring problem from a childhood illness.
206 Roderick Impey Murchison (1792–1871), president of the Royal Geological and Geographic Societies.
207 John 5:8.
208 Roughly halfway between Lake Tanganyika and the ocean in present-day Tanzania.
209 The Malagarasi River, just south of Ujiji.
210 Swahili: Yes, sir.

and they were soon heard welcoming the beautiful flag with cries of "Bindera Kisungu!"—a white man's flag! "Bindera Merikani!"—the American flag!

Then we were surrounded by them: by Wajiji, Wanyamwezi, Wangwana, Warundi, Waguhha, Wamanyuema and Arabs, and were almost deafened with the shouts of "Yambo, yambo, bana! Yambo, bana! Yambo, bana!" ...[211]

We were now about three hundred yards from the village of Ujiji, and the crowds are dense about me. Suddenly I hear a voice on my right say,

"Good morning, sir!"

Startled at hearing this greeting in the midst of such a crowd of black people, I turn sharply around in search of the man, and see him at my side, with the blackest of faces, but animated and joyous—a man dressed in a long white shirt, with a turban of American sheeting around his woolly head, and I ask:

"Who the mischief are you?"

"I am Susi, the servant of Dr. Livingstone," said he, smiling, and showing a gleaming row of teeth.

"What! Is Dr. Livingstone here?"

"Yes, sir."

"In this village?"

"Yes, sir."

"Are you sure?"

"Sure, sure, sir. Why, I leave him just now."

"Good morning, sir," said another voice.

"Hallo," said I, "is this another one?"

"Yes, sir."

"Well, what is your name?"

"My name is Chumah, sir."

"What! are you Chumah, the friend of Wekotani?"

"Yes, sir."

"And is the Doctor well?"

"Not very well, sir."

"Where has he been so long?"

"In Manyuema."

"Now, you Susi, run, and tell the Doctor I am coming."

"Yes, sir," and off he darted like a madman.

But by this time we were within two hundred yards of the village, and the multitude was getting denser, and almost preventing our march. Flags and streamers were out; Arabs and Wangwana were pushing their way through the natives in order to greet us, for, according to their account, we belonged to them. But the great wonder of all was, "How did you come from Unyanyembe?"

Soon Susi came running back, and asked me my name; he had told the Doctor that I was coming, but the Doctor was too surprised to believe him, and, when the Doctor asked him my name, Susi was rather staggered....

---

211 Swahili: Hello, sir!

In the meantime, the head of the Expedition had halted, and the kirangozi was out of the ranks, holding his flag aloft, and Selim said to me, "I see the Doctor, sir. Oh, what an old man! He has got a white beard." And I——what would I not have given for a bit of friendly wilderness, where, unseen, I might vent my joy in some mad freak, such as idiotically biting my hand, turning a somersault, or slashing at trees, in order to allay those exciting feelings that were well-nigh uncontrollable. My heart beats fast, but I must not let my face betray my emotions, lest it shall detract from the dignity of a white man appearing under such extraordinary circumstances.

So I did that which I thought was most dignified. I pushed back the crowds, and, passing from the rear, walked down a living avenue of people, until I came in front of the semicircle of Arabs, in the front of which stood the white man with the grey beard. As I advanced slowly towards him I noticed he was pale, looked wearied, had a grey beard, wore a bluish cap with a faded gold band round it, had on a red-sleeved waistcoat, and a pair of grey tweed trousers. I would have run to him, only I was a coward in the presence of such a mob—would have embraced him, only, he being an Englishman, I did not know how he would receive me; ... so I did what cowardice and false pride suggested was the best thing—walked deliberately to him, took off my hat, and said:

"Dr. Livingstone, I presume?"

"YES," said he, with a kind smile, lifting his cap slightly.

I replace my hat on my head, and he puts on his cap, and we both grasp hands, and I then say aloud: "I thank God, Doctor, I have been permitted to see you."

He answered, "I feel thankful that I am here to welcome you."

I turn to the Arabs, take off my hat to them in response to the saluting chorus of "Yambos" I receive, and the Doctor introduces them to me by name. Then, oblivious of the crowds, oblivious of the men who shared with me my dangers, we—Livingstone and I—turn our faces towards his tembe.[212] He points to the veranda, or, rather, mud platform, under the broad overhanging eaves; he points to his own particular seat, which I see his age and experience in Africa has suggested, namely, a straw mat, with a goatskin over it, and another skin nailed against the wall to protect his back from contact with the cold mud. I protest against taking this seat, which so much more befits him than me, but the Doctor will not yield: I must take it.

We are seated—the Doctor and I—with our backs to the wall. The Arabs take seats on our left. More than a thousand natives are in our front, filling the whole square densely, indulging their curiosity, and discussing the fact of two white men meeting at Ujiji—one just come from Manyuema, in the west, the other from Unyanyembe, in the east.

Conversation began. What about? I declare I have forgotten. Oh! we mutually asked questions of one another, such as: "How did you come here?" and "Where have you been all this long time?—the world has believed you to be dead." Yes, that was the way it began; but whatever the Doctor informed me, and that which I communicated to him, I cannot correctly report, for I found myself gazing at him, conning[213] the wonderful man at whose side I now sat in Central Africa. Every hair of his head and beard, every wrinkle of his face, the wanness of his features, and the slightly wearied look he wore, were all imparting intelligence to me—the knowledge I craved for so much ever since I heard the words, "Take what you want, but find Livingstone." ...

---

212 Swahili: hut.
213 Memorizing.

After giving orders to Bombay and Asmani for the provisioning of the men of the Expedition, I called "Kaif-Halek," or "How-do-ye-do," and introduced him to Dr. Livingstone as one of the soldiers in charge of certain goods left at Unyanyembe, whom I had compelled to accompany me to Ujiji, that he might deliver in person to his master the letter-bag he had been entrusted with by Dr. Kirk.[214] This was that famous letter-bag marked "Nov. 1st, 1870," which was now delivered into the Doctor's hands 365 days after it left Zanzibar![215] How long, I wonder, had it remained at Unyanyembe had I not been despatched into Central Africa in search of the great traveller?

The Doctor kept the letter-bag on his knee, then, presently, opened it, looked at the letters contained there, and read one or two of his children's letters, his face in the meanwhile lighting up.

He asked me to tell him the news. "No, Doctor," said I, "read your letters first, which I am sure you must be impatient to read."

"Ah," said he, "I have waited years for letters, and I have been taught patience. I can surely afford to wait a few hours longer. No, tell me the general news: how is the world getting along?"

"You probably know much already. Do you know that the Suez Canal is a fact—is opened,[216] and a regular trade carried on between Europe and India through it?"

... "Well, that is grand news! What else?"

Shortly I found myself enacting the part of an annual periodical to him.... The world had witnessed and experienced much the last few years. The Pacific Railroad had been completed; Grant had been elected President of the United States; Egypt had been flooded with savans; the Cretan rebellion had terminated; a Spanish revolution had driven Isabella from the throne of Spain, and a Regent had been appointed; ... the Queen of Fashion and the Empress of the French was a fugitive; and the child born in the purple had lost for ever the Imperial crown intended for his head; the Napoleon dynasty was extinguished by the Prussians, Bismarck and Von Moltke; and France, the proud empire, was humbled to the dust.[217]

... What a budget of news it was to one who had emerged from the depths of the primeval forests of Manyuema! The reflection of the dazzling light of civilisation was cast on him while Livingstone was thus listening in wonder to one of the most exciting pages of history ever repeated.... Who could tell under what new phases of uneasy life Europe was laboring even then, while we, two of her lonely children, rehearsed the tale of her late woes and glories? More worthily, perhaps, had the tongue of a lyric Demodocus[218] recounted them; but, in the absence of the poet, the newspaper correspondent performed his part as well and truthfully as he could.

---

214 John Kirk (1832–1922), doctor, explorer, and politician. He had worked with Livingstone on the expedition to Victoria Falls.
215 An island off the northern Tanzanian coast.
216 Completed in 1869, the Suez Canal allowed ships passage from the Indian and Pacific Oceans through to Europe.
217 The Pacific Railroad (completed 1869) crossed the United States; Ulysses Simpson Grant (1822–85), American president; Egypt had become a major fixation for intellectuals (*savants*) in the late nineteenth century; the Cretan Revolt (1866–69) against Ottoman dominion; in the Glorious Revolution, Queen Isabella abdicated in 1868, allowing her son, Alonso XII, to be restored to the throne during the Bourbon Restoration (1874); Eugénia María de Montijo de Guzmán (1826–1920), wife of Napoleon III who fled with him to England after their defeat in the Franco-Prussian war (1870–71) and who led the contemporary fashion for slim dresses; "the child born in the purple" is her child, Eugène Louis Jean Joseph Napoléon (1856–79), Prince Imperial; the Franco-Prussian War (1871–72), which France lost; Otto von Bismarck (1815–98), Prussian and German politician; Helmuth von Moltke "the Elder" (1800–91), German military leader.
218 A singer and poet in Homer, *Odyssey* (c. 630–600 BCE).

Anthony Trollope
from *Australia and New Zealand* (1873)

Prolific writer Anthony Trollope (1815–82) produced 47 novels as well as short stories, travel books, an autobiography, essays, biographies, histories, and sketches. Preoccupied from childhood with financial insecurity, Trollope became a London postal clerk through the connections of his mother (writer Frances Trollope). He worked extensively in Ireland, became post office surveyor of the eastern district, and introduced roadside pillar (mail) boxes in Great Britain before quitting the job in 1867. Though Trollope wrote novels during his early days at the post office, his career as a writer gained traction once he began to write while travelling by train for work. Trollope maintained detailed ledgers of how many pages he wrote per day.

Trollope authored four major travel books: *The West Indies and the Spanish Main* (1859), *North America* (1862), *Australia and New Zealand* (1873), and *South Africa* (1878). This excerpt focuses on Australia, a colony that particularly interested him because his son Frederick lived there.

Chapter 1: Introduction

I have attempted in these volumes to describe the Australian colonies as they at present exist; and to tell, in very brief fashion, the manner in which they were first created. In doing so, it has been impossible to avoid speculations as to their future prospects,—in which is involved the happiness of millions to come of English-speaking men and women. As a group, they are probably the most important of our colonial possessions, as they are certainly the most interesting. Their population is, indeed, still less than half that of the Canadian dominion; but they are very much younger than the Canadas; their increase has been much quicker;—and we made them for ourselves....

When we make mention of "colonies" we should be understood to signify countries outside our own, which by our energies we have made fit for the occupation of our multiplying race....

The Australias and New Zealand have been and still are colonies in every sense; and they are colonies which have been founded by ourselves exclusively,—for the prosperity and the deficiencies of which we and the colonies are solely responsible. No French element, no Dutch element, no Spanish element can be pleaded by us as having interfered with our operations in Australia. And the real colonization of these Eastern lands, which did not in truth commence till the system of using them as penal settlements had been condemned, has been so recent that the colonists and the Government at home have had the advantage of experience, and have taken lessons both from the successes and the failures of earlier enterprises....

... But there are still many in England who have to learn whether Australia is becoming a fitting home for them and their children, and the well-being of Australia still depends in a great degree on the tidings which may reach them. The great object of those who undertake to teach any such lesson, should, I think, be to make the student understand what he, in his condition of life, may be justified in expecting there,—and what are the manner and form of life into which he may probably fall. With this object in view, hoping that by diligence I might be able to do something towards creating a clearer knowledge of these colonies than at present perhaps exists, I have visited them all.... I hope I have done this without prejudice for or against the ways of a country to which I would not willingly migrate myself, being too old for such movement; but in which I have a son who has made his home there.

I should, perhaps, explain to the reader the method in which the different colonies are taken in my narrative. The course has been neither chronological nor geographical,—but has been arranged as I arranged my journey. I went first to Queensland, thence south to New South Wales,—the parent of Queensland; south again to Victoria, one of Queensland's elder sisters, and the most prosperous of the family,—and thence south again across the Straits to Tasmania, a daughter also of New South Wales, and the elder of the three.... I next visited Western Australia, which is far distant from the other colonies, and but little connected with them,—and from thence I went back to South Australia. Neither of these two colonies has sprung from any connection with New South Wales. Having thus visited the six Australian colonies, I went on to New Zealand, and returned home across the United States, journeying always eastwards....

I will venture to say once more that in all that I have written, I have endeavoured to keep in view the conviction that the mother country, in regarding her colonies,—such colonies as those of which I have written,—should think altogether of their welfare, and as little as may be of her own power and glory.

Chapter 4: Aboriginals

From Rockhampton I returned to Maryborough, with the intention of returning thence overland by Gympie to Brisbane....[219] I had touched at Maryborough on my way northwards, and as I saw a greater cluster of Australian black men at Maryborough than elsewhere, and as the question of the treatment of the black men is at present more important in Queensland than in the other colonies, I may as well say here what has to be said on this very disagreeable subject. There is an island—Frazer's Island—at the mouth of the Mary River, in which they are allowed to live without molestation,—no doubt because the place can be converted to no use by white settlers,—and here they seem to be almost amphibious. They live on fish, opossums, iguanas, and whatever can be filched from or may be given to them by their neighbours on the main land. As the steamers run up the river they swim off, thirty or forty of them coming together. A rope is flung out, and the captain generally allows one or two to come on board. These are taken up to Maryborough, where they loaf about, begging for money and tobacco, and return by the same boat on its downward journey. They are not admitted without some article of clothes, and this they bring tied on to their heads. When seen in the water, they are very picturesque,—an effect which is lost altogether on terra firma....[220] To my eyes the deportment of the dignified aboriginal is that of a sapient[221] monkey imitating the gait and manners of a do-nothing white dandy.

... We have some slight account given to us of these aboriginals by Dampier,[222] the buccaneer, who made acquaintance with them on the western coast of Australia in 1688, and again in 1699. He tried to

---

219 Towns or settlements on the east coast of Australia.
220 Latin: firm land.
221 Wise.
222 William Dampier (1651–1715), buccaneer and explorer.

make friends with them; but they attacked his men with spears, wounding some of the party; and at last he shot one of them,—a circumstance which he mentions with great regret. He was good to them, and thought to make them work, but in vain, for, as he says, "they stood like statues, without motion, but grinned like so many monkeys ... so we were forced to carry our water ourselves." This we can imagine very well, remembering that these Australians had never been called upon for an hour's work in their lives. Dampier tried to clothe some of them, but they preferred being naked. But the chiefs were painted. He tells us of one young warrior who was daubed with white paint;—"not for beauty or for ornament, one would think, but, as some wild Indian warriors are said to do, he seemed thereby to design the looking more terrible. This, his painting, added very much to his natural deformity; for they all of them have the most unpleasant looks and worst features of any people I ever saw,—though I have seen great variety of savages."[223]

A hundred years afterwards, in 1770, Cook[224] encountered them at Botany Bay,[225] on the eastern coast, and he endeavoured to make friends with them, and to trade with them,—but in vain. He observes in reference to their nudity, "We thought it remarkable that of all the people we had yet seen, not one had the least appearance of clothing, the old woman herself being destitute even of a fig-leaf."[226] ... Cook, however, certainly endeavoured to treat them well, but without effect. "They did not appear to be numerous," he says, "nor to live in societies, but like other animals, were scattered about along the coasts, and in the woods.... After the first contest at our landing they would never come near enough to parley; nor did they touch a single article of all that we had left at their huts and places they frequented, on purpose for them to take away."[227]

When Governor Phillip,[228]—the first governor,—arrived on Cook's foot-tracks in 1789, he fared a little better with the blacks. He found them still naked,—as a matter of course,—but they took the presents he offered them, and they were at first tractable with him and courteous. When the white men came to settle in numbers round the grand inlet of the sea, which is now Sydney Harbour, the kangaroo ran away, and the fish became scarce in the waters, and the black men lost their usual food. They began to perish from starvation, and of course were not fond of their visitors. They could not depart inland because other tribes would not have them;—for it seems that though no man owned individual property, inland tribes were very jealous of their confines.... Many of the blacks were starved, their accustomed food having been driven away, and others were slaughtered in return for injuries done by them,—which injuries were the natural result of wrongs done to them. And so the quarrel began,—with what result between civilised and savage it is almost needless to say....

... The white man, of course, felt that he was introducing civilisation; but the black man did not want civilisation. He wanted fish, kangaroos, and liberty. And yet is there any one bold enough to go back to the first truth and say that the white man should not have taken the land because it belonged to the black man;—or that if, since the beginning of things, similar justice had prevailed throughout the world, the world would now have been nearer to truth and honesty in its ways than it is?

---

223 William Dampier, *A Voyage to New Holland* (1703).
224 James Cook (1728–79), explorer.
225 Discovered by Cook in 1770, Botany Bay was the location of an early English penal colony.
226 Genesis 3:7.
227 James Cook, "Voyages for Making Discoveries in the Southern Hemisphere" (1773).
228 Arthur Phillip (1738–1814).

These people were in total ignorance of the use of metals, they went naked, they ill-used their women, they had no houses, they produced nothing from the soil. They had not even flint arrow-heads. They practised infanticide. In some circumstances of life they practised cannibalism. They were and are savages of the lowest kind....

Their laws, especially with regard to marriage, are complex and wonderful. Their corroborees, or festival dances, are very wonderful. Their sagacity, especially on the tracking of men or cattle, is very wonderful. The skill with which they use the small appliances of life which they possess is very wonderful. But for years, probably for many centuries, they have made no progress, and the coming of the white man among them has had no tendency to civilise,—only a tendency to exterminate them.

The question I am now endeavouring to discuss is that of the white man's duty in respect to these blacks,—and also the further question whether the white Englishman in Australia has done his duty. There is a strong sect of men in England,—a sect with whom I fully sympathize in their aspirations, though I have sometimes found myself compelled to doubt their information,—who think that the English settler abroad is not to be trusted, except under severe control, with the fate of the poor creatures of inferior races with whom he comes in contact on the distant shores to which his search for wealth may lead him. The settler, as a matter of course, is in quest of fortune, and is one who, living among rough things, is apt to become rough and less scrupulous than his dainty brother at home. When this philanthropy first became loud in its expression in England, we were ourselves the owners of slaves in our own colonies, and the great and glorious task of abolishing that horror for ourselves, so that other nations might afterwards follow in our steps, had to be achieved. Wilberforce, Clarkson, Buxton, Brougham,[229] and others, did achieve it, and it is natural that their spirit should remain with those on whose shoulders their mantle has fallen. When the West Indian blacks were manumitted[230] it was felt to be necessary that they should be defended and protected. Some years since I ventured to express my opinion on that matter.[231] Of all the absurdities in political economy which I ever encountered, that of protecting the labour of the negroes in Jamaica from competition was to my eyes the most gross. And it appeared to me that the idea of training negroes to be magistrates, members of parliament, statesmen, or even merchants, was one destined to failure by the very nature of the man. That a race should have been created so low in its gifts as to be necessarily fit only for savage life or for the life of servants among civilised men was a fact on which I could only speculate ... ; but I could not on that account abstain from forming the opinion. Since that time negroes ... have been made free in the United States, and have then been put in possession of all the privileges belonging to white men. The more I see of the experiment the more convinced I am that the negro cannot live on equal terms with the white man, and that any land, state, or district in which the negro is empowered for awhile to have ascendency over the white man by number of suffrages or other causes, will have but a woful destiny.... White men will quit such land in disgust,—or the white minority will turn, and rend, and trample into dust the black majority. This allusion to the African negro in the western hemisphere would be out of place here, were it not that the mantle of which I have spoken ... is now used,—or a skirt of it is used,—to cover up the nakedness of the poor Australian aboriginal. The idea prevails that he also may be a member of parliament, minister of state, a man and a brother, or what not. That he is infinitely

---

229 William Wilberforce (1759–1833), politician and abolitionist; Thomas Clarkson (1760–1846), abolitionist; Thomas Buxton (1786–1845), politician and abolitionist; Henry Peter Brougham (1778–1868), politician and abolitionist.
230 Freed.
231 Anthony Trollope, *The West Indies and the Spanish Main* (1859).

lower in his gifts than the African negro there can be no doubt. Civilisation among the African tribes is not very high, and our knowledge as to the point which it has reached is still defective. But where he has come within the compass of the white man's power, he has been taught to work for his bread,—which of all teaching is the most important. The Australian black man has not been so taught, and, in spite of a few instances to the contrary, I think I am justified in saying that he cannot be so taught....

I once asked a member of parliament in one of the colonies and a magistrate what he would do,—or rather what he would recommend me to do,—if stress of circumstances compelled me to shoot a black man in the bush. Should I go to some nearest police station, as any one would do who in self-defence had shot a white man;—or should I go on rejoicing as though I had shot a tiger or killed a deadly snake? His advice was clear and explicit. "No one but a fool would say anything about it." The aboriginal therefore whom you are called on to kill,—lest he should kill you or your wife, or because he spears your cattle,—is to be to you the same as a tiger or a snake. But this would be in the back districts, far away from towns, in which the black man has not yet learned to be a fine gentleman with dignified deportment, barely taking the trouble to open his mouth as he asks for sixpence and tobacco....

... I have endeavoured to state the case fairly between the squatter and the aboriginal; for the real question at issue now lies between them. And I find that it resolves itself to this;—had the first English settlers any right to take the country from the black men who were its owners, and have the progressing colonists who still go westward and northward in search of fresh lands the right to drive the black men back, seeing as he does that they cannot live together? If they have no such right,—that is, if they be morally wrong to do it,—then has the whole colonizing system of Great Britain been wrong, not only in Australia, but in every portion of the globe. And had Britain abstained from colonizing under the conviction of conscientious scruples, would it have been better for the human race? Four nations struggled for the possession of Australia, the Portuguese, the Dutch, the French, and ourselves? It fell into our hands, chiefly through the enterprise and skill of Captain Cook. Should we have abstained when we found that it was peopled,—and, so to say, already possessed? And had we done so should we have served the cause of humanity? I doubt whether any philanthropist will say that we should have abstained;—or will think that had we done so the Australian aborigines would at the present moment have fared better with Dutch or French masters than they are now faring with us. It is their fate to be abolished; and they are already vanishing. Nothing short of abstaining from encroaching upon their lands,—abstaining that is from taking possession of Australia could be of any service to them. They have been treated, I think, almost invariably with proffered kindness when first met,—but they have not wanted and have not understood the kindness. For a time they would not submit at all, and now their submission is partial. In 1864 an expedition was made to take cattle from Rockhampton overland to Cape York, the northern extremity of Queensland, by two brothers, Frank and Alexander Jardine.[232] The cattle were then driven up to save the lives of the occupants of a new settlement. The enterprise was carried through with admirable spirit and final success after terrible difficulties. But their progress was one continued battle with black tribes, who knew nothing of them, and who of course regarded them as enemies. Which party was to blame for this bloodshed,—the Messrs. Jardine who were risking their own lives to save the inhabitants of a distant settlement,—or the poor blacks who were struggling against unknown and encroaching enemies? In this

---

232 Francis Lescelles Jardine (1841–1919) and Alexander William Jardine (1843–1920), members of a prominent northern Queensland family.

case there was certainly no cruelty, no thoughtless arrogance, no white man's indifference to the lives of black men. The Messrs. Jardine would have been glad enough to have made their progress without fighting battles, and fought when they did fight simply in self-protection. And yet the blacks were invaded,—most unjustly and cruelly as they must have felt.

Of the Australian black man we may certainly say that he has to go. That he should perish without unnecessary suffering should be the aim of all who are concerned in the matter. But no good can be done by giving to the aboriginal a character which he does not deserve, or by speaking of the treatment which he receives in language which the facts do not warrant.

Florence Dixie
from *Across Patagonia* (1880)

The first female journalist assigned to a war zone, Florence Dixie (1855–1905) published travel narratives, children's stories, novels, dramas, poetry, and (late in life) books against blood sports. She campaigned for women's equality, rejected religious belief, and wrote for the *Agnostic Journal*. Her 1875 marriage brought two children and debt from her husband's gambling. A lover of travel and outdoor sport, Dixie was among the first British women to hunt big game and ride astride a horse (as opposed to sidesaddle). *Across Patagonia* (1880), her bestselling account of her 1878–79 South American trip, brought fame and led to her appointment as war correspondent for the Anglo-Zulu War. Because the war was over upon her 1881 arrival in Cape Town, she instead toured southern Africa and lauded Zulu King Cetewayo. Her brother, John Douglas, Marquess of Queensberry (Alfred Douglas's father), famously provoked the trials of Oscar Wilde (see Life Writing, Aesthetics and Culture).

This excerpt from her Patagonian travels records her encounter with natives whom she expects soon to suffer extinction.

Chapter 1

"Patagonia![233] who would ever think of going to such a place?" "Why, you will be eaten up by cannibals!" "What on earth makes you choose such an outlandish part of the world to go to?" "What can be the attraction?" "Why, it is thousands of miles away, and no one has ever been there before, except Captain Musters,[234] and one or two other adventurous madmen!"

---

233 Patagonia is the southernmost part of South America; it comprises Argentina, south of the Colorado River, and Chile, south of Chiloé Island.
234 George Chaworth Musters (1841–79), naval commander and author of *At Home with the Patagonians: A Year's Wanderings over Untrodden Ground from the Straits of Magellan to the Rio Negro* (1871).

These, and similar questions and exclamations I heard from the lips of my friends and acquaintances, when I told them of my intended trip to Patagonia, the land of the Giants, the land of the fabled Golden City of Manoa.[235] What was the attraction in going to an outlandish place so many miles away? The answer to the question was contained in its own words. Precisely because it was an outlandish place and so far away, I chose it. Palled[236] for the moment with civilisation and its surroundings, I wanted to escape somewhere, where I might be as far removed from them as possible. Many of my readers have doubtless felt the dissatisfaction with oneself, and everybody else, that comes over one at times in the midst of the pleasures of life; … when what was once excitement has become so no longer, and a longing grows up within one to taste a more vigorous emotion than that afforded by the monotonous round of society's so-called "pleasures."

Well, it was in this state of mind that I cast round for some country which should possess the qualities necessary to satisfy my requirements, and finally I decided upon Patagonia as the most suitable. Without doubt there are wild countries more favoured by Nature in many ways. But nowhere else are you so completely alone. Nowhere else is there an area of 100,000 square miles which you may gallop over, and where, whilst enjoying a healthy, bracing climate, you are safe from the persecutions of fevers, friends, savage tribes, obnoxious animals, telegrams, letters, and every other nuisance you are elsewhere liable to be exposed to. To these attractions was added the thought, always alluring to an active mind, that there too I should be able to penetrate into vast wilds, virgin as yet to the foot of man. Scenes of infinite beauty and grandeur might be lying hidden in the silent solitude of the mountains which bound the barren plains of the Pampas,[237] into whose mysterious recesses no one as yet had ever ventured. And I was to be the first to behold them!…

Chapter 6

… After breakfast the horses were saddled, and taking some sugar, tobacco, and other articles for bartering purposes, we set out for the Indian camp, accompanied by Gregorio and Guillaume. I'Aria and Storer were left in charge of our camp, and Francisco[238] went off with the dogs towards Cape Gregorio,[239] in the hope of falling in with some stray ostrich or guanaco.[240] The weather was fine, and for once we were able to rejoice in the absence of the rough winds which were our daily annoyance. We had not gone far when we saw a rider coming slowly towards us, and in a few minutes we found ourselves in the presence of a real Patagonian Indian. We reined in our horses when he got close to us, to have a good look at him, and he doing the same, for a few minutes we stared at him to our hearts' content, receiving in return as minute and careful a scrutiny from him. Whatever he may have thought of us, we thought him a singularly unprepossessing object, and, for the sake of his race, we hoped an unfavourable specimen of it. His dirty brown face, of which the principal feature was a pair of sharp black eyes, was half-hidden by tangled

---

235 Patagonians were fabled to be giants, as they were, on average, over half a foot taller than Europeans; in the El Dorado legend, Manoa is a city of gold.
236 Bored or tired of.
237 The plains of central Argentina.
238 Dixie's guides were Gregorio, an Argentine *gaucho* (cowboy or hunter); Guillaume, a Frenchman whom Dixie disliked intensely; and I'Aria, a Chilean who had accompanied George Musters on his Patagonian trip; her servants were Storer, who was English, and Francisco, a horseman.
239 Cape Gregory, a Protestant mission station on the Strait of Magellan.
240 A wild quadruped; similar to a llama or alpaca.

masses of unkempt hair, held together by a handkerchief tied over his forehead, and his burly body was enveloped in a greasy guanaco-capa,[241] considerably the worse for wear. His feet were bare, but one of his heels was armed with a little wooden spur, of curious and ingenious handiwork. Having completed his survey of our persons, and exchanged a few guttural grunts with Gregorio, of which the purport was that he had lost some horses and was on their search, he galloped away, and, glad to find some virtue in him, we were able to admire the easy grace with which he sat his well-bred looking little horse, which, though considerably below his weight, was doubtless able to do its master good service.

Continuing our way we presently observed several mounted Indians, sitting motionless on their horses, like sentries, on the summit of a tall ridge ahead of us, evidently watching our movements. At our approach they disappeared over the ridge, on the other side of which lay their camping-ground. Cantering forward we soon came in sight of the entire Indian camp, which was pitched in a broad valley-plain, flanked on either side by steep bluffs, and with a little stream flowing down its centre. There were about a dozen big hide tents, in front of which stood crowds of men and women, watching our approach with lazy curiosity.... On our arrival in the camp we were soon encircled by a curious crowd, some of whose number gazed at us with stolid gravity, whilst others laughed and gesticulated as they discussed our appearance in their harsh guttural language, with a vivacious manner which was quite at variance with the received traditions of the solemn bent of the Indian mind. Our accoutrements and clothes seemed to excite great interest.... At first they were content to observe them from a distance, but presently a little boy was delegated by the elders, to advance and give them a closer inspection. This he proceeded to do, coming towards me with great caution, and when near enough, he stretched out his hand and touched the boots gently with the tips of his fingers....

Whilst they were thus occupied I had leisure to observe their general appearance. I was not struck so much by their height as by their extraordinary development of chest and muscle. As regards their stature, I do not think the average height of the men exceeded six feet.... The women were mostly of the ordinary height, though I noticed one who must have been quite six feet, if not more. The features of the pure-bred Tehuelche[242] are extremely regular, and by no means unpleasant to look at. The nose is generally aquiline, the mouth well shaped and beautified by the whitest of teeth, the expression of the eye is intelligent, and the form of the whole head affords a favourable index to their mental capabilities. These remarks do not apply to the Tehuelches in whose veins there is a mixture of Araucanian or Fuegian blood.[243] The flat noses, oblique eyes, and badly proportioned figures of the latter make them most repulsive objects.... Their hair is long and coarse, and is worn parted in the middle, being prevented from falling over their faces by means of a handkerchief, or fillet[244] of some kind, tied round the forehead. They have naturally little hair on the face, and such growth as may appear is carefully eradicated, a painful operation, which many extend even to their eyebrows. Their dress is simple, and consists of a "chiripá," a piece of cloth round the loins, and the indispensable guanaco capa, which is hung loosely over the shoulders and held round the body by the hand, though it would obviously seem more convenient to have it secured round the waist with a belt of some kind. Their horse-hide boots are only worn, for reasons of economy, when hunting.

---

241 Guanaco-skin cape.
242 A group of native peoples in central Argentina.
243 The Mapuche (Araucanians) are a group of native peoples farther to the south; Fuegians are the peoples of the Tierra del Fuego archipelago.
244 Head band.

The women dress like the men except as regards the chiripá, instead of which they wear a loose kind of gown beneath the capa, which they fasten at the neck with a silver brooch or pin. The children are allowed to run about naked till they are five or six years old, and are then dressed like their elders. Partly for ornament, partly also as a means of protection against the wind, a great many Indians paint their faces, their favourite colour, as far as I could see, being red, though one or two I observed had given the preference to a mixture of that colour with black, a very diabolical appearance being the result of this combination.

The Tehuelches are a race that is fast approaching extinction, and even at present it scarcely numbers eight hundred souls. They lead a rambling nomadic existence, shifting their camping places from one region to another, whenever the game in their vicinity gets shy or scarce. It is fortunate for them that the immense numbers of guanaco and ostriches makes it an easy matter for them to find subsistence, as they are extremely lazy, and, plentiful as game is around them, often pass two or three days without food rather than incur the very slight exertion attendant on a day's hunting.

But it is only the men who are cursed or blessed with this indolent spirit. The women are indefatigably industrious. All the work of Tehuelche existence is done by them except hunting. When not employed in ordinary household work they busy themselves in making guanaco capas, weaving gay-coloured garters and fillets for the hair, working silver ornaments, and so forth. Not one of their least arduous tasks is that of collecting firewood, which, always a scarce article, becomes doubly hard to find, except by going great distances, when they camp long in one place....

... There was a trader in the camp who had arrived about the same time as we did, and amongst other wares he had brought a rusty carbine[245] with him for sale. He was called upon by the Indians to produce it and fire it off to compare its qualities with those of my brother's rifle. This he proceeded to do, but seven times in succession the cartridges missed fire. Each time this happened he was greeted with shouts of derisive laughter, and it was evident that both he and his weapon were the objects of most disparaging remarks on the part of the Tehuelches. One of them, a man of some humour, brought out a small piece of ostrich meat and offered it to the trader in exchange for his carbine, saying in broken Spanish, "Your gun never kill piece of meat as big as this. Your gun good to kill dead guanaco." At which witticism there was renewed and prolonged applause, as the newspapers say....

... The Indians had not been out hunting for three days, and there was hardly anything but pemmican[246] in the camp,—a greasy concoction, with which we by no means cared to experiment on our stomachs. With difficulty we at last succeeded in obtaining the leg and breast of an ostrich, and a small piece of half sun-dried guanaco meat, which looked extremely untempting. This transaction having been accomplished, we wandered leisurely about the camp, glancing at the different objects of interest that came in our way.... At one of the tents we saw two remarkably clean and pretty girls, who were engaged on some kind of sewing work; and beside them—probably making love to one (or both)—stood an equally good-looking youth, who struck me by the peculiar neatness of his dress, and his general "*tiré à quatre epingles*"[247] appearance. His hair was brushed and combed, and carefully parted—a bright red silk handkerchief keeping its glossy locks in due subjection. His handsome guanaco capa was new, and brilliantly painted on the outside, and being half opened, displayed a clean white chiripá, fastened at the

---

245 Rifle.
246 A cake of powdered meat, fat, and dried fruits or berries.
247 French: very dapper.

waist by a silver belt of curious workmanship. A pair of neatly fitting horse-hide boots encased his feet, reaching up to the knees, where they were secured by a pair of gay-coloured garters, possibly the gift of one of the fair maidens at his side.

Struck by his graceful bearing and well-bred looking face, I begged Mr. B.,[248] who had brought a sketch-book with him, to make a sketch of this handsome son of the pampa. During the process the young Indian never moved, and preserved a perfectly indifferent demeanour; but when the picture was finished, and given to him for inspection, his forehead contracted with anger, an expression of fear came in his eyes; he gave vent to some angry sounding gutturals, and finally, much to our annoyance, tore the portrait to pieces. He was under the impression that the object of making the sketch was to throw some evil spell over him, and that a misfortune would happen if it were not destroyed....

The Indians were about to make their annual visit to Sandy Point,[249] where they go to obtain the rations of sugar, tobacco, etc., allowed to them by the Chilian Government, and to barter with the inhabitants for the luxuries of civilisation, in exchange for furs and ostrich feathers, at which transactions, as they are seldom sober during their stay outside the colony, they generally get worsted by the cunning white man. Our curiosity regarding the Indians being satisfied, and having obtained all the meat we could from them, we now turned homewards.

Isabella L. Bird

from *Unbeaten Tracks in Japan: An Account of Travels in the Interior, Including Visits to the Aborigines of Yezo and the Shrines of Nikkô and Isé* (1880)

Travel writer Isabella Bird (1831–1904) became the first female Fellow of the Royal Geographical Society and the first woman to address its members. Her life of travel (to North America, China, Hawaii, India, Japan, Korea, Kurdistan, North Africa, Persia, Tibet, and Turkey) was spurred by her evangelicalism and the realization that energetic travel improved her health. She often tackled arduous conditions, occasionally travelling alone. Bird's early publications emerged from letters to her beloved sister Henrietta, which were sometimes published in periodicals before appearing in book form. She supported philanthropic causes, such as buying boats for poor Scottish fishermen, building a shelter for Edinburgh cab men, exposing Edinburgh slum conditions, and building mission hospitals in India.

This excerpt from *Unbeaten Tracks in Japan* (1880) describes Bird's impetus for travel and her hiring of a guide; it also reveals her eye for character and setting, offering the reader a glimpse into the Japanese domestic interior.

---

248 Julius Beerbohm (1854–1906), explorer, writer, and illustrator.
249 Punta Arenas (Sandy Point), on the Strait of Magellan.

Preface.

Having been recommended to leave home, in April 1878, in order to recruit[250] my health by means which had proved serviceable before, I decided to visit Japan.... The climate disappointed me, but though I found the country a study rather than a rapture, its interest exceeded my largest expectations.

This is not a "Book on Japan," but a narrative of travels in Japan, and an attempt to contribute something to the sum of knowledge of the present condition of the country, and it was not till I had travelled for some months in the interior of the main island and in Yezo,[251] that I decided that my materials were novel enough to render the contribution worth making. From Nikkô[252] northwards my route was altogether off the beaten track, and had never been traversed in its entirety by any European. I lived among the Japanese, and saw their mode of living, in regions unaffected by European contact. As a lady travelling alone, and the first European lady who had been seen in several districts through which my route lay, my experiences differed more or less widely from those of preceding travellers....

Letter 6.

... H.B.M.'s Legation, Yedo[253]
June 7....
Several of my kind new acquaintances interested themselves about the (to me) vital matter of a servant interpreter, and many Japanese came to "see after the place." The speaking of intelligible English is a *sine quâ non*,[254] and it was wonderful to find the few words badly pronounced and worse put together, which were regarded by the candidates as a sufficient qualification. Can you speak English? "Yes." What wages do you ask? "Twelve dollars a month." This was always said glibly, and in each case sounded hopeful. Who have you lived with? A foreign name distorted out of all recognition as was natural, was then given. Where have you travelled? This question usually had to be translated into Japanese, and the usual answer was, "The Tokaido, the Nakasendo, to Kiyôto, to Nikkô,"[255] naming the beaten tracks of countless tourists. Do you know anything of Northern Japan and the Hokkaido? "No," with a blank, wondering look. At this stage in every case Dr. Hepburn[256] compassionately stepped in as interpreter, for their stock of English was exhausted. Three were regarded as promising. One was a sprightly youth who came in a well-made European suit of light-coloured tweed, a laid-down collar, a tie with a diamond (?) pin, and a white shirt, so stiffly starched, that he could hardly bend low enough for a bow even of European profundity.... He was a Japanese dandy of the first water.... I was therefore quite relieved when his English broke down at the second question.

---

250 To recover.
251 Now Hokkaido, the second largest and farthest north of Japan's four main islands.
252 A city roughly 150 kilometres north of Tokyo famous for its temples and shrines.
253 Her Britannic Majesty's Embassy, Tokyo.
254 Latin: necessity.
255 The Tokaido and Nakasendo are two of the five major roads of the Edo period (1603–1868), both of which connected Edo (now Tokyo) to Kyoto.
256 James Curtis Hepburn (1815–1911), American physician, missionary, and author of a Japanese-English dictionary.

The second was a most respectable-looking man of thirty-five in a good Japanese dress.... He knew really only a few words of English, and his horror at finding that there was "no master," and that there would be no woman servant, was so great, that I hardly know whether he rejected me, or I him.

The third, sent by Mr. Wilkinson, wore a plain Japanese dress, and had a frank, intelligent face. Though Dr. Hepburn spoke with him in Japanese, he thought that he knew more English than the others, and that what he knew would come out when he was less agitated. He evidently understood what I said, and though I had a suspicion that he would turn out to be the "master," I thought him so prepossessing that I nearly engaged him on the spot....

However, when I had nearly made up my mind in his favour, a creature appeared without any recommendation at all, except that one of Dr. Hepburn's servants was acquainted with him. He is only eighteen, but this is equivalent to twenty-three or twenty-four with us, and only 4 feet 10 inches in height.... He has a round and singularly plain face, good teeth, much elongated eyes, and the heavy droop of his eyelids almost caricatures the usual Japanese peculiarity. He is the most stupid-looking Japanese that I have seen, but, from a rapid, furtive glance in his eyes now and then, I think that the stolidity is partly assumed. He said that he had lived at the American Legation, that he had been a clerk on the Osaka railroad, that he had travelled through northern Japan by the eastern route and in Yezo, with Mr. Maries, a botanical collector,[257] that he ... could write English, that he could walk twenty-five miles a day, and that he thoroughly understood getting through the interior! This would-be paragon had no recommendations, and accounted for this by saying that they had been burned in a recent fire in his father's house. Mr. Maries was not forthcoming, and more than this, I suspected and disliked the boy. However, he understood my English and I his, and being very anxious to begin my travels, I engaged him for twelve dollars a month....

Ever since the solemn night when the contract was signed, I have felt under an incubus.[258] ... He flies up stairs and along the corridors as noiselessly as a cat, and already knows where I keep all my things. Nothing surprises or abashes him, he bows profoundly to Sir Harry and Lady Parkes[259] when he encounters them, but is obviously "quite at home" in a Legation.... He seems as sharp or "smart" as can be, and has already arranged for the first three days of my journey. His name is Ito, and you will doubtless hear much more of him, as he will be my good or evil genius for the next three months.

As no English lady has yet travelled alone through the interior, my project excites a very friendly interest among my friends, and I receive much warning and dissuasion, and a little encouragement. The strongest because the most intelligent dissuasion comes from Dr. Hepburn, who thinks that I ought not to undertake the journey, and that I shall never get through to the Tsugaru Strait.[260] If I accepted much of the advice given to me, as to taking tinned meats and soups, claret, and a Japanese maid, I should need a train of at least six pack-horses!...

On returning here I found that Lady Parkes had made most of the necessary preparations for me, and that they include two light baskets with covers of oiled paper, a travelling bed or stretcher, a folding

---

257 The American Embassy; the Osaka station opened in 1874 on the railway between Osaka and Kobe; the eastern shipping route, along the Pacific coast; Charles Maries (1851–1902), botanist, traveller, and landscaper.
258 An evil male spirit that descends on women in their sleep, seeking intercourse.
259 Harry Smith Parkes (1828–85), British envoy, minister, and consul general of Japan; his wife, Lady Parkes (née Fanny Plumer) (1831/2–79).
260 The strait between the northern island of Hokkaido (Yezo) and the main Japanese island of Honshu, linking the Sea of Japan and the Pacific.

chair, and an india-rubber bath,[261] all which she considers as necessaries for a person in feeble health on a journey of such long duration....

Letter 10.

... Kanaya's, Nikkô, *June* 15.

I don't know what to write about my house. It is a Japanese idyll; there is nothing within or without which does not please the eye, and after the din of *yadoyas*,[262] its silence, musical with the dash of waters and the twitter of birds, is truly refreshing. It is a simple but irregular two-storied pavilion, standing on a stone-faced terrace approached by a flight of stone steps. The garden is well laid out, and, as peonies, irises, and azaleas are now in blossom, it is very bright. The mountain, with its lower part covered with red azaleas, rises just behind, and a stream which tumbles down it supplies the house with water, both cold and pure, and another, after forming a miniature cascade, passes under the house and through a fishpond with rocky islets into the river below. The grey village of Irimichi lies on the other side of the road shut in with the rushing Daiya,[263] and beyond it are high, broken hills, richly wooded, and slashed with ravines and waterfalls.

Kanaya's sister, a very sweet, refined-looking woman, met me at the door and divested me of my boots. The two verandahs are highly polished, so are the entrance and the stairs which lead to my room, and the mats are so fine and white that I almost fear to walk over them even in my stockings. The polished stairs lead to a highly polished, broad verandah with a beautiful view, from which you enter one large room, which, being too large, was at once made into two. Four highly polished steps lead from this into an exquisite room at the back, which Ito occupies, and another polished staircase into the bath-house and garden. The whole front of my room is composed of *shôji*,[264] which slide back during the day.... The panels are of wrinkled sky blue paper splashed with gold. At one end are two alcoves with floors of polished wood, called *tokonoma*.[265] In one hangs a *kakemono*, or wall-picture, a painting of a blossoming branch of the cherry on white silk—a perfect piece of art, which in itself fills the room with freshness and beauty.... I almost wish that the rooms were a little less exquisite, for I am in constant dread of spilling the ink, indenting the mats, or tearing the paper windows....

Kanaya leads the discords at the Shintô shrines;[266] but his duties are few, and he is chiefly occupied in perpetually embellishing his house and garden. His mother, a venerable old lady, and his sister, the sweetest and most graceful Japanese woman but one that I have seen, live with him. She moves about the house like a floating fairy, and her voice has music in its tones.... Kanaya is the chief man in the village, and is very intelligent and apparently well educated. He has divorced his wife, and his sister has practically divorced her husband. Of late, to help his income, he has let these charming rooms to foreigners who have brought letters to him, and he is very anxious to meet their views, while his good taste leads him to avoid Europeanising his beautiful home.

---

261 Portable bath. These folded to about one square foot and were inflated with bellows for use.
262 Japanese: inns.
263 Imaichi, on the bank of the Daiya River, just outside Nikkô.
264 Sliding walls of wooden strips and translucent paper.
265 Traditional alcoves in Japanese reception rooms in which art is displayed.
266 Shinto is an ancient Japanese religion that has melded with Buddhism; the shrines hold spirits of the ancestors and gods.

... It is extremely interesting to live in a private house and to see the externalities at least of domestic life in a Japanese middle-class home.

I.L.B....

Letter 13.

... To-morrow I leave luxury behind, and plunge into the interior, hoping to emerge somehow upon the Sea of Japan. No information can be got here except about the route to Niigata which I have decided not to take, so, after much study of Brunton's map, I have fixed upon one place, and have said positively, "I go to Tajima."[267] If I reach it I can get farther, but all I can learn is, "It's a very bad road, it's all among the mountains." Ito, who has a great regard for his own comforts, tries to dissuade me from going, by saying that I shall lose mine, but as these kind people have ingeniously repaired my bed by doubling the canvas and lacing it into holes in the side poles,[268] and as I have lived for the last three days on rice, eggs, and coarse vermicelli[269] about the thickness and colour of earthworms, this prospect does not appal me!...

My journey will now be entirely over "unbeaten tracks," and will lead through what may be called "Old Japan."...

Letter 15.

... Kurumatogé,[270] *June* 30.
After the hard travelling of six days the rest of Sunday in a quiet place at a high elevation is truly delightful! Mountains and passes, valleys and rice swamps, forests and rice swamps, villages and rice swamps; poverty, industry, dirt, ruinous temples, prostrate Buddhas, strings of straw-shod pack-horses; long, grey, featureless streets, and quiet, staring crowds, are all jumbled up fantastically in my memory. Fine weather accompanied me through beautiful scenery from Ikari to Yokokawa,[271] where I ate my lunch in the street to avoid the innumerable fleas of the tea-house, with a circle round me of nearly all the inhabitants. At first the children, both old and young, were so frightened that they ran away, but by degrees they timidly came back, clinging to the skirts of their parents.... The crowd was filthy and squalid beyond description.... A horse kicked off my saddle before it was girthed, the crowd scattered right and left, and work, which had been suspended for two hours to stare at the foreigner, began again.

A long ascent took us to the top of a pass 2500 feet in height, a projecting spur not 30 feet wide, with a grand view of mountains and ravines, and a maze of involved streams, which unite in a vigorous torrent, whose course we followed for some hours, till it expanded into a quiet river, lounging lazily through a

---

267 Niigata is a mid-western coastal town, north of Tokyo; Richard Henry Brunton (1841–1901), cartographer and engineer who encouraged and oversaw the surveying and mapping of Japan while employed by the Meiji government (1868–76); Tajima is a town north of Tokyo.
268 Author's note: I advise every traveller in the ruder regions of Japan to take a similar stretcher and good mosquito net. With these he may defy all ordinary discomforts.
269 Pasta.
270 A mountain pass near Niigata.
271 In the mountains northwest of Tokyo and south of Niigata.

rice swamp of considerable extent. The map is blank in this region, but I judged, as I afterwards found rightly, that at that pass we had crossed the watershed, and that the streams thenceforward no longer fall into the Pacific, but into the Sea of Japan. At Itosawa the horses produced stumbled so intolerably that I walked the last stage, and reached Kayashima, a miserable village of fifty-seven houses, so exhausted, that I could not go farther, and was obliged to put up with worse accommodation even than at Fujihara,[272] with less strength for its hardships.

The *yadoya* was simply awful. The *daidokoro*[273] had a large wood fire burning in a trench, filling the whole place with stinging smoke, from which my room, which was merely screened off by some dilapidated *shôji*, was not exempt. The rafters were black and shiny with soot and moisture. The house-master, who knelt persistently on the floor of my room till he was dislodged by Ito, apologised for the dirt of his house, as well he might. Stifling, dark, and smoky, as my room was, I had to close the paper windows, owing to the crowd which assembled in the street. There was neither rice nor soy, and Ito, who values his own comfort, began to speak to the house-master and servants loudly and roughly, and to throw my things about, a style of acting which I promptly terminated, for nothing could be more hurtful to a foreigner, or more unkind to the people, than for a servant to be rude and bullying; and the man was most polite, and never approached me but on bended knees....

A little boy, the house-master's son, was suffering from a very bad cough, and a few drops of chlorodyne,[274] which I gave him, allayed it so completely, that the cure was noised abroad in the earliest hours of the next morning, and by five o'clock nearly the whole population was assembled outside my room, with much whispering and shuffling of shoeless feet, and applications of eyes to the many holes in the paper windows. When I drew aside the *shôji*, I was disconcerted by the painful sight which presented itself, for the people were pressing one upon another, fathers and mothers holding naked children covered with skin-disease or with scald-head, or ringworm,[275] daughters leading mothers nearly blind, men exhibiting painful sores, children blinking with eyes infested by flies, and nearly closed with ophthalmia,[276] and all, sick and well, in truly "vile raiment,"[277] lamentably dirty and swarming with vermin, the sick asking for medicine, and the well either bringing the sick or gratifying an apathetic curiosity. Sadly I told them that I did not understand their manifold "diseases and torments,"[278] and that, if I did, I had no stock of medicines, and that in my own country the constant washing of clothes, and the constant application of water to the skin, accompanied by friction with clean cloths, would be much relied upon by doctors for the cure and prevention of similar cutaneous diseases.[279] To pacify them, I made some ointment of animal fat and flowers of sulphur,[280] extracted with difficulty from some man's hoard, and told them how to apply it to some of the worst cases....

---

272 These locations follow the mountain route northwest from Tokyo to Niigata.
273 Japanese: kitchen.
274 A mixture of morphine and chloroform, originally invented to treat cholera by John Collis Browne and later modified to include laudanum and hemp.
275 Scald-head is a term for ringworm, a fungal skin (or hair or nail) infection that sometimes appears as red circles.
276 Eye infection and swelling.
277 Dirty clothing; James 2:2.
278 Matthew 4:24.
279 Skin diseases and infections.
280 Pure, powdered sulphur. Mixing this with animal fat would make a crude approximation of sulphur soap, which helps to treat scabies (lice infestations under the skin, causing a rash), psoriasis, and other complaints.

These people wear no linen,[281] and their clothes, which are seldom washed, are constantly worn, night and day, as long as they will hold together. They seal up their houses as hermetically as they can at night, and herd together in numbers in one sleeping-room, with its atmosphere vitiated to begin with by charcoal and tobacco fumes, huddled up in their dirty garments in wadded quilts, which are kept during the day in close cupboards, and are seldom washed from one year's end to another.... The persons of the people, especially of the children, are infested with vermin, and one fruitful source of skin sores is the irritation arising from this cause. The floors of houses, being concealed by mats, are laid down carelessly with gaps between the boards, and as the damp earth is only eighteen inches or two feet below, emanations of all kinds enter the mats and pass into the rooms....

Kate Marsden

from *On Sledge and Horseback to Outcast Siberian Lepers* (1891)

Travel writer Kate Marsden (1859–1931) was educated at home and boarding school before training as a nurse. Her father's 1873 death left her family poor. Marsden volunteered for an 1877 party to Bulgaria to nurse wounded Russian soldiers, thereby earning a Red Cross medal. Thereafter she assumed a London nursing post, headed a Liverpool convalescent home, superintended Wellington Hospital in New Zealand, and met Queen Victoria. She then committed her life to caring for lepers. She travelled to Siberia by sledge, barge, and horseback, and raised money for a Vilyuysk leprosy hospital (which opened in 1897). One of the Royal Geographical Society's first female fellows, Marsden died in obscurity.

This excerpt from *On Sledge and Horseback to Outcast Siberian Lepers* (1893) vividly and compassionately recounts her meeting with the lepers after a monumental journey.

Chapter 10: Amongst the Lepers

We wended our way through the forest along the 1500 verst-track that the Yakuts had so readily and lovingly marked for us;[282] for they did this work of their own will and without remuneration, though to accomplish it they had to lay aside their summer work in the fields. They knew whither we were bound, and this was the proof of their sympathy for the mission and their pity for the lepers.

Although a path had been marked out for us, the stumps and roots of trees had been left. We rode over a carpet of half-decayed roots, all interlaced with one another. Now and then my horse sank, not this time in mud, but into holes, well hidden amongst the roots, getting his feet entangled in such a way

---

281 Underclothing.
282 A 1,600 kilometre track; a verst is a Russian unit of measurement equivalent to 1.067 kilometres; Yakuts are an indigenous people of northeastern Siberia.

that only a Siberian horse could extricate himself. I had to hang on to the saddle, my body ready for every lurch the horse might give in freeing himself, and prepared to help him at the right moment. We went through miles and miles of forest like this.

At last I thought I could discern ahead a large lake, and beyond that two yourtas.[283] My instinct was true to me; and the peculiar thrill which passed through my whole frame meant that, at last, after all those months of travelling, I had found, thank God! the poor creatures whom I had come to help. A little more zigzag riding along the tedious path, and then I suddenly looked up and saw before me the two yourtas and a little crowd of people. Some of the people came limping, and some leaning on sticks, to catch the first glimpse of us, their faces and limbs distorted by the dreadful ravages of the disease. One poor creature could only crawl by the help of a stool, and all had the same indescribably hopeless expression of the eyes which indicates the disease. I scrambled off the horse, and went quickly amongst the little crowd of the lame, the halt, and the blind. Some were standing, some were kneeling, and some crouching on the ground, and all with eager faces turned towards me. They told me afterwards that they believed God had sent me; and, my friends, if you could all have been there, you would no longer wonder at my having devoted body and soul to this work.

I at once ordered the things to be unpacked, and had them collected on the grass. A prayer of thanksgiving was then offered by the priest, and, next, a prayer for her Imperial Majesty the Empress,[284] in which the poor people heartily joined. As we distributed the gifts, some of the distorted faces half beamed with delight; whilst others changed from a look of fear to one of confidence and rest. Surely such a scene was worth a long journey, and many hardships and perils.

They seemed to know that help was coming, and that although they might not live to enjoy it, other afflicted ones would. The poor fingerless hands, and all the sad contortions with the stamp of hopeless misery on every face—even where a flickering smile had appeared—made me shudder.

The condition of the yourtas is best described by my quoting the documents of two officials, who were sent there by the Government.

The medical inspector, Mr. Smirnoff, says, in his report ... to the Governor: "One is struck at the sight of the smallness of these nomad huts, in which they dwell. Light hardly penetrates, and the atmosphere is so infected by the conglomeration of the lepers, and the exhalations of rotten fish, that one is quite suffocated on entering them. These unfortunates have neither beds nor linen; their clothing consists only of sheep and cow skins, all in rags, and it is under these conditions, without any change, that they are obliged to live tens of years, till at last death releases them from their sufferings. Not far from these huts one perceives graves with crosses on them, indicating the places where the lepers bury each other. The door is so small that one is obliged to bend to be able to enter. The hut is very low, and hardly any light enters, and the atmosphere is so foul that even the fire which is continually burning in the fireplace cannot purify it. The filth of this hovel is disgusting; the dirty table and the few benches covered with filthy skins, in lieu of beds, comprise everything in the place. I found six men and three women huddled together in this infected hovel. It is inexplicable how so many people get to be lodged in so small and low a hut. The clothes of these lepers consisted of skins (of cows) all in rags and holes."

---

283 Russian: a round tent made of hides or felt.
284 Maria Feodorovna (1847–1928), Russian empress married to Alexander III.

The tchinovnick[285] for special services, Mr. Shachourdine, in his report, contained in Protocol No. 3, states:—"The interior of these yourtas is not known to me, as, however much I wanted to get acquainted with the interior of the said huts, I could not get into them, on account of the fearful stench, similar to that coming from a dead body; which was due not only to the lepers themselves, but also to the food that they ate, consisting chiefly of rotten fish."

The yourtas, swarming with vermin of many kinds, were made out of the trunks of trees, fastened with wooden nails, and covered with cow-dung, of which the floor also consisted, mixed with earth. The windows were only one foot square, and were covered with calico. The lepers have no beds. Round the inside of the yourtas were placed trunks of trees, upon which were fixed pieces or planks of wood. On these the lepers slept, closely packed as near to each other as possible, the feet of one to the head of the next. Men, women, and children were all mixed together; calves were also kept there in the summer, and cows during the winter. There was no kind of sanitary arrangements; and, sometimes, in the depth of the winter, none of the inmates venture outside for days together.

In this place the lepers eat, cook, sleep, live, and die. If one of them dies, the body is kept in the hovel for three days. The smoke fills the place—stifling both the lepers and the cattle. Not long ago they had smallpox among them, and four of their number died, and the dead bodies were kept in the same yourta for three days. The dead are buried only a few yards from the dreadful abode, so that the lepers cannot pass their threshold without being reminded of the end daily drawing nearer....

Amongst the lepers was a girl of eighteen, who was perfectly free from disease. Her mother, being infected, was sent off to the yourta, and, before long, gave birth to this girl, who thus had been here all her life—for the Yakuts would never allow her to go amongst them. She pitifully implored us to take compassion on her, and remove her from this horrible place. We held a consultation, and the ispravnick[286] said he was resolved to break the spell of terror that ruled amongst the Yakuts, and then nobly promised to take the girl into his own house as servant. I scarcely knew how to express my admiration of this splendid conduct. All who try to appreciate the full significance and after-effects of the brave chief's decision will not hesitate to class him amongst those whose hearts have the true ring of heroism, and of that charity which is the essence of the Christian religion.

Our return journey was a rather eventful one. My horse became restive, pricked up his ears, shivered and stood still. It was not without much coaxing that I could get him to move. Then other horses became restive, but we managed to go on through the silent forest. The tchinovnick rode forward and reported that he saw a bear crouching in an ominous manner. We were badly armed, there being only two guns and one revolver amongst all the thirty of us. We went on quickly for some distance and then encamped. I was lying down in my tent trying to sleep, but, in reality, wide awake planning the hospital, when suddenly I heard a tremendous stampede—a crashing of branches, horses neighing, and, altogether, a great clamour. I fully expected to see that bear march boldly into my tent; but he had been content, it seemed, with frightening the horses. We started again, and every one was on the alert, feeling sure that the bear would follow us; the cunning fellow might spring from behind a tree at any moment, and the stories I had heard of the doings of these creatures in the woods were not calculated at that moment to fortify one's nerves.

---

285 Russian: a government office clerk in nineteenth-century Russia.
286 Russian: police chief in the nineteenth-century Russian countryside.

Crash, crash, crash! The horses reared—I got off mine, preferring to meet the bear to being dragged through the forest on a mad horse and dashed against the trees. Evidently the bear was somewhere at hand, for one of the baggage horses had flown into the thick of the forest, and was jammed between two trees, causing all this commotion. A little later, whilst we were resting, another of these baggage horses took fright. Its tail was tied to the bridle of another horse, and it dragged its neighbour round and round an open space, the baggage bumping against its hind legs. Then all the other horses got restive, and in another moment would have torn away into the forest had we not quickly quieted them. These untamed Siberian steeds often proved a source of danger to our limbs and lives.

Other alarming incidents occurred, but I will only mention one more. We had to row about twenty versts up the stream, but were unable to make headway against the rapid current. A terrific storm began, and, as the violent gusts tore across the water, they forced the boat against over-hanging trees, and sometimes against the high bank. And whilst we were in this predicament the men shouted, yelled, and screamed as if they were a lot of madmen. The ispravnick managed to get on shore; and I began to think it was high time I did something for self-preservation, for a tumble into that river would have been the end of me. So I quietly watched for an opportunity, and then jumped ashore. The tchinovnick followed, and then we set off to walk ten miles through the forest, one, it was said, in which no human foot had ever been before. Having been without sleep for twenty-four hours, and not having broken my fast for twelve, I was not in exactly good training for that pedestrian feat. I got on tolerably well for about three miles, and then simply dropped. Again I struggled on and again dropped. My very indulgent and patient escort were getting a little tired of this sort of thing, so some of them went forward and sent back two or three soldiers to help me. These sturdy fellows had to drag me into Viluisk,[287] whilst pain seemed to rack every atom of my body. Then I went to bed and slept for twenty-four hours. That rest was, indeed, a godsend, for we had to start in two days on a journey of a thousand versts.

Mary H. Kingsley

from *Travels in West Africa Congo Français, Corisco and Cameroon* (1897)

Travel writer Mary Kingsley (1862–1900) came from a literary family; her uncles Henry and Charles Kingsley and her cousin Mary St. Leger Kingsley (who published under the name Lucas Malet) were novelists. Her love of travel came from her father, who journeyed widely as a personal physician. Mainly self-educated, Kingsley learned German to assist in her father's research and taught herself Latin, Syrian, and Arabic. Caretaker for her parents until their 1892 deaths, Kingsley voyaged twice to West Africa (1893–95), the second time with a commission to collect fish specimens for the British Museum. She usually voyaged alone. Celebrated as a New Woman, Kingsley resisted the title and feminism in general.

---

287 An eastern Siberian town in Russia.

> In this selection from *Travels in West Africa* (1897), Kingsley dismisses contemporary British views of the dangers of Africa, but acknowledges that visitors "either die themselves or get ... accustomed to ... death and fever." She recounts her search for specimens, deploying witty domestic metaphors for her experiences.

Introduction

... I inquired of all my friends as a beginning what they knew of West Africa. The majority knew nothing. A percentage said, "Oh, you can't possibly go there; that's where Sierra Leone[288] is, the white man's grave, you know." If these were pressed further, one occasionally found that they had had relations who had gone out there after having been "sad trials," but, on consideration of their having left not only West Africa, but this world, were now forgiven and forgotten. One lady however kindly remembered a case of a gentleman who had resided some few years at Fernando Po,[289] but when he returned an aged wreck of forty he shook so violently with ague[290] as to dislodge a chandelier, thereby destroying a valuable tea-service and flattening the silver teapot in its midst.

No; there was no doubt about it, the place was not healthy, and although I had not been "a sad trial," yet neither had the chandelier-dislodging Fernando Po gentleman. So I next turned my attention to cross-examining the doctors. "Deadliest spot on earth," they said cheerfully, and showed me maps of the geographical distribution of disease. Now I do not say that a country looks inviting when it is coloured in Scheele's green[291] or a bilious yellow, but these colours may arise from lack of artistic gift in the cartographer. There is no mistaking what he means by black, however, and black you'll find they colour West Africa from above Sierra Leone to below the Congo.[292] "I wouldn't go there if I were you," said my medical friends, "you'll catch something; but if you must go, and you're as obstinate as a mule, just bring me——" and then followed a list of commissions from here to New York....

Chapter 5
Voyage Down Coast

... I should like here to speak of West Coast dangers because I fear you may think that I am careless of, or do not believe in them, neither of which is the case. The more you know of the West Coast of Africa, the more you realise its dangers. For example, on your first voyage out you hardly believe the stories of fever told by the old Coasters.... But a short experience of your own, particularly if you happen on a place having one of its periodic epidemics, soon demonstrates that the underlying horror of the thing

---

288 A sub-Saharan country on the west coast of Africa.
289 Bioko (Fernando Pó), an island off the west coast of Africa that is currently part of Equatorial Guinea.
290 Fever.
291 Invented by German-Swedish chemist Carl Wilhelm Scheele (1742–86), $CuHAsO_3$ was used as a dye and as a pigment to colour paints, cloth, and various types of paper green during the Victorian age; it later fell out of use due to its toxicity.
292 Equatorial Africa was especially known for the dangers with which it threatened Europeans, including diseases, parasites, wild animals, challenging terrain, and clashes with other peoples.

is there, a rotting corpse which the old Coaster has dusted over with jokes to cover it so that it hardly shows at a distance, but which, when you come yourself to live alongside, you soon become cognisant of. Many men, when they have got ashore and settled, realise this, and let the horror get a grip on them; a state briefly and locally described as funk, and a state that usually ends fatally; and you can hardly blame them. Why, I know of a case myself. A young man who had never been outside an English country town before in his life, from family reverses had to take a situation as book-keeper down in the Bights.[293] The factory he was going to was in an isolated out-of-the-way place and not in a settlement, and when the ship called off it, he was put ashore in one of the ship's boats with his belongings, and a case or so of goods. There were only the firm's beach-boys down at the surf, and as the steamer was in a hurry the officer from the ship did not go up to the factory with him, but said good-bye and left him alone with a set of naked savages as he thought, but really of good kindly Kru[294] boys on the beach. He could not understand what they said, nor they what he said, and so he walked up to the house and on to the verandah and tried to find the Agent he had come out to serve under. He looked into the open-ended dining-room and shyly round the verandah, and then sat down and waited for some one to turn up. Sundry natives turned up, and said a good deal, but no one white or comprehensible, so in desperation he made another and a bolder tour completely round the verandah and noticed a most peculiar noise in one of the rooms and an infinity of flies going into the venetian shuttered window. Plucking up courage he went in and found what was left of the white Agent, a considerable quantity of rats, and most of the flies in West Africa. He then presumably had fever, and he was taken off, a fortnight afterwards, by a French boat, to whom the natives signalled, and he is not coming down the Coast again. Some men would have died right out from a shock like this.

But most of the new-comers do not get a shock of this order. They either die themselves or get more gradually accustomed to this sort of thing, when they come to regard death and fever as soldiers, who on a battle-field sit down, and laugh and talk round a camp fire after a day's hard battle, in which they have seen their friends and companions falling round them; all the time knowing that to-morrow the battle comes again and that to-morrow night they themselves may never see....

My main aim in going to Congo Français was to get up above the tide line of the Ogowé River[295] and there collect fishes; for my object on this voyage was to collect fish from a river north of the Congo. I had hoped this river would have been the Niger, for Sir George Goldie[296] had placed at my disposal great facilities for carrying on work there in comfort; but for certain private reasons I was disinclined to go from the Royal Niger Protectorate into the Royal Niger Company's territory;[297] and the Calabar, where

---

293 The Gulf of Guinea includes two bights, or large bays—the Bight of Bonny and the Bight of Benin—and ranges from Ghana to Gabon on Africa's west coast.
294 A native African people whose traditional lands are at the northern tip of the two bights, in Liberia and Côte d'Ivoire.
295 The French Congo was the colony situated where present-day Chad, Gabon, Congo, and the Central African Republic are; the Ogooué (Ogowé) River is the longest river in Gabon, the southernmost country on the bights.
296 The Niger is the largest river in northwestern Africa, the third largest in all Africa (following the Nile and the Congo); George Dashwood Taubman Goldie (1846–1925), a heterodox entrepreneur and explorer, who created the National African Company (later the Royal Niger Company).
297 The Royal Niger Company sold its territory to the British government shortly after this, and the protectorate and former Company territory became Southern Nigeria, now part of Nigeria.

Sir Claude MacDonald[298] did everything he possibly could to assist me, I did not find a good river for me to collect fishes in. These two rivers failing me, from no fault of either of their own presiding genii, my only hope of doing anything now lay on the South West Coast river, the Ogowé, and everything there depended on Mr. Hudson's[299] attitude towards scientific research in the domain of ichthyology.[300] Fortunately for me that gentleman elected to take a favourable view of this affair, and in every way in his power assisted me during my entire stay in Congo Français. But before I enter into a detailed description of this wonderful bit of West Africa, I must give you a brief notice of the manners, habits and customs of West Coast rivers in general, to make the thing more intelligible.

There is an uniformity in the habits of West Coast rivers, from the Volta to the Coanza,[301] which is, when you get used to it, very taking. Excepting the Congo, the really great river comes out to sea with as much mystery as possible; lounging lazily along among its mangrove swamps in a what's-it-matter when-one-comes-out and where's-the-hurry style, through quantities of channels inter-communicating with each other.... High-tide or low-tide, there is little difference in the water; the river, be it broad or narrow, deep or shallow, looks like a pathway of polished metal; for it is as heavy weighted with stinking mud as water e'er can be, ebb or flow, year out and year in....

At high-water you do not see the mangroves displaying their ankles in the way that shocked Captain Lugard.[302] They look most respectable, their foliage rising densely in a wall irregularly striped here and there by the white line of an aërial root, coming straight down into the water from some upper branch as straight as a plummet, in the strange, knowing way an aërial root of a mangrove does, keeping the hard straight line until it gets some two feet above water-level, and then spreading out into blunt fingers with which to dip into the water and grasp the mud. Banks indeed at high water can hardly be said to exist, the water stretching away into the mangrove swamps for miles and miles, and you can then go, in a suitable small canoe, away among these swamps as far as you please.

This is a fascinating pursuit. For people who like that sort of thing it is just the sort of thing they like, as the art critic of a provincial town wisely observed anent[303] an impressionist picture recently acquired for the municipal gallery. But it is a pleasure to be indulged in with caution; for one thing, you are certain to come across crocodiles. Now a crocodile drifting down in deep water, or lying asleep with its jaws open on a sand-bank in the sun, is a picturesque adornment to the landscape when you are on the deck of a steamer, and you can write home about it and frighten your relations on your behalf; but when you are away among the swamps in a small dug-out canoe, and that crocodile and his relations are awake—a thing he makes a point of being at flood tide because of fish coming along—and when he

---

298 The Nigerian port town of Calabar, a district and port in Kingsley's time, is the meeting point for the Cross, Calabar, and Great Qua rivers and also contains several tributaries of the Niger; Claude Maxwell MacDonald (1852–1915), soldier and diplomat, served in both functions in Africa and in the latter only in China and Japan; he was consul general of the Oil Rivers Protectorate (later the Niger Coast Protectorate, part of present-day Nigeria) when Kingsley was travelling in the area.
299 C.G. Hudson, an employee of the Hatton and Cookson trading firm, travelled with Kingsley after the two met in Cabinda in 1893.
300 The study of fish.
301 The Volta is in Ghana, at the north end of the bights; the Cuanza (Coanza) is in Angola, just below Gabon, the southernmost country on the bights.
302 Frederick John Dealtry Lugard (1858–1945), soldier, explorer, agent, and governor general of Nigeria.
303 Regarding.

has got his foot upon his native heath—that is to say, his tail within holding reach of his native mud—he is highly interesting, and you may not be able to write home about him—and you get frightened on your own behalf. For crocodiles can, and often do, in such places, grab at people in small canoes. I have known of several natives losing their lives in this way; some native villages are approachable from the main river by a short cut, as it were, through the mangrove swamps, and the inhabitants of such villages will now and then go across this way with small canoes instead of by the constant channel to the village, which is almost always winding. In addition to this unpleasantness you are liable—until you realise the danger from experience, or have native advice on the point—to get tide-trapped away in the swamps, the water falling round you when you are away in some deep pool or lagoon, and you find you cannot get back to the main river. For you cannot get out and drag your canoe across the stretches of mud that separate you from it, because the mud is of too unstable a nature and too deep, and sinking into it means staying in it, at any rate until some geologist of the remote future may come across you, in a fossilised state, when that mangrove swamp shall have become dry land. Of course if you really want a truly safe investment in Fame, and really care about Posterity, and Posterity's Science, you will jump over into the black batter-like, stinking slime, cheered by the thought of the terrific sensation you will produce 20,000 years hence, and the care you will be taken of then by your fellow-creatures, in a museum. But if you are a mere ordinary person of a retiring nature, like me, you stop in your lagoon until the tide rises again; most of your attention is directed to dealing with an "at home"[304] to crocodiles and mangrove flies, and with the fearful stench of the slime round you…. Twice this chatty little incident, as Lady MacDonald[305] would call it, has happened to me, but never again if I can help it. On one occasion, the last, a mighty Silurian,[306] as *The Daily Telegraph*[307] would call him, chose to get his front paws over the stern of my canoe, and endeavoured to improve our acquaintance. I had to retire to the bows, to keep the balance right, and fetch him a clip on the snout with a paddle, when he withdrew, and I paddled into the very middle of the lagoon, hoping the water there was too deep for him or any of his friends to repeat the performance. Presumably it was, for no one did it again. I should think that crocodile was eight feet long; but don't go and say I measured him, or that this is my outside measurement for crocodiles. I have measured them when they have been killed by other people, fifteen, eighteen, and twenty-one feet odd. This was only a pushing young creature who had not learnt manners….

You often hear the utter lifelessness of mangrove-swamps commented on; why I do not know, for they are fairly heavily stocked with fauna, though the species are comparatively few. There are the crocodiles, more of them than any one wants; there are quantities of flies, particularly the big silent mangrove-fly which lays an egg in you under the skin; the egg becomes a maggot and stays there until it feels fit to enter into external life.[308] Then there are "slimy things that crawl with legs upon a slimy sea,"[309] and any quantity

---

304 A period during which a host or hostess has announced that he or she will be receiving visitors.
305 Ethel MacDonald (née Armstrong) (1857–1941), wife of Claude Maxwell MacDonald, diplomat who served in West Africa, China, and Japan.
306 Crocodile; the Silurian is one of the Paleozoic periods.
307 A popular, affordable daily paper, founded in 1855.
308 Putzi or Tumbu fly larvae make their way under the skin of animals and humans from eggs laid on the ground or on clothing; they create a small boil, with a breathing hole in the centre, in which they gestate for five to ten weeks before ejecting themselves, as pupae, to finish maturing outside of their host.
309 Samuel Taylor Coleridge, "The Rime of the Ancient Mariner" (1798).

of hopping mud-fish, and crabs, and a certain mollusc, and in the water various kinds of cat-fish. Birdless they are save for the flocks of gray parrots that pass over them at evening, hoarsely squarking; and save for this squarking of the parrots the swamps are silent all the day, at least during the dry season; in the wet season there is no silence night or day in West Africa, but that roar of the descending deluge of rain that is more monotonous and more gloomy than any silence can be. In the morning you do not hear the long, low, mellow whistle of the plantain-eaters calling up the dawn, nor in the evening the clock-bird nor the Handel-Festival-sized choruses of frogs,[310] or the crickets, that carry on their vesper[311] controversy of "she did"—"she didn't"[312] so fiercely on hard land.

But the mangrove-swamp follows the general rule for West Africa, and night in it is noisier than the day. After dark it is full of noises; grunts from I know not what, splashes from jumping fish, the peculiar whirr of rushing crabs, and quaint creaking and groaning sounds from the trees; and—above all in eeriness—the strange whine and sighing cough of crocodiles....

---

310 The Handel Festival (which began in 1857 and continued to occur every three years after 1859) was a massive choral festival celebrating the works of George Frideric Handel; the festivals ceased in 1926 due to lack of popularity, but have been revived recently and occur every year in London.
311 Evening.
312 From the folk song "Katy Did"; a traditional rendering of the sound of katydids and other chirping insects.